The Outdoor Art Room

Art for SUMMER

Rita Storey

WINDMILL
BOOKS

Published in 2018 by **Windmill Books**, an Imprint of Rosen Publishing
29 East 21ˢᵗ Street, New York, NY 10010

Series editor: Sarah Peutrill
Art direction: Peter Scoulding
Series designed and created for Franklin Watts by Storeybooks
rita@storeybooks.co.uk
Designer: Rita Storey
Editor: Sarah Ridley
Photography: Tudor Photography, Banbury
Cover images: Tudor Photography, Banbury
Cover design: Cathryn Gilbert

Cataloging-in-Publication Data
Names: Storey, Rita.
Title: Art for summer / Rita Storey.
Description: New York : Windmill Books, 2018. | Series: The outdoor art room | Includes index.
Identifiers: ISBN 9781508194682 (pbk.) | ISBN 9781508194194 (library bound) |
ISBN 9781508194729 (6 pack)
Subjects: LCSH: Handicraft--Juvenile literature. | Summer--Juvenile literature.
Classification: LCC TT160.S76 2018 | DDC 745.5--dc23

Manufactured in China
CPSIA Compliance Information: Batch BW18WM: For Further Information contact
Rosen Publishing, New York, New York at 1-800-237-9932

Before you start

Some of the projects in this book require scissors, strong glue, a butter knife, and paint. When using these things, make sure you are supervised by a responsible adult.

Contents

All about summer

Summer is a wonderful time of the year to be in a garden, park, or backyard. This book is full of art projects and fun things to make and do outside. Have fun!

When is summer?

A year is the amount of time it takes for our planet Earth to go once around the sun. A year is divided into four seasons called spring, summer, fall, and winter. Summer occurs at different times of the year in different parts of the world. In the northern half of the world, summer lasts from June to September. In the southern half, it lasts from December to March. During the summer months, days are long and nights are short.

Summer is the hottest and sunniest season. We wear light clothing to keep cool. The rays from the sun can burn our skin. It is important to remember to wear sunscreen and a hat to avoid sunburn. In summer there is less rain. Sometimes it does not rain for weeks or even months, causing a drought. This can lead to water shortages and forest fires.

What happens in summer?

People look forward to summer. They visit the beach for day trips and vacations during the long school break. Families eat outside, go for hikes, and enjoy the good weather.

Animals in summer

In the summer, food is plentiful. There are lots of insects and lush grass for animals to eat. Animals born in spring have plenty to eat to help them grow strong before winter arrives.

The garden in summer

In the summer, the countryside and our gardens are full of colorful flowers. Bees, butterflies, and other flying insects visit the flowers to pollinate them.

Strawberries, cucumbers, lettuces, green beans, strawberries, and raspberries are all in season in summer.

Shell mobile

On a trip to the beach, it is fun to collect shells. A great way to display them is to make them into a mobile. The shells on this mobile hang from a colorful homemade lighthouse.

1

Put a line of masking tape around the bottom, middle, and top of the paper cup. Paint the cup red between the strips of tape and around the rim. Leave to dry.

You will need:

* white paper cup
* masking tape
* paintbrush and water container
* red paint
* scraps of black paper
* ruler * scissors
* glue
* yellow pom-pom
* clear plastic cup (with the top quarter cut off)
* thick black marker
* 1 piece of string, 8 inches (20 cm) in length
* 4 pieces of string, 10 inches (25 cm) in length
* seashells
* colored beads
* strong glue

2

Peel off the strips of tape. Cut out two pieces of black paper 0.5 inch by 1 inch (2 cm × 3 cm). Cut out one piece of black paper 1.5 inches × 1 inch (4 cm × 3 cm). Glue them onto the cup as shown on the left.

Shell houses

Mollusks are a large group of animals with a soft body and no backbone. They include octopuses, slugs, snails, clams, and limpets. Many types of mollusks have hard shells to protect them. Seashells that we find on the beach were once home to mollusks.

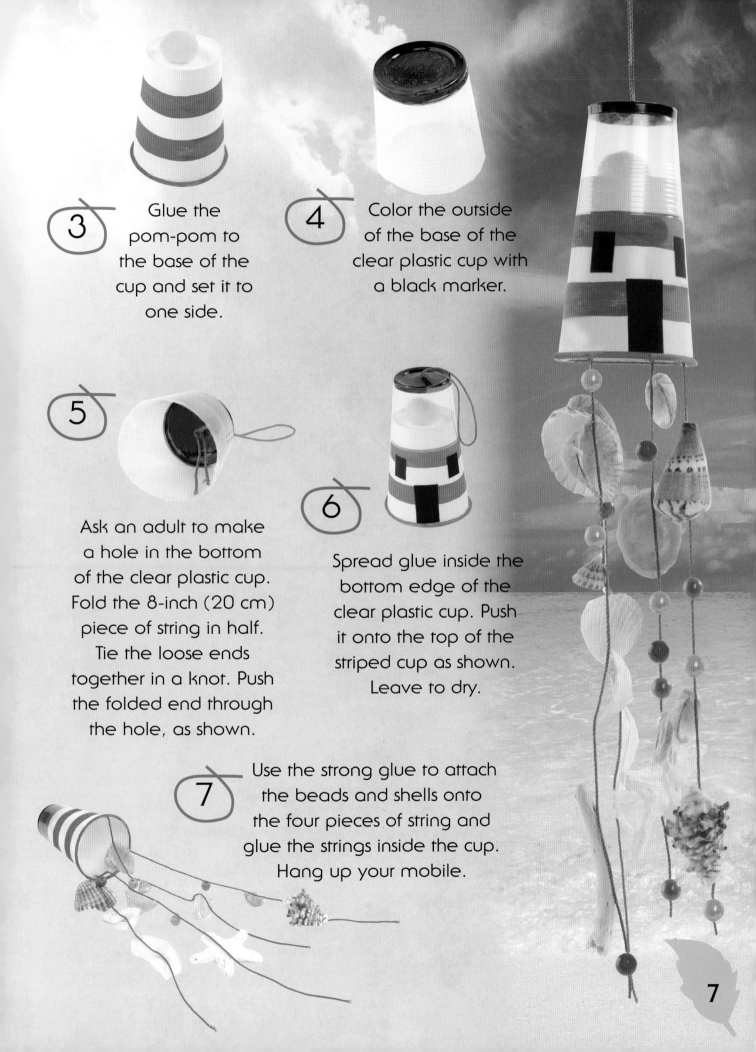

3 Glue the pom-pom to the base of the cup and set it to one side.

4 Color the outside of the base of the clear plastic cup with a black marker.

5 Ask an adult to make a hole in the bottom of the clear plastic cup. Fold the 8-inch (20 cm) piece of string in half. Tie the loose ends together in a knot. Push the folded end through the hole, as shown.

6 Spread glue inside the bottom edge of the clear plastic cup. Push it onto the top of the striped cup as shown. Leave to dry.

7 Use the strong glue to attach the beads and shells onto the four pieces of string and glue the strings inside the cup. Hang up your mobile.

Flower bombs

On a hot day, a water fight is a great way to cool down. These soft sponge flowers are great for drenching your friends.

1 Use scissors to cut three 0.5 inch × 3 inch (2 cm × 8 cm) strips from the blue sponge. Repeat to cut strips from the pink and yellow sponges.

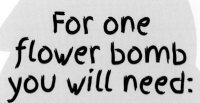

For one flower bomb you will need:
* blue, pink, and yellow sponges
* ruler
* scissors
* strong rubber bands
* bowl
* water

2 Lay sponge strips next to each other, as shown.

3 Put a layer of sponge strips on top, as shown.

4 Stack another layer of sponge strips on top, as shown.

5 Hold all the strips together and slip the rubber band over them.

6 Twist the rubber band until it is tight. Fluff out the ends. Make more flower bombs by repeating steps 1–6.

7 Dip the flower bombs into a bowl of water, divide them in half and find a friend who wants a water fight. Ready, steady, SPLASH!

Garden bunting

For an outdoor party, turn old comics, wrapping paper, and string into colorful bunting to decorate your backyard.

You will need:

* pages from old comics and sheets of used wrapping paper
* scissors
* ruler
* pencil
* glue
* paintbrush
* ball of string

1 Cut the paper into strips that are 4 inches × 12 inches long (10 cm × 30 cm)

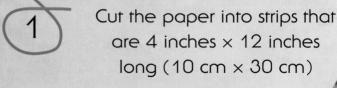

2 Fold each strip in half across its longest side. Make a mark with the pencil halfway along the opposite edge to the fold.

3 Draw a line from the pencil mark to the top left-hand corner of the folded edge.

4 Draw a line from the mark to the bottom left-hand corner of the folded edge.

5 Cut along the lines. Open out. Repeat to make more paper diamond shapes.

6 Lay a paper diamond, pattern-side down, on your work surface. Spread glue on the bottom half of the shape. Lay the string on the fold line.

7 Fold the paper diamond in half, trapping the string. Repeat to add more paper diamonds until the string of bunting is as long as you want it. Leave to dry.

To help the bunting last longer, paint each side with a coat of PVA glue.

Water xylophone

Make this water xylophone and play it outside in the sunshine. Each bottle will make a slightly different sound when tapped with a spoon.

 1 Use the marker and the ruler to draw a line 1 inch (3 cm) from the base of a bottle. Place the funnel in the bottle and fill with water to the line.

You will need:

* 6 glass bottles or glasses the same size
* permanent marker
* ruler
* funnel
* jug of water
* food coloring (green, yellow, red, blue, purple, and orange)
* metal spoon

2 Repeat to fill the other bottles with water after you have marked them as shown above.

 3 Add a few drops of green food coloring to the bottle containing the most water.

 4 Add different food colors to the rest of the bottles, as shown.

 **5** Write the numbers 1 to 6 on the bottles, starting with the bottle of green water. Make the numbers big.

 6 Gently tap the bottles with the spoon to play musical notes.

Play a tune by tapping the numbered bottles in different patterns, for instance: 1,2,3 – 2,3,1 – 1,2,3 – 2,3,1.

sun print

Get outside on a sunny day and use the sunshine to make this stunning leaf print.

1 Make the fabric damp in the plastic bowl.

You will need:

* piece of white or cream cotton fabric, 30 inches by 12 inches (80 cm × 30 cm)

* plastic bowl with a small amount of water in it

* garbage bag

* acrylic paints mixed with the same amount of water

* paintbrush and water container

* a selection of leaves

* small stones

2 Lay the garbage bag on the ground in full sunshine and spread out the wet fabric on top of it. Use the acrylic paints to create a swirling design.

3 Place the leaves on the painted fabric.

sunlight

Light comes from the sun. Sunlight is a source of energy. It warms up the Earth and is used by plants to make food. During the summer, the rays from the sun are at their strongest.

4 Stop the leaves from moving by placing some small stones on top of them. Leave everything in the sunshine for a few hours until the fabric is completely dry.

The fabric under the objects will dry more slowly than the fabric exposed to the sunlight. The areas that dry more quickly pull the paint from under the objects, leaving paler shapes.

5 Peel off the leaves to reveal their shapes.

Very flat leaves work best. Or you could try some other flat objects, such as garden tools or stones.

Fairy ring

Many children's books show pictures of fairies dancing inside a ring of colorful mushrooms on a summer evening. Make a ring of mushrooms for your backyard and imagine fairies dancing inside it.

You will need:

* 18 ounces (500 g) air-dry clay
* ruler
* butter knife
* paintbrush and water container
* white, red, yellow, and blue acrylic paint

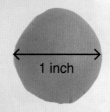

1 inch

1 Roll the clay into six balls, measuring about 1 inch (3 cm) across the widest part.

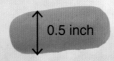

0.5 inch

2 Roll out a long barrel of clay, 0.5 inch (2 cm) across. Using the butter knife, cut six pieces from the clay barrel, each about 1 inch (3 cm) long.

3 Press your fingers into the balls of clay to make dish shapes like the one in the picture.

4 Paint some water onto one end of each piece. Press the wet end into the center of each clay dish to make a mushroom shape.

5 Paint the clay mushrooms white. Leave them to dry.

6   Paint the top of the mushrooms so that you have two red, two blue and two yellow ones. Leave them to dry.

7   Paint on white spots and leave them to dry.

8   Gently push the mushrooms into a lawn or grassy area to create a fairy ring.

To keep the mushrooms looking bright, take them inside if it looks like it's going to rain.

sunflower race

Sunflowers are a wonderful sight in late summer. They can grow very tall. Figure out which is the tallest sunflower using this colorful ladybug measuring stick.

1

Sow the sunflower seeds in your garden or in large flowerpots, following the instructions on the seed packet. Remember to water your sunflowers as they grow.

You will need:

* packet of sunflower seeds (and flowerpots if you need them)
* pencil and thin white paper (for tracing the templates)
* scissors
* sheet of red craft foam
* sewing pin
* sheet of black craft foam
* latex glue and spreader
* black pipe cleaner
* 2 googly eyes
* scraps of blue, yellow, green, and black craft foam
* measuring tape
* long pole
* paintbrush and colored paints
* black marker

2

Use the white paper to trace and cut out the oval template on page 31. Pin it to the red craft foam and cut out the ladybug body.

3

Trace and cut out the semicircle template on page 31. Pin it to the black craft foam and cut around it. Glue the black foam to the red ladybug body, as shown.

4

Fold the black pipe cleaner in half. Curl the ends as shown in the picture below. Glue it to the back of the ladybug body.

6 Use the measuring tape and marker to make marks every 4 inches (10 cm) along the pole. Paint each 4-inch (10 cm) section a different color. When the paint has dried, use the marker to write all the numbers to create a measuring stick.

5 Ask an adult to cut two slits in the ladybug body as shown here. Glue on two googly eyes. Use the templates on page 31 to cut out spots from the craft foam scraps and glue them on. Leave to dry.

7 Slide the foam ladybug onto the pole.

8 Slide the ladybug up the stick as the sunflowers grow. Which sunflower will win?

In dry weather, water the sunflowers every day.

19

Creepy-crawly detective

In the summer, creepy-crawlies like a cool, dark place to hide from the sun. Attract some of them to your mini hotel.

1 Choose a sheltered spot in a semi-shady area. Place the flowerpot upside down, using a small stone to lift up one edge so that creatures can crawl inside.

You will need:

* flowerpot
* a small stone
* leaves * sticks
* a flat stone
* half an orange
* teaspoon
* paintbrush
* paper cups
* pen
* notebook
* magnifying glass

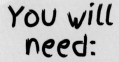

2 Pile up some leaves and sticks next to the flowerpot.

3 Scoop the middle out of half an orange with a teaspoon. Place it next to the flowerpot with its cut side down. Make sure creepy-crawlies can crawl inside it.

Creepy-crawlies

Creepy-crawlies are small animals that don't have backbones. They include spiders, slugs, worms, beetles, centipedes, snails, woodlice, and caterpillars.

4 Put a flat stone next to the flowerpot, leaves, and orange. Leave your new hotel for a few days.

	woodlouse	spider	worm	snail
flowerpot				
leaves				
orange				
stone				

5 Draw a grid like this one in your notebook.

6 Take the mini hotel apart. Use the paintbrush to brush the creepy-crawlies into paper cups. Look very carefully at what you have collected. Count how many of each creature there are. Fill in the grid.

7 When you have counted the creepy-crawlies, gently release them back into the wild close to where you had your mini hotel.

It is best to keep different types of creepy-crawlies apart so that they do not attack each other.

Bees and daisies game

This outdoor game for two players follows the same rules as tic-tac-toe. Use the bees instead of "Os" and the flowers instead of "Xs."

You will need:

* 5 oval stones
* yellow, black, and white acrylic craft paint
* paintbrush
* water (to wash your paintbrush clean)
* 5 round stones
* piece of chalk

Bees

In summer bees, collect nectar from flowers. They take the nectar back to their hive or nest. The nectar collected by all the bees is turned into honey.

 Paint three yellow stripes on an oval stone. Leave to dry.

 Paint three black stripes between the yellow stripes. Leave to dry.

 Use white paint to paint two eyes and a pair of wings.

22

4 Paint a yellow spot in the center of a round stone.

5 Paint white petals around the yellow circle, as shown. Leave to dry.

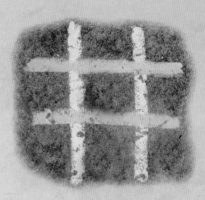

6 Repeat steps 1–5 to make five bee stones and five daisy stones.

7 Draw chalk lines on a sidewalk or driveway, copying this pattern.

8 One player has the bee stones. The other player has the daisy stones. Taking turns, each player places a stone on the chalk grid. The goal is to get three of their own stones in a row, across, down, or diagonal.

Rose perfume

Many roses smell beautiful. This rose-scented perfume is the smell of summer for many people!

You will need:

* scented rose
* small jar
* water
* sieve and bowl
* funnel
* small bottle with lid
* sticker label, colored markers, and ribbon to decorate

1 Ask an adult's permission to cut a rose from their garden. Choose a rose with a strong scent.

2 Gently pull the petals off the rose.

Flowers

Some flowers use scent to attract butterflies, bees, and other flying insects. The insects help to pollinate the flowers by carrying pollen from flower to flower.

3 Put the petals into the jar and fill the jar with water.

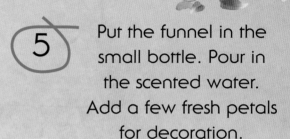

4. Leave the petals in the jar of water for a few days. Hold a sieve over a bowl and pour the petal mixture through the sieve.

5. Put the funnel in the small bottle. Pour in the scented water. Add a few fresh petals for decoration.

6. Write the words "rose petal perfume" on the label and decorate it. Finish by tying a ribbon around the bottle.

This bottle of rose perfume would make a lovely gift. It needs to be used within a month.

rose petal perfume

Flower print picture

Making a colorful flower print picture using real flowers is very easy. The printed paper makes great wrapping paper too.

1 Take the largest flower. Dip the brush into the pink paint. Brush the flower petals with paint.

2 Press the flower head onto the paper to make a print. Carefully lift the flower head and use it to make more prints on different parts of the paper. Leave to dry.

You will need:

* flowers with a flat flower head (1 large, 2 medium and 1 small). Ask permission before cutting flowers.

* paintbrush and water container for cleaning

* pink, yellow, purple, and blue paint

* sheet of white paper

3 Select one of the medium-sized flowers and brush its petals with yellow paint.

colorful flowers

Flower petals are brightly colored so that they attract butterflies, bees, and other insects flying above them.

 4 Print the flower onto the white paper several times. Leave to dry.

 5 Repeat steps 1–4 with the small flower head and purple paint. Leave to dry. Repeat steps 1–4 with the other medium-sized flower head and the blue paint.

Instead of printing the flower heads all over the paper, try making a pattern with them.

Butterfly feeder

Butterflies feed on the nectar from flowers. You can attract butterflies to your backyard by feeding them homemade nectar.

You will need:

* pencil and thin white paper (for tracing the template)

* scissors

* sewing pin

* sheets of yellow, purple, and orange craft foam

* 3 pipe cleaners (green, purple, and orange)

* latex glue and spreader

* plastic bottle cap

* 1 tbsp sugar dissolved in 5 ounces (142 ml) water

* cotton balls

* plastic garden stick

1 Use the pencil and paper to trace the template on page 31 and cut it out. Lay it on the yellow foam, pin in place, and trace around it using a pencil.

2 Cut out the foam flower shape.

3 Twist the end of the green pipe cleaner into a spiral as shown.

4 Spread glue onto the end of the pipe cleaner. Press it onto the foam flower. Leave to dry.

5 Glue the back of the bottle cap onto the other side of the flower shape.

6 Soak a cotton ball in the sugar and water syrup. Push the soaked cotton ball into the bottle cap.

7 Repeat steps 1–6 to make two more flowers using the orange and then the purple craft foam. Twist the pipe cleaner stems around the garden stick.

8 Choose a sunny spot and push the stick into the ground in your garden or in a plant container. Return to the feeder every hour or so to see if butterflies have discovered your feeder.

Butterflies

A butterfly has four different stages to its life cycle: egg, caterpillar, pupa, and butterfly.

Peacock butterflies lay their eggs on nettles in spring. These hatch into caterpillars 10 days later. The caterpillars feed on the nettles and then change into pupa, emerging as butterflies in summer.

Keep the rest of the sugar syrup in a bottle to top up the feeder.

29

summer words

caterpillar the young of a butterfly or moth

drought a long period of time without rainfall

fertilize in plants, when the male and female part of a plant join together to make seeds

hive a shelter for a colony of bees

in season the time of year when a fruit or vegetable is ripe and plentiful

insect a small animal that has three parts to its body, six legs, and often has two pairs of wings

life cycle the series of changes in the life of an animal or plant

nectar a sweet liquid produced in a flower

petal the colorful part of a flower

pollen a fine powder found on flowers

pollinate the way pollen is moved from one plant to another to fertilize it so that it can make seeds

pupa the stage of an insect's life cycle between the young and the adult

scent a strong smell

seed the part of a plant that grows into a new plant

sunlight light from the sun, which travels in straight lines, also called rays

sunscreen a cream or liquid that protects the skin from invisible, harmful sun rays

Templates

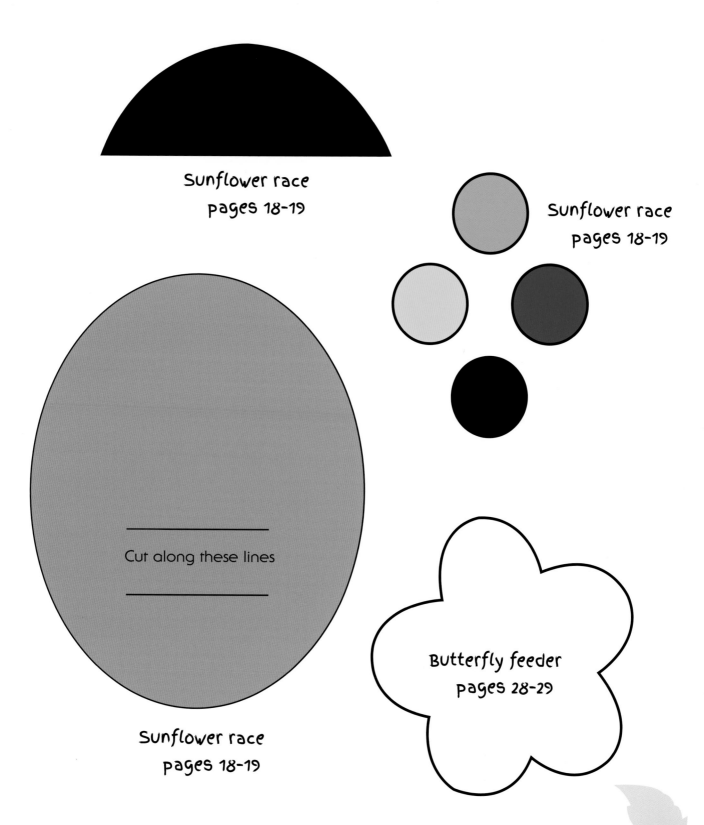

Sunflower race
pages 18-19

Sunflower race
pages 18-19

Cut along these lines

Sunflower race
pages 18-19

Butterfly feeder
pages 28-29

Index

Find out more

For web resources related to the subject of this book, go to: www.windmillbooks.com/weblinks and select this book's title.

INTRODUCTION TO

Operations & Information Management

OPIM 101

Introduction to Management Science
A Modeling and Case Studies Approach
Fourth Edition

Frederick S. Hillier
Stanford University

Mark S. Hillier
University of Washington

Cases developed by
Karl Schmedders
Northwestern University

Molly Stephens
Quinn, Emanuel, Urquhart, Oliver & Hedges LLP

With Addition Material From

Matching Supply with Demand
An Introduction to Operations Management
Third Edition

Gérard Cachon
*The Wharton School,
University of Pennsylvania*

Christian Terwiesch
*The Wharton School,
University of Pennsylvania*

 Learning Solutions

Boston   Burr Ridge, IL   Dubuque, IA   New York   San Francisco   St. Louis
Bangkok   Bogotá   Caracas   Lisbon   London   Madrid
Mexico City   Milan   New Delhi   Seoul   Singapore   Sydney   Taipei   Toronto

The **McGraw-Hill** Companies

Introduction to Operations & Information Management
OPIM 101

This book is a McGraw-Hill Learning Solutions textbook and contains select material from the following sources:
Introduction to Management Science: A Modeling and Case Studies Approach with Spreadsheets, Fourth Edition by Frederick S. Hillier and Mark S. Hillier, with cases developed by Karl Schmedders and Molly Stephens. Copyright © 2011, 2008 by The McGraw-Hill Companies, Inc.
Matching Suppy with Demand: An Introduction to Operations Management, Third Edition by Gérard Cachon and Christian Terwiesch. Copyright © 2013, 2009, 2006 by The McGraw-Hill Companies, Inc.
Both are reprinted with permission of the publisher. Many custom published texts are modified versions or adaptations of our best-selling textbooks. Some adaptations are printed in black and white to keep prices at a minimum, while others are in color.

4 5 6 7 8 9 0 QVS QVS 15

ISBN-13: 978-0-07-781647-6
ISBN-10: 0-07-781647-1

Learning Solutions Consultant: Jennifer Boyle:
Project Manager: Nina Meyer
Cover Designer: Kate Lawler
Printer/Binder: Quad/Graphics
Cover Photo Credits: Cover photos of Philadelphia © Kate Lawler

Brief Contents

Table of Contents

Chapter 2

The Process View of the Organization

Matching supply and demand would be easy if business processes would be instantaneous and could immediately create any amount of supply to meet demand. Understanding the questions of "Why are business processes not instantaneous?" and "What constrains processes from creating more supply?" is thereby at the heart of operations management. To answer these questions, we need to take a detailed look at how business processes actually work. In this chapter, we introduce some concepts fundamental to process analysis. The key idea of the chapter is that it is not sufficient for a firm to create great products and services; the firm also must design and improve its business processes that supply its products and services.

To get more familiar with the process view of a firm, we now take a detailed look behind the scenes of a particular operation, namely the Department of Interventional Radiology at Presbyterian Hospital in Philadelphia.

2.1 Presbyterian Hospital in Philadelphia

Interventional radiology is a subspecialty field of radiology that uses advanced imaging techniques such as real-time X-rays, ultrasound, computed tomography, and magnetic resonance imaging to perform minimally invasive procedures.

Over the past decade, interventional radiology procedures have begun to replace an increasing number of standard "open surgical procedures" for a number of reasons. Instead of being performed in an operating room, interventional radiology procedures are performed in an angiography suite (see Figure 2.1). Although highly specialized, these rooms are less expensive to operate than conventional operating rooms. Interventional procedures are often safer and have dramatically shorter recovery times compared to traditional surgery. Also, an interventional radiologist is often able to treat diseases such as advanced liver cancer that cannot be helped by standard surgery.

Although we may not have been in the interventional radiology unit, many, if not most, of us have been in a radiology department of a hospital at some point in our life. From the perspective of the patient, the following steps need to take place before the patient can go home or return to his or her hospital unit. In process analysis, we refer to these steps as *activities*:

- Registration of the patient.
- Initial consultation with a doctor; signature of the consent form.

FIGURE 2.1
Example of a Procedure in an Interventional Radiology Unit

Reprinted with permission of Arrow International, Inc.

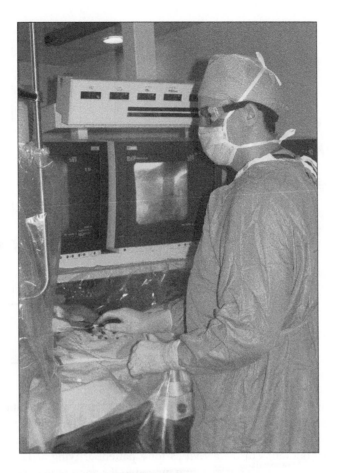

- Preparation for the procedure.
- The actual procedure.
- Removal of all equipment.
- Recovery in an area outside the angiography suite.
- Consultation with the doctor.

Figure 2.2 includes a graphical representation of these steps, called a *Gantt diagram* (named after the 19th-century industrialist Henry Gantt). It provides several useful pieces of information.

First, the Gantt chart allows us to see the process steps and their durations, which are also called *activity times* or *processing times*. The duration simply corresponds to the length of the corresponding bars. Second, the Gantt diagram also illustrates the dependence between the various process activities. For example, the consultation with the doctor can only occur once the patient has arrived and been registered. In contrast, the preparation of the angiography suite can proceed in parallel to the initial consultation.

You might have come across Gantt charts in the context of project management. Unlike process analysis, project management is typically concerned with the completion of one single project (See Chapter 5 for more details on project management.) The most well-known concept of project management is the *critical path*. The critical path is composed of all those activities that—if delayed—would lead to a delay in the overall completion time of the project, or—in this case—the time the patient has completed his or her stay in the radiology unit.

In addition to the eight steps described in the Gantt chart of Figure 2.2, most of us associate another activity with hospital care: waiting. Strictly speaking, waiting is not really

FIGURE 2.2
Gantt Chart
Summarizing the
Activities for
Interventional
Radiology

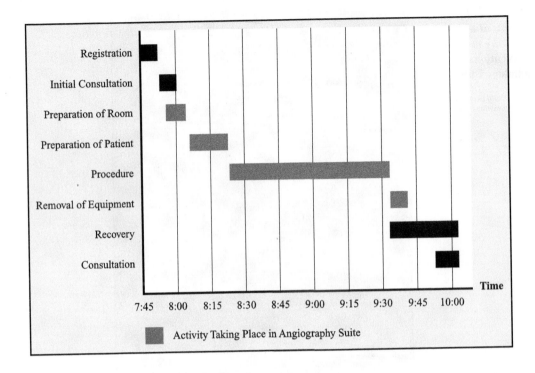

an activity, as it does not add any value to the process. However, waiting is nevertheless relevant. It is annoying for the patient and can complicate matters for the hospital unit. For this reason, waiting times take an important role in operations management. Figure 2.3 shows the actual durations of the activities for a patient arriving at 12:30, as well as the time the patient needs to wait before being moved to the angiography suite.

FIGURE 2.3
Gantt Chart
Summarizing the
Activities for a
Patient Arriving
at 12:30

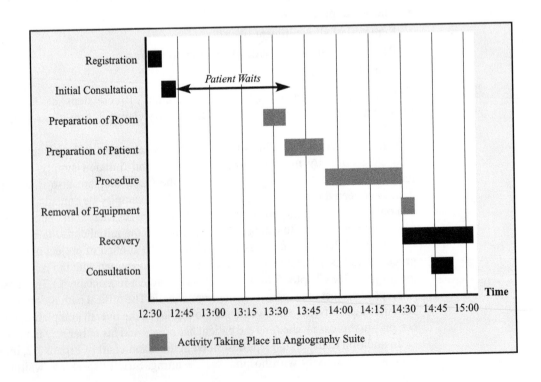

But why is there waiting time? Waiting is—to stay in the medical language for the moment—a symptom of supply–demand mismatch. If supply would be unlimited, our visit to the hospital would be reduced to the duration of the activities outlined in Figure 2.2 (the critical path). Imagine visiting a hospital in which all the nurses, technicians, doctors, and hospital administrators would just care for you!

Given that few of us are in a position to receive the undivided attention of an entire hospital unit, it is important that we not only take the egocentric perspective of the patient, but look at the hospital operations more broadly. From the perspective of the hospital, there are many patients "flowing" through the process.

The people and the equipment necessary to support the interventional radiology process deal with many patients, not just one. We refer to these elements of the process as the *process resources*. Consider, for example, the perspective of the nurse and how she/he spends her/his time in the department of interventional radiology. Obviously, radiology from the viewpoint of the nurse is not an exceptional event, but a rather repetitive endeavor. Some of the nurse's work involves direct interaction with the patient; other work—while required for the patient—is invisible to the patient. This includes the preparation of the angiography suite and various aspects of medical record keeping.

Given this repetitive nature of work, the nurse as well as the doctors, technicians, and hospital administrators think of interventional radiology as a process, not a project. Over the course of the day, they see many patients come and go. Many hospitals, including the Presbyterian Hospital in Philadelphia, have a "patient log" that summarizes at what times patients arrive at the unit. This patient log provides a picture of demand on the corresponding day. The patient log for December 2, is summarized by Table 2.1.

Many of these arrivals were probably scheduled some time in advance. Our analysis here focuses on what happens to the patient once he/she has arrived in the interventional radiology unit. A separate analysis could be performed, looking at the process starting with a request for diagnostics up to the arrival of the patient.

Given that the resources in the interventional radiology unit have to care for 11 patients on December 2, they basically need to complete the work according to 11 Gantt charts of the type outlined in Figure 2.2. This—in turn—can lead to waiting times. Waiting times arise when several patients are "competing" for the same limited resource, which is illustrated by the following two examples.

First, observe that the critical path for a typical patient takes about 2 hours. Note further that we want to care for 11 patients over a 10-hour workday. Consequently, we will have to take care of several patients at once. This would not be a problem if we had unlimited resources, nurses, doctors, space in the angiography suites, and so forth. However,

TABLE 2.1
Patient Log on December 2

Number	Patient Name	Arrival Time	Room Assignment
1		7:35	Main room
2		7:45	
3		8:10	
4		9:30	Main room
5		10:15	Main room
6		10:30	Main room
7		11:05	
8		12:35	Main room
9		14:30	Main room
10		14:35	
11		14:40	

FIGURE 2.4
Time Patient Spent in the Interventional Radiology Unit (for Patients Treated in Main Room Only), Including Room Preparation Time

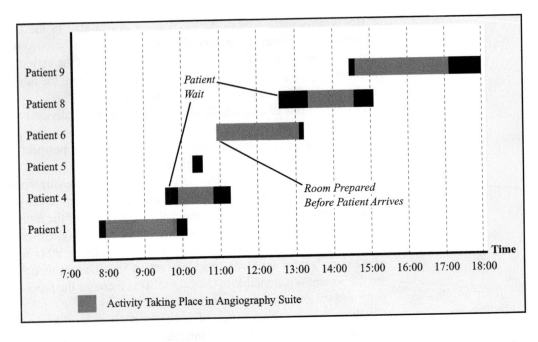

given the resources that we have, if the Gantt charts of two patients are requesting the same resource simultaneously, waiting times result. For example, the second patient might require the initial consultation with the doctor at a time when the doctor is in the middle of the procedure for patient 1. Note also that patients 1, 4, 5, 6, 8, and 9 are assigned to the same room (the unit has a main room and a second room used for simpler cases), and thus they are also potentially competing for the same resource.

A second source of waiting time lies in the unpredictable nature of many of the activities. Some patients will take much longer in the actual procedure than others. For example, patient 1 spent 1:50 hours in the procedure, while patient 9 was in the procedure for 2:30 hours (see Figure 2.4). As an extreme case, consider patient 5, who refused to sign the consent form and left the process after only 15 minutes.

Such uncertainty is undesirable for resources, as it leaves them "flooded" with work at some moments in the day and "starved" for work at other moments. Figure 2.5 summarizes at what moments in time the angiography suite was used on December 2.

By now, we have established two views to the interventional radiology:

• The view of the patient for whom the idealized stay is summarized by Figure 2.2. Mismatches between supply and demand from the patient's perspective mean having a unit of demand (i.e., the patient) wait for a unit of supply (a resource).

• The view of the resources (summarized by Figure 2.5), which experience demand–supply mismatches when they are sometimes "flooded" with work, followed by periods of no work.

As these two perspectives are ultimately two sides of the same coin, we are interested in bringing these two views together. This is the fundamental idea of process analysis.

FIGURE 2.5
Usage of the Main Room

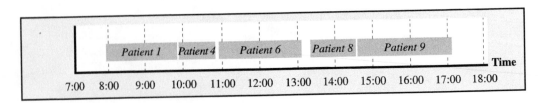

2.2   Three Measures of Process Performance

At the most aggregate level, a process can be thought of as a "black box" that uses *resources* (labor and capital) to transform *inputs* (undiagnosed patients, raw materials, unserved customers) into *outputs* (diagnosed patients, finished goods, served customers). This is shown in Figure 2.6. Chapter 3 explains the details of constructing figures like Figure 2.6, which are called *process flow diagrams*. When analyzing the processes that lead to the supply of goods and services, we first define our unit of analysis.

In the case of the interventional radiology unit, we choose patients as our *flow unit*. Choosing the flow unit is typically determined by the type of product or service the supply process is dealing with; for example, vehicles in an auto plant, travelers for an airline, or gallons of beer in a brewery.

As suggested by the term, flow units flow through the process, starting as input and later leaving the process as output. With the appropriate flow unit defined, we next can evaluate a process based on three fundamental process performance measures:

- The number of flow units contained within the process is called the *inventory* (in a production setting, it is referred to as *work-in-process, WIP*). Given that our focus is not only on production processes, inventory could take the form of the number of insurance claims or the number of tax returns at the IRS. There are various reasons why we find inventory in processes, which we discuss in greater detail below. While many of us might initially feel uncomfortable with the wording, the inventory in the case of the interventional radiology unit is a group of patients.

- The time it takes a flow unit to get through the process is called the *flow time*. The flow time takes into account that the item (flow unit) may have to wait to be processed because there are other flow units (inventory) in the process potentially competing for the same resources. Flow time is an especially important performance metric in service environments or in other business situations that are sensitive to delays, such as make-to-order production, where the production of the process only begins upon the arrival of the customer order. In a radiology unit, flow time is something that patients are likely to care about: it measures the time from their arrival at the interventional radiology unit to the time patients can go home or return to their hospital unit.

- Finally, the rate at which the process is delivering output (measured in [flow units/unit of time], e.g., units per day) is called the *flow rate* or the *throughput rate*. The maximum rate with which the process can generate supply is called the *capacity* of the process. For December 2, the throughput of the interventional radiology unit was 11 patients per day.

Table 2.2 provides several examples of processes and their corresponding flow rates, inventory levels, and flow times.

You might be somewhat irritated that we have moved away from the idea of supply and demand mismatch for a moment. Moreover, we have not talked about profits so far.

FIGURE 2.6
The Process View of an Organization

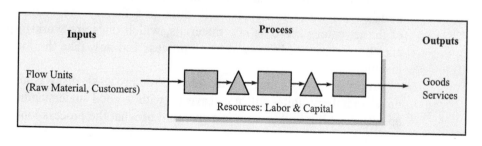

TABLE 2.2
Examples of Flow Rates, Inventories, and Flow Times

	U.S. Immigration	Champagne Industry	MBA Program	Large PC Manufacturer
Flow unit	Application for immigration benefit	Bottle of champagne	MBA student	Computer
Flow rate/ throughput	Approved or rejected visa cases: 6.3 million per year	260 million bottles per year	600 students per year	5,000 units per day
Flow time	Average processing time: 7.6 months	Average time in cellar: 3.46 years	2 years	10 days
Inventory	Pending cases: 4.0 million cases	900 million bottles	1,200 students	50,000 computers

However, note that increasing the maximum flow rate (capacity) avoids situations where we have insufficient supply to match demand. From a profit perspective, a higher flow rate translates directly into more revenues (you can produce a unit faster and thus can produce more units), assuming your process is currently *capacity constrained,* that is, there is sufficient demand that you could sell any additional output you make.

Shorter flow times reduce the time delay between the occurrence of demand and its fulfillment in the form of supply. Shorter flow times therefore also typically help to reduce demand–supply mismatches. In many industries, shorter flow times also result in additional unit sales and/or higher prices, which makes them interesting also from a broader management perspective.

Lower inventory results in lower working capital requirements as well as many quality advantages that we explore later in this book. A higher inventory also is directly related to longer flow times (explained below). Thus, a reduction in inventory also yields a reduction in flow time. As inventory is the most visible indication of a mismatch between supply and demand, we will now discuss it in greater detail.

2.3   Little's Law

Accountants view inventory as an asset, but from an operations perspective, inventory often should be viewed as a liability. This is not a snub on accountants; inventory *should* be an asset on a balance sheet, given how accountants define an asset. But in common speech, the word *asset* means "desirable thing to have" and the dictionary defines *liability* as "something that works to one's disadvantage." In this sense, inventory can clearly be a liability. This is most visible in a service process such as a hospital unit, where patients in the waiting room obviously cannot be counted toward the assets of the health care system.

Let's take another visit to the interventional radiology unit. Even without much medical expertise, we can quickly find out which of the patients are currently undergoing care from some resource and which are waiting for a resource to take care of them. Similarly, if we took a quick walk through a factory, we could identify which parts of the inventory serve as raw materials, which ones are work-in-process, and which ones have completed the production process and now take the form of finished goods inventory.

However, taking a single walk through the process—dishwasher factory or interventional radiology unit—will not leave us with a good understanding of the underlying operations. All it will give us is a snapshot of what the process looked like at one single moment in time. Unfortunately, it is this same snapshot approach that underlies most management (accounting) reports: balance sheets itemize inventory into three categories (raw materials, WIP, finished goods); hospital administrators typically distinguish between pre- and postoperative patients. But such snapshots do not tell us *why* these inventories exist in the first place! Thus, a static, snapshot approach neither helps us to analyze business processes (why is there inventory?) nor helps us to improve them (is this the right amount of inventory?).

Now, imagine that instead of our single visit to the hospital unit, we would be willing to stay for some longer period of time. We arrive early in the morning and make ourselves comfortable at the entrance of the unit. Knowing that there are no patients in the interventional radiology unit overnight, we then start recording any arrival or departure of patients. In other words, we collect data concerning the patient inflow and outflow.

At the end of our stay, we can plot a graph similar to Figure 2.7. The upper of the two curves illustrates the cumulative number of patients who have entered the unit. The curve begins at time zero (7:00) and with zero patients. If we had done the same exercise in a unit with overnight patients, we would have recorded our initial patient count there. The lower of the two curves indicates the cumulative number of patients who have left the unit. Figure 2.7 shows us that by noon, seven patients have arrived, of which five have left the unit again.

At any given moment in time, the *vertical distance* between the upper curve and the lower curve corresponds to the number of patients in the interventional radiology unit, or—abstractly speaking—the inventory level. Thus, although we have not been inside the interventional radiology unit this day, we are able to keep track of the inventory level by comparing the cumulative inflow and outflow. For example, the inventory at noon consisted of two patients.

We also can look at the *horizontal distance* between the two lines. If the patients leave the unit in the same order they entered it, the horizontal gap would measure the exact amount of time each patient spent in the interventional radiology unit. More generally, given that the length of stay might vary across patients and patients do not necessarily leave the unit in the exact same sequence in which they entered it, the average gap between the two lines provides the average length of stay.

FIGURE 2.7
Cumulative Inflow and Outflow

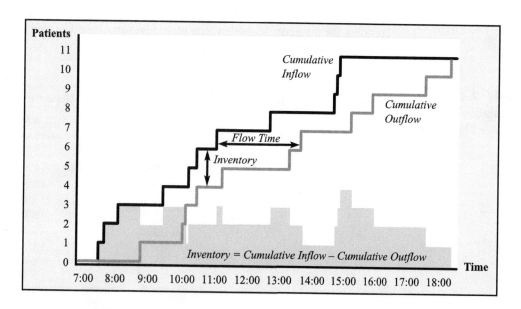

Thus, Figure 2.7 includes all three of the basic process performance measures we discussed on the previous page: flow rate (the slope of the two graphs), inventory (the vertical distance between the two graphs), and flow time (the horizontal distance between the two graphs).

Based on either the graph or the patient log, we can now compute these performance measures for December 2. We already know that the flow rate was 11 patients/day.

Next, consider inventory. Inventory changes throughout the day, reflecting the differences between inflow and outflow of patients. A "brute force" approach to compute average inventory is to count the inventory at every moment in time throughout the day, say every five minutes, and then take the average. For December 2, this computation yields an average inventory of 2.076 patients.

Next, consider the flow time, the time a patient spends in the unit. To compute that information, we need to add to the patient log, Table 2.1, the time each patient left the interventional radiology unit. The difference between arrival time and departure time would be the flow time for a given patient, which in turn would allow us to compute the average flow time across patients. This is shown in Table 2.3 and is in many ways similar to the two graphs in Figure 2.7. We can easily compute that on December 2, the average flow time was 2 hours, 4 minutes, and 33 seconds, or 2.076 hours.

At this point, you might ask: "Does the average inventory always come out the same as the average flow time?" The answer to this question is a resounding *no*. However, the fact that the average inventory was 2.076 patients and the average flow time was 2.076 hours is no coincidence either.

To see how inventory and flow time relate to each other, let us review the three performance measures, flow rate, flow time, and inventory:

- Flow rate = 11 patients per day, which is equal to one patient per hour.
- Flow time = 2.076 hours.
- Inventory = 2.076 patients.

Thus, while inventory and flow time do not have to—and, in fact, rarely are—equal, they are linked in another form. We will now introduce this relationship as Little's Law (named after John D. C. Little).

$$\text{Average inventory} \ = \ \text{Average flow rate} \ \times \ \text{Average flow time} \qquad \text{(Little's Law)}$$

Many people think of this relationship as trivial. However, it is not. Its proof is rather complex for the general case (which includes—among other nasty things—variability) and by mathematical standards is very recent.

TABLE 2.3
Calculation of Average Flow Time

Number	Patient Name	Arrival Time	Departure Time	Flow Time
1		7:35	8:50	1:15
2		7:45	10:05	2:20
3		8:10	10:10	2:00
4		9:30	11:15	1:45
5		10:15	10:30	0:15
6		10:30	13:35	3:05
7		11:05	13:15	2:10
8		12:35	15:05	2:30
9		14:30	18:10	3:40
10		14:35	15:45	1:10
11		14:40	17:20	2:40
			Average	2:04:33

Little's Law is useful in finding the third performance measure when the other two are known. For example, if you want to find out how long patients in a radiology unit spend waiting for their chest X-ray, you could do the following:

1. Observe the inventory of patients at a couple of random points during the day, giving you an average inventory. Let's say this number is seven patients: four in the waiting room, two already changed and waiting in front of the procedure room, and one in the procedure room.

2. Count the procedure slips or any other records showing how many patients were treated that day. This is the day's output. Let's say there were 60 patients over a period of 8 hours; we could say that we have a flow rate of 60/8 = 7.5 patients/hour.

3. Use Little's Law to compute Flow time = Inventory/Flow rate = 7/7.5 = 0.933 hour = 56 minutes. This tells us that, on average, it takes 56 minutes from the time a patient enters the radiology unit to the time his or her chest X-ray is completed. Note that this information would otherwise have to be computed by collecting additional data (e.g., see Table 2.3).

When does Little's Law hold? The short answer is *always*. For example, Little's Law does not depend on the sequence in which the flow units (e.g., patients) are served (remember FIFO and LIFO from your accounting class?). (However, the sequence could influence the flow time of a particular flow unit, e.g., the patient arriving first in the morning, but not the average flow time across all flow units.) Furthermore, Little's Law does not depend on randomness: it does not matter if there is variability in the number of patients or in how long treatment takes for each patient; all that matters is the average flow rate of patients and the average flow time.

In addition to the direct application of Little's Law, for example, in the computation of flow time, Little's Law is also underlying the computation of inventory costs as well as a concept known as inventory turns. This is discussed in the following section.

2.4   Inventory Turns and Inventory Costs

Using physical units as flow units (and, hence, as the inventory measure) is probably the most intuitive way to measure inventory. This could be vehicles at an auto retailer, patients in the hospital, or tons of oil in a refinery.

However, working with physical units is not necessarily the best method for obtaining an aggregate measure of inventory across different products: there is little value to saying you have 2,000 units of inventory if 1,000 of them are paper clips and the remaining 1,000 are computers. In such applications, inventory is often measured in some monetary unit, for example, $5 million worth of inventory.

Measuring inventory in a common monetary unit facilitates the aggregation of inventory across different products. This is why total U.S. inventory is reported in dollars. To illustrate the notion of monetary flow units, consider Kohl's Corp, a large U.S. retailer. Instead of thinking of Kohl's stores as sodas, toys, clothes, and bathroom tissues (physical units), we can think of its stores as processes transforming goods valued in monetary units into sales, which also can be evaluated in the form of monetary units.

As can easily be seen from Kohl's balance sheet, on January 31, 2011, the company held an inventory valued at $3.036 billion (see Table 2.4). Given that our flow unit now is the "individual dollar bill," we want to measure the flow rate through Kohl's operation.

The direct approach would be to take "sales" as the resulting flow. Yet, this measure is inflated by Kohl's gross profit margin; that is, a dollar of sales is measured in sales dol-

TABLE 2.4 Excerpts from Financial Statements of Kohl's and Walmart (All Numbers in Millions)

Source: Taken from 10-K filings.

	2011	2010	2009	2008	2007
Kohl's					
Revenue	$ 18,391	$ 17,178	$ 16,389	$ 16,474	$ 15,544
Cost of Goods Sold	$ 11,359	$ 10,679	$ 10,332	$ 10,459	$ 9,890
Inventory	$ 3,036	$ 2,923	$ 2,799	$ 2,856	$ 2,588
Net Income	$ 1,114	$ 991	$ 885	$ 1,084	$ 1,109
Walmart					
Revenue	$418,952	$ 405,046	$ 401,244	$374,526	$344,992
Cost of Goods Sold	$307,646	$2,97,500	$2,99,419	$280,198	$258,693
Inventory	$ 36,318	$ 33,160	$ 34,511	$ 35,180	$ 33,685
Net Income	$ 16,389	$ 14,335	$ 13,188	$ 12,884	$ 12,036

lars, while a dollar of inventory is measured, given the present accounting practice, in a cost dollar. Thus, the appropriate measure for flow rate is the cost of goods sold, or COGS for short.

With these two measures—flow rate and inventory—we can apply Little's Law to compute what initially might seem a rather artificial measure: how long does the average flow unit (dollar bill) spend within the Kohl's system before being turned into sales, at which point the flow units will trigger a profit intake. This corresponds to the definition of flow time.

$$\text{Flow rate } = \text{ Cost of goods sold } = \$11{,}359 \text{ million/year}$$
$$\text{Inventory } = \$3{,}036 \text{ million}$$

Hence, we can compute flow time via Little's Law as

$$\text{Flow time } = \frac{\text{Inventory}}{\text{Flow rate}}$$
$$= \$3{,}036 \text{ million}/\$11{,}359 \text{ million/year } = 0.267 \text{ year} = 97 \text{ days}$$

Thus, we find that it takes Kohl's—on average—97 days to translate a dollar investment into a dollar of—hopefully profitable—revenues.

This calculation underlies the definition of another way of measuring inventory, namely in terms of *days of supply*. We could say that Kohl's has 97 days of inventory in their process. In other words, the average item we find at Kohl's spends 97 days in Kohl's supply chain.

Alternatively, we could say that Kohl's turns over its inventory 365 days/year/97 days = 3.74 times per year. This measure is called *inventory turns*. Inventory turns is a common benchmark in the retailing environment and other supply chain operations:

$$\text{Inventory turns } = \frac{1}{\text{Flow time}}$$

TABLE 2.5
Inventory Turns and Margins for Selected Retail Segments

Source: Based on Gaur, Fisher, and Raman 2005.

Retail Segment	Examples	Annual Inventory Turns	Gross Margin
Apparel and accessory	Ann Taylor, GAP	4.57	37%
Catalog, mail-order	Spiegel, Lands End	8.60	39%
Department stores	Sears, JCPenney	3.87	34%
Drug and proprietary stores	Rite Aid, CVS	5.26	28%
Food stores	Albertson's, Safeway, Walmart	10.78	26%
Hobby, toy/game stores	Toys R Us	2.99	35%
Home furniture/equipment	Bed Bath & Beyond	5.44	40%
Jewelry	Tiffany	1.68	42%
Radio, TV, consumer electronics	Best Buy, CompUSA	4.10	31%
Variety stores	Kohl's, Walmart, Target	4.45	29%

To illustrate this application of Little's Law further, consider Walmart, one of Kohl's competitors. Repeating the same calculations as outlined on the previous page, we find the following data about Walmart:

$$\text{Cost of goods sold} = \$307,646 \text{ million/year}$$
$$\text{Inventory} = \$36,318 \text{ million}$$
$$\text{Flow time} = \$36,318 \text{ million}/\$307,646 \text{ million/year}$$
$$= 0.118 \text{ year} = 43.1 \text{ days}$$
$$\text{Inventory turns} = 1/43.1 \text{ turns/day}$$
$$= 365 \text{ days/year} \times 1/43.1 \text{ turns/day} = 8.47 \text{ turns per year}$$

Thus, we find that Walmart is able to achieve substantially higher inventory turns than Kohl's. Table 2.5 summarizes inventory turn data for various segments of the retailing industry. Table 2.5 also provides information about gross margins in various retail settings (keep them in mind the next time you haggle for a new sofa or watch!).

Inventory requires substantial financial investments. Moreover, the inventory holding cost is substantially higher than the mere financial holding cost for a number of reasons:

- Inventory might become obsolete (think of the annual holding cost of a microprocessor).
- Inventory might physically perish (you don't want to think of the cost of holding fresh roses for a year).
- Inventory might disappear (also known as theft or shrink).
- Inventory requires storage space and other overhead cost (insurance, security, real estate, etc.).
- There are other less tangible costs of inventory that result from increased wait times (because of Little's Law, to be discussed in Chapter 8) and lower quality (to be discussed in Chapter 11).

Given an annual cost of inventory (e.g., 20 percent per year) and the inventory turn information as computed above, we can compute the per-unit inventory cost that a process (or a supply chain) incurs. To do this, we take the annual holding cost and divide it by the number of times the inventory turns in a year:

$$\text{Per-unit inventory costs} = \frac{\text{Annual inventory costs}}{\text{Annual inventory turns}}$$

Exhibit 2.1

CALCULATING INVENTORY TURNS AND PER-UNIT INVENTORY COSTS

1. Look up the value of inventory from the balance sheet.
2. Look up the cost of goods sold (COGS) from the earnings statement; do *not* use sales!
3. Compute inventory turns as

$$\text{Inventory turns} = \frac{\text{COGS}}{\text{Inventory}}$$

4. Compute per-unit inventory costs as

$$\text{Per-unit inventory costs} \quad \frac{\text{Annual inventory costs}}{\text{Inventory turns}}$$

Note: The annual inventory cost needs to account for the cost of financing the inventory, the cost of depreciation, and other inventory-related costs the firm considers relevant (e.g., storage, theft).

For example, a company that works based on a 20 percent annual inventory cost and that turns its inventory six times per year incurs per-unit inventory costs of

$$\frac{20\% \text{ per year}}{6 \text{ turns per year}} = 3.33\%$$

In the case of Kohl's (we earlier computed that the inventory turns 3.74 times per year), and assuming annual holding costs of 20 percent per year, this translates to inventory costs of about 5.35 percent of the cost of goods sold (20%/3.74 = 5.35). The calculations to obtain per unit inventory costs are summarized in Exhibit 2.1.

To stay in the retailing context a little longer, consider a retailer of consumer electronics who has annual inventory costs of 30 percent (driven by financial costs and obsolescence). Assuming the retailer turns its inventory about four times per year (see Table 2.5.), we obtain a per-unit inventory cost of 30%/4 = 7.5%. Consider a TV in the retailer's assortment that is on the shelf with a price tag of $300 and is procured by the retailer for $200. Based on our calculation, we know that the retailer incurs a $200 × 7.5% = $15 inventory cost for each such TV that is sold. To put this number into perspective, consider Figure 2.8.

Figure 2.8 plots the relationship between gross margin and inventory turns for consumer electronics retailers (based on Gaur, Fisher, and Raman 2005). Note that this graph does not imply causality in this relationship. That is, the model does not imply that if a firm increases its gross margin, its inventory turns will decline automatically. Instead, the way to look at Figure 2.8 is to think of gross margin for a given set of products as being fixed by the competitive environment. We can then make two interesting observations:

- A retailer can decide to specialize in products that turn very slowly to increase its margins. For example, Radio Shack is known for its high margins, as they carry many products in their assortment that turn only once or twice a year. In contrast, Best Buy is carrying largely very popular items, which exposes the company to stiffer competition and lower gross margins.

- For a given gross margin, we observe dramatic differences concerning inventory turns. For example, inventory turns vary between four and nine times for a 15 percent gross margin. Consider retailer A and assume that all retailers work with a 30 percent annual holding cost. Based on the annual inventory turns of 4.5, retailer A faces a 6.66 percent per-unit inventory cost. Now, compare this to competing retailer B, who turns its inventory eight times per year. Thus, retailer B operates with 3.75 percent per-unit inventory

FIGURE 2.8

Relationship between Inventory Turns and Gross Margin

Source: Based on Gaur, Fisher, and Raman 2005.

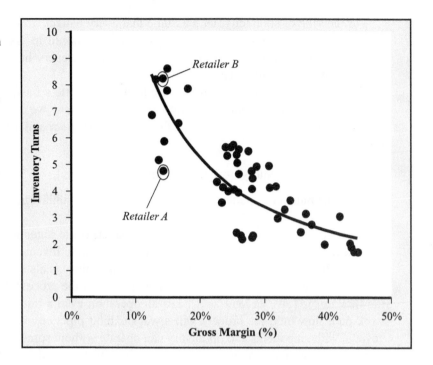

costs, almost a 3 percent cost advantage over retailer A. Given that net profits in this industry segment are around 2 percent of sales, such a cost advantage can make the difference between profits and bankruptcy.

2.5 Five Reasons to Hold Inventory

While Little's Law allows us to compute the average inventory in the process (as long as we know flow time and flow rate), it offers no help in answering the question we raised previously: Why is there inventory in the process in the first place? To understand the need for inventory, we can no longer afford to take the black-box perspective and look at processes from the outside. Instead, we have to look at the process in much more detail.

As we saw from Figure 2.7, inventory reflected a deviation between the inflow into a process and its outflow. Ideally, from an operations perspective, we would like Figure 2.7 to take the shape of two identical, straight lines, representing process inflow and outflow. Unfortunately, such straight lines with zero distance between them rarely exist in the real world. De Groote (1994) discusses five reasons for holding inventory, that is, for having the inflow line differ from the outflow line: (1) the time a flow unit spends in the process, (2) seasonal demand, (3) economies of scale, (4) separation of steps in a process, and (5) stochastic demand. Depending on the reason for holding inventory, inventories are given different names: pipeline inventory, seasonal inventory, cycle inventory, decoupling inventory/ buffers, and safety inventory. It should be noted that these five reasons are not necessarily mutually exclusive and that, in practice, there typically exist more than one reason for holding inventory.

Pipeline Inventory

This first reason for inventory reflects the time a flow unit has to spend in the process in order to be transformed from input to output. Even with unlimited resources, patients still need to spend time in the interventional radiology unit; their flow time would be the length of the critical path. We refer to this basic inventory on which the process operates as *pipeline inventory*.

For the sake of simplicity, let's assume that every patient would have to spend exactly 1.5 hours in the interventional radiology unit, as opposed to waiting for a resource to become available, and that we have one patient arrive every hour. How do we find the pipeline inventory in this case?

The answer is obtained through an application of Little's Law. Because we know two of the three performance measures, flow time and flow rate, we can figure out the third, in this case inventory: with a flow rate of one patient per hour and a flow time of 1.5 hours, the average inventory is

$$\text{Inventory} = 1[\text{patient/hour}] \times 1.5[\text{hours}] = 1.5 \text{ patients}$$

which is the number of patients undergoing some value-adding activity. This is illustrated by Figure 2.9.

In certain environments, you might hear managers make statements of the type "we need to achieve zero inventory in our process." If we substitute Inventory = 0 into Little's Law, the immediate result is that a process with zero inventory is also a process with zero flow rate (unless we have zero flow time, which means that the process does not do anything to the flow unit). Thus, as long as it takes an operation even a minimum amount of time to work on a flow unit, the process will always exhibit pipeline inventory. There can be no hospital without patients and no factory can operate without some work in process!

Little's Law also points us toward the best way to reduce pipeline inventory. As reducing flow rate (and with it demand and profit) is typically not a desirable option, the *only* other way to reduce pipeline inventory is by reducing flow time.

Seasonal Inventory

Seasonal inventory occurs when capacity is rigid and demand is variable. Two examples illustrate this second reason for inventory. Campbell's Soup sells more chicken noodle soup in January than in any other month of the year (see Chapter 17)—not primarily because of cold weather, but because Campbell's discounts chicken noodle soup in January. June is the next biggest sales month, because Campbell's increases its price in July.

So much soup is sold in January that Campbell's starts production several months in advance and builds inventory in anticipation of January sales. Campbell's could wait longer to start production and thereby not build as much inventory, but it would be too costly to assemble the needed capacity (equipment and labor) in the winter only to dismantle that capacity at the end of January when it is no longer needed.

In other words, as long as it is costly to add and subtract capacity, firms will desire to smooth production relative to sales, thereby creating the need for seasonal inventory.

FIGURE 2.9
Pipeline Inventory

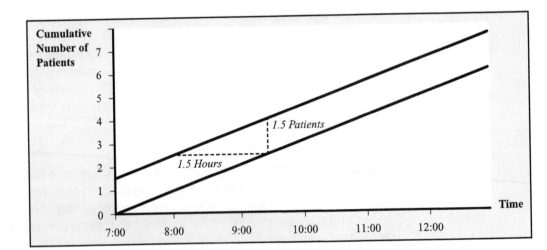

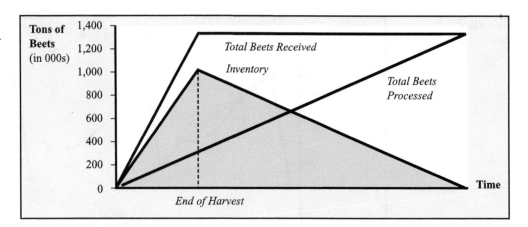

FIGURE 2.10
Seasonal Inventory—
Sugar

An extreme case of seasonal inventory can be found in the agricultural and food processing sector. Due to the nature of the harvesting season, Monitor Sugar, a large sugar cooperative in the U.S. Midwest, collects all raw material for their sugar production over a period of six weeks. At the end of the harvesting season, they have accumulated—in the very meaning of the word—a pile of sugar beets, about 1 million tons, taking the form of a 67-acre sugar beets pile.

Given that food processing is a very capital-intense operation, the process is sized such that the 1.325 million tons of beets received and the almost 1 million tons of inventory that is built allow for a nonstop operation of the production plant until the beginning of the next harvesting season. Thus, as illustrated by Figure 2.10, the production, and hence the product outflow, is close to constant, while the product inflow is zero except for the harvesting season.

Cycle Inventory

Throughout this book, we will encounter many situations in which it is economical to process several flow units collectively at a given moment in time to take advantage of scale economies in operations.

The scale economics in transportation processes provide a good example for the third reason for inventory. Whether a truck is dispatched empty or full, the driver is paid a fixed amount and a sizeable portion of the wear and tear on the truck depends on the mileage driven, not on the load carried. In other words, each truck shipment incurs a fixed cost that is independent of the amount shipped. To mitigate the sting of that fixed cost, it is tempting to load the truck completely, thereby dividing the fixed cost across the largest number of units.

In many cases, this indeed may be a wise decision. But a truck often carries more product than can be immediately sold. Hence, it takes some time to sell off the entire truck delivery. During that interval of time, there will be inventory. This inventory is labeled *cycle inventory* as it reflects that the transportation process follows a certain shipment cycle (e.g., a shipment every week).

Figure 2.11 plots the inventory level of a simple tray that is required during the operation in the interventional radiology unit. As we can see, there exists a "lumpy" inflow of units, while the outflow is relatively smooth. The reason for this is that—due to the administrative efforts related to placing orders for the trays—the hospital only places one order per week.

The major difference between cycle inventory and seasonal inventory is that seasonal inventory is due to temporary imbalances in supply and demand due to variable demand (soup) or variable supply (beets) while cycle inventory is created due to a cost motivation.

FIGURE 2.11
Cycle Inventory

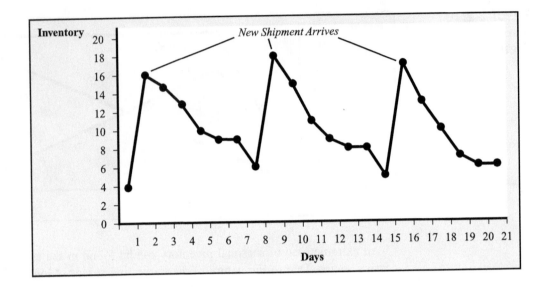

Decoupling Inventory/Buffers

Inventory between process steps can serve as buffers. An inventory buffer allows management to operate steps independently from each other. For example, consider two workers in a garment factory. Suppose the first worker sews the collar onto a shirt and the second sews the buttons. A buffer between them is a pile of shirts with collars but no buttons. Because of that buffer, the first worker can stop working (e.g., to take a break, repair the sewing machine, or change thread color) while the second worker keeps working. In other words, buffers can absorb variations in flow rates by acting as a source of supply for a downstream process step, even if the previous operation itself might not be able to create this supply at the given moment in time.

An automotive assembly line is another example of a production process that uses buffers to decouple the various stations involved with producing the vehicle. In the absence of such buffers, a disruption at any one station would lead to a disruption of all the other stations, upstream and downstream. Think of a bucket brigade to fight a fire: There are no buffers between firefighters in a bucket brigade, so nobody can take a break without stopping the entire process.

Safety Inventory

The final reason for inventory is probably the most obvious, but also the most challenging: stochastic demand. Stochastic demand refers to the fact that we need to distinguish between the predicted demand and the actually realized demand. In other words, we typically face variation in demand relative to our demand prediction. Note that this is different from variations in predictable demand, which is called *seasonality,* like a sales spike of Campbell's chicken noodle soup in January. Furthermore, stochastic demand can be present along with seasonal demand: January sales can be known to be higher than those for other months (seasonal demand) and there can be variation around that known forecast (stochastic demand).

Stochastic demand is an especially significant problem in retailing environments or at the finished goods level of manufacturers. Take a book retailer that must decide how many books to order of a given title. The book retailer has a forecast for demand, but forecasts are (at best) correct on average. Order too many books and the retailer is faced with leftover inventory. Order too few and valuable sales are lost. This trade-off can be managed, as we will discover in Chapter 12, but not eliminated (unless there are zero forecast errors).

FIGURE 2.12
Safety Inventory at
a Blood Bank

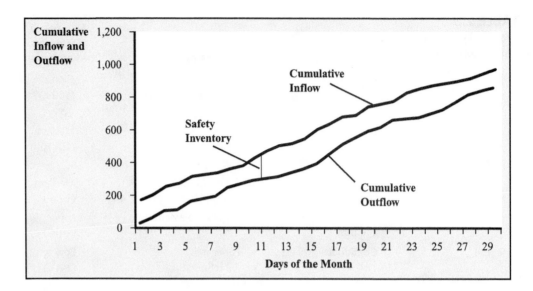

The resulting inventory thereby can be seen as a way to hedge against the underlying demand uncertainty. It might reflect a one-shot decision, for example, in the case of a book retailer selling short-life-cycle products such as newspapers or magazines. If we consider a title with a longer product life cycle (e.g., children's books), the book retailer will be able to replenish books more or less continuously over time.

Figure 2.12 shows the example of the blood bank in the Presbyterian Hospital in Philadelphia. While the detailed inflow and consumption of blood units vary over the course of the month, the hospital always has a couple of days of blood in inventory. Given that blood perishes quickly, the hospital wants to keep only a small inventory at its facility, which it replenishes from the regional blood bank operated by the Red Cross.

2.6   The Product–Process Matrix

Processes leading to the supply of goods or services can take many different forms. Some processes are highly automated, while others are largely manual. Some processes resemble the legendary Ford assembly line, while others resemble more the workshop in your local bike store. Empirical research in operations management, which has looked at thousands of processes, has identified five "clusters" or types of processes. Within each of the five clusters, processes are very similar concerning variables such as the number of different product variants they offer or the production volume they provide. Table 2.6 describes these different types of processes.

By looking at the evolution of a number of industries, Hayes and Wheelwright (1979) observed an interesting pattern, which they referred to as the product–process matrix (see Figure 2.13). The product–process matrix stipulates that over its life cycle, a product typically is initially produced in a job shop process. As the production volume of the product increases, the production process for the product moves from the upper left of the matrix to the lower right.

For example, the first automobiles were produced using job shops, typically creating one product at a time. Most automobiles were unique; not only did they have different colors or add-ons, but they differed in size, geometry of the body, and many other aspects. Henry Ford's introduction of the assembly line corresponded to a major shift along the diagonal of the product–process matrix. Rather than producing a couple of products in a job shop, Ford produced thousands of vehicles on an assembly line.

TABLE 2.6
Process Types and Their Characteristics

	Examples	Number of Different Product Variants	Product Volume (Units/Year)
Job shop	• Design company • Commercial printer • Formula 1 race car	High (100+)	Low (1–100)
Batch process	• Apparel sewing • Bakery • Semiconductor wafers	Medium (10–100)	Medium (100–100k)
Worker-paced line flow	• Auto assembly • Computer assembly	Medium (1–50)	High (10k–1M)
Machine-paced line flow	• Large auto assembly	Low (1–10)	High (10k–1M)
Continuous process	• Paper mill • Oil refinery • Food processing	Low (1–10)	Very high

Note that the "off-diagonals" in the product–process matrix (the lower left and the upper right) are empty. This reflects that it is neither economical to produce very high volumes in a job shop (imagine if all of the millions of new vehicles sold in the United States every year were handcrafted in the same manner as Gottlieb Daimler created the first automobile) nor does it make sense to use an assembly line in order to produce only a handful of products a year.

We have to admit that few companies—if any—would be foolish enough to produce a high-volume product in a job shop. However, identifying a process type and looking at the product–process matrix is more than an academic exercise in industrial history. The usefulness of the product–process matrix lies in two different points:

1. Similar process types tend to have similar problems. For example, as we will discuss in Chapter 4, assembly lines tend to have the problem of line balancing (some workers working harder than others). Batch-flow processes tend to be slow in responding to

FIGURE 2.13
Product–Process Matrix

Source: Hayes and Wheelwright (1979).

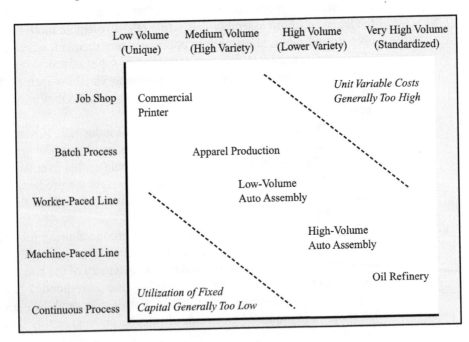

customer demand (see Chapter 7). Thus, once you know a process type, you can quickly determine what type of problems the process is likely to face and what solution methods are most appropriate.

2. The "natural drift" of industries toward the lower right of Figure 2.13 enables you to predict how processes are likely to evolve in a particular industry. Consider, for example, the case of eye surgery. Up until the 1980s, corrective eye surgery was done in large hospitals. There, doctors would perform a large variety of very different eye-related cases. Fifteen years later, this situation had changed dramatically. Many highly specialized eye clinics have opened, most of them focusing on a limited set of procedures. These clinics achieve high volume and, because of the high volume and the lower variety of cases, can operate at much higher levels of efficiency. Similarly, semiconductor production equipment used to be assembled on a one-by-one basis, while now companies such as Applied Materials and Kulicke & Soffa operate worker-paced lines.

2.7 Summary

In this chapter, we emphasized the importance of looking at the operations of a firm not just in terms of the products that the firm supplies, but also at the processes that generate the supply. Looking at processes is especially important with respect to demand–supply mismatches. From the perspective of the product, such mismatches take the form of waiting times; from the perspective of the process, they take the form of inventory.

For any process, we can define three fundamental performance measures: inventory, flow time, and flow rate. The three measures are related by Little's Law, which states that the average inventory is equal to the average flow time multiplied by the average flow rate.

Little's Law can be used to find any of the three performance measures, as long as the other two measures are known. This is specifically important with respect to flow time, which is in practice frequently difficult to observe directly.

A measure related to flow time is inventory turns. Inventory turns, measured by 1/(flow time), captures how fast the flow units are transformed from input to output. It is an important benchmark in many industries, especially retailing. Inventory turns are also the basis of computing the inventory costs associated with one unit of supply.

2.8 Further Reading

De Groote (1994) is a very elegant note describing the basic roles of inventory. This note, as well as many other notes and articles by de Groote, takes a very "lean" perspective to operations management, resembling much more the tradition of economics as opposed to engineering.

Gaur, Fisher, and Raman (2005) provide an extensive study of retailing performance. They present various operational measures, including inventory turns, and show how they relate to financial performance measures.

The Hayes and Wheelwright (1979) reference is widely recognized as a pioneering article linking operations aspects to business strategy. Subsequent work by Hayes, Wheelwright, and Clark (1988) established operations as a key source for a firm's competitive advantage.

2.9 Practice Problems

Q2.1*   **(Dell)** What percentage of cost of a Dell computer reflects inventory costs? Assume Dell's yearly inventory cost is 40 percent to account for the cost of capital for financing the inventory, the warehouse space, and the cost of obsolescence. In other words, Dell incurs a cost of $40 for a $100 component that is in the company's inventory for one entire year. In 2001, Dell's 10-k reports showed that the company had $400 million in inventory and COGS of $26,442 million.

Q2.2   **(Airline)** Consider the baggage check-in of a small airline. Check-in data indicate that from 9 a.m. to 10 a.m., 255 passengers checked in. Moreover, based on counting the number of

(* indicates that the solution is at the end of the book)

passengers waiting in line, airport management found that the average number of passengers waiting for check-in was 35. How long did the average passenger have to wait in line?

Q2.3 **(Inventory Cost)** A manufacturing company producing medical devices reported $60,000,000 in sales over the last year. At the end of the same year, the company had $20,000,000 worth of inventory of ready-to-ship devices.

a. Assuming that units in inventory are valued (based on COGS) at $1,000 per unit and are sold for $2,000 per unit, how fast does the company turn its inventory? The company uses a 25 percent per year cost of inventory. That is, for the hypothetical case that one unit of $1,000 would sit exactly one year in inventory, the company charges its operations division a $250 inventory cost.

b. What—in absolute terms—is the per unit inventory cost for a product that costs $1,000?

Q2.4** **(Apparel Retailing)** A large catalog retailer of fashion apparel reported $100,000,000 in revenues over the last year. On average, over the same year, the company had $5,000,000 worth of inventory in their warehouses. Assume that units in inventory are valued based on cost of goods sold (COGS) and that the retailer has a 100 percent markup on all products.

a. How many times each year does the retailer turn its inventory?

b. The company uses a 40 percent per year cost of inventory. That is, for the hypothetical case that one item of $100 COGS would sit exactly one year in inventory, the company charges itself a $40 inventory cost. What is the inventory cost for a $30 (COGS) item? You may assume that inventory turns are independent of the price.

Q2.5 **(LaVilla)** LaVilla is a village in the Italian Alps. Given its enormous popularity among Swiss, German, Austrian, and Italian skiers, all of its beds are always booked in the winter season and there are, on average, 1,200 skiers in the village. On average, skiers stay in LaVilla for 10 days.

a. How many new skiers are arriving—on average—in LaVilla every day?

b. A study done by the largest hotel in the village has shown that skiers spend on average $50 per person on the first day and $30 per person on each additional day in local restaurants. The study also forecasts that—due to increased hotel prices—the average length of stay for the 2003/2004 season will be reduced to five days. What will be the percentage change in revenues of local restaurants compared to last year (when skiers still stayed for 10 days)? Assume that hotels continue to be fully booked!

Q2.6 **(Highway)** While driving home for the holidays, you can't seem to get Little's Law out of your mind. You note that your average speed of travel is about 60 miles per hour. Moreover, the traffic report from the WXPN traffic chopper states that there is an average of 24 cars going in your direction on a one-quarter mile part of the highway. What is the flow rate of the highway (going in your direction) in cars per hour?

Q2.7 **(Industrial Baking Process)** Strohrmann, a large-scale bakery in Pennsylvania, is laying out a new production process for their packaged bread, which they sell to several grocery chains. It takes 12 minutes to bake the bread. How large an oven is required so that the company is able to produce 4,000 units of bread per hour (measured in the number of units that can be baked simultaneously)?

Q2.8** **(Mt. Kinley Consulting)** Mt. Kinley is a strategy consulting firm that divides its consultants into three classes: associates, managers, and partners. The firm has been stable in size for the last 20 years, ignoring growth opportunities in the 90s, but also not suffering from a need to downsize in the recession at the beginning of the 21st century. Specifically, there have been—and are expected to be—200 associates, 60 managers, and 20 partners.

The work environment at Mt. Kinley is rather competitive. After four years of working as an associate, a consultant goes "either up or out"; that is, becomes a manager or is dismissed from the company. Similarly, after six years, a manager either becomes a partner or is dismissed. The company recruits MBAs as associate consultants; no hires are made at the manager or partner level. A partner stays with the company for another 10 years (a total of 20 years with the company).

    a. How many new MBA graduates does Mt. Kinley have to hire every year?

    b. What are the odds that a new hire at Mt. Kinley will become partner (as opposed to being dismissed after 4 years or 10 years)?

Q2.9   **(Major U.S. Retailers)** The following table shows financial data (year 2004) for Costco Wholesale and Walmart, two major U.S. retailers.

	Costco	Walmart
	($ Millions)	($ Millions)
Inventories	$ 3,643	$ 29,447
Sales (net)	$48,106	$286,103
COGS	$41,651	$215,493

Source: Compustat, WRDS.

Assume that both companies have an average annual holding cost rate of 30 percent (i.e., it costs both retailers $3 to hold an item that they procured for $10 for one entire year).

    a. How many days, on average, does a product stay in Costco's inventory before it is sold? Assume that stores are operated 365 days a year.

    b. How much lower is, on average, the inventory cost for Costco compared to Walmart of a household cleaner valued at $5 COGS? Assume that the unit cost of the household cleaner is the same for both companies and that the price and the inventory turns of an item are independent.

Q2.10   **(McDonald's)** The following figures are taken from the 2003 financial statements of McDonald's and Wendy's.[1] Figures are in million dollars.

	McDonald's	Wendy's
Inventory	$ 129.4	$ 54.4
Revenue	17,140.5	3,148.9
Cost of goods sold	11,943.7	1,634.6
Gross profit	5,196.8	1,514.4

    a. In 2003, what were McDonald's inventory turns? What were Wendy's inventory turns?

    b. Suppose it costs both McDonald's and Wendy's $3 (COGS) per their value meal offerings, each sold at the same price of $4. Assume that the cost of inventory for both companies is 30 percent a year. Approximately how much does McDonald's save in inventory cost *per value meal* compared to that of Wendy's? You may assume the inventory turns are independent of the price.

[1] Example adopted from an About.com article (http://beginnersinvest.about.com/cs/investinglessons/1/blles3mcwen.htm). Financial figures taken from Morningstar.com.

You can view a video of how problems marked with a ** are solved by going on www.cachon-terwiesch.net and follow the links under 'Solved Practice Problems'

Solutions to Selected Practice Problems

Chapter 2

Q2.1 (Dell)

The following steps refer directly to Exhibit 2.1.

Step 1. For 2001, we find in Dell's 10-k: Inventory = \$400 (in millions)

Step 2. For 2001, we find in Dell's 10-k: COGS = \$26,442 (in millions)

Step 3. Inventory turns $= \dfrac{\$26,442/\text{Year}}{\$400} = 66.105$ turns per year

Step 4. Per-unit inventory cost $= \dfrac{40\% \text{ per year}}{66.105 \text{ per year}} = 0.605$ percent per unit

Chapter 3

Understanding the Supply Process: Evaluating Process Capacity

In the attempt to match supply with demand, an important measure is the maximum amount that a process can produce in a given unit of time, a measure referred to as the *process capacity*. To determine the process capacity of an operation, we need to analyze the operation in much greater detail compared to the previous chapter. Specifically, we need to understand the various activities involved in the operation and how these activities contribute toward fulfilling the overall demand.

In this chapter, you will learn how to perform a process analysis. Unlike Chapter 2, where we felt it was sufficient to treat the details of the operation as a black box and merely focus on the performance measures inventory, flow time, and flow rate, we now will focus on the underlying process in great detail.

Despite this increase in detail, this chapter (and this book) is not taking the perspective of an engineer. In fact, in this chapter, you will learn how to take a fairly technical and complex operation and simplify it to a level suitable for managerial analysis. This includes preparing a process flow diagram, finding the capacity and the bottleneck of the process, computing the utilization of various process steps, and computing a couple of other performance measures.

We will illustrate this new material with the Circored plant, a joint venture between the German engineering company Lurgi AG and the U.S. iron ore producer Cleveland Cliffs. The Circored plant converts iron ore (in the form of iron ore fines) into direct reduced iron (DRI) briquettes. Iron ore fines are shipped to the plant from mines in South America; the briquettes the process produces are shipped to various steel mills in the United States.

The example of the Circored process is particularly useful for our purposes in this chapter. The underlying process is complex and in many ways a masterpiece of process engineering (see Terwiesch and Loch [2002] for further details). At first sight, the process is so complex that it seems impossible to understand the underlying process behavior without a detailed background in engineering and metallurgy. This challenging setting allows us to demonstrate how process analysis can be used to "tame the beast" and create a managerially useful view of the process, avoiding any unnecessary technical details.

3.1   How to Draw a Process Flow Diagram

The best way to begin any analysis of an operation is by drawing a *process flow diagram.* A process flow diagram is a graphical way to describe the process and it will help us to structure the information that we collect during the case analysis or process improvement project. Before we turn to the question of how to draw a process flow diagram, first consider alternative approaches to how we could capture the relevant information about a process.

Looking at the plant from above (literally), we get a picture as is depicted in Figure 3.1. At the aggregate level, the plant consists of a large inventory of iron ore (input), the plant itself (the resource), and a large inventory of finished briquettes (output). In many ways, this corresponds to the black box approach to operations taken by economists and many other managerial disciplines.

In an attempt to understand the details of the underlying process, we could turn to the engineering specifications of the plant. Engineers are interested in a detailed description of the various steps involved in the overall process and how these steps are functioning. Such descriptions, typically referred to as specifications, were used in the actual construction of the plant. Figure 3.2 provides one of the numerous specification drawings for the Circored process.

Unfortunately, this attempt to increase our understanding of the Circored process is also only marginally successful. Like the photograph, this view of the process is also a rather static one: It emphasizes the equipment, yet provides us with little understanding of how the iron ore moves through the process. In many ways, this view of a process is similar to taking the architectural drawings of a hospital and hoping that this would lead to insights about what happens to the patients in this hospital.

In a third—and final—attempt to get our hands around this complex process, we change our perspective from the one of the visitor to the plant (photo in Figure 3.1) or the engineers who built the plant (drawing in Figure 3.2) to the perspective of the iron ore itself

FIGURE 3.1
Photo of the Circored Plant

Source: Terwiesch and Loch 2002.

FIGURE 3.2 Engineering Drawing

Source: Terwiesch and Loch 2002.

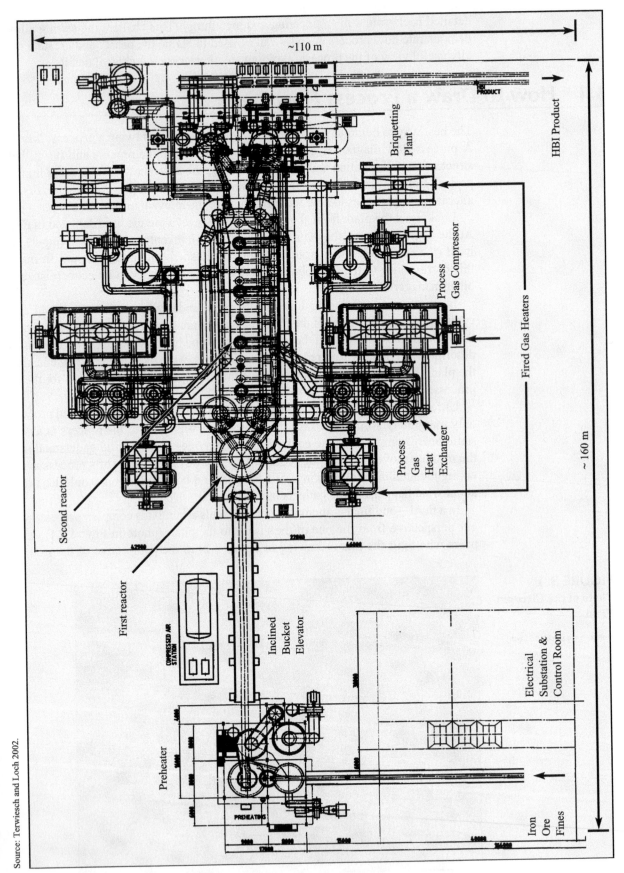

Briquetting Plant

Process Gas Compressor

Fired Gas Heaters

Process Gas Heat Exchanger

HBI Product

Second reactor

First reactor

Inclined Bucket Elevator

COMPRESSED AIR STATION

Preheater

PREHEATING

Electrical Substation & Control Room

Iron Ore Fines

~110 m

~ 160 m

and how it flows through the process. Thus, we define a unit of iron ore—a ton, a pound, or a molecule—as our flow unit and "attach" ourselves to this flow unit as it makes its journey through the process. This is similar to taking the perspective of the patient in a hospital, as opposed to taking the perspective of the hospital resources. For concreteness, we will define our flow unit to be a ton of iron ore.

To draw a process flow diagram, we first need to focus on a part of the process that we want to analyze in greater detail; that is, we need to define the *process boundaries* and an appropriate level of detail. The placement of the process boundaries will depend on the project we are working on. For example, in the operation of a hospital, one project concerned with patient waiting time might look at what happens to the patient waiting for a lab test (e.g., check-in, waiting time, encounter with the nurse). In this project, the encounter with the doctor who requested the lab test would be outside the boundaries of the analysis. Another project related to the quality of surgery, however, might look at the encounter with the doctor in great detail, while either ignoring the lab or treating it with less detail.

A process operates on flow units, which are the entities flowing through the process (e.g., patients in a hospital, cars in an auto plant, insurance claims at an insurance company). A process flow diagram is a collection of boxes, triangles, and arrows (see Figure 3.3). Boxes stand for process activities, where the operation adds value to the flow unit. Depending on the level of detail we choose, a process step (a box) can itself be a process.

Triangles represent waiting areas or *buffers* holding inventory. In contrast to a process step, inventories do not add value; thus, a flow unit does not have to spend time in them. However, as discussed in the previous chapter, there are numerous reasons why the flow unit might spend time in inventory even if it will not be augmented to a higher value there.

FIGURE 3.3
Elements of a Process

Source: Terwiesch and Loch 2002.

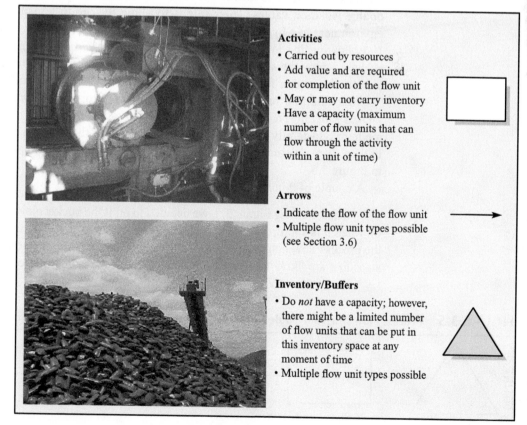

Activities

- Carried out by resources
- Add value and are required for completion of the flow unit
- May or may not carry inventory
- Have a capacity (maximum number of flow units that can flow through the activity within a unit of time)

Arrows

- Indicate the flow of the flow unit
- Multiple flow unit types possible (see Section 3.6)

Inventory/Buffers

- Do *not* have a capacity; however, there might be a limited number of flow units that can be put in this inventory space at any moment of time
- Multiple flow unit types possible

FIGURE 3.4
Process Flow
Diagram, First Step

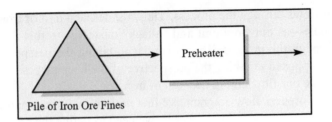

The arrows between boxes and triangles represent the route the flow unit takes through the process. If there are different flow units that take different routes through the process, it can be helpful to use different colors for the different routes. An example of this is given at the end of this chapter.

In the Circored plant, the first step the flow unit encounters in the process is the *preheater*, where the iron ore fines (which have a texture like large-grained sand) are dried and heated. The heating is achieved through an inflow of high-pressured air, which is blown into the preheater from the bottom. The high-speed air flow "fluidizes" the ore, meaning that the mixed air–ore mass (a "sandstorm") circulates through the system as if it was a fluid, while being heated to a temperature of approximately 850–900°C.

However, from a managerial perspective, we are not really concerned with the temperature in the preheater or the chemical reactions happening therein. For us, the preheater is a resource that receives iron ore from the initial inventory and processes it. In an attempt to take record of what the flow unit has experienced up to this point, we create a diagram similar to Figure 3.4.

From the preheater, a large bucket elevator transports the ore to the second process step, the *lock hoppers*. The lock hoppers consist of three large containers, separated by sets of double isolation valves. Their role is to allow the ore to transition from an oxygen-rich environment to a hydrogen atmosphere.

Following the lock hoppers, the ore enters the *circulating fluid bed reactor*, or *first reactor*, where the actual reduction process begins. The reduction process requires the ore to be in the reactor for 15 minutes, and the reactor can hold up to 28 tons of ore.

After this first reduction, the material flows into the *stationary fluid bed reactor*, or *second reactor*. This second reaction takes about four hours. The reactor is the size of a medium two-family home and contains 400 tons of the hot iron ore at any given moment in time. In the meantime, our diagram from Figure 3.4. has extended to something similar to Figure 3.5.

A couple of things are worth noting at this point:

• When creating Figure 3.5, we decided to omit the bucket elevator. There is no clear rule on when it is appropriate to omit a small step and when a step would have to be included in the process flow diagram. A reasonably good rule of thumb is to only include those process steps that are likely to affect the process flow or the economics of the process. The bucket

FIGURE 3.5   Process Flow Diagram (to Be Continued)

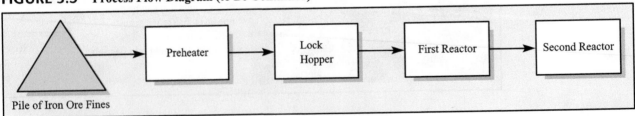

FIGURE 3.6 Completed Process Flow Diagram for the Circored Process

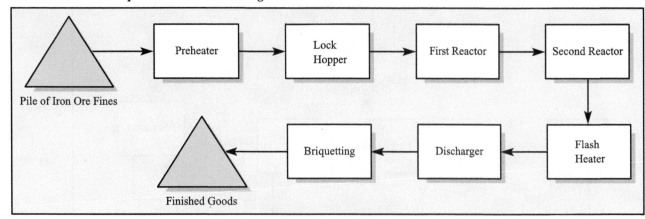

elevator is cheap, the flow units spend little time on it, and this transportation step never becomes a constraint for the process. So it is not included in our process flow diagram.

• The reaction steps are boxes, not triangles, although there is a substantial amount of ore in them, that is, they do hold inventory. The reduction steps are necessary, value-adding steps. No flow unit could ever leave the system without spending time in the reactors. This is why we have chosen boxes over triangles here.

Following the second reactor, the reduced iron enters the *flash heater*, in which a stream of high-velocity hydrogen carries the DRI to the top of the plant while simultaneously reheating it to a temperature of 685°C.

After the flash heater, the DRI enters the *pressure let-down system (discharger)*. As the material passes through the discharger, the hydrogen atmosphere is gradually replaced by inert nitrogen gas. Pressure and hydrogen are removed in a reversal of the lock hoppers at the beginning. Hydrogen gas sensors assure that material leaving this step is free of hydrogen gas and, hence, safe for briquetting.

Each of the three *briquetting* machines contains two wheels that turn against each other, each wheel having the negative of one-half of a briquette on its face. The DRI is poured onto the wheels from the top and is pressed into briquettes, or iron bars, which are then moved to a large pile of finished goods inventory.

This completes our journey of the flow unit through the plant. The resulting process flow diagram that captures what the flow unit has experienced in the process is summarized in Figure 3.6.

When drawing a process flow diagram, the sizes and the exact locations of the arrows, boxes, and triangles do not carry any special meaning. For example, in the context of Figure 3.6, we chose a "U-shaped" layout of the process flow diagram, as otherwise we would have had to publish this book in a larger format.

In the absence of any space constraints, the simplest way to draw a process flow diagram for a process such as Circored's is just as one long line. However, we should keep in mind that there are more complex processes; for example, a process with multiple flow units or a flow unit that visits one and the same resource multiple times. This will be discussed further at the end of the chapter.

Another alternative in drawing the process flow diagram is to stay much closer to the physical layout of the process. This way, the process flow diagram will look familiar for engineers and operators who typically work off the specification drawings (Figure 3.2) and it might help you to find your way around when you are visiting the "real" process. Such an approach is illustrated by Figure 3.7.

FIGURE 3.7 Completed Process Flow Diagram for the Circored Process

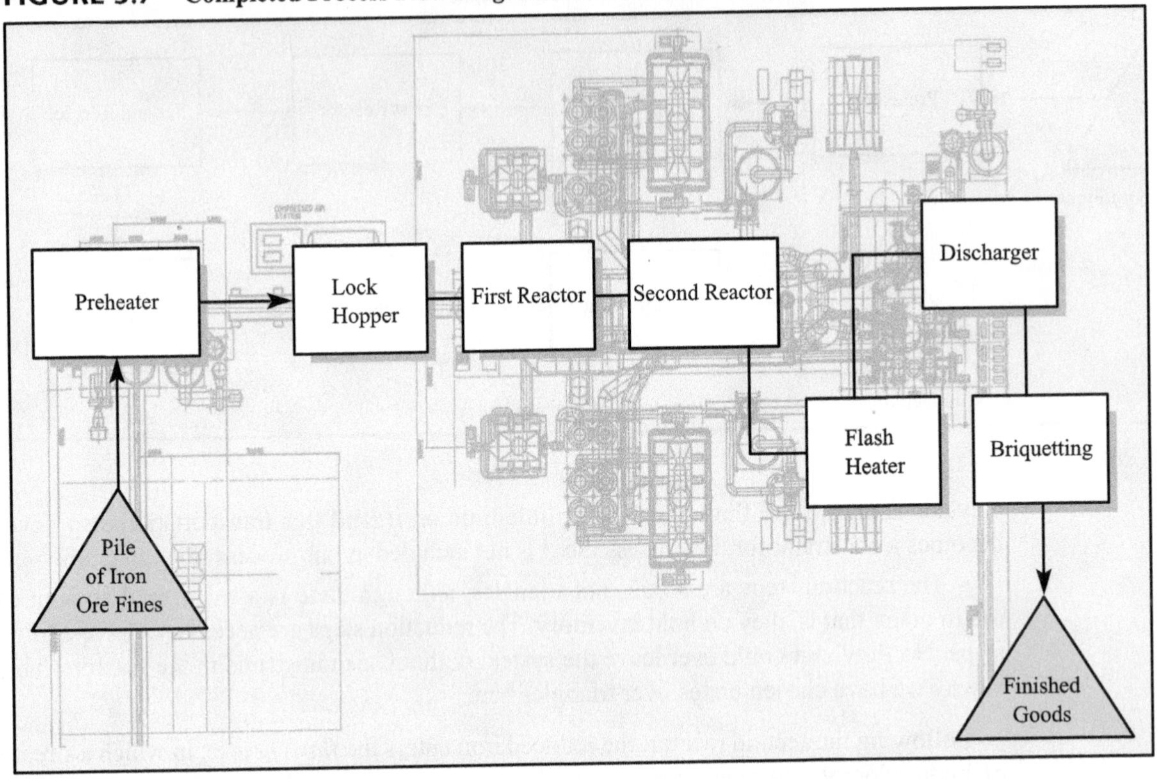

3.2 Bottleneck, Process Capacity, and Flow Rate (Throughput)

From a supply perspective, the most important question that arises is how much direct reduced iron the Circored process can supply in a given unit of time, say one day. This measure is the *capacity* of the process, which we also call the *process capacity*. Not only can capacity be measured at the level of the overall process, it also can be measured at the level of the individual resources that constitute the process. Just as we defined the process capacity, we define the capacity of a resource as the maximum amount the resource can produce in a given time unit.

Note that the process capacity measures how much the process *can* produce, opposed to how much the process actually *does* produce. For example, consider a day where—due to a breakdown or another external event—the process does not operate at all. Its capacity would be unaffected by this, yet the flow rate would reduce to zero. This is similar to your car, which might be able to drive at 130 miles per hour (capacity), but typically—or better, hopefully—only drives at 65 miles per hour (flow rate).

As the completion of a flow unit requires the flow unit to visit every one of the resources in the process, the overall process capacity is determined by the resource with the smallest capacity. We refer to that resource as the *bottleneck*. It provides the weakest link in the overall process chain, and, as we know, a chain is only as strong as its weakest link. More formally, we can write the process capacity as

Process capacity = Minimum{Capacity of resource 1, . . . , Capacity of resource n}

where there are a total of n resources. How much the process actually does produce will depend not only on its capability to create supply (process capacity), but also on the demand for its output as well as the availability of its input. As with capacity, demand and the available input should be measured as rates, that is, as flow units per unit of time. For this process, our flow unit is one ton of ore, so we could define the available input and the demand in terms of tons of ore per hour.

FIGURE 3.8   Supply-Constrained (left) and Demand-Constrained (right) Processes

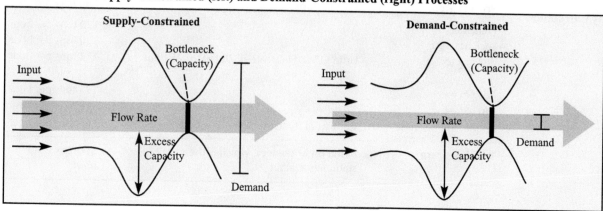

The combination of available input, demand, and process capacity yields the rate at which our flow unit actually flows through the process, called the *flow rate*:

Flow rate = Minimum{Available input, Demand, Process capacity}

If demand is lower than supply (i.e., there is sufficient input available and the process has enough capacity), the process would produce at the rate of demand, independent of the process capacity. We refer to this case as *demand-constrained*. Note that in this definition demand also includes any potential requests for the accumulation of inventory. For example, while the demand for Campbell's chicken noodle soup might be lower than process capacity for the month of November, the process would not be demand-constrained if management decided to accumulate finished goods inventory in preparation for the high sales in the month of January. Thus, demand in our analysis refers to everything that is demanded from the process at a given time.

If demand exceeds supply, the process is *supply-constrained*. Depending on what limits product supply, the process is either input-constrained or capacity-constrained.

Figure 3.8 summarizes the concepts of process capacity and flow rate, together with the notion of demand- versus supply-constrained processes. In the case of the supply-constrained operation, there is sufficient input; thus, the supply constraint reflects a capacity constraint.

To understand how to find the bottleneck in a process and thereby determine the process capacity, consider each of the Circored resources. Note that all numbers are referring to tons of process output. The actual, physical weight of the flow unit might change over the course of the process.

Finding the bottleneck in many ways resembles the job of a detective in a crime story; each activity is a "suspect," in the sense that it could potentially constrain the overall supply of the process:

- The preheater can process 120 tons per hour.
- The lock hoppers can process 110 tons per hour.
- The analysis of the reaction steps is somewhat more complicated. We first observe that at any given moment of time, there can be, at maximum, 28 tons in the first reactor. Given that the iron ore needs to spend 15 minutes in the reactor, we can use Little's Law (see Chapter 2) to see that the maximum amount of ore that can flow through the reactor—and spend 15 minutes in the reactor—is

$$28 \text{ tons} = \text{Flow rate} \times 0.25 \text{ hour} \implies \text{Flow rate} = 112 \text{ tons/hour}$$

Thus, the capacity of the first reactor is 112 tons per hour. Note that a shorter reaction time in this case would translate to a higher capacity.

TABLE 3.1
Capacity Calculation

Process Step	Calculations	Capacity
Preheater		120 tons per hour
Lock hoppers		110 tons per hour
first reactor	Little's Law: Flow rate = 28 tons/0.25 hour	112 tons per hour
Second reactor	Little's Law: Flow rate = 400 tons/4 hours	100 tons per hour
Flash heater		135 tons per hour
Discharger		118 tons per hour
Briquetting machine	Consists of three machines: 3 × 55 tons per hour	165 tons per hour
Total process	Based on bottleneck, which is the stationary reactor	**100 tons per hour**

- We can apply a similar logic for the second reactor, which can hold up to 400 tons:

$$400 \text{ tons} = \text{Flow rate} \times 4 \text{ hours} => \text{Flow rate} = 100 \text{ tons/hour}$$

Thus, the capacity (the maximum possible flow rate through the resource) of the second reactor is 100 tons per hour.

- The flash heater can process 135 tons per hour.
- The discharger has a capacity of 118 tons per hour.
- Each of the three briquetting machines has a capacity of 55 tons per hour. As the briquetting machines collectively form one resource, the capacity at the briquetting machines is simply 3 × 55 tons per hour = 165 tons per hour.

The capacity of each process step is summarized in Table 3.1.

Following the logic outlined above, we can now identify the first reactor as the bottleneck of the Circored process. The overall process capacity is computed as the minimum of the capacities of each resource (all units are in tons per hour):

$$\text{Process capacity} = \text{Minimum} \{120, 110, 112, 100, 135, 118, 165\} = 100$$

3.3 How Long Does It Take to Produce a Certain Amount of Supply?

There are many situations where we need to compute the amount of time required to create a certain amount of supply. For example, in the Circored case, we might ask, "How long does it take for the plant to produce 10,000 tons?" Once we have determined the flow rate of the process, this calculation is fairly straightforward. Let X be the amount of supply we want to fulfill. Then,

$$\text{Time to fullfill } X \text{ units} = \frac{X}{\text{Flow rate}}$$

To answer our question,

$$\text{Time to produce } 10,000 \text{ tons} = \frac{10,000 \text{ tons}}{100 \text{ tons/hour}} = 100 \text{ hours}$$

Note that this calculation assumes the process is already producing output, that is, the first unit in our 10,000 tons flows out of the process immediately. If the process started empty, it would take the first flow unit time to flow through the process. Chapter 4 provides the calculations for that case.

Note that in the previous equation we use flow rate, which in our case is capacity because the system is supply-constrained. However, if our system were demand-constrained, then the flow rate would equal the demand rate.

3.4 Process Utilization and Capacity Utilization

Given the first-of-its-kind nature of the Circored process, the first year of its operation proved to be extremely difficult. In addition to various technical difficulties, demand for the product (reduced iron) was not as high as it could be, as the plant's customers (steel mills) had to be convinced that the output created by the Circored process would be of the high quality required by the steel mills.

While abstracting from details such as scheduled maintenance and inspection times, the plant was designed to achieve a process capacity of 876,000 tons per year (100 tons per hour $\times$ 24 hours/day $\times$ 365 days/year, see above), the demand for iron ore briquettes was only 657,000 tons per year. Thus, there existed a mismatch between demand and potential supply (process capacity).

A common measure of performance that quantifies this mismatch is utilization. We define the *utilization* of a process as

$$\text{Utilization} = \frac{\text{Flow rate}}{\text{Capacity}}$$

Utilization is a measure of how much the process *actually produces* relative to how much it *could produce* if it were running at full speed (i.e., its capacity). This is in line with the example of a car driving at 65 miles per hour (flow rate), despite being able to drive at 130 miles per hour (capacity): the car utilizes 65/130 = 50 percent of its potential.

Utilization, just like capacity, can be defined at the process level or the resource level. For example, the utilization of the process is the flow rate divided by the capacity of the process. The utilization of a particular resource is the flow rate divided by that resource's capacity.

For the Circored case, the resulting utilization is

$$\text{Utilization} = \frac{657,000 \text{ tons per year}}{876,000 \text{ tons per year}} = 0.75 = 75\%$$

In general, there are several reasons why a process might not produce at 100 percent utilization:

- If demand is less than supply, the process typically will not run at full capacity, but only produce at the rate of demand.
- If there is insufficient supply of the input of a process, the process will not be able to operate at capacity.
- If one or several process steps only have a limited availability (e.g., maintenance and breakdowns), the process might operate at full capacity while it is running, but then go into periods of not producing any output while it is not running.

Given that the bottleneck is the resource with the lowest capacity and that the flow rate through all resources is identical, the bottleneck is the resource with the highest utilization.

In the case of the Circored plant, the corresponding utilizations are provided by Table 3.2. Note that all resources in a process with only one flow unit have the same flow

TABLE 3.2
Utilization of the Circored Process Steps Including Downtime

Process Step	Calculations	Utilization
Preheater	657,000 tons/year/[120 tons/hour × 8,760 hours/year]	62.5%
Lock hoppers	657,000 tons/year/[110 tons/hour × 8,760 hours/year]	68.2%
First reactor	657,000 tons/year/[112 tons/hour × 8,760 hours/year]	66.9%
Second reactor	657,000 tons/year/[100 tons/hour × 8,760 hours/year]	75.0%
Flash heater	657,000 tons/year/[135 tons/hour × 8,760 hours/year]	55.6%
Discharger	657,000 tons/year/[118 tons/hour × 8,760 hours/year]	63.6%
Briquetting	657,000 tons/year/[165 tons/hour × 8,760 hours/year]	45.5%
Total process	657,000 tons/year/[100 tons/hour × 8,760 hours/year]	**75%**

rate, which is equal to the overall process flow rate. In this case, this is a flow rate of 657,000 tons per year.

Measuring the utilization of equipment is particularly common in capital-intensive industries. Given limited demand and availability problems, the bottleneck in the Circored process did not operate at 100 percent utilization. We can summarize our computations graphically, by drawing a utilization profile. This is illustrated by Figure 3.9.

Although utilization is commonly tracked, it is a performance measure that should be handled with some care. Specifically, it should be emphasized that the objective of most businesses is to maximize profit, not to maximize utilization. As can be seen in Figure 3.9, there are two reasons in the Circored case for why an individual resource might not achieve 100 percent utilization, thus exhibiting excess capacity.

- First, given that no resource can achieve a higher utilization than the bottleneck, every process step other than the bottleneck will have a utilization gap relative to the bottleneck.

FIGURE 3.9 **Utilization Profile**

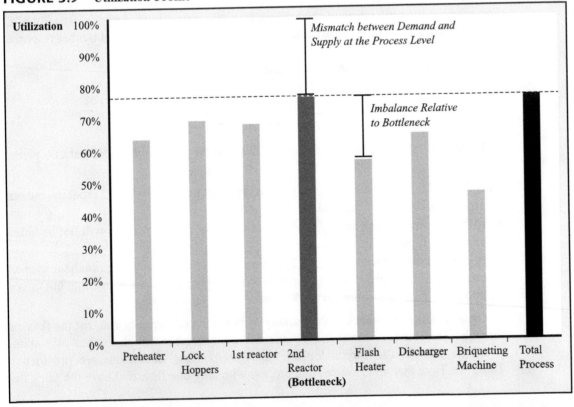

TABLE 3.3
Utilization of the Circored Process Steps Assuming Unlimited Demand and No Downtime

Process Step	Calculations	Utilization
Preheater	100/120	83.3%
Lock hoppers	100/110	90.9%
First reactor	100/112	89.3%
Second reactor	100/100	100.0%
Flash heater	100/135	74.1%
Discharger	100/118	84.7%
Briquetting machine	100/165	60.6%
Total process	**100/100**	**100%**

- Second, given that the process might not always be capacity-constrained, but rather be input- or demand-constrained, even the bottleneck might not be 100 percent utilized. In this case, every resource in the process has a "base level" of excess capacity, corresponding to the difference between the flow rate and the bottleneck capacity.

Note that the second reason disappears if there is sufficient market demand and full resource availability. In this case, only the bottleneck achieves a 100 percent utilization level. If the bottleneck in the Circored plant were utilized 100 percent, we would obtain an overall flow rate of 876,000 tons per year, or, equivalently 100 tons per hour. The resulting utilization levels in that case are summarized in Table 3.3.

3.5   Workload and Implied Utilization

Given the way we defined utilization (the ratio between flow rate and capacity), utilization can never exceed 100 percent. Thus, utilization only carries information about excess capacity, in which case utilization is strictly less than 100 percent. In contrast, we cannot infer from utilization by how much demand exceeds the capacity of the process. This is why we need to introduce an additional measure.

We define the *implied utilization* of a resource as

$$\text{Implied utilization} = \frac{\text{Demand}}{\text{Capacity}}$$

The implied utilization captures the mismatch between what could flow through the resource (demand) and what the resource can provide (capacity). Sometimes the "demand that could flow through a resource" is called the *workload*. So you can also say that the implied utilization of a resource equals its workload divided by its capacity.

Assume that demand for the Circored ore would increase to 1,095,000 tons per year (125 tons per hour). Table 3.4 calculates the resulting levels of implied utilization for the Circored resources.

TABLE 3.4
Implied Utilization of the Circored Process Steps Assuming a Demand of 125 Tons per Hour and No Downtime

Process Step	Calculations	Implied Utilization	Utilization
Preheater	125/120	104.2%	83.3%
Lock hoppers	125/110	113.6%	90.9%
First reactor	125/112	111.6%	89.3%
Second reactor	125/100	125%	100.0%
Flash heater	125/135	92.6%	74.1%
Discharger	125/118	105.9%	84.7%
Briquetting machine	125/165	75.8%	60.6%
Total process	**125/100**	**125%**	**100%**

Several points in the table deserve further discussion:

- Unlike utilization, implied utilization can exceed 100 percent. Any excess over 100 percent reflects that a resource does not have the capacity available to meet demand.
- The fact that a resource has an implied utilization above 100 percent does not make it the bottleneck. As we see in Table 3.4, it is possible to have several resources with an implied utilization above 100 percent. However, there is only one bottleneck in the process! This is the resource where the implied utilization is the highest. In the Circored case, this is—not surprisingly—the first reactor. Would it make sense to say that the process has several bottlenecks? No! Given that we can only operate the Circored process at a rate of 100 tons per hour (the capacity of the first reactor), we have ore flow through every resource of the process at a rate of 100 tons per hour. Thus, while several resources have an implied utilization above 100 percent, all resources other than the first reactor have excess capacity (their utilizations in Table 3.4 are below 100 percent). That is why we should not refer to them as bottlenecks.
- Having said this, it is important to keep in mind that in the case of a capacity expansion of the process, it might be worthwhile to add capacity to these other resources as well, not just to the bottleneck. In fact, depending on the margins we make and the cost of installing capacity, we could make a case to install additional capacity for all resources with an implied utilization above 100 percent. In other words, once we add capacity to the current bottleneck, our new process (with a new bottleneck) could still be capacity-constrained, justifying additional capacity to other resources.

3.6   Multiple Types of Flow Units

Choosing an appropriate flow unit is an essential step when preparing a process flow diagram. While, for the examples we have discussed so far, this looked relatively straightforward, there are many situations that you will encounter where this choice requires more care. The two most common complications are

- The flow of the unit moving through the process breaks up into multiple flows. For example, in an assembly environment, following an inspection step, good units continue to the next processing step, while bad units require rework.
- There are multiple types of flow units, representing, for example, different customer types. In an emergency room, life-threatening cases follow a different flow than less complicated cases.

The critical issue in choosing the flow unit is that you must be able to express all demands and capacities in terms of the chosen flow unit. For example, in the Circored process, we chose one ton of ore to be the flow unit. Thus, we had to express each resource's capacity and the demand in terms of tons of ore. Given that the process only makes ore, the choice of the flow unit was straightforward. However, consider the following example involving multiple product or customer types. An employment verification agency receives resumés from consulting firms and law firms with the request to validate information provided by their job candidates.

Figure 3.10 shows the process flow diagram for this agency. Note that while the three customer types share the first step and the last step in the process (filing and sending confirmation letter), they differ with respect to other steps:

- For internship positions, the agency provides information about the law school/business school the candidate is currently enrolled in as well as previous institutions of higher education and, to the extent possible, provides information about the applicant's course choices and honors.

FIGURE 3.10 Process Flow Diagram with Multiple Product Types

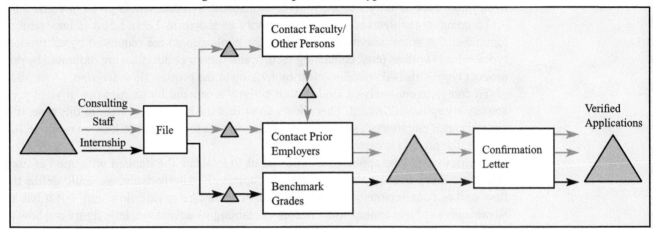

- For staff positions, the agency contacts previous employers and analyzes the letters of recommendation from those employers.
- For consulting/lawyer positions, the agency attempts to call former supervisors and/or colleagues in addition to contacting the previous employers and analyzes the letters of recommendation from those employers.

As far as demand, this process receives 3 consulting, 11 staff, and 4 internship applications per hour. Table 3.5 also provides the capacities of each activity, in applications per hour. Given that the workload on each activity as well as all of the capacities can be expressed in terms of "applications per hour," we can choose "one application" as our flow unit, despite the fact that there are multiple types of applications.

The next step in our process analysis is to find the bottleneck. In this setting this is complicated by the *product mix* (different types of customers flowing through one process). For example, the process step "contact persons" might have a very long processing time, resulting in a low capacity for this activity. However, if the workload on this activity (applications per hour) is also very low, then maybe this low capacity is not an issue.

TABLE 3.5 Finding the Bottleneck in the Multiproduct Case

	Processing Time	Number of Workers	Capacity	Workload [Applications/Hour]				Implied Utilization
				Consulting	Staff	Interns	Total	
File	3 [min./appl.]	1	1/3 [appl./min.] = 20 [appl./hour]	3	11	4	18	18/20 = 90%
Contact persons	20 [min./appl.]	2	2/20 [appl./min.] = 6 [appl./hour]	3	0	0	3	3/6 = 50%
Contact employers	15 [min./appl.]	3	3/15 [appl./min.] = 12 [appl./hour]	3	11	0	14	14/12 = 117%
Grade/school analysis	8 [min./appl.]	2	2/8 [appl./min.] = 15 [appl./hour]	0	0	4	4	4/15 = 27%
Confirmation letter	2 [min./appl.]	1	1/2 [appl./min.] = 30 [appl./hour]	3	11	4	18	18/30 = 60%

To find the bottleneck and to determine capacity in a multiproduct situation, we need to compare each activity's capacity with its demand. The analysis is given in Table 3.5.

To compute the demand on a given activity as shown in Table 3.5, it is important to remember that some activities (e.g., filing the applications) are requested by all product types, whereas others (e.g., contacting faculty and former colleagues) are requested by one product type. This is (hopefully) clear by looking at the process flow diagram.

To complete our analysis, divide each activity's demand by its capacity to yield each activity's implied utilization. This allows us to find the busiest resource. In this case, it is "contact prior employers", so this is our bottleneck. As the implied utilization is above 100 percent, the process is capacity-constrained.

The flow unit "one application" allowed us to evaluate the implied utilization of each activity in this process, but it is not the only approach. Alternatively, we could define the flow unit as "one minute of work." This might seem like an odd flow unit, but it has an advantage over "one application." Before explaining its advantage, let's figure out how to replicate our analysis of implied utilization with this new flow unit.

As before, we need to define our demands and our capacities in terms of our flow unit. In the case of capacity, each worker has "60 minutes of work" available per hour. (By definition, we all do!) So the capacity of an activity is (Number of workers) $\times$ 60 [minutes/hour]. For example "contact persons" has two workers. So its capacity is $2 \times 60 = 120$ minutes of work per hour. Each worker has 60 "minutes of work" available per hour, so two of them can deliver 120 minutes of work.

Now turn to the demands. There are 11 staff applications to be processed each hour and each takes 3 minutes. So the demand for staff applications is $11 \times 3 = 33$ minutes per hour. Now that we know how to express the demands and the capacities in terms of the "minutes of work," the implied utilization of each activity is again the ratio of the amount demanded from the activity to the activity's capacity. Table 3.6 summarizes these calculations. As we would expect, this method yields the same implied utilizations as the "one application" flow unit approach.

So if "one application" and "one minute of work" give us the same answer, how should we choose between these approaches? In this situation, you would work with the approach that you find most intuitive (which is probably "one application," at least initially) because they both allow us to evaluate the implied utilizations. However, the "one minute of work" approach is more robust. To explain why, suppose it took 3 minutes to file a staff application, 5 minutes to file a consulting application, and 2 minutes to file an internship application. In this case, we get into trouble if we define the flow unit to be "one application"—with that flow unit, we cannot express the capacity of the file activity! If we receive only internship applications, then filing could process $60/2 = 30$ applications per hour. However, if we receive only consulting applications, then filing can only process $60/5 = 12$ applications per hour. The number of applications per hour that filing can process depends on the mix of applications! The "minute of work" flow unit completely solves that problem—no matter what mix of applications is sent to filing, with one worker, filing has 60 minutes of work available per hour. Similarly, for a given mix of applications, we can also evaluate the workload on filing in terms of minutes of work (just as is done in Table 3.6).

To summarize, choose a flow unit that allows you to express all demands and capacities in terms of that flow unit. An advantage of the "minute of work" (or "hour of work," "day of work," etc.) approach is that it is possible to do this even if there are multiple types of products or customers flowing through the process.

So what is the next step in our process analysis? We have concluded that it is capacity-constrained because the implied utilization of "contact employers" is greater

TABLE 3.6 Using "One Minute of Work" as the Flow Unit to Find the Bottleneck in the Multiproduct Case

| | Processing Time | Number of Workers | Capacity | Workload [Minutes/Hour] | | | | Implied Utilization |
				Consulting	Staff	Interns	Total	
File	3 [min./appl.]	1	60 [min./hour]	3 × 3	11 × 3	4 × 3	54	54/60 = 90%
Contact persons	20 [min./appl.]	2	120 [min./hour]	3 × 20	0	0	60	60/120 = 50%
Contact employers	15 [min./appl.]	3	180 [min./hour]	3 × 15	11 × 15	0	210	210/180 = 117%
Grade/school analysis	8 [min./appl.]	2	120 [min./hour]	0	0	4 × 8	32	32/120 = 27%
Confirmation letter	2 [min./appl.]	1	60 [min./hour]	3 × 2	11 × 2	4 × 2	36	36/60 = 60%

than 100 percent—it is the bottleneck. Given that it is the only activity with an implied utilization greater than 100 percent, if we are going to add capacity to this process, "contact employers" should be the first candidate—in the current situation, they simply do not have enough capacity to handle the current mix of customers. Notice, if the mix of customers changes, this situation might change. For example, if we started to receive fewer staff applications (which have to flow through "contact employers") and more internship applications (which do not flow through "contact employers") then the workload on "contact employers" would decline, causing its implied utilization to fall as well. Naturally, shifts in the demands requested from a process can alter which resource in the process is the bottleneck.

Although we have been able to conclude something useful with our analysis, one should be cautious to not conclude too much when dealing with multiple types of products or customers. To illustrate some potential complications, consider the following example. At the international arrival area of a major U.S. airport, 15 passengers arrive per minute, 10 of whom are U.S. citizens or permanent residents and 5 are visitors.

The immigration process is organized as follows. Passengers disembark their aircraft and use escalators to arrive in the main immigration hall. The escalators can transport up to 100 passengers per minute. Following the escalators, passengers have to go through immigration. There exist separate immigration resources for U.S. citizens and permanent residents (they can handle 10 passengers per minute) and visitors (which can handle 3 visitors per minute). After immigration, all passengers pick up their luggage. Luggage handling (starting with getting the luggage off the plane and ending with moving the luggage onto the conveyor belts) has a capacity of 10 passengers per minute. Finally, all passengers go through customs, which has a capacity of 20 passengers per minute.

We calculate the implied utilization levels in Table 3.7. Notice when evaluating implied utilization we assume the demand on luggage handling is 10 U.S. citizens and 5 visitors even though we know (or discover via our calculations) that it is not possible for 15 passengers to arrive to luggage handling per minute (there is not enough capacity in immigration). We do this because we want to compare the potential demand on each resource with its capacity to assess its implied utilization. Consequently, we can evaluate each resource's implied utilization in isolation from the other resources.

Based on the values in Table 3.7, the bottleneck is immigration for visitors because it has the highest implied utilization. Furthermore, because its implied utilization is

TABLE 3.7
Calculating Implied Utilization in Airport Example

Resource	Demand for U.S. Citizens and Permanent Residents [Pass./Min.]	Demand for Visitors [Pass./Min.]	Capacity [Pass./Min.]	Implied Utilization
Escalator	10	5	100	15/100 = 15%
Immigration—U.S. residents	10	0	10	10/10 = 100%
Immigration—visitors	0	5	3	5/3 = 167%
Luggage handling	10	5	10	15/10 = 150%
Customs	10	5	20	15/20 = 75%

greater than 100 percent, the process is supply-constrained. Given that there is too little supply, we can expect queues to form. Eventually, those queues will clear because the demand rate of arriving passengers will at some point fall below capacity (otherwise, the queues will just continue to grow, which we know will not happen indefinitely at an airport). But during the times in which the arrival rates of passengers is higher than our capacity, where will the queues form? The answer to this question depends on how we prioritize work.

The escalator has plenty of capacity, so no priority decision needs to be made there. At immigration, there is enough capacity for 10 U.S. citizens and 3 visitors. So 13 passengers may be passed on to luggage handling, but luggage handling can accommodate only 10 passengers. Suppose we give priority to U.S. citizens. In that case, all of the U.S. citizens proceed through luggage handling without interruption, and a queue of visitors will form at the rate of 3 per minute. Of course, there will also be a queue of visitors in front of immigration, as it can handle only 3 per minute while 5 arrive per minute. With this priority scheme, the outflow from this process will be 10 US citizens per minute. However, if we give visitors full priority at luggage handling, then a similar analysis reveals that a queue of U.S. citizens forms in front of luggage handling, and a queue of visitors forms in front of immigration. The outflow is 7 U.S. citizens and 3 visitors.

The operator of the process may complain that the ratio of U.S. citizens to visitors in the outflow (7 to 3) does not match the inflow ratio (2 to 1), even though visitors are given full priority. If we were to insist that those ratios match, then the best we could do is have an outflow of 6 U.S. citizens and 3 visitors—we cannot produce more than 3 visitors per minute given the capacity of immigration, so the 2 to 1 constraint implies that we can "produce" no more than 6 U.S. citizens per minute. Equity surely has a price in this case—we could have an output of 10 passengers per minute, but the equity constraint would limit us to 9 passengers per minute. To improve upon this output while maintaining the equity constraint, we should add more capacity at the bottleneck—immigration for visitors.

3.7 Summary

Figure 3.11 is a summary of the major steps graphically. Exhibits 3.1 and 3.2 summarize the steps required to do the corresponding calculations for a single flow unit and multiple flow units, respectively.

Exhibit 3.1

STEPS FOR BASIC PROCESS ANALYSIS WITH ONE TYPE OF FLOW UNIT

1. Find the capacity of every resource; if there are multiple resources performing the same activity, add their capacities together.
2. The resource with the lowest capacity is called the *bottleneck*. Its capacity determines the capacity of the entire process (*process capacity*).
3. The flow rate is found based on

$$\text{Flow rate} = \text{Minimum \{Available input, Demand, Process capacity\}}$$

4. We find the utilization of the process as

$$\text{Utilization} = \frac{\text{Flow rate}}{\text{Capacity}}$$

The utilization of each resource can be found similarly.

Any process analysis should begin with the creation of a process flow diagram. This is especially important for the case of multiple flow units, as their flows are typically more complex.

Next, we need to identify the bottleneck of the process. As long as there exists only one type of flow unit, this is simply the resource with the lowest capacity. However, for more general cases, we need to perform some extra analysis. Specifically, if there is a product mix, we have to compute the requested capacity (workload) at each resource and then compare it to the available capacity. This corresponds to computing the implied utilization, and we identify the bottleneck as the resource with the highest implied utilization.

Finally, once we have found the bottleneck, we can compute a variety of performance measures. As in the previous chapter, we are interested in finding the flow rate. The flow rate also allows us to compute the process utilization as well as the utilization profile across resources. Utilizations, while not necessarily a business goal by themselves, are important measures in many industries, especially capital-intensive industries.

FIGURE 3.11   **Summary of Process Analysis**

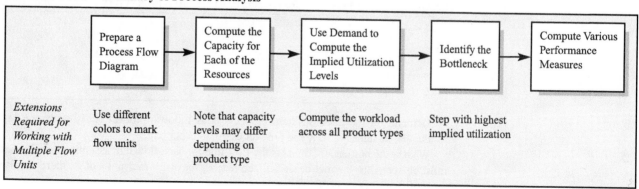

Exhibit 3.2

STEPS FOR BASIC PROCESS ANALYSIS WITH MULTIPLE TYPES OF FLOW UNITS

1. For each resource, compute the number of minutes that the resource can produce; this is 60 [min./hour] × Number of resources within the resource pool.
2. Create a process flow diagram, indicating how the flow units go through the process; use multiple colors to indicate the flow of the different flow units.
3. Create a table indicating how much workload each flow unit is consuming at each resource:

   - The rows of the table correspond to the resources in the process.
   - The columns of the table correspond to the different types of flow units.
   - Each cell of the table should contain one of the following:

   If flow unit does not visit the corresponding resource, 0;
   Otherwise, demand per hour of the corresponding flow unit × processing time.
4. Add up the workload of each resource across all flow units.
5. Compute the implied utilization of each resource as

$$\text{Implied utilization} = \frac{\text{Result of step 4}}{\text{Result of step 1}}$$

The resource with the highest implied utilization is the bottleneck.

The preceding approach is based on Table 3.6; that is, the flow unit is "one minute of work."

3.8 Practice Problems

Q3.1* **(Process Analysis with One Flow Unit)** Consider a process consisting of three resources:

Resource	Processing Time [Min./Unit]	Number of Workers
1	10	2
2	6	1
3	16	3

What is the bottleneck? What is the process capacity? What is the flow rate if demand is eight units per hour? What is the utilization of each resource if demand is eight units per hour?

Q3.2* **(Process Analysis with Multiple Flow Units)** Consider a process consisting of five resources that are operated eight hours per day. The process works on three different products, A, B, and C:

Resource	Number of Workers	Processing Time for A [Min./Unit]	Processing Time for B [Min./Unit]	Processing Time for C [Min./Unit]
1	2	5	5	5
2	2	3	4	5
3	1	15	0	0
4	1	0	3	3
5	2	6	6	6

Demand for the three different products is as follows: product A, 40 units per day; product B, 50 units per day; and product C, 60 units per day.

What is the bottleneck? What is the flow rate for each flow unit assuming that demand must be served in the mix described above (i.e., for every four units of A, there are five units of B and six units of C)?

(* indicates that the solution is at the end of the book)

Q3.3 **(Cranberries)** International Cranberry Uncooperative (ICU) is a competitor to the National Cranberry Cooperative (NCC). At ICU, barrels of cranberries arrive on trucks at a rate of 150 barrels per hour and are processed continuously at a rate of 100 barrels per hour. Trucks arrive at a uniform rate over eight hours, from 6:00 a.m. until 2:00 p.m. Assume the trucks are sufficiently small so that the delivery of cranberries can be treated as a continuous inflow. The first truck arrives at 6:00 a.m. and unloads immediately, so processing begins at 6:00 a.m. The bins at ICU can hold up to 200 barrels of cranberries before overflowing. If a truck arrives and the bins are full, the truck must wait until there is room in the bins.

a. What is the maximum number of barrels of cranberries that are waiting on the trucks at any given time?

b. At what time do the trucks stop waiting?

c. At what time do the bins become empty?

d. ICU is considering using seasonal workers in addition to their regular workforce to help with the processing of cranberries. When the seasonal workers are working, the processing rate increases to 125 barrels per hour. The seasonal workers would start working at 10:00 a.m. and finish working when the trucks stop waiting. At what time would ICU finish processing the cranberries using these seasonal workers?

Q3.4 **(Western Pennsylvania Milk Company)** The Western Pennsylvania Milk Company is producing milk at a fixed rate of 5,000 gallons/hour. The company's clients request 100,000 gallons of milk over the course of one day. This demand is spread out uniformly from 8 a.m. to 6 p.m. If there is no milk available, clients will wait until enough is produced to satisfy their requests.

The company starts producing at 8 a.m. with 25,000 gallons in finished goods inventory. At the end of the day, after all demand has been fulfilled, the plant keeps on producing until the finished goods inventory has been restored to 25,000 gallons.

When answering the following questions, treat trucks/milk as a continuous flow process. Begin by drawing a graph indicating how much milk is in inventory and how much milk is "back-ordered" over the course of the day.

a. At what time during the day will the clients have to start waiting for their requests to be filled?

b. At what time will clients stop waiting?

c. Assume that the milk is picked up in trucks that hold 1,250 gallons each. What is the maximum number of trucks that are waiting?

d. Assume the plant is charged $50 per hour per waiting truck. What are the total waiting time charges on a day?

Q3.5** **(Bagel Store)** Consider a bagel store selling three types of bagels that are produced according to the process flow diagram outlined below. We assume the demand is 180 bagels a day, of which there are 30 grilled veggie, 110 veggie only, and 40 cream cheese. Assume that the workday is 10 hours long and each resource is staffed with one worker.

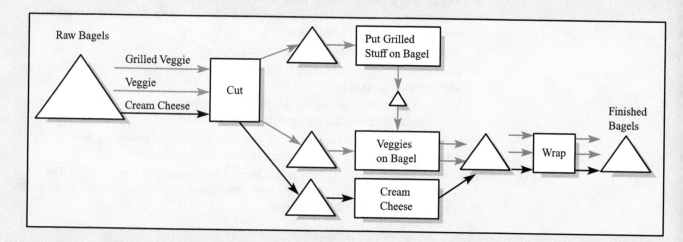

Moreover, we assume the following Processing times:

	Cut	Grilled Stuff	Veggies	Cream Cheese	Wrap
Processing time	3 [min./bagel]	10 [min./bagel]	5 [min./bagel]	4 [min./bagel]	2 [min./bagel]

Processing times are independent of which bagel type is processed at a resource (for example, cutting a bagel takes the same time for a cream cheese bagel as for a veggie bagel).

a. Where in the process is the bottleneck?

b. How many units can the process produce within one hour, assuming the product mix has to remain constant?

Q3.6 **(Valley Forge Income Tax Advice)** VF is a small accounting firm supporting wealthy individuals in their preparation of annual income tax statements. Every December, VF sends out a short survey to their customers, asking for the information required for preparing the tax statements. Based on 24 years of experience, VF categorizes their cases into the following groups:

- Group 1 (new customers, easy): 15 percent of cases
- Group 2 (new customers, complex): 5 percent of cases
- Group 3 (repeat customers, easy): 50 percent of cases
- Group 4 (repeat customers, complex): 30 percent of cases

Here, "easy" versus "complex" refers to the complexity of the customer's earning situation.

In order to prepare the income tax statement, VF needs to complete the following set of activities. Processing times (and even which activities need to be carried out) depend on which group a tax statement falls into. All of the following processing times are expressed in minutes per income tax statement.

Group	Filing	Initial Meeting	Preparation	Review by Senior Accountant	Writing
1	20	30	120	20	50
2	40	90	300	60	80
3	20	No meeting	80	5	30
4	40	No meeting	200	30	60

The activities are carried out by the following three persons:

- Administrative support person: filing and writing.
- Senior accountant (who is also the owner): initial meeting, review by senior accountant.
- Junior accountant: preparation.

Assume that all three persons work eight hours per day and 20 days a month. For the following questions, assume the product mix as described above. Assume that there are 50 income tax statements arriving each month.

a. Which of the three persons is the bottleneck?

b. What is the (implied) utilization of the senior accountant? The junior accountant? The administrative support person?

c. You have been asked to analyze which of the four product groups is the most profitable. Which factors would influence the answer to this?

d. How would the process capacity of VF change if a new word processing system would reduce the time to write the income tax statements by 50 percent?

Q3.7 **(Car Wash Supply Process)** CC Car Wash specializes in car cleaning services. The services offered by the company, the exact service time, and the resources needed for each of them are described in the table following:

Service	Description	Processing Time	Resource Used
A. Wash	Exterior car washing and drying	10 min.	1 automated washing machine
B. Wax	Exterior car waxing	10 min.	1 automated waxing machine
C. Wheel cleaning	Detailed cleaning of all wheels	7 min.	1 employee
D. Interior cleaning	Detailed cleaning inside the car	20 min.	1 employee

The company offers the following packages to their customers:

- Package 1: Includes only car wash (service A).
- Package 2: Includes car wash and waxing (services A and B).
- Package 3: Car wash, waxing, and wheel cleaning (services A, B, and C).
- Package 4: All four services (A, B, C, and D).

Customers of CC Car Wash visit the station at a constant rate (you can ignore any effects of variability) of 40 customers per day. Of these customers, 40 percent buy Package 1, 15 percent buy Package 2, 15 percent buy Package 3, and 30 percent buy Package 4. The mix does not change over the course of the day. The store operates 12 hours a day.

a. What is the implied utilization of the employee doing the wheel cleaning service?

b. Which resource has the highest implied utilization?

For the next summer, CC Car Wash anticipates an increase in the demand to 80 customers per day. Together with this demand increase, there is expected to be a change in the mix of packages demanded: 30 percent of the customers ask for Package 1, 10 percent for Package 2, 10 percent for Package 3, and 50 percent for Package 4. The company will install an additional washing machine to do service A.

c. What will be the new bottleneck in the process?

d. How many customers a day will not be served? Which customers are going to wait? Explain your reasoning!

Q3.8 **(Starbucks)** After an "all night" study session the day before their last final exam, four students decide to stop for some much-needed coffee at the campus Starbucks. They arrive at 8:30 a.m. and are dismayed to find a rather long line.

Fortunately for the students, a Starbucks executive happens to be in line directly in front of them. From her, they learn the following facts about this Starbucks location:

I. There are three employee types:

- There is a single cashier who takes all orders, prepares nonbeverage food items, grinds coffee, and pours drip coffee.
- There is a single frozen drink maker who prepares blended and iced drinks.
- There is a single espresso drink maker who prepares espressos, lattes, and steamed drinks.

II. There are typically four types of customers:

- Drip coffee customers order only drip coffee. This requires 20 seconds of the cashier's time to pour the coffee.
- Blended and iced drink customers order a drink that requires the use of the blender. These drinks take on average 2 minutes of work of the frozen drink maker.
- Espresso drink customers order a beverage that uses espresso and/or steamed milk. On average, these drinks require 1 minute of work of the espresso drink maker.
- Ground coffee customers buy one of Starbucks' many varieties of whole bean coffee and have it ground to their specification at the store. This requires a total of 1 minute of the cashier's time (20 seconds to pour the coffee and 40 seconds to grind the whole bean coffee).

III. The customers arrive uniformly at the following rates from 7 a.m. (when the store opens) until 10 a.m. (when the morning rush is over), with no customers arriving after 10 a.m.:
- Drip coffee customers: 25 per hour.
- Blended and iced drink customers: 20 per hour.
- Espresso drink customers: 70 per hour.
- Ground coffee customers: 5 per hour.

IV. Each customer spends, on average, 20 seconds with the cashier to order and pay.

V. Approximately 25 percent of all customers order food, which requires an additional 20 seconds of the cashier's time per transaction.

While waiting in line, the students reflect on these facts and they answer the following questions:

a. What is the implied utilization of the frozen drink maker?

b. Which resource has the highest implied utilization?

From their conversation with the executive, the students learn that Starbucks is considering a promotion on all scones (half price!), which marketing surveys predict will increase the percentage of customers ordering food to 30 percent (the overall arrival rates of customers will *not* change). However, the executive is worried about how this will affect the waiting times for customers.

c. How do the levels of implied utilization change as a response to this promotion?

Q3.9   **(Paris Airport)** Kim Opim, an enthusiastic student, is on her flight over from Philadelphia (PHL) to Paris. Kim reflects upon how her educational experiences from her operations courses could help explain the long wait time that she experienced before she could enter the departure area of Terminal A at PHL. As an airline representative explained to Kim, there are four types of travelers in Terminal A:

- Experienced short-distance (short-distance international travel destinations are Mexico and various islands in the Atlantic) travelers: These passengers check in online and do not speak with any agent nor do they take any time at the kiosks.
- Experienced long-distance travelers: These passengers spend 3 minutes with an agent.
- Inexperienced short-distance travelers: These passengers spend 2 minutes at a kiosk; however, they do not require the attention of an agent.
- Inexperienced long-distance travelers: These passengers need to talk 5 minutes with an agent.

After a passenger checks in online, or talks with an agent, or uses a kiosk, the passenger must pass through security, where they need 0.5 minutes independent of their type. From historical data, the airport is able to estimate the arrival rates of the different customer types at Terminal A of Philadelphia International:

- Experienced short-distance travelers: 100 per hour
- Experienced long-distance travelers: 80 per hour
- Inexperienced short-distance travelers: 80 per hour
- Inexperienced long-distance travelers: 40 per hour

At this terminal, there are four security check stations, six agents, and three electronic kiosks. Passengers arrive uniformly from 4 p.m. to 8 p.m., with the entire system empty prior to 4 p.m. (the "midafternoon lull") and no customers arrive after 8 p.m. All workers must stay on duty until the last passenger is entirely through the system (e.g., has passed through security).

a. What are the levels of implied utilization at each resource?

b. At what time has the last passenger gone through the system? Note: If passengers of one type have to wait for a resource, passengers that do not require service at the resource can pass by the waiting passengers!

c. Kim, an experienced long-distance traveler, arrived at 6 p.m. at the airport and attempted to move through the check-in process as quickly as she could. How long did she have to wait before she was checked at security?

d. The airline considers showing an educational program that would provide information about the airport's check-in procedures. Passenger surveys indicate that 80 percent of the inexperienced passengers (short or long distance) would subsequently act as experienced passengers (i.e., the new arrival rates would be 164 experienced short-distance, 112 experienced long-distance, 16 inexperienced short-distance, and 8 inexperienced long-distance [passengers/hour]). At what time has the last passenger gone through the system?

You can view a video of how problems marked with a ** are solved by going on www. cachon-terwiesch.net and follow the links under 'Solved Practice Problems'

Solutions to Selected Practice Problems

Chapter 3

Q3.1 (Single Flow Unit)

The following steps refer directly to Exhibit 3.1.

Step 1. We first compute the capacity of the three resources:

$$\text{Resource 1} : \frac{2}{10} \text{ unit per minute} = 0.2 \text{ unit per minute}$$

$$\text{Resource 2} : \frac{1}{6} \text{ unit per minute} = 0.1666 \text{ unit per minute}$$

$$\text{Resource 3} : \frac{3}{16} \text{ unit per minute} = 0.1875 \text{ unit per minute}$$

Step 2. Resource 2 has the lowest capacity; process capacity therefore is 0.1666 unit per minute, which is equal to 10 units per hour.

Step 3. Flow rate = Min{Process capacity, Demand}

$$= \text{Min\{8 units per hour, 10 units per hour\}} = 8 \text{ units per hour}$$

This is equal to 0.1333 unit per minute.

Step 4. We find the utilizations of the three resources as

Resource 1: 0.1333 unit per minute/0.2 unit per minute = 66.66 percent
Resource 2: 0.1333 unit per minute/0.1666 unit per minute = 80 percent
Resource 3: 0.1333 unit per minute/0.1875 unit per minute = 71.11 percent

Q3.2 (Multiple Flow Units)

The following steps refer directly to Exhibit 3.2.

Step 1. Each resource can contribute the following capacity (in minutes of work per day):

Resource	Number of Workers	Minutes per Day
1	2	$2 \times 8 \times 60 = 960$
2	2	$2 \times 8 \times 60 = 960$
3	1	$1 \times 8 \times 60 = 480$
4	1	$1 \times 8 \times 60 = 480$
5	2	$2 \times 8 \times 60 = 960$

Step 2. Process flow diagram:

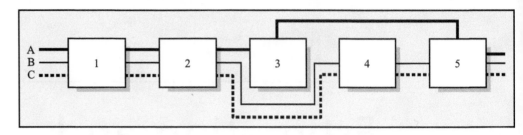

Step 3. We create a table indicating how much capacity will be consumed by the three products at the resources.

Resource	Capacity Requirement from A	Capacity Requirement from B	Capacity Requirement from C
1	5 × 40 = 200	5 × 50 = 250	5 × 60 = 300
2	3 × 40 = 120	4 × 50 = 200	5 × 60 = 300
3	15 × 40 = 600	0 × 50 = 0	0 × 60 = 0
4	0 × 40 = 0	3 × 50 = 150	3 × 60 = 180
5	6 × 40 = 240	6 × 50 = 300	6 × 60 = 360

Step 4. Add up the rows to get the workload for each resource:

Workload for resource 1: 200 + 250 + 300 = 750
Workload for resource 2: 120 + 200 + 300 = 620
Workload for resource 3: 600 + 0 + 0 = 600
Workload for resource 4: 0 + 150 + 180 = 330
Workload for resource 5: 240 + 300 + 360 = 900

Resource	Minutes per Day (see Step 1)	Workload per Day (see Step 4)	Implied Utilization (Step 4/Step 1)
1	960	750	0.78
2	960	620	0.65
3	480	600	1.25
4	480	330	0.69
5	960	900	0.94

Step 5. Compute implied utilization levels. Hence, resource 3 is the bottleneck. Thus, we cannot produce units A at a rate of 40 units per day. Since we are overutilized by 25 percent, we can produce units A at a rate of 32 units per day (four units per hour). Assuming the ratio between A, B, and C is constant (40:50:60), we will produce B at five units per hour and C at six units per hour. If the ratio between A, B, and C is *not* constant, this answer changes. In this case, we would produce 32 units of A and produce products B and C at the rate of demand (50 and 60 units per day respectively).

Chapter

Estimating and Reducing Labor Costs

The objective of any process should be to create value (make profits), not to maximize the utilization of every resource involved in the process. In other words, we should not attempt to produce more than what is demanded from the market, or from the resource downstream in the process, just to increase the utilization measure. Yet, the underutilization of a resource, human labor or capital equipment alike, provides opportunities to improve the process. This improvement can take several forms, including

- If we can reduce the excess capacity at some process step, the overall process becomes more efficient (lower cost for the same output).
- If we can use capacity from underutilized process steps to increase the capacity at the bottleneck step, the overall process capacity increases. If the process is capacity-constrained, this leads to a higher flow rate.

In this chapter, we discuss how to achieve such process improvements. Specifically, we discuss the concept of line balancing, which strives to avoid mismatches between what is supplied by one process step and what is demanded from the following process step (referred to as the process step downstream). In this sense, line balancing attempts to match supply and demand within the process itself.

We use Novacruz Inc. to illustrate the concept of line balancing and to introduce a number of more general terms of process analysis. Novacruz is the producer of a high-end kick scooter, known as the Xootr (pronounced "zooter"), displayed in Figure 4.1.

4.1   Analyzing an Assembly Operation

With the increasing popularity of kick scooters in general, and the high-end market segment for kick scooters in particular, Novacruz faced a challenging situation in terms of organizing their production process. While the demand for their product was not much higher than 100 scooters per week in early March 2000, it grew dramatically, soon reaching 1,200 units per week in the fall of 2000. This demand trajectory is illustrated in Figure 4.2.

First consider March 2000, during which Novacruz faced a demand of 125 units per week. At this time, the assembly process was divided between three workers (resources) as illustrated by Figure 4.3.

The three workers performed the following activities. In the first activity, the first 30 of the overall 80 parts are assembled, including the fork, the steer support, and the t-handle.

56

FIGURE 4.1
The Xootr by
Novacruz

Given the complexity of this assembly operation, it takes about 13 minutes per scooter to complete this activity. We refer to the 13 minutes/unit as the *processing time*. Depending on the context, we will also refer to the processing time as the *activity time* or the *service time* Note that in the current process, each activity is staffed with exactly one worker.

In the second activity, a worker assembles the wheel, the brake, and some other parts related to the steering mechanism. The second worker also assembles the deck. This step is somewhat faster and its processing time is 11 minutes per unit. The scooter is completed by the third worker, who wipes off the product, applies the decals and grip tape, and conducts the final functional test. The processing time is about 8 minutes per unit.

FIGURE 4.2
Lifecycle Demand
Trajectory for Xootrs

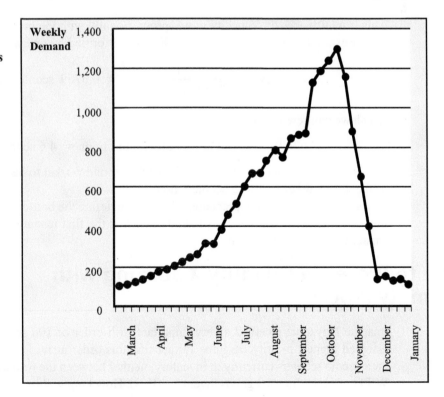

FIGURE 4.3
Current process layout

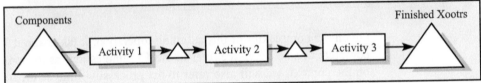

To determine the capacity of an individual resource or a group of resources performing the same activity, we write:

$$\text{Capacity} = \frac{\text{Number of resources}}{\text{Processing time}}$$

This is intuitive, as the capacity grows proportionally with the number of workers.

For example, for the first activity, which is performed by one worker, we write:

$$\text{Capacity} = \frac{1}{13 \text{ minutes/scooter}} = 0.0769 \text{ scooter/minute}$$

which we can rewrite as

$$0.0769 \text{ scooter/minute} \times 60 \text{ minutes/hour} = 4.6 \text{ scooters/hour}$$

Similarly, we can compute capacities of the second worker to be 5.45 scooters/hour and of the third worker to be 7.5 scooters/hour.

As we have done in the preceding chapter, we define the bottleneck as the resource with the lowest capacity. In this case, the bottleneck is the first resource, resulting in a process capacity of 4.6 scooters/hour.

4.2 Time to Process a Quantity *X* Starting with an Empty Process

Imagine Novacruz received a very important rush order of 100 scooters, which would be assigned highest priority. Assume further that this order arrives early in the morning and there are no scooters currently in inventory, neither between the resources (work-in-process, WIP) nor in the finished goods inventory (FGI). How long will it take to fulfill this order?

As we are facing a large order of scooters, we will attempt to move as many scooters through the system as possible. Therefore, we are capacity-constrained and the flow rate of the process is determined by the capacity of the bottleneck (one scooter every 13 minutes). The time between the completions of two subsequent flow units is called the *cycle time* of a process and will be defined more formally in the next section.

We cannot simply compute the time to produce 100 units as 100 units/0.0769 unit/ minute = 1,300 minutes because that calculation assumes the system is producing at the bottleneck rate, one unit every 13 minutes. However, that is only the case once the system is "up and running." In other words, the first scooter of the day, assuming the system starts the day empty (with no work in process inventory), takes even longer than 13 minutes to complete. How much longer depends on how the line is paced.

The current system is called a *worker-paced* line because each worker is free to work at his or her own pace: if the first worker finishes before the next worker is ready to accept the parts, then the first worker puts the completed work in the inventory between them. Eventually the workers need to conform to the bottleneck rate; otherwise, the inventory before the bottleneck would grow too big for the available space. But that concern is not relevant for the first unit moving through the system, so the time to get the first scooter through the system is 13 + 11 + 8 = 32 minutes. More generally:

Time through an empty worker-paced process = Sum of the processing times

An alternative to the worker-paced process is a machine-paced process as depicted in Figure 4.4. In a machine-paced process, all of the steps must work at the same rate even with the first unit through the system. Hence, if a machine-paced process were used, then the first Xootr would be produced after 3 × 13 minutes, as the conveyor belt has the same speed at all three process steps (there is just one conveyor belt, which has to be paced to the slowest step). More generally,

Time through an empty machine-paced process

= Number of resources in sequence × Processing time of the bottleneck step

Now return to our worker-paced process. After waiting 32 minutes for the first scooter, it only takes an additional 13 minutes until the second scooter is produced and from then onwards, we obtain an additional scooter every 13 minutes. Thus, scooter 1 is produced after 32 minutes, scooter 2 after 32 + 13 = 45 minutes, scooter 3 after 32 + (2 × 13) = 58 minutes, scooter 4 after 32 + (3 × 13) = 71 minutes, and so on.

More formally, we can write the following formula. The time it takes to finish X units starting with an empty system is

Time to finish X units starting with an empty system

$$= \text{Time through an empty process} + \frac{X - 1 \text{ unit}}{\text{Flow rate}}$$

You may wonder whether it is always necessary to be so careful about the difference between the time to complete the first unit and all of the rest of the units. In this case, it is because the number of scooters is relatively small, so each one matters. But

FIGURE 4.4

A Machine-Paced Process Layout

(Note: conveyor belt is only shown for illustration)

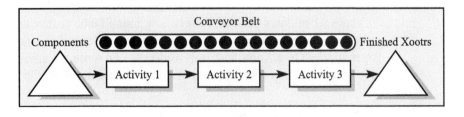

Exhibit 4.1

1. Find the time it takes the flow unit to go through the empty system:
   - In a worker-paced line, this is the sum of the processing times.
   - In a machine-paced line, this is the cycle time $\times$ the number of stations.

2. Compute the capacity of the process (see previous methods). Since we are producing X units as fast as we can, we are capacity-constrained; thus,

$$\text{Flow rate} = \text{Process capacity}$$

3. Time to finish X units

$$= \text{Time through empty process} + \frac{X - 1 \text{ unit}}{\text{Flow rate}}$$

Note: If the process is a continuous process, we can use X instead.

---

imagine a continuous-flow process such as a cranberry processing line. Suppose you want to know how long it takes to produce five tons of cranberries. Let's say a cranberry weighs one gram, so five tons equals five million cranberries. Now how long does it take to produce five million cranberries? Strictly speaking, we would look at the time it takes the first berry to flow through the system and then add the time for the residual 4,999,999 berries. However, for all computational purposes, five million minus one is still five million, so we can make our life a little easier by just ignoring this first berry:

$$\text{Time to finish } X \text{ units with a continuous-flow process}$$

$$= \text{Time through an empty process} + \frac{X \text{ units}}{\text{Flow rate}}$$

Exhibit 4.1 summarizes the calculations leading to the time it takes the process to produce X units starting with an empty system.

4.3 Labor Content and Idle Time

What is the role of labor cost in the production of the Xootr? Let's look first at how much actual labor is involved in the assembly of the Xootr. Towards this end, we define the *labor content* as the sum of the processing times of the three workers. In this case, we compute a labor content of

$$\text{Labor content} = \text{Sum of processing times with labor}$$
$$= 13 \text{ minutes/unit} + 11 \text{ minutes/unit} + 8 \text{ minutes/unit}$$
$$= 32 \text{ minutes per unit}$$

These 32 minutes per unit reflect how much labor is invested into the production of one scooter. We could visualize this measure as follows. Let's say there would be a slip of paper attached to a Xootr and each worker would write the amount of time spent working on the Xootr on this slip. The sum of all numbers entered on the slip is the labor content.

Assume that the average hourly rate of the assembly employees is $12 per hour (and thus $0.20 per minute). Would the resulting cost of labor then be 32 minutes/unit × $0.20/minute = $6.40/unit? The answer is a clear *no*! The reason for this is that the labor content is a measure that takes the perspective of the flow unit but does not reflect any information about how the process is actually operated.

Assume—for illustrative purposes—that we would hire an additional worker for the second activity. As worker 2 is not a constraint on the overall output of the process, this would probably not be a wise thing to do (and that is why we call it an illustrative example). How would the labor content change? Not at all! It would still require the same 32 minutes of labor to produce a scooter. However, we have just increased our daily wages by 33 percent, which should obviously be reflected in our cost of direct labor.

To correctly compute the cost of direct labor, we need to look at two measures:

- The number of scooters produced per unit of time (the flow rate).
- The amount of wages we pay for the same time period.

Above, we found that the process has a capacity of 4.6 scooters an hour, or 161 scooters per week (we assume the process operates 35 hours per week). Given that demand is currently 125 scooters per week (we are demand-constrained), our flow rate is at 125 scooters per week.

Now, we can compute the cost of direct labor as

$$\text{Cost of direct labor} = \frac{\text{Total wages per unit of time}}{\text{Flow rate per unit of time}}$$

$$= \frac{\text{Wages per week}}{\text{Scooters produced per week}}$$

$$= \frac{3 \times \$12/\text{h} \times 35\,\text{h}/\text{week}}{125\ \text{scooters}/\text{week}}$$

$$= \frac{\$1,260/\text{week}}{125\ \text{scooters}/\text{week}} = \$10.08/\text{scooter}$$

Why is this number so much higher than the number we computed based on the direct labor content? The difference between the two numbers reflects underutilization, or what we will refer to as *idle time*. In this case, there are two sources of idle time:

- The process is never able to produce more than its bottleneck. In this case, this means one scooter every 13 minutes. However, if we consider worker 3, who only takes eight minutes on a scooter, this translates into a 5-minute idle time for every scooter built.

- If the process is demand-constrained, even the bottleneck is not operating at its full capacity and, consequently, also exhibits idle time. Given a demand rate of 125 scooters/week, that is, 3.57 scooters/hour or one scooter every 16.8 minutes, all three workers get an extra 3.8 minutes of idle time for every scooter they make.

This reflects the utilization profile and the sources of underutilization that we discussed in Chapter 3 with the Circored process.

Note that this calculation assumes the labor cost is fixed. If it were possible to shorten the workday from the current 7 hours of operations to 5 hours and 25 minutes (25 scooters a day × 1 scooter every 13 minutes), we would eliminate the second type of idle time.

More formally, define the following:

$$\text{Cycle time} = \frac{1}{\text{Flow rate}}$$

Cycle time provides an alternative measure of how fast the process is creating output. As we are producing one scooter every 16.8 minutes, the cycle time is 16.8 minutes. Similar to what we did intuitively above, we can now define the idle time for worker i as the following:

Idle time for a single worker = Cycle time − Processing time of the single worker

Note that this formula assumes that every activity is staffed with exactly one worker. The idle time measures how much unproductive time a worker has for every unit of output produced. These calculations are summarized by Table 4.1.

If we add up the idle time across all workers, we obtain the total idle time that is incurred for every scooter produced:

$$3.8 + 5.8 + 8.8 = 18.4 \text{ minutes/unit}$$

Now, apply the wage rate of $12 per hour ($0.20/minute × 18.4 minutes/unit) and, voilà, we obtain exactly the difference between the labor cost we initially expected based on the direct labor content alone ($6.40 per unit) and the actual cost of direct labor computed above.

As a final measure of process efficiency, we can look at the average labor utilization of the workers involved in the process. We can obtain this number by comparing the labor content with the amount of labor we have to pay for (the labor content and the idle time):

$$\text{Average labor utilization} = \frac{\text{Labor content}}{\text{Labor content} + \text{Sum of idle times across workers}}$$
$$= \frac{32[\text{minutes per unit}]}{32[\text{minutes per unit}] + 18.4[\text{minutes per unit}]} = 63.5\%$$

TABLE 4.1
Basic Calculations Related to Idle Time

	Worker 1	Worker 2	Worker 3
Processing time	13 minutes/unit	11 minutes/unit	8 minutes/unit
Capacity	$\frac{1}{13}$ unit/minute	$\frac{1}{11}$ unit/minute	$\frac{1}{8}$ unit/minute
	= 4.61 units/hour	= 5.45 units/hour	= 7.5 units/hour
Process capacity	Minimum {4.61 units/h, 5.45 units/h, 7.5 units/h} = 4.61 units/hour		
Flow rate	Demand = 125 units/week = 3.57 units/hour Flow rate = Minimum {demand, process capacity} = 3.57 units/hour		
Cycle time	1/3.57 hours/unit = 16.8 minutes/unit		
Idle time	16.8 minutes/unit − 13 minutes/unit = 3.8 minutes/unit	16.8 minutes/unit − 11 minutes/unit = 5.8 minutes/unit	16.8 minutes/unit − 8 minutes/unit = 8.8 minutes/unit
Utilization	3.57/4.61 = 77%	3.57/5.45 = 65.5%	3.57/7.5 = 47.6%

Exhibit 4.2

SUMMARY OF LABOR COST CALCULATIONS

1. Compute the capacity of all resources; the resource with the lowest capacity is the bottleneck (see previous methods) and determines the process capacity.
2. Compute Flow rate = Min{Available input, Demand, Process capacity}; then compute

$$\text{Cycle time} = \frac{1}{\text{Flow rate}}$$

3. Compute the total wages (across all workers) that are paid per unit of time:

$$\text{Cost of direct labor} = \frac{\text{Total wages}}{\text{Flow rate}}$$

4. Compute the idle time across all workers at resource i

Idle time across all workers at resource i = Cycle time × (Number of workers at resource i) − Processing time at resource i

5. Compute the labor content of the flow unit: this is the sum of all processing times involving direct labor.
6. Add up the idle times across all resources (total idle time); then compute

$$\text{Average labor utilization} = \frac{\text{Labor content}}{\text{Labor content} + \text{Total idle time}}$$

An alternative way to compute the same number is by averaging the utilization level across the three workers:

$$\text{Average labor utilization} = \tfrac{1}{3} \times (\text{Utilization}_1 + \text{Utilization}_2 + \text{Utilization}_3) = 63.4\%$$

where Utilization$_i$ denotes the utilization of the ith worker. Exhibit 4.2 summarizes the calculations related to our analysis of labor costs. It includes the possibility that there are multiple workers performing the same activity.

4.4   Increasing Capacity by Line Balancing

Comparing the utilization levels in Table 4.1 reveals a strong imbalance between workers: while worker 1 is working 77 percent of the time, worker 3 is only active about half of the time (47.6 percent to be exact). Imbalances within a process provide micro-level mismatches between what could be supplied by one step and what is demanded by the following steps. *Line balancing* is the act of reducing such imbalances. It thereby provides the opportunity to

- Increase the efficiency of the process by better utilizing the various resources, in this case labor.
- Increase the capacity of the process (without adding more resources to it) by reallocating either workers from underutilized resources to the bottleneck or work from the bottleneck to underutilized resources.

While based on the present demand rate of 125 units per week and the assumption that all three workers are a fixed cost for 35 hours per week, line balancing would change neither the flow rate (process is demand-constrained) nor the cost of direct labor (assuming the 35 hours per week are fixed); this situation changes with the rapid demand growth experienced by Novacruz.

Consider now a week in May, by which, as indicated by Figure 4.1, the demand for the Xootr had reached a level of 200 units per week. Thus, instead of being demand-constrained, the process now is capacity-constrained, specifically, the process now is constrained by worker 1, who can produce one scooter every 13 minutes, while the market demands scooters at a rate of one scooter every 10.5 minutes (200 units/week/35 hours/week = 5.714 units/hour).

Given that worker 1 is the constraint on the system, all her idle time is now eliminated and her utilization has increased to 100 percent. Yet, workers 2 and 3 still have idle time:

- The flow rate by now has increased to one scooter every 13 minutes or $\frac{1}{13}$ unit per minute (equals $\frac{1}{13} \times 60 \times 35 = 161.5$ scooters per week) based on worker 1.

- Worker 2 has a capacity of one scooter every 11 minutes, that is, $\frac{1}{11}$ unit per minute. Her utilization is thus Flow rate/Capacity$_2$ = $\frac{1}{13}/\frac{1}{11} = \frac{11}{13} = 84.6\%$.

- Worker 3 has a capacity of one scooter every 8 minutes. Her utilization is thus $\frac{1}{13}/\frac{1}{8} = \frac{8}{13} = 61.5\%$.

Note that the increase in demand not only has increased the utilization levels across workers (the average utilization is now $\frac{1}{3} \times (100\% + 84.6\% + 61.5\%) = 82\%$), but also has reduced the cost of direct labor to

$$
\begin{aligned}
\text{Cost of direct labor} &= \frac{\text{Total wages per unit of time}}{\text{Flow rate per unit of time}} \\
&= \frac{\text{Wages per week}}{\text{Scooters produced per week}} \\
&= \frac{3 \times \$12/\text{hour} \times 35 \ \text{hours}/\text{week}}{161.5 \ \text{scooters}/\text{week}} \\
&= \frac{\$1,260/\text{week}}{161.5 \ \text{scooters}/\text{week}} = \$7.80/\text{scooter}
\end{aligned}
$$

Now, back to the idea of line balancing. Line balancing attempts to evenly (fairly!) allocate the amount of work that is required to build a scooter across the three process steps.

In an ideal scenario, we could just take the amount of work that goes into building a scooter, which we referred to as the labor content (32 minutes/unit), and split it up evenly between the three workers. Thus, we would achieve a perfect line balance if each worker could take 32/3 minutes/unit; that is, each would have an identical processing time of 10.66 minutes/unit.

Unfortunately, in most processes, it is not possible to divide up the work that evenly. Specifically, the activities underlying a process typically consist of a collection of *tasks* that cannot easily be broken up. A closer analysis of the three activities in our case reveals the task structure shown in Table 4.2.

For example, consider the last task of worker 1 (assemble handle cap), which takes 118 seconds per unit. These 118 seconds per unit of work can only be moved to another worker in their entirety. Moreover, we cannot move this task around freely, as it obviously would not be feasible to move the "assemble handle cap" task to after the "seal carton" task.

TABLE 4.2
Task Durations

Worker	Tasks	Task Duration [seconds/unit]
Worker 1	Prepare cable	30
	Move cable	25
	Assemble washer	100
	Apply fork, threading cable end	66
	Assemble socket head screws	114
	Steer pin nut	49
	Brake shoe, spring, pivot bolt	66
	Insert front wheel	100
	Insert axle bolt	30
	Tighten axle bolt	43
	Tighten brake pivot bolt	51
	Assemble handle cap	118
		Total: 792
Worker 2	Assemble brake lever and cable	110
	Trim and cap cable	59
	Place first rib	33
	Insert axles and cleats	96
	Insert rear wheel	135
	Place second rib and deck	84
	Apply grip tape	56
	Insert deck fasteners	75
		Total: 648
Worker 3	Inspect and wipe off	95
	Apply decal and sticker	20
	Insert in bag	43
	Assemble carton	114
	Insert Xootr and manual	94
	Seal carton	84
		Total: 450

However, we could move the 118 seconds per unit from worker 1 to worker 2. In this case, worker 1 would now have an processing time of 674 seconds per unit and worker 2 (who would become the new bottleneck) would have an processing time of 766 seconds per unit. The overall process capacity is increased, we would produce more scooters, and the average labor utilization would move closer to 100 percent.

But can we do better? Within the scope of this book, we only consider cases where the sequence of tasks is given. Line balancing becomes more complicated if we can resequence some of the tasks. For example, there exists no technical reason why the second to last task of worker 2 (apply grip tape) could not be switched with the subsequent task (insert deck fasteners). There exist simple algorithms and heuristics that support line balancing in such more complex settings. Yet, their discussion would derail us from our focus on managerial issues.

But even if we restrict ourselves to line balancing solutions that keep the sequence of tasks unchanged, we can further improve upon the 766-second cycle time we outlined above. Remember that the "gold standard" of line balancing, the even distribution of the labor content across all resources, suggested an processing time of 10.66 minutes per unit, or 640 seconds per unit.

Moving the "assemble handle cap" task from worker 1 to worker 2 was clearly a substantial step in that direction. However, worker 2 has now 126 seconds per unit (766 seconds/unit − 640 seconds/unit) more than what would be a balanced workload. This situation can be improved if we take the worker's last two tasks (apply grip tape, insert deck fasteners) and move the corresponding 56 + 75 seconds/unit = 131 seconds/unit to worker 3.

The new processing times would be as follows:

- Worker 1: 674 seconds per unit (792 − 118 seconds/unit).
- Worker 2: 635 seconds per unit (648 + 118 − 56 − 75 seconds/unit).
- Worker 3: 581 seconds per unit (450 + 56 + 75 seconds/unit).

Are they optimal? No! We can repeat similar calculations and further move work from worker 1 to worker 2 (tighten brake pivot bolt, 51 seconds per unit) and from worker 2 to worker 3 (place second rib and deck, 84 seconds per unit). The resulting (final) processing times are now

- Worker 1: 623 seconds per unit (674 − 51 seconds/unit).
- Worker 2: 602 seconds per unit (635 + 51 − 84 seconds/unit).
- Worker 3: 665 seconds per unit (581 + 84 seconds/unit).

To make sure we have not "lost" any work on the way, we can add up the three new processing times and obtain the same labor content (1,890 seconds per unit) as before. The resulting labor utilization would be improved to

$$\text{Average labor utilization} = \text{Labor content} / (\text{Labor content} + \text{Total idle time})$$
$$= 1,890 / (1,890 + 42 + 63 + 0) = 94.7\%$$

The process improvement we have implemented based on line balancing is sizeable in its economic impact. Based on the new bottleneck (worker 3), we see that we can produce one Xootr every 665 seconds, thereby having a process capacity of $\frac{1}{665}$ units/second × 3,600 seconds/hour × 35 hours/week = 189.5 units per week. Thus, compared to the unbalanced line (161.5 units per week), we have increased process capacity (and flow rate) by 17 percent (28 units) without having increased our weekly spending rate on labor. Moreover, we have reduced the cost of direct labor to $6.65/unit.

Figure 4.5 summarizes the idea of line balancing by contrasting cycle time and task allocation of the unbalanced line (before) and the balanced line (after).

4.5   Scale Up to Higher Volume

As indicated by Figure 4.2, demand for the Xootr increased dramatically within the next six months and, by July, had reached a level of 700 units per week. Thus, in order to maintain a reasonable match between supply and demand, Novacruz had to increase its process capacity (supply) further.

To increase process capacity for a worker-paced line, in this case from 189.5 units per week (see balanced line with three workers above) to 700 units per week, additional workers are needed. While the fundamental steps involved in building a Xootr remain unchanged, we have several options to lay out the new, high-volume process:

- Using the exact same layout and staffing plan, we could replicate the—now balanced—process and add another (and another, . . .) worker-paced line with three workers each.
- We could assign additional workers to the three process steps, which would increase the capacity of the steps and hence lead to a higher overall process capacity.
- We could divide up the work currently performed by three workers, thereby increasing the specialization of each step (and thus reducing processing times and hence increasing capacity).

FIGURE 4.5
**Graphical
Illustration of
Line Balance**

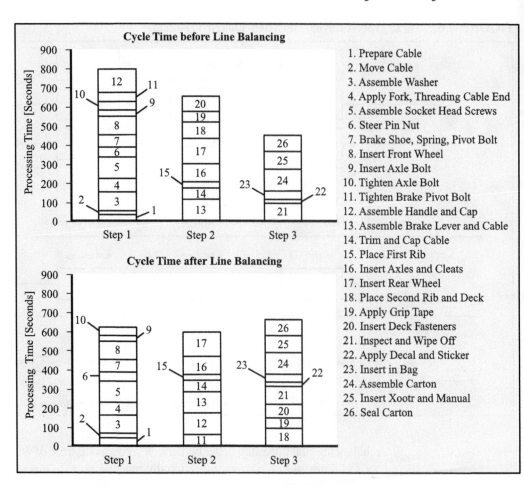

We will quickly go through the computations for all three approaches. The corresponding process flow diagrams are summarized in Figure 4.6.

Increasing Capacity by Replicating the Line

As the capacity of the entire operation grows linearly with the number of replications, we could simply add three replications of the process to obtain a new total capacity of 4×189.5 units/week = 758 units per week.

The advantage of this approach is that it would allow the organization to benefit from the knowledge it has gathered from their initial process layout. The downside of this approach is that it keeps the ratio of workers across the three process steps constant (in total, four people do step 1, four at step 2, and four at step 3), while this might not necessarily be the most efficient way of allocating workers to assembly tasks (it keeps the ratio between workers at each step fixed).

Alternatively, we could just add two replications and obtain a process capacity of 568.5 units per week and make up for the remaining 131.5 units (700 − 568.5 units/week) by adding overtime. Given that the 131.5 units to be produced in overtime would be spread over three lines, each line would have to produce 131.53/3 = 43.84 units per week corresponding to 8.1 hours of overtime per week (43.83 units/week/5.41 units/hour).

Under the assumption that we could use overtime, the average labor utilization would remain unchanged at 94.7 percent.

Increasing Capacity by Selectively Adding Workers

While the first approach assumed the number of workers at each process step to be the same, such a staffing might not necessarily be optimal. Specifically, we observe that (after the

FIGURE 4.6 **Three Process Layouts for High-Volume Production**

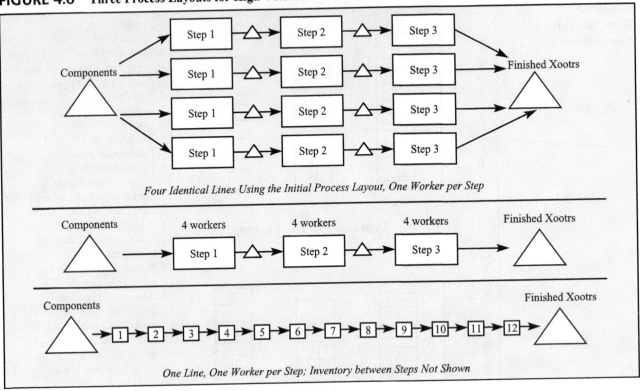

Four Identical Lines Using the Initial Process Layout, One Worker per Step

One Line, One Worker per Step; Inventory between Steps Not Shown

rebalancing) the third step is the bottleneck (processing time of 665 seconds per unit). Thus, we feel tempted to add over-proportionally more workers to this step than to the first two.

Given that we defined the capacity at each resource as the number of workers divided by the corresponding processing time, we can write the following:

$$\text{Requested capacity} = \frac{\text{Number of workers}}{\text{Activity time}}$$

For step 1, this calculation yields (700 units per week at 35 hours per week is 0.00555 unit per second):

$$0.00555 \text{ unit/second} = \frac{\text{Number of workers}}{623 \text{ seconds per unit}}$$

Thus, the number of workers required to meet the current demand is $0.00555 \times 623 = 3.46$ workers. Given that we cannot hire half a worker (and ignoring overtime for the moment), this means we have to hire four workers at step 1. In the same way, we find that we need to hire 3.34 workers at step 2 and 3.69 workers at step 3.

The fact that we need to hire a total of four workers for each of the three steps reflects the good balance that we have achieved above. If we would do a similar computation based on the initial numbers (792,648,450 seconds/unit for workers 1, 2, and 3 respectively; see Table 3.2), we would obtain the following:

- At step 1, we would hire 0.00555 unit/second = Number of workers/792 seconds/unit; therefore, Number of workers = 4.4.
- At step 2, we would hire 0.00555 unit/second = Number of workers/648 seconds/unit; therefore, Number of workers = 3.6.
- At step 3, we would hire 0.00555 unit/second = Number of workers/450 seconds/unit; therefore, Number of workers = 2.5.

Thus, we observe that a staffing that allocates extra resources to activities with longer processing times (5 workers for step 1 versus 4 for step 2 and 3 for step 3) provides an alternative way of line balancing.

Note also that if we had just replicated the unbalanced line, we would have had to add four replications as opposed to the three replications of the balanced line (we need five times step 1). Thus, line balancing, which at the level of the individual worker might look like "hair-splitting," debating about every second of worker time, at the aggregate level can achieve very substantial savings in direct labor cost.

At several places throughout the book, we will discuss the fundamental ideas of the Toyota Production System, of which line balancing is an important element. In the spirit of the Toyota Production System, idle time is considered as waste (*muda*) and therefore should be eliminated from the process to the extent possible.

Increasing Capacity by Further Specializing Tasks

Unlike the previous two approaches to increase capacity, the third approach fundamentally alters the way the individual tasks are assigned to workers. As we noted in our discussion of line balancing, we can think of each activity as a set of individual tasks. Thus, if we increase the level of specialization of workers and now have each worker only be responsible for one or two tasks (as opposed to previously an activity consisting of 5 to 10 tasks), we would be able to reduce processing time and thereby increase the capacity of the line.

Specifically, we begin our analysis by determining a targeted cycle time based on demand: in this case, we want to produce 700 units per week, which means 20 scooters per hour or one scooter every three minutes. How many workers does it take to produce one Xootr every three minutes?

The answer to this question is actually rather complicated. The reason for this complication is as follows. We cannot compute the capacity of an individual worker without knowing which tasks this worker will be in charge of. At the same time, we cannot assign tasks to workers, as we do not know how many workers we have.

To break this circularity, we start our analysis with the staffing we have obtained under the previous approaches, that is, 12 workers for the entire line. Table 4.3 shows how we can assign the tasks required to build a Xootr across these 12 workers.

Following this approach, the amount of work an individual worker needs to master is reduced to a maximum of 180 seconds. We refer to this number as the *span of control*. Given that this span of control is much smaller than under the previous approaches (665 seconds), workers will be able to perform their tasks with significantly less training. Workers are also likely to improve upon their processing times more quickly as specialization can increase the rate of learning.

The downside of this approach is its negative effect on labor utilization. Consider what has happened to labor utilization:

$$\text{Average labor utilization} = \frac{\text{Labor content}}{\text{Labor content} + \text{Sum of idle time}}$$

$$= \frac{1890}{1,890 + 25 + 0 + 65 + 7 + 11 + 11 + 51 + 45 + 40 + 10 + 3 + 2} = 87.5\%$$

Note that average labor utilization was 94.7 percent (after balancing) with three workers. Thus, specialization (smaller spans of control) makes line balancing substantially more complicated. This is illustrated by Figure 4.7.

The reason for this decrease in labor utilization, and thus the poorer line balance, can be found in the granularity of the tasks. Since it is not possible to break up the individual tasks further, moving a task from one worker to the next becomes relatively more significant. For example, when we balanced the three-worker process, moving a 51-second-per-unit

TABLE 4.3
Processing times and Task Allocation under Increased Specialization

Worker	Tasks	Task Duration [seconds/unit]
Worker 1	Prepare cable	30
	Move cable	25
	Assemble washer	100
		Total: 155
Worker 2	Apply fork, threading cable end	66
	Assemble socket head screws	114
		Total: 180
Worker 3	Steer pin nut	49
	Brake shoe, spring, pivot bolt	66
		Total: 115
Worker 4	Insert front wheel	100
	Insert axle bolt	30
	Tighten axle bolt	43
		Total: 173
Worker 5	Tighten brake pivot bolt	51
	Assemble handle cap	118
		Total: 169
Worker 6	Assemble brake lever and cable	110
	Trim and cap cable	59
		Total: 169
Worker 7	Place first rib	33
	Insert axles and cleats	96
		Total: 129
Worker 8	Insert rear wheel	135
		Total: 135
Worker 9	Place second rib and deck	84
	Apply grip tape	56
		Total: 140
Worker 10	Insert deck fasteners	75
	Inspect and wipe off	95
		Total: 170
Worker 11	Apply decal and sticker	20
	Insert in bag	43
	Assemble carton	114
		Total: 177
Worker 12	Insert Xootr and manual	94
	Seal carton	84
		Total: 178
	Total labor content	1,890

task to another step accounted for just 8 percent of the step's work (674 seconds per unit). In a 12-step process, however, moving the same 51-second-per-unit task is now relative to a 169-second-per-unit workload for the step, thereby accounting for 30 percent of work. For this reason, it is difficult to further improve the allocation of tasks to workers relative to what is shown in Figure 4.7.

The observation that line balancing becomes harder with an increase in specialization can best be understood if we "turn this reasoning on its head": line balancing becomes

FIGURE 4.7
Line Balance in a
Highly Specialized
Line
(Different shades
represent different
tasks)

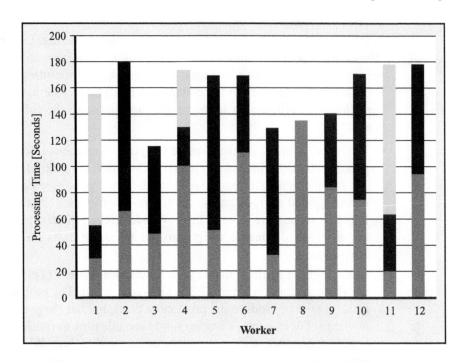

easier with a decrease in specialization. To see this, consider the case of having one single worker do all the tasks in the process. The corresponding labor utilization would be 100 percent (assuming there is enough demand to keep at least one worker busy), as, by definition, this one person also would be the bottleneck.

The idea of having one resource perform all activities of the process is referred to as a work cell. The process flow diagram of a work cell is illustrated by Figure 4.8. Since the processing time at a work cell with one worker is the same as the labor content, we would have a capacity per work cell of $\frac{1}{1,890}$ unit per second = 1.9048 units per hour, or 66.67 units per week. Already 11 work cells would be able to fulfill the demand of 700 Xootrs per week. In other words, the improved balance that comes with a work cell would allow us to further improve efficiency.

Again, the downside of this approach is that it requires one worker to master a span of control of over 30 minutes, which requires a highly trained operator. Moreover, Novacruz found that working with the 12-person line and the corresponding increase in specialization led to a substantial reduction in processing times.

FIGURE 4.8
Parallel Work Cells
(Only three work cells
are shown)

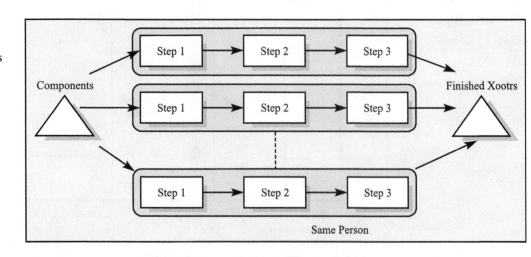

4.6
Summary

In this chapter, we introduced the concept of line balancing. Line balancing attempts to eliminate idle time from the process and thereby increase labor utilization. At first sight, line balancing seems to belong in the same category as "hair-splitting" and "penny-counting." However, it is important to understand the managerial role that line balancing plays in operations. Specifically, it is important to understand the following three managerial benefits:

- First of all, while it is always more tempting to talk about dollars rather than pennies, pennies do matter in many industries. Consider, for example, the computer industry. All PC manufacturers purchase from the same pool of suppliers of processors, disk drives, optical devices, and so forth. Thus, while the $10 of labor cost in a computer might seem small relative to the purchase price of the computer, those $10 are under our managerial control, while most of the other costs are dictated by the market environment.

- Second, in the spirit of the Toyota Production System (TPS), idle time is waste and thereby constitutes what in TPS is known as *muda*. The problem with *muda*/idle time is that it not only adds to the production costs, but has the potential to hide many other problems. For example, a worker might use idle time to finish or rework a task that she could not complete during the allocated processing time. While this does not lead to a direct, out-of-pocket cost, it avoids the root cause of the problem, which, when it surfaces, can be fixed.

- Third, while the $10 labor cost in the assembly operation of a PC manufacturer discussed above might seem like a low number, there is much more labor cost involved in the PC than $10. What appears as procurement cost for the PC maker is to some extent labor cost for the suppliers of the PC maker. If we "roll up" all operations throughout the value chain leading to a PC, we find that the cost of labor is rather substantial. This idea is illustrated in Figure 4.9 for the case of the automotive industry: while for a company like an automotive company assembly labor costs seem to be only a small element of costs, the 70 percent of costs that are procurement costs themselves include assembly labor costs from suppliers, subsuppliers, and so forth. If we look at all costs in the value chain (from an automotive company to their fifth-tier supplier), we see that about a quarter of costs in the automotive supply chain are a result of labor costs. A consequence of this observation is that it is not enough to improve our own operations

FIGURE 4.9
Sources of Cost in the Supply Chain

Source: Whitney 2004.

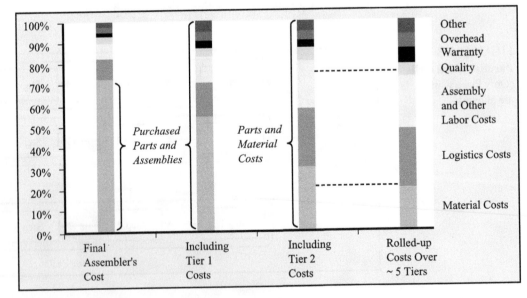

internally, but to spread such improvements throughout the supplier network, as this is where the biggest improvement opportunities are hidden. This concept of supplier development is another fundamental concept of the Toyota Production System.

In addition to these three factors, line balancing also illustrates an important—and from a managerial perspective very attractive—property of operations management. Line balancing improves per-unit labor cost (productivity) and does not require any financial investments in assets! To improve labor productivity, we would typically attempt to automate parts of the assembly, which would lower the per-unit labor cost, but at the same time require a higher investment of capital. Such an approach would be most likely if we operated in a high-wage location such as Germany or France. In contrast, we could try to operate the process with little or no automation but have a lot of labor time invested in the process. Such an approach would be more likely if we moved the process to a low-wage location such as China or Taiwan.

This tension is illustrated by Figure 4.10. The horizontal axis of Figure 4.10. shows the return on the assets tied up in the manufacturing process. High returns are desirable, which could be achieved by using little automation and a lot of labor. The vertical axis shows the productivity of labor, which would be maximized if the process were highly automated. As can be seen in Figure 4.10, there exists a tension (trade-off) between the dimensions, visible in the form of an efficient frontier. Thus, changes with respect to the level of automation would move the process up or down the frontier. One dimension is traded against the other.

In contrast, the effect of line balancing in the context of Figure 4.10 is very different. Line balancing improves labor productivity without any additional investment. To the extent that line balancing allows the firm to eliminate some currently underutilized resources using production equipment, line balancing also reduces the required assets. Thus, what from a strategic perspective seems like a simple, one-dimensional positioning problem along the technology frontier now has an additional dimension. Rather than simply taking the current process as given and finding a good strategic position, the firm should attempt to improve its process capability and improve along both performance dimensions simultaneously.

FIGURE 4.10
Trade-off between Labor Productivity and Capital Investment

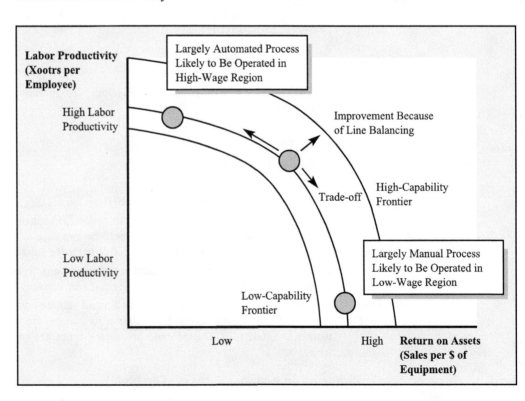

4.7
Further
Reading

Bartholdi and Eisenstein (1996) develop the concept of a bucket brigade, which corresponds to a line operation that is self-balancing. In this concept, workers move between stations and follow relatively simple decision rules that determine which task should be performed next.

Whitney (2004) presents a systematic approach to design and production of mechanical assemblies. This book introduces mechanical and economic models of assemblies and assembly automation. The book takes a system view of assembly, including the notion of product architecture, feature-based design, computer models of assemblies, analysis of mechanical constraint, assembly sequence analysis, tolerances, system-level design for assembly and JIT methods, and economics of assembly automation.

4.8
Practice
Problems

Q4.1*   **(Empty System, Labor Utilization)** Consider a process consisting of three resources in a worker-paced line and a wage rate of $10 per hour. Assume there is unlimited demand for the product.

Resource	Processing time (minutes)	Number of Workers
1	10	2
2	6	1
3	16	3

a. How long does it take the process to produce 100 units starting with an empty system?
b. What is the average labor content?
c. What is the average labor utilization?
d. What is the cost of direct labor?

Q4.2** **(Assign Tasks to Workers)** Consider the following six tasks that must be assigned to four workers on a conveyor-paced assembly line (i.e., a machine-paced line flow). Each worker must perform at least one task.

	Time to Complete Task (seconds)
Task 1	30
Task 2	25
Task 3	35
Task 4	40
Task 5	15
Task 6	30

The current conveyor-paced assembly line configuration assigns the workers in the following way:

- Worker 1: Task 1
- Worker 2: Task 2
- Worker 3: Tasks 3, 4
- Worker 4: Tasks 5, 6

a. What is the capacity of the current line?
b. Now assume that tasks are allocated to maximize capacity of the line, subject to the conditions that (1) a worker can only perform two adjacent operations and (2) all tasks need to be done in their numerical order. What is the capacity of this line now?
c. Now assume that tasks are allocated to maximize capacity of the line and that tasks can be performed in any order. What is the maximum capacity that can be achieved?

Q4.3   **(PowerToys)** PowerToys Inc. produces a small remote-controlled toy truck on a conveyor belt with nine stations. Each station has, under the current process layout, one worker assigned to it. Stations and processing times are summarized in the following table:

(* indicates that the solution is at the end of the book)

Station	Task	Processing Times (seconds)
1	Mount battery units	75
2	Insert remote control receiver	85
3	Insert chip	90
4	Mount front axle	65
5	Mount back axle	70
6	Install electric motor	55
7	Connect motor to battery unit	80
8	Connect motor to rear axle	65
9	Mount plastic body	80

a. What is the bottleneck in this process?

b. What is the capacity, in toy trucks per hour, of the assembly line?

c. What is the direct labor cost for the toy truck with the current process if each worker receives $15/hour, expressed in dollars per toy truck?

d. What would be the direct labor cost for the toy truck if work would be organized in a work cell, that is, one worker performs all tasks? Assume that the processing times would remain unchanged (i.e., there are no specialization gains).

e. What is the utilization of the worker in station 2?

Because of a drastically reduced forecast, the plant management has decided to cut staffing from nine to six workers per shift. Assume that (i) the nine tasks in the preceding table cannot be divided; (ii) the nine tasks are assigned to the six workers in the most efficient way possible; and (iii) if one worker is in charge of two tasks, the tasks have to be adjacent (i.e., one worker cannot work on tasks 1 and 3).

f. How would you assign the nine tasks to the six workers?

g. What is the new capacity of the line (in toy trucks per hour)?

Q4.4 **(12 Tasks to 4 Workers)** Consider the following tasks that must be assigned to four workers on a conveyor-paced assembly line (i.e., a machine-paced line flow). Each worker must perform at least one task. There is unlimited demand.

	Time to Complete Task (seconds)
Task 1	30
Task 2	25
Task 3	15
Task 4	20
Task 5	15
Task 6	20
Task 7	50
Task 8	15
Task 9	20
Task 10	25
Task 11	15
Task 12	20

The current conveyor-paced assembly-line configuration assigns the workers in the following way:

- Worker 1: Tasks 1, 2, 3
- Worker 2: Tasks 4, 5, 6
- Worker 3: Tasks 7, 8, 9
- Worker 4: Tasks 10, 11, 12

a. What is the capacity of the current line?

b. What is the direct labor content?

c. What is the average labor utilization (do not consider any transient effects such as the line being emptied before breaks or shift changes)?

d. How long would it take to produce 100 units, starting with an empty system?

The firm is hiring a fifth worker. Assume that tasks are allocated to the five workers to maximize capacity of the line, subject to the conditions that (i) a worker can only perform adjacent operations and (ii) all tasks need to be done in their numerical order.

e. What is the capacity of this line now?

Again, assume the firm has hired a fifth worker. Assume further that tasks are allocated to maximize capacity of the line and that tasks can be performed in any order.

f. What is the maximum capacity that can be achieved?

g. What is the minimum number of workers that could produce at an hourly rate of 72 units? Assume the tasks can be allocated to workers as described in the beginning (i.e., tasks cannot be done in any order).

Q4.5** (Geneva Watch) The Geneva Watch Corporation manufactures watches on a conveyor belt with six stations. One worker stands at each station and performs the following tasks:

Station	Tasks	Processing Time (seconds)
A: Preparation 1	Heat-stake lens to bezel	14
	Inspect bezel	26
	Clean switch holes	10
	Install set switch in bezel	18
	Total time for A	68
B: Preparation 2	Check switch travel	23
	Clean inside bezel	12
	Install module in bezel	25
	Total time for B	60
C: Battery installation	Install battery clip on module	20
	Heat-stake battery clip on module	15
	Install 2 batteries in module	22
	Check switch	13
	Total time for C	70
D: Band installation	Install band	45
	Inspect band	13
	Total time for D	58
E: Packaging preparation	Cosmetic inspection	20
	Final test	55
	Total time for E	75
F: Watch packaging	Place watch and cuff in display box	20
	Place cover in display box base	14
	Place owner's manual, box into tub	30
	Total time for F	64

These six workers begin their workday at 8:00 a.m. and work steadily until 4:00 p.m. At 4:00, no new watch parts are introduced into station A and the conveyor belt continues until all of the work-in-process inventory has been processed and leaves station F. Thus, each morning the workers begin with an empty system.

a. What is the bottleneck in this process?

b. What is the capacity, in watches per hour, of the assembly line (ignore the time it takes for the first watch to come off the line)?

c. What is the direct labor content for the processes on this conveyor belt?

d. What is the utilization of the worker in station B (ignore the time it takes for the first watch to come off the line)?

e. How many minutes of idle time will the worker in station C have in one hour (ignore the time it takes for the first watch to come off the line)?

f. What time will it be (within one minute) when the assembly line has processed 193 watches on any given day?

Q4.6 **(Yoggo Soft Drink)** A small, privately owned Asian company is producing a private-label soft drink, Yoggo. A machine-paced line puts the soft drinks into plastic bottles and then packages the bottles into boxes holding 10 bottles each. The machine-paced line is comprised of the following four steps: (1) the bottling machine takes 1 second to fill a bottle, (2) the lid machine takes 3 seconds to cover the bottle with a lid, (3) a labeling machine takes 5 seconds to apply a label to a bottle, and (4) the packaging machine takes 4 seconds to place a bottle into a box. When a box has been filled with 10 bottles, a worker tending the packaging machine removes the filled box and replaces it with an empty box. Assume that the time for the worker to remove a filled box and replace it with an empty box is negligible and hence does not affect the capacity of the line. At step 3 there are two labeling machines that each process alternating bottles, that is, the first machine processes bottles 1, 3, 5, . . . and the second machine processes bottles 2, 4, 6, . . . Problem data are summarized in the table following.

Process Step	Number of Machines	Seconds per Bottle
Bottling	1	1
Applying a lid	1	3
Labeling	2	5
Packaging	1	4

a. What is the process capacity (bottles/hour) for the machine-paced line?

b. What is the bottleneck in the process?

c. If one more identical labeling machine is added to the process, how much is the increase in the process capacity going to be (in terms of bottles/hour)?

d. What is the implied utilization of the packaging machine if the demand rate is 60 boxes/hour? Recall that a box consists of 10 bottles.

Q4.7 **(Atlas Inc.)** Atlas Inc. is a toy bicycle manufacturing company producing a five-inch small version of the bike that Lance Armstrong rode to win his first Tour de France. The assembly line at Atlas Inc. consists of seven work stations, each performing a single step. Stations and processing times are summarized here:

- Step 1 (30 sec.): The plastic tube for the frame is cut to size.
- Step 2 (20 sec.): The tube is put together.
- Step 3 (35 sec.): The frame is glued together.
- Step 4 (25 sec.): The frame is cleaned.
- Step 5 (30 sec.): Paint is sprayed onto the frame.
- Step 6 (45 sec.): Wheels are assembled.
- Step 7 (40 sec.): All other parts are assembled to the frame.

Under the current process layout, workers are allocated to the stations as shown here:

- Worker 1: Steps 1, 2
- Worker 2: Steps 3, 4
- Worker 3: Step 5
- Worker 4: Step 6
- Worker 5: Step 7

a. What is the bottleneck in this process?

b. What is the capacity of this assembly line, in finished units/hour?

c. What is the utilization of Worker 4, ignoring the production of the first and last units?

d. How long does it take to finish production of 100 units, starting with an empty process?

e. What is the average labor utilization of the workers, ignoring the production of the first and last units?

f. Assume the workers are paid $15 per hour. What is the cost of direct labor for the bicycle?

g. Based on recommendations of a consultant, Atlas Inc. decides to reallocate the tasks among the workers to achieve maximum process capacity. Assume that if a worker is in charge of two tasks, then the tasks have to be adjacent to each other. Also, assume that the sequence of steps cannot be changed. What is the maximum possible capacity, in units per hour, that can be achieved by this reallocation?

h. Again, assume a wage rate of $15 per hour. What would be the cost of direct labor if one single worker would perform all seven steps? You can ignore benefits of specialization, set-up times, or quality problems.

i. On account of a reduced demand forecast, management has decided to let go of one worker. If work is to be allocated among the four workers such that (i) the tasks can't be divided, (ii) if one worker is in charge of two tasks, the tasks have to be adjacent, (iii) the tasks are assigned in the most efficient way and (iv) each step can only be carried out by one worker, what is the new capacity of the line (in finished units/hour)?

Q4.8 **(Glove Design Challenge)** A manufacturer of women's designer gloves has employed a team of students to redesign her manufacturing unit. They gathered the following information. The manufacturing process consists of four activities: (1) fabric cutting; (2) dyeing; (3) stitching, done by specially designed machines; and (4) packaging. Processing times are shown below. Gloves are moved between activities by a conveyor belt that paces the flow of work (machine-paced line).

Process Step	Number of Machines	Minutes per Glove
Cutting	1	2
Dyeing	1	4
Stitching	1	3
Packaging	1	5

a. What is the process capacity in gloves/hour?

b. Which one of the following statements is true?

   i. The capacity of the process increases by reducing the dyeing time.

   ii. If stitching time increases to 5 min./glove, the capacity of the process remains unchanged, but "time through an empty machine-paced process" increases.

   iii. By reducing packaging time, the process capacity increases.

   iv. By reducing cutting time, the capacity of the process increases.

c. What is the implied utilization of the packaging machine if the demand rate is 10 gloves/hour?

d. What is the flow time for a glove?

Q4.9 **(Worker-Paced Line)**

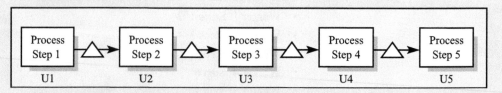

The accompanying diagram depicts a five-step, worker-paced headphone manufacturing plant. The headphones are meant to be used with iPods and DVD players. Step 1 involves a worker bending a metal strip into an arc shape. In step 2, the metal arc is fitted with a plastic sleeve. In step 3, the headphones are fitted at the end of the metal and plastic strips. In step 4, the wires are soldered into the headphones. Step 5 involves a specially designed packaging unit. After the plant has been operational for a couple of hours, the manager inspects the plant. He is particularly interested in cutting labor costs. He observes the following. The process is capacity constrained and the entire process produces 36 units in one hour. U1 through U5 denote the utilization at steps 1 through 5 respectively. Currently, there is a single worker at each step and the utilizations are as follows: U1 = 4/30, U2 = 4/15, U3 = 4/5, U4 = 1, U5 = 2/5.

Answer the following questions based on the given data and information.

a. What is the capacity of step 5?
b. Which step is the bottleneck?
c. Which process step has the highest capacity?
d. If the wage rate is $36 per hour per person, what is the direct labor cost per unit?

You can view a video of how problems marked with a ** are solved by going on www. cachon-terwiesch.net and follow the links under 'Solved Practice Problems'

Solutions to Selected Practice Problems

Chapter 4

Q4.1 (Empty System, Labor Utilization)

Part a

The following computations are based on Exhibit 4.1 in the book. Time to complete 100 units:

Step 1. The process will take $10 + 6 + 16$ minutes $= 32$ minutes to produce the first unit.

Step 2. Resource 2 is the bottleneck and the process capacity is 0.1666 unit per minute.

Step 3. Time to finish 100 units $= 32$ minutes $+ \dfrac{99 \text{ units}}{0.166 \text{ unit/minute}} = 626$ minutes

Parts b, c, and d

We answer these three questions together by using Exhibit 4.2 in the book.

Step 1. Capacities are

$$\text{Resource 1} : \frac{2}{10} \text{ unit/minute} = 0.2 \text{ unit/minute}$$

$$\text{Resource 2} : \frac{1}{6} \text{ unit/minute} = 0.1666 \text{ unit/minute}$$

$$\text{Resource 3} : \frac{3}{16} \text{ unit/minute} = 0.1875 \text{ unit/minute}$$

Resource 2 is the bottleneck and the process capacity is 0.1666 unit/minute.

Step 2. Since there is unlimited demand, the flow rate is determined by the capacity and therefore is 0.1666 unit/minute; this corresponds to a cycle time of 6 minutes/unit.

$$\text{Step 3. Cost of direct labor} = \frac{6 \times \$10/\text{hour}}{60 \text{ minutes/hour} \times 0.1666 \text{ unit/minute}} = \$6/\text{unit}$$

Step 4. Compute the idle time of each worker for each unit:

$$\text{Idle time for workers at resource 1} = 6 \text{ minutes/unit} \times 2 - 10 \text{ minutes/unit}$$
$$= 2 \text{ minutes/unit}$$

$$\text{Idle time for worker at resource 2} = 6 \text{ minutes/unit} \times 1 - 6 \text{ minutes/unit}$$
$$= 0 \text{ minute/unit}$$

$$\text{Idle time for workers at resource 3} = 6 \text{ minutes/unit} \times 3 - 16 \text{ minutes/unit}$$
$$= 2 \text{ minutes/unit}$$

Step 5. Labor content $= 10 + 6 + 16$ minutes/unit $= 32$ minutes/unit

Step 6. Average labor utilization $= \dfrac{32}{32 + 4} = 0.8888$

7

Batching and Other Flow Interruptions: Setup Times and the Economic Order Quantity Model

Up to this point, we were working under the assumption that during every X units of time, one flow unit would enter the process and one flow unit would leave the process. We defined X as the process cycle time. In the scooter example of Chapter 4, we established a cycle time of three minutes in conjunction with Table 4.3, allowing us to fulfill demand of 700 scooters per week.

In an ideal process, a cycle time of three minutes would imply that every resource receives one flow unit as an input each three-minute interval and creates one flow unit of output each three-minute interval. Such a smooth and constant flow of units is the dream of any operations manager, yet it is rarely feasible in practice. There are several reasons for why the smooth process flow is interrupted, the most important ones being setups and variability in processing times or quality levels. The focus of this chapter is on setups, which are an important characteristic of batch-flow operations. Problems related to variability are discussed in Chapters 8 and 9. And quality problems are discussed in Chapter 10.

To discuss setups, we return to the Xootr production process. In particular, we consider the computer numerically controlled (CNC) milling machine which is responsible for making two types of parts on each Xootr—the steer support and two ribs (see Figure 7.1). The steer support attaches the Xootr's deck to the steering column, and the ribs help the deck support the weight of the rider. Once the milling machine starts producing one of these parts, it can produce them reasonably quickly. However, a considerable setup time, or changeover time, is needed before the production of each part type can begin. Our primary objective is to understand how setups like these influence the three basic performance measures of a process: inventory, flow rate, and flow time.

FIGURE 7.1   Milling Machine (left) and Steer Support Parts (right)

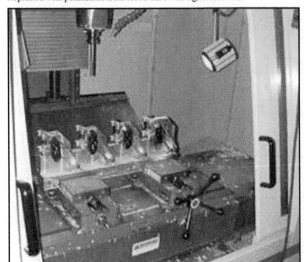 

7.1   The Impact of Setups on Capacity

To evaluate the capacity of the milling machine, we need some more information. Specifically, once set up to produce a part, the milling machine can produce steer supports at the rate of one per minute and can produce ribs at the rate of two per minute. Recall, each Xootr needs one steer support and two ribs. Furthermore, one hour is needed to set up the milling machine to start producing steer supports and one hour is also needed to begin producing ribs. Although no parts are produced during those setup times, it is not quite correct to say that nothing is happening during those times either. The milling machine operator is busy calibrating the milling machine so that it can produce the desired part.

It makes intuitive sense that the following production process should be used with these two parts: set up the machine to make steer supports, make some steer supports, set up the machine to make ribs, make some ribs, and finally, repeat this sequence of setups and production runs. We call this repeating sequence a *production cycle*: one production cycle occurs immediately after another, and all productions cycles "look the same" in the sense that they have the same setups and production runs.

We call this a batch production process because parts are made in batches. Although it may be apparent by what is meant by a "batch", it is useful to provide a precise definition:

A *batch* is a collection of flow units.

Throughout our analysis, we assume that batches are produced in succession. That is, once the production of one batch is completed, the production of the next batch begins and all batches contain the same number and type of flow unit.

Given that a batch is a collection of flow units, we need to define our flow unit in the case of the Xootr. Each Xootr needs one steer support and two ribs, so let's say the flow unit is a "component set" and each component set is composed of those three parts. Hence, each production cycle produces a batch of component sets.

One might ask why we did not define the flow unit to be one of the two types of parts. For example, we could call the steering supports made in a production run a batch of steering supports. However, our interest is not specifically on the capacity to make steering supports or ribs in isolation. We care about the capacity for component sets because one component

FIGURE 7.2 The Impact of Setup Times on Capacity

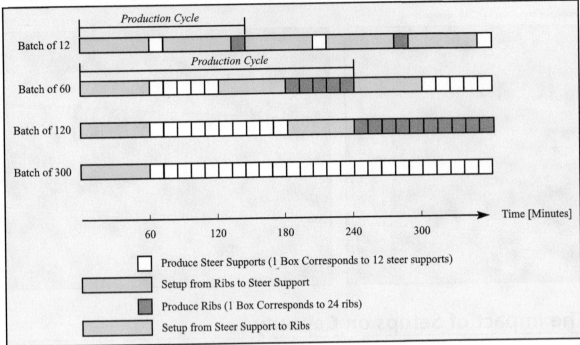

Produce Steer Supports (1 Box Corresponds to 12 steer supports)

Setup from Ribs to Steer Support

Produce Ribs (1 Box Corresponds to 24 ribs)

Setup from Steer Support to Ribs

set is needed for each Xootr. Thus, for the purpose of this analysis, it makes more sense to define the flow unit as a component set and to think in terms of a batch of component sets.

Because no output is produced while the resource is in setup mode, it is fairly intuitive that frequent setups lead to lower capacity. To understand how setups reduce the capacity of a process, consider Figure 7.2. The impact of setups on capacity is fairly intuitive. As nothing is produced at a resource during setup, the more frequently a resource is set up, the lower its capacity. As discussed above, the milling machine underlying the example of Figure 7.2 has the following processing times/setup times:

- It takes one minute to produce one steer support unit (of which there is one per Xootr).
- It takes 60 minutes to change over the milling machine from producing steer supports to producing ribs (setup time).
- It takes 0.5 minute to produce one rib; because there are two ribs in a Xootr, this translates to one minute/per component set.
- Finally, it takes another 60 minutes to change over the milling machine back to producing steer supports.

Now consider the impact that varying the batch size has on capacity. Recall that we defined capacity as the maximum flow rate at which a process can operate. If we produce in small batches of 12 component sets per batch, we spend a total of two hours of setup time (one hour to set up the production for steer supports and one hour to set up the production of ribs) for every 12 component sets we produce. These two hours of setup time are lost from regular production.

The capacity of the resource can be increased by increasing the batch size. If the machine is set up every 60 units, the capacity-reducing impact of setup can be spread out over 60 units. This results in a higher capacity for the milling machine. Specifically, for a batch size of 60, the milling machine could produce at 0.25 component set per minute. Table 7.1 summarizes the capacity calculations for batch sizes of 12, 60, 120, and 300.

TABLE 7.1
The Impact of Setups on Capacity

Batch Size	Time to Complete One Batch [minutes]	Capacity [units/minute]
12	60 minutes (set up steering support)	12/144 = 0.0833
	+ 12 minutes (produce steering supports)	
	+ 60 minutes (set up ribs)	
	+ 12 minutes (produce ribs)	
	144 minutes	
60	60 minutes (set up steering support)	60/240 = 0.25
	+ 60 minutes (produce steering supports)	
	+ 60 minutes (set up ribs)	
	+ 60 minutes (produce ribs)	
	240 minutes	
120	60 minutes (set up steering support)	120/360 = 0.333
	+ 120 minutes (produce steering supports)	
	+ 60 minutes (set up ribs)	
	+ 120 minutes (produce ribs)	
	360 minutes	
300	60 minutes (set up steering support)	300/720 = 0.4166
	+ 300 minutes (produce steering supports)	
	+ 60 minutes (set up ribs)	
	+ 300 minutes (produce ribs)	
	720 minutes	

Generalizing the computations in Table 7.1, we can compute the capacity of a resource with setups as a function of the batch size:

$$\text{Capacity given batch size} = \frac{\text{Batch size}}{\text{Setup time} + \text{Batch size} \times \text{Processing time}}$$

Basically, the above equation is spreading the "unproductive" setup time over the members of a batch. To use the equation, we need to be precise about what we mean by batch size, the setup time, and processing time:

• The batch size is the number of flow units that are produced in one "cycle" (i.e., before the process repeats itself, see Figure 7.2).

• The setup time includes all setups in the production of the batch. In this case, this includes $S = 60$ minutes $+ 60$ minutes $= 120$ minutes. It can also include any other nonproducing time associated with the production of the batch. For example, if the production of each batch requires a 10-minute worker break, then that would be included. Other "setup times" can include scheduled maintenance or forced idled time (time in which literally nothing is happening with the machine—it is neither producing nor being prepped to produce).

• The processing time includes all production time that is needed to produce one complete flow unit of output at the milling machine. In this case, this includes 1 minute/ unit for the steer support as well as two times 0.5 minute/unit for the two ribs. The processing time is thus $p = 1$ minute/unit $+ 2 \times 0.5$ minute/unit $= 2$ minutes/unit. Notice that the processing time is 2 minutes even though no single component set is actually produced over a single period of 2 minutes of length. Due to setups, the processing time for a component set is divided over two periods of one minute each, and those two periods can be separated by a considerable amount of time. Nevertheless, from

FIGURE 7.3
Capacity as a Function of the Batch Size

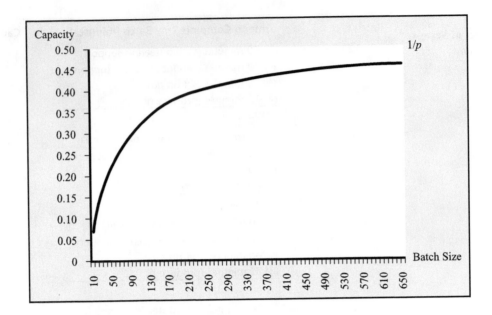

the perspective of calculating the capacity of the milling machine when operated with a given batch size, it does not matter whether each component set is produced over a continuous period of time or disjointed periods of time. All that matters is that a total of 2 minutes is needed for each component set.

Given these definitions, say we operate with a batch size of 100 units. Our capacity in this case would be

$$\text{Capacity (for } B = 100) = \frac{\text{Batch size}}{\text{Setup time} + \text{Batch size} \times \text{Processing time}}$$

$$= \frac{100 \text{ units}}{120 \text{ minutes} + 100 \text{ units} \times 2 \text{ minutes/unit}}$$

$$= 0.3125 \text{ unit/minute}$$

No matter how large a batch size we choose, we will never be able to produce faster than one unit every p units of time. Thus, $1/p$ can be thought of as the maximum capacity the process can achieve. This is illustrated in Figure 7.3.

7.2   Interaction between Batching and Inventory

Given the desirable effect that large batch sizes increase capacity, why not choose the largest possible batch size to maximize capacity? While large batch sizes are desirable from a capacity perspective, they typically require a higher level of inventory, either within the process or at the finished goods level. Holding the flow rate constant, we can infer from Little's Law that such a higher inventory level also will lead to longer flow times. This is why batch-flow operations generally are not very fast in responding to customer orders (remember the last time you bought custom furniture?).

The interaction between batching and inventory is illustrated by the following two examples. First, consider an auto manufacturer producing a sedan and a station wagon on the same assembly line. For simplicity, assume both models have the same demand rate, 400 cars per day each. The metal stamping steps in the process preceding final assembly

FIGURE 7.4 **The Impact of Batch Sizes on Inventory**

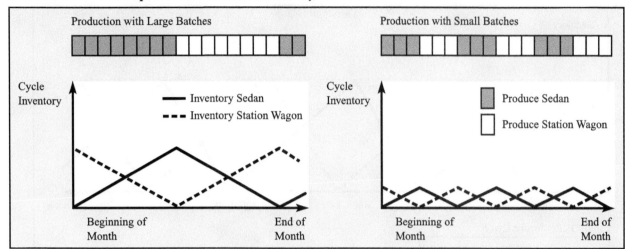

are characterized by especially long setup times. Thus, to achieve a high level of capacity, the plant runs large production batches and produces sedans from the first of a month to the 15th and station wagons from the 16th to the end of the month.

However, it seems fairly unrealistic to assume that customers only demand sedans at the beginning of the month and station wagons at the end of the month. In other words, producing in large batches leads to a mismatch between the rate of supply and the rate of demand.

Thus, in addition to producing enough to cover demand in the first half of the month, to satisfy demand for sedans the company needs to produce 15 days of demand to inventory, which then fulfills demand while the line produces station wagons. This is illustrated by the left side of Figure 7.4. Observe that the average level of inventory is 3,000 cars for each of the two models. Now, ignoring setup times for a moment, consider the case in which the firm produces 400 station wagons and 400 sedans a day. In this setting, one would only need to carry 0.5 day of cycle inventory, a dramatic reduction in inventory. This is illustrated by the right side of Figure 7.4. Thus, smaller batches translate to lower inventory levels!

In the ideal case, which has been propagated by Toyota Production Systems under the word *heijunka* or *mixed-model* production, the company would alternate between producing one sedan and producing one station wagon, thereby producing in batch sizes of one. This way, a much better synchronization of the demand flow and the production flow is achieved and cycle inventory is eliminated entirely.

Second, consider a furniture maker producing chairs in batch sizes of 100. Starting with the wood-cutting step and all the way through the finishing process, the batch of 100 chairs would stay together as one entity.

Now, take the position of one chair in the batch. What is the most dominant activity throughout the process? Waiting! The larger the batch size, the longer the time the flow unit waits for the other "members" of the same batch—a situation comparable with going to the barber with an entire class of children. Given Little's Law, this increase in wait time (and thereby flow time) leads to a proportional increase in inventory.

With these observations, we can turn our attention back to the milling machine at Nova Cruz. Similar to Figure 7.4, we can draw the inventory of components (ribs and steer supports) over the course of a production cycle. Remember that the assembly process following the milling machine requires a supply of one unit every three minutes. This one

FIGURE 7.5 The Impact of Setup Times on Capacity

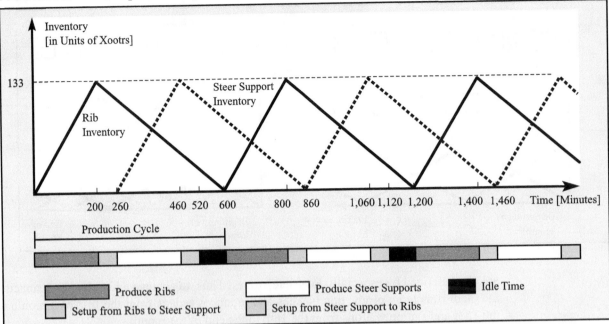

unit consists, from the view of the milling machine, of two ribs and a steer support unit. If we want to ensure a sufficient supply to keep the assembly process operating, we have to produce a sufficient number of ribs such that during the time we do not produce ribs (e.g., setup time and production of steer support) we do not run out of ribs. Say the milling machine operates with a batch size of 200 units, $B = 200$. In that case, the inventory of ribs changes as follows:

- During the production of ribs, inventory accumulates. As we produce ribs for one scooter per minute, but only supply ribs to the assembly line at a rate of one scooter every three minutes, rib inventory accumulates at the rate of two scooters per three minutes, or 2/3 scooters per minute.

- Because we produce for 200 minutes, the inventory of ribs at the end of the production run is 200 minutes × 2/3 scooters per minute = 133 scooters (i.e., 266 ribs).

- How long does the rib inventory for 133 scooters last? The inventory ensures supply to the assembly for 400 minutes (cycle time of assembly operations was three minutes). After these 400 minutes, we need to start producing ribs again. During these 400 minutes, we have to accommodate two setups (together 120 minutes) and 200 minutes for producing the steer supports.

The resulting production plan as well as the corresponding inventory levels are summarized by Figure 7.5. Notice that each production cycle takes 600 minutes, and this includes 80 minutes of idle time. Why do we insert additional idle time into the milling machine's production schedule? The answer is that without the idle time, the milling machine would produce too quickly given our batch size of 200 units. To explain, assembly takes 200 units × 3 minute/unit = 600 minutes to produce a batch of 200 scooters. The milling machine only needs 520 minutes to produce that batch of 600 scooters (120 minutes of setup and 400 minutes of production). Hence, if the milling machine produced one batch after another (without any idle time between them), it would produce 200 components sets every 520 minutes (or 200/520 = 0.3846 components sets per minute), which is faster than assembly can use them (which is 1/3 component sets per minute). This analysis suggests that maybe we want to choose a different batch size, as we see in the next section.

7.3 Choosing a Batch Size in the Presence of Setup Times

When choosing an appropriate batch size for a process flow, it is important to balance the conflicting objectives: capacity and inventory. Large batches lead to large inventory; small batches lead to losses in capacity.

In balancing these two conflicting objectives, we benefit from the following two observations:

• Capacity at the bottleneck step is extremely valuable (as long as the process is capacity-constrained, i.e., there is more demand than capacity) as it constrains the flow rate of the entire process.

• Capacity at a nonbottleneck step is free, as it does not provide a constraint on the current flow rate.

This has direct implications for choosing an appropriate batch size at a process step with setups.

• If the setup occurs at the bottleneck step (and the process is capacity-constrained), it is desirable to increase the batch size, as this results in a larger process capacity and, therefore, a higher flow rate.

• If the setup occurs at a nonbottleneck step (or the process is demand-constrained), it is desirable to decrease the batch size, as this decreases inventory as well as flow time.

The scooter example summarized by Figure 7.6 illustrates these two observations and how they help us in choosing a good batch size. Remember that B denotes the batch size, S the setup time, and p the per unit processing time.

The process flow diagram in Figure 7.6 consists of only two activities: the milling machine and the assembly operations. We can combine the assembly operations into one activity, as we know that its slowest step (bottleneck of assembly) can create one Xootr every three minutes.

To determine the capacity of the milling machine for a batch size of 12, we apply the formula

$$\text{Capacity } (B) = \frac{\text{Batch size}}{\text{Setup time} + \text{Batch size} \times \text{Processing time}}$$

$$= \frac{B}{S + B \times p} = \frac{12}{120 + 12 \times 2} = 0.0833 \text{ unit/minute}$$

The capacity of the assembly operation is easily computed based on its bottleneck capacity of $\frac{1}{3}$ unit per minute. Note that for $B = 12$, the milling machine is the bottleneck.

FIGURE 7.6
Data from the Scooter Case about Setup Times and Batching

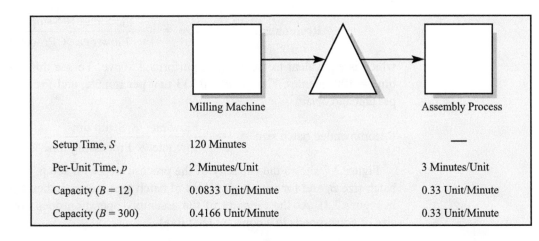

	Milling Machine	Assembly Process
Setup Time, S	120 Minutes	—
Per-Unit Time, p	2 Minutes/Unit	3 Minutes/Unit
Capacity ($B = 12$)	0.0833 Unit/Minute	0.33 Unit/Minute
Capacity ($B = 300$)	0.4166 Unit/Minute	0.33 Unit/Minute

Next consider, what happens to the same calculations if we increase the batch size from 12 to 300. While this does not affect the capacity of the assembly operations, the capacity of the milling machine now becomes

$$\text{Capacity } (B) = \frac{B}{S + B \times p} = \frac{300}{120 + 300 \times 2} = 0.4166 \text{ unit/minute}$$

Thus, we observe that the location of the bottleneck has shifted from the milling machine to the assembly operation, just by modifying the batch size. Now which of the two batch sizes is the "better" one, 12 or 300?

- The batch size of 300 is clearly too large. The milling machine incurs idle time as the overall process is constrained by the (substantially) smaller capacity of the assembly operations (note, based on Figure 7.5, we know that even for the smaller batch size of $B = 200$, there exists idle time at the milling machine). This large batch size is likely to create unnecessary inventory problems as described above.

- The batch size of 12 is likely to be more attractive in terms of inventory. Yet, the process capacity has been reduced to 0.0833 unit per minute, leaving the assembly operation starved for work.

As a batch size of 12 is too small and a batch size of 300 is too large, a good batch size is "somewhere in between." Specifically, we are interested in the smallest batch size that does not adversely affect process capacity.

To find this number, we equate the capacity of the step with setup (in this case, the milling machine) with the capacity of the step from the remaining process that has the smallest capacity (in this case, the assembly operations):

$$\frac{B}{120 + B \times 2} = \frac{1}{3}$$

and solve this equation for B:

$$\frac{B}{120 + B \times 2} = \frac{1}{3}$$

$$3 \times B = 120 + 2 \times B$$

$$B = 120$$

which gives us, in this case, $B = 120$. This algebraic approach is illustrated by Figure 7.7. If you feel uncomfortable with the calculus outlined above (i.e., solving the equation for the batch size B), or you want to program the method directly into Excel or another software package, you can use the following equation:

$$\text{Recommended batch size} = \frac{\text{Flow rate} \times \text{Setup time}}{1 - \text{Flow rate} \times \text{Processing time}}$$

which is equivalent to the analysis performed above. To see this, simply substitute Setup time = 120 minutes, Flow rate = 0.333 unit per minute, and Processing time = 2 minutes per unit and obtain

$$\text{Recommended batch size} = \frac{\text{Flow rate} \times \text{Setup time}}{1 - \text{Flow rate} \times \text{Processing time}} = \frac{0.333 \times 120}{1 - 0.333 \times 2} = 120$$

Figure 7.7 shows the capacity of the process step with setup, which increases with the batch size B, and for very high values of batch size B approaches $1/p$ (similar to the graph in Figure 7.3). As the capacity of the assembly operation does not depend on the batch size, it corresponds to a constant (flat line).

Exhibit 7.1

FINDING A GOOD BATCH SIZE IN THE PRESENCE OF SETUP TIMES

1. Compute Flow rate = Minimum {Available input, Demand, Process capacity}.
2. Define the production cycle, which includes the processing and setups of all flow units in a batch.
3. Compute the time in a production cycle that the resource is in setup; setup times are those times that are independent of the batch size.
4. Compute the time in a production cycle that the resource is processing; this includes all the processing times that are incurred per unit (i.e., are repeated for every member of the batch).
5. Compute the capacity of the resource with setup for a given batch size:

$$\text{Capacity } (B) = \frac{B}{\text{Setup time} + B \times \text{Processing time}}$$

6. We are looking for the batch size that leads to the lowest level of inventory without affecting flow rate; we find this by solving the equation

$$\text{Capacity } (B) = \text{Flow rate}$$

for the batch size B. This also can be done directly using the following formula:

$$\text{Recommended batch size} = \frac{\text{Flow rate} \times \text{Setup time}}{1 - \text{Flow rate} \times \text{Processing time}}$$

The overall process capacity is—in the spirit of the bottleneck idea—the minimum of the two graphs. Thus, before the graphs intersect, the capacity is too low and flow rate is potentially given up. After the intersection point, the assembly operation is the bottleneck and any further increases in batch size yield no return. Exhibit 7.1 provides a summary of the computations leading to the recommended batch size in the presence of setup times.

FIGURE 7.7
Choosing a "Good" Batch Size

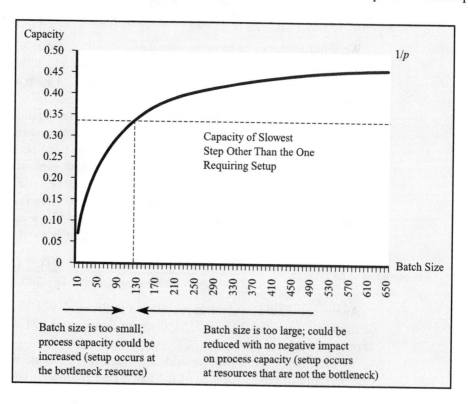

7.4 Setup Times and Product Variety

As we have seen in the case of the Xootr production process, setup times often occur due to the need to change over production from one product to another. This raises the following question: What is the impact of product variety on a process with setup times? To explore this question, let's consider a simple process that makes two kinds of soup: chicken noodle and tomato.

Demand for chicken soup is 100 gallons per hour, while demand for tomato soup is 75 gallons per hour. Switching from one type of soup to another requires 30 minutes to clean the production equipment so that one flavor does not disrupt the flavor of the next soup. Once production begins, the process can make 300 gallons per hour of either type of soup. Given these parameters, let's evaluate a production cycle that minimizes inventory while satisfying demand.

We first need to define our flow unit. In this case, it is natural to let our flow unit be one gallon of soup. Hence, a production cycle of soup contains a certain number of gallons, some chicken and some tomato. In this case, a "batch" is the set of gallons produced in a production cycle. While the plant manager is likely to refer to batches of tomato soup and batches of chicken soup individually, and unlikely to refer to the batch that combines both flavors, we cannot analyze the production process of tomato soup in isolation from the production process of chicken soup. (For example, if we dedicate more time to tomato production, then we will have less time for chicken noodle production.) Because we are ultimately interested in our capacity to make soup, we focus our analysis at the level of the production cycle and refer to the entire production within that cycle as a "batch."

Our desired flow rate is 175 gallons per hour (the sum of demand for chicken and tomato), the setup time is 1 hour (30 minutes per soup and two types of soup) and the processing time is 1/300 hour per gallon. The batch size that minimizes inventory while still meeting our demand is then

$$\text{Recommended batch size} = \frac{\text{Flow rate} \times \text{Setup time}}{1 - \text{Flow rate} \times \text{Processing time}} = \frac{175 \times (2 \times 1/2)}{1 - 175 \times (1/300)} = 420 \text{ gallons}$$

We should produce in proportion to demand (otherwise at least one of the flavors will have too much production and at least one will have too little), so of the 420 gallons, $420 \times 100/(100 + 75) = 240$ gallons should be chicken soup and the remainder, $420 - 240 = 180$ gallons, should be tomato.

To understand the impact of variety on this process, suppose we were to add a third kind of soup to our product offering, onion soup. Furthermore, with onion soup added to the mix, demand for chicken remains 100 gallons per hour, and demand for tomato continues to be 75 gallons per hour, while onion now generates 30 gallons of demand on its own. In some sense, this is an ideal case for adding variety—the new variant adds incrementally to demand without stealing any demand from the existing varieties.

The desired flow rate is now $100 + 75 + 30 = 205$, the setup time is 1.5 hours (three setups per batch), and the inventory minimizing quantity for the production cycle is

$$\text{Recommended batch size} = \frac{\text{Flow rate} \times \text{Setup time}}{1 - \text{Flow rate} \times \text{Processing time}} = \frac{205 \times (3 \times 1/2)}{1 - 205 \times (1/300)} = 971 \text{ gallons}$$

Again, we should produce in proportion to demand: $971 \times (100/205) = 474$ gallons of chicken, $971 \times (75/205) = 355$ gallons of tomato, and $971 \times (30/205) = 142$ gallons of onion.

So what happened when we added to variety? In short, we need more inventory. Our first hint of this is the size of the batch (the amount of soup across all flavors that is produced in a production cycle)—420 gallons without onion, while 971 gallons with onion. We can explore this further by evaluating the maximum inventory of chicken soup in either case. (Average inventory of chicken soup is half of its peak inventory.) In our original case, during production, inventory of chicken soup increases at the rate of $300 - 100 = 200$ gallons per hour. Production of 240 gallons of chicken soup requires 240/300 hours. So, peak inventory of chicken soup is $200 \times (240/300) = 160$ gallons. The analogous calculation with onion included yields a peak inventory of $200 \times (474/300) = 316$ gallons, a 98 percent increase in the amount of inventory needed!

Why did inventory of chicken soup increase when onion soup was added to the mix? Setup times are to blame. With more varieties in the production mix, the production process has to set up more often per production cycle. This reduces the capacity of the production cycle (no soup is made during a setup). To increase the capacity back to the desired flow rate (which is even higher now), we need to operate with larger batches (longer production cycles), and they lead to more inventory.

One may argue that the previous analysis is too optimistic—adding onion soup to the mix should steal some demand away from the other flavors. It turns out that our result is not sensitive to this assumption. To demonstrate, let's consider the opposite extreme—adding onion soup does not expand overall demand, it only steals demand from the other flavors. Specifically, the overall flow rate remains 175 gallons per hour, with or without onion soup. Furthermore, with onion soup, the demand rate for chicken, tomato, and onion are 80, 65, and 30 gallons per hour, respectively. The processing time is still 1/300 gallons per hour, and the setup time per batch is now 1.5 hours (three changeovers due to three types of soup). The batch size that minimizes our inventory while meeting our demand is

$$\text{Recommended batch size} = \frac{\text{Flow rate} \times \text{Setup time}}{1 - \text{Flow rate} \times \text{Processing time}} = \frac{175 \times (3 \times 1/2)}{1 - 175 \times (1/300)} = 630 \text{ gallons}$$

Inventory does not increase as much in this case, but it still increases.

The conclusion from this investigation is that setup times and product variety do not mix very well. Consequently, there are two possible solutions to this challenge. The first is to offer only a limited amount of variety. That was Henry Ford's approach when he famously declared that "You can have any color Model-T you want, as long as it is black." While a convenient solution for a production manager, it is not necessarily the best strategy for satisfying demand in a competitive environment.

The other approach to the incompatibility of setups and variety is to work to eliminate setup times. This is the approach advocated by Shigeo Shingo, one of the most influential thought leader in manufacturing. When he witnessed changeover times of more than an hour in an automobile plant, he responded with the quote, "The flow must go on," meaning that every effort must be made to ensure a smooth flow of production. One way to ensure a smooth flow is to eliminate or reduce setup times. Shigeo Shingo developed a powerful technique for doing exactly that, which we will revisit later in the chapter.

7.5 Setup Time Reduction

Despite improvement potential from the use of "good" batch sizes and smaller transfer batches, setups remain a source of disruption of a smooth process flow. For this reason, rather than taking setups as "God-given" constraints and finding ways to accommodate them, we should find ways that directly address the root cause of the disruption.

This is the basic idea underlying the single minute exchange of die (SMED) method. The creators of the SMED method referred to any setup exceeding 10 minutes as an unacceptable source of process flow disruption. The 10-minute rule is not necessarily meant to be taken literally: the method was developed in the automotive industry, where setup times used to take as much as four hours. The SMED method helps to define an aggressive, yet realistic setup time goal and to identify potential opportunities of setup time reduction.

The basic underlying idea of SMED is to carefully analyze all tasks that are part of the setup time and then divide those tasks into two groups, *internal* setup tasks and *external* setup tasks.

- Internal setup tasks are those tasks that can only be executed while the machine is stopped.
- External setup tasks are those tasks that can be done while the machine is still operating, meaning they can be done *before* the actual changeover occurs.

Experience shows that companies are biased toward using internal setups and that, even without making large investments, internal setups can be translated into external setups.

Similar to our discussion about choosing a good batch size, the biggest obstacles to overcome are ineffective cost accounting procedures. Consider, for example, the case of a simple heat treatment procedure in which flow units are moved on a tray and put into an oven. Loading and unloading of the tray is part of the setup time. The acquisition of an additional tray that can be loaded (or unloaded) while the other tray is still in process (before the setup) allows the company to convert internal setup tasks to external ones. Is this a worthwhile investment?

The answer is, as usual, it depends. SMED applied to nonbottleneck steps is not creating any process improvement at all. As discussed previously, nonbottleneck steps have excessive capacity and therefore setups are entirely free (except for the resulting increase in inventory). Thus, investing in any resource, technical or human, is not only wasteful, but it also takes scarce improvement capacity/funds away from more urgent projects. However, if the oven in the previous example were the bottleneck step, almost any investment in the acquisition of additional trays suddenly becomes a highly profitable investment.

The idea of internal and external setups as well as potential conversion from internal to external setups is best visible in car racing. Any pit stop is a significant disruption of the race car's flow toward the finish line. At any point and any moment in the race, an entire crew is prepared to take in the car, having prepared for any technical problem from tire changes to refueling. While the technical crew might appear idle and underutilized throughout most of the race, it is clear that any second they can reduce from the time the car is in the pit (internal setups) to a moment when the car is on the race track is a major gain (e.g., no race team would consider mounting tires on wheels during the race; they just put on entire wheels).

7.6 Balancing Setup Costs with Inventory Costs: The EOQ Model

Up to now, our focus has been on the role of setup times, as opposed to setup costs. Specifically, we have seen that setup time at the bottleneck leads to an overall reduction in process capacity. Assuming that the process is currently capacity-constrained, setup times thereby carry an opportunity cost reflecting the overall lower flow rate (sales).

Independent of such opportunity costs, setups frequently are associated with direct (out-of-pocket) costs. In these cases, we speak of setup costs (as opposed to setup times). Consider, for example, the following settings:

- The setup of a machine to process a certain part might require scrapping the first 10 parts that are produced after the setup. Thus, the material costs of these 10 parts constitute a setup cost.

- Assume that we are charged a per-time-unit usage fee for a particular resource (e.g., for the milling machine discussed above). Thus, every minute we use the resource, independent of whether we use it for setup or for real production, we have to pay for the resource. In this case, "time is money" and the setup time thereby translates directly into setup costs. However, as we will discuss below, one needs to be very careful when making the conversion from setup times to setup costs.

- When receiving shipments from a supplier, there frequently exists a fixed shipment cost as part of the procurement cost, which is independent of the purchased quantity. This is similar to the shipping charges that a consumer pays at a catalog or online retailer. Shipping costs are a form of setup costs.

All three settings reflect *economies of scale:* the more we order or produce as part of a batch, the more units there are in a batch over which we can spread out the setup costs.

If we can reduce per-unit costs by increasing the batch size, what keeps us from using infinitely (or at least very large) batches? Similar to the case of setup times, we again need to balance our desire for large batches (fewer setups) with the cost of carrying a large amount of inventory.

In the following analysis, we need to distinguish between two cases:

- If the quantity we order is produced or delivered by an outside supplier, all units of a batch are likely to arrive at the same time.
- In other settings, the units of a batch might not all arrive at the same time. This is especially the case when we produce the batch internally.

Figure 7.8 illustrates the inventory levels for the two cases described above. The lower part of Figure 7.8 shows the case of the outside supplier and all units of a batch arriving at the same moment in time. The moment a shipment is received, the inventory level jumps up by the size of the shipment. It then falls up to the time of the next shipment.

The upper part of Figure 7.8 shows the case of units created by a resource with (finite) capacity. Thus, while we are producing, the inventory level increases. Once we stop production, the inventory level falls. Let us consider the case of an outside supplier first (lower part of Figure 7.8). Specifically, consider the case of the Xootr handle caps that Nova Cruz sources from a supplier in Taiwan for $0.85 per unit. Note that the maximum inventory of handle caps occurs at the time we receive a shipment from Taiwan. The inventory is then depleted at the rate of the assembly operations, that is, at a flow rate, R, of 700 units (pairs of handle caps) per week, which is equal to one unit every three minutes.

For the following computations, we make a set of assumptions. We later show that these assumptions do not substantially alter the optimal decisions.

- We assume that production of Xootrs occurs at a constant rate of one unit every three minutes. We also assume our orders arrive on time from Taiwan. Under these two assumptions, we can deplete our inventory all the way to zero before receiving the next shipment.

- There is a fixed setup cost per order that is independent of the amount ordered. In the Xootr case, this largely consists of a $300 customs fee.

- The purchase price is independent of the number of units we order, that is, there are no quantity discounts. We talk about quantity discounts in the next section.

The objective of our calculations is to minimize the cost of inventory and ordering with the constraint that we must never run out of inventory (i.e., we can keep the assembly operation running).

FIGURE 7.8
Different Patterns of
Inventory Levels

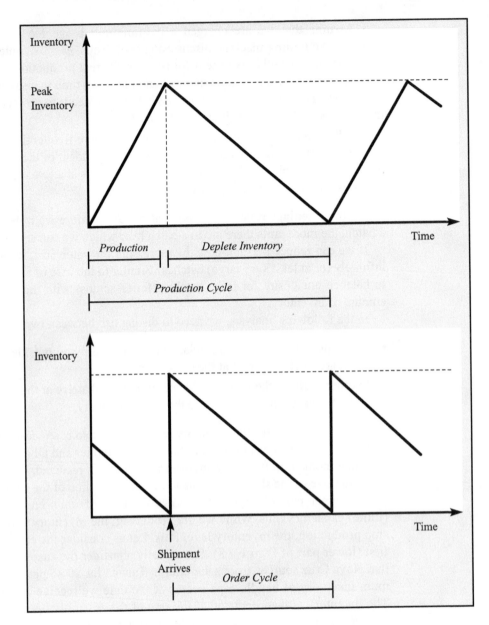

We have three costs to consider: purchase costs, delivery fees, and holding costs. We use 700 units of handle caps each week no matter how much or how frequently we order. Thus, we have no excuse for running out of inventory and there is nothing we can do about our purchase costs of

$$\$0.85/\text{unit} \times 700 \text{ units/week} = \$595 \text{ per week}$$

So when choosing our ordering policy (when and how much to order), we focus on minimizing the sum of the other two costs, delivery fees and inventory costs.

The cost of inventory depends on how much it costs us to hold one unit in inventory for a given period of time, say one week. We can obtain the number by looking at the annual inventory costs and dividing that amount by 52. The annual inventory costs need to account for financing the inventory (cost of capital, especially high for a start-up like Nova Cruz), costs of storage, and costs of obsolescence. Nova Cruz uses an annual inventory cost of 40 percent. Thus, it costs Nova Cruz 0.7692 percent to hold a piece of inventory for one week. Given that a handle cap costs $0.85 per unit, this translates to an inventory cost of $h = 0.007692 \times \$0.85/\text{unit} = \$0.006538$ per unit per week. Note that the annual holding cost needs to include the cost of capital as well as any other cost of inventory (e.g., storage, theft, etc).

How many handle caps will there be, on average, in Nova Cruz's inventory? As we can see in Figure 7.8, the average inventory level is simply

$$\text{Average inventory} = \frac{\text{Order quantity}}{2}$$

If you are not convinced, refer in Figure 7.8 to the "triangle" formed by one order cycle. The average inventory during the cycle is half of the height of the triangle, which is half the order quantity, $Q/2$. Thus, for a given inventory cost, h, we can compute the inventory cost per unit of time (e.g., inventory costs per week):

$$\text{Inventory costs [per unit of time]} = \frac{1}{2}\,\text{Order quantity} \times h = \frac{1}{2}Q \times h$$

Before we turn to the question of how many handle caps to order at once, let's first ask ourselves how frequently we have to place an order. Say at time 0 we have I units in inventory and say we plan our next order to be Q units. The I units of inventory will satisfy demand until time I/R (in other words, we have I/R weeks of supply in inventory). At this time, our inventory will be zero if we don't order before then. We would then again receive an order of Q units (if there is a lead time in receiving this order, we simply would have to place this order earlier).

Do we gain anything by receiving the Q handle caps earlier than at the time when we have zero units in inventory? Not in this model: demand is satisfied whether we order earlier or not and the delivery fee is the same too. But we do lose something by ordering earlier: we incur holding costs per unit of time the Q units are held.

Given that we cannot save costs by choosing the order time intelligently, we must now work on the question of how much to order (the order quantity). Let's again assume that we order Q units with every order and let's consider just one order cycle. The order cycle begins when we order Q units and ends when the last unit is sold, Q/R time units later. For example, with $Q = 1,000$, an order cycle lasts 1,000 units/700 units per week = 1.43 weeks. We incur one ordering fee (setup costs), K, in that order cycle, so our setup costs per week are

$$\text{Setup costs [per unit of time]} = \frac{\text{Setup cost}}{\text{Length of order cycle}}$$
$$= \frac{K}{Q/R} = \frac{K \times R}{Q}$$

Let $C(Q)$ be the sum of our average delivery cost per unit time and our average holding cost per unit time (per week):

$$\text{Per unit of time cost } C(Q) = \text{Setup costs} + \text{Inventory costs}$$
$$= \frac{K \times R}{Q} + \frac{1}{2} \times h \times Q$$

Note that purchase costs are not included in $C(Q)$ for the reasons discussed earlier. From the above we see that the delivery fee per unit time decreases as Q increases: we amortize the delivery fee over more units. But as Q increases, we increase our holding costs.

Figure 7.9 graphs the weekly costs of delivery, the average weekly holding cost, and the total weekly cost, $C(Q)$. As we can see, there is a single order quantity Q that minimizes the total cost $C(Q)$. We call this quantity Q^*, the economic order quantity, or EOQ for short. Hence the name of the model.

FIGURE 7.9   Inventory and Ordering Costs for Different Order Sizes

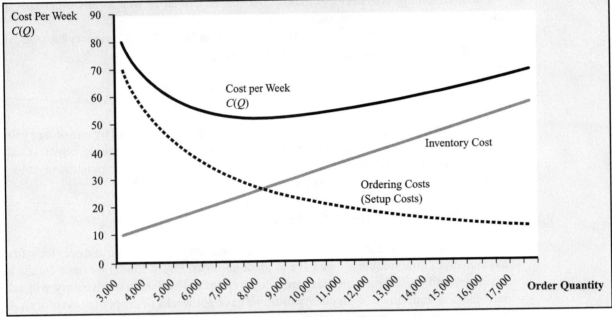

From Figure 7.9 it appears that Q^* is the quantity at which the weekly delivery fee equals the weekly holding cost. In fact, that is true, as can be shown algebraically. Further, using calculus it is possible to show that

$$\text{Economic order quantity} = \sqrt{\frac{2 \times \text{Setup cost} \times \text{Flow rate}}{\text{Holding cost}}}$$

$$Q^* = \sqrt{\frac{2 \times K \times R}{h}}$$

As our intuition suggests, as the setup costs K increase, we should make larger orders, but as holding costs h increase, we should make smaller orders.

We can use the above formula to establish the economic order quantity for handle caps:

$$Q^* = \sqrt{\frac{2 \times \text{Setup cost} \times \text{Flow rate}}{\text{Holding cost}}}$$

$$= \sqrt{\frac{2 \times 300 \times 700}{0.006538}} = 8,014.69$$

The steps required to find the economic order quantity are summarized by Exhibit 7.2.

7.7   Observations Related to the Economic Order Quantity

If we always order the economic order quantity, our cost per unit of time, $C(Q^*)$, can be computed as

$$C(Q^*) = \frac{K \times R}{Q^*} + \frac{1}{2} \times h \times Q^* = \sqrt{2 \times K \times R \times h}$$

Exhibit 7.2

FINDING THE ECONOMIC ORDER QUANTITY

1. Verify the basic assumptions of the EOQ model:

   - Replenishment occurs instantaneously.
   - Demand is constant and not stochastic.
   - There is a fixed setup cost K independent of the order quantity.

2. Collect information on

   - Setup cost, K (only include out-of-pocket cost, not opportunity cost).
   - Flow rate, R.
   - Holding cost, h (not necessarily the yearly holding cost; needs to have the same time unit as the flow rate).

3. For a given order quantity Q, compute

$$\text{Inventory costs [per unit of time]} = \frac{1}{2} Q \times h$$

$$\text{Setup costs [per unit of time]} = \frac{K \times R}{Q}$$

4. The economic order quantity minimizes the sum of the inventory and the setup costs and is

$$Q^* = \sqrt{\frac{2 \times K \times R}{h}}$$

The resulting costs are

$$C(Q^*) = \sqrt{2 \times K \times R \times h}$$

While we have done this analysis to minimize our average cost per unit of time, it should be clear that Q^* would minimize our average cost per unit (given that the rate of purchasing handle caps is fixed). The cost per unit can be computed as

$$\text{Cost per unit} = \frac{C(Q^*)}{R} = \sqrt{\frac{2 \times K \times h}{R}}$$

As we would expect, the per-unit cost is increasing with the ordering fee K as well as with our inventory costs. Interestingly, the per-unit cost is decreasing with the flow rate R. Thus, if we doubled our flow rate, our ordering costs increase by less than a factor of 2. In other words, there are economies of scale in the ordering process: the per-unit ordering cost is decreasing with the flow rate R. Put yet another way, an operation with setup and inventory holding costs becomes more efficient as the demand rate increases.

While we have focused our analysis on the time period when Nova Cruz experienced a demand of 700 units per week, the demand pattern changed drastically over the product life cycle of the Xootr. As discussed in Chapter 4, Nova Cruz experienced a substantial demand growth from 200 units per week to over 1,000 units per week. Table 7.2 shows how increases in demand rate impact the order quantity as well as the per-unit cost of the handle caps. We observe that, due to scale economies, ordering and inventory costs are decreasing with the flow rate R.

TABLE 7.2
Scale Economies in the EOQ Formula

Flow Rate, R	Economic Order Quantity, Q*	Per-Unit Ordering and Inventory Cost, C(Q*)/ R	Ordering and Inventory Costs as a Percentage of Total Procurement Costs
200	4,284	0.14 [$/unit]	14.1%
400	6,058	0.10	10.4%
600	7,420	0.08	8.7%
800	8,568	0.07	7.6%
1,000	9,579	0.06	6.8%

A nice property of the economic order quantity is that the cost function, $C(Q)$, is relatively flat around its minimum Q^* (see graph in Figure 7.9). This suggests that if we were to order Q units instead of Q^*, the resulting cost penalty would not be substantial as long as Q is reasonably close to Q^*. Suppose we order only half of the optimal order quantity, that is, we order $Q^*/2$. In that case, we have

$$C(Q^*/2) = \frac{K \times R}{Q^*/2} + \frac{1}{2} \times h \times Q^*/2 = \frac{5}{4} \times \sqrt{2 \times K \times R \times h} = \frac{5}{4} \times C(Q^*)$$

Thus, if we order only half as much as optimal (i.e., we order twice as frequently as optimal), then our costs increase only by 25 percent. The same holds if we order double the economic order quantity (i.e., we order half as frequently as optimal).

This property has several important implications:

- Consider the optimal order quantity $Q^* = 8,014$ established above. However, now also assume that our supplier is only willing to deliver in predefined quantities (e.g., in multiples of 5,000). The robustness established above suggests that an order of 10,000 will only lead to a slight cost increase (increased costs can be computed as $C(Q = 10,000) = \$53.69$, which is only 2.5 percent higher than the optimal costs).

- Sometimes, it can be difficult to obtain exact numbers for the various ingredients in the EOQ formula. Consider, for example, the ordering fee in the Nova Cruz case. While this fee of $300 was primarily driven by the $300 for customs, it also did include a shipping fee. The exact shipping fee in turn depends on the quantity shipped and we would need a more refined model to find the order quantity that accounts for this effect. Given the robustness of the EOQ model, however, we know that the model is "forgiving" with respect to small misspecifications of parameters.

A particularly useful application of the EOQ model relates to *quantity discounts*. When procuring inventory in a logistics or retailing setting, we frequently are given the opportunity to benefit from quantity discounts. For example:

- We might be offered a discount for ordering a full truckload of supply.
- We might receive a free unit for every five units we order (just as in consumer retailing settings of "buy one, get one free").
- We might receive a discount for all units ordered over 100 units.
- We might receive a discount for the entire order if the order volume exceeds 50 units (or say $2,000).

We can think of the extra procurement costs that we would incur from not taking advantage of the quantity discount—that is, that would result from ordering in smaller quantities—as a setup cost. Evaluating an order discount therefore boils down to a comparison between inventory costs and setup costs (savings in procurement costs), which we can do using the EOQ model.

If the order quantity we obtain from the EOQ model is sufficiently large to obtain the largest discount (the lowest per-unit procurement cost), then the discount has no impact on our order size. We go ahead and order the economic order quantity. The more interesting case occurs when the EOQ is less than the discount threshold. Then we must decide if we wish to order more than the economic order quantity to take advantage of the discount offered to us.

Let's consider one example to illustrate how to think about this issue. Suppose our supplier of handle caps gives us a discount of 5 percent off the entire order if the order exceeds 10,000 units. Recall that our economic order quantity was only 8,014. Thus, the question is "should we increase the order size to 10,000 units in order to get the 5 percent discount, yet incur higher inventory costs, or should we simply order 8,014 units?"

We surely will not order more than 10,000; any larger order does not generate additional purchase cost savings but does increase inventory costs. So we have two choices: either stick with the EOQ or increase our order to 10,000. If we order $Q^* = 8,014$ units, our total cost per unit time is

$$700 \text{ units/week} \times \$0.85/\text{unit} + C(Q^*)$$
$$= \$595/\text{week} + \$52.40/\text{week}$$
$$= \$647.40/\text{week}$$

Notice that we now include our purchase cost per unit time of 700 units/week × \$0.85/unit. The reason for this is that with the possibility of a quantity discount, our purchase cost now depends on the order quantity.

If we increase our order quantity to 10,000 units, our total cost per unit time would be

$$700 \text{ units/week} \times \$0.85/\text{unit} \times 0.95 + C(10,000)$$
$$= \$565.25/\text{week} + \$52.06/\text{week}$$
$$= \$617.31/\text{week}$$

where we have reduced the procurement cost by 5 percent (multiplied by 0.95) to reflect the quantity discount. (*Note:* The 5 percent discount also reduces the holding cost h in $C(.)$) Given that the cost per week is lower in the case of the increased order quantity, we want to take advantage of the quantity discount.

After analyzing the case of all flow units of one order (batch) arriving simultaneously, we now turn to the case of producing the corresponding units internally (upper part of Figure 7.8).

All computations we performed above can be easily transformed to this more general case (see, e.g., Nahmias 2005). Moreover, given the robustness of the economic order quantity, the EOQ model leads to reasonably good recommendations even if applied to production settings with setup costs. Hence, we will not discuss the analytical aspects of this. Instead, we want to step back for a moment and reflect on how the EOQ model relates to our discussion of setup times at the beginning of the chapter.

A common mistake is to rely too much on setup *costs* as opposed to setup *times*. For example, consider the case of Figure 7.6 and assume that the monthly capital cost for the milling machine is \$9,000, which corresponds to \$64 per hour (assuming four weeks of 35 hours each). Thus, when choosing the batch size, and focusing primarily on costs, Nova Cruz might shy away from frequent setups. Management might even consider using the economic order quantity established above and thereby quantify the impact of larger batches on inventory holding costs.

There are two major mistakes in this approach:

• This approach to choosing batch sizes ignores the fact that the investment in the machine is already sunk.

• Choosing the batch size based on cost ignores the effect setups have on process capacity. As long as setup costs are a reflection of the cost of capacity—as opposed to direct financial setup costs—they should be ignored when choosing the batch size. It is the overall process flow that matters, not an artificial local performance measure! From a capacity perspective, setups at nonbottleneck resources are free. And if the setups do occur at the bottleneck, the corresponding setup costs not only reflect the capacity costs of the local resource, but of the entire process!

Thus, when choosing batch sizes, it is important to distinguish between setup costs and setup times. If the motivation behind batching results from setup times (or opportunity costs of capacity), we should focus on optimizing the process flow. Section 7.3 provides the appropriate way to find a good batch size. If we face "true" setup costs (in the sense of out-of-pocket costs) and we only look at a single resource (as opposed to an entire process flow), the EOQ model can be used to find the optimal order quantity.

Finally, if we encounter a combination of setup times and (out-of-pocket) setup costs, we should use both approaches and compare the recommended batch sizes. If the batch size from the EOQ is sufficiently large so that the resource with the setup is not the bottleneck, minimizing costs is appropriate. If the batch size from the EOQ, however, makes the resource with the setups the bottleneck, we need to consider increasing the batch size beyond the EOQ recommendation.

7.8   Other Flow Interruptions: Buffer or Suffer

In addition to illustrating the SMED method, the race car example also helps to illustrate how the concept of batching can be applied to *continuous process flows,* as opposed to discrete manufacturing environments. First of all, we observe that the calculation of the average speed of the race car is nothing but a direct application of the batching formula introduced at the beginning of this chapter:

$$\text{Average speed (number of miles between stops)} = \frac{\text{Number of miles between stops}}{\text{Duration of the stop} + \text{Time to cover one mile} \times \text{Number of miles between stops}}$$

In continuous flow processes, the quantity between two flow interruptions is frequently referred to as a production run.

Consider the production of orange juice, which is produced in a continuous flow process. At an abstract level, orange juice is produced in a three-step process: extraction, filtering, and bottling. Given that the filter at the second process step has to be changed regularly, the process needs to be stopped for 30 minutes following every four hours of production. While operating, the step can produce up to 100 barrels per hour.

To determine the capacity of the filtering step, we use

$$\text{Capacity } (B) = \frac{B}{S + B \times p}$$

$$= \frac{\text{Amount processed between two stops}}{\text{Duration of stop} + \text{Time to produce one barrel} \times \text{Amount processed between two stops}}$$

$$= \frac{400 \text{ barrels}}{30 \text{ minutes} + 60/100 \text{ minutes per barrel} \times 400 \text{ barrels}}$$

$$= \frac{400 \text{ barrels}}{270 \text{ minutes}}$$

$$= 1.48 \ barrels/minute = 88.88 \ barrels/hour$$

FIGURE 7.10
Data for the
Production of
Orange Juice

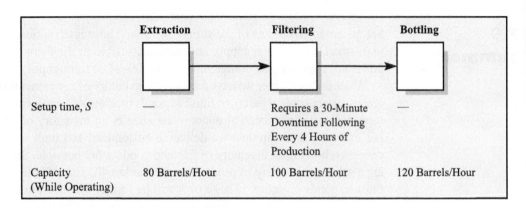

While in the case of batch flow operations we have allowed for substantial buffer sizes between process steps, the process as described in Figure 7.10 is currently operating without buffers. This has substantial implications for the overall flow rate.

Analyzing each step in isolation would suggest that the extraction step is the bottleneck, which would give us a process capacity of 80 barrels per hour. However, in the absence of buffers, the extraction step needs to stop producing the moment the filtering step is shut down. Thus, while running, the process is constrained by the extraction step, producing an output of 80 barrels per hour, and while being shut down, the process step is constrained by the filtering step (at 0 barrel per hour).

Previously, we considered the setup step in isolation from the rest of the process. That is a valid analysis if the setup step indeed works in isolation from the rest of the process, that is, if there is sufficient inventory (buffers) between steps. That assumption is violated here: The filtering step cannot operate at 88 barrels per hour because it is constrained by the extraction step of 80 barrels per hour.

For this reason, when we use our equation

$$\text{Capacity} = \frac{\text{Amount processed between two stops}}{\text{Duration of stop} + \text{Time to produce one barrel} \times \text{Amount processed between two stops}}$$

it is important that we acknowledge that we are producing at a rate of 80 barrels per hour (i.e., $\frac{1}{80}$ hour per barrel) while we are at the filtering step. This leads to the following computation of process capacity:

$$
\begin{aligned}
\text{Capacity} &= \frac{320 \text{ barrels}}{0.5 \text{ hour} + \dfrac{1}{80} \text{ hour per barrel} \times 320 \text{ barrels}} \\
&= 320 \text{ barrels}/4.5 \text{ hours} \\
&= 71.11 \text{ barrels/hour}
\end{aligned}
$$

This prompts the following interesting observation: In the presence of flow interruptions, buffers can increase process capacity. Practitioners refer to this phenomenon as "buffer or suffer," indicating that flow interruptions can be smoothed out by introducing buffer inventories. In the case of Figure 7.10, the buffer would need to absorb the outflow of the extraction step during the downtime of the reduction step. Thus, adding a buffer between these two steps would indeed increase process capacity up to the level where, with 80 barrels per hour, the extraction step becomes the bottleneck.

7.9
Summary

Setups are interruptions of the supply process. These interruptions on the supply side lead to mismatches between supply and demand, visible in the form of inventory and—where this is not possible (see orange juice example)—lost throughput.

While in this chapter we have focused on inventory of components (handle caps), work-in-process (steer support parts), or finished goods (station wagons versus sedans, Figure 7.4), the supply–demand mismatch also can materialize in an inventory of waiting customer orders. For example, if the product we deliver is customized and built to the specifications of the customer, holding an inventory of finished goods is not possible. Similarly, if we are providing a substantial variety of products to the market, the risk of holding completed variants in finished goods inventory is large (this will be further discussed in Chapter 15). Independent of the form of inventory, a large inventory corresponds to long flow times (Little's Law). For this reason, batch processes are typically associated with very long customer lead times.

In this chapter, we discussed tools to choose a batch size. We distinguished between setup times and setup costs. To the extent that a process faces setup times, we need to extend our process analysis to capture the negative impact that setups have on capacity. We then want to look for a batch size that is large enough to not make the process step with the setup the bottleneck, while being small enough to avoid excessive inventory.

To the extent that a process faces (out-of-pocket) setup costs, we need to balance these costs against the cost of inventory. We discussed the EOQ model for the case of supply arriving in one single quantity (sourcing from a supplier), as well as the case of internal production. Figure 7.11 provides a summary of the major steps you should take when analyzing processes with flow interruptions, including setup times, setup costs, or machine downtimes. There are countless extensions to the EOQ model to capture, among other things, quantity discounts, perishability, learning effects, inflation, and quality problems.

Our ability to choose a "good" batch size provides another example of process improvement. Consider a process with significant setup times at one resource. As a manager of this process, we need to balance the conflicting objectives of

- Fast response to customers (short flow times, which correspond, because of Little's Law, to low inventory levels), which results from using small batch sizes.
- Cost benefits that result from using large batch sizes. The reason for this is that large batch sizes enable a high throughput, which in turn allows the firm to spread out its fixed costs over a maximum number of flow units.

FIGURE 7.11 **Summary of Batching**

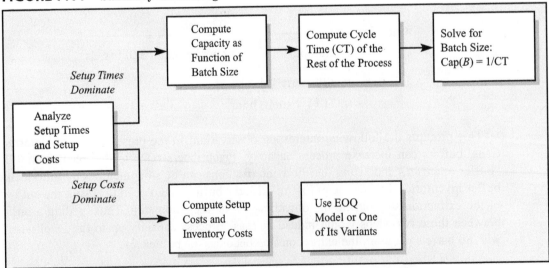

FIGURE 7.12
Choosing a Batch Size

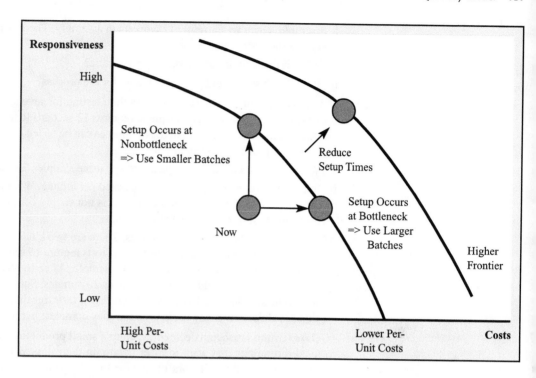

This tension is illustrated by Figure 7.12. Similar to the case of line balancing, we observe that adjustments in the batch size are not trading in one performance measure against the other, but allow us to improve by reducing current inefficiencies in the process.

Despite our ability to choose batch sizes that mitigate the tension between inventory (responsiveness) and costs, there ultimately is only one way to handle setups: eliminate them wherever possible or at least shorten them. Setups do not add value and are therefore wasteful.

Methods such as SMED are powerful tools that can reduce setup times substantially. Similarly, the need for transfer batches can be reduced by locating the process resources according to the flow of the process.

7.10
Further
Reading

Nahmias (2005) is a widely used textbook in operations management that discusses, among other things, many variants of the EOQ model.

7.11
Practice
Problems

Q7.1*   **(Window Boxes)** Metal window boxes are manufactured in two process steps: stamping and assembly. Each window box is made up of three pieces: a base (one part A) and two sides (two part Bs).

The parts are fabricated by a single stamping machine that requires a setup time of 120 minutes whenever switching between the two part types. Once the machine is set up, the processing time for each part A is one minute while the processing time for each part B is only 30 seconds.

Currently, the stamping machine rotates its production between one batch of 360 for part A and one batch of 720 for part B. Completed parts move from the stamping machine to the assembly only after the entire batch is complete.

At assembly, parts are assembled manually to form the finished product. One base (part A) and two sides (two part Bs), as well as a number of small purchased components, are required for each unit of final product. Each product requires 27 minutes of labor time

(* indicates that the solution is at the end of the book)

to assemble. There are currently 12 workers in assembly. There is sufficient demand to sell every box the system can make.

   a. What is the capacity of the stamping machine?

   b. What batch size would you recommend for the process?

Q7.2** **(PTests)** Precision Testing (PTests) does fluid testing for several local hospitals. Consider their urine testing process. Each sample requires 12 seconds to test, but after 300 samples, the equipment must be recalibrated. No samples can be tested during the recalibration process and that process takes 30 minutes.

   a. What is PTest's maximum capacity to test urine samples (in samples per hour)?

   b. Suppose 2.5 urine samples need to be tested per minute. What is the smallest batch size (in samples) that ensures that the process is not supply constrained? (Note; A batch is the number of tests between calibrations.)

   c. PTest also needs to test blood samples. There are two kinds of tests that can be done—a "basic" test and a "complete" test. Basic tests require 15 seconds per sample, whereas "complete" tests require 1.5 minutes per sample. After 100 tests, the equipment needs to be cleaned and recalibrated, which takes 20 minutes. Suppose PTest runs the following cyclic schedule: 70 basic tests, 30 complete tests, recalibrate, and then repeat. With this schedule, how many *basic* tests can they complete per minute on average?

Q7.3 **(Gelato)** Bruno Fruscalzo decided to set up a small production facility in Sydney to sell to local restaurants that want to offer gelato on their dessert menu. To start simple, he would offer only three flavors of gelato: fragola (strawberry), chocolato (chocolate), and bacio (chocolate with hazelnut). After a short time he found his demand and setup times to be

	Fragola	Chocolato	Bacio
Demand (kg/hour)	10	15	5
Setup time (hours)	3/4	1/2	1/6

Bruno first produces a batch of fragola, then a batch of chocolato, then a batch of bacio and then he repeats that sequence. For example, after producing bacio and before producing fragola, he needs 45 minutes to set up the ice cream machine, but he needs only 10 minutes to switch from chocolato to bacio. When running, his ice cream machine produces at the rate of 50 kg per hour no matter which flavor it is producing (and, of course, it can produce only one flavor at a time).

   a. Suppose Bruno wants to minimize the amount of each flavor produced at one time while still satisfying the demand for each of the flavors. (He can choose a different quantity for each flavor.) If we define a batch to be the quantity produced in a single run of each flavor, how many kilograms should he produce in each batch?

   b. Given your answer in part (a), how many kilograms of fragola should he make with each batch?

   c. Given your answer in part (a), what is the maximum inventory of chocolato? (Assume production and demand occur at constant rates.)

Q7.4 **(Two-step)** Consider the following two step process:

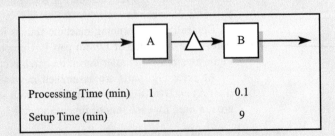

Step A has a processing time of 1 minute per unit, but no setup is required. Step B has an processing time of 0.1 minute per unit, but a setup time of 9 minutes is require per batch. A buffer with ample inventory is allowed between the two steps.

a. Suppose units are produced in batches of 5 (i.e., after each set of 5 units are produced, step B must incur a setup of 9 minutes). What is the capacity of the process (in units per minute)?

b. What is the batch size that maximizes the flow rate of this process with minimal inventory? Assume there is ample demand.

c. Now suppose the inventory buffer is removed between steps A and B:

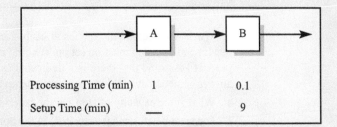

Processing Time (min)	1	0.1
Setup Time (min)	—	9

Thus, when B is being set up, A cannot work because there is no place to put its completed units. Once B has finished its setup and is ready to work on units, A can resume its work because B is now ready to accept A's output. What batch size achieves a flow rate of 0.82 unit per minute?

Q7.5   **(Simple Setup)** Consider the following batch flow process consisting of three process steps performed by three machines:

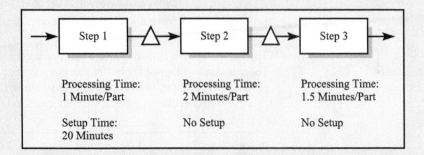

Step 1		Step 2		Step 3
Processing Time: 1 Minute/Part		Processing Time: 2 Minutes/Part		Processing Time: 1.5 Minutes/Part
Setup Time: 20 Minutes		No Setup		No Setup

Work is processed in batches at each step. Before a batch is processed at step 1, the machine has to be set up. During a setup, the machine is unable to process any product.

a. Assume that the batch size is 50 parts. What is the capacity of the process?

b. For a batch size of 10 parts, which step is the bottleneck for the process?

c. Using the current production batch size of 50 parts, how long would it take to produce 20 parts starting with an empty system? Assume that the units in the batch have to stay together (no smaller transfer batches allowed) when transferred to step 2 and to step 3. A unit can leave the system the moment it is completed at step 3. Assume step 1 needs to be set up before the beginning of production.

d. Using the current production batch size of 50 parts, how long would it take to produce 20 parts starting with an empty system? Assume that the units in the batch do *not* have to stay together; specifically, units are transferred to the next step the moment they are completed at any step. Assume step 1 needs to be set up before the beginning of production.

e. What batch size would you choose, assuming that all units of a batch stay together for the entire process?

Q7.6   **(Setup Everywhere)** Consider the following batch-flow process consisting of three process steps performed by three machines:

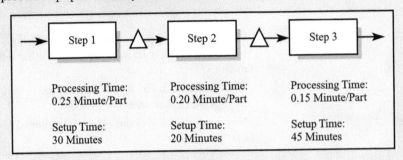

Work is processed in batches at each step. Before a batch is processed at a step, the machine at that step must be set up. (During a setup, the machine is unable to process any product.) Assume that there is a dedicated setup operator for each machine (i.e., there is always someone available to perform a setup at each machine.)

a. What is the capacity of step 1 if the batch size is 35 parts?

b. For what batch sizes is step 1 (2, 3) the bottleneck?

Q7.7   **(JCL Inc.)** JCL Inc. is a major chip manufacturing firm that sells its products to computer manufacturers like Dell, HP, and others. In simplified terms, chip making at JCL Inc. involves three basic operations: depositing, patterning, and etching.

- **Depositing:** Using chemical vapor deposition (CVD) technology, an insulating material is deposited on the wafer surface, forming a thin layer of solid material on the chip.

- **Patterning:** Photolithography projects a microscopic circuit pattern on the wafer surface, which has a light-sensitive chemical like the emulsion on photographic film. It is repeated many times as each layer of the chip is built.

- **Etching:** Etching removes selected material from the chip surface to create the device structures.

The following table lists the required processing times and setup times at each of the steps. There is unlimited space for buffer inventory between these steps. Assume that the unit of production is a wafer, from which individual chips are cut at a later stage.

Note: A Setup can only begin once the batch has arrived at the machine.

Process Step	1 Depositing	2 Patterning	3 Etching
Setup time	45 min.	30 min.	20 min.
Processing time	0.15 min./unit	0.25 min./unit	0.20 min./unit

a. What is the process capacity in units per hour with a batch size of 100 wafers?

b. For the current batch size of 100 wafers, how long would it take to produce 50 wafers? Assume that the batch needs to stay together during deposition and patterning (i.e., the firm does not work with transfer batches that are less than the production batch). However, the 50 wafers can leave the process the moment all 50 wafers have passed through the etching stage. Recall that a setup can only be started upon the arrival of the batch at the machine.

c. For what batch size is step 3 (etching) the bottleneck?

d. Suppose JCL Inc. came up with a new technology that eliminated the setup time for step 1 (deposition), but increased the processing time to 0.45 min./unit. What would be the batch size you would choose so as to maximize the overall capacity of the process, assuming all units of a batch stay together for the entire process?

Q7.8   **(Kinga Doll Company)** Kinga Doll Company manufactures eight versions of its popular girl doll, Shari. The company operates on a 40-hour work week. The eight versions differ in doll skin, hair, and eye color, enabling most children to have a doll with a similar appearance to them. It currently sells an average of 4,000 dolls (spread equally among its eight versions) per week to boutique toy retailers. In simplified terms, doll making at Kinga involves three basic operations: molding the body and hair, painting the face, and dressing the doll. Changing over between versions requires setup time at the molding and painting stations due to the different colors of plastic pellets, hair, and eye color paint required. The table below lists the setup times for a batch and the processing times for each unit at each step. Unlimited space for buffer inventory exists between these steps.

Assume that (i) setups need to be completed first, (ii) a setup can only start once the batch has arrived at the resource, and (iii) all flow units of a batch need to be processed at a resource before any of the units of the batch can be moved to the next resource.

Process Step	1 Molding	2 Painting	3 Dressing
Setup time	15 min.	30 min.	No setup
Processing time	0.25 min./unit	0.15 min./unit	0.30 min./unit

a. What is the process capacity in units per hour with a batch size of 500 dolls?
b. What is the time it takes for the first batch of 500 dolls to go through an empty process?
c. Which batch size would minimize inventory without decreasing the process capacity?
d. Which batch size would minimize inventory without decreasing the current flow rate?

Q7.9 **(Bubba Chump Shrimp)** The Bubba Chump Shrimp Company processes and packages shrimp for sale to wholesale seafood distributors. The shrimp are transported to the main plant by trucks that carry 1,000 pounds (lb) of shrimp. Once the continuous flow processing of the shrimp begins, *no* inventory is allowed in buffers due to spoilage and all of the shrimp must be processed within 12 hours to prevent spoilage. The processing begins at the sorter, where the trucks dump the shrimp onto a conveyor belt that feeds into the sorter, which can sort up to 500 lb per hour. The shrimp then proceed to the desheller, which can process shrimp at the rate of 400 lb per hour. However, after 3 hours and 45 minutes of processing, the desheller must be stopped for 15 minutes to clean out empty shrimp shells that have accumulated. The veins of the shrimp are then removed in the deveining area at a maximum rate of 360 lb per hour. The shrimp proceed to the washing area, where they are processed at 750 lb per hour. Finally, the shrimp are packaged and frozen.

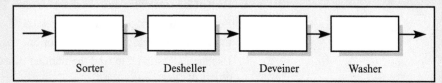

Note: All unit weights given are in "final processed shrimp." You do *not* need to account for the weight of the waste in the deshelling area. The plant operates continuously for 12 hours per day beginning at 8:00 a.m. Finally, there is negligible time to fill the system in the morning.

a. What is the daily process capacity of the desheller (in isolation from the other processes)?
b. What is the daily process capacity of the deveiner (in isolation from the other processes)?
c. What is the daily process capacity of the processing plant (excluding the packaging and freezing)?
d. If five trucks arrive one morning at 8:00 a.m., what is the total number of pounds of shrimp that must be wasted?

Q7.10* **(Cat Food)** Cat Lovers Inc. (CLI) is the distributor of a very popular blend of cat food that sells for $1.25 per can. CLI experiences demand of 500 cans per week on average. They order the cans of cat food from the Nutritious & Delicious Co. (N&D). N&D sells cans to CLI at $0.50 per can and charges a flat fee of $7 per order for shipping and handling.

CLI uses the economic order quantity as their fixed order size. Assume that the opportunity cost of capital and all other inventory cost is 15 percent annually and that there are 50 weeks in a year.

    a. How many cans of cat food should CLI order at a time?

    b. What is CLI's total order cost for one year?

    c. What is CLI's total holding cost for one year?

    d. What is CLI's weekly inventory turns?

Q7.11* **(Beer Distributor)** A beer distributor finds that it sells on average 100 cases a week of regular 12-oz. Budweiser. For this problem assume that demand occurs at a constant rate over a 50-week year. The distributor currently purchases beer every two weeks at a cost of $8 per case. The inventory-related holding cost (capital, insurance, etc.) for the distributor equals 25 percent of the dollar value of inventory per year. Each order placed with the supplier costs the distributor $10. This cost includes labor, forms, postage, and so forth.

    a. Assume the distributor can choose any order quantity it wishes. What order quantity minimizes the distributor's total inventory-related costs (holding and ordering)?

    For the next three parts, assume the distributor selects the order quantity specified in part (a).

    b. What are the distributor's inventory turns per year?

    c. What is the inventory-related cost per case of beer sold?

    d. Assume the brewer is willing to give a 5 percent quantity discount if the distributor orders 600 cases or more at a time. If the distributor is interested in minimizing its total cost (i.e., purchase and inventory-related costs), should the distributor begin ordering 600 or more cases at a time?

Q7.12** **(Millennium Liquors)** Millennium Liquors is a wholesaler of sparkling wines. Their most popular product is the French Bete Noire. Weekly demand is for 45 cases. Assume demand occurs over 50 weeks per year. The wine is shipped directly from France. Millennium's annual cost of capital is 15 percent, which also includes all other inventory-related costs. Below are relevant data on the costs of shipping, placing orders, and refrigeration.

- Cost per case: $120
- Shipping cost (for any size shipment): $290
- Cost of labor to place and process an order: $10
- Fixed cost for refrigeration: $75/week

    a. Calculate the weekly holding cost for one case of wine.

    b. Use the EOQ model to find the number of cases per order and the average number of orders per year.

    c. Currently orders are placed by calling France and then following up with a letter. Millennium and its supplier may switch to a simple ordering system using the Internet. The new system will require much less labor. What would be the impact of this system on the ordering pattern?

Q7.13 **(Powered by Koffee)** Powered by Koffee (PBK) is a new campus coffee store. PBK uses 50 bags of whole bean coffee every month, and you may assume that demand is perfectly steady throughout the year.

PBK has signed a year-long contract to purchase its coffee from a local supplier, Phish Roasters, for a price of $25 per bag and an $85 fixed cost for every delivery independent

(* indicates that the solution is at the end of the book)

of the order size. The holding cost due to storage is $1 per bag per month. PBK managers figure their cost of capital is approximately 2 percent per month.

a. What is the optimal order size, in bags?

b. Given your answer in (a), how many times a year does PBK place orders?

c. Given your answer in (a), how many months of supply of coffee does PBK have on average?

d. On average, how many dollars per month does PBK spend to hold coffee (including cost of capital)?

Suppose that a South American import/export company has offered PBK a deal for the next year. PBK can buy a years' worth of coffee directly from South America for $20 per bag and a fixed cost for delivery of $500. Assume the estimated cost for inspection and storage is $1 per bag per month and the cost of capital is approximately 2 percent per month.

e. Should PBK order from Phish Roasters or the South American import/export company? Quantitatively justify your answer.

You can view a video of how problems marked with a ** are solved by going on www. cachon-terwiesch.net and follow the links under 'Solved Practice Problems'

Solutions to Selected Practice Problems

Chapter 7

Q7.1 (Window Boxes)

The following computations are based on Exhibit 7.1.

Part a

Step 1. Since there is sufficient demand, the step (other than the stamping machine) that determines flow rate is assembly. Capacity at assembly is $\frac{12}{27}$ unit/minute.

Step 2. The production cycle consists of the following parts:
- Setup for A (120 minutes).
- Produce parts A (360 × 1 minute).
- Setup for B (120 minutes).
- Produce parts B (720 × 0.5 minute).

Step 3. There are two setups in the production cycle, so the setup time is 240 minutes.

Step 4. Every completed window box requires one part A (one minute per unit) and two parts B (2 × 0.5 minute per unit). Thus, the per-unit activity time is two minutes per unit.

Step 5. Use formula

$$\text{Capacity given batch size} = \frac{360 \text{ units}}{240 \text{ minutes} + 360 \text{ units} \times 2 \text{ minutes/unit}}$$
$$= 0.375 \text{ unit/minute}$$

Step 6. Capacity at stamping for a general batch size is

$$\frac{\text{Batch size}}{240 \text{ minutes} + \text{Batch size} \times 2 \text{ minutes/unit}}$$

We need to solve the equation

$$\frac{\text{Batch size}}{240 \text{ minutes} + \text{Batch size} \times 2 \text{ minutes/unit}} = \frac{12}{27}$$

for the batch size. The batch size solving this equation is Batch size = 960. We can obtain the same number directly by using

$$\text{Recommended batch size} = \frac{\text{Flow rate} \times \text{Setup time}}{1 - \text{Flow rate} \times \text{Time per unit}} = \frac{\frac{12}{27} \times 240}{1 - \frac{12}{27} \times 2} = 960$$

Q7.10 (Cat Food)

$$\frac{7 \times 500}{EOQ} = 1.62$$

Part a

Holding costs are $0.50 \times 15\%/50 = 0.0015$ per can per week. Note, each can is purchased for $0.50, so that is the value tied up in inventory and therefore determines the holding cost. The EOQ is then

Part b

The ordering cost is $7 per order. The number of orders per year is 500/EOQ. Thus, order cost = $/week = 81$/year

Part c

The average inventory level is EOQ/2. Inventory costs per week are thus $0.5 \times EOQ \times 0.0015 = \$1.62$. Given 50 weeks per year, the inventory cost per year is $81

Part d

Inventory turns 5 Flow rate/Inventory

   Flow Rate 5 500 cans per week

   Inventory 5 0.5 3 EOQ

   Thus, Inventory Turns = R/(0.5×EOQ) = 0.462 turns per week = 23.14 turns per year

Q7.11 (Beer Distributor)

The holding costs are 25% per year = 0.5% per week = 8*0.005 = $0.04 per week

$$\frac{7 \times 500}{EOQ} = 1.62$$

Part a

EOQ=

Part b

Inventory turns = Flow Rate/Inventory = $100 \times 50/(0.5 \times EOQ)$ = 5000/EOQ = 44.7 turns per year

Part c

Per unit inventory cost =

Part d

You would never order more than Q = 600

   For Q = 600, we would get the following costs: $0.5 \times 600 \times 0.04 \times 0.95 + 10 \times 100/600 = 13.1$

   The cost per unit would be 13.1/100 = $0.131

   The quantity discount would save us 5%, which is $0.40 per case. However, our operating costs increase by $0.131 - 0.089 = \$0.042$. Hence, the savings outweigh the cost increase and it is better to order 600 units at a time.

Chapter  8

Variability and Its Impact on Process Performance: Waiting Time Problems

For consumers, one of the most visible—and probably annoying—forms of supply–demand mismatches is waiting time. As consumers, we seem to spend a significant portion of our life waiting in line, be it in physical lines (supermarkets, check-in at airports) or in "virtual" lines (listening to music in a call center, waiting for a response e-mail).

It is important to distinguish between different types of waiting time:

• Waiting time predictably occurs when the expected demand rate exceeds the expected supply rate for some limited period of time. This happens especially in cases of constant capacity levels and demand that exhibits seasonality. This leads to implied utilization levels of over 100 percent for some time period. Queues forming at the gate of an airport after the flight is announced are an example of such queues.

• As we will see in the next section, in the presence of variability, queues also can arise if the implied utilization is below 100 percent. Such queues can thereby be fully attributed to the presence of variability, as there exists, on average, enough capacity to meet demand.

While the difference between these two types of waiting time probably does not matter much to the customer, it is of great importance from the perspective of operations management. The root cause for the first type of waiting time is a capacity problem; variability is only a secondary effect. Thus, when analyzing this type of a problem, we first should use the tools outlined in Chapters 3, 4, and 7 instead of focusing on variability.

The root cause of the second type of waiting time is variability. This makes waiting time unpredictable, both from the perspective of the customer as well as from the perspective of the operation. Sometimes, it is the customer (demand) waiting for service (supply) and, sometimes, it is the other way around. Demand just never seems to match supply in these settings.

Analyzing waiting times and linking these waiting times to variability require the introduction of new analytical tools, which we present in this chapter. We will discuss the tools for analyzing waiting times based on the example of An-ser Services, a call-center operation in

Wisconsin that specializes in providing answering services for financial services, insurance companies, and medical practices. Specifically, the objective of this chapter is to

- Predict waiting times and derive some performance metrics capturing the service quality provided to the customer.
- Recommend ways of reducing waiting time by choosing appropriate capacity levels, redesigning the service system, and outlining opportunities to reduce variability.

8.1 Motivating Example: A Somewhat Unrealistic Call Center

For illustrative purposes, consider a call center with just one employee from 7 A.M. to 8 A.M. Based on prior observations, the call-center management estimates that, on average, a call takes 4 minutes to complete (e.g., giving someone driving directions) and there are, on average, 12 calls arriving in a 60-minute period, that is, on average, one call every 5 minutes.

What will be the average waiting time for a customer before talking to a customer service representative? From a somewhat naïve perspective, there should be no waiting time at all. Since the call center has a capacity of serving 60/4 = 15 calls per hour and calls arrive at a rate of 12 calls per hour, supply of capacity clearly exceeds demand. If anything, there seems to be excess service capacity in the call center since its utilization, which we defined previously (Chapter 3) as the ratio between flow rate and capacity, can be computed as

$$\text{Utilization} = \frac{\text{Flow rate}}{\text{Capacity}} = \frac{12 \text{ calls per hour}}{15 \text{ calls per hour}} = 80\%$$

First, consider the arrivals and processing times as depicted in Figure 8.1. A call arrives exactly every 5 minutes and then takes exactly 4 minutes to be served. This is probably the weirdest call center that you have ever seen! No need to worry, we will return to "real operations" momentarily, but the following thought experiment will help you grasp how variability can lead to waiting time.

Despite its almost robotlike processing times and the apparently very disciplined customer service representative ("sorry, 4 minutes are over; thanks for your call"), this call center has one major advantage: no incoming call ever has to wait.

FIGURE 8.1
A Somewhat Odd Service Process

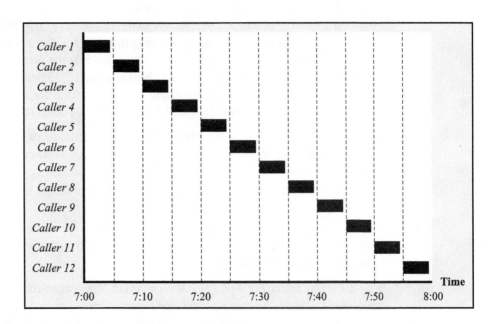

FIGURE 8.2
Data Gathered at a Call Center

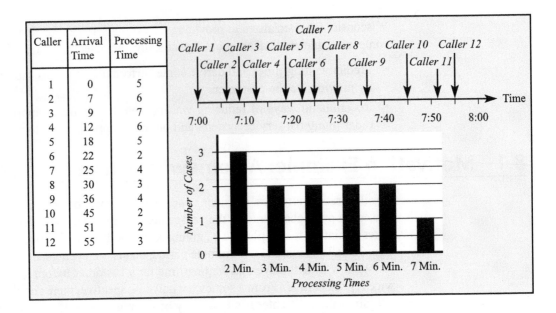

Caller	Arrival Time	Processing Time
1	0	5
2	7	6
3	9	7
4	12	6
5	18	5
6	22	2
7	25	4
8	30	3
9	36	4
10	45	2
11	51	2
12	55	3

Assuming that calls arrive like kick scooters at an assembly line and are then treated by customer service representatives that act like robots reflects a common mistake managers make when calculating process performance. These calculations look at the process at an aggregate level and consider how much capacity is available over the entire hour (day, month, quarter), yet ignore how the requests for service are spaced out within the hour.

If we look at the call center on a minute-by-minute basis, a different picture emerges. Specifically, we observe that calls do not arrive like kick scooters appear at the end of the assembly line, but instead follow a much less systematic pattern, which is illustrated by Figure 8.2.

Moreover, a minute-by-minute analysis also reveals that the actual service durations also vary across calls. As Figure 8.2 shows, while the average processing time is 4 minutes, there exist large variations across calls, and the actual processing times range from 2 minutes to 7 minutes.

Now, consider how the hour from 7:00 A.M. to 8:00 A.M. unfolds. As can be seen in Figure 8.2, the first call comes in at 7:00 A.M. This call will be served without waiting time, and it takes the customer service representative 5 minutes to complete the call. The following 2 minutes are idle time from the perspective of the call center (7:05–7:07). At 7:07, the second call comes in, requiring a 6-minute processing time. Again, the second caller does not have to wait and will leave the system at 7:13. However, while the second caller is being served, at 7:09 the third caller arrives and now needs to wait until 7:13 before beginning the service.

Figure 8.3 shows the waiting time and processing time for each of the 12 customers calling between 7:00 A.M. and 8:00 A.M. Specifically, we observe that

- Most customers do have to wait a considerable amount of time (up to 10 minutes) before being served. This waiting occurs, although, on average, there is plenty of capacity in the call center.
- The call center is not able to provide a consistent service quality, as some customers are waiting, while others are not.
- Despite long waiting times and—because of Little's Law—long queues (see lower part of Figure 8.3), the customer service representative incurs idle time repeatedly over the time period from 7 A.M. to 8 A.M.

Why does variability not average out over time? The reason for this is as follows. In the call center example, the customer service representative can only serve a customer if there is capacity *and* demand at the same moment in time. Therefore, capacity can never "run

FIGURE 8.3
**Detailed Analysis of
Call Center**

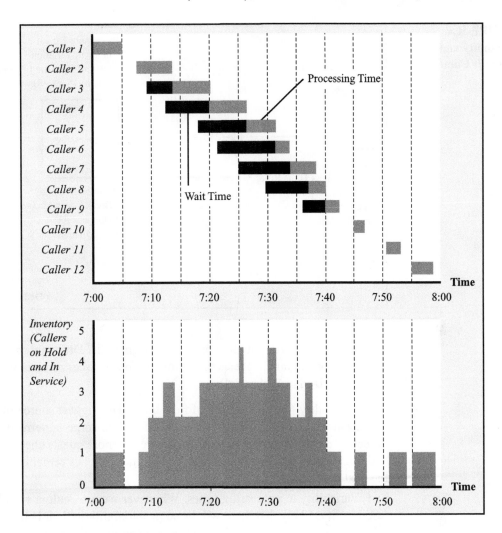

ahead" of demand. However, demand can "run ahead" of capacity, in which case the queue builds up. The idea that inventory can be used to decouple the supply process from demand, thereby restoring the flow rate to the level achievable in the absence of variability, is another version of the "buffer or suffer" principle that we already encountered in Chapter 7. Thus, if a service organization attempts to achieve the flow-rate levels feasible based on averages, long waiting times will result (unfortunately, in those cases, it is the customer who gets "buffered" and "suffers").

Taking the perspective of a manager attempting to match supply and demand, our objectives have not changed. We are still interested in calculating the three fundamental performance measures of an operation: inventory, flow rate, and flow time. Yet, as the above example illustrated, we realize that the process analysis tools we have discussed up to this point in the book need to be extended to appropriately deal with variability.

8.2 Variability: Where It Comes From and How It Can Be Measured

As a first step toward restoring our ability to understand a process's basic performance measures in the presence of variability, we take a more detailed look at the concept of variability itself. Specifically, we are interested in the sources of variability and how to measure variability.

FIGURE 8.4
Variability and Where It Comes From

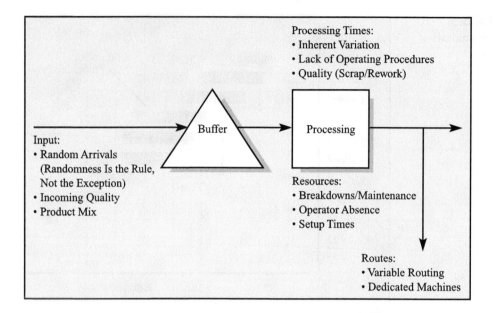

Why is there variability in a process to begin with? Drawing a simple (the most simple) process flow diagram suggests the following four sources of variability (these four sources are summarized in Figure 8.4):

• Variability from the inflow of flow units. The biggest source of variability in service organizations comes from the market itself. While some patterns of the customer-arrival process are predictable (e.g., in a hotel there are more guests checking out between 8 A.M. and 9 A.M. than between 2 P.M. and 3 P.M.), there always remains uncertainty about when the next customer will arrive.

• Variability in processing times. Whenever we are dealing with human operators at a resource, it is likely that there will be some variability in their behavior. Thus, if we would ask a worker at an assembly line to repeat a certain activity 100 times, we would probably find that some of these activities were carried out faster than others. Another source of variability in processing times that is specific to a service environment is that in most service operations, the customer him/herself is involved in many of the tasks constituting the processing time. At a hotel front desk, some guests might require extra time (e.g., the guest requires an explanation for items appearing on his or her bill), while others check out faster (e.g., simply use the credit card that they used for the reservation and only return their room key).

• Random availability of resources. If resources are subject to random breakdowns, for example, machine failures in manufacturing environments or operator absenteeism in service operations, variability is created.

• Random routing in case of multiple flow units in the process. If the path a flow unit takes through the process is itself random, the arrival process at each individual resource is subject to variability. Consider, for example, an emergency room in a hospital. Following the initial screening at the admissions step, incoming patients are routed to different resources. A nurse might handle easy cases, more complex cases might be handled by a general doctor, and severe cases are brought to specific units in the hospital (e.g., trauma center). Even if arrival times and processing times are deterministic, this random routing alone is sufficient to introduce variability.

In general, any form of variability is measured based on the standard deviation. In our case of the call center, we could measure the variability of call durations based on collecting some data and then computing the corresponding standard deviation. The problem with this approach is that the standard deviation provides an *absolute* measure of variability. Does a standard deviation of 5 minutes indicate a high variability? A 5-minute standard deviation for call durations (processing times) in the context of a call center seems like a large number. In the context of a 2-hour surgery in a trauma center, a 5-minute standard deviation seems small.

For this reason, it is more appropriate to measure variability in *relative* terms. Specifically, we define the *coefficient of variation* of a random variable as

$$\text{Coefficient of variation} = \text{CV} = \frac{\text{Standard deviation}}{\text{Mean}}$$

As both the standard deviation and the mean have the same measurement units, the coefficient of variation is a unitless measure.

8.3 Analyzing an Arrival Process

Any process analysis we perform is only as good as the information we feed into our analysis. For this reason, Sections 8.3 and 8.4 focus on data collection and data analysis for the upcoming mathematical models. As a manager intending to apply some of the following tools, this data analysis is essential. However, as a student with only a couple of hours left to the final exam, you might be better off jumping straight to Section 8.5.

Of particular importance when dealing with variability problems is an accurate representation of the demand, which determines the timing of customer arrivals.

Assume we got up early and visited the call center of An-ser; say we arrived at their offices at 6:00 A.M. and we took detailed notes of what takes place over the coming hour. We would hardly have had the time to settle down when the first call comes in. One of the An-ser staff takes the call immediately. Twenty-three seconds later, the second call comes in; another 1:24 minutes later, the third call; and so on.

We define the time at which An-ser receives a call as the *arrival time*. Let AT_i denote the arrival time of the ith call. Moreover, we define the time between two consecutive arrivals as the *interarrival time*, IA. Thus, $\text{IA}_i = \text{AT}_{i+1} - \text{AT}_i$. Figure 8.5 illustrates these two definitions.

If we continue this data collection, we accumulate a fair number of arrival times. Such data are automatically recorded in call centers, so we could simply download a file that looks like Table 8.1.

Before we can move forward and introduce a mathematical model that predicts the effects of variability, we have to invest in some simple, yet important, data analysis. A major risk related to any mathematical model or computer simulation is that these tools always provide

FIGURE 8.5 **The Concept of Interarrival Times**

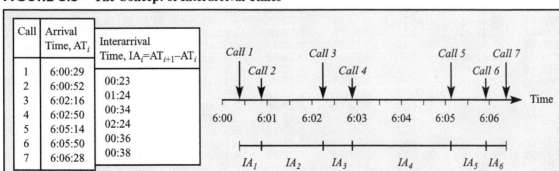

Call	Arrival Time, AT_i	Interarrival Time, $\text{IA}_i=\text{AT}_{i+1}-\text{AT}_i$
1	6:00:29	
2	6:00:52	00:23
3	6:02:16	01:24
4	6:02:50	00:34
5	6:05:14	02:24
6	6:05:50	00:36
7	6:06:28	00:38

TABLE 8.1   Call Arrivals at An-ser on April 2, from 6:00 A.M. to 10:00 A.M.

6:00:29	6:52:39	7:17:57	7:33:51	7:56:16	8:17:33	8:28:11	8:39:25	8:55:56	9:21:58
6:00:52	6:53:06	7:18:10	7:34:05	7:56:24	8:17:42	8:28:12	8:39:47	8:56:17	9:22:02
6:02:16	6:53:07	7:18:17	7:34:19	7:56:24	8:17:50	8:28:13	8:39:51	8:57:42	9:22:02
6:02:50	6:53:24	7:18:38	7:34:51	7:57:39	8:17:52	8:28:17	8:40:02	8:58:45	9:22:30
6:05:14	6:53:25	7:18:54	7:35:10	7:57:51	8:17:54	8:28:43	8:40:09	8:58:49	9:23:13
6:05:50	6:54:18	7:19:04	7:35:13	7:57:55	8:18:03	8:28:59	8:40:23	8:58:49	9:23:29
6:06:28	6:54:24	7:19:40	7:35:21	7:58:26	8:18:12	8:29:06	8:40:34	8:59:32	9:23:45
6:07:37	6:54:36	7:19:41	7:35:44	7:58:41	8:18:21	8:29:34	8:40:35	8:59:38	9:24:10
6:08:05	6:55:06	7:20:10	7:35:59	7:59:12	8:18:23	8:29:38	8:40:46	8:59:45	9:24:30
6:10:16	6:55:19	7:20:11	7:36:37	7:59:20	8:18:34	8:29:40	8:40:51	9:00:14	9:24:42
6:12:13	6:55:31	7:20:26	7:36:45	7:59:22	8:18:46	8:29:45	8:40:58	9:00:52	9:25:07
6:12:48	6:57:25	7:20:27	7:37:07	7:59:22	8:18:53	8:29:46	8:41:12	9:00:53	9:25:15
6:14:04	6:57:38	7:20:38	7:37:14	7:59:36	8:18:54	8:29:47	8:41:26	9:01:09	9:26:03
6:14:16	6:57:44	7:20:52	7:38:01	7:59:50	8:18:58	8:29:47	8:41:32	9:01:31	9:26:04
6:14:28	6:58:16	7:20:59	7:38:03	7:59:54	8:19:20	8:29:54	8:41:49	9:01:55	9:26:23
6:17:51	6:58:34	7:21:11	7:38:05	8:01:22	8:19:25	8:30:00	8:42:23	9:02:25	9:26:34
6:18:19	6:59:41	7:21:14	7:38:18	8:01:42	8:19:28	8:30:01	8:42:51	9:02:30	9:27:02
6:19:11	7:00:50	7:21:46	7:39:00	8:01:56	8:20:09	8:30:08	8:42:53	9:02:38	9:27:04
6:20:48	7:00:54	7:21:56	7:39:17	8:02:08	8:20:23	8:30:23	8:43:24	9:02:51	9:27:27
6:23:33	7:01:08	7:21:58	7:39:35	8:02:26	8:20:27	8:30:23	8:43:28	9:03:29	9:28:25
6:24:25	7:01:31	7:23:03	7:40:06	8:02:29	8:20:44	8:30:31	8:43:47	9:03:33	9:28:37
6:25:08	7:01:39	7:23:16	7:40:23	8:02:39	8:20:54	8:31:02	8:44:23	9:03:38	9:29:09
6:25:19	7:01:56	7:23:19	7:41:34	8:02:47	8:21:12	8:31:11	8:44:49	9:03:51	9:29:15
6:25:27	7:04:52	7:23:48	7:42:20	8:02:52	8:21:12	8:31:19	8:45:05	9:04:11	9:29:52
6:25:38	7:04:54	7:24:01	7:42:33	8:03:06	8:21:25	8:31:20	8:45:10	9:04:33	9:30:47
6:25:48	7:05:37	7:24:09	7:42:51	8:03:58	8:21:28	8:31:22	8:45:28	9:04:42	9:30:58
6:26:05	7:05:39	7:24:45	7:42:57	8:04:07	8:21:43	8:31:23	8:45:31	9:04:44	9:30:59
6:26:59	7:05:42	7:24:56	7:43:23	8:04:27	8:21:44	8:31:27	8:45:32	9:04:44	9:31:03
6:27:37	7:06:37	7:25:01	7:43:34	8:05:53	8:21:53	8:31:45	8:45:39	9:05:22	9:31:55
6:27:46	7:06:46	7:25:03	7:43:43	8:05:54	8:22:19	8:32:05	8:46:24	9:06:01	9:33:08
6:29:32	7:07:11	7:25:18	7:43:44	8:06:43	8:22:44	8:32:13	8:46:27	9:06:12	9:33:45
6:29:52	7:07:24	7:25:39	7:43:57	8:06:47	8:23:00	8:32:19	8:46:40	9:06:14	9:34:07
6:30:26	7:07:46	7:25:40	7:43:57	8:07:07	8:23:02	8:32:59	8:46:41	9:06:41	9:35:15
6:30:32	7:09:17	7:25:46	7:45:07	8:07:43	8:23:12	8:33:02	8:47:00	9:06:44	9:35:40
6:30:41	7:09:34	7:25:48	7:45:32	8:08:28	8:23:30	8:33:27	8:47:04	9:06:48	9:36:17
6:30:53	7:09:38	7:26:30	7:46:22	8:08:31	8:24:04	8:33:30	8:47:06	9:06:55	9:36:37
6:30:56	7:09:53	7:26:38	7:46:38	8:09:05	8:24:17	8:33:40	8:47:15	9:06:59	9:37:23
6:31:04	7:09:59	7:26:49	7:46:48	8:09:15	8:24:19	8:33:47	8:47:27	9:08:03	9:37:37
6:31:45	7:10:29	7:27:30	7:47:00	8:09:48	8:24:26	8:34:19	8:47:40	9:08:33	9:37:38
6:33:49	7:10:37	7:27:36	7:47:15	8:09:57	8:24:39	8:34:20	8:47:46	9:09:32	9:37:42
6:34:03	7:10:54	7:27:50	7:47:53	8:10:39	8:24:48	8:35:01	8:47:53	9:10:32	9:39:03
6:34:15	7:11:07	7:27:50	7:48:01	8:11:16	8:25:03	8:35:07	8:48:27	9:10:46	9:39:10
6:36:07	7:11:30	7:27:56	7:48:14	8:11:30	8:25:04	8:35:25	8:48:48	9:10:53	9:41:37
6:36:12	7:12:02	7:28:01	7:48:14	8:11:38	8:25:07	8:35:29	8:49:14	9:11:32	9:42:58
6:37:21	7:12:08	7:28:17	7:48:50	8:11:49	8:25:16	8:36:13	8:49:19	9:11:37	9:43:27
6:37:23	7:12:18	7:28:25	7:49:00	8:12:00	8:25:22	8:36:14	8:49:20	9:11:50	9:43:37
6:37:57	7:12:18	7:28:26	7:49:04	8:12:07	8:25:31	8:36:23	8:49:40	9:12:02	9:44:09
6:38:20	7:12:26	7:28:47	7:49:48	8:12:17	8:25:32	8:36:23	8:50:19	9:13:19	9:44:21
6:40:06	7:13:16	7:28:54	7:49:50	8:12:40	8:25:32	8:36:29	8:50:38	9:14:00	9:44:32
6:40:11	7:13:21	7:29:09	7:49:59	8:12:41	8:25:45	8:36:35	8:52:11	9:14:04	9:44:37
6:40:59	7:13:22	7:29:27	7:50:13	8:12:42	8:25:48	8:36:37	8:52:29	9:14:07	9:44:44
6:42:17	7:14:04	7:30:02	7:50:27	8:12:47	8:25:49	8:37:05	8:52:40	9:15:15	9:45:10
6:43:01	7:14:07	7:30:07	7:51:07	8:13:40	8:26:01	8:37:11	8:52:41	9:15:26	9:46:15
6:43:05	7:14:49	7:30:13	7:51:31	8:13:41	8:26:04	8:37:12	8:52:43	9:15:27	9:46:44
6:43:57	7:15:19	7:30:50	7:51:40	8:13:52	8:26:11	8:37:35	8:53:03	9:15:36	9:49:48
6:44:02	7:15:38	7:30:55	7:52:05	8:14:04	8:26:15	8:37:44	8:53:08	9:15:40	9:50:19
6:45:04	7:15:41	7:31:24	7:52:25	8:14:41	8:26:28	8:38:01	8:53:19	9:15:40	9:52:53
6:46:13	7:15:57	7:31:35	7:52:32	8:15:15	8:26:28	8:38:02	8:53:30	9:15:40	9:53:13
6:47:01	7:16:28	7:31:41	7:53:10	8:15:25	8:26:37	8:38:10	8:53:32	9:15:41	9:53:15
6:47:10	7:16:36	7:31:45	7:53:18	8:15:39	8:26:58	8:38:15	8:53:44	9:15:46	9:53:50
6:47:35	7:16:40	7:31:46	7:53:19	8:15:48	8:27:07	8:38:39	8:54:25	9:16:12	9:54:24
6:49:23	7:16:45	7:32:13	7:53:51	8:16:09	8:27:09	8:38:40	8:54:28	9:16:34	9:54:48
6:50:54	7:16:50	7:32:16	7:53:52	8:16:10	8:27:17	8:38:44	8:54:49	9:18:02	9:54:51
6:51:04	7:17:08	7:32:16	7:54:04	8:16:18	8:27:26	8:38:49	8:55:05	9:18:06	9:56:40
6:51:17	7:17:09	7:32:34	7:54:16	8:16:26	8:27:29	8:38:57	8:55:05	9:20:19	9:58:25
6:51:48	7:17:09	7:32:34	7:54:26	8:16:39	8:27:35	8:39:07	8:55:14	9:20:42	9:59:19
6:52:17	7:17:19	7:32:57	7:54:51	8:17:16	8:27:54	8:39:20	8:55:22	9:20:44	
6:52:17	7:17:22	7:33:13	7:55:13	8:17:24	8:27:57	8:39:20	8:55:25	9:20:54	
6:52:31	7:17:22	7:33:36	7:55:35	8:17:28	8:27:59	8:39:21	8:55:50	9:21:55	

us with a number (or a set of numbers), independent of the accuracy with which the inputs we enter into the equation reflect the real world.

Answering the following two questions before proceeding to any other computations improves the predictions of our models substantially.

- Is the arrival process *stationary;* that is, is the expected number of customers arriving in a certain time interval constant over the period we are interested in?
- Are the interarrival times *exponentially distributed,* and therefore form a so-called *Poisson* arrival process?

We now define the concepts of stationary arrivals and exponentially distributed interarrival times. We also describe how these two questions can be answered, both in general as well as in the specific setting of the call center described previously. We also discuss the importance of these two questions and their impact on the calculations in this and the next chapter.

Stationary Arrivals

Consider the call arrival pattern displayed in Table 8.1. How tempting it is to put these data into a spreadsheet, compute the mean and the standard deviation of the interarrival times over that time period, and end the analysis of the arrival pattern at this point, assuming that the mean and the standard deviation capture the entire behavior of the arrival process. Five minutes with Excel, and we could be done!

However, a simple graphical analysis (Figure 8.6) of the data reveals that there is more going on in the arrival process than two numbers can capture. As we can see graphically in Figure 8.6, the average number of customers calling within a certain time interval (e.g., 15 minutes) is not constant over the day.

To capture such changes in arrival processes, we introduce the following definitions:

- An arrival process is said to be *stationary* if, for any time interval (e.g., an hour), the expected number of arrivals in this time interval only depends on the length of the time interval, not on the starting time of the interval (i.e., we can move a time interval of a fixed length back and forth on a time line without changing the expected number of arrivals). In the context of Figure 8.6, we see that the arrival process is not stationary. For example, if we take a 3-hour interval, we see that there are many more customers arriving from 6 A.M. to 9 A.M. than there are from 1 A.M. to 4 A.M.
- An arrival process exhibits *seasonality* if it is not stationary.

FIGURE 8.6
Seasonality over the Course of a Day

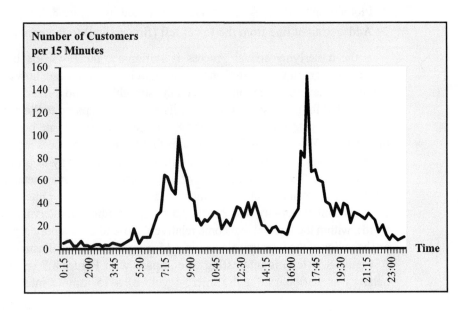

FIGURE 8.7   **Test for Stationary Arrivals**

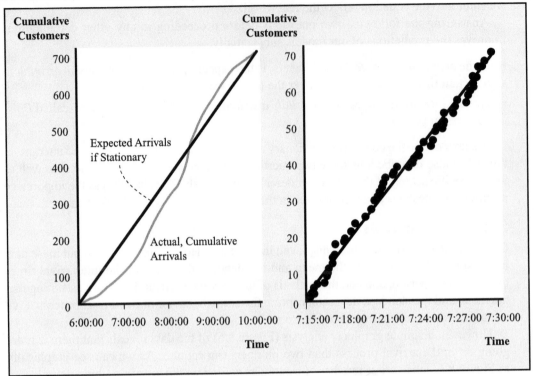

When analyzing an arrival process, it is important that we distinguish between changes in demand (e.g., the number of calls in 15 minutes) that are a result of variability and changes in demand that are a result of seasonality. Both variability and seasonality are unpleasant from an operations perspective. However, the effect of seasonality alone can be perfectly predicted ex ante, while this is not possible for the case of variability (we might know the expected number of callers for a day, but the actual number is a realization of a random variable).

Based on the data at hand, we observe that the arrival process is not stationary over a period of several hours. In general, a simple analysis determines whether a process is stationary.

1. Sort all arrival times so that they are increasing in time (label them as $AT_1 \ldots AT_n$).
2. Plot a graph with ($x \, AT_i; \, y = i$) as illustrated by Figure 8.7.
3. Add a straight line from the lower left (first arrival) to the upper right (last arrival).

If the underlying arrival process is stationary, there will be no significant deviation between the graph you plotted and the straight line. In this case, however, in Figure 8.7 (left) we observe several deviations between the straight line and the arrival data. Specifically, we observe that for the first hour, fewer calls come in compared to the average arrival rate from 6 A.M. to 10 A.M. In contrast, around 8:30 A.M., the arrival rate becomes much higher than the average. Thus, our analysis indicates that the arrival process we face is not stationary.

When facing nonstationary arrival processes, the best way to proceed is to divide up the day (the week, the month) into smaller time intervals and have a separate arrival rate for each interval. If we then look at the arrival process within the smaller intervals—in our case, we use 15-minute intervals—we find that the seasonality within the interval is relatively low. In other words, within the interval, we come relatively close to a stationary arrival stream. The stationary behavior of the interarrivals within a 15-minute interval is illustrated by Figure 8.7 (right).

Figure 8.7 (left) is interesting to compare with Figure 8.7 (right): the arrival process behaves as stationary "at the micro-level" of a 15-minute interval, yet exhibits strong seasonality over the course of the entire day, as we observed in Figure 8.6. Note that the peaks in Figure 8.6 correspond to those time slots where the line of "actual, cumulative arrivals" in Figure 8.7 grows faster than the straight line "predicted arrivals."

In most cases in practice, the context explains this type of seasonality. For example, in the case of An-ser, the spike in arrivals corresponds to people beginning their day, expecting that the company they want to call (e.g., a doctor's office) is already "up and running." However, since many of these firms are not handling calls before 9 A.M., the resulting call stream is channeled to the answering service.

Exponential Interarrival Times

Interarrival times commonly are distributed following an *exponential distribution.* If IA is a random interarrival time and the interarrival process follows an exponential distribution, we have

$$\text{Probability } \{IA \leq t\} = 1 - e^{-\frac{t}{a}}$$

where a is the average interarrival time as defined above. Exponential functions are frequently used to model interarrival time in theory as well as practice, both because of their good fit with empirical data as well as their analytical convenience. If an arrival process has indeed exponential interarrival times, we refer to it as a *Poisson arrival process.*

It can be shown analytically that customers arriving independently from each other at the process (e.g., customers calling into a call center) form a demand pattern with exponential interarrival times. The shape of the cumulative distribution function for the exponential distribution is given in Figure 8.8. The average interarrival time is in minutes. An important property of the exponential distribution is that the standard deviation is also equal to the average, a.

Another important property of the exponential distribution is known as the *memoryless property.* The memoryless property simply states that the number of arrivals in the next time slot (e.g., 1 minute) is independent of when the last arrival has occurred.

To illustrate this property, consider the situation of an emergency room. Assume that, on average, a patient arrives every 10 minutes and no patients have arrived for the last

FIGURE 8.8 **Distribution Function of the Exponential Distribution (left) and an Example of a Histogram (right)**

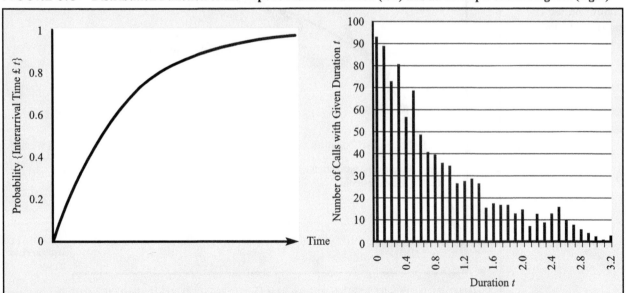

20 minutes. Does the fact that no patients have arrived in the last 20 minutes increase or decrease the probability that a patient arrives in the next 10 minutes? For an arrival process with exponential interarrival times, the answer is *no*.

Intuitively, we feel that this is a reasonable assumption in many settings. Consider, again, an emergency room. Given that the population of potential patients for the ER is extremely large (including all healthy people outside the hospital), we can treat new patients as arriving independently from each other (the fact that Joan Wiley fell off her mountain bike has nothing to do with the fact that Joe Hoop broke his ankle when playing basketball).

Because it is very important to determine if our interarrival times are exponentially distributed, we now introduce the following four-step diagnostic procedure:

1. Compute the interarrival times $IA_1 \ldots IA_n$.
2. Sort the interarrival times in increasing order; let a_i denote the ith smallest interarrival time (a_1 is the smallest interarrival time; a_n is the largest).
3. Plot pairs ($x = a_i$, $y = i/n$). The resulting graph is called an empirical distribution function.
4. Compare the graph with an exponential distribution with "appropriately chosen parameter." To find the best value for the parameter, we set the parameter of the exponential distribution equal to the average interarrival time we obtain from our data. If a few observations from the sample are substantially remote from the resulting curve, we might adjust the parameter for the exponential distribution "manually" to improve fit.

Figure 8.9 illustrates the outcome of this process. If the underlying distribution is indeed exponential, the resulting graph will resemble the analytical distribution as in the case of Figure 8.9. Note that this procedure of assessing the goodness of fit works also for any other distribution function.

Nonexponential Interarrival Times

In some cases, we might find that the interarrival times are not exponentially distributed. For example, we might encounter a situation where arrivals are scheduled (e.g., every hour), which typically leads to a lower amount of variability in the arrival process.

FIGURE 8.9
Empirical versus Exponential Distribution for Interarrival Times

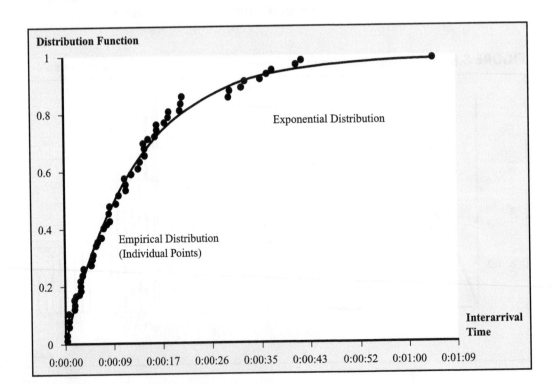

FIGURE 8.10

How to Analyze a Demand/Arrival Process

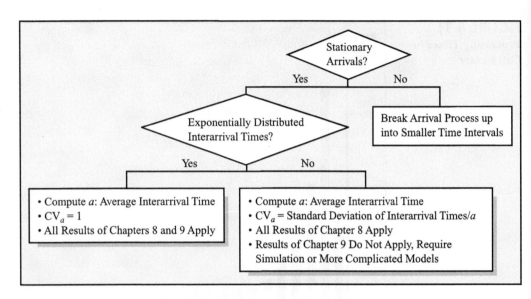

While in the case of the exponential distribution the mean interarrival time is equal to the standard deviation of interarrival times and, thus, one parameter is sufficient to characterize the entire arrival process, we need more parameters to describe the arrival process if interarrival times are not exponentially distributed.

Following our earlier definition of the coefficient of variation, we can measure the variability of an arrival (demand) process as

$$CV_a = \frac{\text{Standard deviation of interarrival time}}{\text{Average interarrival time}}$$

Given that for the exponential distribution the mean is equal to the standard deviation, its coefficient of variation is equal to 1.

Summary: Analyzing an Arrival Process

Figure 8.10 provides a summary of the steps required to analyze an arrival process. It also shows what to do if any of the assumptions required for the following models (Chapters 8 and 9) are violated.

8.4 Processing Time Variability

Just as exact arrival time of an individual call is difficult to predict, so is the actual duration of the call. Thus, service processes also have a considerable amount of variability from the supply side. Figure 8.11 provides a summary of call durations for the case of the An-ser call center. From the perspective of the customer service representative, these call durations are the processing times. As mentioned previously, we will use the words *processing time, processing time,* and *processing time* interchangeably.

We observe that the variability in processing times is substantial. While some calls were completed in less than a minute, others took more than 10 minutes! Thus, in addition to the variability of demand, variability also is created within the process.

There have been reports of numerous different shapes of processing time distributions. For the purposes of this book, we focus entirely on their mean and standard deviation. In other words, when we collect data, we do not explicitly model the distribution of the processing times, but assume that the mean and standard deviation capture all the relevant information. This information is sufficient for all computations in Chapters 8 and 9.

FIGURE 8.11
Processing Times in Call Center

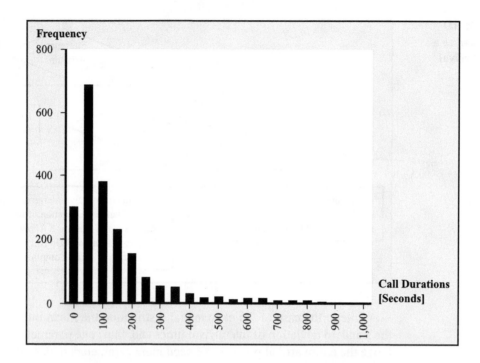

Based on the data summarized in Figure 8.11, we compute the mean processing time as 120 seconds and the corresponding standard deviation as 150 seconds. As we have done with the interarrival times, we can now define the coefficient of variation, which we obtain by

$$CV_p = \frac{\text{Standard deviation of processing time}}{\text{Average processing time}}$$

Here, the subscript p indicates that the CV measures the variability in the processing times. As with the arrival process, we need to be careful not to confuse variability with seasonality. Seasonality in processing times refers to known patterns of call durations as a function of the day of the week or the time of the day (as Figure 8.12 shows, calls take significantly longer on weekends than during the week). Call durations also differ depending on the time of the day.

FIGURE 8.12
Average Call Durations: Weekday versus Weekend

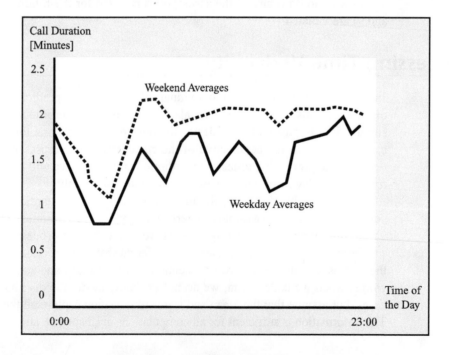

The models we introduce in Chapters 8 and 9 require a stationary service process (in the case of seasonality in the service process, just divide up the time line into smaller intervals, similar to what we did with the arrival process) but do not require any other properties (e.g., exponential distribution of processing time). Thus, the standard deviation and mean of the processing time are all we need to know.

8.5 Predicting the Average Waiting Time for the Case of One Resource

Based on our measures of variability, we now introduce a simple formula that restores our ability to predict the basic process performance measures: inventory, flow rate, and flow time.

In this chapter, we restrict ourselves to the most basic process diagram, consisting of one buffer with unlimited space and one single resource. This process layout corresponds to the call center example discussed above. Figure 8.13 shows the process flow diagram for this simple system.

Flow units arrive to the system following a demand pattern that exhibits variability. On average, a flow unit arrives every a time units. We labeled a as the average interarrival time. This average reflects the mean of interarrival times IA_1 to IA_n. After computing the standard deviation of the IA_1 to IA_n interarrival times, we can compute the coefficient of variation CV_a of the arrival process as discussed previously.

Assume that it takes on average p units of time to serve a flow unit. Similar to the arrival process, we can define p_1 to p_n as the empirically observed processing times and compute the coefficient of variation for the processing times, CV_p, accordingly. Given that there is only one single resource serving the arriving flow units, the capacity of the server can be written as $1/p$.

As discussed in the introduction to this chapter, we are considering cases in which the capacity exceeds the demand rate; thus, the resulting utilization is strictly less than 100 percent. If the utilization were above 100 percent, inventory would predictably build up and we would not need any sophisticated tools accounting for variability to predict that flow units will incur waiting times. However, the most important insight of this chapter is that flow units incur waiting time even if the server utilization is below 100 percent.

Given that capacity exceeds demand and assuming we never lose a customer (i.e., once a customer calls, he or she never hangs up), we are demand-constrained and, thus, the flow rate R is the demand rate. (Chapter 9 deals with the possibility of lost customers.) Specifically, since a customer arrives, on average, every a units of time, the flow rate $R = 1/a$. Recall that we can compute utilization as

$$\text{Utilization} = \frac{\text{Flow rate}}{\text{Capacity}} = \frac{1/a}{1/p} = p/a < 100\%$$

Note that, so far, we have not applied any concept that went beyond the deterministic process analysis we discussed in Chapters 3 to 7.

FIGURE 8.13

A Simple Process with One Queue and One Server

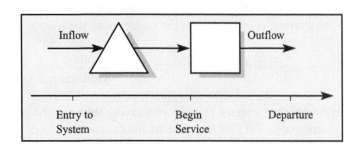

FIGURE 8.14

A Simple Process with One Queue and One Server

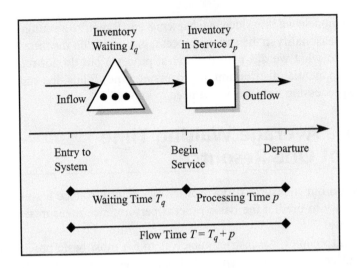

Now, take the perspective of a flow unit moving through the system (see Figure 8.14). A flow unit can spend time waiting in the queue (in a call center, this is the time when you listen to Music of the '70s). Let T_q denote the time the flow unit has to spend in the queue waiting for the service to begin. The subscript q denotes that this is only the time the flow unit waits in the queue. Thus, T_q does *not* include the actual processing time, which we defined as p. Based on the waiting time in the queue T_q and the average processing time p, we can compute the flow time (the time the flow unit will spend in the system) as

$$\text{Flow time} = \text{Time in queue} + \text{Processing time}$$
$$T = T_q + p$$

Instead of taking the perspective of the flow unit, we also can look at the system as a whole, wondering how many flow units will be in the queue and how many will be in service. Let I_q be defined as the inventory (number of flow units) that are in the queue and I_p be the number of flow units in process. Since the inventory in the queue I_q and the inventory in process I_p are the only places we can find inventory, we can compute the overall inventory in the system as $I = I_q + I_p$.

As long as there exists only one resource, I_p is a number between zero and one: sometimes there is a flow unit in service ($I_p = 1$); sometimes there is not ($I_p = 0$). The probability that at a random moment in time the server is actually busy, working on a flow unit, corresponds to the utilization. For example, if the utilization of the process is 30 percent, there exists a .3 probability that at a random moment in time the server is busy. Alternatively, we can say that over the 60 minutes in an hour, the server is busy for

$$.3 \times 60 \ [\text{minutes/hour}] = 18 \ \text{minutes}$$

While the inventory in service I_p and the processing time p are relatively easy to compute, this is unfortunately not the case for the inventory in the queue I_q or the waiting time in the queue T_q.

Based on the processing time p, the utilization, and the variability as measured by the coefficients of variation for the interarrival time CV_a and the processing time CV_p, we can compute the average waiting time in the queue using the following formula:

$$\text{Time in queue} = \text{Processing time} \times \left(\frac{\text{Utilization}}{1 - \text{Utilization}} \right) \times \left(\frac{CV_a^2 + CV_p^2}{2} \right)$$

The formula does not require that the processing times or the interarrival times follow a specific distribution. Yet, for the case of nonexponential interarrival times, the formula only approximates the expected time in the queue, as opposed to being 100 percent exact. The formula should be used only for the case of a stationary process (see Section 8.3 for the definition of a stationary process as well as for what to do if the process is not stationary).

The above equation states that the waiting time in the queue is the product of three factors:

- The waiting time is expressed as multiples of the processing time. However, it is important to keep in mind that the processing time also directly influences the utilization (as Utilization = Processing time/Interarrival time). Thus, one should not think of the waiting time as increasing linearly with the processing time.

- The second factor captures the utilization effect. Note that the utilization has to be less than 100 percent. If the utilization is equal to or greater than 100 percent, the queue continues to grow. This is not driven by variability, but simply by not having the requested capacity. We observe that the utilization factor is nonlinear and becomes larger and larger as the utilization level is increased closer to 100 percent. For example, for Utilization = 0.8, the utilization factor is $0.8/(1 - 0.8) = 4$; for Utilization = 0.9, it is $0.9/(1 - 0.9) = 9$; and for Utilization = 0.95, it grows to $0.95/(1 - 0.95) = 19$.

- The third factor captures the amount of variability in the system, measured by the average of the squared coefficient of variation of interarrival times CV_a and processing times CV_p. Since CV_a and CV_p affect neither the average processing time p nor the utilization u, we observe that the waiting time grows with the variability in the system.

The best way to familiarize ourselves with this newly introduced formula is to apply it and "see it in action." Toward that end, consider the case of the An-ser call center at 2:00 A.M. in the morning. An-ser is a relatively small call center and they receive very few calls at this time of the day (see Section 8.3 for detailed arrival information), so at 2:00 A.M., there is only one person handling incoming calls.

From the data we collected in the call center, we can quickly compute that the average processing time at An-ser at this time of the day is around 90 seconds. Given that we found in the previous section that the processing time does depend on the time of the day, it is important that we use the processing time data representative for these early morning hours: Processing time $p = 90$ seconds.

Based on the empirical processing times we collected in Section 8.4, we now compute the standard deviation of the processing time to be 120 seconds. Hence, the coefficient of variation for the processing time is

$$CV_p = 120 \text{ seconds}/90 \text{ seconds} = 1.3333$$

From the arrival data we collected (see Figure 8.6), we know that at 2:00 A.M. there are 3 calls arriving in a 15-minute interval. Thus, the interarrival time is $a = 5$ minutes = 300 seconds. Given the processing time and the interarrival time, we can now compute the utilization as

$$\text{Utilization} = \text{Processing time/Interarrival time} \ (= p/a)$$
$$= 90 \text{ seconds}/300 \text{ seconds} = 0.3$$

Concerning the coefficient of variation of the interarrival time, we can take one of two approaches. First, we could take the observed interarrival times and compute the standard deviation empirically. Alternatively, we could view the arrival process during the time period as random. Given the good fit between the data we collected and the exponential distribution (see Figure 8.9), we assume that arrivals follow a Poisson process (interarrival times are exponentially distributed). This implies a coefficient of variation of

$$CV_a = 1$$

Substituting these values into the waiting time formula yields

$$\text{Time in queue} = \text{Processing time} \times \left(\frac{\text{Utilization}}{1 - \text{Utilization}} \right) \times \left(\frac{CV_a^2 + CV_p^2}{2} \right)$$

$$= 90 \times \frac{0.3}{1 - 0.3} \times \frac{1^2 + 1.3333^2}{2}$$

$$= 53.57 \text{ seconds}$$

Note that this result captures the average waiting time of a customer before getting served. To obtain the customer's total time spent for the call, including waiting time and processing time, we need to add the processing time p for the actual service. Thus, the flow time can be computed as

$$T = T_q + p = 53.57 \text{ seconds} + 90 \text{ seconds} = 143.57 \text{ seconds}$$

It is important to point out that the value 53.57 seconds provides the average waiting time. The actual waiting times experienced by individual customers vary. Some customers get lucky and receive service immediately; others have to wait much longer than 53.57 seconds. This is discussed further below.

Waiting times computed based on the methodology outlined above need to be seen as long-run averages. This has the following two practical implications:

- If the system would start empty (e.g., in a hospital lab, where there are no patients before the opening of the waiting room), the first couple of patients are less likely to experience significant waiting time. This effect is transient: Once a sufficient number of patients have arrived, the system reaches a "steady-state." Note that given the 24-hour operation of An-ser, this is not an issue in this specific case.

- If we observe the system for a given time interval, it is unlikely that the average waiting time we observe within this interval is exactly the average we computed. However, the longer we observe the system, the more likely the expected waiting time T_q will indeed coincide with the empirical average. This resembles a casino, which cannot predict how much money a specific guest will win (or typically lose) in an evening, yet can well predict the economics of the entire guest population over the course of a year.

Now that we have accounted for the waiting time T_q (or the flow time T), we are able to compute the resulting inventory. With $1/a$ being our flow rate, we can use Little's Law to compute the average inventory I as

$$I = R \times T = \frac{1}{a} \times (T_q + p)$$

$$= 1/300 \times (53.57 + 90) = 0.479$$

Thus, there is, on average, about half a customer in the system (it is 2:00 A.M. after all . . .). This inventory includes the two subsets we defined as inventory in the queue (I_q) and inventory in process (I_p):

- I_q can be obtained by applying Little's Law, but this time, rather than applying Little's Law to the entire system (the waiting line and the server), we apply it only to the waiting line in isolation. If we think of the waiting line as a mini process in itself (the corresponding process flow diagram consists only of one triangle), we obtain a flow time of T_q. Hence,

$$I_q = 1/a \times T_q = 1/300 \times 53.57 = 0.179$$

- At any given moment in time, we also can look at the number of customers that are currently talking to the customer service representative. Since we assumed there would only be one representative at this time of the day, there will never be more than one caller at this stage. However, there are moments in time when no caller is served, as the utilization of the employee is well below 100 percent. The average number of callers in service can thus be computed as

$$I_p = \text{Probability}\{0 \text{ callers talking to representative}\} \times 0$$
$$+ \text{Probability}\{1 \text{ caller talking to representative}\} \times 1$$
$$I_p = (1 - u) \times 0 + u \times 1 = u$$

In this case, we obtain $I_p = 0.3$.

8.6 Predicting the Average Waiting Time for the Case of Multiple Resources

After analyzing waiting time in the presence of variability for an extremely simple process, consisting of just one buffer and one resource, we now turn to more complicated operations. Specifically, we analyze a waiting time model of a process consisting of one waiting area (queue) and a process step performed by multiple, identical resources.

We continue our example of the call center. However, now we consider time slots at more busy times over the course of the day, when there are many more customer representatives on duty in the An-ser call center. The basic process layout is illustrated in Figure 8.15.

Let m be the number of parallel servers we have available. Given that we have m servers working in parallel, we now face a situation where the average processing time is likely to be much longer than the average interarrival time. Taken together, the m resources have a capacity of m/p, while the demand rate continues to be given by $1/a$. We can compute the utilization u of the service process as

$$\text{Utilization} = \frac{\text{Flow rate}}{\text{Capacity}} = \frac{1/\text{Interarrival time}}{(\text{Number of resources}/\text{Processing time})}$$
$$= \frac{1/a}{m/p} = \frac{p}{a \times m}$$

Similar to the case with one single resource, we are only interested in the cases of utilization levels below 100 percent.

FIGURE 8.15
A Process with One Queue and Multiple, Parallel Servers ($m = 5$)

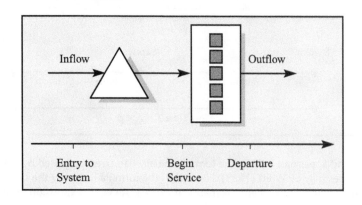

The flow unit will initially spend T_q units of time waiting for service. It then moves to the next available resource, where it spends p units of time for service. As before, the total flow time is the sum of waiting time and processing time:

$$\text{Flow time} = \text{Waiting time in queue} + \text{Processing time}$$
$$T = T_q + p$$

Based on the processing time p, the utilization u, the coefficients of variation for both service (CV_p) and arrival process (CV_a) as well as the number of resources in the system (m), we can compute the average waiting time T_q using the following formula:[1]

$$\text{Time in queue} = \left(\frac{\text{Processing time}}{m}\right) \times \left(\frac{\text{Utilization}^{\sqrt{2(m+1)}-1}}{1-\text{Utilization}}\right) \times \left(\frac{CV_a^2 + CV_p^2}{2}\right)$$

As in the case of one single resource, the waiting time is expressed as the product of the processing time, a utilization factor, and a variability factor. We also observe that for the special case of $m = 1$, the above formula is exactly the same as the waiting time formula for a single resource. Note that all other performance measures, including the flow time (T), the inventory in the system (I), and the inventory in the queue (I_q), can be computed as discussed before.

While the above expression does not necessarily seem an inviting equation to use, it can be programmed without much effort into a spreadsheet. Furthermore, it provides the average waiting time for a system that otherwise could only be analyzed with much more sophisticated software packages.

Unlike the waiting time formula for the single resource case, which provides an exact quantification of waiting times as long as the interarrival times follow an exponential distribution, the waiting time formula for multiple resources is an approximation. The formula works well for most settings we encounter, specifically if the ratio of utilization u to the number of servers m is large (u/m is high).

Now that we have computed waiting time, we can again use Little's Law to compute the average number of flow units in the waiting area I_q, the average number of flow units in service I_p, and the average number of flow units in the entire system $I = I_p + I_q$. Figure 8.16 summarizes the key performance measures.

FIGURE 8.16
Summary of Key Performance Measures

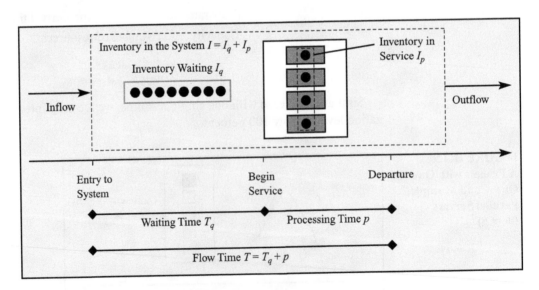

[1] Hopp and Spearman (1996); the formula initially had been proposed by Sakasegawa (1977) and used successfully by Whitt (1983). For $m = 1$, the formula is exactly the same as in the previous section. The formula is an approximation for $m > 1$. An exact expression for this case does not exist.

SUMMARY OF WAITING TIME CALCULATIONS

1. Collect the following data:

   - Number of servers, m
   - Processing time, p
   - Interarrival time, a
   - Coefficient of variation for interarrival (CV_a) and processing time (CV_p)

2. Compute utilization: $u = \dfrac{p}{a \times m}$

3. Compute expected waiting time:

$$T_q = \left(\frac{\text{Processing time}}{m} \right) \times \left(\frac{\text{Utilization}^{\sqrt{2(m+1)}-1}}{1 - \text{Utilization}} \right) \times \left(\frac{CV_a^2 + CV_p^2}{2} \right)$$

4. Based on T_q, we can compute the remaining performance measures as

$$\text{Flow time } T = T_q + p$$
$$\text{Inventory in service } I_p = m \times u$$
$$\text{Inventory in the queue } I_q = T_q/a$$
$$\text{Inventory in the system } I = I_p + I_q$$

Note that in the presence of multiple resources serving flow units, there can be more than one flow unit in service simultaneously. If u is the utilization of the process, it is also the utilization of each of the m resources, as they process demand at the same rate. We can compute the expected number of flow units at any of the m resources *in isolation* as

$$u \times 1 + (1 - u) \times 0 = u$$

Adding up across the m resources then yields

$$\text{Inventory in process} = \text{Number of resources} \times \text{Utilization}$$
$$I_p = m \times u$$

We illustrate the methodology using the case of An-ser services. Assuming we would work with a staff of 10 customer service representatives (CSRs) for the 8:00 A.M. to 8:15 A.M. time slot, we can compute the utilization as follows:

$$\text{Utilization } u = \frac{p}{a \times m} = \frac{90 \,[\text{seconds}/\text{call}]}{11.39 \times 10 \,[\text{seconds}/\text{call}]} = 0.79$$

where we obtained the interarrival time of 11.39 seconds between calls by dividing the length of the time interval (15 minutes = 900 seconds) by the number of calls received over the interval (79 calls). This now allows us to compute the average waiting time as

$$T_q = \left(\frac{p}{m} \right) \times \left(\frac{u^{\sqrt{2(m+1)}-1}}{1 - u} \right) \times \left(\frac{CV_a^2 + CV_p^2}{2} \right)$$
$$= \left(\frac{90}{10} \right) \times \left(\frac{0.79^{\sqrt{2(10+1)}-1}}{1 - 0.79} \right) \times \left(\frac{1 + 1.3333^2}{2} \right) = 24.98 \text{ seconds}$$

The most important calculations related to waiting times caused by variability are summarized in Exhibit 8.1.

8.7 Service Levels in Waiting Time Problems

So far, we have focused our attention on the average waiting time in the process. However, a customer requesting service from our process is not interested in the average time he or she waits in queue or the average total time to complete his or her request (waiting time T_q and flow time T respectively), but in the wait times that he or she experiences personally.

Consider, for example, a caller who has just waited for 15 minutes listening to music while on hold. This caller is likely to be unsatisfied about the long wait time. Moreover, the response from the customer service representative of the type "we are sorry for your delay, but our average waiting time is only 4 minutes" is unlikely to reduce this dissatisfaction.

Thus, from a managerial perspective, we not only need to analyze the average wait time, but also the likelihood that the wait time exceeds a certain *target wait time* (*TWT*). More formally, we can define the *service level* for a given target wait time as the percentage of customers that will begin service in TWT or less units of waiting time:

$$\text{Service level} = \text{Probability\{Waiting time} \leq \text{TWT\}}$$

This service level provides us with a way to measure to what extent the service is able to respond to demand within a consistent waiting time. A service level of 95 percent for a target waiting time of TWT = 2 minutes means that 95 percent of the customers are served in less than 2 minutes of waiting time.

Figure 8.17 shows the empirical distribution function (see Section 8.3 on how to create this graph) for waiting times at the An-ser call center for a selected time slot. Based on the graph, we can distinguish between two groups of customers. About 65 percent of the customers did not have to wait at all and received immediate service. The remaining 35 percent of the customers experienced a waiting time that strongly resembles an exponential distribution.

We observe that the average waiting time for the entire calling population (not just the ones who had to wait) was, for this specific sample, about 10 seconds. For a target wait time TWT = 30 seconds, we find a service level of 90 percent; that is, 90 percent of the callers had to wait 30 seconds or less.

FIGURE 8.17
Empirical Distribution of Waiting Times at An-ser

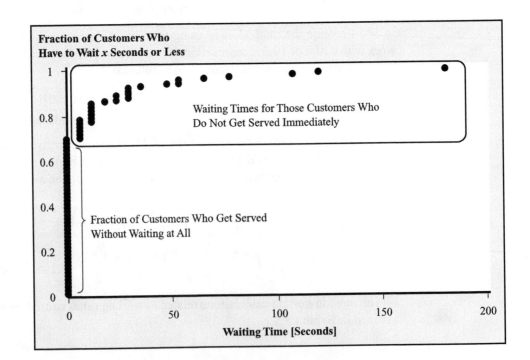

Service levels as defined above are a common performance measure for service operations in practice. They are used internally by the firm in charge of delivering a certain service. They also are used frequently by firms that want to outsource a service, such as a call center, as a way to contract (and track) the responsiveness of their service provider.

There is no universal rule of what service level is right for a given service operation. For example, responding to large public pressure, the German railway system (Deutsche Bundesbahn) has recently introduced a policy that 80 percent of the calls to their customer complaint number should be handled within 20 seconds. Previously, only 30 percent of the calls were handled within 20 seconds. How fast you respond to calls depends on your market position and the importance of the incoming calls for your business. A service level that worked for the German railway system (30 percent within 20 seconds) is likely to be unacceptable in other, more competitive environments.

8.8   Economic Implications: Generating a Staffing Plan

So far, we have focused purely on analyzing the call center for a given number of customer service representatives (CSRs) on duty and predicted the resulting waiting times. This raises the managerial question of how many CSRs An-ser should have at work at any given moment in time over the day. The more CSRs we schedule, the shorter the waiting time, but the more we need to pay in terms of wages.

When making this trade-off, we need to balance the following two costs:

- Cost of waiting, reflecting increased line charges for 1-800 numbers and customer dissatisfaction (line charges are incurred for the actual talk time as well as for the time the customer is on hold).
- Cost of service, resulting from the number of CSRs available.

Additional costs that could be factored into the analysis are

- Costs related to customers calling into the call center but who are not able to gain access even to the waiting line, that is, they receive a busy signal (blocked customers; this will be discussed further in Chapter 9).
- Costs related to customers who hang up while waiting for service.

In the case of An-ser, the average salary of a CSR is $10 per hour. Note that CSRs are paid independent of being idle or busy. Variable costs for a 1-800 number are about $0.05 per minute. A summary of various costs involved in managing a call center—or service operations in general—is given by Figure 8.18.

FIGURE 8.18
Economic Consequences of Waiting

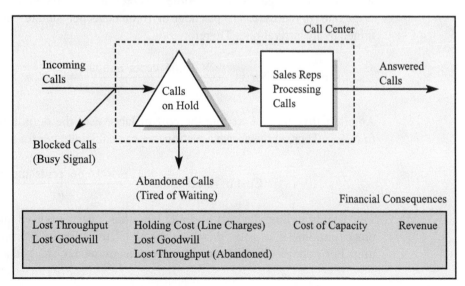

TABLE 8.2
Determining the Number of CSRs to Support Target Wait Time

Number of CSRs, *m*	Utilization $u = p/(a \times m)$	Expected Wait Time T_q [seconds] Based on Waiting Time Formula
8	0.99	1221.23
9	0.88	72.43
10	0.79	24.98
11	0.72	11.11
12	0.66	5.50
13	0.61	2.89
14	0.56	1.58

When deciding how many CSRs to schedule for a given time slot, we first need to decide on how responsive we want to be to our customers. For the purpose of our analysis, we assume that the management of An-ser wants to achieve an average wait time of 10 seconds. Alternatively, we also could set a service level and then staff according to a TWT constraint, for example, 95 percent of customers to be served in 20 seconds or less.

Now, for a given arrival rate, we need to determine the number of CSRs that will correspond to an average wait time of 10 seconds. Again, consider the time interval from 8:00 A.M. to 8:15 A.M. Table 8.2 shows the utilization level as well as the expected wait time for different numbers of customer service representatives. Note that using fewer than 8 servers would lead to a utilization above one, which would mean that queues would build up independent of variability, which is surely not acceptable.

Table 8.2 indicates that adding CSRs leads to a reduction in waiting time. For example, while a staff of 8 CSRs would correspond to an average waiting time of about 20 minutes, the average waiting time falls below 10 seconds once a twelfth CSR has been added. Thus, working with 12 CSRs allows An-ser to meet its target of an average wait time of 10 seconds. In this case, the actual service would be even better and we expect the average wait time for this specific time slot to be 5.50 seconds.

Providing a good service level does come at the cost of increased labor. The more CSRs are scheduled to serve, the lower is their utilization. In Chapter 4 we defined the cost of direct labor as

$$\text{Cost of direct labor} = \frac{\text{Total wages per unit of time}}{\text{Flow rate per unit of time}}$$

where the total wages per unit of time are determined by the number of CSRs *m* times their wage rate (in our case, $10 per hour or 16.66 cents per minute) and the flow rate is determined by the arrival rate. Therefore,

$$\text{Cost of direct labor} = \frac{m \times 16.66 \text{ cents/minute}}{1/a} = a \times m \times 16.66 \text{ cents/minute}$$

An alternative way of writing the cost of labor uses the definition of utilization ($u = p/(a \times m)$). Thus, in the above equation, we can substitute p/u for $a \times m$ and obtain

$$\text{Cost of direct labor} = \frac{p \times 16.66 \text{ cents/minute}}{u}$$

This way of writing the cost of direct labor has a very intuitive interpretation: The actual processing time *p* is inflated by a factor of 1/Utilization to appropriately account for idle time. For example, if utilization were 50 percent, we are charged a $1 of idle time penalty

TABLE 8.3
Economic Implications of Various Staffing Levels

Number of Servers	Utilization	Cost of Labor per Call	Cost of Line Charges per Call	Total Cost per Call
8	0.988	0.2531	1.0927	1.3458
9	0.878	0.2848	0.1354	0.4201
10	0.790	0.3164	0.0958	0.4122
11	0.718	0.3480	0.0843	0.4323
12	0.658	0.3797	0.0796	0.4593
13	0.608	0.4113	0.0774	0.4887
14	0.564	0.4429	0.0763	0.5193
15	0.527	0.4746	0.0757	0.5503

for every $1 we spend on labor productively. In our case, the utilization is 66 percent; thus, the cost of direct labor is

$$\text{Cost of direct labor} = \frac{1.5 \ \text{minutes/call} \times 16.66 \ \text{cents/minute}}{0.66} = 38 \ \text{cents/call}$$

This computation allows us to extend Table 8.2 to include the cost implications of the various staffing scenarios (our calculations do not consider any cost of lost goodwill). Specifically, we are interested in the impact of staffing on the cost of direct labor per call as well as in the cost of line charges.

Not surprisingly, we can see in Table 8.3 that moving from a very high level of utilization of close to 99 percent (using 8 CSRs) to a more responsive service level, for example, as provided by 12 CSRs, leads to a significant increase in labor cost.

At the same time, though, line charges drop from over $1 per call to almost $0.075 per call. Note that $0.075 per call is the minimum charge that can be achieved based on staffing changes, as it corresponds to the pure talk time.

Adding line charges and the cost of direct labor allows us to obtain total costs. In Table 8.3, we observe that total costs are minimized when we have 10 CSRs in service.

However, we need to be careful in labeling this point as the optimal staffing level, as the total cost number is a purely internal measure and does not take into account any information about the customer's cost of waiting. For this reason, when deciding on an appropriate staffing level, it is important to set acceptable service levels for waiting times as done in Table 8.2 and then staffing up to meet these service levels (opposed to minimizing internal costs).

If we repeat the analysis that we have conducted for the 8:00 A.M. to 8:15 A.M. time slot over the 24 hours of the day, we obtain a staffing plan. The staffing plan accounts for both the seasonality observed throughout the day as well as the variability and the resulting need for extra capacity. This is illustrated by Figure 8.19.

When we face a nonstationary arrival process as in this case, a common problem is to decide into how many intervals one should break up the time line to have close to a stationary arrival process within a time interval (in this case, 15 minutes). While we cannot go into the theory behind this topic, the basic intuition is this: It is important that the time intervals are large enough so that

- We have enough data to come up with reliable estimates for the arrival rate of the interval (e.g., if we had worked with 30-second intervals, our estimates for the number of calls arriving within a 30-second time interval would have been less reliable).
- Over the course of an interval, the queue needs sufficient time to reach a "steady state"; this is achieved if we have a relatively large number of arrivals and service completions within the duration of a time interval (more than 10).

FIGURE 8.19
**Staffing and
Incoming Calls over
the Course of a Day**

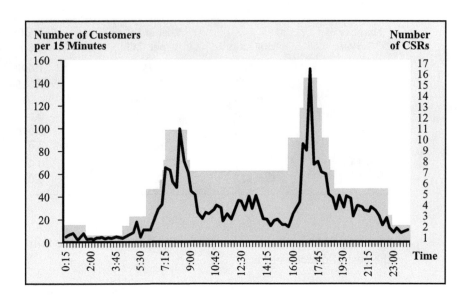

In practice, finding a staffing plan can be somewhat more complicated, as it needs to account for

- Breaks for the operators.
- Length of work period. It is typically not possible to request an operator to show up for work for only a one-hour time slot. Either one has to provide longer periods of time or one would have to temporarily route calls to other members of the organization (supervisor, back-office employees).

Despite these additional complications, the analysis outlined above captures the most important elements typical for making supply-related decisions in service environments.

8.9   Impact of Pooling: Economies of Scale

Consider a process that currently corresponds to two (m) demand arrival processes that are processed by two (m) identical servers. If demand cannot be processed immediately, the flow unit waits in front of the server where it initially arrived. An example of such a system is provided in Figure 8.20 (left).

Here is an interesting question: Does combining the two systems into a single system with one waiting area and two (m) identical servers lead to lower average waiting times? We refer to such a combination of multiple resources into one "mega-resource" as *pooling*.

FIGURE 8.20
**The Concept of
Pooling**

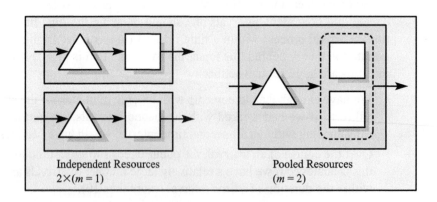

Consider, for example, two small food services at an airport. For simplicity, assume that both of them have a customer arrival stream with an average interarrival time a of 4 minutes and a coefficient of variation equal to one. The processing time p is three minutes per customer and the coefficient of variation for the service process also is equal to one. Consequently, both food services face a utilization of $p/a = 0.75$.

Using our waiting time formula, we compute the average waiting time as

$$T_q = \text{Processing time} \times \left(\frac{\text{Utilization}}{1 - \text{Utilization}} \right) \times \left(\frac{CV_a^2 + CV_p^2}{2} \right)$$

$$= 3 \times \left(\frac{0.75}{1 - 0.75} \right) \times \left(\frac{1 + 1}{2} \right)$$

$$= 3 \times (0.75/0.25) = 9 \text{ minutes}$$

Now compare this with the case in which we combine the capacity of both food services to serve the demand of both services. The capacity of the pooled process has increased by a factor of two and now is $\frac{2}{3}$ unit per minute. However, the demand rate also has doubled: If there was one customer every four minutes arriving for service 1 and one customer every four minutes arriving for service 2, the pooled service experiences an arrival rate of one customer every $a = 2$ minutes (i.e., two customers every four minutes is the same as one customer every two minutes).

We can compute the utilization of the pooled process as

$$u = \frac{p}{a \times m}$$

$$= 3/(2 \times 2) = 0.75$$

Observe that the utilization has not changed compared to having two independent services. Combining two processes with a utilization of 75 percent leads to a pooled system with a 75 percent utilization. However, a different picture emerges when we look at the waiting time of the pooled system. Using the waiting time formula for multiple resources, we can write

$$T_q = \left(\frac{\text{Processing time}}{m} \right) \times \left(\frac{\text{Utilization}^{\sqrt{2(m+1)}-1}}{1 - \text{Utilization}} \right) \times \left(\frac{CV_a^2 + CV_p^2}{2} \right)$$

$$= \left(\frac{3}{2} \right) \times \left(\frac{0.75^{\sqrt{2(2+1)}-1}}{1 - 0.75} \right) \times \left(\frac{1 + 1}{2} \right) = 3.95 \text{ minutes}$$

In other words, the pooled process on the right of Figure 8.20 can serve the same number of customers using the same processing time (and thereby having the same utilization), but in only *half* the waiting time!

While short of being a formal proof, the intuition for this result is as follows. The pooled process uses the available capacity more effectively, as it prevents the case that one resource is idle while the other faces a backlog of work (waiting flow units). Thus, pooling identical resources balances the load for the servers, leading to shorter waiting times. This behavior is illustrated in Figure 8.21.

Figure 8.21 illustrates that for a given level of utilization, the waiting time decreases with the number of servers in the resource pool. This is especially important for higher levels of utilization. While for a system with one single server waiting times tend to "go

FIGURE 8.21
How Pooling Can
Reduce Waiting Time

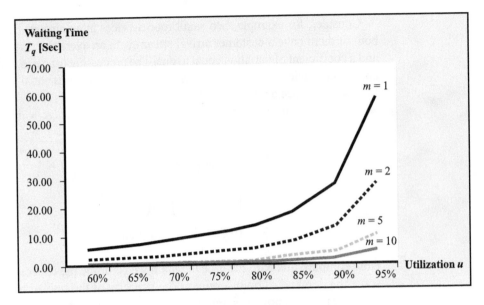

through the roof" once the utilization exceeds 85 percent, a process consisting of 10 identical servers can still provide reasonable service even at utilizations approaching 95 percent.

Given that a pooled system provides better service than individual processes, a service organization can benefit from pooling identical branches or work groups in one of two forms:

- The operation can use pooling to reduce customer waiting time without having to staff extra workers.
- The operation can reduce the number of workers while maintaining the same responsiveness.

These economic benefits of pooling can be illustrated nicely within the context of the An-ser case discussed above. In our analysis leading to Table 8.2, we assumed that there would be 79 calls arriving per 15-minute time interval and found that we would need 12 CSRs to serve customers with an average wait time of 10 seconds or less.

Assume we could pool An-ser's call center with a call center of comparable size; that is, we would move all CSRs to one location and merge both call centers' customer populations. Note that this would not necessarily require the two call centers to "move in" with each other; they could be physically separate as long as the calls are routed through one joint network.

Without any consolidation, merging the two call centers would lead to double the number of CSRs and double the demand, meaning 158 calls per 15-minute interval. What would be the average waiting time in the pooled call center? Or, alternatively, if we maintained an average waiting time of 10 seconds or less, how much could we reduce our staffing level? Table 8.4 provides the answers to these questions.

First, consider the row of 24 CSRs, corresponding to pooling the entire staff of the two call centers. Note specifically that the utilization of the pooled call center is not any different from what it was in Table 8.2. We have doubled the number of CSRs, but we also have doubled the number of calls (and thus cut the interarrival time by half). With 24 CSRs, we expect an average waiting time of 1.2 seconds (compared to almost 6 seconds before).

Alternatively, we could take the increased efficiency benefits resulting from pooling by reducing our labor cost. We also observe from Table 8.4 that a staff of 20 CSRs would be able to answer calls with an average wait time of 10 seconds. Thus, we could increase

TABLE 8.4
Pooling Two Call
Centers

Number of CSRs	Utilization	Expected Wait Time [seconds]	Labor Cost per Call	Line Cost per Call	Total Cost
16	0.988	588.15	0.2532	0.5651	0.8183
17	0.929	72.24	0.2690	0.1352	0.4042
18	0.878	28.98	0.2848	0.0992	0.3840
19	0.832	14.63	0.3006	0.0872	0.3878
20	0.790	8.18	0.3165	0.0818	0.3983
21	0.752	4.84	0.3323	0.0790	0.4113
22	0.718	2.97	0.3481	0.0775	0.4256
23	0.687	1.87	0.3639	0.0766	0.4405
24	0.658	1.20	0.3797	0.0760	0.4558
25	0.632	0.79	0.3956	0.0757	0.4712
26	0.608	0.52	0.4114	0.0754	0.4868
27	0.585	0.35	0.4272	0.0753	0.5025
28	0.564	0.23	0.4430	0.0752	0.5182
29	0.545	0.16	0.4589	0.0751	0.5340
30	0.527	0.11	0.4747	0.0751	0.5498

utilization to almost 80 percent, which would lower our cost of direct labor from $0.3797 to $0.3165. Given an annual call volume of about 700,000 calls, such a saving would be of significant impact for the bottom line.

Despite the nice property of pooled systems outlined above, pooling should not be seen as a silver bullet. Specifically, pooling benefits are much lower than expected (and potentially negative) in the following situations:

• Pooling benefits are significantly lower when the systems that are pooled are not truly independent. Consider, for example, the idea of pooling waiting lines before cash registers in supermarkets, similar to what is done at airport check-ins. In this case, the individual queues are unlikely to be independent, as customers in the current, nonpooled layout will intelligently route themselves to the queue with the shortest waiting line. Pooling in this case will have little, if any, effect on waiting times.

• Similar to the concept of line balancing we introduced earlier in this book, pooling typically requires the service workforce to have a broader range of skills (potentially leading to higher wage rates). For example, an operator sufficiently skilled that she can take orders for hiking and running shoes, as well as provide answering services for a local hospital, will likely demand a higher wage rate than someone who is just trained to do one of these tasks.

• In many service environments, customers value being treated consistently by the same person. Pooling several lawyers in a law firm might be desirable from a waiting-time perspective but ignores the customer desire to deal with one point of contact in the law firm.

• Similarly, pooling can introduce additional setups. In the law-firm example, a lawyer unfamiliar with the situation of a certain client might need a longer time to provide some quick advice on the case and this extra setup time mitigates the operational benefits from pooling.

• Pooling can backfire if pooling combines different customer classes because this might actually increase the variability of the service process. Consider two clerks working in a retail bank, one of them currently in charge of simple transactions (e.g., processing time of 2 minutes per customer), while the other one is in charge of more complex cases (e.g., processing time of 10 minutes). Pooling these two clerks makes the service process more variable and might actually increase waiting time.

8.10 Priority Rules in Waiting Lines

Choosing an appropriate level of capacity helps to prevent waiting lines from building up in a process. However, in a process with variability, it is impossible to eliminate waiting lines entirely. Given, therefore, that at some point in time some customers will have to wait before receiving service, we need to decide on the order in which we permit them access to the server. This order is determined by a *priority rule,* sometimes also referred to as a queuing discipline.

Customers are assigned priorities by adding a (small) step at the point in the process where customers arrive. This process step is called the *triage step*. At triage, we collect information about some of the characteristics of the arriving customer, which we use as input for the priority rule. Below we discuss priority rules based on the following characteristics:

- The processing time or the expected processing time of the customer (processing-time-dependent priority rules).
- Processing-time-independent priority rules, including priority rules based on customer arrival time and priority rules based on customer importance or urgency.

Processing-Time-Dependent Priority Rules

If it is possible to observe the customer's processing time or his or her expected processing time prior to initiating the service process, this information should be incorporated when assigning a priority to the customer. The most commonly used service-time-dependent priority rule is the shortest processing time (SPT) rule.

Under the SPT rule, the next available server is allocated to the customer with the shortest (expected) processing time of all customers currently in the waiting line. The SPT rule is extremely effective and performs well, with respect to the expected waiting time as well as to the variance of the waiting time. If the processing times are not dependent on the sequence with which customers are processed, the SPT rule can be shown to lead to the shortest average flow time. Its basic intuition is summarized by Figure 8.22.

Processing-Time-Independent Priority Rules

In many cases, it is difficult or impossible to assess the processing time or even the expected processing time prior to initiating the service process. Moreover, if customers are able to misrepresent their processing time, then they have an incentive to suggest that their processing time is less than it really is when the SPT rule is applied (e.g., "Can I just ask a quick question? . . ."). In contrast, the customer arrival time is easy to observe and difficult for the customer to manipulate.

For example, a call center receiving calls for airline reservations knows the sequence with which callers arrive but does not know which customer has already gathered all relevant information and is ready to order and which customer still requires explanation and discussion.

FIGURE 8.22 **The Shortest Processing time (SPT) Rule (used in the right case)**

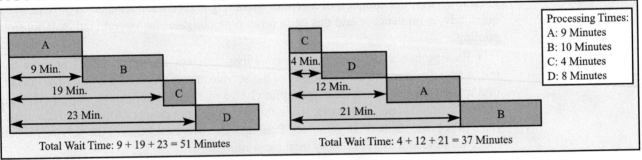

Total Wait Time: 9 + 19 + 23 = 51 Minutes   Total Wait Time: 4 + 12 + 21 = 37 Minutes

The most commonly used priority rule based on arrival times is the first-come, first-served (FCFS) rule. With the FCFS rule, the next available server is allocated to the customer in the waiting line with the earliest arrival time.

In addition to using arrival time information, many situations in practice require that characteristics such as the urgency or the importance of the case are considered in the priority rule. Consider the following two examples:

- In an emergency room, a triage nurse assesses the urgency of each case and then assigns a priority to the patient. Severely injured patients are given priority, independent of their arrival times.

- Customers calling in for investor services are likely to experience different priorities, depending on the value of their invested assets. Customers with an investment of greater than $5 million are unlikely to wait, while customers investing only several thousand dollars might wait for 20 minutes or more.

Such urgency-based priority rules are also independent of the processing time. In general, when choosing a service-time-independent priority rule, the following property should be kept in mind: Whether we serve customers in the order of their arrival, in the reverse order of their arrival (last-come, first-served), or even in alphabetical order, the expected waiting time does not change. Thus, higher priority service (shorter waiting time) for one customer always requires lower priority (longer waiting time) for other customers.

From an implementation perspective, one last point is worth noting. Using priority rules other than FCFS might be perceived as unfair by the customers who arrived early and are already waiting the longest. Thus, while the average waiting time does not change, serving latecomers first increases the variance of the waiting time. Since variability in waiting time is not desirable from a service-quality perspective, the following property of the FCFS rule is worth remembering: Among service-time-independent priority rules, the FCFS rule minimizes the variance of waiting time and flow time.

8.11   Reducing Variability

In this chapter, we have provided some new methods to evaluate the key performance measures of flow rate, flow time, and inventory in the presence of variability. We also have seen that variability is the enemy of all operations (none of the performance measures improves as variability increases). Thus, in addition to just taking variability as given and adjusting our models to deal with variability, we should always think about ways to reduce variability.

Ways to Reduce Arrival Variability

One—somewhat obvious—way of achieving a match between supply and demand is by "massaging" demand such that it corresponds exactly to the supply process. This is basically the idea of *appointment systems* (also referred to as reservation systems in some industries).

Appointment systems have the potential to reduce the variability in the arrival process as they encourage customers to arrive at the rate of service. However, one should not overlook the problems associated with appointment systems, which include

- Appointment systems do not eliminate arrival variability. Customers do not perfectly arrive at the scheduled time (and some might not arrive at all, "no-shows"). Consequently, any good appointment system needs ways to handle these cases (e.g., extra charge or extra waiting time for customers arriving late). However, such actions are typically very difficult to implement, due to what is perceived to be "fair" and/or "acceptable," or because variability in processing times prevents service providers from always keeping on schedule (and if the doctor has the right to be late, why not the patient?).

- What portion of the available capacity should be reserved in advance. Unfortunately, the customers arriving at the last minute are frequently the most important ones: emergency operations in a hospital do not come through an appointment system and business travelers paying 5 to 10 times the fare of low-price tickets are not willing to book in advance (this topic is further explored in the revenue management chapter, Chapter 16).

The most important limitation, however, is that appointment systems might reduce the variability of the arrival process as seen by the operation, but they do not reduce the variability of the true underlying demand. Consider, for example, the appointment system of a dental office. While the system (hopefully) reduces the time the patient has to wait before seeing the dentist on the day of the appointment, this wait time is not the only performance measure that counts, as the patient might already have waited for three months between requesting to see the dentist and the day of the appointment. Thus, appointment systems potentially hide a much larger supply–demand mismatch and, consequently, any good implementation of an appointment system includes a continuous measurement of both of the following:

- The inventory of customers who have an appointment and are now waiting for the day they are scheduled to go to the dentist.
- The inventory of customers who wait for an appointment in the waiting room of the dentist.

In addition to the concept of appointment systems, we can attempt to influence the customer arrival process (though, for reasons similar to the ones discussed, not the true underlying demand pattern) by providing incentives for customers to avoid peak hours. Frequently observed methods to achieve this include

- Early-bird specials at restaurants or bars.
- Price discounts for hotels during off-peak days (or seasons).
- Price discounts in transportation (air travel, highway tolls) depending on the time of service.
- Pricing of air travel depending on the capacity that is already reserved.

It is important to point out that, strictly speaking, the first three items do not reduce variability; they level expected demand and thereby reduce seasonality (remember that the difference between the two is that seasonality is a pattern known already ex ante). The fourth item refers to the concept of revenue management, which is discussed in Chapter 16.

Ways to Reduce Processing Time Variability

In addition to reducing variability by changing the behavior of our customers, we also should consider how to reduce internal variability. However, when attempting to standardize activities (reducing the coefficient of variation of the processing times) or shorten processing times, we need to find a balance between operational efficiency (call durations) and the quality of service experienced by the customer (perceived courtesy).

Figure 8.23 compares five of An-ser's operators for a specific call service along these two dimensions. We observe that operators NN, BK, and BJ are achieving relatively short call durations while being perceived as friendly by the customers (based on recorded calls). Operator KB has shorter call durations, yet also scores lower on courtesy. Finally, operator NJ has the longest call durations and is rated medium concerning courtesy.

Based on Figure 8.23, we can make several interesting observations. First, observe that there seems to exist a frontier capturing the inherent trade-off between call duration and courtesy. Once call durations for this service go below 2.5 minutes, courtesy seems hard to maintain. Second, observe that operator NJ is away from this frontier, as he is neither

FIGURE 8.23
Operator
Performance
Concerning Call
Duration and
Courtesy

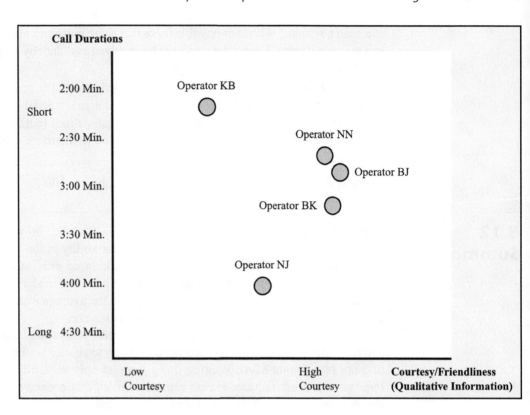

overly friendly nor fast. Remarkably, this operator also has the highest variability in call durations, which suggests that he is not properly following the operating procedures in place (this is not visible in the graph).

To reduce the inefficiencies of operators away from the frontier (such as NJ), call centers invest heavily in training and technology. For example, technology allows operators to receive real-time instruction of certain text blocks that they can use in their interaction with the customer (scripting). Similarly, some call centers have instituted training programs in which operators listen to audio recordings of other operators or have operators call other operators with specific service requests. Such steps reduce both the variability of processing times as well as their means and, therefore, represent substantial improvements in operational performance.

There are other improvement opportunities geared primarily toward reducing the variability of the processing times:

• Although in a service environment (or in a make-to-order production setting) the operator needs to acknowledge the idiosyncrasy of each customer, the operator still can follow a consistent process. For example, a travel agent in a call center might use predefined text blocks (scripts) for his or her interaction with the customer (welcome statement, first question, potential up-sell at the end of the conversation). This approach allowed operators NN, BK, and BJ in Figure 8.23 to be fast and friendly. Thus, being knowledgeable about the process (when to say what) is equally important as being knowledgeable about the product (what to say).

• Processing times in a service environment—unlike processing times in a manufacturing context—are not under the complete control of the resource. The customer him/herself plays a crucial part in the activity at the resource, which automatically introduces a certain amount of variability (e.g., having the customer provide his or her credit card number, having the customer bag the groceries, etc.) What is the consequence of this? At least from a variability perspective, the answer is clear: Reduce the involvement of the customer during the service at a scarce resource wherever possible (note that if the customer involvement does not occur at a scarce resource, having the customer be involved and thereby do part of the work might be very desirable, e.g., in a self-service setting).

• Variability in processing times frequently reflects quality problems. In manufacturing environments, this could include reworking a unit that initially did not meet specifications. However, rework also occurs in service organizations (e.g., a patient who is released from the intensive care unit but later on readmitted to intensive care can be thought of as rework).

Many of these concepts are discussed further in Chapter 10.

8.12 Summary

In this chapter, we have analyzed the impact of variability on waiting times. As we expected from our more qualitative discussion of variability in the beginning of this chapter, variability causes waiting times, even if the underlying process operates at a utilization level of less than 100 percent. In this chapter, we have outlined a set of tools that allows us to quantify this waiting time, with respect to both the average waiting time (and flow time) as well as the service level experienced by the customer.

There exists an inherent tension between resource utilization (and thereby cost of labor) and responsiveness: Adding service capacity leads to shorter waiting times but higher costs of labor (see Figure 8.24). Waiting times grow steeply with utilization levels. Thus, any responsive process requires excess capacity. Given that capacity is costly, it is important that only as much capacity is installed as is needed to meet the service objective in place for the process. In this chapter, we have outlined a method that allows a service operation to find the point on the frontier that best supports their business objectives (service levels).

However, our results should be seen not only as a way to predict/quantify the waiting time problem. They also outline opportunities for improving the process. Improvement opportunities can be broken up into capacity-related opportunities and system-design-related opportunities, as summarized below.

FIGURE 8.24
Balancing Efficiency with Responsiveness

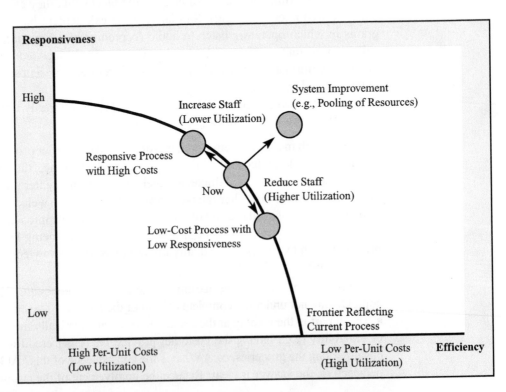

Capacity-Related Improvements

Operations benefit from flexibility in capacity, as this allows management to adjust staffing levels to predicted demand. For example, the extent to which a hospital is able to have more doctors on duty at peak flu season is crucial in conducting the staffing calculations outlined in this chapter. A different form of flexibility is given by the operation's ability to increase capacity in the case of unpredicted demand. For example, the extent to which a bank can use supervisors and front-desk personnel to help with unexpected spikes in inbound calls can make a big difference in call center waiting times. This leads to the following two improvement opportunities:

- Demand (and sometimes supply) can exhibit seasonality over the course of the day. In such cases, the waiting time analysis should be done for individual time intervals over which the process behaves relatively stationary. System performance can be increased to the extent the organization is able to provide time-varying capacity levels that mirror the seasonality of demand (e.g., Figure 8.19).

- In the presence of variability, a responsive process cannot avoid excess capacity, and thereby will automatically face a significant amount of idle time. In many operations, this idle time can be used productively for tasks that are not (or at least are less) time critical. Such work is referred to as background work. For example, operators in a call center can engage in outbound calls during times of underutilization.

System-Design-Related Improvements

Whenever we face a trade-off between two conflicting performance measures, in this case between responsiveness and efficiency, finding the right balance between the measures is important. However, at least equally important is the attempt to improve the underlying process, shifting the frontier and allowing for higher responsiveness and lower cost (see Figure 8.24). In the context of services suffering from variability-induced waiting times, the following improvement opportunities should be considered:

- By combining similar resources into one joint resource pool (pooling resources), we are able to either reduce wait times for the same amount of capacity or reduce capacity for the same service level. Processes that face variability thereby exhibit very strong scale economies.

- Variability is not exogenous and we should remember to reduce variability wherever possible.

- By introducing a triage step before the actual service process that sequences incoming flow units according to a priority rule (service-time-dependent or service-time-independent), we can reduce the average wait time, assign priority to the most important flow units, or create a waiting system that is perceived as fair by customers waiting in line.

8.13 Further Reading

Gans, Koole, and Mandelbaum (2003) is a recent overview on call-center management from a queuing theory perspective. Further quantitative tools on queueing can be found in Hillier and Lieberman (2002).

Hall (1997) is a very comprehensive and real-world-focused book that provides numerous tools related to variability and its consequences in services and manufacturing.

8.14 Practice Problems

Q8.1*   **(Online Retailer)** Customers send e-mails to a help desk of an online retailer every 2 minutes, on average, and the standard deviation of the interarrival time is also 2 minutes. The online retailer has three employees answering e-mails. It takes on average 4 minutes to write a response e-mail. The standard deviation of the processing times is 2 minutes.

(* indicates that the solution is at the end of the book)

a. Estimate the average customer wait before being served.

b. How many e-mails would there be, on average, that have been submitted to the online retailer but not yet answered?

Q8.2** **(My-law.com)** My-law.com is a recent start-up trying to cater to customers in search of legal services who are intimidated by the idea of talking to a lawyer or simply too lazy to enter a law office. Unlike traditional law firms, My-law.com allows for extensive interaction between lawyers and their customers via telephone and the Internet. This process is used in the upfront part of the customer interaction, largely consisting of answering some basic customer questions prior to entering a formal relationship.

In order to allow customers to interact with the firm's lawyers, customers are encouraged to send e-mails to my-lawyer@My-law.com. From there, the incoming e-mails are distributed to the lawyer who is currently "on call." Given the broad skills of the lawyers, each lawyer can respond to each incoming request.

E-mails arrive from 8 A.M. to 6 P.M. at a rate of 10 e-mails per hour (coefficient of variation for the arrivals is 1). At each moment in time, there is exactly one lawyer "on call," that is, sitting at his or her desk waiting for incoming e-mails. It takes the lawyer, on average, 5 minutes to write the response e-mail. The standard deviation of this is 4 minutes.

a. What is the average time a customer has to wait for the response to his/her e-mail, ignoring any transmission times? *Note:* This includes the time it takes the lawyer to start writing the e-mail *and* the actual writing time.

b. How many e-mails will a lawyer have received at the end of a 10-hour day?

c. When not responding to e-mails, the lawyer on call is encouraged to actively pursue cases that potentially could lead to large settlements. How much time on a 10-hour day can a My-law.com lawyer dedicate to this activity (assume the lawyer can instantly switch between e-mails and work on a settlement)?

To increase the responsiveness of the firm, the board of My-law.com proposes a new operating policy. Under the new policy, the response would be highly standardized, reducing the standard deviation for writing the response e-mail to 0.5 minute. The average writing time would remain unchanged.

d. How would the amount of time a lawyer can dedicate to the search for large settlement cases change with this new operating policy?

e. How would the average time a customer has to wait for the response to his/her e-mail change? *Note:* This includes the time until the lawyer starts writing the e-mail *and* the actual writing time.

Q8.3** **(Car Rental Company)** The airport branch of a car rental company maintains a fleet of 50 SUVs. The interarrival time between requests for an SUV is 2.4 hours, on average, with a standard deviation of 2.4 hours. There is no indication of a systematic arrival pattern over the course of a day. Assume that, if all SUVs are rented, customers are willing to wait until there is an SUV available. An SUV is rented, on average, for 3 days, with a standard deviation of 1 day.

a. What is the average number of SUVs parked in the company's lot?

b. Through a marketing survey, the company has discovered that if it reduces its daily rental price of $80 by $25, the average demand would increase to 12 rental requests per day and the average rental duration will become 4 days. Is this price decrease warranted? Provide an analysis!

c. What is the average time a customer has to wait to rent an SUV? Please use the initial parameters rather than the information in part (b).

d. How would the waiting time change if the company decides to limit all SUV rentals to *exactly* 4 days? Assume that if such a restriction is imposed, the average interarrival time will increase to 3 hours, with the standard deviation changing to 3 hours.

Q8.4 **(Tom Opim)** The following situation refers to Tom Opim, a first-year MBA student. In order to pay the rent, Tom decides to take a job in the computer department of a local department store. His only responsibility is to answer telephone calls to the department, most of which are inquiries about store hours and product availability. As Tom is the only person answering calls, the manager of the store is concerned about queuing problems.

Currently, the computer department receives an average of one call every 3 minutes, with a standard deviation in this interarrival time of 3 minutes.

Tom requires an average of 2 minutes to handle a call. The standard deviation in this processing time is 1 minute.

The telephone company charges $5.00 per hour for the telephone lines whenever they are in use (either while a customer is in conversation with Tom or while waiting to be helped).

Assume that there are no limits on the number of customers that can be on hold and that customers do not hang up even if forced to wait a long time.

a. For one of his courses, Tom has to read a book (*The Pole,* by E. Silvermouse). He can read 1 page per minute. Tom's boss has agreed that Tom could use his idle time for studying, as long as he drops the book as soon as a call comes in. How many pages can Tom read during an 8-hour shift?

b. How long does a customer have to wait, on average, before talking to Tom?

c. What is the average total cost of telephone lines over an 8-hour shift? Note that the department store is billed whenever a line is in use, including when a line is used to put customers on hold.

Q8.5 **(Atlantic Video)** Atlantic Video, a small video rental store in Philadelphia, is open 24 hours a day, and—due to its proximity to a major business school—experiences customers arriving around the clock. A recent analysis done by the store manager indicates that there are 30 customers arriving every hour, with a standard deviation of interarrival times of 2 minutes. This arrival pattern is consistent and is independent of the time of day. The checkout is currently operated by one employee, who needs on average 1.7 minutes to check out a customer. The standard deviation of this check-out time is 3 minutes, primarily as a result of customers taking home different numbers of videos.

a. If you assume that every customer rents at least one video (i.e., has to go to the checkout), what is the average time a customer has to wait in line before getting served by the checkout employee, not including the actual checkout time (within 1 minute)?

b. If there are no customers requiring checkout, the employee is sorting returned videos, of which there are always plenty waiting to be sorted. How many videos can the employee sort over an 8-hour shift (assume no breaks) if it takes exactly 1.5 minutes to sort a single video?

c. What is the average number of customers who are at the checkout desk, either waiting or currently being served (within 1 customer)?

d. Now assume *for this question only* that 10 percent of the customers do not rent a video at all and therefore do not have to go through checkout. What is the average time a customer has to wait in line before getting served by the checkout employee, not including the actual checkout time (within 1 minute)? Assume that the coefficient of variation for the arrival process remains the same as before.

e. As a special service, the store offers free popcorn and sodas for customers waiting in line at the checkout desk. (*Note:* The person who is currently being served is too busy with paying to eat or drink.) The store owner estimates that every minute of customer waiting time costs the store 75 cents because of the consumed food. What is the optimal number of employees at checkout? Assume an hourly wage rate of $10 per hour.

Q8.6 **(RentAPhone)** RentAPhone is a new service company that provides European mobile phones to American visitors to Europe. The company currently has 80 phones available at Charles de Gaulle Airport in Paris. There are, on average, 25 customers per day requesting a phone. These requests arrive uniformly throughout the 24 hours the store is open. (*Note:* This means customers arrive at a faster rate than 1 customer per hour.) The corresponding coefficient of variation is 1.

Customers keep their phones on average 72 hours. The standard deviation of this time is 100 hours.

Given that RentAPhone currently does not have a competitor in France providing equally good service, customers are willing to wait for the telephones. Yet, during the waiting period, customers are provided a free calling card. Based on prior experience, RentAPhone found that the company incurred a cost of $1 per hour per waiting customer, independent of day or night.

a. What is the average number of telephones the company has in its store?

b. How long does a customer, on average, have to wait for the phone?

c. What are the total monthly (30 days) expenses for telephone cards?

d. Assume RentAPhone could buy additional phones at $1,000 per unit. Is it worth it to buy one additional phone? Why?

e. How would waiting time change if the company decides to limit all rentals to *exactly* 72 hours? Assume that if such a restriction is imposed, the number of customers requesting a phone would be reduced to 20 customers per day.

Q8.7 **(Webflux Inc.)** Webflux is an Internet-based DVD rental business specializing in hard-to-find, obscure films. Its operating model is as follows. When a customer finds a film on the Webflux Web site and decides to watch it, she puts it in the virtual shopping cart. If a DVD is available, it is shipped immediately (assume it can be shipped during weekends and holidays, too). If not available, the film remains in the customer's shopping cart until a rented DVD is returned to Webflux, at which point it is shipped to the customer if she is next in line to receive it. Webflux maintains an internal queue for each film and a returned DVD is shipped to the first customer in the queue (first-in, first-out).

Webflux has one copy of the 1990 film *Sundown, the Vampire in Retreat,* starring David Carradine and Bruce Campbell. The average time between requests for the DVD is 10 days, with a coefficient of variation of 1. On average, a customer keeps the DVD for 5 days before returning it. It also takes 1 day to ship the DVD to the customer and 1 day to ship it from the customer back to Webflux. The standard deviation of the time between shipping the DVD out from Webflux and receiving it back is 7 days (i.e., it takes on average 7 days to (a) ship it, (b) have it with the customer, and (c) ship it back); hence, the coefficient of variation of this time is 1.

a. What is the average time that a customer has to wait to receive *Sundown, the Vampire in Retreat* DVD after the request? Recall it takes 1 day for a shipped DVD to arrive at a customer address (i.e., in your answer, you have to include the 1-day shipping time).

b. On average, how many customers are in Webflux's internal queue for *Sundown?* Assume customers do not cancel their items in their shopping carts.

Thanks to David Carradine's renewed fame after the recent success of *Kill Bill Vol. I* and *II* which he starred in, the demand for *Sundown* has spiked. Now the average interarrival time for the DVD requests at Webflux is 3 days. Other numbers (coefficient of variation, time in a customer's possession, shipping time) remain unchanged. *For the following question only,* assume sales are lost for customers who encounter stockouts; that is those who cannot find a DVD on the Webflux Web site simply navigate away without putting it in the shopping cart.

c. To satisfy the increased demand, Webflux is considering acquiring a second copy of the *Sundown* DVD. If Webflux owns a total of two copies of *Sundown* DVDs (whether in Webflux's internal stock, in customer's possession, or in transit), what percentage of the customers are turned away because of a stockout? (*Note:* To answer this question, you will need material from Chapter 9.)

Q8.8 **(Security Walking Escorts)** A university offers a walking escort service to increase security around campus. The system consists of specially trained uniformed professional security officers that accompany students from one campus location to another. The service is operated 24 hours a day, seven days a week. Students request a walking escort by phone. Requests for escorts are received, on average, every 5 minutes with a coefficient of variation of 1. After receiving a request, the dispatcher contacts an available escort (via a mobile phone), who immediately proceeds to pick up the student and walk her/him to her/his destination. If there are no escorts available (that is, they are all either walking a student to her/his destination or walking to pick up a student), the dispatcher puts the request in a queue until an escort becomes available. An escort takes, on average, 25 minutes for picking up a student and taking her/him to her/his desired location (the coefficient of variation of this time is also 1). Currently, the university has 8 security officers who work as walking escorts.

a. How many security officers are, on average, available to satisfy a new request?

b. How much time does it take—on average—from the moment a student calls for an escort to the moment the student arrives at her/his destination?

For the next two questions, consider the following scenario. During the period of final exams, the number of requests for escort services increases to 19.2 per hour (one request every 3.125 minutes). The coefficient of variation of the time between successive requests equals 1. However, if a student requesting an escort finds out from the dispatcher that her/his request would have to be put in the queue (i.e., all security officers are busy walking other students), the student cancels the request and proceeds to walk on her/his own.

c. How many students per hour who called to request an escort end up canceling their request and go walking on their own? (*Note:* To answer this question, you will need material from Chapter 9.)

d. University security regulations require that at least 80 percent of the students' calls to request walking escorts have to be satisfied. What is the minimum number of security officers that are needed in order to comply with this regulation?

Q8.9 **(Mango Electronics Inc.)** Mango Electronics Inc. is a *Fortune* 500 company that develops and markets innovative consumer electronics products. The development process proceeds as follows.

Mango researches new technologies to address unmet market needs. Patents are filed for products that have the requisite market potential. Patents are granted for a period of 20 years starting from the date of issue. After receiving a patent, the patented technologies are then developed into marketable products at five independent development centers. Each product is only developed at one center. Each center has all the requisite skills to bring any of the products to market (a center works on one product at a time). On average, Mango files a patent every 7 months (with standard deviation of 7 months). The average development process lasts 28 months (with standard deviation of 56 months).

a. What is the utilization of Mango's development facilities?

b. How long does it take an average technology to go from filing a patent to being launched in the market as a commercial product?

c. How many years of patent life are left for an average product launched by Mango Electronics?

Q8.10 **(UPS Shipping)** A UPS employee, Davis, packs and labels three types of packages: basic packages, business packages, and oversized packages. Business packages take priority over basic packages and oversized packages because those customers paid a premium to have guaranteed two-day delivery. During his nine-hour shift, he has, on average, one container of packages containing a variety of basic, business, and oversized packages to process every 3 hours. As soon as Davis processes a package, he passes it to the next employee, who loads it onto a truck. The times it takes him to process the three different types of packages and the average number of packages per container are shown in the table below.

	Basic	Business	Oversized
Average number of minutes to label and package each unit	5 minutes	4 minutes	6 minutes
Average number of units per container	10	10	5

Davis currently processes packages from each container as follows. First, he processes all business packages in the container. Then he randomly selects either basic packages or oversized packages for processing until the container is empty. However, his manager suggested to Davis that, for each container, he should process all the business packages first, second the basic packages, and last the oversized packages.

a. If Davis follows his supervisor's advice, what will happen to Davis's utilization?

b. What will happen to the average time that a package spends in the container?

You can view a video of how problems marked with a ** are solved by going on www. cachon-terwiesch.net and follow the links under 'Solved Practice Problems'

Solutions to Selected Practice Problems

Chapter 8

Q8.1 (Online Retailer)

Part a

We use Exhibit 8.1 for our computations.

Step 1. We collect the basic ingredients for the waiting time formula:

Activity time = 4 minutes

$$CV_p = \frac{2}{4}$$

Interarrival time = 2 minutes

$CV_a = 1$

Number of resources = 3

Step 2. This allows us to compute utilization as

$$p/am = 4/(2 \times 3) = 0.6666$$

Step 3. We then use the waiting time formula

$$T_q \approx \left(\frac{4}{3}\right) \times \left(\frac{0.666^{\sqrt{2(3+1)}-1}}{1-0.6666}\right) \times \left(\frac{1^2 + 0.5^2}{2}\right) = 1.19 \text{ minutes}$$

Step 4. We find the

Inventory in service: $I_p = m \times u = 3 \times 0.666 = 2$
Inventory in the queue: $I_q = T_q/a = 1.19/2 = 0.596$
Inventory in the system: $I = I_p + I_q = 2.596$

Part b

The number of e-mails that have been received but not yet answered corresponds to the total inventory of e-mails. We find this to be 2.596 e-mails (see Step 4 above).

Glossary

A

abandoning   Refers to flow units leaving the process because of lengthy waiting times.

activity   Value-adding steps in a process where resources process flow units.

activity on node (AON) representation   A way to graphically illustrate the project dependencies in which activities correspond to nodes in a graph.

activity time   The duration that a flow unit has to spend at a resource, not including any waiting time; also referred to as service time or processing time.

A/F ratio   The ratio of actual demand (A) to forecasted demand (F). Used to measure forecast accuracy.

Andon cord   A cord running adjacent to assembly lines that enables workers to stop production if they detect a defect. Just like the jidoka automatic shut-down of machines, this procedure dramatizes manufacturing problems and acts as a pressure for process improvements.

appointment   Predefined times at which the flow unit supposedly enters the process; used to reduce variability (and seasonality) in the arrival process.

assemble-to-order   Also known as make-to-order. A manufacturing system in which final assembly of a product only begins once a firm order has been received. Dell Inc. uses assemble-to-order with personal computers.

asset turns   See capital turns.

assignable causes of variation   Those effects that result in changes of the parameters of the underlying statistical distribution of the process. Thus, for assignable causes, a change in process performance is not driven simply by common-cause variation.

attribute-based control charts   A special form of control chart that only distinguishes between defective and nondefective items. Such control charts should be used if it is not possible to capture the quality conformance of a process outcome in one variable.

authorization level   For a fare class, the percentage of capacity that is available to that fare class or lower. An authorization level is equivalent to a booking limit expressed as a percentage of capacity.

availability   The proportion of a time a process (single resource or buffer) is able to either process (in the case of a resource) or admit (in the case of a buffer) incoming flow units.

average labor utilization   Measures the percentage of paid labor time that is spent on actual production as opposed to idle time; measures the efficiency of the process as well as the balance of work across workers.

B

back order   If demand occurs and inventory is not available, then the demand can be back-ordered until inventory becomes available.

back-order penalty cost   The cost incurred by a firm per back order. This cost can be explicit or implicit (e.g., lost goodwill and future business).

balancing resources   Attempting to achieve an even utilization across the resources in a process. This is equivalent to minimizing idle time by reallocating work from one resource to another.

base stock level   Also known as the order-up-to level. In the implementation of an order-up-to policy, inventory is ordered so that inventory position equals the base stock level.

batch   A collection of flow units.

batch flow operation   Those processes where flow units are batched to benefit from scale economies of production and/or transportation. Batch flow operations are known to have long flow times.

batch ordering   A firm batch orders when it orders in integer multiples of a fixed batch size. For example, if a firm's batch size is 20 cases, then the firm orders either 0, 20, 40, 60, . . . cases.

bid price   With bid price control, a bid price is assigned to each segment of capacity and a reservation is accepted only if its fare exceeds the bid prices of the segments of capacity that it uses.

bid price control   A method for controlling whether or not to accept a reservation. This method explicitly recognizes that not all customers paying the same fare for a segment of capacity are equally valuable to the firm.

blocking   The situation in which a resource has completed its work on a flow unit, yet cannot move the flow unit to the next step (resource or inventory) downstream as there is not space available.

booking limit   The maximum number of reservations that are allowed for a fare class or lower.

bottleneck   The resource with the lowest capacity in the process.

buckets   A booking limit is defined for a bucket that contains multiple fare class–itinerary combinations.

buffer   Another word for inventory, which is used especially if the role of the buffer is to maintain a certain throughput level despite the presence of variability.

buffer inventory   Allows resources to operate independent from each other, thereby avoiding blocking and starving (in which case we speak of a decoupling buffer).

buffer-or-suffer principle The inherent tension between inventory and flow rate. In a process that suffers from setup times or variability, adding inventory can increase the flow rate.

bullwhip effect The propagation of demand variability up the supply chain.

business model Articulates how a firm aims to create a positive net utility to the customer while making a profit. Typically involves choices with respect to the process timing, the process location, and the process standardization.

business model innovation A substantial shift in a firm's business model either relative to others in the industry or to its previous practice.

buy-back contract A contract in which a supplier agrees to purchase leftover inventory from a retailer at the end of the selling season.

C

capability index The ratio between the tolerance level and the actual variation of the process.

capacity Measures the maximum flow rate that can be supported by a resource.

capacity-constrained A process for which demand exceeds the process capacity.

capacity pooling The practice of combining multiple capacities to deliver one or more products or services.

capital turns The ratio between revenues and invested capital; measures how much capital is needed to support a certain size of a company.

carbon dioxide equivalent (CO_2e) For a given gas, the weight of CO_2 that has the equivalent warming potential as 1 kilogram of that gas.

carbon footprint The total creation of carbon dioxide equivalents an organization is responsible for. Can be analyzed in the form of scope 1, 2, or 3.

channel assembly The practice in the PC industry of having final assembly completed by a distributor (e.g., Ingram Micron) rather than the manufacturer (e.g., IBM).

channel stuffing The practice of inducing retailers to carry more inventory than needed to cover short-term needs.

coefficient of variation A measure of variability. Coefficient of variation = Standard deviation divided by the mean; that is, the ratio of the standard deviation of a random variable to the mean of the random variable. This is a relative measure of the uncertainty in a random variable.

collaborative planning, forecasting, and replenishment A set of practices designed to improve the exchange of information within a supply chain.

common causes of variation Constant variation reflecting pure randomness in the process. Such causes are hence a result of pure randomness as opposed to being the result of an assignable cause.

conservation-of-matter law A law that states that, on average, the flow into a system must equal the flow out of the system, otherwise the quantity within the system will not be stable.

consignment inventory Inventory that is kept at a customer's location but is owned by the supplier.

consolidated distribution The practice of delivering from a supplier to multiple locations (e.g., retail stores) via a distribution center.

continuous process A process in which the flow unit continuously flows from one resource to the next; different from discrete process, in which the flow units are separate entities.

contract manufacturer A firm that manufactures or assembles a product for another firm. Contract manufacturers typically manufacture products from multiple competitors, they are generally responsible for procurement, but they do not design or distribute the products they assemble.

control charts Graphical tools to statistically distinguish between assignable and common causes of variation. Control charts visualize variation, thereby enabling the user to judge whether the observed variation is due to common causes or assignable causes.

control limits Part of control charts that indicate to what extent a process outcome falls in line with the common cause variation of the process versus being a result of an assignable cause. Outcomes above the upper control limit (UCL) or below the lower control limit (LCL) indicate the presence of an assignable cause.

cost of direct labor Measures the per-unit cost of labor, which includes both the labor content (the actual labor going into completing a flow unit) and the idle time that occurs across all workers per completed flow unit.

critical path A project management term that refers to all those activities that—if delayed—would delay the overall completion of the project.

critical ratio The ratio of the underage cost to the sum of the overage and underage costs. It is used in the newsvendor model to choose the expected profit-maximizing order quantity.

cross docking The practice of moving inventory in a distribution facility from the inbound dock directly to the outbound loading dock without placing the inventory in storage within the distribution facility.

cycle inventory The inventory that results from receiving (producing) several flow units in one order (batch) that are then used over a time period of no further inflow of flow units.

cycle time The time that passes between two consecutive flow units leaving the process. Cycle time = 1/Flow rate.

D

decision tree A scenario-based approach to map out the discrete outcomes of a particular uncertainty.

decoupling inventory See buffer inventory.

demand pooling combining demands from multiple sources to reduce overall variability.

discovery-driven planning A process that emphasizes learning about unknown variables related to a project with the goal of deciding whether or not to invest further resources in the project.

demand aggregation The idea to supply multiple demand streams with the same resource and thereby generate economies of scale.

demand-constrained A process for which the flow rate is limited by demand.

demand-pull An inventory policy in which demand triggers the ordering of replenishments.

density function The function that returns the probability the outcome of a random variable will exactly equal the inputted value.

dependency matrix Describes the dependencies among the activities in a project.

design specifications Establish how much a process outcome is allowed to vary before it is labeled a defect. Design specifications are driven by customer requirements, not by control limits.

distribution function The function that returns the probability the outcome of a random variable will equal the inputted value or lower.

diversion The practice by retailers of purchasing product from a supplier only to resell the product to another retailer.

diverters Firms that practice diversion.

double marginalization The phenomenon in a supply chain in which one firm takes an action that does not optimize supply chain performance because the firm's margin is less than the supply chain's total margin.

DuPont model A financial framework built around the idea that the overall ROIC of a business can be decomposed into two financial ratios, the margins and the asset turns.

E

earliest completion time (ECT) The earliest time a project activity can be completed, which can be computed as the sum of the earliest start time and the duration of the activity.

earliest start time (EST) The earliest time a project activity can start, which requires that all information providing activities are completed.

economies of scale Obtaining lower cost per unit based on a higher flow rate. Can happen, among other reasons, because of a spread of fixed cost, learning, statistical reasons (pooling), or the usage of dedicated resources.

Efficient Consumer Response The collective name given to several initiatives in the grocery industry to improve the efficiency of the grocery supply chain.

efficient frontier All locations in a space of performance measures (e.g., time and cost) that are efficient, that is,

improvement along one dimension can occur only if the level of another dimension is reduced.

electronic data interchange (EDI) A technology standard for the communication between firms in the supply chain.

elimination of flow units Discarding defective flow units instead of reworking them.

e-lot system A decoupling buffer that is tracked to detect any systemic variation that could suggest a defect in the process; it is thereby a way to direct managerial attention toward defects in the process that would otherwise be hidden by inventory without immediately losing flow rate.

empirical distribution function A distribution function constructed with historical data.

EOQ (economic order quantity) The quantity that minimizes the sum of inventory costs and fixed ordering cost.

erlang loss formula Computes the proportion of time a resource has to deny access to incoming flow units in a system of multiple parallel servers and no space for inventory.

expected leftover inventory The expected amount of inventory left over at the end of the season when a fixed quantity is chosen at the start of a single selling season with random demand.

expected lost sales The expected amount of demand that is not satisfied when a fixed quantity is chosen at the start of a single selling season and demand is random.

Expected Marginal Seat Analysis A technique developed by Peter Belobaba of MIT to assign booking limits to multiple fare classes.

expected sales The expected amount of demand that is satisfied when a fixed quantity is chosen at the start of a single selling season and demand is random.

exponential distribution Captures a random variable with distribution $\text{Prob}\{x < t\} = 1 - \exp(-t/a)$, where a is the mean as well as the standard deviation of the distribution. If interarrival times are exponentially distributed, we speak of a Poisson arrival process. The exponential distribution is known for the memoryless property; that is, if an exponentially distributed service time with mean five minutes has been going on for five minutes, the expected remaining duration is still five minutes.

external setups Those elements of setup times that can be conducted while the machine is processing; an important element of setup time reduction/SMED.

F

FCFS (first-come, first-served) Rule that states that flow units are processed in the order of their arrivals.

fences Restrictions imposed on a low-fare class to prevent high-fare customers from purchasing the low fare. Examples include advanced purchase requirements and Saturday night stay over.

FIFO (first-in, first out) See FCFS.

fill rate   The fraction of demand that is satisfied; that is, that is able to purchase a unit of inventory.

flexibility   The ability of a process to meet changes in demand and/or a high amount of product variety.

flow rate (R)   Also referred to as throughput. Flow rate measures the number of flow units that move through the process in a given unit of time. *Example:* The plant produces at a flow rate of 20 scooters per hour. Flow rate = Min{Demand, Capacity}.

flow time (T)   Measures the time a flow unit spends in the process, which includes the time it is worked on at various resources as well as any time it spends in inventory. *Example:* A customer spends a flow time of 30 minutes on the phone in a call center.

flow unit   The unit of analysis that we consider in process analysis; for example, patients in a hospital, scooters in a kick-scooter plant, and callers in a call center.

forecast   The estimate of demand and potentially also of the demand distribution.

forward buying   If a retailer purchases a large quantity during a trade promotion, then the retailer is said to forward buy.

G

gamma distribution   A continuous distribution. The sum of exponential distributions is a gamma distribution. This is a useful distribution to model demands with high coefficients of variation (say about 0.5).

Gantt chart   A graphical way to illustrate the durations of activities as well as potential dependencies between the activities.

H

heijunka   A principle of the Toyota Production System, proposing that models are mixed in the production process according to their mix in customer demand.

hockey stick phenomenon   A description of the demand pattern that a supplier can receive when there is a substantial amount of order synchronization among its customers.

holding cost rate   The cost incurred to hold one unit of inventory for one period of time.

horizontal pooling   Combining a sequence of resources in a queuing system that the flow unit would otherwise visit sequentially; increases the span of control; also related to the concept of a work cell.

I

idle time   The time a resource is not processing a flow unit. Idle time should be reduced as it is a non-value-adding element of labor cost.

ikko-nagashi   An element of the Toyota Production System. It advocates the piece-by-piece transfer of flow units (transfer batches of one).

implied utilization   The workload imposed by demand of a resource relative to its available capacity. Implied utilization = Demand rate/Capacity.

incentive conflicts   In a supply chain, firms may have conflicting incentives with respect to which actions should be taken.

independent arrivals   A requirement for both the waiting time and the loss formulas. Independent arrivals mean that the probability of having an arrival occur in the next x minutes is independent of how many arrivals have occurred in the last y minutes.

information turnaround time (ITAT)   The delay between the occurrence of a defect and its detection.

innovation   A novel match between a solution and a need that creates value.

in-stock probability   The probability all demand is satisfied over an interval of time.

integrated supply chain   The supply chain considered as a single integrated unit, that is, as if the individual firms were owned by a single entity.

interarrival time   The time that passes between two consecutive arrivals.

internal setups   Those elements of setup times that can only be conducted while the machine is not producing. Internal setups should be reduced as much as possible and/or converted to external setups wherever possible (SMED).

inventory (I)   The number of flow units that are in the process (or in a particular resource). Inventory can be expressed in (a) flow units (e.g., scooters), (b) days of supply (e.g., three days of inventory), or (c) monetary units ($1 million of inventory).

inventory cost   The cost a process incurs as a result of inventory. Inventory costs can be computed on a per-unit basis (see Exhibit 2.1) or on a per-unit-of-time basis.

inventory level   The on-hand inventory minus the number of units back-ordered.

inventory policy   The rule or method by which the timing and quantity of inventory replenishment are decided.

inventory position   The inventory level plus the number of units on order.

inventory turns   How often a company is able to turn over its inventory. Inventory turns = 1/Flow time, which—based on Little's Law—is COGS/Inventory.

Ishikawa diagram   Also known as fishbone diagram or cause–effect diagram; graphically represents variables that are causally related to a specific outcome.

J

jidoka   In the narrow sense, a specific type of machine that can automatically detect defects and automatically shut down itself. The basic idea is that shutting down the machine forces human intervention in the process, which in turn triggers process improvement.

just-in-time   The idea of producing units as close as possible to demand, as opposed to producing the units earlier and then leaving them in inventory or producing them later and thereby leaving the unit of demand waiting. Just-in-time is a fundamental part of the Toyota Production System as well as of the matching supply with demand framework postulated by this book.

K

kaizen   The continuous improvement of processes, typically driven by the persons directly involved with the process on a daily basis.

kanban   A production and inventory control system in which the production and delivery of parts are triggered by the consumption of parts downstream (pull system).

key performance indicator   An operational variable with a strong marginal impact on ROIC (value driver) that is used as an indicator of current operational performance.

L

labor content   The amount of labor that is spent on a flow unit from the beginning to the end of the process. In a purely manual process, we find labor content as the sum of all the activity times.

labor productivity   The ratio between revenue and labor cost.

labor utilization   How well a process uses the labor involved in the process. Labor utilization can be found based on activity times and idle times.

latest completion time (LCT)   The latest time a project activity has to be completed by to avoid delaying the overall completion time of the project.

latest start time (LST)   The latest time a project activity can start without delaying the overall completion time of the project.

lead time   The time between when an order is placed and when it is received. Process lead time is frequently used as an alternative word for flow time.

lean operations   An operations paradigm built around the idea of waste reduction; inspired by the Toyota Production System.

line balancing   The process of evenly distributing work across the resources of a process. Line balancing reduces idle time and can (a) reduce cycle time or (b) reduce the number of workers that are needed to support a given flow rate.

Little's Law   The average inventory is equal to the average flow rate times the average flow time ($I = R \times T$).

location pooling   The combination of inventory from multiple locations into a single location.

loss function   A function that returns the expected number of units by which a random variable exceeds the inputted value.

M

machine-paced line   A process design in which flow units are moved from one resource to another by a constant speed dictated by the conveyor belt. There is typically no inventory between the resources connected by a conveyor belt.

make-to-order   A production system, also known as assemble-to-order, in which flow units are produced only once the customer order for that flow unit has been received. Make-to-order production typically requires wait times for the customer, which is why it shares many similarities with service operations. Dell Inc. uses make-to-order with personal computers.

make-to-stock   A production system in which flow units are produced in anticipation of demand (forecast) and then held in finished goods inventory.

margin arithmetic   Equations that evaluate the percentage increase in profit as a function of the gross margin and the percentage increase in revenue.

marginal cost pricing   The practice of setting the wholesale price to the marginal cost of production.

materials requirement planning   A system to control the timing and quantity of component inventory replenishment based on forecasts of future demand and production schedules.

maximum profit   In the context of the newsvendor model, the expected profit earned if quantity can be chosen after observing demand. As a result, there are no lost sales and no leftover inventory.

mean   The expected value of a random variable.

mismatch cost   The sum of the underage cost and the overage cost. In the context of the newsvendor model, the mismatch cost is the sum of the lost profit due to lost sales and the total loss on leftover inventory.

mixed model production   See heijunka.

MRP jitters   The phenomenon in which multiple firms operate their MRP systems on the same cycle, thereby creating order synchronization.

muda   One specific form of waste, namely waste in the form of non-value-adding activities. Muda also refers to unnecessary inventory (which is considered the worst form of muda), as unnecessary inventory costs money without adding value and can cover up defects and other problems in the process.

multiple flow units   Used in a process that has a mix of products or customers flowing through it. Most computations, including the location of the bottleneck, depend on the mix of products.

N

negative binomial distribution   A discrete distribution function with two parameters that can independently change the mean of the distribution as well as the standard deviation. In contrast, the Poisson distribution has only one parameter and can only regulate its mean.

nested booking limits Booking limits for multiple fare classes are nested if each booking limit is defined for a fare class or lower. With nested booking limits, it is always the case that an open fare class implies all higher fare classes are open and a closed fare class implies all lower fare classes are closed.

newsvendor model A model used to choose a single order quantity before a single selling season with stochastic demand.

nonlinear The relationship between variables if the graph of the two variables is not a straight line.

normal distribution A continuous distribution function with the well-known bell-shaped density function.

no-show A customer that makes a reservation but cancels or fails to arrive for service.

O

on allocation A product whose total amount demanded exceeds available capacity.

on-hand inventory The number of units currently in inventory.

on-order inventory Also known as pipeline inventory. The number of units of inventory that have been ordered but have not been received.

one-for-one ordering policy Another name for an order-up-to policy. (With this policy, one unit is ordered for every unit of demand.)

options contract With this contract, a buyer pays a price per option purchased from a supplier and then pays an additional price later on to exercise options. The supplier is responsible for building enough capacity to satisfy all of the options purchased in case they are all exercised.

order batching A cause of the bullwhip effect. A firm order batches when it orders only in integer multiples of some batch quantity.

order inflation The practice of ordering more than desired in anticipation of receiving only a fraction of the order due to capacity constraints upstream.

order synchronization A cause of the bullwhip effect. This describes the situation in which two or more firms submit orders at the same moments in time.

order-up-to level Also known as the base stock level. In the implementation of an order-up-to policy, inventory is ordered so that inventory position equals the order-up-to level.

order-up-to model A model used to manage inventory with stochastic demand, positive lead times, and multiple replenishments.

origin-destination control A revenue management system in the airline industry that recognizes passengers that request the same fare on a particular segment may not be equally valuable to the firm because they differ in their itinerary and hence total revenue.

out-of-stock When a firm has no inventory.

overage cost In the newsvendor model, the cost of purchasing one too many units. In other words, it is the increase in profit if the firm had purchased one fewer unit without causing a lost sale (i.e., thereby preventing one additional unit of leftover inventory).

overbooking The practice of accepting more reservations than can be accommodated with available capacity.

P

pallet Literally the platform used (often wood) by a forklift to move large quantities of material.

par level Another name for the order-up-to level in the order-up-to model.

Pareto principle Principle that postulates that 20 percent of the causes account for 80 percent of all problems (also known as the 80-20 rule).

period In the order-up-to model, time is divided into periods of time of equal length. Typical period lengths include one day, one week, and one month.

phantom orders An order that is canceled before delivery is taken.

pipeline inventory The minimum amount of inventory that is required to operate the process. Since there is a minimum flow time that can be achieved (i.e., sum of the activity times), because of Little's Law, there is also a minimum required inventory in the process. Also known as on-order inventory, it is the number of units of inventory that have been ordered but have not been received.

point-of-sale (POS) Data on consumer transactions.

Poisson distribution A discrete distribution function that often provides an accurate representation of the number of events in an interval of time when the occurrences of the events are independent of each other. In other words, it is a good distribution to model demand for slow-moving items.

Poisson process An arrival process with exponentially distributed interarrival times.

poka-yoke A Toyota technique of "fool-proofing" many assembly operations, that is, by making mistakes in assembly operations physically impossible.

pooling The concept of combining several resources (including their buffers and their arrival processes) into one joint resource. In the context of waiting time problems, pooling reduces the expected wait time.

preference fit The firm's ability to provide consumers with the product or service they want or need.

price protection The practice in the PC industry of compensating distributors due to reductions in a supplier's wholesale price. As a result of price protection, the price a distributor pays to purchase inventory is effectively always the current price; that is, the supplier rebates the distributor whenever a price reduction occurs for each unit the distributor is holding in inventory.

precedence relationship The connection between two activities in a project in which one activity must be completed before the other can begin.

priority rules Used to determine the sequence with which flow units waiting in front of the same resource are served. There are two types of priority rules: service time independent (e.g., FCFS rule) and service time dependent (e.g., SPT rule).

process Resources, inventory locations, and a flow that describe the path of a flow unit from its transformation as input to output.

process analysis Concerned with understanding and improving business processes. This includes determining the location of the bottleneck and computing the basic performance measures inventory, flow rate, and flow time.

process capability The tolerance level of the process relative to its current variation in outcomes. This is frequently measured in the form of the capability index.

process capacity Capacity of an entire process, which is the maximum flow rate that can be achieved in the process. It is based on the capacity of the bottleneck.

process flow diagram Maps resources and inventory and shows graphically how the flow unit travels through the process in its transformation from input to output.

process utilization To what extent an entire process uses its capacity when supporting a given flow rate. Process utilization = Flow rate/Process capacity.

processing time The duration that a flow unit has to spend at a resource, not including any waiting time; also referred to as activity time or service time.

product pooling The practice of using a single product to serve two demand segments that were previously served by their own product version.

production batch The collection of flow units that are produced within a production cycle.

production cycle The processing and setups of all flow units before the resource starts to repeat itself.

production smoothing The practice of smoothing production relative to demand. Used to manage seasonality. In anticipation of a peak demand period production is maintained above the current flow rate, building up inventory. During the peak demand, production is not increased substantially, but rather, the firm satisfies the gap by drawing down previously accumulated inventory.

productivity ratio The ratio between revenue as a measure of output and some cost (for example labor cost) as a measure of input.

project A temporary (and thus nonrepetitive) operation consisting of a set of activities; different from a process, which is a repetitive operation.

protection level The number of reservations that must always be available for a fare class or higher. For example, if a flight has 120 seats and the protection level is 40 for the high-fare class, then it must always be possible to have 40 high-fare reservations.

pull system A manufacturing system in which production is initiated by the occurrence of demand.

push system A manufacturing system in which production is initiated in anticipation of demand.

Q

quality at the source The idea of fixing defects right when and where they occur. This is a fundamental idea of the Toyota Production System. Fixing defects later on in the process is difficult and costly.

quantity discount Reduced procurement costs as a result of large order quantities. Quantity discounts have to be traded off against the increased inventory costs.

quantity flexibility contracts With this contract, a buyer provides an initial forecast to a supplier. Later on the buyer is required to purchase at least a certain percentage of the initial forecast (e.g., 75 percent), but the buyer also is allowed to purchase a certain percentage above the forecast (e.g., 125 percent of the forecast). The supplier must build enough capacity to be able to cover the upper bound.

quartile analysis A technique to empirically analyze worker productivity (e.g., in the form of their processing times) by comparing the performance of the top quartile with the performance of the bottom quartile.

queue The accumulation of flow units waiting to be processed or served.

queuing system A sequence of individual queues in which the outflow of one buffer/server is the inflow to the next buffer/server.

Quick Response A series of practices in the apparel industry used to improve the efficiency of the apparel supply chain.

R

random variable A variable that represents a random event. For example, the random variable X could represent the number of times the value 7 is thrown on two dice over 100 tosses.

range of a sample The difference between the highest and the lowest value in the sample.

R-bar charts Track the variation in the outcome of a process. R-bar charts require that the outcome of a process be evaluated based on a single variable.

reactive capacity Capacity that can be used after useful information regarding demand is learned; that is, the capacity can be used to react to the learned demand information.

resource The entity of a process that the flow unit has to visit as part of its transformation from input to output.

returns policy See buy-back contract.

revenue management   Also known as yield management. The set of tools used to maximize revenue given a fixed supply.

revenue-sharing contracts   With this contract, a retailer pays a supplier a wholesale price per unit purchased plus a fraction of the revenue the retailer realizes from the unit.

rework   An approach of handling defective flow units that attempts to invest further resource time into the flow unit in the attempt to transform it into a conforming (nondefective) flow unit.

rework loops   An iteration/repetition of project or process activities done typically because of quality problems.

ROIC   Return on invested capital, defined as the ratio between financial returns (profits) and the invested capital.

round-up rule   When looking for a value inside a table, it often occurs that the desired value falls between two entries in the table. The round-up rule chooses the entry that leads to the larger quantity.

S

safety inventory   The inventory that a firm holds to protect itself from random fluctuations in demand.

salvage value   The value of leftover inventory at the end of the selling season in the newsvendor model.

scale economies   Cost savings that can be achieved in large operations. Examples are pooling benefits in waiting time problems and lower per-unit setup costs in batch flow operations.

scope 1 emissions   All direct emissions of an organization, such as fuel burned in its own trucks, or oil burned in its own machines.

scope 2 emissions   All emissions of an organization associated with purchased electricity, heat, steam, or other forms of energy.

scope 3 emissions   All emissions of an organization, including emissions created upstream in the value chain (suppliers) as well as downstream in the value chain (customers using the product or service).

seasonal arrivals   Systemic changes in the interarrival times (e.g., peak times during the day, the week, or the year).

seasonal inventory   Arises if the flow rate exceeds the demand rate in anticipation of a time period when the demand rate exceeds the flow rate.

second buy   An opportunity to request a second replenishment, presumably after some demand information is learned.

service level   The probability with which a unit of incoming demand will receive service as planned. In the context of waiting time problems, this means having a waiting time less than a specified target wait time; in other contexts, this also can refer to the availability of a product.

service time   The duration that a flow unit has to spend at a resource, not including any waiting time; also referred to as activity time or processing time.

setup cost   Costs that are incurred in production whenever a resource conducts a setup and in transportation whenever a shipment is done. Setup costs drive batching. It is important to include only out-of-pocket costs in the setup costs, not opportunity costs.

setup time   The duration of time a resource cannot produce as it is either switched from one setting to the other (e.g., from producing part A to producing part B, in which case we speak of a changeover time) or not available for production for other reasons (e.g., maintenance step). Setup times reduce capacity and therefore create an incentive to produce in batches.

setup time reduction   See SMED.

shortage gaming   A cause of the bullwhip effect. In situations with a capacity constraint, retailers may inflate their orders in anticipation of receiving only a portion of their order.

single segment control   A revenue management system in the airline industry in which all passengers on the same segment paying the same fare class are treated equally.

six sigma   In its narrow sense, refers to a process capability of two. This means that a process outcome can fall six standard deviations above or below the mean and still be within tolerance (i.e., still not be a defect). In its broader meaning, refers to quality improvement projects that are using statistical process control.

slack time   The difference between the earliest completion time and the latest completion time; measures by how much an activity can be delayed without delaying the overall project.

SMED (single minute exchange of dies)   The philosophy of reducing setup times instead of just finding optimal batch sizes for given setup times.

span of control   The scope of activities a worker or a resource performs. If the resource is labor, having a high span of control requires extensive training. Span of control is largest in a work cell.

specification levels   The cut-off points above (in the case of upper specification level) and below (in the case of lower specification level) which a process outcome is labeled a defect.

SPT (shortest processing time) rule   A priority rule that serves flow units with the shortest processing time first. The SPT rule is known to minimize the overall waiting time.

standard deviation   A measure of the absolute variability around a mean. The square of the standard deviation equals the variance.

standard normal   A normal distribution with mean 0 and standard deviation 1.

starving   The situation in which a resource has to be idle as there is no flow unit completed in the step (inventory, resource) upstream from it.

stationary arrivals   When the arrival process does not vary systemically over time; opposite of seasonal arrivals.

statistical process control (SPC)   A set of statistical tools that is used to measure the capability of a process and to help monitor the process, revealing potential assignable causes of variation.

stochastic   An event that is random, that is, its outcome cannot be predicted with certainty.

stockout   Occurs if a customer demands a unit but a unit of inventory is not available. This is different from "being out of stock," which merely requires that there is no inventory available.

stockout probability   The probability a stockout occurs over a predefined interval of time.

supply chain   The series of firms that deliver a good or service from raw materials to customer fulfillment.

supply chain efficiency   The ratio of the supply chain's actual profit to the supply chain's optimal profit.

supply-constrained   A process for which the flow rate is limited by either capacity or the availability of input.

sustainable operations   An operations paradigm built around the idea of not depleting or destroying scarce resources, including the atmosphere, water, materials, land, and people.

T

takotei-mochi   A Toyota technique to reduce worker idle time. The basic idea is that a worker can load one machine and while this machine operates, the worker—instead of being idle—operates another machine along the process flow.

tandem queue   A set of queues aligned in a series so that the output of one server flows to only one other server.

target wait time (TWT)   The wait time that is used to define a service level concerning the responsiveness of a process.

tasks   The atomic pieces of work that together constitute activities. Tasks can be moved from one activity/resource to another in the attempt to improve line balance.

throughput   See flow rate.

tolerance levels   The range of acceptable outcomes of a process. See also design specifications.

Toyota Production System   A collection of practices related to production, product development, and supply chain management as developed by the Toyota Motor Corporation. Important elements discussed in this book are the idea of permanent improvement (kaizen), the reduction of waste (muda), inventory reduction (just-in-time, kanban), mixed model production (heijunka), and reduction of setup times (SMED).

trade promotion   A temporary price discount off the wholesale price that a supplier offers to its retailer customers.

transactional efficiency   Measures how easy it is to do business with a firm. Consists of the subdimension customer effort and the elapsed time between need articulation and need fulfillment.

transfer batch   A collection of flow units that are transferred as a group from one resource to the next.

trunk inventory   The inventory kept by sales representatives in the trunk of their vehicles.

tsukurikomi   The Toyota idea of integrating quality inspection throughout the process. This is therefore an important enabler of the quality-at-the-source idea.

turn-and-earn   An allocation scheme in which scarce capacity is allocated to downstream customers proportional to their past sales.

U

underage cost   In the newsvendor model, the profit loss associated with ordering one unit too few. In other words, it is the increase in profit if one additional unit had been ordered and that unit is sold.

universal design/product   A product that is designed to serve multiple functions and/or multiple customer segments.

unknown unknowns (unk-unks)   Project management parlance to refer to uncertainties in a project that are not known at the outset of the project.

utilization   The extent to which a resource uses its capacity when supporting a given flow rate. Utilization = Flow rate/Capacity.

V

value chain   See supply chain.

value curve   A graphical depiction of the key attributes of a product or service. Can be used to compare a new business model with an incumbent solution. Common attributes are the transactional efficiency, the preference fit, as well as price and quality.

value driver   An operational variable that has a strong marginal effect on the ROIC.

variance   A measure of the absolute variability around a mean. The square root of the variance equals the standard deviation.

vendor-managed inventory   The practice of switching control of inventory management from a retailer to a supplier.

virtual nesting   A revenue management system in the airline industry in which passengers on different itineraries and paying different fare classes may nevertheless be included in the same bucket for the purchase of capacity controls.

virtual pooling The practice of holding inventory in multiple physical locations that share inventory information data so that inventory can be moved from one location to another when needed.

W

waiting time The part of flow time in which the flow unit is not processed by a resource.

waiting time formula The average wait time, T_q, that a flow unit spends in a queue before receiving service.

waste An abstract word that refers to any inefficiencies that exist in the process; for example, line imbalances, inadequate batch sizes, variability in service times, and so forth. Waste can be seen as the distance between the current performance of a process and the efficient frontier. Waste is called "muda" in the Toyota Production System.

win–win A situation in which both parties in a negotiation are better off.

work cell A resource where several activities that were previously done by separate resources (workers, machines) are combined into a single resource (team of workers). Work cells have several quality advantages, as they have a short ITAT; they are also—by definition—more balanced.

work in process (WIP) The inventory that is currently in the process (as opposed to inventory that is finished goods or raw material).

worker-paced line A process layout in which a worker moves the flow unit to the next resource or buffer when he or she has completed processing it; in contrast to a machine-paced line, where the flow unit moves based on a conveyor belt.

workload The request for capacity created by demand. Workload drives the implied utilization.

X

X-bar charts Track the mean of an outcome of a process. X-bar charts require that the outcome of a process be evaluated based on a single variable.

Y

yield management Also known as revenue management. The set of tools used to maximize revenue given a fixed supply.

yield of a resource The percentage of flow units processed correctly at the resource. More generally, we also can speak of the yield of an entire process.

Z

zero-sum game A game in which the total payoff to all players equals a constant no matter what outcome occurs.

z-statistic Given quantity and any normal distribution, that quantity has a unique z-statistic such that the probability the outcome of the normal distribution is less than or equal to the quantity equals the probability the outcome of a standard normal distribution equals the z-statistic.

Chapter Two

Linear Programming: Basic Concepts

Learning objectives

After completing this chapter, you should be able to

1. Explain what linear programming is.
2. Identify the three key questions to be addressed in formulating any spreadsheet model.
3. Name and identify the purpose of the four kinds of cells used in linear programming spreadsheet models.
4. Formulate a basic linear programming model in a spreadsheet from a description of the problem.
5. Present the algebraic form of a linear programming model from its formulation on a spreadsheet.
6. Apply the graphical method to solve a two-variable linear programming problem.
7. Use Excel to solve a linear programming spreadsheet model.

The management of any organization regularly must make decisions about how to allocate its resources to various activities to best meet organizational objectives. Linear programming is a powerful problem-solving tool that aids management in making such decisions. It is applicable to both profit-making and not-for-profit organizations, as well as governmental agencies. The resources being allocated to activities can be, for example, money, different kinds of personnel, and different kinds of machinery and equipment. In many cases, a wide variety of resources must be allocated simultaneously. The activities needing these resources might be various production activities (e.g., producing different products), marketing activities (e.g., advertising in different media), financial activities (e.g., making capital investments), or some other activities. Some problems might even involve activities of *all* these types (and perhaps others), because they are competing for the same resources.

You will see as we progress that even this description of the scope of linear programming is not sufficiently broad. Some of its applications go beyond the allocation of resources. However, activities always are involved. Thus, a recurring theme in linear programming is the need to find the *best mix* of activities—which ones to pursue and at what levels.

Like the other management science techniques, linear programming uses a *mathematical model* to represent the problem being studied. The word *linear* in the name refers to the form of the mathematical expressions in this model. *Programming* does not refer to computer programming; rather, it is essentially a synonym for planning. Thus, linear programming means the *planning of activities* represented by a *linear* mathematical model.

Because it comprises a major part of management science, linear programming takes up several chapters of this book. Furthermore, many of the lessons learned about how to apply linear programming also will carry over to the application of other management science techniques.

This chapter focuses on the basic concepts of linear programming.

2.1 A CASE STUDY: THE WYNDOR GLASS CO. PRODUCT-MIX PROBLEM

Jim Baker has had an excellent track record during his seven years as manager of new product development for the Wyndor Glass Company. Although the company is a small one, it has been experiencing considerable growth largely because of the innovative new products developed by Jim's group. Wyndor's president, John Hill, has often acknowledged publicly the key role that Jim has played in the recent success of the company.

Therefore, John felt considerable confidence six months ago in asking Jim's group to develop the following new products:

- An 8-foot glass door with aluminum framing.
- A 4-foot × 6-foot double-hung, wood-framed window.

Although several other companies already had products meeting these specifications, John felt that Jim would be able to work his usual magic in introducing exciting new features that would establish new industry standards.

Background

The **Wyndor Glass Co.** produces high-quality glass products, including windows and glass doors that feature handcrafting and the finest workmanship. Although the products are expensive, they fill a market niche by providing the highest quality available in the industry for the most discriminating buyers. The company has three plants.

Plant 1 produces aluminum frames and hardware.
Plant 2 produces wood frames.
Plant 3 produces the glass and assembles the windows and doors.

Because of declining sales for certain products, top management has decided to revamp the company's product line. Unprofitable products are being discontinued, releasing production capacity to launch the two new products developed by Jim Baker's group if management approves their release.

The 8-foot glass door requires some of the production capacity in Plants 1 and 3, but not Plant 2. The 4-foot × 6-foot double-hung window needs only Plants 2 and 3.

Management now needs to address two issues:

1. Should the company go ahead with launching these two new products?
2. If so, what should be the *product mix*—the number of units of each produced per week—for the two new products?

Management's Discussion of the Issues

Having received Jim Baker's memorandum describing the two new products, John Hill now has called a meeting to discuss the current issues. In addition to John and Jim, the meeting includes Bill Tasto, vice president for manufacturing, and Ann Lester, vice president for marketing.

Let's eavesdrop on the meeting.

John Hill (president): Bill, we will want to rev up to start production of these products as soon as we can. About how much production output do you think we can achieve?

Bill Tasto (vice president for manufacturing): We do have a little available production capacity, because of the products we are discontinuing, but not a lot. We should be able to achieve a production rate of a few units per week for each of these two products.

John: Is that all?

Bill: Yes. These are complicated products requiring careful crafting. And, as I said, we don't have much production capacity available.

John: Ann, will we be able to sell several of each per week?

Ann Lester (vice president for marketing): Easily.

John: Good. Now there's one more issue to resolve. With this limited production capacity, we need to decide how to split it between the two products. Do we want to produce the same

Swift & Company is a diversified protein-producing business based in Greeley, Colorado. With annual sales of over $8 billion, beef and related products are by far the largest portion of the company's business.

To improve the company's sales and manufacturing performance, upper management concluded that it needed to achieve three major objectives. One was to enable the company's customer service representatives to talk to their more than 8,000 customers with accurate information about the availability of current and future inventory while considering requested delivery dates and maximum product age upon delivery. A second was to produce an efficient shift-level schedule for each plant over a 28-day horizon. A third was to accurately determine whether a plant can ship a requested order-line-item quantity on the requested date and time given the availability of cattle and constraints on the plant's capacity.

To meet these three challenges, a management science team developed an *integrated system of 45 linear programming models* based on three model formulations to dynamically schedule its beef-fabrication operations at five plants in real time as it receives orders. *The total audited benefits realized in the first year* of operation of this system were **$12.74 million**, including $12 million due to *optimizing the product mix.* Other benefits include a reduction in orders lost, a reduction in price discounting, and better on-time delivery.

Source: A. Bixby, B. Downs, and M. Self, "A Scheduling and Capable-to-Promise Application for Swift & Company, *Interfaces* 36, no. 1 (January–February 2006), pp. 69–86. (A link to this article is provided on our Web site, www.mhhe.com/hillier4e.)

number of both products? Or mostly one of them? Or even just produce as much as we can of one and postpone launching the other one for a little while?

Jim Baker (manager of new product development): It would be dangerous to hold one of the products back and give our competition a chance to scoop us.

Ann: I agree. Furthermore, launching them together has some advantages from a marketing standpoint. Since they share a lot of the same special features, we can combine the advertising for the two products. This is going to make a big splash.

John: OK. But which mixture of the two products is going to be most profitable for the company?

Bill: I have a suggestion.

John: What's that?

Bill: A couple times in the past, our Management Science Group has helped us with these same kinds of product-mix decisions, and they've done a good job. They ferret out all the relevant data and then dig into some detailed analysis of the issue. I've found their input very helpful. And this is right down their alley.

John: Yes, you're right. That's a good idea. Let's get our Management Science Group working on this issue. Bill, will you coordinate with them?

The meeting ends.

> The issue is to find the most profitable mix of the two new products.

The Management Science Group Begins Its Work

At the outset, the Management Science Group spends considerable time with Bill Tasto to clarify the general problem and specific issues that management wants addressed. A particular concern is to ascertain the appropriate objective for the problem from management's viewpoint. Bill points out that John Hill posed the issue as determining which mixture of the two products is going to be most profitable for the company.

Therefore, with Bill's concurrence, the group defines the key issue to be addressed as follows.

> **Question:** Which combination of *production rates* (the number of units produced per week) for the two new products would *maximize the total profit* from both of them?

The group also concludes that it should consider *all* possible combinations of production rates of both new products permitted by the available production capacities in the three plants. For example, one alternative (despite Jim Baker's and Ann Lester's objections) is to forgo producing one of the products for now (thereby setting its production rate equal to zero) in order to produce as

TABLE 2.1
Data for the Wyndor
Glass Co. Product-Mix
Problem

	Production Time Used for Each Unit Produced		
Plant	Doors	Windows	Available per Week
1	1 hour	0	4 hours
2	0	2 hours	12 hours
3	3 hours	2 hours	18 hours
Unit profit	$300	$500	

much as possible of the other product. (We must not neglect the possibility that maximum profit from both products might be attained by producing none of one and as much as possible of the other.)

The Management Science Group next identifies the information it needs to gather to conduct this study:

1. Available production capacity in each of the plants.
2. How much of the production capacity in each plant would be needed by each product.
3. Profitability of each product.

Concrete data are not available for any of these quantities, so estimates have to be made. Estimating these quantities requires enlisting the help of key personnel in other units of the company.

Bill Tasto's staff develops the estimates that involve production capacities. Specifically, the staff estimates that the production facilities in Plant 1 needed for the new kind of doors will be available approximately four hours per week. (The rest of the time Plant 1 will continue with current products.) The production facilities in Plant 2 will be available for the new kind of windows about 12 hours per week. The facilities needed for both products in Plant 3 will be available approximately 18 hours per week.

The amount of each plant's production capacity actually used by each product depends on its production rate. It is estimated that each door will require one hour of production time in Plant 1 and three hours in Plant 3. For each window, about two hours will be needed in Plant 2 and two hours in Plant 3.

By analyzing the cost data and the pricing decision, the Accounting Department estimates the profit from the two products. The projection is that the profit per unit will be $300 for the doors and $500 for the windows.

Table 2.1 summarizes the data now gathered.

The Management Science Group recognizes this as being a classic **product-mix problem.** Therefore, the next step is to develop a *mathematical model*—that is, a *linear programming model*—to represent the problem so that it can be solved mathematically. The next four sections focus on how to develop this model and then how to solve it to find the most profitable mix between the two products, assuming the estimates in Table 2.1 are accurate.

Review
Questions

1. What were the two issues addressed by management?
2. The Management Science Group was asked to help analyze which of these issues?
3. How did this group define the key issue to be addressed?
4. What information did the group need to gather to conduct its study?

2.2 FORMULATING THE WYNDOR PROBLEM ON A SPREADSHEET

Spreadsheets provide a powerful and intuitive tool for displaying and analyzing many management problems. We now will focus on how to do this for the Wyndor problem with the popular spreadsheet package Microsoft Excel.[1]

[1] Other spreadsheet packages with similar capabilities also are available, and the basic ideas presented here are still applicable.

Formulating a Spreadsheet Model for the Wyndor Problem

Excel Tip: Cell shading and borders can be added by using the borders button and the fill color button in the Font Group of the Home tab (Excel 2007 or 2010) or the formatting toolbar (other versions).

Figure 2.1 displays the Wyndor problem by transferring the data in Table 2.1 onto a spreadsheet. (Columns E and F are being reserved for later entries described below.) We will refer to the cells showing the data as **data cells.** To distinguish the data cells from other cells in the spreadsheet, they are shaded light blue. (In the textbook figures, the light blue shading appears as light gray.) The spreadsheet is made easier to interpret by using *range names*. (As mentioned in Section 1.2, a **range name** is simply a descriptive name given to a cell or range of cells that immediately identifies what is there. Excel allows you to use range names instead of the corresponding cell addresses in Excel equations, since this usually makes the equations much easier to interpret at a glance.) The data cells in the Wyndor Glass Co. problem are given the range names UnitProfit (C4:D4), HoursUsedPerUnitProduced (C7:D9), and Hours Available (G7:G9). To enter a range name, first select the range of cells, then click in the name box on the left of the formula bar above the spreadsheet and type a name. (See Appendix B for further details about defining and using range names.)

Excel Tip: See the margin notes in Section 1.2 for tips on adding range names.

Three questions need to be answered to begin the process of using the spreadsheet to formulate a mathematical model (in this case, a **linear programming model**) for the problem.

These are the three key questions to be addressed in formulating any spreadsheet model.

1. What are the *decisions* to be made?
2. What are the *constraints* on these decisions?
3. What is the overall *measure of performance* for these decisions?

The preceding section described how Wyndor's Management Science Group spent considerable time with Bill Tasto, vice president for manufacturing, to clarify management's view of their problem. These discussions provided the following answers to these questions.

1. The decisions to be made are the *production rates* (number of units produced per week) for the two new products.

Some students find it helpful to organize their thoughts by answering these three key questions before beginning to formulate the spreadsheet model.

2. The constraints on these decisions are that the number of hours of production time used per week by the two products in the respective plants cannot exceed the number of hours available.
3. The overall measure of performance for these decisions is the *total profit* per week from the two products.

Figure 2.2 shows how these answers can be incorporated into the spreadsheet. Based on the first answer, the *production rates* of the two products are placed in cells C12 and D12 to locate them in the columns for these products just under the data cells. Since we don't know yet what these production rates should be, they are just entered as zeroes in Figure 2.2. (Actually, any trial solution can be entered, although *negative* production rates should be excluded since they are impossible.) Later, these numbers will be changed while seeking the best mix of production rates. Therefore, these cells containing the decisions to be made are called **changing cells.** To highlight the changing cells, they are shaded bright yellow with a light border. (In the textbook figures, the bright yellow appears as gray.) The changing cells are given the range name UnitsProduced (C12:D12).

The changing cells contain the decisions to be made.

FIGURE 2.1

The initial spreadsheet for the Wyndor problem after transferring the data in Table 2.1 into data cells.

	A	B	C	D	E	F	G
1		**Wyndor Glass Co. Product-Mix Problem**					
2							
3			**Doors**	**Windows**			
4		Unit Profit	$300	$500			
5							Hours
6			Hours Used per Unit Produced				Available
7		Plant 1	1	0			4
8		Plant 2	0	2			12
9		Plant 3	3	2			18

FIGURE 2.2

The complete spreadsheet for the Wyndor problem with an initial trial solution (both production rates equal to zero) entered into the changing cells (C12 and D12).

	A	B	C	D	E	F	G
1	**Wyndor Glass Co. Product-Mix Problem**						
2							
3			**Doors**	**Windows**			
4		Unit Profit	$300	$500			
5					Hours		Hours
6			Hours Used per Unit Produced		Used		Available
7		Plant 1	1	0	0	≤	4
8		Plant 2	0	2	0	≤	12
9		Plant 3	3	2	0	≤	18
10							
11			**Doors**	**Windows**			**Total Profit**
12		Units Produced	0	0			$0

Using the second answer, the total number of hours of production time used per week by the two products in the respective plants is entered in cells E7, E8, and E9, just to the right of the corresponding data cells. The total number of production hours depends on the production rates of the two products, so this total is zero when the production rates are zero. With positive production rates, the total number of production hours used per week in a plant is the sum of the production hours used per week by the respective products. The production hours used by a product is the number of hours needed for *each* unit of the product *times* the number of units being produced. Therefore, when positive numbers are entered in cells C12 and D12 for the number of doors and windows to produce per week, the data in cells C7:D9 are used to calculate the total production hours per week as follows:

The colon in C7:D9 is Excel shorthand for the *range from* C7 to D9; that is, the entire block of cells in column C or D and in row 7, 8, or 9.

Production hours in Plant 1 = 1(# of doors) + 0(# of windows)

Production hours in Plant 2 = 0(# of doors) + 2(# of windows)

Production hours in Plant 3 = 3(# of doors) + 2(# of windows)

Consequently, the Excel equations for the three cells in column E are

E7 = C7*C12 + D7*D12

E8 = C8*C12 + D8*D12

E9 = C9*C12 + D9*D12

where each asterisk denotes multiplication. Since each of these cells provides output that depends on the changing cells (C12 and D12), they are called **output cells.**

Output cells show quantities that are calculated from the changing cells.

Notice that each of the equations for the output cells involves the sum of two products. There is a function in Excel called SUMPRODUCT that will sum up the product of each of the individual terms in two different ranges of cells when the two ranges have the same number of rows and the same number of columns. Each product being summed is the product of a term in the first range and the term in the corresponding location in the second range. For example, consider the two ranges, C7:D7 and C12:D12, so that each range has one row and two columns. In this case, SUMPRODUCT (C7:D7, C12:D12) takes each of the individual terms in the range C7:D7, multiplies them by the corresponding term in the range C12:D12, and then sums up these individual products, just as shown in the first equation above. Applying the range name for UnitsProduced (C12:D12), the formula becomes SUMPRODUCT(C7:D7, Units-Produced). Although optional with such short equations, this function is especially handy as a shortcut for entering longer equations.

The SUMPRODUCT function is used extensively in linear programming spreadsheet models.

The formulas in the output cells E7:E9 are very similar. Rather than typing each of these formulas separately into the three cells, it is quicker (and less prone to typos) to type the formula just once in E7 and then copy the formula down into cells E8 and E9. To do this, first enter the formula =SUMPRODUCT(C7:D7, UnitsProduced) in cell E7. Then select cell E7 and drag the fill handle (the small box on the lower right corner of the cell cursor) down through cells E8 and E9.

When copying formulas, it is important to understand the difference between relative and absolute references. In the formula in cell E7, the reference to cells C7:D7 is based upon the relative position to the cell containing the formula. In this case, this means the two cells in the same row and immediately to the left. This is known as a **relative reference.** When this formula is copied to new cells using the fill handle, the reference is automatically adjusted to refer to the new cell(s) at the same relative location (the two cells in the same row and immediately to the left). The formula in E8 becomes =SUMPRODUCT(C8:D8, UnitsProduced) and the formula in E9 becomes =SUMPRODUCT(C9:D9, UnitsProduced). This is exactly what we want, since we always want the hours used at a given plant to be based upon the hours used per unit produced at that same plant (the two cells in the same row and immediately to the left).

In contrast, the reference to the UnitsProduced in E7 is called an **absolute reference.** These references do not change when they are filled into other cells but instead always refer to the same absolute cell locations.

You can make the column absolute and the row relative (or vice versa) by putting a $ sign in front of only the letter (or number) of the cell reference.

To make a relative reference, simply enter the cell address (e.g., C7:D7). References referred to by a range name are treated as absolute references. Another way to make an absolute reference to a range of cells is to put $ signs in front of the letter and number of the cell reference (e.g., $C$12:$D$12). See Appendix B for more details about relative and absolute referencing and copying formulas.

Excel tip: After entering a cell reference, repeatedly pressing the F4 key (or command-T on a Mac) will rotate among the four possibilities of relative and absolute references (e.g., C12, $C$12, C$12, $C12).

Next, ≤ signs are entered in cells F7, F8, and F9 to indicate that each total value to their left cannot be allowed to exceed the corresponding number in column G. (On the computer ≤ (or ≥) is often represented as <= (or >=), since there is no ≤ (or ≥) key on the keyboard.) The spreadsheet still will allow you to enter trial solutions that violate the ≤ signs. However, these ≤ signs serve as a reminder that such trial solutions need to be rejected if no changes are made in the numbers in column G.

One easy way to enter a ≤ (or ≥) in a spreadsheet is to type < (or >) with underlining turned on.

Finally, since the answer to the third question is that the overall measure of performance is the total profit from the two products, this profit (per week) is entered in cell G12. Much like the numbers in column E, it is the sum of products. Since cells C4 and D4 give the profit from *each* door and window produced, the total profit per week from these products is

$$\text{Profit} = \$300(\# \text{ of doors}) + \$500(\# \text{ of windows})$$

Hence, the equation for cell G12 is

$$\text{G12} = \text{SUMPRODUCT(C4:D4, C12:D12)}$$

Utilizing range names of TotalProfit (G12), UnitProfit (C4:D4), and UnitsProduced (C12:D12), this equation becomes

$$\text{TotalProfit} = \text{SUMPRODUCT(UnitProfit, UnitsProduced)}$$

This is a good example of the benefit of using range names for making the resulting equation easier to interpret.

TotalProfit (G12) is a special kind of output cell. It is the particular cell that is being targeted to be made as large as possible when making decisions regarding production rates. Therefore, TotalProfit (G12) is referred to as the **objective** or **target cell.** This cell is shaded orange with a heavy border. (In the textbook figures, the orange appears as gray and is distinguished from the changing cells by its darker shading and heavy border.)

The objective or target cell contains the overall measure of performance for the decisions in the changing cells.

The bottom of Figure 2.3 summarizes all the formulas that need to be entered in the Hours Used column and in the Total Profit cell. Also shown is a summary of the range names (in alphabetical order) and the corresponding cell addresses.

This completes the formulation of the spreadsheet model for the Wyndor problem.

With this formulation, it becomes easy to analyze any trial solution for the production rates. Each time production rates are entered in cells C12 and D12, Excel immediately calculates the output cells for hours used and total profit. For example, Figure 2.4 shows the spreadsheet when the production rates are set at four doors per week and three windows per week. Cell G12 shows that this yields a total profit of $2,700 per week. Also note that E7 = G7, E8 < G8, and E9 = G9, so the ≤ signs in column F are all satisfied. Thus, this trial

FIGURE 2.3

The spreadsheet model for the Wyndor problem, including the formulas for the target cell TotalProfit (G12) and the other output cells in column E, where the objective is to maximize the target cell.

	A	B	C	D	E	F	G
1		**Wyndor Glass Co. Product-Mix Problem**					
2							
3			**Doors**	**Windows**			
4		Unit Profit	$300	$500			
5					Hours		Hours
6			Hours Used per Unit Produced		Used		Available
7		Plant 1	1	0	0	≤	4
8		Plant 2	0	2	0	≤	12
9		Plant 3	3	2	0	≤	18
10							
11			**Doors**	**Windows**			**Total Profit**
12		Units Produced	0	0			$0

Range Name	Cell
HoursAvailable	G7:G9
HoursUsed	E7:E9
HoursUsedPerUnitProduced	C7:D9
TotalProfit	G12
UnitProfit	C4:D4
UnitsProduced	C12:D12

	E
5	Hours
6	Used
7	=SUMPRODUCT(C7:D7, UnitsProduced)
8	=SUMPRODUCT(C8:D8, UnitsProduced)
9	=SUMPRODUCT(C9:D9, UnitsProduced)

	G
11	Total Profit
12	=SUMPRODUCT(UnitProfit, UnitsProduced)

FIGURE 2.4

The spreadsheet for the Wyndor problem with a new trial solution entered into the changing cells, UnitsProduced (C12:D12).

	A	B	C	D	E	F	G
1		**Wyndor Glass Co. Product-Mix Problem**					
2							
3			**Doors**	**Windows**			
4		Unit Profit	$300	$500			
5					Hours		Hours
6			Hours Used per Unit Produced		Used		Available
7		Plant 1	1	0	4	≤	4
8		Plant 2	0	2	6	≤	12
9		Plant 3	3	2	18	≤	18
10							
11			**Doors**	**Windows**			**Total Profit**
12		Units Produced	4	3			$2,700

solution is *feasible*. However, it would *not* be feasible to further increase both production rates, since this would cause E7 > G7 and E9 > G9.

Does this trial solution provide the best mix of production rates? Not necessarily. It might be possible to further increase the total profit by simultaneously increasing one production rate and decreasing the other. However, it is not necessary to continue using trial and error to explore such possibilities. We shall describe in Section 2.5 how the Excel Solver can be used to quickly find the best (optimal) solution.

This Spreadsheet Model Is a Linear Programming Model

The spreadsheet model displayed in Figure 2.3 is an example of a *linear programming* model. The reason is that it possesses all the following characteristics.

Characteristics of a Linear Programming Model on a Spreadsheet

1. Decisions need to be made on the levels of a number of activities, so *changing cells* are used to display these levels. (The two activities for the Wyndor problem are the production of the two new products, so the changing cells display the number of units produced per week for each of these products.)

2. These activity levels can have any value (including fractional values) that satisfy a number of constraints. (The production rates for Wyndor's new products are restricted only by the constraints on the number of hours of production time available in the three plants.)

3. Each **constraint** describes a restriction on the feasible values for the levels of the activities, where a constraint commonly is displayed by having an output cell on the left, a mathematical sign ($\leq$, $\geq$, or $=$) in the middle, and a data cell on the right. (Wyndor's three constraints involving hours available in the plants are displayed in Figures 2.2–2.4 by having output cells in column E, $\leq$ signs in column F, and data cells in column G.)

4. The decisions on activity levels are to be based on an overall measure of performance, which is entered in the *objective* or *target cell.* The objective is to either *maximize* the target cell or *minimize* the target cell, depending on the nature of the measure of performance. (Wyndor's overall measure of performance is the total profit per week from the two new products, so this measure has been entered in the target cell G12, where the objective is to maximize this target cell.)

5. The Excel equation for each *output cell* (including the target cell) can be expressed as a SUMPRODUCT function,[2] where each term in the sum is the product of a *data cell* and a *changing cell.* (The bottom of Figure 2.3 shows how a SUMPRODUCT function is used for each output cell for the Wyndor problem.)

Characteristics 2 and 5 are key ones for differentiating a linear programming model from other kinds of mathematical models that can be formulated on a spreadsheet.

Characteristic 2 rules out situations where the activity levels need to have *integer* values. For example, such a situation would arise in the Wyndor problem if the decisions to be made were the *total* numbers of doors and windows to produce (which must be integers) rather than the numbers per week (which can have fractional values since a door or window can be started in one week and completed in the next week). When the activity levels do need to have integer values, a similar kind of model (called an *integer programming* model) is used instead by making a small adjustment on the spreadsheet, as will be illustrated in Section 3.2.

Characteristic 5 prohibits those cases where the Excel equation for an output cell cannot be expressed as a SUMPRODUCT function. To illustrate such a case, suppose that the weekly profit from producing Wyndor's new windows can be *more* than doubled by doubling the production rate because of economies in marketing larger amounts. This would mean that the Excel equation for the target cell would need to be more complicated than a SUMPRODUCT function. Consideration of how to formulate such models will be deferred to Chapter 8.

Summary of the Formulation Procedure

The procedure used to formulate a linear programming model on a spreadsheet for the Wyndor problem can be adapted to many other problems as well. Here is a summary of the steps involved in the procedure.

1. Gather the data for the problem (such as summarized in Table 2.1 for the Wyndor problem).

2. Enter the data into *data cells* on a spreadsheet.

3. Identify the decisions to be made on the levels of activities and designate *changing cells* for displaying these decisions.

4. Identify the constraints on these decisions and introduce *output cells* as needed to specify these constraints.

---

[2] There also are some special situations where a SUM function can be used instead because all the numbers that would have gone into the corresponding data cells are 1's.

5. Choose the overall measure of performance to be entered into the *objective* or *target cell*.
6. Use a SUMPRODUCT function to enter the appropriate value into each output cell (including the objective or target cell).

This procedure does not spell out the details of how to set up the spreadsheet. There generally are alternative ways of doing this rather than a single "right" way. One of the great strengths of spreadsheets is their flexibility for dealing with a wide variety of problems.

Review Questions

1. What are the three questions that need to be answered to begin the process of formulating a linear programming model on a spreadsheet?
2. What are the roles for the data cells, the changing cells, the output cells, and the objective or target cell when formulating such a model?
3. What is the form of the Excel equation for each output cell (including the objective or target cell) when formulating such a model?

2.3 THE MATHEMATICAL MODEL IN THE SPREADSHEET

A linear programming model can be formulated either as a spreadsheet model or as an algebraic model.

There are two widely used methods for formulating a linear programming model. One is to formulate it directly on a spreadsheet, as described in the preceding section. The other is to use algebra to present the model. The two versions of the model are equivalent. The only difference is whether the language of spreadsheets or the language of algebra is used to describe the model. Both versions have their advantages, and it can be helpful to be bilingual. For example, the two versions lead to different, but complementary, ways of analyzing problems like the Wyndor problem (as discussed in the next two sections). Since this book emphasizes the spreadsheet approach, we will only briefly describe the algebraic approach.

Formulating the Wyndor Model Algebraically

The reasoning for the algebraic approach is similar to that for the spreadsheet approach. In fact, except for making entries on a spreadsheet, the initial steps are just as described in the preceding section for the Wyndor problem.

1. Gather the relevant data (Table 2.1 in Section 2.1).
2. Identify the decisions to be made (the production rates for the two new products).
3. Identify the constraints on these decisions (the production time used in the respective plants cannot exceed the amount available).
4. Identify the overall measure of performance for these decisions (the total profit from the two products).
5. Convert the verbal description of the constraints and measure of performance into quantitative expressions in terms of the data and decisions (see below).

To start performing step 5, note that Table 2.1 indicates that the number of hours of production time available per week for the two new products in the respective plants are 4, 12, and 18. Using the data in this table for the number of hours used per door or window produced then leads to the following quantitative expressions for the constraints:

$$\text{Plant 1:} \quad (\text{\# of doors}) \leq 4$$
$$\text{Plant 2:} \quad 2(\text{\# of windows}) \leq 12$$
$$\text{Plant 3:} \quad 3(\text{\# of doors}) + 2(\text{\# of windows}) \leq 18$$

In addition, negative production rates are impossible, so two other constraints on the decisions are

$$(\text{\# of doors}) \geq 0 \quad (\text{\# of windows}) \geq 0$$

The overall measure of performance has been identified as the total profit from the two products. Since Table 2.1 gives the unit profits for doors and windows as \$300 and \$500, respectively, the expression obtained in the preceding section for the total profit per week from these products is

$$\text{Profit} = \$300(\text{\# of doors}) + \$500(\text{\# of windows})$$

The objective is to make the decisions (number of doors and number of windows) so as to maximize this profit, subject to satisfying all the constraints identified above.

To state this objective in a compact algebraic model, we introduce algebraic symbols to represent the measure of performance and the decisions. Let

P = Profit (total profit per week from the two products, in dollars)

D = # of doors (number of the special new doors to be produced per week)

W = # of windows (number of the special new windows to be produced per week)

Substituting these symbols into the above expressions for the constraints and the measure of performance (and dropping the dollar signs in the latter expression), the linear programming model for the Wyndor problem now can be written in algebraic form as shown below.

Algebraic Model

Choose the values of D and W so as to maximize

$$P = 300D + 500W$$

subject to satisfying all the following constraints:

$$
\begin{aligned}
D &\leq 4 \\
2W &\leq 12 \\
3D + 2W &\leq 18
\end{aligned}
$$

and

$$D \geq 0 \qquad W \geq 0$$

Terminology for Linear Programming Models

Much of the terminology of algebraic models also is sometimes used with spreadsheet models. Here are the key terms for both kinds of models in the context of the Wyndor problem.

1. D and W (or C12 and D12 in Figure 2.3) are the **decision variables.**
2. $300D + 500W$ [or SUMPRODUCT (UnitProfit, UnitsProduced)] is the **objective function.**
3. P (or G12) is the *value of the objective function* (or *objective value* for short).
4. $D \geq 0$ and $W \geq 0$ (or C12 ≥ 0 and D12 ≥ 0) are called the **nonnegativity constraints** (or *nonnegativity conditions*).
5. The other constraints are referred to as **functional constraints** (or *structural constraints*).
6. The **parameters** of the model are the constants in the algebraic model (the numbers in the data cells).
7. *Any* choice of values for the decision variables (regardless of how desirable or undesirable the choice) is called a **solution** for the model.
8. A **feasible solution** is one that satisfies all the constraints, whereas an **infeasible solution** violates at least one constraint.
9. The *best* feasible solution, the one that maximizes P (or G12), is called the **optimal solution.** (It is possible to have a *tie* for the best feasible solution, in which case all the tied solutions are called optimal solutions.)

Management scientists often use algebraic models, but managers generally prefer spreadsheet models.

Comparisons

So what are the relative advantages of algebraic models and spreadsheet models? An algebraic model provides a very concise and explicit statement of the problem. Sophisticated software packages that can solve huge problems generally are based on algebraic models because of both their compactness and their ease of use in rescaling the size of a problem. Management science practitioners with an extensive mathematical background find algebraic models very useful. For others, however, spreadsheet models are far more intuitive. Many very intelligent people (including many managers and business students) find algebraic models overly abstract. Spreadsheets lift this "algebraic curtain." Both managers and business students training to be managers generally live with spreadsheets, not algebraic models. Therefore, the emphasis throughout this book is on spreadsheet models.

Review Questions

1. When formulating a linear programming model, what are the initial steps that are the same with either a spreadsheet formulation or an algebraic formulation?
2. When formulating a linear programming model algebraically, algebraic symbols need to be introduced to represent which kinds of quantities in the model?
3. What are decision variables for a linear programming model? The objective function? Non-negativity constraints? Functional constraints?
4. What is meant by a feasible solution for the model? An optimal solution?

2.4 THE GRAPHICAL METHOD FOR SOLVING TWO-VARIABLE PROBLEMS

Linear programming problems having only two decision variables, like the Wyndor problem, can be solved by a **graphical method.**

graphical method
The graphical method provides helpful intuition about linear programming.

Although this method cannot be used to solve problems with more than two decision variables (and most linear programming problems have far more than two), it still is well worth learning. The procedure provides geometric intuition about linear programming and what it is trying to achieve. This intuition is helpful in analyzing larger problems that cannot be solved directly by the graphical method.

It is more convenient to apply the graphical method to the *algebraic version* of the linear programming model rather than the spreadsheet version. We shall briefly illustrate the method by using the algebraic model obtained for the Wyndor problem in the preceding section. (A far more detailed description of the graphical method, including its application to the Wyndor problem, is provided in the supplement to this chapter on the CD-ROM.) For this purpose, keep in mind that

D = Production rate for the special new doors (the number in changing cell C12 of the spreadsheet)

W = Production rate for the special new windows (the number in changing cell D12 of the spreadsheet)

The key to the graphical method is the fact that possible solutions can be displayed as points on a two-dimensional graph that has a horizontal axis giving the value of D and a vertical axis giving the value of W. Figure 2.5 shows some sample points.

Notation: Either $(D, W) = (2, 3)$ or just $(2, 3)$ refers to the solution where $D = 2$ and $W = 3$, as well as to the corresponding point in the graph. Similarly, $(D, W) = (4, 6)$ means $D = 4$ and $W = 6$, whereas the origin $(0, 0)$ means $D = 0$ and $W = 0$.

To find the optimal solution (the best feasible solution), we first need to display graphically where the feasible solutions are. To do this, we must consider each constraint, identify the solutions graphically that are permitted by that constraint, and then combine this information to identify the solutions permitted by all the constraints. The solutions permitted by all the constraints are the feasible solutions and the portion of the two-dimensional graph where the feasible solutions lie is referred to as the **feasible region.**

feasible region
The points in the feasible region are those that satisfy *every* constraint.

The shaded region in Figure 2.6 shows the feasible region for the Wyndor problem. We now will outline how this feasible region was identified by considering the five constraints one at a time.

FIGURE 2.5

Graph showing the points $(D, W) = (2, 3)$ and $(D, W) = (4, 6)$ for the Wyndor Glass Co. product-mix problem.

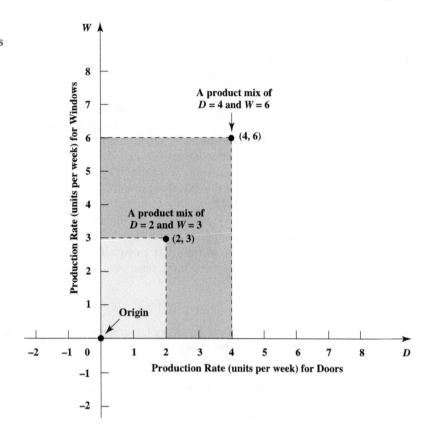

To begin, the constraint $D \geq 0$ implies that consideration must be limited to points that lie on or to the right of the W axis. Similarly, the constraint $W \geq 0$ restricts consideration to the points on or above the D axis.

FIGURE 2.6

Graph showing how the feasible region is formed by the constraint boundary lines, where the arrows indicate which side of each line is permitted by the corresponding constraint.

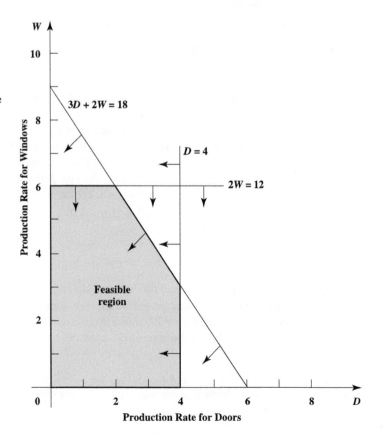

Next, consider the first functional constraint, $D \leq 4$, which limits the usage of Plant 1 for producing the special new doors to a maximum of four hours per week. The solutions permitted by this constraint are those that lie on, or to the left of, the vertical line that intercepts the D axis at $D = 4$, as indicated by the arrows pointing to the left from this line in Figure 2.6.

The second functional constraint, $2W \leq 12$, has a similar effect, except now the boundary of its permissible region is given by a *horizontal* line with the equation, $2W = 12$ (or $W = 6$), as indicated by the arrows pointing downward from this line in Figure 2.6. The line forming the boundary of what is permitted by a constraint is sometimes referred to as a **constraint boundary line,** and its equation may be called a **constraint boundary equation.** Frequently, a *constraint boundary line* is identified by its equation.

For any constraint with an inequality sign, its constraint boundary equation is obtained by replacing the inequality sign by an equality sign.

For each of the first two functional constraints, $D \leq 4$ and $2W \leq 12$, note that the equation for the constraint boundary line ($D = 4$ and $2W = 12$, respectively) is obtained by replacing the inequality sign with an equality sign. For *any* constraint with an inequality sign (whether a functional constraint or a nonnegativity constraint), the general rule for obtaining its constraint boundary equation is to substitute an equality sign for the inequality sign.

We now need to consider one more functional constraint, $3D + 2W \leq 18$. Its constraint boundary equation

$$3D + 2W = 18$$

includes both variables, so the boundary line it represents is neither a vertical line nor a horizontal line. Therefore, the boundary line must intercept (cross through) both axes somewhere. But where?

> When a constraint boundary line is neither a vertical line nor a horizontal line, the line *intercepts* the D axis at the point on the line where $W = 0$. Similarly, the line *intercepts* the W axis at the point on the line where $D = 0$.

Hence, the constraint boundary line $3D + 2W = 18$ intercepts the D axis at the point where $W = 0$.

When $W = 0$, $3D + 2W = 18$ becomes $3D = 18$
so the intercept with the D axis is at $\qquad D = 6$

The location of a slanting constraint boundary line is found by identifying where it intercepts each of the two axes.

Similarly, the line intercepts the W axis where $D = 0$.

When $D = 0$, $3D + 2W = 18$ becomes $2W = 18$
so the intercept with the D axis is at $\qquad W = 9$

Consequently, the constraint boundary line is the line that passes through these two intercept points, as shown in Figure 2.6.

Checking whether (0, 0) satisfies a constraint indicates which side of the constraint boundary line satisfies the constraint.

As indicated by the arrows emanating from this line in Figure 2.6, the solutions permitted by the constraint $3D + 2W \leq 18$ are those that lie on the *origin* side of the constraint boundary line $3D + 2W = 18$. The easiest way to verify this is to check whether the origin itself, $(D, W) = (0, 0)$, satisfies the constraint.[3] If it does, then the permissible region lies on the side of the constraint boundary line where the origin is. Otherwise, it lies on the other side. In this case,

$$3(0) + 2(0) = 0$$

so $(D, W) = (0, 0)$ satisfies

$$3D + 2W \leq 18$$

(In fact, the origin satisfies *any* constraint with a $\leq$ sign and a positive right-hand side.)

A feasible solution for a linear programming problem must satisfy *all* the constraints *simultaneously.* The arrows in Figure 2.6 indicate that the nonnegative solutions permitted by each of these constraints lie on the side of the constraint boundary line where the origin is

---

[3] The one case where using the origin to help determine the permissible region does *not* work is if the constraint boundary line passes through the origin. In this case, any other point *not* lying on this line can be used just like the origin.

(or on the line itself). Therefore, the *feasible solutions* are those that lie nearer to the origin than *all three* constraint boundary lines (or on the line nearest the origin).

Having identified the feasible region, the final step is to find which of these feasible solutions is the best one—the *optimal solution*. For the Wyndor problem, the objective happens to be to *maximize* the total profit per week from the two products (denoted by P). Therefore, we want to find the feasible solution (D, W) that makes the value of the objective function

$$P = 300D + 500W$$

as large as possible.

To accomplish this, we need to be able to locate all the points (D, W) on the graph that give a specified value of the objective function. For example, consider a value of $P = 1{,}500$ for the objective function. Which points (D, W) give $300D + 500W = 1{,}500$?

This equation is the equation of a *line*. Just as when plotting constraint boundary lines, the location of this line is found by identifying its intercepts with the two axes. When $W = 0$, this equation yields $D = 5$, and similarly, $W = 3$ when $D = 0$, so these are the two intercepts, as shown by the bottom slanting line passing through the feasible region in Figure 2.7.

$P = 1{,}500$ is just one sample value of the objective function. For any other specified value of P, the points (D, W) that give this value of P also lie on a line called an *objective function line*.

> An **objective function line** is a line whose points all have the same value of the objective function.

For the bottom objective function line in Figure 2.7, the points on this line that lie in the feasible region provide alternate ways of achieving an objective function value of $P = 1{,}500$. Can we do better? Let us try doubling the value of P to $P = 3{,}000$. The corresponding objective function line

$$300D + 500W = 3{,}000$$

is shown as the middle line in Figure 2.7. (Ignore the top line for the moment.) Once again, this line includes points in the feasible region, so $P = 3{,}000$ is achievable.

Let us pause to note two interesting features of these objective function lines for $P = 1{,}500$ and $P = 3{,}000$. First, these lines are *parallel*. Second, *doubling* the value of P from 1,500 to 3,000 also *doubles* the value of W at which the line intercepts the W axis from $W = 3$ to $W = 6$. These features are no coincidence, as indicated by the following properties.

FIGURE 2.7

Graph showing three objective function lines for the Wyndor Glass Co. product-mix problem, where the top one passes through the optimal solution.

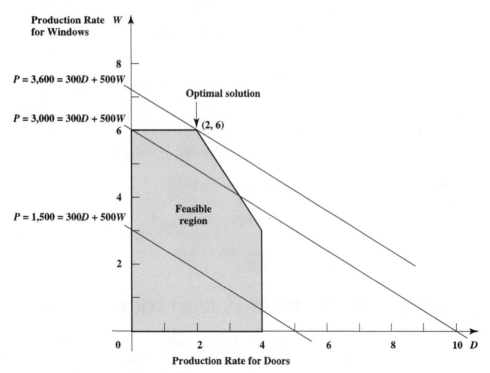

Key Properties of Objective Function Lines: All objective function lines for the same problem are *parallel.* Furthermore, the value of W at which an objective function line intercepts the W axis is *proportional* to the value of P.

These key properties of objective function lines suggest the strategy to follow to find the optimal solution. We already have tried $P = 1,500$ and $P = 3,000$ in Figure 2.7 and found that their objective function lines include points in the feasible region. Increasing P again will generate another parallel objective function line farther from the origin. The objective function line of special interest is the one farthest from the origin that still includes a point in the feasible region. This is the third objective function line in Figure 2.7. The point on this line that is in the feasible region, $(D, W) = (2, 6)$, is the optimal solution since no other feasible solution has a larger value of P.

Optimal Solution

$D = 2$ (Produce 2 special new doors per week)

$W = 6$ (Produce 6 special new windows per week)

These values of D and W can be substituted into the objective function to find the value of P.

$$P = 300D + 500W = 300(2) + 500(6) = 3,600$$

Check out this module in the Interactive Management Science Modules to learn more about the graphical method.

The Interactive Management Science Modules (available at **www.mhhe.com/hillier4e** or in your CD-ROM) includes a module that is designed to help increase your understanding of the graphical method. This module, called *Graphical Linear Programming and Sensitivity Analysis,* enables you to immediately see the constraint boundary lines and objective function lines that result from any linear programming model with two decision variables. You also can see how the objective function lines lead you to the optimal solution. Another key feature of the module is the ease with which you can use the graphical method to perform *what-if analysis* to see *what* happens *if* any changes occur in the data for the problem. (We will focus on what-if analysis for linear programming, including the role of the graphical method for this kind of analysis, in Chapter 5.)

Summary of the Graphical Method

The graphical method can be used to solve any linear programming problem having only two decision variables. The method uses the following steps:

1. Draw the constraint boundary line for each functional constraint. Use the origin (or any point not on the line) to determine which side of the line is permitted by the constraint.
2. Find the feasible region by determining where all constraints are satisfied simultaneously.
3. Determine the slope of one objective function line. All other objective function lines will have the same slope.
4. Move a straight edge with this slope through the feasible region in the direction of improving values of the objective function. Stop at the last instant that the straight edge still passes through a point in the feasible region. This line given by the straight edge is the optimal objective function line.
5. A feasible point on the optimal objective function line is an optimal solution.

Review Questions

1. The graphical method can be used to solve linear programming problems with how many decision variables?
2. What do the axes represent when applying the graphical method to the Wyndor problem?
3. What is a constraint boundary line? A constraint boundary equation?
4. What is the easiest way of determining which side of a constraint boundary line is permitted by the constraint?

2.5   USING EXCEL TO SOLVE LINEAR PROGRAMMING PROBLEMS

The graphical method is very useful for gaining geometric intuition about linear programming, but its practical use is severely limited by only being able to solve tiny problems with two decision variables. Another procedure that will solve linear programming problems of any

Excel Tip: If you select cells by clicking on them, they will first appear in the dialogue box with their cell addresses and with dollar signs (e.g., $C$9:$D$9). You can ignore the dollar signs. Solver eventually will replace both the cell addresses and the dollar signs with the corresponding range name (if a range name has been defined for the given cell addresses), but only after either adding a constraint or closing and reopening the Solver dialogue box.

Solver Tip: To select changing cells, click and drag across the range of cells. If the changing cells are not contiguous, you can type a comma and then select another range of cells. Up to 200 changing cells can be selected with the basic version of Solver that comes with Excel.

The Add Constraint dialogue box is used to specify all the functional constraints.

When solving a linear programming problem, be sure to specify that non-negativity constraints are needed and that the model is linear by choosing Simplex LP (for Excel 2010) or Assume Linear Model (for earlier versions).

reasonable size is needed. Fortunately, Excel includes a tool called **Solver** that will do this once the spreadsheet model has been formulated as described in Section 2.2. To access Solver the first time, you need to install it. For Excel 2007 and 2010, click the Office Button, choose Excel Options, then click on Add-Ins on the left side of the window, select Manage Excel Add-Ins at the bottom of the window, and then press the Go button. Make sure Solver is selected in the Add-Ins dialogue box, and then it should appear on the Data tab. For Excel 2008 (for the Mac), go to **www.solver.com/mac** to download and install the Solver application. For versions of Excel prior to 2007, choose Add-Ins from the Tools menu and make sure Solver is selected. Solver should then appear in the Tools menu.

Figure 2.3 in Section 2.2 shows the spreadsheet model for the Wyndor problem. The values of the decision variables (the production rates for the two products) are in the *changing cells,* UnitsProduced (C12:D12), and the value of the objective function (the total profit per week from the two products) is in the *objective* or *target cell* TotalProfit (G12). To get started, an arbitrary trial solution has been entered by placing zeroes in the changing cells. The Solver will then change these to the optimal values after solving the problem.

This procedure is started by choosing Solver on the Data tab (for Excel 2007 or 2010), or opening the Solver application (for Excel 2008 for the Mac), or choosing Solver in the Tools menu (for versions of Excel prior to 2007). Figure 2.8 shows the Excel 2010 Solver dialogue box on top and the Solver dialogue box for earlier versions on the bottom. These are used to tell Solver where each component of the model is located on the spreadsheet. Note that the Solver dialogue box for Excel 2010 looks somewhat different than for earlier versions of Excel. One notable difference is in the terminology used for the first entry. Excel 2010 refers to this as the *objective* while earlier versions refer to it as the *target cell.* We have used both terms to this point in the text, but to simplify the exposition, we normally will refer to this as simply the target cell hereafter.

You have the choice of typing the range names, typing the cell addresses, or clicking on the cells in the spreadsheet. Figure 2.8 shows the result of using the first choice, so TotalProfit (rather than G12) has been entered for the target cell. Since the goal is to maximize the target cell, Max also has been selected. The next entry in the Solver dialogue box identifies the *changing cells,* which are UnitsProduced (C12:D12) for the Wyndor problem. (Excel 2010 refers to these as *changing variable cells,* but we will continue to use the shorter term *changing cells* used by earlier versions of Excel.)

Next, the cells containing the functional constraints need to be specified. This is done by clicking on the Add button on the Solver dialogue box. This brings up the Add Constraint dialogue box shown in Figure 2.9. The ≤ signs in cells F7, F8, and F9 of Figure 2.3 are a reminder that the cells in HoursUsed (E7:E9) all need to be less than or equal to the corresponding cells in HoursAvailable (G7:G9). These constraints are specified for the Solver by entering HoursUsed (or E7:E9) on the left-hand side of the Add Constraint dialogue box and HoursAvailable (or G7:G9) on the right-hand side. For the sign between these two sides, there is a menu to choose between <= , =, or >= , so <= has been chosen. This choice is needed even though ≤ signs were previously entered in column F of the spreadsheet because the Solver only uses the constraints that are specified with the Add Constraint dialogue box.

If there were more functional constraints to add, you would click on Add to bring up a new Add Constraint dialogue box. However, since there are no more in this example, the next step is to click on OK to go back to the Solver dialogue box.

Before asking Solver to solve the model, two more steps need to be taken. We need to tell Solver that nonnegativity constraints are needed for the changing cells to reject negative production rates. We also need to specify that this is a *linear* programming problem so the simplex method (the standard method used by Solver to solve linear programming problems) can be used. When using versions of Excel prior to 2010, we start by clicking on the Options button to bring up the dialogue box shown in Figure 2.10. The two steps then are executed by checking both the *Assume Non-Negative* option and the *Assume Linear Model* option (as has been done in Figure 2.10) and then clicking OK to return to the Solver dialogue box. Regarding the other options (which are also available in the Excel 2010 Solver by clicking on the Options button), accepting the default values shown in the figure usually is fine for small problems. When using Excel 2010, there is no need to bring up its Solver Options dialogue box because the two steps now are executed directly on the Solver dialogue box. This is demonstrated in the top half of

FIGURE 2.8

The Solver dialogue box for Excel 2010 (top) and earlier versions (bottom) after specifying the first components of the model for the Wyndor problem. Although different terminology is used, the entries are the same— TotalProfit (G12) is being maximized by changing UnitsProduced (C12:D12). Figure 2.9 will demonstrate the addition of constraints and then Figure 2.10 and 2.11 will demonstrate the changes needed to specify that the problem being considered is a linear programming problem. (The default *Solving Method* shown here—*GRG Nonlinear*—is not applicable to linear programming problems.)

The Incomplete Solver Dialogue Box for Excel 2010

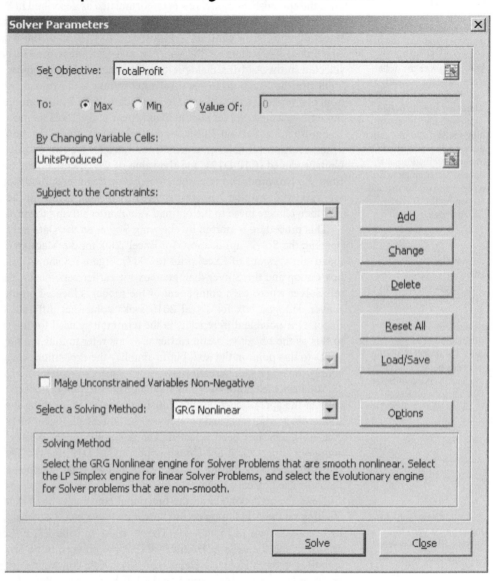

The Incomplete Solver Dialogue Box for Earlier Versions of Excel

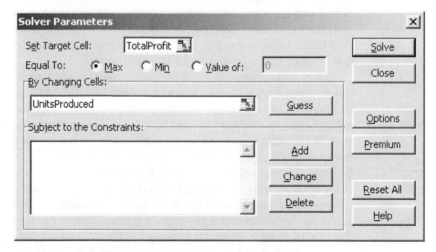

FIGURE 2.9

The Add Constraint dialogue box after specifying that cells E7, E8, and E9 in Figure 2.3 are required to be less than or equal to cells G7, G8, and G9, respectively.

FIGURE 2.10

The Solver Options dialogue box for versions of Excel prior to 2010 after checking the Assume Linear Model and Assume Non-Negative options to indicate that we wish to solve a linear programming model that has nonnegativity constraints.

Solver Tip: The message "Solver could not find a feasible solution" means that there are no solutions that satisfy all the constraints. The message "The Objective Cell values do not converge" means that Solver could not find a best solution, because better solutions always are available (e.g., if the constraints do not prevent infinite profit). In Excel 2010, the message "The linearity conditions required by this LP Solver are not satisfied" means Simplex LP was chosen as the Solving Method, but the model is not linear. In earlier versions of Excel, the message "The conditions for Assume Linear Model are not satisfied" means that the Assume Linear Model checkbox was checked, but the model is not linear.

Figure 2.11, where the *Make Unconstrained Variables Non-Negative* option has been checked and the *Solving Method* chosen is *Simplex LP* (rather than *GRG Nonlinear* or *Evolutionary*, which are used for solving nonlinear problems). With either Excel 2010 or prior versions, the Solver dialogue boxes shown in Figure 2.11 now summarize the complete model.

Now you are ready to click on Solve in the Solver dialogue box, which will start the solving of the problem in the background. After a few seconds (for a small problem), Solver will then indicate the results. Typically, it will indicate that it has found an optimal solution, as specified in the Solver Results dialogue box shown in Figure 2.12. If the model has no feasible solutions or no optimal solution, the dialogue box will indicate that instead by stating that "Solver could not find a feasible solution" or that "The Objective Cell values do not converge." (Section 14.1 will describe how these possibilities can occur.) The dialogue box also presents the option of generating various reports. One of these (the Sensitivity Report) will be discussed in detail in Chapter 5.

After solving the model and clicking OK in the Solver Results dialogue box, the Solver replaces the original numbers in the changing cells with the optimal numbers, as shown in Figure 2.13. Thus, the optimal solution is to produce two doors per week and six windows per week, just as was found by the graphical method in the preceding section. The spreadsheet also indicates the corresponding number in the target cell (a total profit of $3,600 per week), as well as the numbers in the output cells HoursUsed (E7:E9).

The entries needed for the Solver dialogue box are summarized in the *Solver Parameters* box shown on the bottom left of Figure 2.13. Rather than showing screenshots of the two different Solver dialogue boxes (one for Excel 2010 and the other for earlier versions), each with somewhat different terminology, this summary provides the information that needs to be entered for either of these dialogue boxes and combines the terminology seen in both versions. This more compact summary of the Solver Parameters will be shown for all of the many models that involve the Solver throughout the book.

FIGURE 2.11

The completed Solver dialogue box for Excel 2010 (top) and earlier versions (bottom) after specifying the entire model in terms of the spreadsheet.

The Completed Solver Dialogue Box for Excel 2010

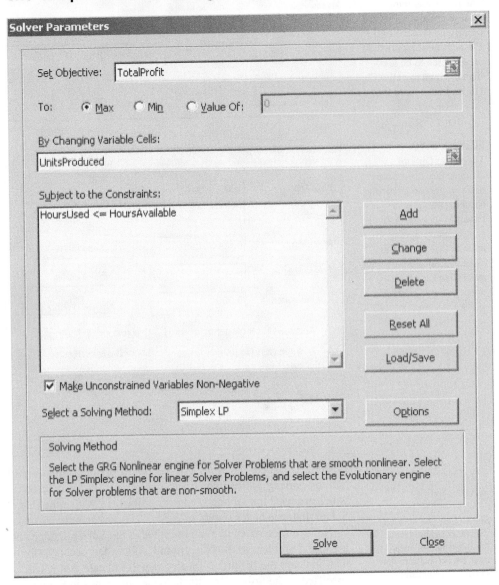

The Completed Solver Dialogue Box for Earlier Versions of Excel

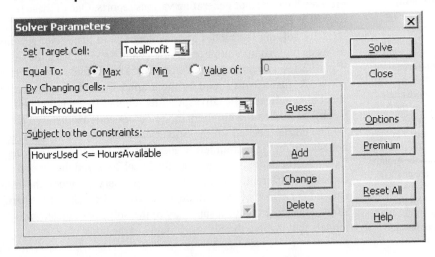

FIGURE 2.12
The Solver Results dialogue box that indicates that an optimal solution has been found.

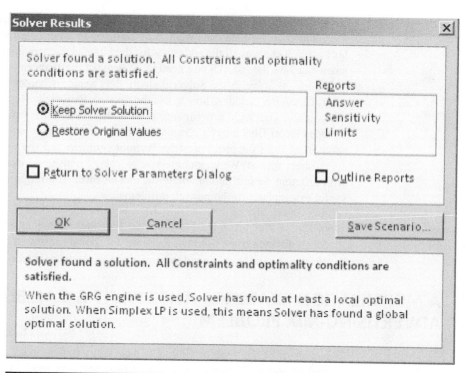

Solver Results

Solver found a solution. All Constraints and optimality conditions are satisfied.

○ Keep Solver Solution
○ Restore Original Values

Reports
Answer
Sensitivity
Limits

☐ Return to Solver Parameters Dialog   ☐ Outline Reports

OK   Cancel   Save Scenario...

Solver found a solution. All Constraints and optimality conditions are satisfied.

When the GRG engine is used, Solver has found at least a local optimal solution. When Simplex LP is used, this means Solver has found a global optimal solution.

FIGURE 2.13
The spreadsheet obtained after solving the Wyndor problem.

	A	B	C	D	E	F	G
1		**Wyndor Glass Co. Product-Mix Problem**					
2							
3			**Doors**	**Windows**			
4		Unit Profit	$300	$500			
5					Hours		Hours
6			Hours Used per Unit Produced		Used		Available
7		Plant 1	1	0	2	≤	4
8		Plant 2	0	2	12	≤	12
9		Plant 3	3	2	18	≤	18
10							
11			**Doors**	**Windows**			**Total Profit**
12		Units Produced	2	6			$3,600

Solver Parameters
Set Objective (Target Cell): Total Profit
To: Max
By Changing (Variable) Cells:
 UnitsProduced
Subject to the Constraints:
 HoursUsed <= HoursAvailable

Solver Options (Excel 2010):
 Make Variables Nonnegative
 Solving Method: Simplex LP
Solver Options: (older Excel)
 Assume Nonnegative
 Assume Linear Model

	E
5	Hours
6	Used
7	=SUMPRODUCT(C7:D7, UnitsProduced)
8	=SUMPRODUCT(C8:D8, UnitsProduced)
9	=SUMPRODUCT(C9:D9, UnitsProduced)

	G
11	Total Profit
12	=SUMPRODUCT(UnitProfit, UnitsProduced)

Range Name	Cell
HoursAvailable	G7:G9
HoursUsed	E7:E9
HoursUsedPerUnitProduced	C7:D9
TotalProfit	G12
UnitProfit	C4:D4
UnitsProduced	C12:D12

At this point, you might want to check what would happen to the optimal solution if any of the numbers in the data cells were to be changed to other possible values. This is easy to do because Solver saves all the addresses for the target cell, changing cells, constraints, and so on when you save the file. All you need to do is make the changes you want in the data cells and then click on Solve in the Solver dialogue box again. (Chapter 5 will focus on this kind of *what-if analysis*, including how to use the Solver's Sensitivity Report to expedite the analysis.)

To assist you with experimenting with these kinds of changes, your MS Courseware includes Excel files for this chapter (as for others) that provide a complete formulation and solution of the examples here (the Wyndor problem and the one in the next section) in a spreadsheet format. We encourage you to "play" with these examples to see what happens with different data, different solutions, and so forth. You might also find these spreadsheets useful as templates for homework problems.

Review
Questions

1. Which dialogue box is used to enter the addresses for the target cell and the changing cells?
2. Which dialogue box is used to specify the functional constraints for the model?
3. Which options normally need to be chosen to solve a linear programming model?

2.6 A MINIMIZATION EXAMPLE—THE PROFIT & GAMBIT CO. ADVERTISING-MIX PROBLEM

The analysis of the Wyndor Glass Co. case study in Sections 2.2 and 2.5 illustrated how to formulate and solve one type of linear programming model on a spreadsheet. The same general approach can be applied to many other problems as well. The great flexibility of linear programming and spreadsheets provides a variety of options for how to adapt the formulation of the spreadsheet model to fit each new problem. Our next example illustrates some options not used for the Wyndor problem.

Planning an Advertising Campaign

The **Profit & Gambit Co.** produces cleaning products for home use. This is a highly competitive market, and the company continually struggles to increase its small market share. Management has decided to undertake a major new advertising campaign that will focus on the following three key products:

- A spray prewash stain remover.
- A liquid laundry detergent.
- A powder laundry detergent.

This campaign will use both television and the print media. A commercial has been developed to run on national television that will feature the liquid detergent. The advertisement for the print media will promote all three products and will include cents-off coupons that consumers can use to purchase the products at reduced prices. The general goal is to increase the sales of each of these products (but especially the liquid detergent) over the next year by a significant percentage over the past year. Specifically, management has set the following goals for the campaign:

- Sales of the stain remover should increase by at least 3 percent.
- Sales of the liquid detergent should increase by at least 18 percent.
- Sales of the powder detergent should increase by at least 4 percent.

Table 2.2 shows the estimated increase in sales for each *unit* of advertising in the respective outlets.[4] (A *unit* is a standard block of advertising that Profit & Gambit commonly purchases, but other amounts also are allowed.) The reason for -1 percent for the powder detergent in the Television column is that the TV commercial featuring the new liquid detergent will take away some sales from the powder detergent. The bottom row of the table shows the cost per unit of advertising for each of the two outlets.

[4] A simplifying assumption is being made that each additional unit of advertising in a particular outlet will yield the same increase in sales regardless of how much advertising already is being done. This becomes a poor assumption when the levels of advertising under consideration can reach a saturation level (as in Case 8.1), but is a reasonable approximation for the small levels of advertising being considered in this problem.

TABLE 2.2
**Data for the Profit &
Gambit Co. Advertising-
Mix Problem**

| Product | Increase in Sales per Unit of Advertising | | Minimum Required Increase |
	Television	Print Media	
Stain remover	0%	1%	3%
Liquid detergent	3	2	18
Powder detergent	−1	4	4
Unit cost	$1 million	$2 million	

Management's objective is to determine how much to advertise in each medium to meet the sales goals at a minimum total cost.

Formulating a Spreadsheet Model for This Problem

The procedure summarized at the end of Section 2.2 can be used to formulate the spreadsheet model for this problem. Each step of the procedure is repeated below, followed by a description of how it is performed here.

1. Gather the data for the problem. This has been done as presented in Table 2.2.
2. Enter the data into *data cells* on a spreadsheet. The top half of Figure 2.14 shows this spreadsheet. The data cells are in columns C and D (rows 4 and 8 to 10), as well as in cells G8:G10. Note how this particular formatting of the spreadsheet has facilitated a direct transfer of the data from Table 2.2.
3. Identify the decisions to be made on the levels of activities and designate *changing cells* for making these decisions. In this case, the activities of concern are *advertising on television* and *advertising in the print media,* so the *levels* of these activities refer to the *amount* of advertising in these media. Therefore, the decisions to be made are

> Decision 1: TV = Number of units of advertising on television
>
> Decision 2: PM = Number of units of advertising in the print media

The two gray cells with light borders in Figure 2.14—C14 and D14—have been designated as the changing cells to hold these numbers:

$$TV \rightarrow \text{cell C14} \qquad PM \rightarrow \text{cell D14}$$

with AdvertisingUnits as the range name for these cells. (See the bottom of Figure 2.14 for a list of all the range names.) These are natural locations for the changing cells, since each one is in the column for the corresponding advertising medium. To get started, an arbitrary trial solution (such as all zeroes) is entered into these cells. (Figure 2.14 shows the optimal solution after having already applied the Solver.)

4. Identify the constraints on these decisions and introduce *output cells* as needed to specify these constraints. The three constraints imposed by management are the goals for the increased sales for the respective products, as shown in the rightmost column of Table 2.2. These constraints are

Unlike the Wyndor problem, we need to use ≥ signs for these constraints.

Stain remover:	Total increase in sales ≥ 3%
Liquid detergent:	Total increase in sales ≥ 18%
Powder detergent:	Total increase in sales ≥ 4%

The second and third columns of Table 2.2 indicate that the *total* increases in sales from both forms of advertising are

Total for stain remover	=1% of PM
Total for liquid detergent	= 3% of TV + 2% of PM
Total for powder detergent	= −1% of TV + 4% of PM

FIGURE 2.14

The spreadsheet model for the Profit & Gambit problem, including the formulas for the target cell TotalCost (G14) and the other output cells in column E, as well as the specifications needed to set up the Solver. The changing cells, AdvertisingUnits (C14:D14), show the optimal solution obtained by the Solver.

	A	B	C	D	E	F	G
1		**Profit & Gambit Co. Advertising-Mix Problem**					
2							
3			**Television**	**Print Media**			
4		Unit Cost ($millions)	1	2			
5							
6					Increased		Minimum
7			Increase in Sales per Unit of Advertising		Sales		Increase
8		Stain Remover	0%	1%	3%	≥	3%
9		Liquid Detergent	3%	2%	18%	≥	18%
10		Powder Detergent	-1%	4%	8%	≥	4%
11							
12							**Total Cost**
13			**Television**	**Print Media**			**($millions)**
14		Advertising Units	4	3			10

Solver Parameters

Set Objective (Target Cell): TotalCost
To: Min
By Changing (Variable) Cells:
  AdvertisingUnits
Subject to the Constraints:
IncreasedSales >= MinimumIncrease

Solver Options (Excel 2010):
  Make Variables Nonnegative
  Solving Method: Simplex LP
Solver Options (older Excel):
  Assume Nonnegative
  Assume Linear Model

	E
6	Increased
7	Sales
8	=SUMPRODUCT(C8:D8, AdvertisingUnits)
9	=SUMPRODUCT(C9:D9, AdvertisingUnits)
10	=SUMPRODUCT(C10:D10, AdvertisingUnits)

	G
12	Total Cost
13	($millions)
14	=SUMPRODUCT(UnitCost, AdvertisingUnits)

Range Name	Cells
AdvertisingUnits	C14: D14
IncreasedSales	E8: E10
IncreasedSalesPerUnitAdvertising	C8: D10
MinimumIncrease	G8: G10
TotalCost	G14
UnitCost	C4: D4

Consequently, since rows 8, 9, and 10 in the spreadsheet are being used to provide information about the three products, cells E8, E9, and E10 are introduced as output cells to show the total increase in sales for the respective products. In addition, ≥ signs have been entered in column F to remind us that the increased sales need to be at least as large as the numbers in column G. (The use of ≥ signs here rather than ≤ signs is one key difference from the spreadsheet model for the Wyndor problem in Figure 2.3.)

Unlike the Wyndor problem, the objective now is to minimize the target cell.

5. Choose the overall measure of performance to be entered into the *target cell*. Management's stated objective is to determine how much to advertise in each medium to meet the sales goals at a *minimum total cost*. Therefore, the *total cost* of the advertising is entered in the target cell TotalCost(G14). G14 is a natural location for this cell since it is in the same row as the changing cells. The bottom row of Table 2.2 indicates that the number going into this cell is

$$\text{Cost} = (\$1 \text{ million}) \, TV + (\$2 \text{ million}) \, PM \rightarrow \text{cell G14}$$

6. Use a SUMPRODUCT function to enter the appropriate value into each output cell (including the target cell). Based on the above expressions for cost and total increases in sales, the SUMPRODUCT functions needed here for the output cells are those shown

Samsung Electronics Corp., Ltd. (SEC), is a leading merchant of dynamic and static random access memory devices and other advanced digital integrated circuits. Its site at Kiheung, South Korea (probably the largest semiconductor fabrication site in the world), fabricates more than 300,000 silicon wafers per month and employs over 10,000 people.

Cycle time is the industry's term for the elapsed time from the release of a batch of blank silicon wafers into the fabrication process until completion of the devices that are fabricated on those wafers. Reducing cycle times is an ongoing goal since it both decreases costs and enables offering shorter lead times to potential customers, a real key to maintaining or increasing market share in a very competitive industry.

Three factors present particularly major challenges when striving to reduce cycle times. One is that the product mix changes continually. Another is that the company often needs to make substantial changes in the fab-out schedule inside the target cycle time as it revises forecasts of customer demand. The third is that the machines of a general type are not homogeneous so only a small number of machines are qualified to perform each device step.

A management science team developed a *huge linear programming model with tens of thousands of decision variables and functional constraints* to cope with these challenges. The objective function involved minimizing back-orders and finished-goods inventory.

The ongoing implementation of this model enabled the company to reduce manufacturing cycle times to fabricate dynamic random access memory devices from more than 80 days to less than 30 days. This tremendous improvement and the resulting reduction in both manufacturing costs and sale prices enabled Samsung to capture *an additional* **$200 million** *in annual sales revenue.*

Source: R. C. Leachman, J. Kang, and Y. Lin, "SLIM: Short Cycle Time and Low Inventory in Manufacturing at Samsung Electronics," *Interfaces* 32, no.1 (January–February 2002), pp. 61–77. (A link to this article is provided on our Web site, **www.mhhe.com/hillier4e.**)

under the right side of the spreadsheet in Figure 2.14. Note that each of these functions involves the relevant data cells and the changing cells, AdvertisingUnits(C14:D14).

This spreadsheet model is a linear programming model, since it possesses all the characteristics of such models enumerated in Section 2.2.

Applying the Solver to This Model

The procedure for using the Excel Solver to obtain an optimal solution for this model is basically the same as described in Section 2.5. The Solver parameters are shown below the left-hand side of the spreadsheet in Figure 2.14. In addition to specifying the target cell and changing cells, the constraints that IncreasedSales $\geq$ MinimumIncrease have been specified in this box by using the Add Constraint dialogue box. Since the objective is to *minimize* total cost, Min also has been selected. (This is in contrast to the choice of Max for the Wyndor problem.)

Two options are also specified at the bottom of the Solver Parameters box on the lower left-hand side of Figure 2.14. The changing cells need nonnegativity constraints (specified in the main Solver dialogue box in Excel 2010 and after clicking Options in earlier versions of Excel) because negative values of advertising levels are not possible alternatives. Choosing the Simplex LP solving method (Excel 2010) or the Assume Linear Model option (after clicking Options in earlier versions of Excel) specifies that this is a linear programming model.

After clicking on Solve in the Solver dialogue box and then clicking OK in the Solver Results dialogue box, the optimal solution shown in the changing cells of the spreadsheet in Figure 2.14 is obtained.

Optimal Solution

C14 = 4 (Undertake 4 units of advertising on television)
D14 = 3 (Undertake 3 units of advertising in the print media)

The target cell indicates that the total cost of this advertising plan would be $10 million.

The Mathematical Model in the Spreadsheet

When performing step 5 of the procedure for formulating a spreadsheet model, the total cost of advertising was determined to be

$$\text{Cost} = \text{TV} + 2\,\text{PM} \quad (\text{in millions of dollars})$$

where the objective is to choose the values of TV (number of units of advertising on television) and PM (number of units of advertising in the print media) so as to minimize this cost. Step 4 identified three functional constraints:

Stain remover:	1% of PM $\geq$ 3%
Liquid detergent:	3% of TV + 2% of PM $\geq$ 18%
Powder detergent:	−1% of TV + 4% of PM $\geq$ 4%

Choosing the Assume Non-Negative option with the Solver recognized that TV and PM cannot be negative. Therefore, after dropping the percentage signs from the functional constraints, the complete mathematical model in the spreadsheet can be stated in the following succinct form.

$$\text{Minimize } \text{Cost} = \text{TV} + 2\,\text{PM} \quad \text{(in millions of dollars)}$$

subject to

Stain remover increased sales:	PM $\geq$ 3
Liquid detergent increased sales:	3 TV + 2 PM $\geq$ 18
Powder detergent increased sales:	−TV + 4 PM $\geq$ 4

and

$$\text{TV} \geq 0 \qquad \text{PM} \geq 0$$

Implicit in this statement is "Choose the values of TV and PM so as to. . . ." The term "subject to" is shorthand for "Choose these values *subject to* the requirement that the values satisfy all the following constraints."

This model is the *algebraic* version of the *linear programming* model in the spreadsheet. Note how the parameters (constants) of this algebraic model come directly from the numbers in Table 2.2. In fact, the entire model could have been formulated directly from this table.

The differences between this algebraic model and the one obtained for the Wyndor problem in Section 2.3 lead to some interesting changes in how the graphical method is applied to solve the model. To further expand your geometric intuition about linear programming, we briefly describe this application of the graphical method next.

Since this linear programming model has only two decision variables, it can be solved by the graphical method described in Section 2.4. The method needs to be adapted in two ways to fit this particular problem. First, because all the functional constraints now have a $\geq$ sign with a positive right-hand side, after obtaining the constraint boundary lines in the usual way, the arrows indicating which side of each line satisfies that constraint now all point *away* from the origin. Second, the method is adapted to *minimization* by moving the objective function lines in the direction that *reduces* Cost and then stopping at the last instant that an objective function line still passes through a point in the feasible region, where such a point then is an optimal solution. The supplement to this chapter includes a description of how the graphical method is applied to the Profit & Gambit problem in this way.

Review Questions

1. What kind of product is produced by the Profit & Gambit Co.?
2. Which advertising media are being considered for the three products under consideration?
3. What is management's objective for the problem being addressed?
4. What was the rationale for the placement of the target cell and the changing cells in the spreadsheet model?
5. The algebraic form of the linear programming model for this problem differs from that for the Wyndor Glass Co. problem in which two major ways?

2.7 LINEAR PROGRAMMING FROM A BROADER PERSPECTIVE

Linear programming is an invaluable aid to managerial decision making in all kinds of companies throughout the world. The emergence of powerful spreadsheet packages has helped to further spread the use of this technique. The ease of formulating and solving small linear programming models on a spreadsheet now enables some managers with a very modest background in management science to do this themselves on their own desktop.

Many linear programming studies are major projects involving decisions on the levels of many hundreds or thousands of activities. For such studies, sophisticated software packages that go beyond spreadsheets generally are used for both the formulation and solution processes. These studies normally are conducted by technically trained teams of management scientists, sometimes called operations research analysts, at the instigation of management. Management needs to keep in touch with the management science team to ensure that the study reflects management's objectives and needs. However, management generally does not get involved with the technical details of the study.

Consequently, there is little reason for a manager to know the details of how linear programming models are solved beyond the rudiments of using the Excel Solver. (Even most management science teams will use commercial software packages for solving their models on a computer rather than developing their own software.) Similarly, a manager does not need to know the technical details of how to formulate complex models, how to validate such a model, how to interact with the computer when formulating and solving a large model, how to efficiently perform what-if analysis with such a model, and so forth. Therefore, these technical details are de-emphasized in this book. A student who becomes interested in conducting technical analyses as part of a management science team should plan to take additional, more technically oriented courses in management science.

So what does an enlightened manager need to know about linear programming? A manager needs to have a good intuitive feeling for what linear programming is. One objective of this chapter is to begin to develop that intuition. That's the purpose of studying the graphical method for solving two-variable problems. It is rare to have a *real* linear programming problem with as few as two decision variables. Therefore, the graphical method has essentially no practical value for solving real problems. However, it has great value for conveying the basic notion that linear programming involves pushing up against constraint boundaries and moving objective function values in a favorable direction as far as possible. You also will see in Chapter 14 that this approach provides considerable geometric insight into how to analyze larger models by other methods.

A manager must also have an appreciation for the relevance and power of linear programming to encourage its use where appropriate. For *future* managers using this book, this appreciation is being promoted by using application vignettes and their linked articles to describe *real* applications of linear programming and the resulting impact, as well as by including (in miniature form) various realistic examples and case studies that illustrate what can be done.

Certainly a manager must be able to recognize situations where linear programming is applicable. We focus on developing this skill in Chapter 3, where you will learn how to recognize the *identifying features* for each of the major types of linear programming problems (and their mixtures).

In addition, a manager should recognize situations where linear programming should *not* be applied. Chapter 8 will help to develop this skill by examining certain underlying assumptions of linear programming and the circumstances that violate these assumptions. That chapter also describes other approaches that *can* be applied where linear programming should not.

A manager needs to be able to distinguish between competent and shoddy studies using linear programming (or any other management science technique). Therefore, another goal of the upcoming chapters is to demystify the overall process involved in conducting a management science study, all the way from first studying a problem to final implementation of the managerial decisions based on the study. This is one purpose of the case studies throughout the book.

Finally, a manager must understand how to interpret the results of a linear programming study. He or she especially needs to understand what kinds of information can be obtained through *what-if analysis,* as well as the implications of such information for managerial decision making. Chapter 5 focuses on these issues.

Review Questions

1. Does management generally get heavily involved with the technical details of a linear programming study?
2. What is the purpose of studying the graphical method for solving problems with two decision variables when essentially all real linear programming problems have more than two?
3. List the things that an enlightened manager should know about linear programming.

2.8 Summary

Linear programming is a powerful technique for aiding managerial decision making for certain kinds of problems. The basic approach is to formulate a mathematical model called a linear programming model to represent the problem and then to analyze this model. Any linear programming model includes decision variables to represent the decisions to be made, constraints to represent the restrictions on the feasible values of these decision variables, and an objective function that expresses the overall measure of performance for the problem.

Spreadsheets provide a flexible and intuitive way of formulating and solving a linear programming model. The data are entered into data cells. Changing cells display the values of the decision variables, and a target cell shows the value of the objective function. Output cells are used to help specify the constraints. After formulating the model on the spreadsheet and specifying it further with the Solver dialogue box, the Solver is used to quickly find an optimal solution.

The graphical method can be used to solve a linear programming model having just two decision variables. This method provides considerable insight into the nature of linear programming models and optimal solutions.

Glossary

absolute reference A reference to a cell (or a column or a row) with a fixed address, as indicated either by using a range name or by placing a $ sign in front of the letter and number of the cell reference. (Section 2.2), 27

changing cells The cells in the spreadsheet that show the values of the decision variables. (Section 2.2), 25

constraint A restriction on the feasible values of the decision variables. (Sections 2.2 and 2.3), 29

constraint boundary equation The equation for the constraint boundary line. (Section 2.4), 34

constraint boundary line For linear programming problems with two decision variables, the line forming the boundary of the solutions that are permitted by the constraint. (Section 2.4), 34

data cells The cells in the spreadsheet that show the data of the problem. (Section 2.2), 25

decision variable An algebraic variable that represents a decision regarding the level of a particular activity. The value of the decision variable appears in a changing cell on the spreadsheet. (Section 2.3), 31

feasible region The geometric region that consists of all the feasible solutions. (Section 2.4), 32

feasible solution A solution that simultaneously satisfies all the constraints in the linear programming model. (Section 2.3), 31

functional constraint A constraint with a function of the decision variables on the left-hand side. All constraints in a linear programming model that are not nonnegativity constraints are called functional constraints. (Section 2.3), 31

graphical method A method for solving linear programming problems with two decision variables on a two-dimensional graph. (Section 2.4), 32

infeasible solution A solution that violates at least one of the constraints in the linear programming model. (Section 2.3), 31

linear programming model The mathematical model that represents a linear programming problem. (Sections 2.2 and 2.3), 25

nonnegativity constraint A constraint that expresses the restriction that a particular decision variable must be nonnegative (greater than or equal to zero). (Section 2.3), 31

objective Another name for target cell as defined below. (Section 2.2), 27

objective function The part of a linear programming model that expresses what needs to be either maximized or minimized, depending on the objective for the problem. The value of the objective function appears in the target cell on the spreadsheet. (Section 2.3), 31

objective function line For a linear programming problem with two decision variables, a line whose points all have the same value of the objective function. (Section 2.4), 35

optimal solution The best feasible solution according to the objective function. (Section 2.3), 31

output cells The cells in the spreadsheet that provide output that depends on the changing cells. These cells frequently are used to help specify constraints. (Section 2.2), 26

parameter The parameters of a linear programming model are the constants (coefficients or right-hand sides) in the functional constraints and the objective function. Each parameter represents a quantity (e.g., the amount available of a resource) that is of importance for the analysis of the problem. (Section 2.3), 31

product-mix problem A type of linear programming problem where the objective is to find the most profitable mix of production levels for the products under consideration. (Section 2.1), 24

range name A descriptive name given to a cell or range of cells that immediately identifies what is there. (Section 2.2), 25

relative reference A reference to a cell whose address is based upon its position relative to the cell containing the formula. (Section 2.2), 27

solution Any single assignment of values to the decision variables, regardless of whether the assignment is a good one or even a feasible one. (Section 2.3), 31

Solver The spreadsheet tool that is used to specify the model in the spreadsheet and then to obtain an optimal solution for that model. (Section 2.5), 37

target cell The cell in the spreadsheet that shows the overall measure of performance of the decisions. (Section 2.2), 27

Learning Aids for This Chapter in Your MS Courseware

Chapter 2 Excel Files:

Wyndor Example

Profit & Gambit Example

Interactive Management Science Modules:

Module for Graphical Linear Programming and Sensitivity Analysis

Excel Add-ins:

Premium Solver for Education

Supplement to Chapter 2 on the CD-ROM:

More About the Graphical Method for Linear Programming

Solved Problems (See the CD-ROM or Web site for the Solution)

2.S1. Back Savers Production Problem

Back Savers is a company that produces backpacks primarily for students. They are considering offering some combination of two different models—the Collegiate and the Mini. Both are made out of the same rip-resistant nylon fabric. Back Savers has a long-term contract with a supplier of the nylon and receives a 5,000-square-foot shipment of the material each week. Each Collegiate requires 3 square feet while each Mini requires 2 square feet. The sales forecasts indicate that at most 1,000 Collegiates and 1,200 Minis can be sold per week. Each Collegiate requires 45 minutes of labor to produce and generates a unit profit of $32. Each Mini requires 40 minutes of labor and generates a unit profit of $24. Back Savers has 35 laborers that each provides 40 hours of labor per week. Management wishes to know what quantity of each type of backpack to produce per week.

a. Formulate and solve a linear programming model for this problem on a spreadsheet.

b. Formulate this same model algebraically.

c. Use the graphical method by hand to solve this model.

2.S2. Conducting a Marketing Survey

The marketing group for a cell phone manufacturer plans to conduct a telephone survey to determine consumer attitudes toward a new cell phone that is currently under development. In order to have a sufficient sample size to conduct the analysis, they need to contact at least 100 young males (under age 40), 150 older males (over age 40), 120 young females (under age 40), and 200 older females (over age 40). It costs $1 to make a daytime phone call and $1.50 to make an evening phone call (because of higher labor costs). This cost is incurred whether or not anyone answers the phone. The table below shows the likelihood of a given customer type answering each phone call. Assume the survey is conducted with whoever first answers the phone. Also, because of limited evening staffing, at most one-third of phone calls placed can be evening phone calls. How should the marketing group conduct the telephone survey so as to meet the sample size requirements at the lowest possible cost?

a. Formulate and solve a linear programming model for this problem on a spreadsheet.

b. Formulate this same model algebraically.

Who Answers?	Daytime Calls	Evening Calls
Young male	10%	20%
Older male	15%	30%
Young female	20%	20%
Older female	35%	25%
No answer	20%	5%

Problems

We have inserted the symbol E* (for Excel) to the left of each problem or part where Excel should be used. An asterisk on the problem number indicates that at least a partial answer is given in the back of the book.

2.1.   Read the referenced article that fully describes the management science study summarized in the application vignette presented in Section 2.1. Briefly describe how linear programming was applied in this study. Then list the various financial and nonfinancial benefits that resulted from this study.

2.2.   Reconsider the Wyndor Glass Co. case study introduced in Section 2.1. Suppose that the estimates of the unit profits for the two new products now have been revised to $600 for the doors and $300 for the windows.

E*   a. Formulate and solve the revised linear programming model for this problem on a spreadsheet.

b. Formulate this same model algebraically.

c. Use the graphical method to solve this revised model.

2.3.   Reconsider the Wyndor Glass Co. case study introduced in Section 2.1. Suppose that Bill Tasto (Wyndor's vice president for manufacturing) now has found a way to provide a little additional production time in Plant 2 to the new products.

a. Use the graphical method to find the new optimal solution and the resulting total profit if *one* additional hour per week is provided.

b. Repeat part *a* if *two* additional hours per week are provided instead.

c. Repeat part *a* if *three* additional hours per week are provided instead.

d. Use these results to determine how much each additional hour per week would be worth in terms of increasing the total profit from the two new products.

E*2.4. Use the Excel Solver to do Problem 2.3.

2.5. The following table summarizes the key facts about two products, A and B, and the resources, Q, R, and S, required to produce them.

| | Resource Usage per Unit Produced | | |
Resource	Product A	Product B	Amount of Resource Available
Q	2	1	2
R	1	2	2
S	3	3	4
Profit/unit	$3,000	$2,000	

All the assumptions of linear programming hold.

E* a. Formulate and solve a linear programming model for this problem on a spreadsheet.

b. Formulate this same model algebraically.

2.6.* This is your lucky day. You have just won a $10,000 prize. You are setting aside $4,000 for taxes and partying expenses, but you have decided to invest the other $6,000. Upon hearing this news, two different friends have offered you an opportunity to become a partner in two different entrepreneurial ventures, one planned by each friend. In both cases, this investment would involve expending some of your time next summer as well as putting up cash. Becoming a *full* partner in the first friend's venture would require an investment of $5,000 and 400 hours, and your estimated profit (ignoring the value of your time) would be $4,500. The corresponding figures for the second friend's venture are $4,000 and 500 hours, with an estimated profit to you of $4,500. However, both friends are flexible and would allow you to come in at any *fraction* of a full partnership you would like. If you choose a fraction of a full partnership, all the above figures given for a full partnership (money investment, time investment, and your profit) would be multiplied by this same fraction.

Because you were looking for an interesting summer job anyway (maximum of 600 hours), you have decided to participate in one or both friends' ventures in whichever combination would maximize your total estimated profit. You now need to solve the problem of finding the best combination.

a. Describe the analogy between this problem and the Wyndor Glass Co. problem discussed in Section 2.1. Then construct and fill in a table like Table 2.1 for this problem, identifying both the activities and the resources.

b. Identify verbally the decisions to be made, the constraints on these decisions, and the overall measure of performance for the decisions.

c. Convert these verbal descriptions of the constraints and the measure of performance into quantitative expressions in terms of the data and decisions.

E* d. Formulate a spreadsheet model for this problem. Identify the data cells, the changing cells, and the target cell. Also show the Excel equation for each output cell expressed as a SUMPRODUCT function. Then use the Excel Solver to solve this model.

e. Indicate why this spreadsheet model is a linear programming model.

f. Formulate this same model algebraically.

g. Identify the decision variables, objective function, nonnegativity constraints, functional constraints, and parameters in both the algebraic version and spreadsheet version of the model.

h. Use the graphical method by hand to solve this model. What is your total estimated profit?

i. Use the Graphical Linear Programming and Sensitivity Analysis module in your Interactive Management Science Modules to apply the graphical method to this model.

2.7. You are given the following linear programming model in algebraic form, where x_1 and x_2 are the decision variables and Z is the value of the overall measure of performance.

Maximize $Z = x_1 + 2x_2$

subject to

Constraint on resource 1: $x_1 + x_2 \le 5$ (amount available)
Constraint on resource 2: $x_1 + 3x_2 \le 9$ (amount available)

and

$$x_1 \ge 0 \qquad x_2 \ge 0$$

a. Identify the objective function, the functional constraints, and the nonnegativity constraints in this model.

E* b. Incorporate this model into a spreadsheet.

c. Is $(x_1, x_2) = (3, 1)$ a feasible solution?

d. Is $(x_1, x_2) = (1, 3)$ a feasible solution?

E* e. Use the Excel Solver to solve this model.

2.8. You are given the following linear programming model in algebraic form, where x_1 and x_2 are the decision variables and Z is the value of the overall measure of performance.

Maximize $Z = 3x_1 + 2x_2$

subject to

Constraint on resource 1: $3x_1 + x_2 \le 9$ (amount available)
Constraint on resource 2: $x_1 + 2x_2 \le 8$ (amount available)

and

$$x_1 \ge 0 \qquad x_2 \ge 0$$

a. Identify the objective function, the functional constraints, and the nonnegativity constraints in this model.

E* b. Incorporate this model into a spreadsheet.

c. Is $(x_1, x_2) = (2, 1)$ a feasible solution?

d. Is $(x_1, x_2) = (2, 3)$ a feasible solution?

e. Is $(x_1, x_2) = (0, 5)$ a feasible solution?

E* f. Use the Excel Solver to solve this model.

2.9.   The Whitt Window Company is a company with only three employees that makes two different kinds of handcrafted windows: a wood-framed and an aluminum framed window. They earn $60 profit for each wood-framed window and $30 profit for each aluminum-framed window. Doug makes the wood frames and can make 6 per day. Linda makes the aluminum frames and can make 4 per day. Bob forms and cuts the glass and can make 48 square feet of glass per day. Each wood-framed window uses 6 square feet of glass and each aluminum-framed window uses 8 square feet of glass.

The company wishes to determine how many windows of each type to produce per day to maximize total profit.

a. Describe the analogy between this problem and the Wyndor Glass Co. problem discussed in Section 2.1. Then construct and fill in a table like Table 2.1 for this problem, identifying both the activities and the resources.

b. Identify verbally the decisions to be made, the constraints on these decisions, and the overall measure of performance for the decisions.

c. Convert these verbal descriptions of the constraints and the measure of performance into quantitative expressions in terms of the data and decisions.

E* d. Formulate a spreadsheet model for this problem. Identify the data cells, the changing cells, and the target cell. Also show the Excel equation for each output cell expressed as a SUMPRODUCT function. Then use the Excel Solver to solve this model.

e. Indicate why this spreadsheet model is a linear programming model.

f. Formulate this same model algebraically.

g. Identify the decision variables, objective function, nonnegativity constraints, functional constraints, and parameters in both the algebraic version and spreadsheet version of the model.

h. Use the graphical method to solve this model.

i. A new competitor in town has started making wood-framed windows as well. This may force the company to lower the price it charges and so lower the profit made for each wood-framed window. How would the optimal solution change (if at all) if the profit per wood-framed window decreases from $60 to $40? From $60 to $20?

j. Doug is considering lowering his working hours, which would decrease the number of wood frames he makes per day. How would the optimal solution change if he only makes 5 wood frames per day?

2.10.   The Apex Television Company has to decide on the number of 27" and 20" sets to be produced at one of its factories. Market research indicates that at most 40 of the 27" sets and 10 of the 20" sets can be sold per month. The maximum number of work-hours available is 500 per month. A 27" set requires 20 work-hours and a 20" set requires 10 work-hours. Each 27" set

sold produces a profit of $120 and each 20" set produces a profit of $80. A wholesaler has agreed to purchase all the television sets produced if the numbers do not exceed the maxima indicated by the market research.

E* a. Formulate and solve a linear programming model for this problem on a spreadsheet.

b. Formulate this same model algebraically.

c. Solve this model by using the Graphical Linear Programming and Sensitivity Analysis module in your Interactive Management Science Modules to apply the graphical method.

2.11.   The WorldLight Company produces two light fixtures (products 1 and 2) that require both metal frame parts and electrical components. Management wants to determine how many units of each product to produce so as to maximize profit. For each unit of product 1, one unit of frame parts and two units of electrical components are required. For each unit of product 2, three units of frame parts and two units of electrical components are required. The company has 200 units of frame parts and 300 units of electrical components. Each unit of product 1 gives a profit of $1, and each unit of product 2, up to 60 units, gives a profit of $2. Any excess over 60 units of product 2 brings no profit, so such an excess has been ruled out.

a. Identify verbally the decisions to be made, the constraints on these decisions, and the overall measure of performance for the decisions.

b. Convert these verbal descriptions of the constraints and the measure of performance into quantitative expressions in terms of the data and decisions.

E* c. Formulate and solve a linear programming model for this problem on a spreadsheet.

d. Formulate this same model algebraically.

e. Solve this model by using the Graphical Linear Programming and Sensitivity Analysis module in your Interactive Management Science Modules to apply the graphical method. What is the resulting total profit?

2.12.   The Primo Insurance Company is introducing two new product lines: special risk insurance and mortgages. The expected profit is $5 per unit on special risk insurance and $2 per unit on mortgages.

Management wishes to establish sales quotas for the new product lines to maximize total expected profit. The work requirements are shown below:

a. Identify verbally the decisions to be made, the constraints on these decisions, and the overall measure of performance for the decisions.

b. Convert these verbal descriptions of the constraints and the measure of performance into quantitative expressions in terms of the data and decisions.

Department	Work-Hours per Unit		Work-Hours Available
	Special Risk	Mortgage	
Underwriting	3	2	2,400
Administration	0	1	800
Claims	2	0	1,200

E*   *c.* Formulate and solve a linear programming model for this problem on a spreadsheet.

   d. Formulate this same model algebraically.

2.13.* You are given the following linear programming model in algebraic form, with x_1 and x_2 as the decision variables and constraints on the usage of four resources:

$$\text{Maximize} \quad \text{Profit} = 2x_1 + x_2$$

subject to

$$
\begin{aligned}
x_2 &\le 10 \quad &\text{(resource 1)} \\
2x_1 + 5x_2 &\le 60 \quad &\text{(resource 2)} \\
x_1 + x_2 &\le 18 \quad &\text{(resource 3)} \\
3x_1 + x_2 &\le 44 \quad &\text{(resource 4)}
\end{aligned}
$$

and

$$x_1 \ge 0 \qquad x_2 \ge 0$$

   a. Use the graphical method to solve this model.

E*   *b.* Incorporate this model into a spreadsheet and then use the Excel Solver to solve this model.

2.14. Because of your knowledge of management science, your boss has asked you to analyze a product mix problem involving two products and two resources. The model is shown below in algebraic form, where x_1 and x_2 are the production rates for the two products and P is the total profit.

$$\text{Maximize} \quad P = 3x_1 + 2x_2$$

subject to

$$
\begin{aligned}
x_1 + x_2 &\le 8 \quad &\text{(resource 1)} \\
2x_1 + x_2 &\le 10 \quad &\text{(resource 2)}
\end{aligned}
$$

and

$$x_1 \ge 0 \qquad x_2 \ge 0$$

   a. Use the graphical method to solve this model.

E*   *b.* Incorporate this model into a spreadsheet and then use the Excel Solver to solve this model.

2.15. Weenies and Buns is a food processing plant that manufactures hot dogs and hot dog buns. They grind their own flour for the hot dog buns at a maximum rate of 200 pounds per week. Each hot dog bun requires 0.1 pound of flour. They currently have a contract with Pigland, Inc., which specifies that a delivery of 800 pounds of pork product is delivered every Monday. Each hot dog requires 1/4 pound of pork product. All the other ingredients in the hot dogs and hot dog buns are in plentiful supply. Finally, the labor force at Weenies and Buns consists of five employees working full time (40 hours per week each). Each hot dog requires three minutes of labor, and each hot dog bun requires two minutes of labor. Each hot dog yields a profit of $0.20, and each bun yields a profit of $0.10.

Weenies and Buns would like to know how many hot dogs and how many hot dog buns they should produce each week so as to achieve the highest possible profit.

   a. Identify verbally the decisions to be made, the constraints on these decisions, and the overall measure of performance for the decisions.

   b. Convert these verbal descriptions of the constraints and the measure of performance into quantitative expressions in terms of the data and decisions.

E*   *c.* Formulate and solve a linear programming model for this problem on a spreadsheet.

   d. Formulate this same model algebraically.

   e. Use the graphical method to solve this model. Decide yourself whether you would prefer to do this by hand or by using the Graphical Linear Programming and Sensitivity Analysis module in your Interactive Management Science Modules.

2.16. The Oak Works is a family-owned business that makes handcrafted dining room tables and chairs. They obtain the oak from a local tree farm, which ships them 2,500 pounds of oak each month. Each table uses 50 pounds of oak while each chair uses 25 pounds of oak. The family builds all the furniture itself and has 480 hours of labor available each month. Each table or chair requires six hours of labor. Each table nets Oak Works $400 in profit, while each chair nets $100 in profit. Since chairs are often sold with the tables, they want to produce *at least* twice as many chairs as tables.

The Oak Works would like to decide how many tables and chairs to produce so as to maximize profit.

   a. Formulate and solve a linear programming model for this problem on a spreadsheet.

   b. Formulate this same model algebraically.

2.17. Read the referenced article that fully describes the management science study summarized in the application vignette presented in Section 2.6. Briefly describe how linear programming was applied in this study. Then list the various financial and nonfinancial benefits that resulted from this study.

2.18. Nutri-Jenny is a weight-management center. It produces a wide variety of frozen entrees for consumption by its clients. The entrees are strictly monitored for nutritional content to ensure that the clients are eating a balanced diet. One new entree will be a "beef sirloin tips dinner." It will consist of beef tips and gravy, plus some combination of peas, carrots, and a dinner roll. Nutri-Jenny would like to determine what quantity of each item to include in the entree to meet the nutritional requirements, while costing as little as possible. The nutritional information for each item and its cost are given in the following table.

Item	Calories (per oz.)	Calories from Fat (per oz.)	Vitamin A (IU per oz.)	Vitamin C (mg per oz.)	Protein (gr. per oz.)	Cost (per oz.)
Beef tips	54	19	0	0	8	40¢
Gravy	20	15	0	1	0	35¢
Peas	15	0	15	3	1	15¢
Carrots	8	0	350	1	1	18¢
Dinner roll	40	10	0	0	1	10¢

The nutritional requirements for the entree are as follows: (1) it must have between 280 and 320 calories, (2) calories from fat should be no more than 30 percent of the total number of calories, and (3) it must have at least 600 IUs of vitamin A, 10 milligrams of vitamin C, and 30 grams of protein. Furthermore, for practical reasons, it must include at least 2 ounces of beef, and it must have at least half an ounce of gravy per ounce of beef.

E* a. Formulate and solve a linear programming model for this problem on a spreadsheet.

    b. Formulate this same model algebraically.

2.19. Ralph Edmund loves steaks and potatoes. Therefore, he has decided to go on a steady diet of only these two foods (plus some liquids and vitamin supplements) for all his meals. Ralph realizes that this isn't the healthiest diet, so he wants to make sure that he eats the right quantities of the two foods to satisfy some key nutritional requirements. He has obtained the following nutritional and cost information:

Grams of Ingredient per Serving

Ingredient	Steak	Potatoes	Daily Requirement (grams)
Carbohydrates	5	15	≥ 50
Protein	20	5	≥ 40
Fat	15	2	≤ 60
Cost per serving	$4	$2	

Ralph wishes to determine the number of daily servings (may be fractional) of steak and potatoes that will meet these requirements at a minimum cost.

    a. Identify verbally the decisions to be made, the constraints on these decisions, and the overall measure of performance for the decisions.

    b. Convert these verbal descriptions of the constraints and the measure of performance into quantitative expressions in terms of the data and decisions.

    c. Formulate and solve a linear programming model for this problem on a spreadsheet.

    d. Formulate this same model algebraically.

    e. Use the graphical method by hand to solve this model.

    f. Use the Graphical Linear Programming and Sensitivity Analysis module in your Interactive Management Science Modules to apply the graphical method to this model.

2.20. Dwight is an elementary school teacher who also raises pigs for supplemental income. He is trying to decide what to feed his pigs. He is considering using a combination of pig feeds available from local suppliers. He would like to feed the pigs at minimum cost while also making sure each pig receives an adequate supply of calories and vitamins. The cost, calorie content, and vitamin content of each feed is given in the table below.

Contents	Feed Type A	Feed Type B
Calories (per pound)	800	1,000
Vitamins (per pound)	140 units	70 units
Cost (per pound)	$0.40	$0.80

Each pig requires at least 8,000 calories per day and at least 700 units of vitamins. A further constraint is that no more than 1/3 of the diet (by weight) can consist of Feed Type A, since it contains an ingredient that is toxic if consumed in too large a quantity.

    a. Identify verbally the decisions to be made, the constraints on these decisions, and the overall measure of performance for the decisions.

    b. Convert these verbal descriptions of the constraints and the measure of performance into quantitative expressions in terms of the data and decisions.

E* c. Formulate and solve a linear programming model for this problem on a spreadsheet.

    d. Formulate this same model algebraically.

2.21. Reconsider the Profit & Gambit Co. problem described in Section 2.6. Suppose that the estimated data given in Table 2.2 now have been changed as shown in the table that accompanies this problem.

E* a. Formulate and solve a linear programming model on a spreadsheet for this revised version of the problem.

    b. Formulate this same model algebraically.

    c. Use the graphical method to solve this model.

    d. What were the key changes in the data that caused your answer for the optimal solution to change from the one for the original version of the problem?

    e. Write a paragraph to the management of the Profit & Gambit Co. presenting your conclusions from the above parts. Include the potential effect of further refining the key data in the below table. Also point out the leverage that your results might provide to management in negotiating a decrease in the unit cost for either of the advertising media.

	Increase in Sales per Unit of Advertising		
Product	Television	Print Media	Minimum Required Increase
Stain remover	0%	1.5%	3%
Liquid detergent	3	4	18
Powder detergent	−1	2	4
Unit cost	$1 million	$2 million	

2.22. You are given the following linear programming model in algebraic form, with x_1 and x_2 as the decision variables:

Minimize $\quad \text{Cost} = 40x_1 + 50x_2$

subject to

Constraint 1: $\quad 2x_1 + 3x_2 \geq 30$

Constraint 2: $\quad x_1 + x_2 \geq 12$

Constraint 3: $\quad 2x_1 + x_2 \geq 20$

and

$$x_1 \geq 0 \qquad x_2 \geq 0$$

reduce the center's operating costs to avoid having to raise the tuition fee. Elizabeth is currently planning what to feed the children for lunch. She would like to keep costs to a minimum, but also wants to make sure she is meeting the nutritional requirements of the children. She has already decided to go with peanut butter and jelly sandwiches, and some combination of apples, milk, and/or cranberry juice. The nutritional content of each food choice and its cost are given in the table that accompanies this problem.

The nutritional requirements are as follows. Each child should receive between 300 and 500 calories, but no more than 30 percent of these calories should come from fat. Each child

Food Item	Calories from Fat	Total Calories	Vitamin C (mg)	Fiber (g)	Cost (¢)
Bread (1 slice)	15	80	0	4	6
Peanut butter (1 tbsp)	80	100	0	0	5
Jelly (1 tbsp)	0	70	4	3	8
Apple	0	90	6	10	35
Milk (1 cup)	60	120	2	0	20
Cranberry juice (1 cup)	0	110	80	1	40

a. Use the graphical method to solve this model.

b. How does the optimal solution change if the objective function is changed to $\text{Cost} = 40x_1 + 70x_2$?

c. How does the optimal solution change if the third functional constraint is changed to $2x_1 + x_2 \geq 15$?

E* *d.* Now incorporate the original model into a spreadsheet and use the Excel Solver to solve this model.

E* *e.* Use Excel to do parts *b* and *c*.

2.23. The Learning Center runs a day camp for 6–10 year olds during the summer. Its manager, Elizabeth Reed, is trying to

should receive at least 60 milligrams (mg) of vitamin C and at least 10 grams (g) of fiber.

To ensure tasty sandwiches, Elizabeth wants each child to have a minimum of 2 slices of bread, 1 tablespoon (tbsp) of peanut butter, and 1 tbsp of jelly, along with at least 1 cup of liquid (milk and/or cranberry juice).

Elizabeth would like to select the food choices that would minimize cost while meeting all these requirements.

E* *a.* Formulate and solve a linear programming model for this problem on a spreadsheet.

b. Formulate this same model algebraically.

Partial Answers to Selected Problems

CHAPTER 2

2.6. *d.* Fraction of $1^{\text{st}} = 0.667$, fraction of $2^{\text{nd}} = 0.667$. Profit $= \$6,000$.

2.13. *b.* $x_1 = 13$, $x_2 = 5$. Profit $= \$31$.

2.S1 Back Savers Production Problem

Back Savers is a company that produces backpacks primarily for students. They are considering offering some combination of two different models—the Collegiate and the Mini. Both are made out of the same rip-resistant nylon fabric. Back Savers has a long-term contract with a supplier of the nylon and receives a 5000 square-foot shipment of the material each week. Each Collegiate requires 3 square feet while each Mini requires 2 square feet. The sales forecasts indicate that at most 1000 Collegiates and 1200 Minis can be sold per week. Each Collegiate requires 45 minutes of labor to produce and generates a unit profit of $32. Each Mini requires 40 minutes of labor and generates a unit profit of $24. Back Savers has 35 laborers that each provides 40 hours of labor per week. Management wishes to know what quantity of each type of backpack to produce per week.

a. *Formulate and solve a linear programming model for this problem on a spreadsheet.*

To build a spreadsheet model for this problem, start by entering the data. The data for this problem are the unit profit of each type of backpack, the resource requirements (square feet of nylon and labor hours required), the availability of each resource, 5400 square feet of nylon and (35 laborers)(40 hours/laborer) = 1400 labor hours, and the sales forecast for each type of backpack (1000 Collegiates and 1200 Minis). In order to keep the units consistent in row 8 (hours), the labor required for each backpack (in cells C8 and D8) are converted from minutes to hours (0.75 hours = 45 minutes, 0.667 hours = 40 minutes). The range names UnitProfit (C4:D4), Available (G7:G8), and SalesForecast (C13:D13) are added for these data.

	B	C	D	E	F	G
3		Collegiate	Mini			
4	Unit Profit	$32	$24			
5						
6		Resource Used per Unit Produced				Available
7	Nylon (sq. ft.)	3	2			5400
8	Labor (hours)	0.75	0.667			1400
9						
10						
11						
12						
13	Sales Forecast	1000	1200			

The decision to be made in this problem is how many of each type of backpack to make. Therefore, we add two changing cells with range name UnitsProduced (C11:D11). The values in CallsPlaced will eventually be determined by the Solver. For now, arbitrary values of 10 and 10 are entered.

	B	C	D	E	F	G
3		Collegiate	Mini			
4	Unit Profit	$32	$24			
5						
6		Resource Used per Unit Produced				Available
7	Nylon (sq. ft.)	3	2			5400
8	Labor (hours)	0.75	0.667			1400
9						
10						
11	Units Produced	10	10			
12						
13	Sales Forecast	1000	1200			

The goal is to produce backpacks so as to achieve the highest total profit. Thus, the target cell should calculate the total profit, where the objective will be to maximize this target cell. In this case, the total profit will be

Total Profit = ($32)(# of Collegiates) + ($24)(# of Minis)

or

Total Cost = SUMPRODUCT(UnitProfit, UnitsProduced).

This formula is entered into cell G11 and given a range name of TotalProfit. With 10 Collegiates and 10 Minis produced, the total profit would be ($32)(10) + ($24)(10) = $560.

	B	C	D	E	F	G
3		Collegiate	Mini			
4	Unit Profit	$32	$24			
5						
6		Resource Used per Unit Produced				Available
7	Nylon (sq. ft.)	3	2			5400
8	Labor (hours)	0.75	0.667			1400
9						
10						Total Profit
11	Units Produced	10	10			$560
12						
13	Sales Forecast	1000	1200			

	G
10	Total Profit
11	=SUMPRODUCT(UnitProfit,UnitsProduced)

The first set of constraints in this problem involve the limited available resources (nylon and labor hours). Given the number of units produced (UnitsProduced in C11:D11), we calculate the total resources required. For nylon, this will be =SUMPRODUCT(C7:D7, UnitsProduced) in cell E7. By using a range name or an absolute reference for the units produced, this formula can be copied into cell E8 to calculate the labor hours required. The total resources used (TotalResources in E7:E8) must be <= Available (in cells G7:G8), as indicated by the <= in F7:F8.

	B	C	D	E	F	G
3		Collegiate	Mini			
4	Unit Profit	$32	$24			
5				Total		
6		Resource Used per Unit Produced		Required		Available
7	Nylon (sq. ft.)	3	2	50	<=	5400
8	Labor (hours)	0.75	0.667	14.166667	<=	1400
9						
10						Total Profit
11	Units Produced	10	10			$560

	E
5	Total
6	Required
7	=SUMPRODUCT(C7:D7,UnitsProduced)
8	=SUMPRODUCT(C8:D8,UnitsProduced)

The final constraint is that it does not make sense to produce more backpacks than can be sold (as predicted by the sales forecast). Therefore UnitsProduced (C11:D11) should be less-than-or-equal-to the SalesForecast (C13:D13), as indicated by the <= in C12:D12

	B	C	D	E	F	G
3		Collegiate	Mini			
4	Unit Profit	$32	$24			
5				Total		
6		Resource Used per Unit Produced		Required		Available
7	Nylon (sq. ft.)	3	2	50	<=	5400
8	Labor (hours)	0.75	0.667	14.16666667	<=	1400
9						
10						Total Profit
11	Units Produced	10	10			$560
12		<=	<=			
13	Sales Forecast	1000	1200			

The Solver information and solved spreadsheet are shown below.

	B	C	D	E	F	G
3		Collegiate	Mini			
4	Unit Profit	$32	$24			
5				Total		
6		Resource Used per Unit Produced		Required		Available
7	Nylon (sq. ft.)	3	2	4950	<=	5400
8	Labor (hours)	0.75	0.667	1400	<=	1400
9						
10						Total Profit
11	Units Produced	1000	975			$55,400
12		<=	<=			
13	Sales Forecast	1000	1200			

Solver Parameters

Set Objective (Target Cell): TotalProfit
To: Max
By Changing (Variable) Cells:
   UnitsProduced
Subject to the Constraints:
   TotalRequired <= Available
   UnitsProduced <= SalesForecast

Solver Options (Excel 2010):
   Make Variables Nonnegative
   Solving Method: Simplex LP
Solver Options (older Excel):
   Assume Nonnegative
   Assume Linear Model

Range Name	Cells
Available	G7:G8
SalesForecast	C13:D13
TotalProfit	G11
TotalRequired	E7:E8
UnitProfit	C4:D4
UnitsProduced	C11:D11

	E
5	Total
6	Required
7	=SUMPRODUCT(C7:D7,UnitsProduced)
8	=SUMPRODUCT(C8:D8,UnitsProduced)

	G
10	Total Profit
11	=SUMPRODUCT(UnitProfit,UnitsProduced)

Thus, they should produce 1000 Collegiates and 975 Minis to achieve the maximum total profit of $55,400.

b. *Formulate this same model algebraically.*

To build an algebraic model for this problem, start by defining the decision variables. In this case, the two decisions are how many Collegiates to produce and how many Minis to produce. These variables are defined below:

Let C = Number of Collegiates to produce,
       M = Number of Minis to produce.

4

Next determine the goal of the problem. In this case, the goal is to produce the number of each type of backpack to achieve the highest possible total profit. Each Collegiate yields a unit profit of $32 while each Mini yields a unit profit of $24. The objective function is therefore

Maximize Total Profit = $32C + $24M$.

The first set of constraints in this problem involve the limited resources (nylon and labor hours). Given the number of backpacks produced, C and M, and the required nylon and labor hours for each, the total resources used can be calculated. These total resources used need to be less than or equal to the amount available. Since the labor available is in units of hours, the labor required for each backpack needs to be in units of hours (3/4 hour and 2/3 hour) rather than minutes (45 minutes and 40 minutes). These constraints are as follows:

Nylon:	$3C + 2M \leq 5400$ square feet,
Labor Hours:	$(3/4)C + (2/3)M \leq 1400$ hours.

The final constraint is that they should not produce more of each backpack than the sales forecast. Therefore,

Sales Forecast:	$C \leq 1000$
	$M \leq 1200$.

After adding nonnegativity constraints, the complete algebraic formulation is given below:

Let C = Number of Collegiates to produce,
       M = Number of Minis to produce.

Maximize Total Profit = $32C + $24M$,

subject to

Nylon:	$3C + 2M \leq 5400$ square feet,
Labor Hours:	$(3/4)C + (2/3)M \leq 1400$ hours,
Sales Forecast:	$C \leq 1000$
	$M \leq 1200$.

and $C \geq 0$, $M \geq 0$.

c. *Use the graphical method by hand to solve this model.*

Start by plotting a graph with Collegiates (C) on the horizontal axis and Minis (M) on the vertical axis, as shown below.

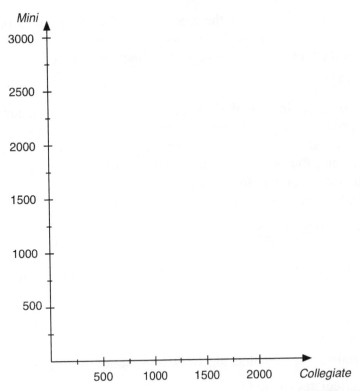

Next, the four constraint boundary lines (where the left-hand-side of the constraint exactly equals the right-hand-side) need to be plotted. The easiest way to do this is by determining where these lines intercepts the two axes. For the Nylon constraint boundary line ($3C + 2M = 5400$), setting $M = 0$ yields a C-intercept of 1800 while setting $C = 0$ yields an M-intercept of 2700. For the Labor constraint boundary line ($(3/4)C + (2/3)M = 1400$), setting $M = 0$ yields a C-intercept of 1866.67 while setting $C = 0$ yields an M-intercept of 2100. The sales forecast constraints are a horizontal line at $M = 1200$ and a vertical line at $C = 1000$. These constraint boundary lines are plotted below.

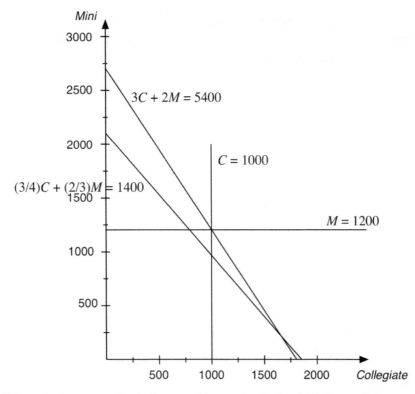

A feasible solution must be below and/or to the left of all four of these constraints while being above the Collegiate axis (since $C \geq 0$) and to the right of the Mini axis (since $M \geq 0$). This yields the feasible region shown below.

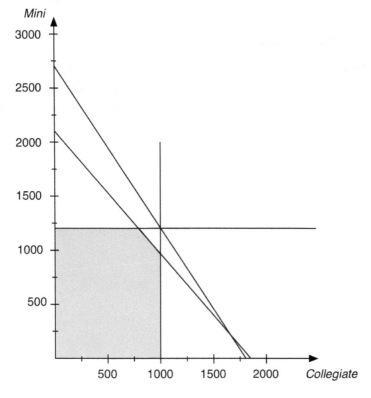

To find the optimal solution, an objective function line is plotted by setting the objective function equal to a value. For example, the objective function line when the value of the objective function is $48,000 is plotted as a dashed line below.

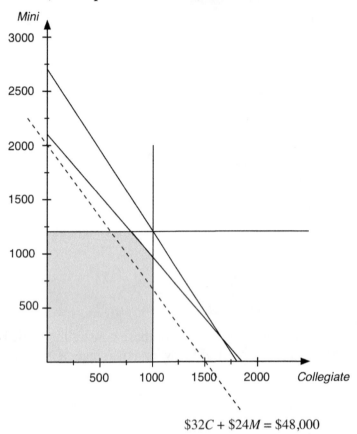

$$\$32C + \$24M = \$48,000$$

All objective function lines will be parallel to this one. To find the feasible solution that maximizes profit, slide this line out as far as possible while still touching the feasible region. This occurs when the profit is $55,400, and the objective function line intersect the feasible region at the single point with $(C, M) = (1000, 975)$ as shown below.

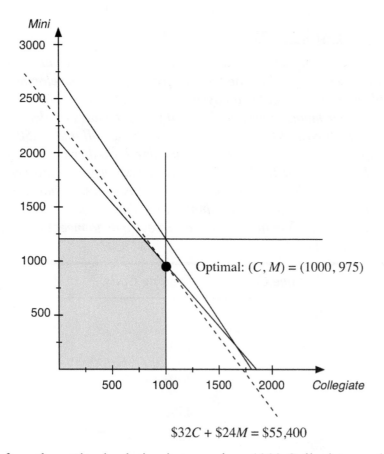

$$\$32C + \$24M = \$55{,}400$$

Therefore, the optimal solution is to produce 1000 Collegiates and 975 Minis, yielding a total profit of $55,400.

2.S2 Conducting a Marketing Survey

The marketing group for a cell phone manufacturer plans to conduct a telephone survey to determine consumer attitudes toward a new cell phone that is currently under development. In order to have a sufficient sample size to conduct the analysis, they need to contact at least 100 young males (under age 40), 150 older males (over age 40), 120 young females (under age 40), and 200 older females (over age 40). It costs $1 to make a daytime phone call and $1.50 to make an evening phone call (due to higher labor costs). This cost is incurred whether or not anyone answers the phone. The table below shows the likelihood of a given customer type answering each phone call. Assume the survey is conducted with whoever first answers the phone. Also, because of limited evening staffing, at most one-third of phone calls placed can be evening phone calls. How should the marketing group conduct the telephone survey so as to meet the sample size requirements at the lowest possible cost?

Who Answers?	Daytime Calls	Evening Calls
Young Male	10%	20%
Older Male	15%	30%
Young Female	20%	20%
Older Female	35%	25%
No Answer	20%	5%

a. *Formulate and solve a linear programming model for this problem on a spreadsheet.*

To build a spreadsheet model for this problem, start by entering the data. The data for this problem are the cost of each type of phone call, the percentages of each customer type answering each type of phone call, and the total number of each customer type needed for the survey.

	B	C	D	E	F	G
3		Daytime Call	Evening Call			
4	Unit Cost	$1.00	$1.50			
5						Responses
6	Respondent					Needed
7	Young Male	10%	20%			100
8	Older Male	15%	30%			150
9	Young Female	20%	20%			120
10	Older Female	35%	25%			200

The decision to be made in this problem is how many of each type of phone call to make. Therefore, we add two changing cells with range name CallsPlaced (C13:D13). The values in CallsPlaced will eventually be determined by the Solver. For now, arbitrary values of 10 and 5 are entered.

	B	C	D	E	F	G
3		Daytime Call	Evening Call			
4	Unit Cost	$1.00	$1.50			
5						Responses
6	**Respondent**					Needed
7	Young Male	10%	20%			100
8	Older Male	15%	30%			150
9	Young Female	20%	20%			120
10	Older Female	35%	25%			200
11						
12						
13	Calls Placed	10	5			

The goal of the marketing group is to conduct the survey at the lowest possible cost. Thus, the target cell should calculate the total cost, where the objective will be to minimize this target cell. In this case, the total cost will be

Total Cost = ($1)(# of daytime calls) + ($1.50)(# of evening calls)

or

Total Cost = SUMPRODUCT(UnitCost, CallsPlaced).

This formula is entered into cell G13 and given a range name of TotalCost. With 10 daytime phone calls and 5 evening calls, the total cost would be ($1)(10) + ($1.50)(5) = $17.50.

	B	C	D	E	F	G
3		Daytime Call	Evening Call			
4	Unit Cost	$1.00	$1.50			
5						Responses
6	**Respondent**					Needed
7	Young Male	10%	20%			100
8	Older Male	15%	30%			150
9	Young Female	20%	20%			120
10	Older Female	35%	25%			200
11						
12						Total Cost
13	Calls Placed	10	5			$17.50

	G
12	Total Cost
13	=SUMPRODUCT(UnitCost,CallsPlaced)

The first set of constraints in this problem involve the minimum responses required from each customer group. Given the number of calls placed (CallsPlaced in C13:D13), we calculate the total responses by each customer type. For young males, this will be =SUMPRODUCT(C7:D7, CallsPlaced). By using a range name or an absolute reference for the calls placed, this formula can be copied into cells E8-E10 to calculate the number of older males, young females, and older females reached. The total responses of each customer type (Total Responses in E7:E10) must be >= ResponsesNeeded (in cells G7:G10), as indicated by the >= in F7:F10.

	B	C	D	E	F	G
3		Daytime Call	Evening Call			
4	Unit Cost	$1.00	$1.50			
5				Total		Responses
6	**Respondent**			Responses		Needed
7	Young Male	10%	20%	2	>=	100
8	Older Male	15%	30%	3	>=	150
9	Young Female	20%	20%	3	>=	120
10	Older Female	35%	25%	4.75	>=	200
11						
12						Total Cost
13	Calls Placed	10	5			$17.50

	E
5	Total
6	Responses
7	=SUMPRODUCT(C7:D7,CallsPlaced)
8	=SUMPRODUCT(C8:D8,CallsPlaced)
9	=SUMPRODUCT(C9:D9,CallsPlaced)
10	=SUMPRODUCT(C10:D10,CallsPlaced)

The final constraint is that at most one third of the total calls placed can be evening calls. In other words:

Evening Calls <= (1/3)(Total Calls Placed)

The two sides of this constraint (i.e., evening calls and 1/3 of total calls placed) are calculated in cells C15 and E15. Enter <= in D15 to show that C15 <= E15.

	B	C	D	E	F	G
3		Daytime Call	Evening Call			
4	Unit Cost	$1.00	$1.50			
5				Total		Responses
6	**Respondent**			Responses		Needed
7	Young Male	10%	20%	2	>=	100
8	Older Male	15%	30%	3	>=	150
9	Young Female	20%	20%	3	>=	120
10	Older Female	35%	25%	4.75	>=	200
11						
12						Total Cost
13	Calls Placed	10	5			$17.50
14						
15	Evening Calls	5	<=	5	33.33%	of Total Calls

	B	C	D	E	F	G
15	Evening Calls	=D13	<=	=F15*(C13+D13)	0.333333:	of Total Calls

The Solver information and solved spreadsheet are shown below.

	A	B	C	D	E	F	G
1		**Conducting a Marketing Survey**					
2							
3			Daytime Call	Evening Call			
4		Unit Cost	$1.00	$1.50			
5					Total		Responses
6		**Respondent**			Responses		Needed
7		Young Male	10%	20%	100	>=	100
8		Older Male	15%	30%	150	>=	150
9		Young Female	20%	20%	150	>=	120
10		Older Female	35%	25%	237.5	>=	200
11							
12							Total Cost
13		Calls Placed	500	250			$875.00
14							
15		Evening Calls	250	<=	250	33.33%	of Total Calls

Solver Parameters

Set Objective (Target Cell): TotalCost
To: Min
By Changing (Variable) Cells:
   CallsPlaced
Subject to the Constraints:
   EveningCalls <= E15
   TotalResponses >= ResponsesNeeded

Solver Options (Excel 2010):
   Make Variables Nonnegative
   Solving Method: Simplex LP
Solver Options (older Excel):
   Assume Nonnegative
   Assume Linear Model

Range Name	Cells
CallsPlaced	C13:D13
EveningCalls	C15
ResponsesNeeded	G7:G10
TotalCost	G13
TotalResponses	E7:E10
UnitCost	C4:D4

	E
5	Total
6	Responses
7	=SUMPRODUCT(C7:D7,CallsPlaced)
8	=SUMPRODUCT(C8:D8,CallsPlaced)
9	=SUMPRODUCT(C9:D9,CallsPlaced)
10	=SUMPRODUCT(C10:D10,CallsPlaced)

	G
12	Total Cost
13	=SUMPRODUCT(UnitCost,CallsPlaced)

	B	C	D	E	F	G
15	Evening Calls	=D13	<=	=F15*(C13+D13)	0.333333	of Total Calls

Thus, the marketing group should place 500 daytime calls and 250 evening calls at a total cost of $875.

b. *Formulate this same model algebraically.*

To build an algebraic model for this problem, start by defining the decision variables. In this case, the two decisions are how many daytime calls and how many evening calls to place. These variables are defined below:

Let D = Number of daytime calls to place
E = Number of evening calls to place.

Next determine the goal of the problem. In this case, the goal is to conduct the marketing survey at the lowest possible cost. Each daytime call costs \$1 while each evening call costs \$1.50. The objective function is therefore

Minimize Total Cost = $\$1D + \$1.50E$.

The first set of constraints in this problem involve the minimum responses required from each customer group. Given the number of calls place, D and E, and the percentage of calls answered by each customer group, the total responses for each customer group is calculated. These total responses need to be greater than or equal to the minimum responses required. These constraints are as follows:

Young Males:	$(10\%)D + (20\%)E \geq 100$
Older Males:	$(15\%)D + (30\%)E \geq 150$
Young Females:	$(20\%)D + (20\%)E \geq 120$
Older Females:	$(35\%)D + (25\%)E \geq 200$.

The final constraint is that at most one third of the total calls placed can be evening calls. In other words:

Evening Calls <= (1/3)(Total Calls Placed)

Substituting E for Evening Calls, and $D + E$ for Total Calls Placed yields the following constraint:

$E \leq (1/3)(D + E)$.

After adding nonnegativity constraints, the complete algebraic formulation is given below:

Let D = Number of daytime calls to place
E = Number of evening calls to place.

Minimize Total Cost = $\$1D + \$1.50E$.

subject to

Young Males:	$(10\%)D + (20\%)E \geq 100$
Older Males:	$(15\%)D + (30\%)E \geq 150$
Young Females:	$(20\%)D + (20\%)E \geq 120$
Older Females:	$(35\%)D + (25\%)E \geq 200$
Evening Call Ratio:	$E \leq (1/3)(D + E)$

and $D \geq 0$, $E \geq 0$.

Linear Programming: Formulation and Applications

Learning objectives

After completing this chapter, you should be able to

1. Recognize various kinds of managerial problems to which linear programming can be applied.
2. Describe the five major categories of linear programming problems, including their identifying features.
3. Formulate a linear programming model from a description of a problem in any of these categories.
4. Describe the difference between resource constraints and benefit constraints, including the difference in how they arise.
5. Describe fixed-requirement constraints and where they arise.
6. Identify the kinds of Excel functions that linear programming spreadsheet models use for the output cells, including the target cell.
7. Identify the four components of any linear programming model and the kind of spreadsheet cells used for each component.
8. Recognize managerial problems that can be formulated and analyzed as linear programming problems.
9. Understand the flexibility that managers have in prescribing key considerations that can be incorporated into a linear programming model.

Linear programming problems come in many guises. And their models take various forms. This diversity can be confusing to both students and managers, making it difficult to recognize when linear programming can be applied to address a managerial problem. Since managers instigate management science studies, the ability to recognize the applicability of linear programming is an important managerial skill. This chapter focuses largely on developing this skill.

The usual textbook approach to trying to teach this skill is to present a series of diverse examples of linear programming applications. The weakness of this approach is that it emphasizes differences rather than the common threads between these applications. Our approach will be to emphasize these common threads—the **identifying features**—that tie together linear programming problems even when they arise in very different contexts. We will describe some broad categories of linear programming problems and the identifying features that characterize them. Then we will use diverse examples, but with the purpose of illustrating and emphasizing the common threads among them.

We will focus on five key categories of linear programming problems: resource-allocation problems, cost–benefit–trade-off problems, mixed problems, transportation problems, and assignment problems. In each case, an important identifying feature is the nature of the restrictions on what decisions can be made, and thus the nature of the resulting functional constraints in the linear programming model. For each category, you will see how the basic data for a problem lead directly to a linear programming model with a certain distinctive form. Thus, model formulation becomes a by-product of proper problem formulation.

The chapter begins with a case study that initially involves a resource-allocation problem. We then return to the case study in Section 3.4, where additional managerial considerations turn the problem into a mixed problem.

Sections 3.2 to 3.6 focus on the five categories of linear programming problems in turn. Section 3.7 then takes a broader look at the formulation of linear programming models from a managerial perspective. This section (along with Section 3.4) highlights the importance of having the model accurately reflect the managerial view of the problem. These (and other) sections also describe the flexibility available to managers for having the model structured to best fit their view of the important considerations.

3.1   A CASE STUDY: THE SUPER GRAIN CORP. ADVERTISING-MIX PROBLEM

Claire Syverson, vice president for marketing of the **Super Grain Corporation,** is facing a daunting challenge: how to break into an already overly crowded breakfast cereal market in a big way. Fortunately, the company's new breakfast cereal—*Crunchy Start*—has a lot going for it: Great taste. Nutritious. Crunchy from start to finish. She can recite the litany in her sleep now. It has the makings of a winning promotional campaign.

However, Claire knows that she has to avoid the mistakes she made in her last campaign for a breakfast cereal. That had been her first big assignment since she won this promotion, and what a disaster! She thought she had developed a really good campaign. But somehow it had failed to connect with the most crucial segments of the market—young children and parents of young children. She also has concluded that it was a mistake not to include cents-off coupons in the magazine and newspaper advertising. Oh well. Live and learn.

But she had better get it right this time, especially after the big stumble last time. The company's president, David Sloan, already has impressed on her how important the success of Crunchy Start is to the future of the company. She remembers exactly how David concluded the conversation. "The company's shareholders are not happy. We need to get those earnings headed in the right direction again." Claire had heard this tune before, but she saw in David's eyes how deadly serious he is this time.

Claire often uses spreadsheets to help organize her planning. Her management science course in business school impressed upon her how valuable spreadsheet modeling can be. She regrets that she did not rely more heavily on spreadsheet modeling for the last campaign. That was a mistake that she is determined not to repeat.

Now it is time for Claire to carefully review and formulate the problem in preparation for formulating a spreadsheet model.

The Problem

Claire already has employed a leading advertising firm, Giacomi & Jackowitz, to help design a nationwide promotional campaign that will achieve the largest possible exposure for Crunchy Start. Super Grain will pay this firm a fee based on services performed (not to exceed $1 million) and has allocated an additional $4 million for advertising expenses.

Giacomi & Jackowitz has identified the three most effective advertising media for this product:

Medium 1:   Television commercials on Saturday morning programs for children.

Medium 2:   Advertisements in food and family-oriented magazines.

Medium 3:   Advertisements in Sunday supplements of major newspapers.

TABLE 3.1
Cost and Exposure Data for the Super Grain Corp. Advertising-Mix Problem

Cost Category	Costs		
	Each TV Commercial	Each Magazine Ad	Each Sunday Ad
Ad budget	$300,000	$150,000	$100,000
Planning budget	90,000	30,000	40,000
Expected number of exposures	1,300,000	600,000	500,000

The problem now is to determine which *levels* should be chosen for these *advertising activities* to obtain the most effective *advertising mix.*

To determine the *best mix of activity levels* for this particular advertising problem, it is necessary (as always) to identify the *overall measure of performance* for the problem and then the contribution of each activity toward this measure. An ultimate goal for Super Grain is to maximize its profits, but it is difficult to make a direct connection between advertising exposure and profits. Therefore, as a rough surrogate for profit, Claire decides to use *expected number of exposures* as the overall measure of performance, where each viewing of an advertisement by some individual counts as one exposure.

Giacomi & Jackowitz has made preliminary plans for advertisements in the three media. The firm also has estimated the expected number of exposures for each advertisement in each medium, as given in the bottom row of Table 3.1.

The number of advertisements that can be run in the different media are restricted by both the advertising budget (a limit of $4 million) and the planning budget (a limit of $1 million for the fee to Giacomi & Jackowitz). Another restriction is that there are only five commercial spots available for running different commercials (one commercial per spot) on children's television programs Saturday morning (medium 1) during the time of the promotional campaign. (The other two media have an ample number of spots available.)

Consequently, the three *resources* for this problem are:

Resource 1: Advertising budget ($4 million).

Resource 2: Planning budget ($1 million).

Resource 3: TV commercial spots available (5).

Table 3.1 shows how much of the advertising budget and the planning budget would be used by each advertisement in the respective media.

- The first row gives the cost per advertisement in each medium.
- The second row shows Giacomi & Jackowitz's estimates of its total cost (including overhead and profit) for designing and developing each advertisement for the respective media.[1] (This cost represents the billable fee from Super Grain.)
- The last row then gives the expected number of exposures per advertisement.

Analysis of the Problem

Claire decides to formulate and solve a linear programming model for this problem on a spreadsheet. The formulation procedure summarized at the end of Section 2.2 guides this process. Like any linear programming model, this model will have four components:

1. The data
2. The decisions
3. The constraints
4. The measure of performance

---

[1] When presenting its estimates in this form, the firm is making two simplifying assumptions. One is that its cost for designing and developing each additional advertisement in a medium is roughly the same as for the first advertisement in that medium. The second is that its cost when working with one medium is unaffected by how much work it is doing (if any) with the other media.

The spreadsheet needs to be formatted to provide the following kinds of cells for these components:

Four kinds of cells are needed for these four components of a spreadsheet model.

Data → data cells

Decisions → changing cells

Constraints → output cells

Measure of performance → target cell

Figure 3.1 shows the spreadsheet model formulated by Claire. Let us see how she did this by considering each of the components of the model individually.

FIGURE 3.1

The spreadsheet model for the Super Grain problem (Section 3.1), including the target cell TotalExposures (H13) and the other output cells BudgetSpent (F8:F9), as well as the specifications needed to set up the Solver. The changing cells NumberOfAds (C13:E13) show the optimal solution obtained by the Solver.

	A	B	C	D	E	F	G	H
1		**Super Grain Corp. Advertising-Mix Problem**						
2								
3			TV Spots	Magazine Ads	SS Ads			
4		Exposures per Ad	1,300	600	500			
5		(thousands)						
6						Budget		Budget
7			Cost per Ad ($thousands)			Spent		Available
8		Ad Budget	300	150	100	4,000	≤	4,000
9		Planning Budget	90	30	40	1,000	≤	1,000
10								
11								Total Exposures
12			TV Spots	Magazine Ads	SS Ads			(thousands)
13		Number of Ads	0	20	10			17,000
14			≤					
15		Max TV Spots	5					

Set Objective (Target Cell): TotalExposures
To: Max
By Changing (Variable) Cells:
  NumberOfAds
Subject to the Constraints:
  BudgetSpent <= BudgetAvailable
  TVSpots <= MaxTVSpots

Solver Options (Excel 2010):
  Make Variables Nonnegative
  Solving Method: Simplex LP
Solver Options (older Excel):
  Assume Nonnegative
  Assume Linear Model

	F
6	Budget
7	Spent
8	=SUMPRODUCT(C8:E8,NumberOfAds)
9	=SUMPRODUCT(C9:E9,NumberOfAds)

	H
11	Total Exposures
12	(thousands)
13	=SUMPRODUCT(ExposuresPerAd,NumberOfAds)

Range Name	Cells
BudgetAvailable	H8: H9
BudgetSpent	F8: F9
CostPerAd	C8: E9
ExposuresPerAd	C4: E4
MaxTVSpots	C15
NumberOfAds	C13: E13
TotalExposures	H13
TVSpots	C13

The Data

One important kind of data is the information given earlier about the amounts available of the three resources for the problem (the advertising budget, the planning budget, and the commercial spots available). Table 3.1 provides the other key data for the problem. Using units of thousands of dollars, these data have been transferred directly into data cells in the spreadsheet in Figure 3.1 and given these range names: ExposuresPerAd (C4:E4), CostPerAd (C8:E9), BudgetAvailable (H8:H9), and MaxTVSpots (C15).

The Decisions

The problem has been defined as determining the most effective advertising mix among the three media selected by Giacomi & Jackowitz. Therefore, there are three decisions:

Decision 1: TV = Number of commercials for separate spots on television.

Decision 2: M = Number of advertisements in magazines.

Decision 3: SS = Number of advertisements in Sunday supplements.

The changing cells to hold these numbers have been placed in row 13 in the columns for these media:

$$TV \rightarrow \text{cell C13} \qquad M \rightarrow \text{cell D13} \qquad SS \rightarrow \text{cell E13}$$

These changing cells are collectively referred to by the range name NumberOfAds (C13:E13).

The Constraints

These changing cells need to be nonnegative. In addition, constraints are needed for the three resources. The first two resources are the ad budget and planning budget. The amounts available for these two budgets are shown in the range BudgetAvailable (H8:H9). As suggested by the $\leq$ signs entered into column G, the corresponding constraints are

Total spending on advertising $\leq$ 4,000 (Ad budget in $1,000s)

Total cost of planning $\leq$ 1,000 (Planning budget in $1,000s)

Using the data in columns C, D, and E for the resources, these totals are

Total spending on advertising = $300TV + 150M + 100SS$

Total cost of planning = $90TV + 30M + 40SS$

These sums of products on the right-hand side are entered into the output cells BudgetSpent (F8:F9) by using the SUMPRODUCT functions shown in the lower right-hand side of Figure 3.1. Although the $\leq$ signs entered in column G are only cosmetic (trial solutions still can be entered in the changing cells that violate these inequalities), they will serve as a reminder later to use these same $\leq$ signs when entering the constraints in the Solver dialogue box.

Excel Tip: Range names may overlap. For instance, we have used NumberOfAds to refer to the whole range of changing cells, C13:E13, and TVSpots to refer to the single cell, C13.

The third resource is TV spots for different commercials. Five such spots are available for purchase. The number of spots used is one of the changing cells (C13). Since this cell will be used in a constraint, we assign the cell its own range name: TVSpots (C13). The maximum number of TV spots available is in the data cell MaxTVSpots (C15). Thus, the required constraint is TVSpots $\leq$ MaxTVSpots.

The Measure of Performance

Claire Syverson is using *expected number of exposures* as the overall measure of performance, so let

Exposure = Expected number of exposures (in thousands) from all the advertising

The data cells ExposuresPerAd (C4:E4) provide the expected number of exposures (in thousands) per advertisement in the respective media and the changing cells NumberOfAds (C13:E13) give the number of each type of advertisement. Therefore,

$$\text{Exposure} = 1{,}300TV + 600M + 500SS$$

$$= \text{SUMPRODUCT (ExposuresPerAd, NumberOfAds)}$$

is the formula that needs to be entered into the target cell, TotalExposures (H13).

Summary of the Formulation

The above analysis of the four components of the model has formulated the following linear programming model (in algebraic form) on the spreadsheet:

$$\text{Maximize} \quad \text{Exposure} = 1{,}300TV + 600M + 500SS$$

subject to

Ad spending:	$300TV + 150M + 100SS \leq 4{,}000$
Planning costs:	$90TV + 30M + 40SS \leq 1{,}000$
Number of television spots:	$TV \qquad\qquad\qquad \leq \quad 5$

and

$$TV \geq 0 \quad M \geq 0 \quad SS \geq 0$$

The difficult work of defining the problem and gathering all the relevant data in Table 3.1 leads directly to this formulation.

Solving the Model

To solve the spreadsheet model formulated above, some key information needs to be entered into the Solver dialogue box. The lower left-hand side of Figure 3.1 shows the needed entries: the target cell (TotalExposures), the changing cells (NumberOfAds), the objective of maximizing the target cell, and the constraints BudgetSpent ≤ BudgetAvailable and TVSpots ≤ MaxTVSpots. Two options are also specified at the bottom of the Solver Parameters box on the lower left-hand side of Figure 3.1. The changing cells need nonnegativity constraints (specified in the main Solver dialogue box in Excel 2010 and after clicking Options in earlier versions of Excel) because negative values of advertising are not possible. Choose the Simplex LP solving method (Excel 2010) or the Assume Linear Model option (after clicking Options in earlier versions of Excel), because this is a linear programming model. Clicking on the Solve button then tells the Solver to find an optimal solution for the model and display it in the changing cells.

The optimal solution given in row 13 of the spreadsheet provides the following plan for the promotional campaign:

Do not run any television commercials.

Run 20 advertisements in magazines.

Run 10 advertisements in Sunday supplements.

Since TotalExposures (H13) gives the expected number of exposures in thousands, this plan would be expected to provide 17,000,000 exposures.

Evaluation of the Adequacy of the Model

When she chose to use a linear programming model to represent this advertising-mix problem, Claire recognized that this kind of model does not provide a perfect match to this problem. However, a mathematical model is intended to be only an approximate representation of the real problem. Approximations and simplifying assumptions generally are required to have a workable model. All that is really needed is that there be a reasonably high correlation between the prediction of the model and what would actually happen in the real problem. The team now needs to check whether this criterion is satisfied.

Linear programming models allow fractional solutions.

One assumption of linear programming is that *fractional* solutions are allowed. For the current problem, this means that a fractional number (e.g., 3½) of television commercials (or of ads in magazines or Sunday supplements) should be allowed. This is technically true, since a commercial can be aired for less than a normal run, or an ad can be run in just a fraction of the usual magazines or Sunday supplements. However, one defect of the model is that it assumes that Giacomi & Jackowitz's cost for planning and developing a commercial or ad that receives only a fraction of its usual run is only that fraction of its usual cost, even though the actual cost would be the same as for a full run. Fortunately, the optimal solution obtained was an *integer* solution (0 television commercials, 20 ads in magazines, and 10 ads in Sunday supplements), so the assumption that fractional solutions are allowed was not even needed.

Although it is possible to have a fractional number of a normal run of commercials or ads, a normal run tends to be much more effective than a fractional run. Therefore, it would have been reasonable for Claire to drop the assumption that fractional solutions are allowed. If Claire had done this and the optimal solution for the linear programming model had not turned out to be integer, constraints can be added to require the changing cells to be integer. (The TBA Airlines example in the next section provides an illustration of this type of constraint.) After adding such constraints, the model is called an *integer programming model* instead of a linear programming model, but it still can be readily solved by the Excel Solver.

Another key assumption of linear programming is that the appropriate equation for each of the output cells, including the target cell, is one that can be expressed as a SUMPRODUCT of data cells and changing cells (or occasionally just a SUM of changing cells). For the target cell (cell H13) in Figure 3.1, this implies that the expected number of exposures to be obtained from each advertising medium is *proportional* to the number of advertisements in that medium. This proportionality seems true, since each viewing of the advertisements by some individual counts as another exposure. Another implication of using a SUMPRODUCT function is that the expected number of exposures to be obtained from an advertising medium is unaffected by the number of advertisements in the other media. Again, this implication seems valid, since viewings of advertisements in different media count as separate exposures.

> Linear programming models should use SUM or SUMPRODUCT functions for the output cells, including the target cell.

Although a SUMPRODUCT function is appropriate for calculating the expected number of exposures, the choice of this number for the overall measure of performance is somewhat questionable. Management's real objective is to maximize the profit generated as a result of the advertising campaign, but this is difficult to measure so *expected number of exposures* was selected to be a surrogate for profit. This would be valid if profit were proportional to the expected number of exposures. However, proportionality is only an approximation in this case because too many exposures for the same individual reach a saturation level where the impact (potential profit) from one more exposure is substantially less than for the first exposure. (When proportionality is not a reasonable approximation, Chapter 8 will describe nonlinear models that can be used instead.)

To check how reasonable it is to use expected number of exposures as a surrogate for profit, Claire meets with Sid Jackowitz, one of the senior partners of Giacomi & Jackowitz. Sid indicates that the contemplated promotional campaign (20 advertisements in magazines and 10 in Sunday supplements) is a relatively modest one well below saturation levels. Most readers will only notice these ads once or twice, and a second notice is very helpful for reinforcing the first one. Furthermore, the readership of magazines and Sunday supplements is sufficiently different that the interaction of the advertising impact in these two media should be small. Consequently, Claire concludes that using expected number of exposures for the target cell in Figure 3.1 provides a reasonable approximation. (A continuation of this case study in Case 8-1 will delve into the more complicated analysis that is required in order to use profit directly as the measure of performance to be recorded in the target cell instead of making this approximation.)

Next, Claire quizzes Sid about his firm's costs for planning and developing advertisements in these media. Is it reasonable to assume that the cost in a given medium is proportional to the number of advertisements in that medium? Is it reasonable to assume that the cost of developing advertisements in one medium would not be substantially reduced if the firm had just finished developing advertisements in another medium that might have similar themes? Sid acknowledges that there is some carryover in ad planning from one medium to another, especially if both are print media (e.g., magazines and Sunday supplements), but that the carryover is quite limited because of the distinct differences in these media. Furthermore, he feels that the proportionality assumption is quite reasonable for any given medium since the amount of work involved in planning and developing each additional advertisement in the medium is nearly the same as for the first one in the medium. The total fee that Super Grain will pay Giacomi & Jackowitz will eventually be based on a detailed accounting of the amount of work done by the firm. Nevertheless, Sid feels that the cost estimates previously provided by the firm (as entered in cells C9, D9, and E9 in units of thousands of dollars) give a reasonable basis for roughly projecting what the fee will be for any given plan (the entries in the changing cells) for the promotional campaign.

Based on this information, Claire concludes that using a SUMPRODUCT function for cell F9 provides a reasonable approximation. Doing the same for cell F8 is clearly justified. Given her earlier conclusions as well, Claire decides that the linear programming model incorporated into Figure 3.1 (plus any expansions of the model needed later for the detailed planning) is a sufficiently accurate representation of the real advertising-mix problem. It will not be necessary to refine the results from this model by turning next to a more complicated kind of mathematical model (such as those to be described in Chapter 8).

Therefore, Claire sends a memorandum to the company's president, David Sloan, describing a promotional campaign that corresponds to the optimal solution from the linear programming model (no TV commercials, 20 ads in magazines, and 10 ads in Sunday supplements). She also requests a meeting to evaluate this plan and discuss whether some modifications should be made.

We will pick up this story again in Section 3.4.

Review
Questions

1. What is the problem being addressed in this case study?
2. What overall measure of performance is being used?
3. What are the assumptions of linear programming that need to be checked to evaluate the adequacy of using a linear programming model to represent the problem under consideration?

3.2 RESOURCE-ALLOCATION PROBLEMS

In the opening paragraph of Chapter 2, we described managerial problems involving the allocation of an organization's resources to its various productive activities. Those were *resource-allocation* problems.

> **Resource-allocation problems** are linear programming problems involving the *allocation of resources to activities*. The *identifying feature* for any such problem is that each functional constraint in the linear programming model is a **resource constraint,** which has the form,
>
> Amount of resource used ≤ Amount of resource available
>
> for one of the resources.

The amount of a resource used depends on which activities are undertaken, the levels of those activities, and how heavily those activities need to use the resource. Thus, the resource constraints place limits on the levels of the activities. The objective is to choose the levels of the activities so as to maximize some overall measure of performance (such as total profit) from the activities while satisfying all the resource constraints.

Beginning with the case study and then the familiar Wyndor Glass Co. product-mix problem, we will look at four examples that illustrate the characteristics of resource-allocation problems. These examples also demonstrate how this type of problem can arise in a variety of contexts.

The Super Grain Corp. Advertising-Mix Problem

The linear programming model formulated in Section 3.1 for the Super Grain case study is one example of a resource-allocation problem. The three *activities* under consideration are the advertising in the three types of media chosen by Giacomi & Jackowitz.

Activity 1: TV commercials.

Activity 2: Magazine ads.

Activity 3: Sunday ads.

The decisions being made are the *levels* of these activities, that is, the *number* of TV commercials, magazine ads, and Sunday ads to run.

An initial step in formulating any resource-allocation problem is to identify the activities and the resources.

The *resources* to be allocated to these activities are

Resource 1:   Advertising budget ($4 million).

Resource 2:   Planning budget ($1 million).

Resource 3:   TV spots available for different commercials (5).

where the *amounts available* of these resources are given in parentheses. Thus, this problem has three resource constraints:

Advertising budget used	≤ $4 million
Planning budget used	≤ $1 million
TV spots used	≤ 5

Rows 8–9 and cells C13:C15 in Figure 3.1 show these constraints in a spreadsheet. Cells C8:E9 give the amount of the advertising budget and the planning budget used by *each unit* of each activity, that is, the amount used by one TV spot, one magazine ad, and one Sunday ad, respectively.

Cells C4, D4, and E4 on this spreadsheet give the *contribution per unit of each activity* to the overall measure of performance (expected number of exposures).

Characteristics of Resource-Allocation Problems

For each proposed activity, a decision needs to be made as to how much of the activity to do. In other words, what should the level of the activity be?

Other resource-allocation problems have the same kinds of characteristics as the Super Grain problem. In each case, there are activities where the decisions to be made are the *levels* of these activities. The contribution of each activity to the overall measure of performance is proportional to the level of that activity. Commonly, this measure of performance is the *total profit* from the activities, but occasionally it is something else (as in the Super Grain problem).

Every problem of this type has a resource constraint for each resource. The amounts of the resources used depend on the levels of the activities. For each resource, the amount used by each activity is proportional to the level of that activity.

These three kinds of data are needed for any resource-allocation problem.

The manager or management science team studying a resource allocation problem needs to gather (with considerable help) three kinds of data:

1. The *amount available* of each resource.
2. The amount of each resource needed by each activity. Specifically, for each combination of resource and activity, the *amount of the resource used per unit of the activity* must be estimated.
3. The *contribution per unit of each activity* to the overall measure of performance.

Generally there is considerable work involved in developing these data. A substantial amount of digging and consultation is needed to obtain the best estimates available in a timely fashion. This step is critical. Well-informed estimates are needed to obtain a valid linear programming model for guiding managerial decisions. The dangers involved in inaccurate estimates are one reason why *what-if analysis* (Chapter 5) is such an important part of most linear programming studies.

The Wyndor Glass Co. Product-Mix Problem

The product-mix problem facing the management of the Wyndor Glass Co. in Section 2.1 is to determine the most profitable mix of production rates for the two new products, considering the limited availability of spare production capacity in the company's three plants. This is a resource-allocation problem.

The *activities* under consideration are

Activity 1:   Produce the special new doors.

Activity 2:   Produce the special new windows.

The decisions being made are the *levels* of these activities, that is, the production rates for the doors and windows. Production rate is being measured as the number of units (doors or windows) produced per week. Management's objective is to maximize the total profit generated by the two new products, so the overall measure of performance is total profit. The contribution of each product to profit is proportional to the production rate for that product.

The *resources* to be allocated to these activities are

Resource 1:   Production capacity in Plant 1.
Resource 2:   Production capacity in Plant 2.
Resource 3:   Production capacity in Plant 3.

Each of the three functional constraints in the linear programming model formulated in Section 2.2 (see rows 7–9 of the spreadsheet in Figure 2.3 or 2.4) is a *resource constraint* for one of these three resources. Column E shows the amount of production capacity used in each plant and column G gives the amount available.

Table 2.1 in Section 2.1 provides the data for the Wyndor problem. You already have seen how the numbers in Table 2.1 become the parameters in the linear programming model in either its spreadsheet formulation (Section 2.2) or its algebraic form (Section 2.3).

The TBA Airlines Problem

TBA Airlines is a small regional company that specializes in short flights in small passenger airplanes. The company has been doing well and management has decided to expand its operations.

The Problem

The basic issue facing management now is whether to purchase more small airplanes to add some new short flights or to start moving into the national market by purchasing some large airplanes for new cross-country flights (or both). Many factors will go into management's final decision, but the most important one is which strategy is likely to be most profitable.

The first row of Table 3.2 shows the estimated net annual profit (inclusive of capital recovery costs) from each type of airplane purchased. The second row gives the purchase cost per airplane and also notes that the total amount of capital available for airplane purchases is $250 million. The third row records the fact that management does not want to purchase more than five small airplanes because of limited possibilities for adding lucrative short flights, whereas they have not specified a maximum number for large airplanes (other than that imposed by the limited capital available).

How many airplanes of each type should be purchased to maximize the total net annual profit?

Formulation

This is a *resource-allocation problem*. The activities under consideration are

Activity 1:   Purchase small airplanes.
Activity 2:   Purchase large airplanes.

The decisions to be made are the levels of these activities, that is,

S = Number of small airplanes to purchase
L = Number of large airplanes to purchase

The one resource to be allocated to these activities is

Resource: Investment capital ($250 million).

Thus, there is a single resource constraint:

$$\text{Investment capital spent} \leq \$250 \text{ million}$$

In addition, management has specified one side constraint,

$$\text{Number of small airplanes purchased} \leq 5$$

Figure 3.2 shows the formulation of a spreadsheet model for this problem, where the data in Table 3.2 have been transferred into the data cells—UnitProfit (C4:D4), CapitalPerUnitPurchased

TABLE 3.2
Data for the TBA Airlines Problem

	Small Airplane	Large Airplane	Capital Available
Net annual profit per airplane	$7 million	$22 million	
Purchase cost per airplane	$25 million	$75 million	$250 million
Maximum purchase quantity	5	No maximum	

FIGURE 3.2

A spreadsheet model for the TBA Airlines integer programming problem where the changing cells, UnitsProduced (C12:D12), show the optimal airplane purchases obtained by the Solver, and the target cell, TotalProfit (G12), gives the resulting total profit in millions of dollars.

	A	B	C	D	E	F	G
1		TBA Airlines Airplane Purchasing Problem					
2							
3			Small Airplane	Large Airplane			
4		Unit Profit ($millions)	7	22			
5							
6					Capital		Capital
7			Capital per Unit Purchased		Spent		Available
8		Capital ($millions)	25	75	250	<=	250
9							
10							Total Profit
11			Small Airplane	Large Airplane			($millions)
12		Number Purchased	1	3			73
13			<=				
14		Maximum Small Airplanes	5				

	E
6	Capital
7	Spent
8	=SUMPRODUCT(CapitalPerUnitPurchased,NumberPurchased)

	G
10	Total Profit
11	($millions)
12	=SUMPRODUCT(UnitProfit,NumberPurchased)

Solver Parameters

Set Objective (Target Cell): TotalProfit
To: Max
By Changing (Variable) Cells:
    NumberPurchased
Subject to the Constraints:
    CapitalSpent <= CapitalAvailable
    NumberPurchased = integer
    SmallAirplanes <= MaxSmallAirplanes

Solver Options (Excel 2010):
    Make Variables Nonnegative
    Solving Method: Simplex LP
Solver Options (older Excel):
    Assume Nonnegative
    Assume Linear Model

Range Name	Cells
Capital Available	G8
CapitalPerUnitPurchased	C8:D8
CapitalSpent	E8
MaxSmallAirplanes	C14
NumberPurchased	C12:D12
SmallAirplanes	C12
TotalProfit	G12
UnitProfit	C4:D4

(C8:D8), CapitalAvailable (G8), and MaxSmallAirplanes (C14). The resource constraint then appears in cells C8:G8 while C12:C14 shows the side constraint. The objective for this problem is to maximize the total net annual profit, so the equation for the target cell is

TotalProfit (G12) = SUMPRODUCT (UnitProfit, UnitsPurchased)

Since the TBA Airlines problem is a resource-allocation problem, this spreadsheet model has essentially the same form as the Super Grain and Wyndor problems except for one small difference. The changing cells in this case must have *integer* values since it is not feasible for the company to purchase and operate a fraction of an airplane. Therefore, constraints that the changing cells need to be integer are added in the Add Constraint dialogue box. Choose the range of these cells (C12:D12) as the left-hand side and then choose int from the pop-up menu between the left-hand and right-hand side.[2]

[2] On most versions of Excel, Solver will automatically fill in "integer" in the right-hand side of the Add Constraint dialogue box after choosing int from the pop-up menu. Macintosh versions prior to Excel 2008 leave the right-hand side of the Add Constraint dialogue box blank and then give an error message if you click OK. Typing "integer" into the right-hand side before clicking OK is a workaround.

These changing cells in Figure 3.2 show the optimal solution, $(S, L) = (1, 3)$, obtained after clicking on the Solve button.

One of the assumptions of linear programming is that the changing cells are allowed to have *any* values, including *fractional* values, that satisfy the functional and nonnegativity constraints. Therefore, technically speaking, the TBA problem is not a linear programming problem because of adding the constraints,

$$\text{UnitsProduced} = \text{Integer}$$

Excel Tip: To constrain a range of changing cells to be integer, choose the range of cells in the left-hand side of the Add Constraint dialogue box and choose int from the pop-up menu. Clicking OK then enters the constraint that these cells = integer in the Solver dialogue box.

that are displayed in the Solver Parameters box in Figure 3.2. Such a problem that fits linear programming except for adding such constraints is called an **integer programming problem.** The method used by Solver to solve integer programming problems is quite different from that for solving linear programming problems. In fact, integer programming problems tend to be much more difficult to solve than linear programming problems so there is considerably more limitation on the size of the problem. However, this doesn't matter to a spreadsheet modeler dealing with small problems. From his or her viewpoint, there is virtually no distinction between linear programming and integer programming problems. They are formulated in exactly the same way. Then, at the very end, a decision needs to be made as to whether any of the changing cells need to be restricted to integer values. If so, those constraints are added as described above. Keep this option in mind as we continue to discuss the formulation of various types of linear programming problems throughout the chapter.

Summary of the Formulation

The above formulation of a model with one resource constraint and one side constraint for the TBA Airlines problem now can be summarized (in algebraic form) as follows.

$$\text{Maximize} \quad \text{Profit} = 7S + 22L$$

subject to

$$25S + 75L \leq 250$$
$$S \qquad \leq \quad 5$$

and

$$S \geq 0 \qquad L \geq 0$$

Excel Tip: Even when a changing cell is constrained to be integer, rounding errors occasionally will cause Excel to return a noninteger value very close to an integer (e.g., 1.23E-10, meaning 0.000000000123). To make the spreadsheet cleaner, you may replace these "ugly" representations by their proper integer values in the changing cells.

Excel Tip: In the Solver Options of Excel 2010, the *Integer Optimality* (%) setting (1 percent by default) causes Solver to stop solving an integer programming problem when it finds a feasible solution whose objective function value is within the specified percentage of being optimal. (In earlier versions of Excel, this option is referred to as *Tolerance,* and the default is 5 percent.) This is useful to speed up solving large problems. For smaller problems (e.g., homework problems), this option should be set to 0 to guarantee finding an optimal solution.

Capital Budgeting

Financial planning is one of the most important areas of application for resource-allocation problems. The resources being allocated in this area are quite different from those for applications in the *production planning* area (such as the Wyndor Glass Co. product-mix problem), where the resources tend to be *production facilities* of various kinds. For financial planning, the resources tend to be *financial assets* such as cash, securities, accounts receivable, lines of credit, and so forth. Our specific example involves *capital budgeting,* where the resources are amounts of investment capital available at different points in time.

The Problem

The **Think-Big Development Co.** is a major investor in commercial real-estate development projects. It currently has the opportunity to share in three large construction projects:

Project 1:   Construct a high-rise office building.
Project 2:   Construct a hotel.
Project 3:   Construct a shopping center.

Each project requires each partner to make investments at four different points in time: a down payment now, and additional capital after one, two, and three years. Table 3.3 shows for each project the *total* amount of investment capital required from all the partners at these four points in time. Thus, a partner taking a certain percentage share of a project is obligated to invest that percentage of each of the amounts shown in the table for the project.

TABLE 3.3
Financial Data for
the Projects Being
Considered for Partial
Investment by the
Think-Big
Development Co.

	Investment Capital Requirements		
Year	**Office Building**	**Hotel**	**Shopping Center**
0	$40 million	$80 million	$90 million
1	60 million	80 million	50 million
2	90 million	80 million	20 million
3	10 million	70 million	60 million
Net present value	$45 million	$70 million	$50 million

All three projects are expected to be very profitable in the long run. So the management of Think-Big wants to invest as much as possible in some or all of them. Management is willing to commit all the company's investment capital currently available, as well as all additional investment capital expected to become available over the next three years. The objective is to determine the *investment mix* that will be most profitable, based on current estimates of profitability.

Since it will be several years before each project begins to generate income, which will continue for many years thereafter, we need to take into account the *time value of money* in evaluating how profitable it might be. This is done by *discounting* future cash outflows (capital invested) and cash inflows (income), and then adding discounted net cash flows, to calculate a project's *net present value*.

Based on current estimates of future cash flows (not included here except for outflows), the estimated net present value for each project is shown in the bottom row of Table 3.3. All the investors, including Think-Big, then will split this net present value in proportion to their share of the total investment.

For each project, *participation shares* are being sold to major investors, such as Think-Big, who become the partners for the project by investing their proportional shares at the four specified points in time. For example, if Think-Big takes a 10 percent share of the office building, it will need to provide $4 million now, and then $6 million, $9 million, and $1 million in 1 year, 2 years, and 3 years, respectively.

The company currently has $25 million available for capital investment. Projections are that another $20 million will become available after one year, $20 million more after two years, and another $15 million after three years. What share should Think-Big take in the respective projects to maximize the total net present value of these investments?

Formulation

This is a *resource-allocation problem*. The activities under consideration are

Activity 1: Invest in the construction of an office building.

Activity 2: Invest in the construction of a hotel.

Activity 3: Invest in the construction of a shopping center.

Thus, the decisions to be made are the levels of these activities, that is, what participation share to take in investing in each of these projects. A participation share can be expressed as either a fraction or a percentage of the entire project, so the entire project is considered to be one "unit" of that activity.

The resources to be allocated to these activities are the funds available at the four investment points. Funds not used at one point are available at the next point. (For simplicity, we will ignore any interest earned on these funds.) Therefore, the *resource constraint* for each point must reflect the cumulative funds to that point.

Resource 1: Total investment capital available now.

Resource 2: Cumulative investment capital available by the end of one year.

Resource 3: Cumulative investment capital available by the end of two years.

Resource 4: Cumulative investment capital available by the end of three years.

TABLE 3.4
Resource Data for the
Think-Big Development
Co. Investment-Mix
Problem

	Cumulative Investment Capital Required for an Entire Project			
Resource	**Office Building**	**Hotel**	**Shopping Center**	**Amount of Resource Available**
1 (Now)	$ 40 million	$ 80 million	$ 90 million	$25 million
2 (End of year 1)	100 million	160 million	140 million	45 million
3 (End of year 2)	190 million	240 million	160 million	65 million
4 (End of year 3)	200 million	310 million	220 million	80 million

Since the amount of investment capital available is $25 million now, another $20 million in one year, another $20 million in two years, and another $15 million in three years, the amounts available of the resources are the following.

Amount of resource 1 available = $25 million

Amount of resource 2 available = $(25 + 20) million = $45 million

Amount of resource 3 available = $(25 + 20 + 20) million = $65 million

Amount of resource 4 available = $(25 + 20 + 20 + 15) million = $80 million

Table 3.4 shows all the data involving these resources. The rightmost column gives the amounts of resources available calculated above. The middle columns show the *cumulative* amounts of the investment capital requirements listed in Table 3.3. For example, in the Office Building column of Table 3.4, the second number ($100 million) is obtained by adding the first two numbers ($40 million and $60 million) in the Office Building column of Table 3.3.

The Data   As with any resource-allocation problem, three kinds of data need to be gathered. One is the amounts available of the resources, as given in the rightmost column of Table 3.4. A second is the amount of each resource needed by each project, which is given in the middle columns of this table. A third is the contribution of each project to the overall measure of performance (net present value), as given in the bottom row of Table 3.3.

The first step in formulating the spreadsheet model is to enter these data into data cells in the spreadsheet. In Figure 3.3, the data cells (and their range names) are NetPresentValue (C5:E5), CapitalRequired (C9:E12), and CapitalAvailable (H9:H12). To save space on the spreadsheet, these numbers are entered in units of millions of dollars.

The Decisions   With three activities under consideration, there are three decisions to be made.

Decision 1:   *OB* = Participation share in the office building

Decision 2:   *H* = Participation share in the hotel

Decision 3:   *SC* = Participation share in the shopping center

For example, if Think-Big management were to decide to take a one-tenth participation share (i.e., a 10 percent participation share) in each of these projects, then

$OB = 0.1 = 10\%$

$H = 0.1 = 10\%$

$SC = 0.1 = 10\%$

However, it may not be desirable to take the same participation share (expressed as either a fraction or a percentage) in each of the projects, so the idea is to choose the best combination of values of *OB, H,* and *SC.* In Figure 3.3, the participation shares (expressed as percentages) have been placed in changing cells under the data cells (row 16) in the columns for the three projects, so

$$OB \rightarrow \text{cell C16} \qquad H \rightarrow \text{D16} \qquad SC \rightarrow \text{cell E16}$$

where these cells are collectively referred to by the range name ParticipationShare (C16:E16).

The Constraints The numbers in these changing cells make sense only if they are nonnegative, so the *Assume Non-Negative* option will need to be selected in the Solver dialogue box. In addition, the four resources require resource constraints:

Total invested now	≤ 25	(millions of dollars available)
Total invested within 1 year	≤ 45	(millions of dollars available)
Total invested within 2 years	≤ 65	(millions of dollars available)
Total invested within 3 years	≤ 80	(millions of dollars available)

The data in columns C, D, and E indicate that (in millions of dollars)

$$\text{Total invested now} = 40\, OB + 80\, H + 90\, SC$$
$$\text{Total invested within 1 year} = 100\, OB + 160\, H + 140\, SC$$
$$\text{Total invested within 2 years} = 190\, OB + 240\, H + 160\, SC$$
$$\text{Total invested within 3 years} = 200\, OB + 310\, H + 220\, SC$$

These totals are calculated in the output cells CapitalSpent (F9:F12) using the SUMPRODUCT function, as shown below the spreadsheet in Figure 3.3. Finally, $\leq$ signs are entered into column G to indicate the resource constraints that will need to be entered in the Solver dialogue box.

FIGURE 3.3

The spreadsheet model for the Think-Big problem, including the formulas for the target cell TotalNPV (H16) and the other output cells CapitalSpent (F9:F12), as well as the specifications needed to set up the Solver. The changing cells ParticipationShare (C16:E16) show the optimal solution obtained by the Solver.

	A	B	C	D	E	F	G	H
1		**Think-Big Development Co. Capital Budgeting Program**						
2								
3			Office		Shopping			
4			Building	Hotel	Center			
5		Net Present Value	45	70	50			
6		($millions)				Cumulative		Cumulative
7						Capital		Capital
8			Cumulative Capital Required ($millions)			Spent		Available
9		Now	40	80	90	25	$\leq$	25
10		End of Year 1	100	160	140	44.76	$\leq$	45
11		End of Year 2	190	240	160	60.58	$\leq$	65
12		End of Year 3	200	310	220	80	$\leq$	80
13								
14			Office		Shopping			Total NPV
15			Building	Hotel	Center			($millions)
16		Participation Share	0.00%	16.50%	13.11%			18.11

Range Name	Cells
CapitalAvailable	H9:H12
CapitalRequired	C9:E12
CapitalSpent	F9:F12
ParticipationShare	C16:E16
NetPresentValue	C5:E5
TotalNPV	H16

	F
6	Cumulative
7	Capital
8	Spent
9	=SUMPRODUCT(C9:E9,ParticipationShare)
10	=SUMPRODUCT(C10:E10,ParticipationShare)
11	=SUMPRODUCT(C11:E11,ParticipationShare)
12	=SUMPRODUCT C12:E12,ParticipationShare)

	H
14	Total NPV
15	($millions)
16	=SUMPRODUCT(NetPresentValue,ParticipationShare)

The Measure of Performance   The objective is to

$$\text{Maximize} \quad NPV = \text{total } \textit{net present value} \text{ of the investments}$$

NetPresentValue (C5:E5) shows the net present value of each entire project, while Participation-Share (C16:E16) shows the participation share for each of the projects. Therefore, the total net present value of all the participation shares purchased in all three projects is (in millions of dollars)

$$NPV = 45 \, OB + 70 \, H + 50 \, SC$$
$$= \text{SUMPRODUCT (NetPresentValue, ParticipationShare)}$$
$$\rightarrow \text{ cell H16}$$

Summary of the Formulation   This completes the formulation of the linear programming model on the speadsheet, as summarized below (in algebraic form).

$$\text{Maximize} \quad NPV = 45 \, OB + 70 \, H + 50 \, SC$$

subject to

Total invested now:	$40 \, OB + 80 \, H + 90 \, SC \leq 25$
Total invested within 1 year:	$100 \, OB + 160 \, H + 140 \, SC \leq 45$
Total invested within 2 years:	$190 \, OB + 240 \, H + 160 \, SC \leq 65$
Total invested within 3 years:	$200 \, OB + 310 \, H + 220 \, SC \leq 80$

and

$$OB \geq 0 \quad H \geq 0 \quad SC \geq 0$$

where all these numbers are in units of millions of dollars.

Note that this model possesses the key *identifying feature* for resource-allocation problems, namely, each functional constraint is a *resource constraint* that has the form

$$\text{Amount of resource used} \leq \text{Amount of resource available}$$

Solving the Model   The lower left-hand side of Figure 3.3 shows the entries needed in the Solver dialogue box to specify the model, along with the selection of the usual two options. The spreadsheet shows the resulting optimal solution in row 16, namely,

Invest nothing in the office building.
Invest in 16.50 percent of the hotel.
Invest in 13.11 percent of the shopping center.

TotalNPV (H16) indicates that this investment program would provide a total net present value of $18.11 million.

This amount actually is only an estimate of what the total net present value would turn out to be, depending on the accuracy of the financial data given in Table 3.3. There is some uncertainty about the construction costs for the three real estate projects, so the actual investment capital requirements for years 1, 2, and 3 may deviate somewhat from the amounts specified in this table. Because of the risk involved in these projects, the net present value for each one also might deviate from the amounts given at the bottom of the table. Chapter 5 describes one approach to analyzing the effect of such deviations. Chapters 12 and 13 will present another technique, called *computer simulation,* for systematically taking future uncertainties into account. Section 13.5 will focus on further analysis of this same example.

Another Look at Resource Constraints

These examples of resource-allocation problems illustrate a variety of resources: financial allocations for advertising and planning purposes, TV commercial spots available for purchase, available production capacities of different plants, the total amount of capital available for investment, and cumulative investment capital available by certain times. However, these illustrations only scratch the surface of the realm of possible resources that need to be allocated to activities in resource-allocation problems. In fact, by interpreting *resource* sufficiently broadly, *any* restriction on the decisions to be made that has the form

Amount used ≤ Amount available

can be thought of as a *resource constraint,* where the thing whose amount is being measured is the corresponding "resource." Since *any* functional constraint with a ≤ sign in a linear programming model (including the side constraint in the TBA Airlines example) can be verbalized in this form, any such constraint can be thought of as a resource constraint.

> Hereafter, we will use **resource constraint** to refer to *any* functional constraint with a ≤ sign in a linear programming model. The constant on the right-hand side represents the *amount available* of a resource. Therefore, the left-hand side represents the *amount used* of this resource. In the algebraic form of the constraint, the coefficient (positive or negative) of each decision variable is the *resource usage per unit* of the corresponding activity.

Summary of the Formulation Procedure for Resource-Allocation Problems

The four examples illustrate that the following steps are used for any resource-allocation problem to define the specific problem, gather the relevant data, and then formulate the linear programming model.

1. Since any linear programming problem involves finding the *best mix* of levels of various activities, identify these *activities* for the problem at hand. The decisions to be made are the levels of these activities.
2. From the viewpoint of management, identify an appropriate *overall measure of performance* (commonly *profit,* or a surrogate for profit) for solutions of the problem.
3. For each activity, estimate the *contribution per unit of the activity* to this overall measure of performance.
4. Identify the *resources* that must be allocated to the activities.
5. For each resource, identify the *amount available* and then the *amount used per unit of each activity.*
6. Enter the data gathered in steps 3 and 5 into *data cells* in a spreadsheet. A convenient format is to have the data associated with each activity in a separate column, the data for the unit profit and each constraint in a separate row, and to leave two blank columns between the *activity* columns and the *amount of resource available* column. Figure 3.4 shows a template of the overall format of a spreadsheet model for resource-allocation problems.

FIGURE 3.4

A template of a spreadsheet model for pure resource-allocation problems.

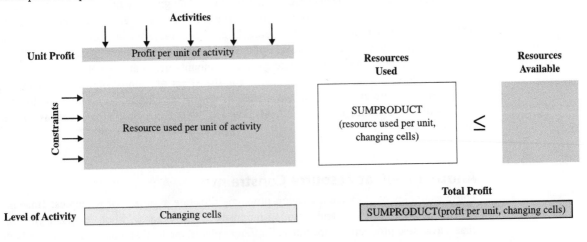

7. Designate *changing cells* for displaying the decisions on activity levels.

8. For the two blank columns created in step 6, use the left one as a *Totals* column for *output cells* and enter ≤ signs into the right one for all the resources. In the row for each resource, use the SUMPRODUCT function to enter the *total amount used* in the Totals column.

9. Designate a *target cell* for displaying the overall measure of performance. Use a SUMPRODUCT function to enter this measure of performance.

All the functional constraints in this linear programming model in a spreadsheet are *resource constraints,* that is, constraints with a ≤ sign. This is the *identifying feature* that classifies the problem as being a resource-allocation problem.

Review
Questions

1. What is the identifying feature for a resource-allocation problem?
2. What is the form of a resource constraint?
3. What are the three kinds of data that need to be gathered for a resource-allocation problem?
4. Compare the types of activities for the four examples of resource-allocation problems.
5. Compare the types of resources for the four examples of resource-allocation problems.

3.3   COST–BENEFIT–TRADE-OFF PROBLEMS

Cost–benefit–trade-off problems have a form that is very different from resource-allocation problems. The difference arises from *managerial objectives* that are very different for the two kinds of problems.

For resource-allocation problems, limits are set on the use of various resources (including financial resources), and then the objective is to make the most effective use (according to some overall measure of performance) of these given resources.

For cost–benefit–trade-off problems, management takes a more aggressive stance, prescribing what *benefits* must be achieved by the activities under consideration (regardless of the resulting resource usage), and then the objective is to achieve all these benefits with *minimum cost.* By prescribing a *minimum acceptable level* for each kind of benefit, and then minimizing the cost needed to achieve these levels, management hopes to obtain an appropriate *trade-off* between cost and benefits. (You will see in Chapter 5 that *what-if analysis* plays a key role in providing the additional information needed for management to choose the best trade-off between cost and benefits.)

A cost–benefit–trade-off formulation enables management to specify minimum goals for the benefits that need to be achieved by the activities.

> **Cost–benefit–trade-off problems** are linear programming problems where the mix of levels of various activities is chosen to achieve minimum acceptable levels for various benefits at a minimum cost. The *identifying feature* is that each functional constraint is a **benefit constraint,** which has the form

$$\text{Level achieved} \geq \text{Minimum acceptable level}$$

for one of the benefits.

Interpreting *benefit* broadly, we can think of *any* functional constraint with a ≥ sign as a *benefit constraint.* In most cases, the *minimum acceptable level* will be prescribed by management as a policy decision, but occasionally this number will be dictated by other circumstances.

For any cost–benefit–trade-off problem, a major part of the study involves identifying all the activities and benefits that should be considered and then gathering the data relevant to these activities and benefits.

These three kinds of data are needed for any cost–benefit–trade-off problem.

Three kinds of data are needed:

1. The *minimum acceptable level* for each benefit (a managerial policy decision).
2. For each benefit, the *contribution of each activity* to that benefit (per unit of the activity).
3. The *cost* per unit of each activity.

Let's examine two examples of cost–benefit–trade-off problems.

The Profit & Gambit Co. Advertising-Mix Problem

As described in Section 2.6, the Profit & Gambit Co. will be undertaking a major new advertising campaign focusing on three cleaning products. The two kinds of advertising to be used are television and the print media. Management has established minimum goals—the minimum acceptable increase in sales for each product—to be gained by the campaign.

The problem is to determine how much to advertise in each medium to meet all the sales goals at a minimum total cost.

An initial step in formulating any cost–benefit–trade-off problem is to identify the activities and the benefits.

The activities in this cost–benefit–trade-off problem are:

Activity 1:   Advertise on television.

Activity 2:   Advertise in the print media.

The benefits being sought from these activities are:

Benefit 1:   Increased sales for a spray prewash stain remover.

Benefit 2:   Increased sales for a liquid laundry detergent.

Benefit 3:   Increased sales for a powder laundry detergent.

Management wants these increased sales to be at least 3 percent, 18 percent, and 4 percent, respectively. As shown in Section 2.6, each benefit leads to a *benefit constraint* that incorporates the managerial goal for the *minimum acceptable level* of increase in the sales for the corresponding product, namely,

Level of benefit 1 achieved $\geq 3\%$

Level of benefit 2 achieved $\geq 18\%$

Level of benefit 3 achieved $\geq 4\%$

The data for this problem are given in Table 2.2 (Section 2.6). Section 2.6 describes how the linear programming model is formulated directly from the numbers in this table.

This example provides an interesting contrast with the Super Grain Corp. case study in Section 3.1, which led to a formulation as a resource-allocation problem. Both are advertising-mix problems, yet they lead to entirely different linear programming models. They differ because of the differences in the managerial view of the key issues in each case:

- As the vice president for marketing of Super Grain, Claire Syverson focused first on how much to spend on the advertising campaign and then set limits (an advertising budget of $4 million and a planning budget of $1 million) that led to resource constraints.
- The management of Profit & Gambit instead focused on what it wanted the advertising campaign to accomplish and then set goals (minimum required increases in sales) that led to benefit constraints.

From this comparison, we see that it is not the nature of the *application* that determines the classification of the resulting linear programming formulation. Rather, it is the nature of the *restrictions* imposed on the decisions regarding the mix of activity levels. If the restrictions involve *limits* on the usage of resources, that identifies a resource-allocation problem. If the restrictions involve *goals* on the levels of benefits, that characterizes a cost–benefit–trade-off problem. Frequently, the nature of the restrictions arise from the way management frames the problem.

However, we don't want you to get the idea that every linear programming problem falls entirely and neatly into either one type or the other. In the preceding section and this one, we are looking at *pure* resource-allocation problems and *pure* cost–benefit–trade-off problems. Although many *real* problems tend to be either one type or the other, it is fairly common to have *both* resource constraints and benefit constraints, even though one may predominate. (In the next section, you will see an example of how both types of constraints can arise in the same problem when the management of the Super Grain Corporation introduces additional considerations into the analysis of their advertising-mix problem.) Furthermore, we still need to consider additional categories of linear programming problems in the remaining sections of this chapter.

Now, another example of a pure cost–benefit–trade-off problem.

Personnel Scheduling

One of the common applications of cost–benefit–trade-off analysis involves personnel scheduling for a company that provides some kind of service, where the objective is to schedule the

An Application Vignette

Cost control is essential for survival in the airline industry. Therefore, upper management of **United Airlines** initiated a management science study to improve the utilization of personnel at the airline's reservations offices and airports by matching work schedules to customer needs more closely. The number of employees needed at each location to provide the required level of service varies greatly during the 24-hour day and might fluctuate considerably from one half hour to the next.

Trying to design the work schedules for all the employees at a given location to meet these service requirements most efficiently is a nightmare of combinatorial considerations. Once an employee arrives, he or she will be there continuously for the entire shift (2 to 10 hours, depending on the employee), *except* for either a meal break or short rest breaks every two hours. Given the *minimum* number of employees needed on duty for *each* half-hour interval over a 24-hour day (this minimum changes from day to day over a seven-day week), *how many* employees of *each shift length* should begin work at *what start time* over *each* 24-hour day of a seven-day week? Fortunately, linear programming thrives on such combinatorial nightmares. The linear programming model for some of the locations scheduled involves over 20,000 decisions!

This application of linear programming was credited with *saving United Airlines more than* **$6 million** *annually* in just direct salary and benefit costs. Other benefits included improved customer service and reduced workloads for support staff.

Source: T. J. Holloran and J. E. Bryne, "United Airlines Station Manpower Planning System," *Interfaces* 16, no. 1 (January–February 1986), pp. 39–50. (A link to this article is provided on our Web site, **www.mhhe.com/hillier4e.**)

work times of the company's employees so as to minimize the cost of providing the level of service specified by management. The following example illustrates how this can be done.

The Problem

Union Airways is adding more flights to and from its hub airport and so needs to hire additional customer service agents. However, it is not clear just how many more should be hired. Management recognizes the need for cost control while also consistently providing a satisfactory level of service to the company's customers, so a desirable trade-off between these two factors is being sought. Therefore, a management science team is studying how to schedule the agents to provide satisfactory service with the smallest personnel cost.

Based on the new schedule of flights, an analysis has been made of the *minimum* number of customer service agents that need to be on duty at different times of the day to provide a satisfactory level of service. (The queueing models presented in Chapter 11 can be used to determine the minimum numbers of agents needed to keep customer waiting times reasonable.) These numbers are shown in the last column of Table 3.5 for the time periods given in the first column. The other entries in this table reflect one of the provisions in the company's current contract with the union that represents the customer service agents. The provision is that each agent works an eight-hour shift. The authorized shifts are

Shift 1:	6:00 AM to 2:00 PM.
Shift 2:	8:00 AM to 4:00 PM.
Shift 3:	Noon to 8:00 PM.
Shift 4:	4:00 PM to midnight.
Shift 5:	10:00 PM to 6:00 AM.

TABLE 3.5
Data for the Union Airways Personnel Scheduling Problem

Time Period	Time Periods Covered by Shift					Minimum Number of Agents Needed
	1	2	3	4	5	
6:00 AM to 8:00 AM	✔					48
8:00 AM to 10:00 AM	✔	✔				79
10:00 AM to noon	✔	✔				65
Noon to 2:00 PM	✔	✔	✔			87
2:00 PM to 4:00 PM		✔	✔			64
4:00 PM to 6:00 PM			✔	✔		73
6:00 PM to 8:00 PM			✔	✔		82
8:00 PM to 10:00 PM				✔		43
10:00 PM to midnight				✔	✔	52
Midnight to 6:00 AM					✔	15
Daily cost per agent	$170	$160	$175	$180	$195	

Check marks in the main body of Table 3.5 show the time periods covered by the respective shifts. Because some shifts are less desirable than others, the wages specified in the contract differ by shift. For each shift, the daily compensation (including benefits) for each agent is shown in the bottom row. The problem is to determine how many agents should be assigned to the respective shifts each day to minimize the *total* personnel cost for agents, based on this bottom row, while meeting (or surpassing) the service requirements given in the last column.

Formulation

This problem is, in fact, a pure cost–benefit–trade-off problem. To formulate the problem, we need to identify the *activities* and *benefits* involved.

Activities correspond to shifts.

The *level* of each activity is the number of agents assigned to that shift.

A *unit* of each activity is one agent assigned to that shift.

Thus, the general description of a linear programming problem as finding the *best mix of activity levels* can be expressed for this specific application as finding the *best mix of shift sizes*.

Benefits correspond to time periods.

For each time period, the *benefit* provided by the activities is the service that agents provide customers during that period.

The *level* of a benefit is measured by the number of agents on duty during that time period.

Once again, a careful formulation of the problem, including gathering all the relevant data, leads rather directly to a spreadsheet model. This model is shown in Figure 3.5, and we outline its formulation below.

The Data As indicated in this figure, all the data in Table 3.5 have been entered directly into the data cells CostPerShift (C5:G5), ShiftWorksTimePeriod (C8:G17), and MinimumNeeded (J8:J17). For the ShiftWorksTimePeriod (C8:G17) data, an entry of 1 indicates that the corresponding shift includes that time period whereas 0 indicates not. Like any cost–benefit–trade-off problem, these numbers indicate the contribution of each activity to each benefit. Each agent working a shift contributes either 0 or 1 toward the minimum number of agents needed in a time period.

The Decisions Since the activities in this case correspond to the five shifts, the decisions to be made are

S_1 = Number of agents to assign to Shift 1 (starts at 6 AM)

S_2 = Number of agents to assign to Shift 2 (starts at 8 AM)

S_3 = Number of agents to assign to Shift 3 (starts at noon)

S_4 = Number of agents to assign to Shift 4 (starts at 4 PM)

S_5 = Number of agents to assign to Shift 5 (starts at 10 PM)

The changing cells to hold these numbers have been placed in the activity columns in row 21, so

$$S_1 \rightarrow \text{cell C21} \qquad S_2 \rightarrow \text{cell D21} \qquad \ldots \qquad S_5 \rightarrow \text{cell G21}$$

where these cells are collectively referred to by the range name NumberWorking (C21:G21).

The Constraints These changing cells need to be nonnegative. In addition, we need 10 *benefit constraints,* where each one specifies that the *total* number of agents serving in the corresponding time period listed in column B must be no less than the minimum acceptable number given in column J. Thus, these constraints are

Total number of agents serving 6–8 AM	≥ 48 (min. acceptable)
Total number of agents serving 8–10 AM	≥ 79 (min. acceptable)

.

.

.

Total number of agents serving midnight–6 AM	≥ 15 (min. acceptable)

FIGURE 3.5

The spreadsheet model for the Union Airways problem, including the formulas for the target cell TotalCost (J21) and the other output cells TotalWorking (H8:H17), as well as the specifications needed to set up the Solver. The changing cells NumberWorking (C21:G21) show the optimal solution obtained by the Solver.

	A	B	C	D	E	F	G	H	I	J
1		**Union Airways Personnel Scheduling Problem**								
2										
3			6AM–2PM	8AM–4PM	Noon–8PM	4PM–Midnight	10PM–6AM			
4			Shift	Shift	Shift	Shift	Shift			
5		Cost per Shift	$170	$160	$175	$180	$195			
6								Total		Minimum
7		Time Period			Shift Works Time Period? (1=yes, 0=no)			Working		Needed
8		6AM–8AM	1	0	0	0	0	48	≥	48
9		8AM–10AM	1	1	0	0	0	79	≥	79
10		10AM–12PM	1	1	0	0	0	79	≥	65
11		12PM–2PM	1	1	1	0	0	118	≥	87
12		2PM–4PM	0	1	1	0	0	70	≥	64
13		4PM–6PM	0	0	1	1	0	82	≥	73
14		6PM–8PM	0	0	1	1	0	82	≥	82
15		8PM–10PM	0	0	0	1	0	43	≥	43
16		10PM–12AM	0	0	0	1	1	58	≥	52
17		12AM–6AM	0	0	0	0	1	15	≥	15
18										
19			6AM–2PM	8AM–4PM	Noon–8PM	4PM–Midnight	10PM–6AM			
20			Shift	Shift	Shift	Shift	Shift			Total Cost
21		Number Working	48	31	39	43	15			$30,610

Solver Parameters

Set Objective (Target Cell): TotalCost
To: Min
By Changing (Variable) Cells:
  NumberWorking
Subject to the Constraints:
  NumberWorking = integer
  TotalWorking >= MinimumNeeded

Solver Options (Excel 2010):
  Make Variables Nonnegative
  Solving Method: Simplex LP
Solver Options (older Excel):
  Assume Nonnegative
  Assume Linear Model

Range Name	Cells
CostPerShift	C5:G5
MinimumNeeded	J8:J17
NumberWorking	C21:G21
ShiftWorksTimePeriod	C8:G17
TotalCost	J21
TotalWorking	H8:H17

	H
6	Total
7	Working
8	=SUMPRODUCT(C8:G8,NumberWorking)
9	=SUMPRODUCT(C9:G9,NumberWorking)
10	=SUMPRODUCT(C10:G10,NumberWorking)
11	=SUMPRODUCT(C11:G11,NumberWorking)
12	=SUMPRODUCT(C12:G12,NumberWorking)
13	=SUMPRODUCT(C13:G13,NumberWorking)
14	=SUMPRODUCT(C14:G14,NumberWorking)
15	=SUMPRODUCT(C15:G15,NumberWorking)
16	=SUMPRODUCT(C16:G16,NumberWorking)
17	=SUMPRODUCT(C17:G17,NumberWorking)

	J
20	Total Cost
21	=SUMPRODUCT(CostPerShift,NumberWorking)

Since columns C to G indicate which of the shifts serve each of the time periods, these totals are

Total number of agents serving 6–8 AM	$= S_1$
Total number of agents serving 8–10 AM	$= S_1 + S_2$

.

.

.

Total number of agents serving midnight–6 AM	$= S_5$

These totals are calculated in the output cells TotalWorking (H8:H17) using the SUMPRODUCT functions shown below the spreadsheet in Figure 3.5.

One other type of constraint is that the number of agents assigned to each shift must have an integer value. These constraints for the five shifts should be added in the same way as described for the TBA Airlines problem in Section 3.2. In particular, they are added in the Add Constraint dialogue box by entering Number Working on the left-hand side and then choosing int from the pop-up menu between the left-hand side and the right-hand side. The set of constraints, NumberWorking = integer, then appears in the Solver dialogue box, as shown in Figure 3.5.

The Measure of Performance   The objective is to

$$\text{Minimize} \quad \text{Cost} = \text{Total daily personnel cost for all agents}$$

Since CostPerShift (C5:G5) gives the daily cost per agent on each shift and NumberWorking (C21:G21) gives the number of agents working each shift,

$$\text{Cost} = 170S_1 + 160S_2 + 175S_3 + 180S_4 + 195S_5 \quad (\text{in dollars})$$
$$= \text{SUMPRODUCT (CostPerShift, NumberWorking)}$$
$$\rightarrow \text{cell J21}$$

Summary of the Formulation   The above steps provide the complete formulation of the linear programming model on a spreadsheet, as summarized below (in algebraic form).

$$\text{Minimize} \quad \text{Cost} = 170S_1 + 160S_2 + 175S_3 + 180S_4 + 195S_5 \quad (\text{in dollars})$$

subject to

Total agents 6–8 AM:	S_1	≥ 48
Total agents 8–10 AM:	$S_1 + S_2$	≥ 79

.

.

.

Total agents midnight–6 AM:	$S_5 \geq 15$

and

$$S_1 \geq 0 \quad S_2 \geq 0 \quad S_3 \geq 0 \quad S_4 \geq 0 \quad S_5 \geq 0$$

Solving the Model   The lower left-hand corner of Figure 3.5 shows the entries needed in the Solver dialogue box, along with the selection of the usual two options. After solving, NumberWorking (C21:G21) in the spreadsheet shows the resulting optimal solution for the number of agents that should be assigned to each shift. TotalCost (J21) indicates that this plan would cost $30,610 per day.

FIGURE 3.6

A template of a spreadsheet model for pure cost–benefit–trade-off problems.

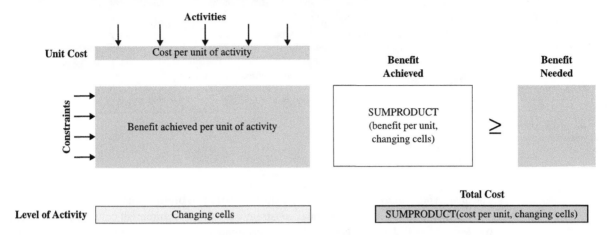

Summary of the Formulation Procedure for Cost–Benefit–Trade-off Problems

The nine steps in formulating any cost–benefit–trade-off problem follow the same pattern as presented at the end of the preceding section for resource-allocation problems, so we will not repeat them here. The main differences are that the overall measure of performance now is the total cost of the activities (or some surrogate of total cost chosen by management) in steps 2 and 3, benefits now replace resources in steps 4 and 5, and ≥ signs now are entered to the right of the output cells for benefits in step 8. Figure 3.6 shows a template of the format of a spreadsheet model for cost–benefit–trade-off problems.

All the functional constraints in the resulting model are *benefit constraints,* that is, constraints with a ≥ sign. This is the *identifying feature* of a pure cost–benefit–trade-off problem.

Review Questions

1. What is the difference in managerial objectives between resource-allocation problems and cost–benefit–trade-off problems?
2. What is the identifying feature of a cost–benefit–trade-off problem?
3. What is the form of a benefit constraint?
4. What are the three kinds of data that need to be gathered for a cost–benefit–trade-off problem?
5. Compare the types of activities for the two examples of cost–benefit–trade-off problems.
6. Compare the types of benefits for the two examples of cost–benefit–trade-off problems.

3.4 MIXED PROBLEMS

Sections 3.2 and 3.3 each described a broad category of linear programming problems—resource-allocation and cost–benefit–trade-off problems. As summarized in Table 3.6, each features one of the first two types of functional constraints shown there. In fact, the *identifying feature* of a *pure* resource-allocation problem is that *all* its functional constraints are *resource constraints*. The *identifying feature* of a *pure* cost–benefit–trade-off problem is that *all* its functional constraints are *benefit constraints*. (Keep in mind that the functional constraints include *all* the constraints of a problem *except* its nonnegativity constraints.)

The bottom row of Table 3.6 shows the last of the three types of functional constraints, namely, **fixed-requirement constraints,** which require that the left-hand side of each such constraint must exactly equal some fixed amount. Thus, since the left-hand side represents the amount provided of some quantity, the form of a fixed-requirement constraint is

$$\text{Amount provided} = \text{Required amount}$$

TABLE 3.6 **Types of Functional Constraints**

Type	Form*	Typical Interpretation	Main Usage
Resource constraint	LHS ≤ RHS	For some resource, Amount used ≤ Amount available	Resource-allocation problems and mixed problems
Benefit constraint	LHS ≥ RHS	For some benefit, Level achieved ≥ Minimum acceptable level	Cost–benefit–trade-off problems and mixed problems
Fixed-requirement constraint	LHS = RHS	For some quantity, Amount provided = Required amount	Fixed-requirements problems and mixed problems

*LHS = Left-hand side (a SUMPRODUCT function).
RHS = Right-hand side (a constant).

The *identifying feature* of a *pure* **fixed-requirements problem** is that it is a linear programming problem where *all* its functional constraints are fixed-requirement constraints. The next two sections will describe two particularly prominent types of fixed-requirement problems called *transportation problems* and *assignment problems*.

However, before turning to these types of problems, we first will use a continuation of the Super Grain case study from Section 3.1 to illustrate how many linear programming problems fall into another broad category called *mixed problems*.

> Many linear programming problems do not fit completely into any of the previously discussed categories (pure resource-allocation problems, cost–benefit–trade-off problems, and fixed-requirement problems) because the problem's functional constraints include more than one of the types shown in Table 3.6. Such problems are called *mixed problems*.

Now let us see how a more careful analysis of the Super Grain case study turns this resource-allocation problem into a mixed problem that includes all three types of functional constraints shown in Table 3.6.

Super Grain Management Discusses Its Advertising-Mix Problem

The description of the Super Grain case study in Section 3.1 ends with Clair Syverson (Super Grain's vice president for marketing) sending a memorandum to the company's president, David Sloan, requesting a meeting to evaluate her proposed promotional campaign for the company's new breakfast cereal.

Soon thereafter, Claire Syverson and David Sloan meet to discuss plans for the campaign.

David Sloan (president):   Thanks for your memo, Claire. The plan you outline for the promotional campaign looks like a reasonable one. However, I am surprised that it does not make any use of TV commercials. Why is that?

Claire Syverson (vice president for marketing):   Well, as I described in my memo, I used a spreadsheet model to see how to maximize the number of exposures from the campaign and this turned out to be the plan that does this. I also was surprised that it did not include TV commercials, but the model indicated that introducing commercials would provide less exposures on a dollar-for-dollar basis than magazine ads and Sunday supplement ads. Don't you think it makes sense to use the plan that maximizes the number of exposures?

David: Not necessarily. Some exposures are a lot less important than others. For example, we know that middle-aged adults are not big consumers of our cereals, so we don't care very much how many of those people see our ads. On the other hand, young children are big consumers. Having TV commercials on the Saturday morning programs for children is our primary method of reaching young children. You know how important it will be to get young children to ask their parents for Crunchy Start. That is our best way of generating first-time sales. Those commercials also get seen by a lot of parents who are watching the programs with their kids. What we need is a commercial that is appealing to both parents and kids, and that gets the kids immediately bugging their parents to go buy Crunchy Start. I think that is a real key to a successful campaign.

Claire: Yes, that makes a lot of sense. In fact, I already have set some goals regarding the number of young children and the number of parents of young children that need to be reached by this promotional campaign.

David: Good. Did you include those goals in your spreadsheet model?

Claire: No, I didn't.

David: Well, I suggest that you incorporate them directly into your model. I suspect that maximizing exposures while also meeting your goals will give us a high impact plan that includes some TV commercials.

Claire: Good idea. I'll try it.

David: Are there any other factors that the plan in your memo doesn't take into account as well as you would like?

Claire: Well, yes, one. The plan doesn't take into account my budget for cents-off coupons in magazines and newspapers.

David: You should be able to add that to your model as well. Why don't you go back and see what happens when you incorporate these additional considerations?

Claire: OK, will do. You seem to have had a lot of experience with spreadsheet modeling.

David: Yes. It is a great tool as long as you maintain some healthy skepticism about what comes out of the model. No model can fully take into account everything that we must consider when dealing with managerial problems. This is especially true the first time or two you run the model. You need to keep asking, what are the missing quantitative considerations that I still should add to the model? Then, after you have made the model as complete as possible and obtained a solution, you still need to use your best managerial judgment to weigh intangible considerations that cannot be incorporated into the model.

Incorporating Additional Managerial Considerations into the Super Grain Model

Therefore, David and Claire conclude that the spreadsheet model needs to be expanded to incorporate some additional considerations. In particular, since the promotional campaign is for a breakfast cereal that should have special appeal to young children, they feel that two audiences should be targeted—*young children* and *parents of young children*. (This is why one of the three advertising media recommended by Giacomi & Jackowitz is commercials on children's television programs Saturday morning.) Consequently, Claire now has set two new goals for the campaign.

Goal 1:   The advertising should be seen by at least five million young children.

Goal 2:   The advertising should be seen by at least five million parents of young children.

In effect, these two goals are *minimum acceptable levels* for two special *benefits* to be achieved by the advertising activities.

Benefit 1:   Promoting the new breakfast cereal to young children.

Benefit 2:   Promoting the new breakfast cereal to parents of young children.

Because of the way the goals have been articulated, the *level* of each of these benefits is measured by the *number of people* in the specified category that are reached by the advertising.

To enable constructing the corresponding *benefit constraints* (as described in Section 3.3), Claire asks Giacomi & Jackowitz to estimate how much each advertisement in each of the media will contribute to each benefit, as measured by the number of people reached in the specified category. These estimates are given in Table 3.7.

It is interesting to observe that management wants special consideration given to these two kinds of benefits even though the original spreadsheet model (Figure 3.1) already takes them into account to some extent. As described in Section 3.1, the *expected number of exposures* is the overall measure of performance to be maximized. This measure counts up all the times

TABLE 3.7 Benefit Data for the Revised Super Grain Corp. Advertising-Mix Problem

	Number Reached in Target Category (in millions)			
Target Category	Each TV Commercial	Each Magazine Ad	Each Sunday Ad	Minimum Acceptable Level
Young children	1.2	0.1	0	5
Parents of young children	0.5	0.2	0.2	5

that an advertisement is seen by any individual, including all those individuals in the target audiences. However, maximizing this *general* measure of performance does *not* ensure that the two *specific goals* prescribed by management (Claire Syverson) will be achieved. Claire feels that achieving these goals is essential to a successful promotional campaign. Therefore, she complements the general objective with specific benefit constraints that *do* ensure that the goals will be achieved. Having benefit constraints added to incorporate managerial goals into the model is a prerogative of management.

Benefit constraints are useful for incorporating managerial goals into the model.

Claire has one more consideration she wants to incorporate into the model. She is a strong believer in the promotional value of *cents-off coupons* (coupons that shoppers can clip from printed advertisements to obtain a refund of a designated amount when purchasing the advertised item). Consequently, she always earmarks a major portion of her annual marketing budget for the redemption of these coupons. She still has $1,490,000 left from this year's allotment for coupon redemptions. Because of the importance of Crunchy Start to the company, she has decided to use this entire remaining allotment in the campaign promoting this cereal.

This *fixed amount* for coupon redemptions is a *fixed requirement* that needs to be expressed as a *fixed-requirement constraint*. As described at the beginning of this section, the form of a fixed-requirement constraint is that, for some type of quantity,

$$\text{Amount provided} = \text{Required amount}$$

In this case, the quantity involved is the amount of money provided for the redemption of cents-off coupons. To specify this constraint in the spreadsheet, we need to estimate how much each advertisement in each of the media will contribute toward fulfilling the required amount for the quantity. Both medium 2 (advertisements in food and family-oriented magazines) and medium 3 (advertisements in Sunday supplements of major newspapers) will feature cents-off coupons. The estimates of the amount of coupon redemption per advertisement in each of these media is given in Table 3.8.

Formulation of the Revised Spreadsheet Model

Figure 3.7 shows one way of formatting the spreadsheet to expand the original spreadsheet model in Figure 3.1 to incorporate the additional managerial considerations. We outline the four components of the revised model below.

The Data

Additional data cells in NumberReachedPerAd (C11:E12), MinimumAcceptable (H11:H12), CouponRedemptionPerAd (C15:E15), and RequiredAmount (H15) give the data in Tables 3.7 and 3.8.

TABLE 3.8 Data for the Fixed-Requirement Constraint for the Revised Super Grain Corp. Advertising-Mix Problem

	Contribution toward Required Amount			
Requirement	Each TV Spot	Each Magazine Ad	Each Sunday Ad	Required Amount
Coupon redemption	0	$40,000	$120,000	$1,490,000

FIGURE 3.7

The spreadsheet model for the revised Super Grain problem, including the formulas for the target cell TotalExposures (H19) and the other output cells in column F, as well as the specifications needed to set up the Solver.

The changing cells NumberOfAds (C19:E19) show the optimal solution obtained by the Solver.

	A	B	C	D	E	F	G	H
1		**Super Grain Corp. Advertising-Mix Problem**						
2								
3			TV Spots	Magazine Ads	SS Ads			
4		Exposures per Ad	1,300	600	500			
5		(thousands)						
6			Cost per Ad ($thousands)			Budget Spent		Budget Available
7		Ad Budget	300	150	100	3,775	≤	4,000
8		Planning Budget	90	30	40	1,000	≤	1,000
9								
10			Number Reached per Ad (millions)			Total Reached		Minimum Acceptable
11		Young Children	1.2	0.1	0	5	≥	5
12		Parents of Young Children	0.5	0.2	0.2	5.85	≥	5
13								
14			TV Spots	Magazine Ads	SS Ads	Total Redeemed		Required Amount
15		Coupon Redemption	0	40	120	1,490	=	1,490
16		per Ad ($thousands)						
17								Total Exposures
18			TV Spots	Magazine Ads	SS Ads			(thousands)
19		Number of Ads	3	14	7.75			16,175
20			≤					
21		Maximum TV Spots	5					

Solver Parameters

Set Objective (Target Cell): TotalExposures
To: Max
By Changing (Variable) Cells:
　NumberOfAds
Subject to the Constraints:
　BudgetSpent <= Budget Available
　TVSpots <= MaxTVSpots
　TotalReached >= MinimumAcceptable
　TotalRedeemed = RequiredAmount

Solver Options (Excel 2010):
　Make Variables Nonnegative
　Solving Method: Simplex LP
Solver Options (older Excel):
　Assume Nonnegative
　Assume Linear Model

Range Name	Cells
BudgetAvailable	H7:H8
BudgetSpent	F7:F8
CostPerAd	C7:E8
CouponRedemptionPerAd	C15:E15
ExposuresPerAd	C4:E4
MaxTVSpots	C21
MinimumAcceptable	H11:H12
NumberOfAds	C19:E19
NumberReachedPerAd	C11:E12
RequiredAmount	H15
TotalExposures	H19
TotalReached	F11:F12
TotalRedeemed	F15
TVSpots	C19

	F
6	Budget Spent
7	=SUMPRODUCT(C7:E7,NumberOfAds)
8	=SUMPRODUCT(C8:E8,NumberOfAds)
9	
10	Total Reached
11	=SUMPRODUCT(C11:E11,NumberOfAds)
12	=SUMPRODUCT(C12:E12,NumberOfAds)
13	
14	Total Redeemed
15	=SUMPRODUCT(CouponRedemptionPerAd, NumberOfAds)

	H
17	Total Exposures
18	(thousands)
19	=SUMPRODUCT(ExposuresPerAd,NumberOfAds)

The Decisions

Recall that, as before, the decisions to be made are

TV = Number of commercials on television

M = Number of advertisements in magazines

SS = Number of advertisements in Sunday supplements

The changing cells to hold these numbers continue to be in NumberOfAds (C19:E19).

The Constraints

In addition to the original constraints, we now have two benefit constraints and one fixed-requirement constraint. As specified in rows 11 and 12, columns F to H, the benefit constraints are

| Total number of young children reached | ≥ 5 | (goal 1 in millions) |
| Total number of parents reached | ≥ 5 | (goal 2 in millions) |

Using the data in columns C to E of these rows,

Total number of young children reached $= 1.2TV + 0.1M + 0SS$

$\qquad\qquad\qquad\qquad\qquad\qquad = $ SUMPRODUCT (C11:E11, NumberOfAds)

$\qquad\qquad\qquad\qquad\qquad\qquad \rightarrow$ cell F11

Total number of parents reached $\qquad = 0.5TV + 0.2M + 0.2SS$

$\qquad\qquad\qquad\qquad\qquad\qquad = $ SUMPRODUCT (C12:E12, NumberOfAds)

$\qquad\qquad\qquad\qquad\qquad\qquad \rightarrow$ cell F12

These output cells are given the range name TotalReached (F11:F12).

The fixed-requirement constraint indicated in row 15 is that

$$\text{Total coupon redemption} = 1{,}490 \qquad \text{(allotment in \$1,000s)}$$

CouponRedemptionPerAd (C15:E15) gives the number of coupons redeemed per ad, so

Total coupon redemption $= 0TV + 40M + 120SS$

$\qquad\qquad\qquad\qquad\qquad\qquad = $ SUMPRODUCT (CouponRedemptionPerAd, NumberOfAds)

$\qquad\qquad\qquad\qquad\qquad\qquad \rightarrow$ cell F15

These same constraints are specified for the Solver in the Solver dialogue box, along with the original constraints, in Figure 3.7.

The Measure of Performance

The measure of performance continues to be

Exposure $= 1{,}300TV + 600M + 500SS$

$\qquad\qquad\qquad = $ SUMPRODUCT (ExposuresPerAd, NumberOfAds)

$\qquad\qquad\qquad \rightarrow$ cell H19

so the target cell is again TotalExposures (H19).

Summary of the Formulation

The above steps have resulted in formulating the following linear programming model (in algebraic form) on a spreadsheet.

$$\text{Maximize} \quad \text{Exposure} = 1{,}300TV + 600M + 500SS$$

subject to the following constraints:

1. *Resource constraints:*

$$300TV + 150M + 100SS \leq 4{,}000 \quad \text{(ad budget in \$1,000s)}$$
$$90TV + 30M + 40SS \leq 1{,}000 \quad \text{(planning budget in \$1,000s)}$$
$$TV \qquad\qquad\qquad \leq \quad 5 \quad \text{(television spots available)}$$

2. *Benefit constraints:*

$$1.2TV + 0.1M \qquad\quad \geq \quad 5 \quad \text{(millions of young children)}$$
$$0.5TV + 0.2M + 0.2SS \geq \quad 5 \quad \text{(millions of parents)}$$

3. *Fixed-requirement constraint:*

$$40M + 120SS = 1{,}490 \quad \text{(coupon budget in \$1,000s)}$$

4. *Nonnegativity constraints:*

$$TV \geq 0 \quad M \geq 0 \quad SS \geq 0$$

Solving the Model

The lower left-hand corner of Figure 3.7 shows the entries needed in the Solver dialogue box, along with the selection of the usual two options. The Solver then finds the optimal solution given in row 19. This optimal solution provides the following plan for the promotional campaign:

Run 3 television commercials.

Run 14 advertisements in magazines.

Run 7.75 advertisements in Sunday supplements (so the eighth advertisement would appear in only 75 percent of the newspapers).

Although the expected number of exposures with this plan is only 16,175,000, versus the 17,000,000 with the first plan shown in Figure 3.1, both Claire Syverson and David Sloan feel that the new plan does a much better job of meeting all of management's goals for this campaign. They decide to adopt the new plan.

A model may need to be modified a number of times before it adequately incorporates all the important considerations.

This case study illustrates a common theme in real applications of linear programming—the continuing evolution of the linear programming model. It is common to make later adjustments in the initial version of the model, perhaps even many times, as experience is gained in using the model. Frequently, these adjustments are made to more adequately reflect some important managerial considerations. This may result in a mixed problem because the new functional constraints needed to incorporate the managerial considerations may be of a different type from those in the original model.

Summary of the Formulation Procedure for Mixed Linear Programming Problems

The procedure for formulating mixed problems is similar to the one outlined at the end of Section 3.2 for resource-allocation problems. However, pure resource-allocation problems only have resource constraints whereas mixed problems can include all three types of functional constraints (resource constraints, benefit constraints, and fixed-requirement constraints). Therefore, the following summary for formulating mixed problems includes separate steps for dealing with these different types of constraints. Also see Figure 3.8 for a template of the format for a spreadsheet model of mixed problems. (This format works well for most mixed problems, including those encountered in this chapter, but more flexibility is occasionally needed, as will be illustrated in the next chapter.)

1. Since any linear programming problem involves finding the *best mix* of levels of various activities, identify these *activities* for the problem at hand. The decisions to be made are the *levels* of these activities.

FIGURE 3.8

A template of a spreadsheet model for mixed problems.

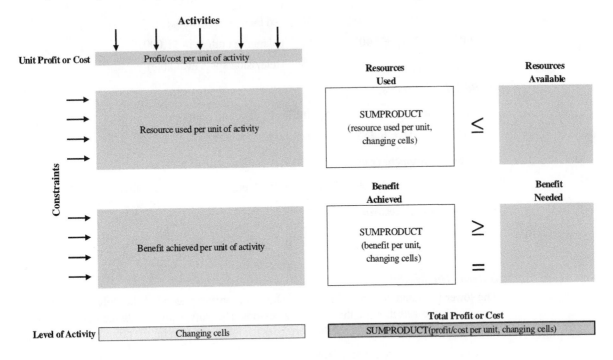

2. From the viewpoint of management, identify an appropriate *overall measure of performance* for solutions of the problem.

3. For each activity, estimate the *contribution per unit* of the activity to this overall measure of performance.

4. Identify any *resources* that must be allocated to the activities (as described in Section 3.2). For each one, identify the *amount available* and then the *amount used per unit of each activity*.

5. Identify any *benefits* to be obtained from the activities (as described in Section 3.3). For each one, identify the *minimum acceptable level* prescribed by management and then the *benefit contribution per unit of each activity*.

6. Identify any *fixed requirements* that, for some type of quantity, the amount provided must equal a required amount (as described in Section 3.4). For each fixed requirement, identify the *required amount* and then the *contribution toward this required amount per unit of each activity*.

7. Enter the data gathered in steps 3–6 into *data cells* in a spreadsheet.

8. Designate *changing cells* for displaying the decisions on activity levels.

9. Use *output cells* to specify the constraints on resources, benefits, and fixed requirements.

10. Designate a *target cell* for displaying the overall measure of performance.

Review Questions

1. What types of functional constraints can appear in a mixed linear programming problem?

2. What managerial goals needed to be incorporated into the expanded linear programming model for the Super Grain Corp. problem?

3. Which categories of functional constraints are included in the new linear programming model?

4. Why did management adopt the new plan even though it provides a smaller expected number of exposures than the original plan recommended by the original linear programming model?

3.5 TRANSPORTATION PROBLEMS

One of the most common applications of linear programming involves optimizing a shipping plan for transporting goods. In a typical application, a company has several plants producing a certain product that needs to be shipped to the company's customers (or perhaps to distribution centers). How much should each plant ship to each customer in order to minimize the total cost? Linear programming can provide the answer. This type of linear programming problem is called a **transportation problem.**

This kind of application normally needs two kinds of functional constraints. One kind specifies that the amount of the product produced at each plant must equal the total amount shipped to customers. The other kind specifies that the total amount received from the plants by each customer must equal the amount ordered. These are *fixed-requirement constraints,* which makes the problem a *fixed-requirements problem.* However, there also are variations of this problem where resource constraints or benefit constraints are needed.

Transportation problems and assignment problems (described in the next section) are such important types of linear programming problems that the entire Chapter 15 on the CD-ROM is devoted to further describing these two related types of problems and providing examples of a wide variety of applications.

We provide below an example of a typical transportation problem.

The Big M Company Transportation Problem

The **Big M Company** produces a variety of heavy duty machines at two factories. One of its products is a large turret lathe. Orders have been received from three customers to purchase some of these turret lathes next month. These lathes will be shipped individually, and Table 3.9 shows what the cost will be for shipping each lathe from each factory to each customer. This table also shows how many lathes have been ordered by each customer and how many will be produced by each factory. The company's distribution manager now wants to determine how many machines to ship from each factory to each customer to minimize the total shipping cost.

Figure 3.9 depicts the distribution network for this problem. This network ignores the geographical layout of the factories and customers and instead lines up the two factories in one column on the left and the three customers in one column on the right. Each arrow shows one of the shipping lanes through this distribution network.

Formulation of the Problem in Linear Programming Terms

We need to identify the *activities* and *requirements* of this transportation problem to formulate it as a linear programming problem. In this case, two kinds of activities have been mentioned—the *production* of the turret lathes at the two factories and the *shipping* of these lathes along the various shipping lanes. However, we know the specific amounts to be produced at each factory, so no decisions need to be made about the production activities. The decisions to be made concern the levels of the *shipping activities*—how many lathes to ship through each shipping lane. Therefore, we need to focus on the shipping activities for the linear programming formulation.

The *activities* correspond to shipping lanes, depicted by arrows in Figure 3.9.

The *level* of each activity is the number of lathes shipped through the corresponding shipping lane.

TABLE 3.9
Some Data for the Big M Company Distribution-Network Problem

To From	Customer 1	Customer 2	Customer 3	Output
	Shipping Cost for Each Lathe			
Factory 1	$700	$900	$800	12 lathes
Factory 2	800	900	700	15 lathes
Order size	10 lathes	8 lathes	9 lathes	

FIGURE 3.9

The distribution network
for the Big M Company
problem.

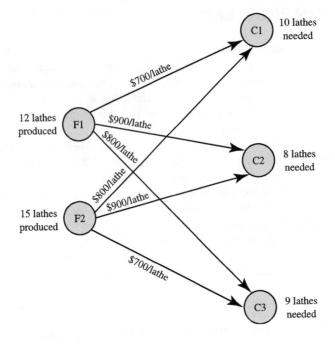

Just as any linear programming problem can be described as finding the best mix of activity levels, this one involves finding the *best mix of shipping amounts* for the various shipping lanes. The decisions to be made are

$S_{\text{F1-C1}}$ = Number of lathes shipped from Factory 1 to Customer 1

$S_{\text{F1-C2}}$ = Number of lathes shipped from Factory 1 to Customer 2

$S_{\text{F1-C3}}$ = Number of lathes shipped from Factory 1 to Customer 3

$S_{\text{F2-C1}}$ = Number of lathes shipped from Factory 2 to Customer 1

$S_{\text{F2-C2}}$ = Number of lathes shipped from Factory 2 to Customer 2

$S_{\text{F2-C3}}$ = Number of lathes shipped from Factory 2 to Customer 3

so six changing cells will be needed in the spreadsheet.

The objective is to

$$\text{Minimize} \quad \text{Cost} = \text{Total cost for shipping the lathes}$$

Using the shipping costs given in Table 3.9,

$$\text{Cost} = 700S_{\text{F1-C1}} + 900S_{\text{F1-C2}} + 800S_{\text{F1-C3}} + 800S_{\text{F2-C1}} + 900S_{\text{F2-C2}} + 700S_{\text{F2-C3}}$$

is the quantity in dollars to be entered into the target cell. (We will use a SUMPRODUCT function to do this a little later.)

The spreadsheet model also will need five constraints involving *fixed requirements*. Both Table 3.9 and Figure 3.9 show these requirements.

Requirement 1: Factory 1 must ship 12 lathes.

Requirement 2: Factory 2 must ship 15 lathes.

Requirement 3: Customer 1 must receive 10 lathes.

Requirement 4: Customer 2 must receive 8 lathes.

Requirement 5: Customer 3 must receive 9 lathes.

Thus, there is a specific requirement associated with each of the five locations in the distribution network shown in Figure 3.9.

All five of these requirements can be expressed in constraint form as

$$\text{Amount provided} = \text{Required amount}$$

For example, Requirement 1 can be expressed algebraically as

$$S_{\text{F1-C1}} + S_{\text{F1-C2}} + S_{\text{F1-C3}} = 12$$

where the left-hand side gives the total number of lathes shipped from Factory 1, and 12 is the required amount to be shipped from Factory 1. Therefore, this constraint restricts $S_{\text{F1-C1}}$, $S_{\text{F1-C2}}$, and $S_{\text{F1-C3}}$ to values that sum to the required amount of 12. In contrast to the $\leq$ form for resource constraints and the $\geq$ form for benefit constraints, the constraints express *fixed requirements* that must hold with equality, so this transportation problem falls into the category of fixed-requirements problems introduced in the preceding section. However, Chapter 15 (on the CD-ROM) gives several examples that illustrate how variants of transportation problems can have resource constraints or benefit constraints as well. For example, if 12 lathes represent the manufacturing capacity of Factory 1 (the maximum number that can be shipped) rather than a requirement for how many must be shipped, the constraint just given for Requirement 1 would become a $\leq$ resource constraint instead. Such variations can be incorporated readily into the spreadsheet model.

Formulation of the Spreadsheet Model

Careful *problem* formulation needs to precede *model* formulation.

In preparation for formulating the *model,* the *problem* has been formulated above by identifying the decisions to be made, the constraints on these decisions, and the overall measure of performance, as well as gathering all the important data displayed in Table 3.9. All this information leads to the spreadsheet model shown in Figure 3.10. The data cells include ShippingCost (C5:E6), Output (H11:H12), and OrderSize (C15:E15), incorporating all the data from Table 3.9. The changing cells are UnitsShipped (C11:E12), which give the decisions on the amounts to be shipped through the respective shipping lanes. The output cells are Total-

Here is an example where SUM functions are used for output cells instead of SUMPRODUCT functions.

ShippedOut (F11:F12) and TotalToCustomer (C13:E13), where the SUM functions entered into these cells are shown below the spreadsheet in Figure 3.10. The constraints are that TotalShippedOut is required to equal Output and TotalToCustomer is required to equal OrderSize. These constraints have been specified on the spreadsheet and entered into the Solver dialogue box. The target cell is TotalCost (H15), where its SUMPRODUCT function gives the total shipping cost. The lower left-hand corner of Figure 3.10 shows the entries needed in the Solver dialogue box, along with the selection of the usual two options.

The layout of the spreadsheet is different than for all the prior linear programming examples in the book. Rather than a separate column for each activity and a separate row for each constraint, the cost data and changing cells are laid out in a table format. This format provides a more natural and compact way of displaying the constraints and results.

FIGURE 3.10

The spreadsheet model for the Big M Company problem, including the formulas for the target cell TotalCost (H15) and the other output cells TotalShippedOut (F11:F12) and TotalToCustomer (C13:E13), as well as the specifications needed to set up the Solver. The changing cells UnitsShipped (C11:E12) show the optimal solution obtained by the Solver.

	A	B	C	D	E	F	G	H
1		**Big M Company Distribution Problem**						
2								
3		**Shipping Cost**						
4		**(per Lathe)**	Customer 1	Customer 2	Customer 3			
5		Factory 1	$700	$900	$800			
6		Factory 2	$800	$900	$700			
7								
8						Total		
9						Shipped		
10		**Units Shipped**	Customer 1	Customer 2	Customer 3	Out		Output
11		Factory 1	10	2	0	12	=	12
12		Factory 2	0	6	9	15	=	15
13		Total to Customer	10	8	9			
14			=	=	=			**Total Cost**
15		Order Size	10	8	9			$20,500

Solver Parameters

Set Objective (Target Cell): TotalCost
To: Min
By Changing (Variable) Cells:
   UnitsShipped
Subject to the Constraints:
   TotalShippedOut = Output
   TotalToCustomer = OrderSize

Solver Options (Excel 2010):
   Make Variables Nonnegative
   Solving Method: Simplex LP
Solver Options (older Excel):
   Assume Nonnegative
   Assume Linear Model

Range Name	Cells
OrderSize	C15:E15
Output	H11:H12
ShippingCost	C5:E6
TotalCost	H15
TotalShippedOut	F11:F12
TotalToCustomer	C13:E13
UnitsShipped	C11:E12

	F
8	Total
9	Shipped
10	Out
11	=SUM(C11:E11)
12	=SUM(C12:E12)

	B	C	D	E
13	Total to Customer	=SUM(C11:C12)	=SUM(D11:D12)	=SUM(E11:E12)

	H
14	Total Cost
15	=SUMPRODUCT(ShippingCost,UnitsShipped)

UnitsShipped (C11:E12) in the spreadsheet in Figure 3.10 shows the result of applying the Solver to obtain an optimal solution for the number of lathes to ship through each shipping lane. TotalCost (H15) indicates that the total shipping cost for this shipping plan is $20,500.

Since any transportation problem is a special type of linear programming problem, it makes the standard assumption that fractional solutions are allowed. However, we actually don't want this assumption for this particular application since only *integer* numbers of lathes can be shipped from a factory to a customer. Fortunately, even while making the standard assumption, the numbers in the optimal solution shown in UnitsShipped (C11:E12) only have integer values. This is no coincidence. Because of the form of its model, almost any transportation problem (including this one) is guaranteed in advance to have an optimal solution that has only integer values despite the fact that fractional solutions also are allowed. In particular, as long as the data for the problem includes only integer values for all the supplies and demands (which are the outputs and order sizes in the Big M Company problem), any transportation problem with feasible solutions is guaranteed to have an optimal solution with integer values for all its decision variables. Therefore, it is not necessary to add constraints to the model that require these variables to have only integer values.

To summarize, here is the algebraic form of the linear programming model that has been formulated in the spreadsheet.

$$\text{Minimize} \quad \text{Cost} = 700S_{\text{F1-C1}} + 900S_{\text{F1-C2}} + 800S_{\text{F1-C3}} + 800S_{\text{F2-C1}}$$
$$+ 900S_{\text{F2-C2}} + 700S_{\text{F2-C3}}$$

subject to the following constraints:

1. *Fixed-requirement constraints:*

$$
\begin{array}{llll}
S_{\text{F1-C1}} + S_{\text{F1-C2}} + S_{\text{F1-C3}} & & = 12 & \text{(Factory 1)} \\
& S_{\text{F2-C1}} + S_{\text{F2-C2}} + S_{\text{F2-C3}} = 15 & & \text{(Factory 2)} \\
S_{\text{F1-C1}} & + S_{\text{F2-C1}} & = 10 & \text{(Customer 1)} \\
\quad S_{\text{F1-C2}} & + S_{\text{F2-C2}} & = 8 & \text{(Customer 2)} \\
\quad\quad S_{\text{F1-C3}} & + S_{\text{F2-C3}} & = 9 & \text{(Customer 3)}
\end{array}
$$

2. *Nonnegativity constraints:*

$$S_{\text{F1-C1}} \geq 0 \quad S_{\text{F1-C2}} \geq 0 \quad S_{\text{F1-C3}} \geq 0 \quad S_{\text{F2-C1}} \geq 0 \quad S_{\text{F2-C2}} \geq 0 \quad S_{\text{F2-C3}} \geq 0$$

Review Questions

1. Why are transportation problems given this name?
2. What is an identifying feature of transportation problems?
3. How does the form of a fixed-requirement constraint differ from that of a resource constraint? A benefit constraint?
4. What are the quantities with fixed requirements in the Big M Company problem?

3.6 ASSIGNMENT PROBLEMS

We now turn to another special type of linear programming problem called **assignment problems.** As the name suggests, this kind of problem involves making *assignments.* Frequently, these are assignments of people to jobs. Thus, many applications of the assignment problem involve aiding managers in matching up their personnel with tasks to be performed. Other applications might instead involve assigning machines, vehicles, or plants to tasks.

Here is a typical example.

An Example: The Sellmore Company Problem

The marketing manager of the **Sellmore Company** will be holding the company's annual sales conference soon for sales regional managers and personnel. To assist in the administration of the conference, he is hiring four temporary employees (Ann, Ian, Joan, and Sean), where each will handle one of the following four tasks:

1. Word processing of written presentations.
2. Computer graphics for both oral and written presentations.
3. Preparation of conference packets, including copying and organizing written materials.
4. Handling of advance and on-site registrations for the conference.

He now needs to decide which person to assign to each task.

Decisions need to be made regarding which person to assign to each task.

Although each temporary employee has at least the minimal background necessary to perform any of the four tasks, they differ considerably in how efficiently they can handle the different types of work. Table 3.10 shows how many hours each would need for each task. The rightmost column gives the hourly wage based on the background of each employee.

Formulation of a Spreadsheet Model

Using Cost (D15:G18), the objective is to minimize the total cost of the assignments.

Figure 3.11 shows a spreadsheet model for this problem. Table 3.10 is entered at the top. Combining these required times and wages gives the cost (cells D15:G18) for each possible assignment of a temporary employee to a task, using equations shown at the bottom of

TABLE 3.10
Data for the Sellmore
Co. Problem

| Temporary Employee | Required Time per Task (Hours) | | | | Hourly Wage |
	Word Processing	Graphics	Packets	Registrations	
Ann	35	41	27	40	$14
Ian	47	45	32	51	12
Joan	39	56	36	43	13
Sean	32	51	25	46	15

Figure 3.11. This *cost table* is just the way that any assignment problem is displayed. The objective is to determine which assignments should be made to minimize the sum of the associated costs.

A value of 1 in a changing cell indicates that the corresponding assignment is being made, whereas 0 means that the assignment is not being made.

The values of 1 in Supply (J24:J27) indicate that each person (assignee) listed in column C must perform exactly one task. The values of 1 in Demand (D30:G30) indicate that each task must be performed by exactly one person. These requirements then are specified in the constraints given in the Solver dialogue box.

Each of the changing cells Assignment (D24:G27) is given a value of 1 when the corresponding assignment is being made, and a value of 0 otherwise. Therefore, the Excel equation for the target cell, TotalCost = SUMPRODUCT(Cost, Assignment), gives the total cost for the assignments being made. The Solver Parameters box specifies that the objective is to minimize this target cell.

Excel Tip: When solving an assignment problem, rounding errors occasionally will cause Excel to return a noninteger value very close to 0 (e.g., 1.23 E-10, meaning 0.000000000123) or very close to 1 (e.g., 0.9999912). To make the spreadsheet cleaner, you may replace these "ugly" representations by their proper value of 0 or 1 in the changing cells.

The changing cells in Figure 3.11 show the optimal solution obtained after clicking on the Solve button. This solution is

Assign Ann to prepare conference packets.

Assign Ian to do the computer graphics.

Assign Joan to handle registrations.

Assign Sean to do the word processing.

The total cost given in cell J30 is $1,957.

Characteristics of Assignment Problems

Note that all the functional constraints of the Sellmore Co. problem (as shown in cells H24:J27 and D28:G30 of Figure 3.11) are fixed-requirement constraints which require each person to perform exactly one task and require each task to be performed by exactly one person. Thus, like the Big M Company transportation problem, the Sellmore Co. is a fixed-requirements problem. This is a characteristic of all pure assignment problems. However, Chapter 15 (on the CD-ROM) gives some examples of variants of assignment problems where this is not the case.

Like the changing cells Assignment (D24:G27) in Figure 3.11, the changing cells in the spreadsheet model for any pure assignment problem gives a value of 1 when the corresponding assignment is being made, and a value of 0 otherwise. Since the fixed-requirement constraints require only each row or column of changing cells to add up to 1 (which could happen, e.g., if two of the changing cells in the same row or column had a value of 0.5 and the rest 0), this would seem to necessitate adding the constraints that each of the changing cells must be *integer*. After choosing the Solver option to make the changing cells nonnegative, this then would force each of the changing cells to be 0 or 1. However, it turned out to be unnecessary to add the constraints that require the changing cells to have values of 0 or 1 in Figure 3.11 because Solver gave an optimal solution that had only values of 0 or 1 anyway. In fact, a general characteristic of pure assignment problems is that Solver always provides such an optimal solution without needing to add these additional constraints.

Review Questions

1. Why are assignment problems given this name?
2. Pure assignment problems have what type of functional constraints?
3. What is the interpretation of the changing cells in the spreadsheet model of a pure assignment problem?

FIGURE 3.11

A spreadsheet formulation of the Sellmore Co. problem as an assignment problem, including the target cell TotalCost (J30) and the other output cells Cost (D15:G18), TotalAssignments (H24:H27), and TotalAssigned (D28:G28), as well as the specifications needed to set up the model. The values of 1 in the changing cells Assignment (D24:G27) show the optimal plan obtained by the Solver for assigning the people to the tasks.

	A	B	C	D	E	F	G	H	I	J
1		**Sellmore Co. Assignment Problem**								
2										
3					**Task**					
4		**Required Time**			Word				Hourly	
5		**(Hours)**			Processing	Graphics	Packets	Registrations	Wage	
6			Ann		35	41	27	40	$14	
7		Assignee	Ian		47	45	32	51	$12	
8			Joan		39	56	36	43	$13	
9			Sean		32	51	25	46	$15	
10										
11										
12					**Task**					
13					Word					
14		**Cost**			Processing	Graphics	Packets	Registrations		
15			Ann		$490	$574	$378	$560		
16		Assignee	Ian		$564	$540	$384	$612		
17			Joan		$507	$728	$468	$559		
18			Sean		$480	$765	$375	$690		
19										
20										
21					**Task**					
22		**Assignment**			Word				Total	
23					Processing	Graphics	Packets	Registrations	Assignments	Supply
24			Ann		0	0	1	0	1	=	1
25		Assignee	Ian		0	1	0	0	1	=	1
26			Joan		0	0	0	1	1	=	1
27			Sean		1	0	0	0	1	=	1
28			Total Assigned		1	1	1	1			
29					=	=	=	=			Total Cost
30			Demand		1	1	1	1			$1,957

	B	C	D	E	F	G
13			Word			
14	Cost		Processing	Graphics	Packets	Registrations
15		Ann	=D6*I6	=E6*I6	=F6*I6	=G6*I6
16	Assignee	Ian	=D7*I7	=E7*I7	=F7*I7	=G7*I7
17		Joan	=D8*I8	=E8*I8	=F8*I8	=G8*I8
18		Sean	=D9*I9	=E9*I9	=F9*I9	=G9*I9

	H
22	Total
23	Assignments
24	=SUM(D24:G24)
25	=SUM(D25:G25)
26	=SUM(D26:G26)
27	=SUM(D27:G27)

Solver Parameters

Set Objective (Target Cell): TotalCost
To: Min
By Changing (Variable) Cells:
 Assignment
Subject to the Constraints:
 TotalAssigned = Demand
 TotalAssignments = Supply

Solver Options (Excel 2010):
 Make Variables Nonnegative
 Solving Method: Simplex LP
Solver Options (older Excel):
 Assume Nonnegative
 Assume Linear Model

	J
29	Total Cost
30	=SUMPRODUCT(Cost,Assignment)

Range Name	Cells
Assignment	D24:G27
Cost	D15:G18
Demand	D30:G30
HourlyWage	I6:I9
RequiredTime	D6:G9
Supply	J24:J27
TotalAssigned	D28:G28
TotalAssignments	H24:H27
TotalCost	J30

	C	D	E	F	G
28	Total Assigned	=SUM(D24:D27)	=SUM(E24:E27)	=SUM(F24:F27)	=SUM(G24:G27)

3.7 MODEL FORMULATION FROM A BROADER PERSPECTIVE

Formulating and analyzing a linear programming model provides information to help managers make their decisions. That means the model must accurately reflect the managerial view of the problem:

Both the measure of performance and the constraints in a model need to reflect the managerial view of the problem.

- The overall *measure of performance* must capture what management wants accomplished.
- When management limits the amounts of resources that will be made available to the activities under consideration, these limitations should be expressed as *resource constraints.*
- When management establishes minimum acceptable levels for benefits to be gained from the activities, these managerial goals should be incorporated into the model as *benefit constraints.*
- If management has fixed requirements for certain quantities, then *fixed-requirement constraints* are needed.

With the help of spreadsheets, some managers now are able to formulate and solve small linear programming models themselves. However, larger linear programming models may be formulated by *management science teams,* not managers. When this is done, the management science team must thoroughly understand the managerial view of the problem. This requires clear communication with management from the very beginning of the study and maintaining effective communication as new issues requiring managerial guidance are identified. Management needs to clearly convey its view of the problem and the important issues involved. A manager cannot expect to obtain a helpful linear programming study without making clear just what help is wanted.

Linear programming studies need strong managerial input and support.

As is necessary in any textbook, the examples in this chapter are far smaller, simpler, and more clearly spelled out than is typical of real applications. Many real studies require formulating complicated linear programming models involving hundreds or thousands of decisions and constraints. In these cases, there usually are many ambiguities about just what should be incorporated into the model. Strong managerial input and support are vital to the success of a linear programming study for such complex problems.

When dealing with huge real problems, there is no such thing as "the" correct linear programming model for the problem. The model continually evolves throughout the course of the study. Early in the study, various techniques are used to test initial versions of the model to identify the errors and omissions that inevitably occur when constructing such a large model. This testing process is referred to as **model validation.**

Once the basic formulation has been validated, there are many reasonable variations of the model that might be used. Which variation to use depends on such factors as the assumptions about the problem that seem most reasonable, the estimates of the parameters of the model that seem most reliable, and the degree of detail desired in the model.

In large linear programming studies, a good approach is to begin with a relatively simple version of the model and then use the experience gained with this model to evolve toward more elaborate models that more nearly reflect the complexity of the real problem. This process of **model enrichment** continues only as long as the model remains reasonably easy to solve. It must be curtailed when the study's results are needed by management. Managers often need to curb the natural instinct of management science teams to continue adding "bells and whistles" to the model rather than winding up the study in a timely fashion with a less elegant but adequate model.

When managers study the output of the current model, they often detect some undesirable characteristics that point toward needed model enrichments. These enrichments frequently take the form of new *benefit constraints* to satisfy some managerial goals not previously articulated. (Recall that this is what happened in the Super Grain case study.)

What-if analysis addresses some key questions that remain after formulating and solving a model.

Even though many reasonable variations of the model could be used, an *optimal solution* can be solved for only with respect to one specific version of the model at a time. This is why *what-if analysis* is such an important part of a linear programming study. After obtaining an optimal solution with respect to one specific model, management will have many what-if questions:

- What if the estimates of the parameters in the model are incorrect?
- How do the conclusions change if different plausible assumptions are made about the problem?
- What happens when certain managerial options are pursued that are not incorporated into the current model?

Chapter 5 is devoted primarily to describing how what-if analysis addresses these and related issues, as well as how managers use this information.

Because managers *instigate* management science studies, they need to know enough about linear programming models and their formulation to be able to recognize managerial problems to which linear programming can be applied. Furthermore, since managerial input is so important for linear programming studies, managers need to understand the kinds of managerial concerns that can be incorporated into the model. Developing these two skills have been the most important goals of this chapter.

Review *Questions*

1. A linear programming model needs to reflect accurately whose view of the problem?
2. What is meant by *model validation?*
3. What is meant by the process of *model enrichment?*
4. Why is what-if analysis an important part of a linear programming study?

3.8 Summary

Functional constraints with a $\le$ sign are called *resource constraints,* because they require that the *amount used* of some resource must be *less than or equal to* the *amount available* of that resource. The identifying feature of *resource-allocation problems* is that all their functional constraints are resource constraints.

Functional constraints with a $\ge$ sign are called *benefit constraints,* since their form is that the *level achieved* for some benefit must be *greater than or equal to* the *minimum acceptable level* for that benefit. Frequently, benefit constraints express goals prescribed by management. If every functional constraint is a benefit constraint, then the problem is a *cost–benefit–trade-off problem.*

Functional constraints with an = sign are called *fixed-requirement constraints,* because they express the fixed requirement that, for some quantity, the *amount provided* must be *equal to* the *required amount.* The identifying feature of *fixed-requirements problems* is that their functional constraints are fixed-requirement constraints. One prominent type of fixed-requirements problem is transportation problems, which typically involve finding a shipping plan that minimizes the total cost of transporting a product from a number of plants to a number of customers. Another prominent type is assignment problems, which typically involves assigning people to tasks so as to minimize the total cost of performing these tasks.

Linear programming problems that do not fit into any of these three categories are called *mixed problems.*

In many real applications, management science teams formulate and analyze large linear programming models to help guide managerial decision making. Such teams need strong managerial input and support to help ensure that their work really meets management's needs.

Glossary

assignment problem   A type of linear programming problem that typically involves assigning people to tasks so as to minimize the total cost of performing these tasks. (Section 3.6), 93

benefit constraint   A functional constraint with a $\ge$ sign. The left-hand side is interpreted as the level of some benefit that is achieved by the activities under consideration, and the right-hand side is the minimum acceptable level for that benefit. (Section 3.3), 75

cost–benefit–trade-off problem   A type of linear programming problem involving the trade-off between the total cost of the activities under consideration and the benefits to be achieved by these activities. Its identifying feature is that each functional constraint in the linear programming model is a benefit constraint. (Section 3.3), 75

fixed-requirement constraint   A functional constraint with an = sign. The left-hand side represents the amount provided of some type of quantity, and the right-hand side represents the required amount for that quantity. (Section 3.4), 81

fixed-requirements problem   A type of linear programming problem concerned with optimizing how to meet a number of fixed requirements. Its identifying feature is that each functional constraint in its model is a fixed-requirement constraint. (Section 3.4), 82

identifying feature   A feature of a model that identifies the category of linear programming problem it represents. (Chapter introduction), 58

integer programming problem   A variation of a linear programming problem that has the additional restriction that some or all of the decision variables must have integer values. (Section 3.2), 69

mixed problem Any linear programming problem that includes at least two of the three types of functional constraints (resource constraints, benefit constraints, and fixed-requirement constraints). (Section 3.4), 82

model enrichment The process of using experience with a model to identify and add important details that will provide a better representation of the real problem. (Section 3.7), 96

model validation The process of checking and testing a model to develop a valid model. (Section 3.7), 96

resource-allocation problem A type of linear programming problem concerned with allocating

resources to activities. Its identifying feature is that each functional constraint in its model is a resource constraint. (Section 3.2), 65

resource constraint A functional constraint with a ≤ sign. The left-hand side represents the amount of some resource that is used by the activities under consideration, and the right-hand side represents the amount available of that resource. (Section 3.2), 65

transportation problem A type of linear programming problem that typically involves finding a shipping plan that minimizes the total cost of transporting a product from a number of plants to a number of customers. (Section 3.5), 89

Learning Aids for This Chapter in Your MS Courseware

Chapter 3 Excel Files:

Super Grain Example

TBA Airlines Example

Think-Big Example

Union Airways Example

Big M Example

Revised Super Grain Example

Sellmore Example

Solved Problems (See the CD-ROM or Web site for the Solutions)

3.S1. Farm Management

Dwight and Hattie have run the family farm for over 30 years. They are currently planning the mix of crops to plant on their 120-acre farm for the upcoming season. The table below gives the labor-hours and fertilizer required per acre, as well as the total expected profit per acre for each of the potential crops under consideration. Dwight, Hattie, and their children can work at most 6,500 total hours during the upcoming season. They have 200 tons of fertilizer available. What mix of crops should be planted to maximize the family's total profit?

a. Formulate and solve a linear programming model for this problem in a spreadsheet.

b. Formulate this same model algebraically.

Crop	Labor Required (hours per acre)	Fertilizer Required (tons per acre)	Expected Profit (per acre)
Oats	50	1.5	$500
Wheat	60	2	$600
Corn	105	4	$950

3.S2. Diet Problem

The kitchen manager for Sing Sing prison is trying to decide what to feed its prisoners. She would like to offer some combination of milk, beans, and oranges. The goal is to minimize

cost, subject to meeting the minimum nutritional requirements imposed by law. The cost and nutritional content of each food, along with the minimum nutritional requirements, are shown below. What diet should be fed to each prisoner?

a. Formulate and solve a linear programming model for this problem in a spreadsheet.

b. Formulate this same model algebraically.

	Milk (gallons)	Navy Beans (cups)	Oranges (large Calif. Valencia)	Minimum Daily Requirement
Niacin (mg)	3.2	4.9	0.8	13.0
Thiamin (mg)	1.12	1.3	0.19	1.5
Vitamin C (mg)	32.0	0.0	93.0	45.0
Cost ($)	2.00	0.20	0.25	

3.S3. Cutting Stock Problem

Decora Accessories manufactures a variety of bathroom accessories, including decorative towel rods and shower curtain rods. Each of the accessories includes a rod made out of stainless steel. However, many different lengths are needed: 12, 18, 24, 40, and 60 inches. Decora purchases 60-inch rods from an outside supplier and then cuts the rods as needed for their products.

Each 60-inch rod can be used to make a number of smaller rods. For example, a 60-inch rod could be used to make a 40-inch and an 18-inch rod (with 2 inches of waste), or five 12-inch rods (with no waste). For the next production period, Decora needs twenty-five 12-inch rods, fifty-two 18-inch rods, forty-five 24-inch rods, thirty 40-inch rods, and twelve 60-inch rods. What is the fewest number of 60-inch rods that can be purchased to meet their production needs? Formulate and solve an integer programming model in a spreadsheet.

3.S4. Producing and Distributing AEDs at Heart Start

Heart Start produces automated external defibrillators in each of two different plants (A and B). The unit production costs and monthly production capacity of the two plants are indicated in the table below. The automated external defibrillators are sold through three wholesalers. The shipping cost from each plant to the warehouse of each wholesaler along with the monthly demand from each wholesaler are also indicated in the table. The management of Heart Start now has asked their top management scientist (you) to address the following two questions. How many automated external defibrillators should be produced in each plant, and how should they be distributed to each of the three wholesaler warehouses so as to minimize the combined cost of production and shipping? Formulate and solve a linear programming model in a spreadsheet.

3.S5. Bidding for Classes

In the MBA program at a prestigious university in the Pacific Northwest, students bid for electives in the second year of their program. Each student has 100 points to bid (total) and must take two electives. There are four electives available: Management Science (MS), Finance (Fin), Operations Management (OM), and Marketing (Mkt). Each class is limited to 5 students. The bids submitted for each of the 10 students are shown in the table below.

Student Bids for Classes				
Student	MS	Fin	OM	Mkt
George	60	10	10	20
Fred	20	20	40	20
Ann	45	45	5	5
Eric	50	20	5	25
Susan	30	30	30	10
Liz	50	50	0	0
Ed	70	20	10	0
David	25	25	35	15
Tony	35	15	35	15
Jennifer	60	10	10	20

a. Formulate and solve a spreadsheet model to determine an assignment of students to classes so as to maximize the total bid points of the assignments.

b. Does the resulting solution seem like a fair assignment?

c. Which alternative objectives might lead to a fairer assignment?

	Unit Shipping Cost			Unit Production Cost	Monthly Production Capacity
	Warehouse 1	Warehouse 2	Warehouse 3		
Plant A	$22	$14	$30	$600	100
Plant B	$16	$20	$24	$625	120
Monthly Demand	80	60	70		

Problems

We have inserted the symbol E* to the left of each problem (or its parts) where Excel should be used (unless your instructor gives you contrary instructions). An asterisk on the problem number indicates that at least a partial answer is given in the back of the book.

3.1.   Reconsider the Super Grain Corp. case study as presented in Section 3.1. The advertising firm, Giacomi & Jackowitz, now has suggested a fourth promising advertising medium—radio commercials—to promote the company's new breakfast cereal, Crunchy Start. Young children are potentially major consumers of this cereal, but parents of young children (the major potential purchasers) often are too busy to do much reading (so may miss the

company's advertisements in magazines and Sunday supplements) or even to watch the Saturday morning programs for children where the company's television commercials are aired. However, these parents do tend to listen to the radio during the commute to and from work. Therefore, to better reach these parents, Giacomi & Jackowitz suggests giving consideration to running commercials for Crunchy Start on nationally syndicated radio programs that appeal to young adults during typical commuting hours.

Giacomi & Jackowitz estimates that the cost of developing each new radio commercial would be $50,000, and that the expected number of exposures per commercial would be 900,000. The firm has determined that 10 spots are available for different radio commercials, and each one would cost $200,000 for a normal run.

E*   a. Formulate and solve a spreadsheet model for the revised advertising-mix problem that includes this fourth advertising medium. Identify the data cells, the changing cells, and the target cell. Also show the Excel equation for each output cell expressed as a SUMPRODUCT function.

b. Indicate why this spreadsheet model is a linear programming model.

c. Express this model in algebraic form.

3.2.* Consider a resource-allocation problem having the following data:

Resource	Resource Usage per Unit of Each Activity		Amount of Resource Available
	1	2	
1	2	1	10
2	3	3	20
3	2	4	20
Contribution per unit	$20	$30	

Contribution per unit = profit per unit of the activity.

E*   a. Formulate a linear programming model for this problem on a spreadsheet.

E*   b. Use the spreadsheet to check the following solutions: $(x_1, x_2) = (2, 2), (3, 3), (2, 4), (4, 2), (3, 4), (4, 3)$. Which of these solutions are feasible? Which of these feasible solutions has the best value of the objective function?

E*   c. Use the Solver to find an optimal solution.

d. Express this model in algebraic form.

e. Use the graphical method to solve this model.

3.3. Consider a resource-allocation problem having the following data.

Resource	Resource Usage per Unit of Each Activity			Amount of Resource Available
	1	2	3	
A	30	20	0	500
B	0	10	40	600
C	20	20	30	1,000
Contribution per unit	$50	$40	$70	

Contribution per unit = profit per unit of the activity.

E*   a. Formulate and solve a linear programming model for this problem on a spreadsheet.

b. Express this model in algebraic form.

E*3.4. Consider a resource-allocation problem having the following data:

Resource	Resource Usage per Unit of Each Activity				Amount of Resource Available
	1	2	3	4	
P	3	5	−2	4	400
Q	4	−1	3	2	300
R	6	3	2	−1	400
S	−2	2	5	3	300
Contribution per unit	$11	$9	$8	$9	

Contribution per unit = profit per unit of the activity.

a. Formulate a linear programming model for this problem on a spreadsheet.

b. Make five guesses of your own choosing for the optimal solution. Use the spreadsheet to check each one for feasibility and, if feasible, for the value of the objective function. Which feasible guess has the best objective function value?

c. Use the Solver to find an optimal solution.

3.5.* The Omega Manufacturing Company has discontinued the production of a certain unprofitable product line. This act created considerable excess production capacity. Management is considering devoting this excess capacity to one or more of three products, products 1, 2, and 3. The available capacity of the machines that might limit output is summarized in the following table:

Machine Type	Available Time (in Machine-Hours per Week)
Milling machine	500
Lathe	350
Grinder	150

The number of machine-hours required for each unit of the respective products is as follows:

Productivity Coefficient (in Machine-Hours per Unit)

Machine Type	Product 1	Product 2	Product 3
Milling machine	9	3	5
Lathe	5	4	0
Grinder	3	0	2

The Sales Department indicates that the sales potential for products 1 and 2 exceeds the maximum production rate and that the sales potential for product 3 is 20 units per week. The unit profit would be $50, $20, and $25, respectively, for products 1, 2, and 3. The objective is to determine how much of each product Omega should produce to maximize profit.

a. Indicate why this is a resource-allocation problem by identifying both the activities and the limited resources to be allocated to these activities.

b. Identify verbally the decisions to be made, the constraints on these decisions, and the overall measure of performance for the decisions.

c. Convert these verbal descriptions of the constraints and the measure of performance into quantitative expressions in terms of the data and decisions.

E*   d. Formulate a spreadsheet model for this problem. Identify the data cells, the changing cells, the target cell, and the other output cells. Also show the Excel equation for each output cell expressed as a SUMPRODUCT function. Then use the Excel Solver to solve the model.

e. Summarize the model in algebraic form.

3.6.   Ed Butler is the production manager for the Bilco Corporation, which produces three types of spare parts for automobiles. The manufacture of each part requires processing on each of two machines, with the following processing times (in hours):

Machine	Part		
	A	B	C
1	0.02	0.03	0.05
2	0.05	0.02	0.04

Each machine is available 40 hours per month. Each part manufactured will yield a unit profit as follows:

	Part		
	A	B	C
Profit	$50	$40	$30

Ed wants to determine the mix of spare parts to produce to maximize total profit.

a. Identify both the activities and the resources for this resource-allocation problem.

E*   b. Formulate a linear programming model for this problem on a spreadsheet.

E*   c. Make three guesses of your own choosing for the optimal solution. Use the spreadsheet to check each one for feasibility and, if feasible, for the value of the objective function. Which feasible guess has the best objective function value?

E*   d. Use the Solver to find an optimal solution.

e. Express the model in algebraic form.

E*3.7.   Consider the following algebraic formulation of a resource-allocation problem with three resources, where the decisions to be made are the levels of three activities (A_1, A_2, and A_3).

Maximize   Profit $= 20A_1 + 40A_2 + 30A_3$

subject to

Resource 1: $3A_1 + 5A_2 + 4A_3 \le 400$ (amount available)

Resource 2: $A_1 + A_2 + A_3 \le 100$ (amount available)

Resource 3: $A_1 + 3A_2 + 2A_3 \le 200$ (amount available)

and

$$A_1 \ge 0 \quad A_2 \ge 0 \quad A_3 \ge 0$$

Formulate and solve the spreadsheet model for this problem.

3.8.   Read the referenced article that fully describes the management science study summarized in the application vignette presented in Section 3.3. Briefly describe how linear programming was applied in this study. Then list the various financial and nonfinancial benefits that resulted from this study.

3.9.   Consider a cost–benefit–trade-off problem having the following data:

	Benefit Contribution per Unit of Each Activity		
Benefit	1	2	Minimum Acceptable Level
1	5	3	60
2	2	2	30
3	7	9	126
Unit cost	$60	$50	

E*   a. Formulate a linear programming model for this problem on a spreadsheet.

E*   b. Use the spreadsheet to check the following solutions: $(x_1, x_2) = (7, 7), (7, 8), (8, 7), (8, 8), (8, 9), (9, 8)$. Which of these solutions are feasible? Which of these feasible solutions has the best value of the objective function?

E*   c. Use the Solver to find an optimal solution.

d. Express the model in algebraic form.

e. Use the graphical method to solve this model.

E*3.10. Consider a cost–benefit–trade-off problem having the following data:

	Benefit Contribution per Unit of Each Activity			
Benefit	1	2	3	4	Minimum Acceptable Level
P	2	−1	4	3	80
Q	1	4	−1	2	60
R	3	5	4	−1	110
Unit cost	$400	$600	$500	$300	

a. Formulate a linear programming model for this problem on a spreadsheet.

b. Make five guesses of your own choosing for the optimal solution. Use the spreadsheet to check each one for feasibility and, if feasible, for the value of the objective function. Which feasible guess has the best objective function value?

c. Use the Solver to find an optimal solution.

3.11.*   Fred Jonasson manages a family-owned farm. To supplement several food products grown on the farm, Fred also raises pigs for market. He now wishes to determine the quantities of the available types of feed (corn, tankage, and alfalfa) that should be given to each pig. Since pigs will eat any mix of these feed types, the objective is to determine which mix will meet certain nutritional requirements at a *minimum cost*. The number of units of each type of basic nutritional ingredient contained within a kilogram of each feed type is given in the following table, along with the daily nutritional requirements and feed costs:

Nutritional Ingredient	Kilogram of Corn	Kilogram of Tankage	Kilogram of Alfalfa	Minimum Daily Requirement
Carbohydrates	90	20	40	200
Protein	30	80	60	180
Vitamins	10	20	60	150
Cost (¢)	84	72	60	

E*   *a.* Formulate a linear programming model for this problem on a spreadsheet.

E*   *b.* Use the spreadsheet to check if $(x_1, x_2, x_3) = (1, 2, 2)$ is a feasible solution and, if so, what the daily cost would be for this diet. How many units of each nutritional ingredient would this diet provide daily?

E*   *c.* Take a few minutes to use a trial-and-error approach with the spreadsheet to develop your best guess for the optimal solution. What is the daily cost for your solution?

E*   *d.* Use the Solver to find an optimal solution.

       e. Express the model in algebraic form.

3.12. Maureen Laird is the chief financial officer for the Alva Electric Co., a major public utility in the Midwest. The company has scheduled the construction of new hydroelectric plants 5, 10, and 20 years from now to meet the needs of the growing population in the region served by the company. To cover the construction costs, Maureen needs to invest some of the company's money now to meet these future cash flow needs. Maureen may purchase only three kinds of financial assets, each of which costs $1 million per unit. Fractional units may be purchased. The assets produce income 5, 10, and 20 years from now, and that income is needed to cover minimum cash flow requirements in those years, as shown in the following table.

		Income per Unit of Asset		
Year	Asset 1	Asset 2	Asset 3	Minimum Cash Flow Required
5	$2 million	$1 million	$0.5 million	$400 million
10	0.5 million	0.5 million	1 million	100 million
20	0	1.5 million	2 million	300 million

Maureen wishes to determine the mix of investments in these assets that will cover the cash flow requirements while minimizing the total amount invested.

E*   *a.* Formulate a linear programming model for this problem on a spreadsheet.

E*   *b.* Use the spreadsheet to check the possibility of purchasing 100 units of asset 1, 100 units of asset 2, and 200 units of asset 3. How much cash flow would this mix of investments generate 5, 10, and 20 years from now? What would be the total amount invested?

E*   *c.* Take a few minutes to use a trial-and-error approach with the spreadsheet to develop your best guess for the optimal solution. What is the total amount invested for your solution?

E*   *d.* Use the Solver to find an optimal solution.

       e. Summarize the model in algebraic form.

3.13. Web Mercantile sells many household products through an online catalog. The company needs substantial warehouse space for storing its goods. Plans now are being made for leasing warehouse storage space over the next five months. Just how much space will be required in each of these months is known. However, since these space requirements are quite different, it may be most economical to lease only the amount needed each month on a month-by-month basis. On the other hand, the additional cost for leasing space for additional months is much less than for the first month, so it may be less expensive to lease the maximum amount needed for the entire five months. Another option is the intermediate approach of changing the total amount of space leased (by adding a new lease and/or having an old lease expire) at least once but not every month.

The space requirement and the leasing costs for the various leasing periods are as follows:

Month	Required Space (Square Feet)
1	30,000
2	20,000
3	40,000
4	10,000
5	50,000

Leasing Period (Months)	Cost per Sq. Ft. Leased
1	$ 65
2	100
3	135
4	160
5	190

The objective is to minimize the total leasing cost for meeting the space requirements.

    a. Indicate why this is a cost–benefit–trade-off problem by identifying both the activities and the benefits being sought from these activities.

    b. Identify verbally the decisions to be made, the constraints on these decisions, and the overall measure of performance for the decisions.

    c. Convert these verbal descriptions of the constraints and the measure of performance into quantitative expressions in terms of the data and decisions.

E*   *d.* Formulate a spreadsheet model for this problem. Identify the data cells, the changing cells, the target cell, and the other output cells. Also show the Excel equation for each output cell expressed as a SUMPRODUCT function. Then use the Excel Solver to solve the model.

    e. Summarize the model in algebraic form.

E*3.14. Consider the following algebraic formulation of a cost–benefit–trade-off problem involving three benefits, where the decisions to be made are the levels of four activities (A_1, A_2, A_3, and A_4):

$$\text{Minimize} \quad \text{Cost} = 2A_1 + A_2 - A_3 + 3A_4$$

subject to

Benefit 1: $3A_1 + 2A_2 - 2A_3 + 5A_4 \geq 80$ (minimum acceptable level)

Benefit 2: $A_1 - A_2 \qquad + A_4 \geq 10$ (minimum acceptable level)

Benefit 3: $A_1 + A_2 - A_3 + 2A_4 \geq 30$ (minimum acceptable level)

and

$$A_1 \geq 0 \quad A_2 \geq 0 \quad A_3 \geq 0 \quad A_4 \geq 0$$

Formulate and solve the spreadsheet model for this problem.

Time of Day	Minimum Number of Consultants Required to Be on Duty
8 AM–noon	6
Noon–4 PM	8
4 PM–8 PM	12
8 PM–midnight	6

Two types of computer consultants can be hired: full-time and part-time. The full-time consultants work for eight consecutive hours in any of the following shifts: morning (8 AM–4 PM), afternoon (noon–8 PM), and evening (4 PM–midnight). Full-time consultants are paid $14 per hour.

Part-time consultants can be hired to work any of the four shifts listed in the table. Part-time consultants are paid $12 per hour.

An additional requirement is that during every time period, there must be at least two full-time consultants on duty for every part-time consultant on duty.

Larry would like to determine how many full-time and part-time consultants should work each shift to meet the above requirements at the minimum possible cost.

    a. Which category of linear programming problem does this problem fit? Why?

E*   *b.* Formulate and solve a linear programming model for this problem on a spreadsheet.

    c. Summarize the model in algebraic form.

3.16.* The Medequip Company produces precision medical diagnostic equipment at two factories. Three medical centers have placed orders for this month's production output. The following table shows what the cost would be for shipping each unit from each factory to each of these customers. Also shown are the number of units that will be produced at each factory and the number of units ordered by each customer.

A decision now needs to be made about the shipping plan for how many units to ship from each factory to each customer.

	Unit Shipping Cost			
From \ To	Customer 1	Customer 2	Customer 3	Output
Factory 1	$600	$800	$700	400 units
Factory 2	400	900	600	500 units
Order size	300 units	200 units	400 units	

    a. Which category of linear programming problem does this problem fit? Why?

E*   *b.* Formulate and solve a linear programming model for this problem on a spreadsheet.

    c. Summarize this formulation in algebraic form.

3.15. Larry Edison is the Director of the Computer Center for Buckly College. He now needs to schedule the staffing of the center. It is open from 8 AM until midnight. Larry has monitored the usage of the center at various times of the day and determined that the following number of computer consultants are required:

3.17. The Fagersta Steelworks currently is working two mines to obtain its iron ore. This iron ore is shipped to either of two storage facilities. When needed, it then is shipped on to the company's steel plant. The diagram below depicts this distribution network, where M1 and M2 are the two mines, S1 and S2 are the two storage facilities, and P is the steel plant. The diagram also shows the monthly amounts produced at the mines and needed at the plant, as well as the shipping cost and the maximum amount that can be shipped per month through each shipping lane.

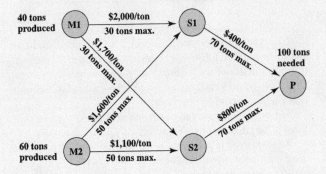

Management now wants to determine the most economical plan for shipping the iron ore from the mines through the distribution network to the steel plant.

 a. Identify all the requirements that will need to be expressed in fixed-requirement constraints.

E* b. Formulate and solve a linear programming model for this problem on a spreadsheet.

 c. Express this model in algebraic form.

3.18.* Al Ferris has $60,000 that he wishes to invest now in order to use the accumulation for purchasing a retirement annuity in five years. After consulting with his financial advisor, he has been offered four types of fixed-income investments, which we will label as investments A, B, C, and D.

Investments A and B are available at the beginning of each of the next five years (call them years 1 to 5). Each dollar invested in A at the beginning of a year returns $1.40 (a profit of $0.40) two years later (in time for immediate reinvestment). Each dollar invested in B at the beginning of a year returns $1.70 three years later.

Investments C and D will each be available at one time in the future. Each dollar invested in C at the beginning of year 2 returns $1.90 at the end of year 5. Each dollar invested in D at the beginning of year 5 returns $1.30 at the end of year 5.

Al wishes to know which investment plan maximizes the amount of money that can be accumulated by the beginning of year 6.

 a. For this problem, all its functional constraints can be expressed as fixed-requirement constraints. To do this, let A_t, B_t, C_t, and D_t be the amounts invested in investments A, B, C, and D, respectively, at the beginning of year t for each t where the investment is available and will mature by the end of year 5. Also let R_t be the number of available dollars *not* invested at the beginning of year t (and so available for investment in a later year). Thus, the amount invested at the beginning of year t *plus* R_t must equal the number of dollars available for investment at that time. Write such an equation in terms of the relevant variables

above for the beginning of each of the five years to obtain the five fixed-requirement constraints for this problem.

 b. Formulate a complete linear programming model for this problem in algebraic form.

E* c. Formulate and solve this model on a spreadsheet.

3.19. The Metalco Company desires to blend a new alloy of 40 percent tin, 35 percent zinc, and 25 percent lead from several available alloys having the following properties:

Property	Alloy				
	1	2	3	4	5
Percentage of tin	60	25	45	20	50
Percentage of zinc	10	15	45	50	40
Percentage of lead	30	60	10	30	10
Cost ($/lb)	22	20	25	24	27

The objective is to determine the proportions of these alloys that should be blended to produce the new alloy at a minimum cost.

 a. Identify all the requirements that will need to be expressed in fixed-requirement constraints.

E* b. Formulate and solve a linear programming model for this problem on a spreadsheet.

 c. Express this model in algebraic form.

3.20. The Weigelt Corporation has three branch plants with excess production capacity. Fortunately, the corporation has a new product ready to begin production, and all three plants have this capability, so some of the excess capacity can be used in this way. This product can be made in three sizes—large, medium, and small—that yield a net unit profit of $420, $360, and $300, respectively. Plants 1, 2, and 3 have the excess capacity to produce 750, 900, and 450 units per day of this product, respectively, regardless of the size or combination of sizes involved.

The amount of available in-process storage space also imposes a limitation on the production rates of the new product. Plants 1, 2, and 3 have 13,000, 12,000, and 5,000 square feet, respectively, of in-process storage space available for a day's production of this product. Each unit of the large, medium, and small sizes produced per day requires 20, 15, and 12 square feet, respectively.

Sales forecasts indicate that if available, 900, 1,200, and 750 units of the large, medium, and small sizes, respectively, would be sold per day.

At each plant, some employees will need to be laid off unless most of the plant's excess production capacity can be used to produce the new product. To avoid layoffs if possible, management has decided that the plants should use the same percentage of their excess capacity to produce the new product.

Management wishes to know how much of each of the sizes should be produced by each of the plants to maximize profit.

E* a. Formulate and solve a linear programming model for this mixed problem on a spreadsheet.

 b. Express the model in algebraic form.

3.21.* A cargo plane has three compartments for storing cargo: front, center, and back. These compartments have capacity limits on both *weight* and *space,* as summarized below:

Compartment	Weight Capacity (Tons)	Space Capacity (Cubic Feet)
Front	12	7,000
Center	18	9,000
Back	10	5,000

Furthermore, the weight of the cargo in the respective compartments must be the same proportion of that compartment's weight capacity to maintain the balance of the airplane.

The following four cargoes have been offered for shipment on an upcoming flight as space is available:

Cargo	Weight (Tons)	Volume (Cubic Feet/Ton)	Profit ($/Ton)
1	20	500	320
2	16	700	400
3	25	600	360
4	13	400	290

Any portion of these cargoes can be accepted. The objective is to determine how much (if any) of each cargo should be accepted and how to distribute each among the compartments to maximize the total profit for the flight.

E*   a. Formulate and solve a linear programming model for this mixed problem on a spreadsheet.

b. Express the model in algebraic form.

3.22.   Comfortable Hands is a company that features a product line of winter gloves for the entire family—men, women, and children. They are trying to decide what mix of these three types of gloves to produce.

Comfortable Hands's manufacturing labor force is unionized. Each full-time employee works a 40-hour week. In addition, by union contract, the number of full-time employees can never drop below 20. Nonunion, part-time workers also can be hired with the following union-imposed restrictions: (1) each part-time worker works 20 hours per week and (2) there must be at least two full-time employees for each part-time employee.

All three types of gloves are made out of the same 100 percent genuine cowhide leather. Comfortable Hands has a long-term contract with a supplier of the leather and receives a 5,000-square-foot shipment of the material each week. The material requirements and labor requirements, along with the *gross profit* per glove sold (not considering labor costs), are given in the following table.

Glove	Material Required (Square Feet)	Labor Required (Minutes)	Gross Profit (per Pair)
Men's	2	30	$ 8
Women's	1.5	45	10
Children's	1	40	6

Each full-time employee earns $13 per hour, while each part-time employee earns $10 per hour. Management wishes to know what mix of each of the three types of gloves to produce per week, as well as how many full-time and part-time workers to employ. They would like to maximize their *net profit*—their gross profit from sales minus their labor costs.

E*   a. Formulate and solve a linear programming model for this problem on a spreadsheet.

b. Summarize this formulation in algebraic form.

E*3.23. Oxbridge University maintains a powerful mainframe computer for research use by its faculty, Ph.D. students, and research associates. During all working hours, an operator must be available to operate and maintain the computer, as well as to perform some programming services. Beryl Ingram, the director of the computer facility, oversees the operation.

It is now the beginning of the fall semester and Beryl is confronted with the problem of assigning different working hours to her operators. Because all the operators are currently enrolled in the university, they are available to work only a limited number of hours each day.

There are six operators (four undergraduate students and two graduate students). They all have different wage rates because of differences in their experience with computers and in their programming ability. The following table shows their wage rates, along with the maximum number of hours that each can work each day.

Operators	Wage Rate	Maximum Hours of Availability				
		Mon.	Tue.	Wed.	Thurs.	Fri.
K. C.	$10.00/hour	6	0	6	0	6
D. H.	$10.10/hour	0	6	0	6	0
H. B.	$9.90/hour	4	8	4	0	4
S. C.	$9.80/hour	5	5	5	0	5
K. S.	$10.80/hour	3	0	3	8	0
N. K.	$11.30/hour	0	0	0	6	2

Each operator is guaranteed a certain minimum number of hours per week that will maintain an adequate knowledge of the operation. This level is set arbitrarily at 8 hours per week for the undergraduate students (K. C., D. H., H. B., and S. C.) and 7 hours per week for the graduate students (K. S. and N. K.).

The computer facility is to be open for operation from 8 AM to 10 PM Monday through Friday with exactly one operator on duty during these hours. On Saturdays and Sundays, the computer is to be operated by other staff.

Because of a tight budget, Beryl has to minimize cost. She wishes to determine the number of hours she should assign to each operator on each day. Formulate and solve a spreadsheet model for this problem.

3.24.   Slim-Down Manufacturing makes a line of nutritionally complete, weight-reduction beverages. One of its products is a strawberry shake that is designed to be a complete meal. The strawberry shake consists of several ingredients. Some information about each of these ingredients is given next.

Ingredient	Calories from Fat (per tbsp.)	Total Calories (per tbsp.)	Vitamin Content (mg/tbsp.)	Thickeners (mg/tbsp.)	Cost (¢/tbsp.)
Strawberry flavoring	1	50	20	3	10
Cream	75	100	0	8	8
Vitamin supplement	0	0	50	1	25
Artificial sweetener	0	120	0	2	15
Thickening agent	30	80	2	25	6

The nutritional requirements are as follows. The beverage must total between 380 and 420 calories (inclusive). No more than 20 percent of the total calories should come from fat. There must be at least 50 milligrams (mg) of vitamin content. For taste reasons, there must be at least two tablespoons (tbsp.) of strawberry flavoring for each tbsp. of artificial sweetener. Finally, to maintain proper thickness, there must be exactly 15 mg of thickeners in the beverage.

Management would like to select the quantity of each ingredient for the beverage that would minimize cost while meeting the above requirements.

    a. Identify the requirements that lead to resource constraints, to benefit constraints, and to fixed-requirement constraints.

E*   *b.* Formulate and solve a linear programming model for this problem on a spreadsheet.

    c. Summarize this formulation in algebraic form.

3.25. Joyce and Marvin run a day care for preschoolers. They are trying to decide what to feed the children for lunches. They would like to keep their costs down, but they also need to meet the nutritional requirements of the children. They have already decided to go with peanut butter and jelly sandwiches, and some combination of graham crackers, milk, and orange juice. The nutritional content of each food choice and its cost are given in the table below.

Food Item	Calories from Fat	Total Calories	Vitamin C (mg)	Protein (g)	Cost (¢)
Bread (1 slice)	10	70	0	3	5
Peanut butter (1 tbsp.)	75	100	0	4	4
Strawberry jelly (1 tbsp.)	0	50	3	0	7
Graham cracker (1 cracker)	20	60	0	1	8
Milk (1 cup)	70	150	2	8	15
Juice (1 cup)	0	100	120	1	35

The nutritional requirements are as follows. Each child should receive between 400 and 600 calories. No more than 30 percent of the total calories should come from fat. Each child should consume at least 60 milligrams (mg) of vitamin C and 12 grams (g) of protein. Furthermore, for practical reasons, each child needs exactly 2 slices of bread (to make the sandwich), at least twice as much peanut butter as jelly, and at least 1 cup of liquid (milk and/or juice).

Joyce and Marvin would like to select the food choices for each child that minimize cost while meeting the above requirements.

    a. Identify the requirements that lead to resource constraints, to benefit constraints, and to fixed-requirement constraints.

E*   *b.* Formulate and solve a linear programming model for this problem on a spreadsheet.

    c. Express the model in algebraic form.

3.26. Read the referenced article that fully describes the management science study summarized in the application vignette presented in Section 3.5. Briefly describe how the model for the transportation problem was applied in this study. Then list the various financial and nonfinancial benefits that resulted from this study.

E*3.27. The Cost-Less Corp. supplies its four retail outlets from its four plants. The shipping cost per shipment from each plant to each retail outlet is given below.

	Unit Shipping Cost			
Retail Outlet:	1	2	3	4
Plant				
1	$500	$600	$400	$200
2	200	900	100	300
3	300	400	200	100
4	200	100	300	200

Plants 1, 2, 3, and 4 make 10, 20, 20, and 10 shipments per month, respectively. Retail outlets 1, 2, 3, and 4 need to receive 20, 10, 10, and 20 shipments per month, respectively.

The distribution manager, Randy Smith, now wants to determine the best plan for how many shipments to send from each plant to the respective retail outlets each month. Randy's objective is to minimize the total shipping cost.

Formulate this problem as a transportation problem on a spreadsheet and then use the Excel Solver to obtain an optimal solution.

E*3.28. The Childfair Company has three plants producing child push chairs that are to be shipped to four distribution centers. Plants 1, 2, and 3 produce 12, 17, and 11 shipments per month, respectively. Each distribution center needs to receive 10 shipments per month. The distance from each plant to the respective distribution centers is given below:

	Distance to Distribution Center (Miles)			
	1	2	3	4
Plant				
1	800	1,300	400	700
2	1,100	1,400	600	1,000
3	600	1,200	800	900

The freight cost for each shipment is $100 plus 50 cents/mile.

How much should be shipped from each plant to each of the distribution centers to minimize the total shipping cost?

Formulate this problem as a transportation problem on a spreadsheet and then use the Excel Solver to obtain an optimal solution.

E*3.29.   The Onenote Co. produces a single product at three plants for four customers. The three plants will produce 60, 80, and 40 units, respectively, during the next week. The firm has made a commitment to sell 40 units to customer 1, 60 units to customer 2, and at least 20 units to customer 3. Both customers 3 and 4 also want to buy as many of the remaining units as possible. The net profit associated with shipping a unit from plant i for sale to customer j is given by the following table:

	Customer			
	1	2	3	4
Plant				
1	$800	$700	$500	$200
2	500	200	100	300
3	600	400	300	500

Management wishes to know how many units to sell to customers 3 and 4 and how many units to ship from each of the plants to each of the customers to maximize profit. Formulate and solve a spreadsheet model for this problem.

E*3.30. The Move-It Company has two plants building forklift trucks that then are shipped to three distribution centers. The production costs are the same at the two plants, and the cost of shipping each truck is shown below for each combination of plant and distribution center:

	Distribution Center		
	1	2	3
Plant			
A	$800	$700	$400
B	600	800	500

A total of 60 forklift trucks are produced and shipped per week. Each plant can produce and ship any amount up to a maximum of 50 trucks per week, so there is considerable flexibility on how to divide the total production between the two plants so

as to reduce shipping costs. However, each distribution center must receive exactly 20 trucks per week.

Management's objective is to determine how many forklift trucks should be produced at each plant, and then what the overall shipping pattern should be to minimize total shipping cost. Formulate and solve a spreadsheet model for this problem.

E*3.31. Redo Problem 3.30 when any distribution center may receive any quantity between 10 and 30 forklift trucks per week in order to further reduce total shipping cost, provided only that the total shipped to all three distribution centers must still equal 60 trucks per week.

E*3.32. Consider the assignment problem having the following cost table:

	Job		
	1	2	3
Person			
A	$5	$7	$4
B	3	6	5
C	2	3	4

The optimal solution is A-3, B-1, C-2, with a total cost of $10.

Formulate this problem on a spreadsheet and then use the Excel Solver to obtain the optimal solution identified above.

3.33.   Four cargo ships will be used for shipping goods from one port to four other ports (labeled 1, 2, 3, 4). Any ship can be used for making any one of these four trips. However, because of differences in the ships and cargoes, the total cost of loading, transporting, and unloading the goods for the different ship–port combinations varies considerably, as shown in the following table:

	Port			
	1	2	3	4
Ship				
1	$500	$400	$600	$700
2	600	600	700	500
3	700	500	700	600
4	500	400	600	600

The objective is to assign the four ships to four different ports in such a way as to minimize the total cost for all four shipments.

    a. Describe how this problem fits into the format for an assignment problem.

E* *b.* Formulate and solve this problem on a spreadsheet.

E*3.34. Reconsider Problem 3.30. Now distribution centers 1, 2, and 3 must receive exactly 10, 20, and 30 units per week, respectively. For administrative convenience, management has decided that each distribution center will be supplied totally by a single plant, so that one plant will supply one distribution center and the other plant will supply the other two distribution centers. The choice of these assignments of plants to distribution centers is to be made solely on the basis of minimizing total shipping cost.

Formulate and solve a spreadsheet model for this problem.

3.35. Vincent Cardoza is the owner and manager of a machine shop that does custom order work. This Wednesday afternoon, he has received calls from two customers who would like to place rush orders. One is a trailer hitch company that would like some custom-made heavy-duty tow bars. The other is a mini-car-carrier company that needs some customized stabilizer bars. Both customers would like as many as possible by the end of the week (two working days). Since both products would require the use of the same two machines, Vincent needs to decide and inform the customers this afternoon about how many of each product he will agree to make over the next two days.

Each tow bar requires 3.2 hours on machine 1 and 2 hours on machine 2. Each stabilizer bar requires 2.4 hours on machine 1 and 3 hours on machine 2. Machine 1 will be available for 16 hours over the next two days and machine 2 will be available for 15 hours. The profit for each tow bar produced would be $130 and the profit for each stabilizer bar produced would be $150.

Vincent now wants to determine the mix of these production quantities that will maximize the total profit.

    a. Formulate an integer programming model in algebraic form for this problem.

E*   *b.* Formulate and solve the model on a spreadsheet.

3.36. Pawtucket University is planning to buy new copier machines for its library. Three members of its Management Science Department are analyzing what to buy. They are considering two different models: Model A, a high-speed copier, and Model B, a lower speed but less expensive copier. Model A can handle 20,000 copies a day and costs $6,000. Model B can handle 10,000 copies a day but only costs $4,000. They would like to have at least six copiers so that they can spread them throughout the library. They also would like to have at least one high-speed copier. Finally, the copiers need to be able to handle a capacity of at least 75,000 copies per day. The objective is to determine the mix of these two copiers that will handle all these requirements at minimum cost.

E*   *a.* Formulate and solve a spreadsheet model for this problem.

    b. Formulate this same model in algebraic form.

3.37. Northeastern Airlines is considering the purchase of new long-, medium-, and short-range jet passenger airplanes. The purchase price would be $67 million for each long-range plane, $50 million for each medium-range plane, and $35 million for each short-range plane. The board of directors has authorized a maximum commitment of $1.5 billion for these purchases. Regardless of which airplanes are purchased, air travel of all distances is expected to be sufficiently large that these planes would be utilized at essentially maximum capacity. It is estimated that the net annual profit (after capital recovery costs are subtracted) would be $4.2 million per long-range plane, $3 million per medium-range plane, and $2.3 million per short-range plane.

It is predicted that enough trained pilots will be available to the company to crew 30 new airplanes. If only short-range planes were purchased, the maintenance facilities would be able to handle 40 new planes. However, each medium-range plane is equivalent to 1 1/3 short-range planes, and each long-range plane is equivalent to 12/3 short-range planes in terms of their use of the maintenance facilities.

The information given here was obtained by a preliminary analysis of the problem. A more detailed analysis will be conducted subsequently. However, using the preceding data as a first approximation, management wishes to know how many planes of each type should be purchased to maximize profit.

E*   *a.* Formulate and solve a spreadsheet model for this problem.

    b. Formulate this model in algebraic form.

Partial Answers to Selected Problems

CHAPTER 3

3.2. *c.* 3.333 of Activity 1, 3.333 of Activity 2. Profit = $166.67.

3.5. *d.* 26 of Product 1, 54.76 of Product 2, 20 of Product 3. Profit = $2,904.76.

3.11. *d.* 1.14 kg of corn, 2.43 kg of alfalfa. Cost = $2.42.

3.16. *b.* Cost = $410,000.

Shipment Quantities	Customer 1	Customer 2	Customer 3
Factory 1	300	0	100
Factory 2	0	200	300

3.18. *c.* $60,000 in Investment A (year 1), $84,000 in Investment A (year 3), $117,600 in Investment D (year 5). Total accumulation in year 6 = $152,880.

3.21. *a.* Profit = $13,330.

Cargo Placement	Front	Center	Back
Cargo 1	0	5	10
Cargo 2	7.333	4.167	0
Cargo 3	0	0	0
Cargo 4	4.667	8.333	0

3.S1 Farm Management

Dwight and Hattie have run the family farm for over thirty years. They are currently planning the mix of crops to plant on their 120-acre farm for the upcoming season. The table below gives the labor hours and fertilizer required per acre, as well as the total expected profit per acre for each of the potential crops under consideration. Dwight, Hattie, and their children can work at most 6,500 total hours during the upcoming season. They have 200 tons of fertilizer available. What mix of crops should be planted to maximize the family's total profit.

a. *Formulate and solve a linear programming model for this problem in a spreadsheet.*

Crop	Labor Required (hours per acre)	Fertilizer Required (tons per acre)	Expected Profit (per acre)
Oats	50	1.5	$500
Wheat	60	2	$600
Corn	105	4	$950

This is a resource-allocation problem. The activities are the planting of the three crops and the limited resources are land, labor, and fertilizer. We will therefore build a spreadsheet following the template for resource-allocation problems in Figure 3.4. Start by entering the data. The data for this problem are the labor required, fertilizer required, and expected profit for each crop (per acre). Following the template, the data in the spreadsheet would be entered as displayed below, where range names of ProfitPerAcre (C4:E4) and TotalAvailable (H7:H9) are assigned to the corresponding data cells.

	B	C	D	E	F	G	H
3		Oats	Wheat	Corn			
4	Profit (per acre)	$500	$600	$950			
5							Total
6	**Resources**	Resources Used per Acre					Available
7	Land (acres)	1	1	1			120
8	Labor (hours)	50	60	105			6500
9	Fertilizer (tons)	1.5	2	4			200

The decisions to be made in this problem are how many acres of each crop to plant. Therefore, we add three changing cells in C12:E12 with range name AcresPlanted. The values in AcresPlanted (C12:E12) will eventually be determined by the Solver. For now, an arbitrary value of 1 is entered for each crop.

	B	C	D	E	F	G	H
3		Oats	Wheat	Corn			
4	Profit (per acre)	$500	$600	$950			
5							Total
6	**Resources**	Resources Used per Acre					Available
7	Land (acres)	1	1	1			120
8	Labor (hours)	50	60	105			6500
9	Fertilizer (tons)	1.5	2	4			200
10							
11							
12	Acres Planted	1	1	1			

The goal is to maximize the family's total profit. Thus, the target cell should calculate the total profit. In this case, the total profit will be

Total Profit = ($500)(acres of oats) + ($600)(acres of wheat) + ($950)(acres of corn)

or

Total Profit = SUMPRODUCT(ProfitPerAcre, AcresPlanted).

This formula is entered into cell H12. With 1 acre of each crop planted, the total cost would be ($500)(1) + ($600)(1) + ($950)(1) = $2,050.

	B	C	D	E	F	G	H
3		Oats	Wheat	Corn			
4	Profit (per acre)	$500	$600	$950			
5							Total
6	**Resources**	Resources Used per Acre					Available
7	Land (acres)	1	1	1			120
8	Labor (hours)	50	60	105			6500
9	Fertilizer (tons)	1.5	2	4			200
10							
11							Total Profit
12	Acres Planted	1	1	1			$2,050

	H
11	Total Profit
12	=SUMPRODUCT(ProfitPerAcre,AcresPlanted)

The functional constraints in this problem involve the limited resources of land, labor, and fertilizer. Given the AcresPlanted (the changing cells in C12:E12), we calculate the total resources used in TotalUsed (cells F7:F9). For land, this will be =SUMPRODUCT(C7:E7, AcresPlanted). Using a range name or an absolute reference for the acres planted, this formula can be copied into cells F8:F9 to calculate the amount of labor and fertilizer used. The total resources used must be <= TotalAvailable (H7:H9), as indicated by the <= in G7:G9.

	B	C	D	E	F	G	H
3		Oats	Wheat	Corn			
4	Profit (per acre)	$500	$600	$950			
5					Total		Total
6	Resources	Resources Used per Acre			Used		Available
7	Land (acres)	1	1	1	3	<=	120
8	Labor (hours)	50	60	105	215	<=	6500
9	Fertilizer (tons)	1.5	2	4	8	<=	200
10							
11							Total Profit
12	Acres Planted	1	1	1			$2,050

	F
5	Total
6	Used
7	=SUMPRODUCT(C7:E7,AcresPlanted)
8	=SUMPRODUCT(C8:E8,AcresPlanted)
9	=SUMPRODUCT(C9:E9,AcresPlanted)

3

The Solver information and solved spreadsheet are shown below.

	A	B	C	D	E	F	G	H
1		**Farm Management**						
2								
3			Oats	Wheat	Corn			
4		Profit (per acre)	$500	$600	$950			
5						Total		Total
6		**Resources**	Resources Used per Acre			Used		Available
7		Land (acres)	1	1	1	120	<=	120
8		Labor (hours)	50	60	105	6,400	<=	6500
9		Fertilizer (tons)	1.5	2	4	200	<=	200
10								
11								Total Profit
12		Acres Planted	80	40	0			$64,000

Solver Parameters

Set Objective (Target Cell): TotalProfit
To: Max
By Changing (Variable) Cells:
  AcresPlanted
Subject to the Constraints:
  TotalUsed <= TotalAvailable

Solver Options (Excel 2010):
  Make Variables Nonnegative
  Solving Method: Simplex LP
Solver Options (older Excel):
  Assume Nonnegative
  Assume Linear Model

Range Name	Cells
AcresPlanted	C12:E12
ProfitPerAcre	C4:E4
TotalAvailable	H7:H9
TotalProfit	H12
TotalUsed	F7:F9

	F
5	Total
6	Used
7	=SUMPRODUCT(C7:E7,AcresPlanted)
8	=SUMPRODUCT(C8:E8,AcresPlanted)
9	=SUMPRODUCT(C9:E9,AcresPlanted)

	H
11	Total Profit
12	=SUMPRODUCT(ProfitPerAcre,AcresPlanted)

Thus, oats should be planted on 80 acres and wheat on 40 acres, while not planting any corn, with a resulting total profit of $64,000.

b. *Formulate this same model algebraically.*

To build an algebraic model for this problem, start by defining the decision variables. In this case, the three decisions are how many acres of oats, wheat, and corn to plant. These variables are defined below:

Let O = Acres of oats planted,
  W = Acres of wheat planted,
  C = Acres of corn planted.

Next determine the goal of the problem. In this case, the goal is to achieve the highest possible total profit. Each acre of oats yields a profit of $500, each acre of wheat yields a profit of $600, while each acre of corn yields a profit of $950. The objective function is therefore

Maximize Total Profit = $500O + $600W + $950C.

There are three limited resources in this problem: 120 acres of land, 6500 hours of labor, and 200 tons of fertilizer. Each acre of a given crop that is planted uses up one available acre. The data for labor hours used and fertilizer used per acre planted can be used to calculate the total resources used as a function of the decision variables. The total resources used need to be less than or equal to the amount available. These constraints are therefore as follows:

Land: $O + W + C \leq 120$ acres,
Labor: $50O + 60W + 105C \leq 6500$ hours,
Fertilizer: $1.5O + 2W + 4C \leq 200$ tons

After adding nonnegativity constraints, the complete algebraic formulation is given below:

Let O = Acres of Oats planted,
        W = Acres of Wheat planted,
        C = Acres of Corn planted.

Maximize Total Profit = $500O + $600W + $950C.

subject to

Land: $O + W + C \leq 120$ acres,
Labor: $50O + 60W + 105C \leq 6500$ hours,
Fertilizer: $1.5O + 2W + 4C \leq 200$ tons

and $O \geq 0$, $W \geq 0$, $C \geq 0$.

3.S2 Diet Problem

The kitchen manager for Sing Sing Prison is trying to decide what to feed its prisoners. She would like to offer some combination of milk, beans, and oranges. The goal is to minimize cost, subject to meeting the minimum nutritional requirements imposed by law. The cost and nutritional content of each food, along with the minimum nutritional requirements, are shown below. What diet should be fed to each prisoner?

a. *Formulate and solve a linear programming model for this problem in a spreadsheet.*

	Milk (gallons)	Navy Beans (cups)	Oranges (large Calif. Valencia)	Minimum Daily Requirement
Niacin (mg)	3.2	4.9	0.8	13.0
Thiamin (mg)	1.12	1.3	0.19	1.5
Vitamin C (mg)	32.0	0.0	93.0	45.0
Cost ($)	2.00	0.20	0.25	

This is a cost-benefit-trade-off problem. The activities are the quantities of food to feed each prisoner and the required benefits are the minimum nutritional requirements. We will therefore build a spreadsheet following the template for cost-benefit-trade-off problems in Figure 3.6. Start by entering the data. The data for this problem are the nutrient content of each food, the minimum daily requirement for each nutrient, and the cost of each food. Following the template, the data in the spreadsheet would be entered as displayed below, where range names of UnitCost (C5:E5), NutritionalContents (C9:E11), and MinimumRequirement (H9:H11) are assigned to the corresponding data cells.

	B	C	D	E	F	G	H
3		Milk	Beans				
4		(gal.)	(cups)	Oranges			
5	Unit Cost	$2.00	$0.20	$0.25			
6							
7							Minimum
8		Nutritional Contents (mg)					Requirement
9	Niacin	3.2	4.9	0.8			13
10	Thiamin	1.12	1.3	0.19			1.5
11	Vitamin C	32	0	93			45

The decisions to be made in this problem are how much of each food type should be fed to each prisoner. Therefore, we add three changing cells in C13:E13, with range name Quantity. The values in Quantity (C13:E13) will eventually be determined by the Solver. For now, an arbitrary value of 1 is entered for each food type.

The goal is to minimize the total cost per prisoner. Thus, the target cell should calculate this cost:
        Total Cost = ($2)(gallons of milk) + ($0.20)(cups of beans) + ($0.25)(number of oranges)
or
        Total Cost = SUMPRODUCT(UnitCost, Quantity).
This formula is entered into cell H14.

	B	C	D	E	F	G	H
3		Milk	Beans				
4		(gal.)	(cups)	Oranges			
5	Unit Cost	$2.00	$0.20	$0.25			
6							
7							Minimum
8			Nutritional Contents (mg)				Requirement
9	Niacin	3.2	4.9	0.8			13
10	Thiamin	1.12	1.3	0.19			1.5
11	Vitamin C	32	0	93			45
12							
13	Quantity	1	1	1			Total Cost
14	(per prisoner)						$2.45

	H
13	Total Cost
14	=SUMPRODUCT(UnitCost,Quantity)

The functional constraints in this problem involve the minimum daily requirement of each nutrient. Given the amount of food fed each prisoner (the changing cells in C13:E13), we calculate the total resources used in F9:F11. For niacin, this will be =SUMPRODUCT(C9:E9, $C$13:$E$13). Using an absolute reference for the acres planted, this formula can be copied into cells F10-F11 to calculate the thiamin and vitamin C. The benefit achieved (total of each nutrient) must be >= the minimum needed (H9:H11), as indicated by the >= in G9:G11.

	B	C	D	E	F	G	H
3		Milk	Beans				
4		(gal.)	(cups)	Oranges			
5	Unit Cost	$2.00	$0.20	$0.25			
6							
7					Total		Minimum
8		Nutritional Contents (mg)			Nutrients		Requirement
9	Niacin	3.2	4.9	0.8	8.9	>=	13
10	Thiamin	1.12	1.3	0.19	2.610	>=	1.5
11	Vitamin C	32	0	93	125	>=	45
12							
13	Quantity	1	1	1			Total Cost
14	(per prisoner)						$2.45

	F
7	Total
8	Nutrients
9	=SUMPRODUCT(C9:E9,Quantity)
10	=SUMPRODUCT(C10:E10,Quantity)
11	=SUMPRODUCT(C11:E11,Quantity)

The Solver information and solved spreadsheet are shown below.

	A	B	C	D	E	F	G	H
1		**The Prison Diet Problem**						
2								
3			Milk	Beans				
4			(gal.)	(cups)	Oranges			
5		Unit Cost	$2.00	$0.20	$0.25			
6								
7						Total		Minimum
8			Nutritional Contents (mg)			Nutrients		Requirement
9		Niacin	3.2	4.9	0.8	13	>=	13
10		Thiamin	1.12	1.3	0.19	3.438	>=	1.5
11		Vitamin C	32	0	93	45	>=	45
12								
13		Quantity	0	2.574	0.484			Total Cost
14		(per prisoner)						$0.64

Solver Parameters

Set Objective (Target Cell): TotalCost
To: Min
By Changing (Variable) Cells:
    Quantity
Subject to the Constraints:
    TotalNutrients >= MinimumRequirement

Solver Options (Excel 2010):
    Make Variables Nonnegative
    Solving Method: Simplex LP
Solver Options (older Excel):
    Assume Nonnegative
    Assume Linear Model

Range Name	Cells
MinimumRequirement	H9:H11
NutritionalContents	C9:E11
Quantity	C13:E13
TotalCost	H14
TotalNutrients	F9:F11
UnitCost	C5:E5

	F
7	Total
8	Nutrients
9	=SUMPRODUCT(C9:E9,Quantity)
10	=SUMPRODUCT(C10:E10,Quantity)
11	=SUMPRODUCT(C11:E11,Quantity)

	H
13	Total Cost
14	=SUMPRODUCT(UnitCost,Quantity)

Thus, each prisoner should be fed a daily average of 2.574 cups of beans and 0.484 oranges for a total cost of $0.64.

b. *Formulate this same model algebraically.*

To build an algebraic model for this problem, start by defining the decision variables. In this case, the three decisions are how many gallons of milk, cups of beans, and how many oranges to feed each prisoner. These variables are defined below:

Let M = gallons of milk fed to each prisoner,
      B = cups of beans fed to each prisoner,
      O = number of oranges fed to each prisoner.

Next determine the goal of the problem. In this case, the goal is to meet the nutritional requirements at the lowest possible cost. Each gallon of milk costs $2, each cup of beans costs $0.20, and each orange costs $0.25. The objective function is therefore

Minimize Total Cost = $2.00M + \$0.20B + \$0.25O$.

The nutritional requirements include minimum requirements for niacin, thiamin, and vitamin C. The data for the nutritional contents of each type of food can be used to calculate the total level of each nutrient achieved as a function of the decision variables. The total nutrients need to be greater than or equal to the minimum requirement. These constraints are therefore as follows:

Niacin: $3.2M + 4.9B + 0.8O \geq 13$mg,
Thiamin: $1.12M + 1.3B + 0.19O \geq 1.5$mg,
Vitamin C: $32M + 93O \geq 45$mg.

After adding nonnegativity constraints, the complete algebraic formulation is given below:

Let M = gallons of milk fed to each prisoner,
      B = cups of beans fed to each prisoner,
      O = number of oranges fed to each prisoner.

Minimize Total Cost = $2.00M + \$0.20B + \$0.25O$.

subject to

Niacin: $3.2M + 4.9B + 0.8O \geq 13$mg,
Thiamin: $1.12M + 1.3B + 0.19O \geq 1.5$mg,
Vitamin C: $32M + 93O \geq 45$mg.

and $M \geq 0, B \geq 0, O \geq 0$.

3.S3 Cutting Stock Problem

Decora Accessories manufactures a variety of bathroom accessories, including decorative towel rods and shower curtain rods. Each of the accessories includes a rod made out of stainless steel. However, many different lengths are needed: 12", 18", 24", 40", and 60". Decora purchases 60" rods from an outside supplier and then cuts the rods as needed for their products. Each 60" rod can be used to make a number of smaller rods. For example, a 60" rod could be used to make a 40" and an 18" rod (with 2" of waste), or 5 12" rods (with no waste). For the next production period, Decora needs 25 12" rods, 52 18" rods, 45 24" rods, 30 40" rods, and 12 60" rods. What is the fewest number of 60" rods that can be purchased to meet their production needs? Formulate and solve an integer programming model in a spreadsheet.

This is a cost-benefit-trade-off problem. For each length of rod, the required benefit is obtaining the minimum number needed of those rods. Each possible way of cutting a 60" rod will represent an activity. For example, a 60" rod can be cut into 5 12" rods, or 3 12" rods and an 18" rod (with 6" scrap), or 3 12" rods and a 24" rod, etc. We will build a spreadsheet following the template for cost-benefit-trade-off problems in Figure 3.6. Start by entering the data. The data for this problem are the total length of the uncut rods, the minimum number of each rod length required and, for each possible pattern of cutting a 60" rod, the number of each length rod created. There are 11 possible patterns of cutting a 60" rod that either leave no scrap or an unusable piece of scrap (i.e., less than 12"). Following the template, the data in the spreadsheet would be entered as displayed, where range names of UncutRodLength (F3), MinimumRequirement (P7:P11), and Waste (C12:M12) are assigned to the corresponding data cells.

	B	C	D	E	F	G	H	I	J	K	L	M	N	O	P
3	Length of Uncut Rods				60										
4															
5	Length of					Pattern									Minimum
6	Cut Rod	1	2	3	4	5	6	7	8	9	10	11			Requirement
7	12	5	3	3	2	1	1	1							25
8	18		1		2	1			3	2	1				52
9	24			1		1	2			1					45
10	40							1			1				30
11	60											1			12
12	Waste	0	6	0	0	6	0	8	6	0	2	0			

	B	C
12	Waste	=UncutRodLength-SUMPRODUCT($B$7:$B$11,C7:C11)

The decisions to be made in this problem are how many rods should be cut into each of the possible patterns. Therefore, we add 11 changing cells in C14:M14, with range name PatternQuantity. The values in PatternQuantity (C14:M14) will eventually be determined by the Solver. For now, an arbitrary value of 1 is entered for each pattern.

	B	C	D	E	F	G	H	I	J	K	L	M	N	O	P
3	Length of Uncut Rods				60										
4															
5	Length of					Pattern									Minimum
6	Cut Rod	1	2	3	4	5	6	7	8	9	10	11			Needed
7	12	5	3	3	2	1	1	1							25
8	18		1		2	1			3	2	1				52
9	24			1		1	2			1					45
10	40							1			1				30
11	60											1			12
12	Waste	0	6	0	0	6	0	8	6	0	2	0			
13															
14	Pattern Quantity	1	1	1	1	1	1	1	1	1	1	1			

The goal is to minimize the total number of 60" (uncut) rods needed. This is just the sum of the changing cells:

Total Uncut Rods needed = SUM(PatternQuantity).

This formula is entered into cell P14.

	B	C	D	E	F	G	H	I	J	K	L	M	N	O	P
3	Length of Uncut Rods				60										
4															
5	Length of					Pattern									Minimum
6	Cut Rod	1	2	3	4	5	6	7	8	9	10	11			Needed
7	12	5	3	3	2	1	1	1							25
8	18		1		2	1			3	2	1				52
9	24			1		1	2			1					45
10	40							1			1				30
11	60											1			12
12	Waste	0	6	0	0	6	0	8	6	0	2	0			
13															Total Uncut Rods Needed
14	Pattern Quantity	1	1	1	1	1	1	1	1	1	1	1			11

	P
13	Total Uncut Rods Needed
14	=SUM(PatternQuantity)

The functional constraints in this problem require that the number of cut rods of each length must be at least the minimum number needed. Given PatternQuantity (the changing cells in C14:M14), we calculate the total number of each rod length produced in TotalProduced (N7:N11). For 12" rods, this will be =SUMPRODUCT(C7:M7, PatternQuantity). Using a range name or absolute reference for the quantity of each pattern, this formula can be copied into cells N8:N11 to calculate the total number of other lengths created. For each rod length, the benefit achieved (the total number of that rod length cut) must be >= MinimumRequirement (P7:P11), as indicated by the >= in O7:O11.

	B	C	D	E	F	G	H	I	J	K	L	M	N	O	P
3	Length of Uncut Rods				60										
4															
5	Length of					Pattern							Total		Minimum
6	Cut Rod	1	2	3	4	5	6	7	8	9	10	11	Produced		Needed
7	12	5	3	3	2	1	1	1					16	>=	25
8	18		1		2	1			3	2	1		10	>=	52
9	24			1		1	2			1			5	>=	45
10	40							1			1		2	>=	30
11	60											1	1	>=	12
12	Waste	0	6	0	0	6	0	8	6	0	2	0			
13													Total Uncut Rods Needed		
14	Pattern Quantity	1	1	1	1	1	1	1	1	1	1	1			11

	N
5	Total
6	Produced
7	=SUMPRODUCT(C7:M7,PatternQuantity)
8	=SUMPRODUCT(C8:M8,PatternQuantity)
9	=SUMPRODUCT(C9:M9,PatternQuantity)
10	=SUMPRODUCT(C10:M10,PatternQuantity)
11	=SUMPRODUCT(C11:M11,PatternQuantity)

Also, an integer number of each pattern must be cut. Therefore, we constrain the changing cells to be integer. The Solver information and solved spreadsheet are shown below.

	A	B	C	D	E	F	G	H	I	J	K	L	M	N	O	P
1		**Cutting Stock Problem**														
2																
3		Length of Uncut Rods				60										
4																
5		Length of					Pattern							Total		Minimum
6		Cut Rod	1	2	3	4	5	6	7	8	9	10	11	Produced		Needed
7		12	5	3	3	2	1	1	1					27	>=	25
8		18		1		2	1			3	2	1		52	>=	52
9		24			1		1	2			1			45	>=	45
10		40							1			1		30	>=	30
11		60											1	12	>=	12
12		Waste	0	6	0	0	6	0	8	6	0	2	0			
13															Total Uncut Rods Needed	
14		Pattern Quantity	2	0	0	0	0	17	0	0	11	30	12			72

Solver Parameters

Set Objective (Target Cell): TotalRodsNeeded
To: Min
By Changing (Variable) Cells:
    PatternQuantity
Subject to the Constraints:
    PatternQuantity = integer
    TotalProduced >= MinimumNeeded

Solver Options (Excel 2010):
    Make Variables Nonnegative
    Solving Method: Simplex LP
Solver Options (older Excel):
    Assume Nonnegative
    Assume Linear Model

Range Name	Cells
MinimumNeeded	P7:P11
PatternQuantity	C14:M14
TotalProduced	N7:N11
TotalRodsNeeded	P14
UncutRodLength	F3
Waste	C12:M12

	N
5	Total
6	Produced
7	=SUMPRODUCT(C7:M7,PatternQuantity)
8	=SUMPRODUCT(C8:M8,PatternQuantity)
9	=SUMPRODUCT(C9:M9,PatternQuantity)
10	=SUMPRODUCT(C10:M10,PatternQuantity)
11	=SUMPRODUCT(C11:M11,PatternQuantity)

	P
13	Total Uncut Rods Needed
14	=SUM(PatternQuantity)

	B	C
12	Waste	=UncutRodLength-SUMPRODUCT($B$7:$B$11,C7:C11)

Thus, PatternQuantity (C14:M14) show the number of rods that should be cut into the respective patterns. TotalRodsNeeded (P14) indicates that a total of 72 uncut rods are needed.

3.S4 Producing and Distributing AEDs at Heart Start

Heart Start produces automated external defibrillators (AEDs) in each of two different plants (A and B). The unit production costs and monthly production capacity of the two plants are indicated in the table below. The AEDs are sold through three wholesalers. The shipping cost from each plant to the warehouse of each wholesaler along with the monthly demand from each wholesaler are also indicated in the table. How many AEDs should be produced in each plant, and how should they be distributed to each of the three wholesaler warehouses so as to minimize the combined cost of production and shipping? Formulate and solve a linear programming model in a spreadsheet.

	Unit Shipping Cost			Unit Production Cost	Monthly Production Capacity
	Warehouse 1	*Warehouse 2*	*Warehouse 3*		
Plant A	$22	$14	$30	$600	100
Plant B	$16	$20	$24	$625	120
Monthly Demand	80	60	70		

This is a transportation problem as described in Section 3.5 of the text. Start by entering the data. The data for this problem are the unit shipping cost, the unit production cost and monthly production capacity at each plant, and the monthly demand at each warehouse. The data are shown below, where range names of UnitProductionCost (H5:H6), MonthlyCapacity (H11:H12), and MonthlyDemand (C15:E15) are assigned to the corresponding data cells. Note that space has been reserved in the middle of the spreadsheet (C11:E12) for the changing cells.

	A	B	C	D	E	F	G	H
1		**AED Production and Distribution**						
2								Unit
3		Shipping						Production
4		Cost (per unit)	Warehouse 1	Warehouse 2	Warehouse 3			Cost
5		Plant A	$22	$14	$30			$600
6		Plant B	$16	$20	$24			$625
7								
8								Monthly
9								Capacity
10								100
11								120
12								
13								
14								
15		Monthly Demand	80	60	70			

15

The decisions to be made in this problem are how many units to ship from each plant to each warehouse. Therefore, we add a table of changing cells with range name UnitsShipped (C11:E12). The values in UnitsShipped (C11:E12) will eventually be determined by the Solver. For now, zeroes are entered.

	A	B	C	D	E	F	G	H
1		**AED Production and Distribution**						
2								Unit
3		**Shipping**						Production
4		**Cost (per unit)**	Warehouse 1	Warehouse 2	Warehouse 3			Cost
5		Plant A	$22	$14	$30			$600
6		Plant B	$16	$20	$24			$625
7								
8								
9		**Units**						Monthly
10		**Shipped**	Warehouse 1	Warehouse 2	Warehouse 3			Capacity
11		Plant A	0	0	0			100
12		Plant B	0	0	0			120
13								
14								
15		Monthly Demand	80	60	70			

The goal is to minimize the total cost, including production costs and shipping costs. The total production costs and the total shipping costs are calculated as follows.

Total Production Cost = SUMPRODUCT(UnitProductionCost, UnitsShipped),

Total Shipping Cost = SUMPRODUCT(ShippingCost, UnitsShipped).

These formulas are entered into H16 and H17, with the overall total cost calculated by summing these two costs in H18, as shown in the spreadsheet below.

	A	B	C	D	E	F	G	H
1		**AED Production and Distribution**						
2								Unit
3		**Shipping**						Production
4		**Cost (per unit)**	Warehouse 1	Warehouse 2	Warehouse 3			Cost
5		Plant A	$22	$14	$30			$600
6		Plant B	$16	$20	$24			$625
7								
8								
9		**Units**						Monthly
10		**Shipped**	Warehouse 1	Warehouse 2	Warehouse 3			Capacity
11		Plant A	0	0	0			100
12		Plant B	0	0	0			120
13								
14								
15		Monthly Demand	80	60	70			
16						Total Production Cost		$0
17						Total Shipping Cost		$0
18						Overall Cost		$0

	G	H
16	Total Production Cost	=SUMPRODUCT(UnitProductionCost,TotalShippedOut)
17	Total Shipping Cost	=SUMPRODUCT(ShippingCost,UnitsShipped)
18	Overall Cost	=TotalProductionCost+TotalShippingCost

The functional constraints in this problem are that each plant can't ship out more than its monthly capacity, and each warehouse needs to receive its monthly demand. The units shipped out of each plant are calculated by summing each row of changing cells, while the units shipped to each warehouse are caculated by summing each column of changing cells. These constraints are shown in the spreadsheet below.

	A	B	C	D	E	F	G	H
1		**AED Production and Distribution**						
2								Unit
3		**Shipping**						Production
4		**Cost (per unit)**	Warehouse 1	Warehouse 2	Warehouse 3			Cost
5		Plant A	$22	$14	$30			$600
6		Plant B	$16	$20	$24			$625
7								
8						Total		
9		**Units**				Shipped		Monthly
10		**Shipped**	Warehouse 1	Warehouse 2	Warehouse 3	Out		Capacity
11		Plant A	0	0	0	0	<=	100
12		Plant B	0	0	0	0	<=	120
13		Total to Warehouse	0	0	0			
14			=	=	=			
15		Monthly Demand	80	60	70			
16						Total Production Cost		$0
17						Total Shipping Cost		$0
18						Overall Cost		$0

	F
8	Total
9	Shipped
10	Out
11	=SUM(C11:E11)
12	=SUM(C12:E12)

	B	C	D	E
13	Total to Warehouse	=SUM(C11:C12)	=SUM(D11:D12)	=SUM(E11:E12)

The Solver information and solved spreadsheet are shown below.

	A	B	C	D	E	F	G	H
1		**AED Production and Distribution**						
2								
3		Shipping						Unit
4		Cost (per unit)	Warehouse 1	Warehouse 2	Warehouse 3			Production
5		Plant A	$22	$14	$30			Cost
6		Plant B	$16	$20	$24			$600
								$625
7								
8						Total		
9		Units				Shipped		Monthly
10		Shipped	Warehouse 1	Warehouse 2	Warehouse 3	Out		Capacity
11		Plant A	40	60	0	100	<=	100
12		Plant B	40	0	70	110	<=	120
13		Total to Warehouse	80	60	70			
14			=	=	=			
15		Monthly Demand	80	60	70			
16						Total Production Cost		$128,750
17						Total Shipping Cost		$4,040
18						Overall Cost		$132,790

Solver Parameters

Set Objective (Target Cell): OverallCost
To: Min
By Changing (Variable) Cells:
    UnitsShipped
Subject to the Constraints:
    TotalShippedOut <= MonthlyCapacity
    TotalToWarehouse = MonthlyDemand

Solver Options (Excel 2010):
    Make Variables Nonnegative
    Solving Method: Simplex LP
Solver Options (older Excel):
    Assume Nonnegative
    Assume Linear Model

Range Name	Cells
MonthlyCapacity	H11:H12
MonthlyDemand	C15:E15
OverallCost	H18
UnitShippingCost	C5:E6
TotalProductionCost	H16
TotalShippedOut	F11:F12
TotalShippingCost	H17
TotalToWarehouse	C13:E13
UnitProductionCost	H5:H6
UnitsShipped	C11:E12

	F
8	Total
9	Shipped
10	Out
11	=SUM(C11:E11)
12	=SUM(C12:E12)

	B	C	D	E
13	Total to Warehouse	=SUM(C11:C12)	=SUM(D11:D12)	=SUM(E11:E12)

	G	H
16	Total Production Cost	=SUMPRODUCT(UnitProductionCost,TotalShippedOut)
17	Total Shipping Cost	=SUMPRODUCT(ShippingCost,UnitsShipped)
18	Overall Cost	=TotalProductionCost+TotalShippingCost

Thus, from Plant A they should ship 40 to Warehouse 1 and 60 units to Warehouse 2, from Plant B they should ship 40 units to Warehouse 1 and 70 units to Warehouse 3, giving an overall total cost of $132,790.

3.S5 Bidding for Classes

In the MBA program at a prestigious university in the Pacific Northwest, students bid for electives in the second year of their program. Each student has 100 points to bid (total) and must take two electives. There are four electives available: Management Science, Finance, Operations Management, and Marketing. Each class is limited to 5 students. The bids submitted for each of the 10 students are shown in the table below.

Student	Management Science	Finance	Operations Management	Marketing
George	60	10	10	20
Fred	20	20	40	20
Ann	45	45	5	5
Eric	50	20	5	25
Susan	30	30	30	10
Liz	50	50	0	0
Ed	70	20	10	0
David	25	25	35	15
Tony	35	15	35	15
Jennifer	60	10	10	20

a. *Formulate and solve a spreadsheet model to determine an assignment of students to classes so as to maximize the total bid points of the assignments.*

This is a special kind of assignment problem. The assignees are the students and the tasks are the classes. Each student is assigned to take two classes. Each class has a limit of five students. Start by entering the data. The data for this problem are the bid points for each student for each class, where the corresponding data cells are assigned a range name of Points (C5:F14).

	B	C	D	E	F
3		Management		Operations	
4	**Points**	Science	Finance	Management	Marketing
5	George	60	10	10	20
6	Fred	20	20	40	20
7	Ann	45	45	5	5
8	Eric	50	20	5	25
9	Susan	30	30	30	10
10	Liz	50	50	0	0
11	Ed	70	20	10	0
12	David	25	25	35	15
13	Tony	35	15	35	15
14	Jennifer	60	10	10	20

The decisions to be made in this problem are whether or not to assign each student to each class. Therefore, a table of changing cells is created for each student and class combination in C18:F27, and given a range name of Assignment. The values in Assignment (C18:F27) will eventually be determined by the Solver. For now, arbitrary values of 0 and 1 are entered.

	B	C	D	E	F
3		Management		Operations	
4	**Points**	Science	Finance	Management	Marketing
5	George	60	10	10	20
6	Fred	20	20	40	20
7	Ann	45	45	5	5
8	Eric	50	20	5	25
9	Susan	30	30	30	10
10	Liz	50	50	0	0
11	Ed	70	20	10	0
12	David	25	25	35	15
13	Tony	35	15	35	15
14	Jennifer	60	10	10	20
15					
16		Management		Operations	
17	**Assignment**	Science	Finance	Management	Marketing
18	George	1	0	1	0
19	Fred	0	1	0	1
20	Ann	1	0	1	0
21	Eric	0	1	0	1
22	Susan	1	0	1	0
23	Liz	0	1	0	1
24	Ed	1	0	1	0
25	David	0	1	0	1
26	Tony	1	0	1	0
27	Jennifer	0	1	0	1

The goal is to maximize the total bid points of the assignments.

Total Bid Points = SUMPRODUCT(Points, Assignment).

This formula is entered into cell I29.

	B	C	D	E	F	G	H	I
3		Management		Operations				
4	**Points**	Science	Finance	Management	Marketing			
5	George	60	10	10	20			
6	Fred	20	20	40	20			
7	Ann	45	45	5	5			
8	Eric	50	20	5	25			
9	Susan	30	30	30	10			
10	Liz	50	50	0	0			
11	Ed	70	20	10	0			
12	David	25	25	35	15			
13	Tony	35	15	35	15			
14	Jennifer	60	10	10	20			
15								
16		Management		Operations				
17	**Assignment**	Science	Finance	Management	Marketing			
18	George	1	0	1	0			
19	Fred	0	1	0	1			
20	Ann	1	0	1	0			
21	Eric	0	1	0	1			
22	Susan	1	0	1	0			
23	Liz	0	1	0	1			
24	Ed	1	0	1	0			
25	David	0	1	0	1			
26	Tony	1	0	1	0			
27	Jennifer	0	1	0	1			
28								
29							Total Points	535

	H	I
29	Total Points	=SUMPRODUCT(Points,Assignment)

21

The functional constraints in this problem are that each student must be assigned to two classes, each class is limited to five students, and each student can take each class at most once. The number of classes a student is assigned to is just the sum of the row of changing cells for each student. For example, for George it is =SUM(C18:F18). This formula is copied into G18:G27. The number of students assigned to a class is the sum of the column of changing cells for each class. For example, for Management Science it is =SUM(C18:C27). This formula is copied into C28:F28.

	B	C	D	E	F	G	H	I
3		Management		Operations				
4	**Points**	Science	Finance	Management	Marketing			
5	George	60	10	10	20			
6	Fred	20	20	40	20			
7	Ann	45	45	5	5			
8	Eric	50	20	5	25			
9	Susan	30	30	30	10			
10	Liz	50	50	0	0			
11	Ed	70	20	10	0			
12	David	25	25	35	15			
13	Tony	35	15	35	15			
14	Jennifer	60	10	10	20			
15								
16		Management		Operations		Total		Classes
17	**Assignment**	Science	Finance	Management	Marketing	Classes		to Take
18	George	1	0	1	0	2	=	2
19	Fred	0	1	0	1	2	=	2
20	Ann	1	0	1	0	2	=	2
21	Eric	0	1	0	1	2	=	2
22	Susan	1	0	1	0	2	=	2
23	Liz	0	1	0	1	2	=	2
24	Ed	1	0	1	0	2	=	2
25	David	0	1	0	1	2	=	2
26	Tony	1	0	1	0	2	=	2
27	Jennifer	0	1	0	1	2	=	2
28		5	5	5	5			
29		<=	<=	<=	<=		Total Points	535
30	Capacity	5	5	5	5			

	K
16	Total
17	Classes
18	=SUM(C18:F18)
19	=SUM(C19:F19)
20	=SUM(C20:F20)
21	=SUM(C21:F21)
22	=SUM(C22:F22)
23	=SUM(C23:F23)
24	=SUM(C24:F24)
25	=SUM(C25:F25)
26	=SUM(C26:F26)
27	=SUM(C27:F27)

	B	C	D	E	F
28	Total in Class	=SUM(C18:C27)	=SUM(D18:D27)	=SUM(E18:E27)	=SUM(F18:F27)

The Solver information and solved spreadsheet are shown below.

	A	B	C	D	E	F	G	H	I	J	K
1		**Bidding for Classes**									
2											
3			Management		Operations						
4		**Points**	Science	Finance	Management	Marketing					
5		George	60	10	10	20					
6		Fred	20	20	40	20					
7		Ann	45	45	5	5					
8		Eric	50	20	5	25					
9		Susan	30	30	30	10					
10		Liz	50	50	0	0					
11		Ed	70	20	10	0					
12		David	25	25	35	15					
13		Tony	35	15	35	15					
14		Jennifer	60	10	10	20					
15											
16			Management		Operations		Total		Classes		Student
17		**Assignment**	Science	Finance	Management	Marketing	Classes		to Take		Points
18		George	1	0	0	1	2	=	2		80
19		Fred	0	0	1	1	2	=	2		60
20		Ann	1	1	0	0	2	=	2		90
21		Eric	0	1	0	1	2	=	2		45
22		Susan	0	1	1	0	2	=	2		60
23		Liz	1	1	0	0	2	=	2		100
24		Ed	1	0	1	0	2	=	2		80
25		David	0	1	1	0	2	=	2		60
26		Tony	0	0	1	1	2	=	2		50
27		Jennifer	1	0	0	1	2	=	2		80
28		Total in Class	5	5	5	5					
29			<=	<=	<=	<=	Total Points		705		
30		Capacity	5	5	5	5					

Solver Parameters

Set Objective (Target Cell): TotalPoints
To: Max
By Changing (Variable) Cells:
    Assignment
Subject to the Constraints:
    Assignment <= 1
    TotalClasses = ClassesToTake
    TotalInClass <= Capacity

Solver Options (Excel 2010):
    Make Variables Nonnegative
    Solving Method: Simplex LP
Solver Options (older Excel):
    Assume Nonnegative
    Assume Linear Model

Range Name	Cells
Assignment	C18:F27
Capacity	C30:F30
ClassesToTake	I18:I27
Points	C5:F14
StudentPoints	K18:K27
TotalClasses	G18:G27
TotalInClass	C28:F28
TotalPoints	I29

	G
16	Total
17	Classes
18	=SUM(C18:F18)
19	=SUM(C19:F19)
20	=SUM(C20:F20)
21	:
22	:

	K
16	Student
17	Points
18	=SUMPRODUCT(C5:F5,C18:F18)
19	=SUMPRODUCT(C6:F6,C19:F19)
20	=SUMPRODUCT(C7:F7,C20:F20)
21	:
22	:

	B	C	D	E	F
28	Total in Class	=SUM(C18:C27)	=SUM(D18:D27)	=SUM(E18:E27)	=SUM(F18:F27)

	H	I
29	Total Points	=SUMPRODUCT(Points,Assignment)

Thus, the 1's in Assignment (C18:F27) show the assignments that should be made, achieving a total of 705 points.

b. *Does the resulting solution seem like a fair assignment?*
No. For example, Eric did not get into Management Science despite bidding 50 points, while Ann got in with only 45 points. Also, Eric got into classes worth only 45 total bid points to him while Liz got classes worth 100 bid points to her.

c. *Which alternative objectives might lead to a fairer assignment?*
Perhaps maximizing the minimum total number of bid points achieved by each student.

The Art of Modeling with Spreadsheets

Learning objectives

After completing this chapter, you should be able to

1. Describe the general process for modeling in spreadsheets.
2. Describe some guidelines for building good spreadsheet models.
3. Apply both the general process for modeling in spreadsheets and the guidelines in this chapter to develop your own spreadsheet model from a description of the problem.
4. Identify some deficiencies in a poorly formulated spreadsheet model.
5. Apply a variety of techniques for debugging a spreadsheet model.

Nearly all managers now make extensive use of spreadsheets to analyze business problems. What they are doing is *modeling* with spreadsheets.

Spreadsheet modeling is a major emphasis throughout this book. Section 1.2 in Chapter 1 introduced a spreadsheet model for performing break-even analysis. Section 2.2 in Chapter 2 described how to use spreadsheets to formulate linear programming models. Chapter 3 focused on spreadsheet models for five key categories of linear programming problems: resource-allocation problems, cost–benefit–trade-off problems, mixed problems, transportation problems, and assignment problems. Many kinds of spreadsheet models are discussed in subsequent chapters as well. However, those presentations focus mostly on the characteristics of spreadsheet models that fit the management science techniques (such as linear programming) being covered in those chapters. We devote this chapter instead to the general *process* of building models with spreadsheets.

Modeling in spreadsheets is more an art than a science. There is no systematic procedure that invariably will lead to a single correct spreadsheet model. For example, if two managers were given exactly the same business problem to analyze with a spreadsheet, their spreadsheet models would likely look quite different. There is no one right way of modeling any given problem. However, some models will be better than others.

Although no completely systematic procedure is available for modeling in spreadsheets, there is a general process that should be followed. This process has four major steps: (1) *plan* the spreadsheet model, (2) *build* the model, (3) *test* the model, and (4) *analyze* the model and its results. After introducing a case study in Section 4.1, the next section will describe this plan-build-test-analyze process in some detail and illustrate the process in the context of the case study. Section 4.2 also will discuss some ways of overcoming common stumbling blocks in the modeling process.

Unfortunately, despite its logical approach, there is no guarantee that the plan-build-test-analyze process will lead to a "good" spreadsheet model. A good spreadsheet model is easy to understand, easy to debug, and easy to modify. Section 4.3 presents some guidelines for building such models. This section also uses the case study in Section 4.1 to illustrate the difference between appropriate formulations and poor formulations of a model.

Even with an appropriate formulation, the initial versions of large spreadsheet models commonly will include some small but troublesome errors, such as inaccurate references to cell addresses or typographical errors when entering equations into cells. Indeed, some studies have shown that a surprisingly large number of errors typically occur in the first version of such models. These errors often can be difficult to track down. Section 4.4 presents some helpful ways to debug a spreadsheet model and root out such errors.

The overriding goal of this chapter is to provide a solid foundation for becoming a successful spreadsheet modeler. However, this chapter by itself will not turn you into a highly skilled modeler. Ultimately, to reach this point you also will need to study various examples of good spreadsheet models in the different areas of management science and then have lots of practice in formulating your own models. This process will continue throughout the remainder of this book.

4.1   A CASE STUDY: THE EVERGLADE GOLDEN YEARS COMPANY CASH FLOW PROBLEM

The **Everglade Golden Years Company** operates upscale retirement communities in certain parts of southern Florida. The company was founded in 1946 by Alfred Lee, who was in the right place at the right time to enjoy many successful years during the boom in the Florida economy as many wealthy retirees flooded into the area. Today, the company continues to be run by the Lee family, with Alfred's grandson, Sheldon Lee, as the CEO.

The past few years have been difficult ones for Everglade. The demand for retirement community housing has been light and Everglade has been unable to maintain full occupancy. However, this market has picked up recently and the future is looking brighter. Everglade has recently broken ground for the construction of a new retirement community and has more new construction planned over the next 10 years (2011 to 2020).

With only $1 million in cash reserves and negative cash flows looming soon, loans will be needed to observe the company policy of maintaining a balance of at least $500,000 at all times.

Julie Lee is the chief financial officer (CFO) at Everglade. She has spent the last week in front of her computer trying to come to grips with the company's imminent cash flow problem. Julie has projected Everglade's net cash flows over the next 10 years as shown in Table 4.1. With less money currently coming in than would be provided by full occupancy and with all the construction costs for the new retirement community, Everglade will have negative cash flow for the next few years. With only $1 million in cash reserves, it appears that Everglade will need to take out some loans in order to meet its financial obligations. Also, to protect against uncertainty, company policy dictates maintaining a balance of at least $500,000 in cash reserves at all times.

The company's bank has offered two types of loans to Everglade. The first is a 10-year loan with interest-only payments made annually and then the entire principal repaid in a single balloon payment after 10 years. The interest rate on this long-term loan is a favorable 7 percent per year. The second option is a series of one-year loans. These loans can be taken out each year as needed, but each must be repaid (with interest) the following year. Each new loan can be used to help repay the loan for the preceding year if needed. The interest rate for these short-term loans currently is projected to be 10 percent per year.

Armed with her cash flow projections and the loan options from the bank, Julie schedules a meeting with the CEO, Sheldon Lee. Their discussion is as follows:

Julie: Well, we really seem to be in a pickle. There is no way to meet our cash flow problems without borrowing money.

TABLE 4.1
Projected Net Cash Flows for the Everglade Golden Years Company over the Next Ten Years

Year	Projected Net Cash Flow (millions of dollars)
2011	−8
2012	−2
2013	−4
2014	3
2015	6
2016	3
2017	−4
2018	7
2019	−2
2020	10

Sheldon: I was afraid of that. What are our options?

Julie: I've talked to the bank, and we can take out a 10-year loan with an interest rate of 7 percent, or a series of one-year loans at a projected rate of 10 percent.

Sheldon: Wow. That 7 percent rate sounds good. Can we just borrow all that we need using the 10-year loan?

Julie: That was my initial reaction as well. However, after looking at the cash flow projections I'm not sure the answer is so clear-cut. While we have negative cash flow for the next few years, the situation looks much brighter down the road. With a 10-year loan, we are obligated to keep the loan and make the interest payments for 10 years. The one-year loans are more flexible. We can borrow the money only in the years we need it. This way we can save on interest payments in the future.

Sheldon: Okay. I can see how the flexibility of the one-year loans could save us some money. Those loans also will look better if interest rates come down in future years.

Julie: Or they could go higher instead. There's no way to predict future interest rates, so we might as well just plan on the basis of the current projection of 10 percent per year.

Sheldon: Yes, you're right. So which do you recommend, a 10-year loan or a series of one-year loans?

Julie: Well, there's actually another option as well. We could consider a combination of the two types of loans. We could borrow some money long-term to get the lower interest rate and borrow some money short-term to retain flexibility.

The objective is to develop a financial plan that will keep the company solvent and then maximize the cash balance in 2021, after all the loans are paid off.

Sheldon: That sounds complicated. What we want is a plan that will keep us solvent throughout the 10 years and then leave us with as large a cash balance as possible at the end of the 10 years after paying off all the loans. Could you set this up on a spreadsheet to figure out the best plan?

Julie: You bet. I'll try that and get back to you.

Sheldon: Great. Let's plan to meet again next week when you have your report ready.

You'll see in the next two sections how Julie carefully develops her spreadsheet model for this cash flow problem.

Review Questions

1. What is the advantage of the long-term loan for Everglade?
2. What is the advantage of the series of short-term loans for Everglade?
3. What is the objective for the financial plan that needs to be developed?

4.2 OVERVIEW OF THE PROCESS OF MODELING WITH SPREADSHEETS

You will see later that a linear programming model can be incorporated into a spreadsheet to solve this problem. However, you also will see that the format of this spreadsheet model does not fit readily into any of the categories of linear programming models described in Chapter 3. Even the template given in Figure 3.8 that shows the format for a spreadsheet model of *mixed problems* (the broadest category of linear programming problems) does not help in formulating the model for the current problem. The reason is that the Everglade cash flow management problem is an example of a more complicated type of linear programming problem (a *dynamic problem* with many time periods) that requires starting from scratch in carefully formulating the spreadsheet model. Therefore, this example will nicely illustrate the process of modeling with spreadsheets when dealing with complicated problems of any type, including those discussed later in the book that do not fit linear programming.

Spaghetti code is a term from computer programming. It refers to computer code that is not logically organized and thus jumps all over the place, so it is jumbled like a plate of spaghetti.

When presented with a problem like the Everglade problem, the temptation is to jump right in, launch Excel, and start entering a model. Resist this urge. Developing a spreadsheet model without proper planning inevitably leads to a model that is poorly organized and filled with "spaghetti code."

FIGURE 4.1

A flow diagram for the general plan-build-test-analyze process for modeling with spreadsheets.

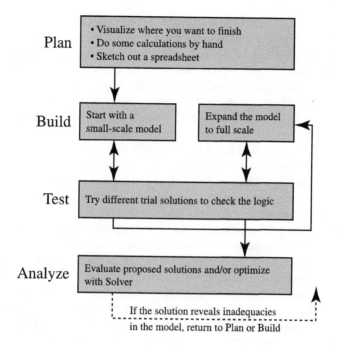

Part of the challenge of planning and developing a spreadsheet model is that there is no standard procedure to follow. It is more an art than a science. However, to provide you with some structure as you begin learning this art, we suggest that you follow the modeling process depicted in Figure 4.1.

As suggested by the figure, the four major steps in this process are to (1) plan, (2) build, (3) test, and (4) analyze the spreadsheet model. The process mainly flows in this order. However, the two-headed arrows between Build and Test indicate a back-and-forth process where testing frequently results in returning to the Build step to fix some problems discovered during the Test step. This back and forth movement between Build and Test may occur several times until the modeler is satisfied with the model. At the same time that this back and forth movement is occurring, the modeler may be involved with further building of the model. One strategy is to begin with a small version of the model to establish its basic logic and then, after testing verifies its accuracy, to expand to a full-scale model. Even after completing the testing and then the analyzing of the model, the process may return to the Build step or even the Plan step if the Analysis step reveals inadequacies in the model.

Each of these four major steps may also include some detailed steps. For example, Figure 4.1 lists three detailed steps within the Plan step. Initially, when dealing with a fairly complicated problem, it is helpful to take some time to perform each of these detailed steps manually one at a time. However, as you become more experienced with modeling in spreadsheets, you may find yourself merging some of the detailed steps and quickly performing them mentally. An experienced modeler often is able to do some of these steps mentally, without working them out explicitly on paper. However, if you find yourself getting stuck, it is likely that you are missing a key element from one of the previous detailed steps. You then should go back a step or two and make sure that you have thoroughly completed those preceding steps.

We now describe the various components of the modeling process in the context of the Everglade cash flow problem. At the same time, we also point out some common stumbling blocks encountered while building a spreadsheet model and how these can be overcome.

A modeler might go back and forth between the Build and Test steps several times.

Plan: Visualize Where You Want to Finish

One common stumbling block in the modeling process occurs right at the very beginning. Given a complicated situation like the one facing Julie at Everglade, sometimes it can be difficult to decide how to even get started. At this point, it can be helpful to think about where you want to end up. For example, what information should Julie provide in her report to Sheldon? What should the "answer" look like when presenting the recommended approach to the problem? What kinds of numbers need to be included in the recommendation? The answers to these questions can quickly lead you to the heart of the problem and help get the modeling process started.

The question that Julie is addressing is *which loan,* or combination of loans, to use and in *what amounts.* The long-term loan is taken in a single lump sum. Therefore, the "answer" should include a single number indicating how much money to borrow now at the long-term rate. The short-term loan can be taken in any or all of the 10 years, so the "answer" should include 10 numbers indicating how much to borrow at the short-term rate in each given year. These will be the changing cells in the spreadsheet model.

What other numbers should Julie include in her report to Sheldon? The key numbers would be the projected cash balance each year, the amount of the interest payments, and when loan payments are due. These will be output cells in the spreadsheet model.

It is important to distinguish between the numbers that represent decisions (changing cells) and those that represent results (output cells). For instance, it may be tempting to include the cash balances as changing cells. These cells clearly change depending on the decisions made. However, the cash balances are a *result* of how much is borrowed, how much is paid, and all of the other cash flows. They cannot be chosen independently but instead are a function of the other numbers in the spreadsheet. The distinguishing characteristic of changing cells (the loan amounts) is that they do not depend on anything else. They represent the independent decisions being made. They impact the other numbers, but not vice versa.

At this point, you should know what changing cells and output cells are needed.

At this stage in the process, you should have a clear idea of what the answer will look like, including what and how many changing cells are needed, and what kind of results (output cells) should be obtained.

Plan: Do Some Calculations by Hand

When building a model, another common stumbling block can arise when trying to enter a formula in one of the output cells. For example, just how does Julie keep track of the cash balances in the Everglade cash flow problem? What formulas need to be entered? There are a lot of factors that enter into this calculation, so it is easy to get overwhelmed.

If you are getting stuck at this point, it can be a very useful exercise to do some calculations by hand. Just pick some numbers for the changing cells and determine with a calculator or pencil and paper what the results should be. For example, pick some loan amounts for Everglade and then calculate the company's resulting cash balance at the end of the first couple of years. Let's say Everglade takes a long-term loan of $6 million and then adds short-term loans of $2 million in 2011 and $5 million in 2012. How much cash would the company have left at the end of 2011 and at the end of 2012?

These two quantities can be calculated by hand as follows. In 2011, Everglade has some initial money in the bank ($1 million), a negative cash flow from its business operations (−$8 million), and a cash inflow from the long-term and short-term loans ($6 million and $2 million, respectively). Thus, the ending balance for 2011 would be:

Ending balance (2011) = Starting balance	$1 million
+ Cash flow (2011)	−$8 million
+ LT loan (2011)	+ $6 million
+ ST loan (2011)	+ $2 million
	$1 million

The calculations for the year 2012 are a little more complicated. In addition to the starting balance left over from 2011 ($1 million), negative cash flow from business operations for 2012 (−$2 million), and a new short-term loan for 2012 ($5 million), the company will need to make interest payments on its 2011 loans as well as pay back the short-term loan from 2011. The ending balance for 2012 is therefore:

Ending balance (2012) = Starting balance (from end of 2011)	$1 million
+ Cash flow (2012)	−$2 million
+ ST loan (2012)	+ $5 million
−LT interest payment	−(7%)($6 million)

−ST interest payment	−(10%)($2 million)
−ST loan payback (2011)	− $2 million
	$1.38 million

Doing calculations by hand can help in a couple of ways. First, it can help clarify what formula should be entered for an output cell. For instance, looking at the by-hand calculations above, it appears that the formula for the ending balance for a particular year should be

$$\text{Ending balance} = \text{Starting balance} + \text{Cash flow} + \text{Loans} - \text{Interest payments} - \text{Loan paybacks}$$

Hand calculations can clarify what formulas are needed for the output cells.

It now will be a simple exercise to enter the proper cell references in the formula for the ending balance in the spreadsheet model. Second, hand calculations can help to verify the spreadsheet model. By plugging in a long-term loan of $6 million, along with short-term loans of $2 million in 2011 and $5 million in 2012, into a completed spreadsheet, the ending balances should be the same as calculated above. If they're not, this suggests an error in the spreadsheet model (assuming the hand calculations are correct).

Plan: Sketch Out a Spreadsheet

Any model typically has a large number of different elements that need to be included on the spreadsheet. For the Everglade problem, these would include some data cells (interest rates, starting balance, minimum balances, and cash flows), some changing cells (loan amounts), and a number of output cells (interest payments, loan paybacks, and ending balances). Therefore, a potential stumbling block can arise when trying to organize and lay out the spreadsheet model. Where should all the pieces fit on the spreadsheet? How do you begin putting together the spreadsheet?

Before firing up Excel and blindly entering the various elements, it can be helpful to sketch a layout of the spreadsheet. Is there a logical way to arrange the elements? A little planning at this stage can go a long way toward building a spreadsheet that is well organized. Don't bother with numbers at this point. Simply sketch out blocks on a piece of paper for the various data cells, changing cells, and output cells, and label them. Concentrate on the layout. Should a block of numbers be laid out in a row or a column, or as a two-dimensional table? Are there common row or column headings for different blocks of cells? If so, try to arrange the blocks in consistent rows or columns so they can utilize a single set of headings. Try to arrange the spreadsheet so that it starts with the data at the top and progresses logically toward the target cell at the bottom. This will be easier to understand and follow than if the data cells, changing cells, output cells, and target cell are all scattered throughout the spreadsheet.

Plan where the various blocks of data cells, changing cells, and output cells should go on the spreadsheet by sketching your layout ideas on paper.

A sketch of a potential spreadsheet layout for the Everglade problem is shown in Figure 4.2. The data cells for the interest rates, starting balance, and minimum cash balance are at the top

FIGURE 4.2

Sketch of the spreadsheet for Everglade's cash flow problem.

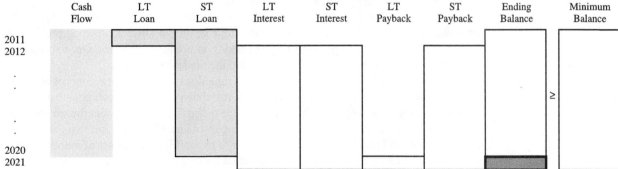

of the spreadsheet. All of the remaining elements in the spreadsheet then follow the same structure. The rows represent the different years (from 2011 through 2021). All the various cash inflows and outflows are then broken out in the columns, starting with the projected cash flow from the business operations (with data for each of the 10 years), continuing with the loan inflows, interest payments, and loan paybacks, and culminating with the ending balance (calculated for each year). The long-term loan is a one-time loan (in 2011), so it is sketched as a single cell. The short-term loan can occur in any of the 10 years (2011 through 2020), so it is sketched as a block of cells. The interest payments start one year after the loans. The long-term loan is paid back 10 years later (2021).

Organizing the elements with a consistent structure, like in Figure 4.2, not only saves having to retype the year labels for each element, but also makes the model easier to understand. Everything that happens in a given year is arranged together in a single row.

It is generally easiest to start sketching the layout with the data. The structure of the rest of the model should then follow the structure of the data cells. For example, once the projected cash flows data are sketched as a vertical column (with each year in a row), then it follows that the other cash flows should be structured the same way.

The sketch of a spreadsheet in Figure 4.2 has a logical progression, starting with the data on the top left and then moving through the calculations toward the target cell on the bottom right.

There is also a logical progression to the spreadsheet. The data for the problem are located at the top and left of the spreadsheet. Then, since the cash flow, loan amounts, interest payments, and loan paybacks are all part of the calculation for the ending balance, the columns are arranged this way, with the ending balance directly to the right of all these other elements. Since Sheldon has indicated that the objective is to maximize the ending balance in 2021, this cell is designated to be the target cell.

Each year, the balance must be greater than the minimum required balance ($500,000). Since this will be a constraint in the model, it is logical to arrange the balance and minimum balance blocks of numbers adjacent to each other in the spreadsheet. You can put the ≥ signs on the sketch to remind yourself that these will be constraints.

Build: Start with a Small Version of the Spreadsheet

Once you've thought about a logical layout for the spreadsheet, it is finally time to open a new worksheet in Excel and start building the model. If it is a complicated model, you may want to start by building a small, readily manageable version of the model. The idea is to first make sure that you've got the logic of the model worked out correctly for the small version before expanding the model to full scale.

Work out the logic for a small version of the spreadsheet model before expanding to full size.

For example, in the Everglade problem, we could get started by building a model for just the first two years (2011 and 2012), like the spreadsheet shown in Figure 4.3.

This spreadsheet is set up to follow the layout suggested in the sketch of Figure 4.2. The loan amounts are in columns D and E. Since the interest payments are not due until the following year, the formulas in columns F and G refer to the loan amounts from the preceding year (LTLoan, or D11, for the long-term loan, and E11 for the short-term loan). The loan payments are calculated in columns H and I. Column H is blank because the long-term loan does not need to be repaid until 2021. The short-term loan is repaid one year later, so the formula in cell I12 refers to the short-term loan taken the preceding year (cell E11). The ending balance in 2011 is the starting balance plus the sum of all the various cash flows that occur in 2011 (cells C11:I11). The ending balance in 2012 is the ending balance in 2011 (cell J11) plus the sum of all the various cash flows that occur in 2012 (cells C12:I12). All these formulas are summarized below the spreadsheet in Figure 4.3.

Building a small version of the spreadsheet works very well for spreadsheets that have a time dimension. For example, instead of jumping right into a 10-year planning problem, we can start with the simpler problem of just looking at a couple of years. Once this smaller model is working correctly, you then can expand the model to 10 years.

Even if a spreadsheet model does not have a time dimension, the same concept of starting small can be applied. For example, if certain constraints considerably complicate a problem, start by working on a simpler problem without the difficult constraints. Get the simple model working and then move on to tackle the difficult constraints. If a model has many sets of output cells, you can build up a model piece by piece by working on one set of output cells at a time, making sure each set works correctly before moving on to the next.

Test: Test the Small Version of the Model

If you do start with a small version of the model first, be sure to test this version thoroughly to make sure that all the logic is correct. It is far better to fix a problem early, while the spreadsheet is still a manageable size, rather than later after an error has been propagated throughout a much larger spreadsheet.

Try entering numbers in the changing cells for which you know what the values of the output cells should be.

To test the spreadsheet, try entering values in the changing cells for which you know what the values of the output cells should be, and then see if the spreadsheet gives the results that you expect. For example, in Figure 4.3, if zeroes are entered for the loan amounts, then the interest payments and loan payback quantities also should be zero. If $1 million is borrowed for both the long-term loan and the short-term loan, then the interest payments the following year should be $70,000 and $100,000, respectively. (Recall that the interest rates are 7 percent and 10 percent, respectively.) If Everglade takes out a $6 million long-term loan and a $2 million short-term loan in 2011, plus a $5 million short-term loan in 2012, then the ending balances should be $1 million for 2011 and $1.38 million for 2012 (based on the calculations done earlier by hand). All these tests work correctly for the spreadsheet in Figure 4.3, so we can be fairly certain that it is correct.

If the output cells are not giving the results that you expect, then carefully look through the formulas to see if you can determine and fix the problem. Section 4.4 will give further guidance on some ways to debug a spreadsheet model.

Build: Expand the Model to Full-Scale Size

Once a small version of the spreadsheet has been tested to make sure all the formulas are correct and everything is working properly, the model can be expanded to full-scale size. Excel's fill commands often can be used to quickly copy the formulas into the remainder of the model.

FIGURE 4.3

A small version (years 2011 and 2012 only) of the spreadsheet for the Everglade cash flow management problem.

	A	B	C	D	E	F	G	H	I	J	K	L
1		**Everglade Cash Flow Management Problem (Years 2011 and 2012)**										
2												
3		LT Rate	7%									
4		ST Rate	10%									
5					(all cash figures in millions of dollars)							
6		Start Balance	1									
7		Minimum Cash	0.5									
8												
9			Cash	LT	ST	LT	ST	LT	ST	Ending		Minimum
10		Year	Flow	Loan	Loan	Interest	Interest	Payback	Payback	Balance		Balance
11		2011	–8	6	2					1.00	≥	0.50
12		2012	–2		5	–0.42	–0.20		–2.00	1.38	≥	0.50

	F	G	H	I	J	K	L
9	LT	ST	LT	ST	Ending		Minimum
10	Interest	Interest	Payback	Payback	Balance		Balance
11					=StartBalance+SUM(C11:I11)	≥	=MinimumCash
12	= –LTRate*LTLoan	= –STRate*E11		= –E11	=J11+SUM(C12:I12)	≥	=MinimumCash

Range Name	Cell
LTLoan	D11
LTRate	C3
MinimumCash	C7
StartBalance	C6
STRate	C4

Excel Tip: A shortcut for filling down or filling across to the right is to select the cell you want to copy, click on the fill handle (the small box in the lower right-hand corner of the selection rectangle), and drag through the cells you want to fill.

For Figure 4.3, the formulas in columns F, G, I, J, and L can be copied using the Fill Down command in the Editing Group of the Home tab (for Excel 2007 or 2010) or in the Edit menu (for other versions of Excel) to obtain all the formulas shown in Figure 4.4. For example, selecting cells G12:G21 and choosing Fill Down will take the formula in cell G12 and copy it (after adjusting the cell address in Column E for the formula) into cells G13 through G21.

Before using the fill commands to copy formulas, be sure that the relative and absolute references have been used appropriately. (Appendix B provides details about relative and absolute references.) For example, in G12 ($=-$STRate*E11) using a range name for STRate makes this an absolute reference. When copied into cells G13:G21, the short-term loan interest rate used will always be the value in STRate (C4). The reference to E11 (the loan amount from the previous year) is a relative reference. E11 is two cells to the left and one cell up. When the formula is copied from G12 into G13:G21, the reference in each of these cells will continue to be two cells to the left and one cell up. This is exactly what we want, since we always want the interest payment to be based on the short-term loan that was taken one year ago (two cells to the left and one cell up).

Excel Tip: A shortcut for changing a cell reference from relative to absolute is to press the F4 key on a PC or command-T on a Mac.

After using the Fill Down command to copy the formulas in columns F, G, I, J, and L and entering the LT loan payback into cell H21, the complete model appears as shown in Figure 4.4.

Test: Test the Full-Scale Version of the Model

Just as it was important to test the small version of the model, it needs to be tested again after it is expanded to full-scale size. The procedure is the same one followed for testing the small version, including the ideas that will be presented in Section 4.4 for debugging a spreadsheet model.

Analyze: Analyze the Model

Before using the Solver dialogue box to prepare for applying Solver, the spreadsheet in Figure 4.4 is merely an evaluative model for Everglade. It can be used to evaluate any proposed solution, including quickly determining what interest and loan payments will be required and what the resulting balances will be at the end of each year. For example, LTLoan (D11) and STLoan (E11:E20) in Figure 4.4 show one possible plan, which turns out to be unacceptable because EndingBalance (J11:J21) indicates that a negative ending balance would result in four of the years.

To optimize the model, the Solver dialogue box is used as shown in Figure 4.5 to specify the target cell, the changing cells, and the constraints. Everglade management wants to find a combination of loans that will keep the company solvent throughout the next 10 years (2011–2020) and then will leave as large a cash balance as possible in 2021 after paying off all the loans. Therefore, the target cell to be maximized is EndBalance (J21) and the changing cells are the loan amounts LTLoan (D11) and STLoan (E11:E20). To assure that Everglade maintains a minimum balance of at least $500,000 at the end of each year, the constraints for the model are EndingBalance (J11:J21) $\geq$ MinimumBalance (L11:L21).

After running Solver, the optimal solution is shown in Figure 4.5. The changing cells, LTLoan (D11) and STLoan (E11:E20) give the loan amounts in the various years. The target cell EndBalance (J21) indicates that the ending balance in 2021 will be $2.92 million.

Conclusion of the Case Study

The spreadsheet model developed by Everglade's CFO, Julie Lee, is the one shown in Figure 4.5. Her next step is to submit a report to her CEO, Sheldon Lee, that recommends the plan obtained by this model.

Soon thereafter, Sheldon and Julie meet to discuss her report.

Sheldon: Thanks for your report, Julie. Excellent job. Your spreadsheet really lays everything out in a very understandable way.

Julie: Thanks. It took a little while to get the spreadsheet organized properly and to make sure it was operating correctly, but I think the time spent was worthwhile.

Sheldon: Yes, it was. You can't rush those things. But one thing is still bothering me.

Julie: What's that?

Sheldon: It has to do with our forecasts for the company's future cash flows. We have been assuming that the cash flows in the coming years will be the ones shown in column C of

FIGURE 4.4

A complete spreadsheet model for the Everglade cash flow management problem, including the equations entered into the target cell EndBalance (J21) and all the other output cells, to be used before calling on the Excel Solver. The entries in the changing cells, LTLoan (D11) and STLoan (E11:E20), are only a trial solution at this stage.

	A	B	C	D	E	F	G	H	I	J	K	L
1		**Everglade Cash Flow Management Problem**										
2												
3		LT Rate	7%									
4		ST Rate	10%									
5						(all cash figures in millions of dollars)						
6		Start Balance	1									
7		Minimum Cash	0.5									
8												
9			Cash	LT	ST	LT	ST	LT	ST	Ending		Minimum
10		Year	Flow	Loan	Loan	Interest	Interest	Payback	Payback	Balance		Balance
11		2011	−8	6	2					1.00	≥	0.5
12		2012	−2		5	−0.42	−0.20		−2	1.38	≥	0.5
13		2013	−4		0	−0.42	−0.50		−5	−8.54	≥	0.5
14		2014	3		0	−0.42	0		0	−5.96	≥	0.5
15		2015	6		0	−0.42	0		0	−0.38	≥	0.5
16		2016	3		0	−0.42	0		0	2.20	≥	0.5
17		2017	−4		0	−0.42	0		0	−2.22	≥	0.5
18		2018	7		0	−0.42	0		0	4.36	≥	0.5
19		2019	−2		0	−0.42	0		0	1.94	≥	0.5
20		2020	10		0	−0.42	0		0	11.52	≥	0.5
21		2021				−0.42	0	−6	0	5.10	≥	0.5

	F	G	H	I	J	K	L
9	LT	ST	LT	ST	Ending		Minimum
10	Interest	Interest	Payback	Payback	Balance		Balance
11					=StartBalance+SUM(C11:I11)	≥	=MinimumCash
12	=−LTRate*LTLoan	=−STRate*E11		=−E11	=J11+SUM(C12:I12)	≥	=MinimumCash
13	=−LTRate*LTLoan	=−STRate*E12		=−E12	=J12+SUM(C13:I13)	≥	=MinimumCash
14	=−LTRate*LTLoan	=−STRate*E13		=−E13	=J13+SUM(C14:I14)	≥	=MinimumCash
15	=−LTRate*LTLoan	=−STRate*E14		=−E14	=J14+SUM(C15:I15)	≥	=MinimumCash
16	=−LTRate*LTLoan	=−STRate*E15		=−E15	=J15+SUM(C16:I16)	≥	=MinimumCash
17	=−LTRate*LTLoan	=−STRate*E16		=−E16	=J16+SUM(C17:I17)	≥	=MinimumCash
18	=−LTRate*LTLoan	=−STRate*E17		=−E17	=J17+SUM(C18:I18)	≥	=MinimumCash
19	=−LTRate*LTLoan	=−STRate*E18		=−E18	=J18+SUM(C19:I19)	≥	=MinimumCash
20	=−LTRate*LTLoan	=−STRate*E19		=−E19	=J19+SUM(C20:I20)	≥	=MinimumCash
21	=−LTRate*LTLoan	=−STRate*E20	=−LTLoan	=−E20	=J20+SUM(C21:I21)	≥	=MinimumCash

Range Name	Cells
CashFlow	C11:C20
EndBalance	J21
EndingBalance	J11:J21
LTLoan	D11
LTRate	C3
MinimumBalance	L11:L21
MinimumCash	C7
StartBalance	C6
STLoan	E11:E20
STRate	C4

FIGURE 4.5

A complete spreadsheet model for the Everglade cash flow management problem after calling on the Excel Solver to obtain the optimal solution shown in the changing cells, LTLoan (D11) and STLoan (E11:E20). The target cell EndBalance (J21) indicates that the resulting cash balance in 2021 will be $2.92 million if all the data cells prove to be accurate.

	A	B	C	D	E	F	G	H	I	J	K	L
1		**Everglade Cash Flow Management Problem**										
2												
3		LT Rate	7%									
4		ST Rate	10%									
5						(all cash figures in millions of dollars)						
6		Start Balance	1									
7		Minimum Cash	0.5									
8												
9			Cash	LT	ST	LT	ST	LT	ST	Ending		Minimum
10		Year	Flow	Loan	Loan	Interest	Interest	Payback	Payback	Balance		Balance
11		2011	–8	6.65	0.85					0.50	≥	0.50
12		2012	–2		3.40	–0.47	–0.09		–0.85	0.50	≥	0.50
13		2013	–4		8.21	–0.47	–0.34		–3.40	0.50	≥	0.50
14		2014	3		6.49	–0.47	–0.82		–8.21	0.50	≥	0.50
15		2015	6		1.61	–0.47	–0.65		–6.49	0.50	≥	0.50
16		2016	3		0	–0.47	–0.16		–1.61	1.27	≥	0.50
17		2017	–4		3.70	–0.47	0		0	0.50	≥	0.50
18		2018	7		0	–0.47	–0.37		–3.70	2.97	≥	0.50
19		2019	–2		0	–0.47	0		0	0.50	≥	0.50
20		2020	10		0	–0.47	0		0	10.03	≥	0.50
21		2021				–0.47	0	–6.65	0	2.92	≥	0.50

	F	G	H	I	J	K	L
9	LT	ST	LT	ST	Ending		Minimum
10	Interest	Interest	Payback	Payback	Balance		Balance
11					= StartBalance+SUM(C11:I11)	≥	=MinimumCash
12	=–LTRate*LTLoan	=–STRate*E11		=–E11	=J11+SUM(C12:I12)	≥	=MinimumCash
13	=–LTRate*LTLoan	=–STRate*E12		=–E12	=J12+SUM(C13:I13)	≥	=MinimumCash
14	=–LTRate*LTLoan	=–STRate*E13		=–E13	=J13+SUM(C14:I14)	≥	=MinimumCash
15	=–LTRate*LTLoan	=–STRate*E14		=–E14	=J14+SUM(C15:I15)	≥	=MinimumCash
16	=–LTRate*LTLoan	=–STRate*E15		=–E15	=J15+SUM(C16:I16)	≥	=MinimumCash
17	=–LTRate*LTLoan	=–STRate*E16		=–E16	=J16+SUM(C17:I17)	≥	=MinimumCash
18	=–LTRate*LTLoan	=–STRate*E17		=–E17	=J17+SUM(C18:I18)	≥	=MinimumCash
19	=–LTRate*LTLoan	=–STRate*E18		=–E18	=J18+SUM(C19:I19)	≥	=MinimumCash
20	=–LTRate*LTLoan	=–STRate*E19		=–E19	=J19+SUM(C20:I20)	≥	=MinimumCash
21	=–LTRate*LTLoan	=–STRate*E20	=–LTLoan	=–E20	=J20+SUM(C21:I21)	≥	=MinimumCash

Solver Parameters

Set Objective (Target Cell) : EndBalance
To: Max
By Changing (Variable) Cells:
 LTLoan, STLoan
Subject to the Constraints:
 EndingBalance >= MinimumBalance

Solver Options (Excel 2010):
 Make Variables Nonnegative
 Solving Method: Simplex LP
Solver Options (older Excel):
 Assume Nonnegative
 Assume Linear Model

Range Name	Cells
CashFlow	C11:C20
EndBalance	J21
EndingBalance	J11:J21
LTLoan	D11
LTRate	C3
MinimumBalance	L11:L21
MinimumCash	C7
StartBalance	C6
STLoan	E11:E20
STRate	C4

your spreadsheet. Those are good estimates, but we both know that they are only estimates. A lot of changes that we can't foresee now are likely to occur over the next 10 years. When there is a shift in the economy, or when other unexpected developments occur that impact the company, those cash flows can change a lot. How do we know if your recommended plan will still be a good one if those kinds of changes occur?

Julie: A very good question. To answer it, we should do some *what-if analysis* to see what would happen if those kinds of changes occur. Now that the spreadsheet is set up properly, it will be very easy to do that by simply changing some of the cash flows in column C and seeing what would happen with the current plan. You can try out any change or changes you want and immediately see the effect. Each time you change a future cash flow, you also have the option of trying out changes on short-term loan amounts to see what kind of adjustments would be needed to maintain a balance of at least $500,000 in every year.

OK, are you ready? Shall we do some what-if analysis now?

Sheldon: Let's do.

Fortunately, Julie had set up the spreadsheet properly (providing a data cell for the cash flow in each of the next 10 years) to enable performing *what-if analysis* immediately by simply trying different numbers in some of these data cells. (The next chapter will focus on describing the importance of what-if analysis and alternative ways of performing this kind of analysis.) After spending half an hour trying different numbers, Sheldon and Julie conclude that the plan in Figure 4.5 will be a sound initial financial plan for the next 10 years, even if future cash flows deviate somewhat from current forecasts. If deviations do occur, adjustments will of course need to be made in the short-term loan amounts. At any point, Julie also will have the option of returning to the company's bank to try to arrange another long-term loan for the remainder of the 10 years at a lower interest rate than that offered for short-term loans. If so, essentially the same spreadsheet model as in Figure 4.5 can be used, along with the Excel Solver, to find the optimal adjusted financial plan for the remainder of the 10 years.

A management science technique called *computer simulation* provides another effective way of taking the uncertainty of future cash flows into account. Chapters 12 and 13 will describe this technique and Section 13.4 will be devoted to continuing the analysis of this same case study.

> *Providing a data cell for each piece of data makes it easy to check what would happen if the correct value for a piece of data differs from its initial estimate.*

Review Questions

1. What is a good way to get started with a spreadsheet model if you don't even know where to begin?
2. What are two ways in which doing calculations by hand can help you?
3. Describe a useful way to get started organizing and laying out a spreadsheet.
4. What types of values should be put into the changing cells to test the model?
5. What is the difference between an absolute cell reference and a relative cell reference?

4.3 SOME GUIDELINES FOR BUILDING "GOOD" SPREADSHEET MODELS

There are many ways to set up a model on a spreadsheet. While one of the benefits of spreadsheets is the flexibility they offer, this flexibility also can be dangerous. Although Excel provides many features (such as range names, shading, borders, etc.) that allow you to create "good" spreadsheet models that are easy to understand, easy to debug, and easy to modify, it is also easy to create "bad" spreadsheet models that are difficult to understand, difficult to debug, and difficult to modify. The goal of this section is to provide some guidelines that will help you to create "good" spreadsheet models.

Enter the Data First

> *All the data should be laid out on the spreadsheet before beginning to formulate the rest of the spreadsheet model.*

Any spreadsheet model is driven by the data in the spreadsheet. The form of the entire model is built around the structure of the data. Therefore, it is always a good idea to enter and carefully lay out all the data before you begin to set up the rest of the model. The model structure then can conform to the layout of the data as closely as possible.

An Application Vignette

Welch's, Inc., is the world's largest processor of Concord and Niagara grapes with annual sales surpassing $550 million per year. Such products as Welch's grape jelly and Welch's grape juice have been enjoyed by generations of American consumers.

Every September, growers begin delivering grapes to processing plants that then press the raw grapes into juice. Time must pass before the grape juice is ready for conversion into finished jams, jellies, juices, and concentrates.

Deciding how to use the grape crop is a complex task given changing demand and uncertain crop quality and quantity. Typical decisions include what recipes to use for major product groups, the transfer of grape juice between plants, and the mode of transportation for these transfers.

Because Welch's lacked a formal system for optimizing raw material movement and the recipes used for production, a management science team developed a preliminary linear programming model. This was a large model with 8,000 decision variables that focused on the component level of detail. Small-scale testing proved that the model worked.

To make the model more useful, the team then revised it by aggregating demand by product group rather than by component. This reduced its size to 324 decision variables and 361 functional constraints. *The model then was incorporated into a spreadsheet.*

The company has run the continually updated version of this *spreadsheet model* each month since 1994 to provide senior management with information on the optimal logistics plan generated by the Solver. The *savings* from using and optimizing this model were *approximately $150,000 in the first year alone.* A major advantage of incorporating the linear programming model into a spreadsheet has been the ease of explaining the model to managers with differing levels of mathematical understanding. This has led to a widespread appreciation of the management science approach for both this application and others.

Source: E. W. Schuster and S. J. Allen, "Raw Material Management at Welch's, Inc.," *Interfaces* 28, no. 5 (September–October 1998), pp. 13–24. (A link to this article is provided on our Web site, www.mhhe.com/hillier4e.)

Often, it is easier to set up the rest of the model when the data are already on the spreadsheet. In the Everglade problem (see Figure 4.5), the data for the cash flows have been laid out in the first columns of the spreadsheet (B and C), with the year labels in column B and the data in cells C11:C20. Once the data are in place, the layout for the rest of the model quickly falls into place around the structure of the data. It is only logical to lay out the changing cells and output cells using the same structure, with each of the various cash flows in columns that utilize the same row labels from column B.

Now reconsider the spreadsheet model developed in Section 2.2 for the Wyndor Glass Co. problem. The spreadsheet is repeated here in Figure 4.6. The data for the Hours Used per Unit Produced have been laid out in the center of the spreadsheet in cells C7:D9. The output cells, HoursUsed (E7:E9), then have been placed immediately to the right of these data and to the left of the data on HoursAvailable(G7:G9), where the row labels for these output cells are the same as for all these data. This makes it easy to interpret the three constraints being laid out in rows 7–9 of the spreadsheet model. Next, the changing cells and target cell have been placed together in row 12 below the data, where the column labels for the changing cells are the same as for the columns of data above.

The locations of the data occasionally will need to be shifted somewhat to better accommodate the overall model. However, with this caveat, the model structure generally should conform to the data as closely as possible.

Organize and Clearly Identify the Data

Related data should be grouped together in a convenient format and entered into the spreadsheet with labels that clearly identify the data. For data that are laid out in tabular form, the table should have a heading that provides a general description of the data and then each row and column should have a label that will identify each entry in the table. The units of the data also should be identified. Different types of data should be well separated in the spreadsheet. However, if two tables need to use the same labels for either their rows or columns, then be consistent in making them either rows in both tables or columns in both tables.

Provide labels in the spreadsheet that clearly identify all the data.

In the Wyndor Glass Co. problem (Figure 4.6), the three sets of data have been grouped into tables and clearly labeled Unit Profit, Hours Used per Unit Produced, and Hours Available. The units of the data are identified (dollar signs are included in the unit profit data and hours are indicated in the labels of the time data). Finally, all three data tables make consistent use of rows and columns. Since the Unit Profit data have their product labels (Doors and Windows) in

FIGURE 4.6
The spreadsheet model formulated in Section 2.2 for the Wyndor Glass Co. product-mix problem.

	A	B	C	D	E	F	G
1		Wyndor Glass Co. Product-Mix Problem					
2							
3			Doors	Windows			
4		Unit Profit	$300	$500			
5					Hours		Hours
6			Hours Used per Unit Produced		Used		Available
7		Plant 1	1	0	2	≤	4
8		Plant 2	0	2	12	≤	12
9		Plant 3	3	2	18	≤	18
10							
11			Doors	Windows			Total Profit
12		Units Produced	2	6			$3,600

Solver Parameters
Set Objective (Target Cell): TotalProfit
To: Max
By Changing (Variable) Cells:
  UnitsProduced
Subject to the Constraints:
  HoursUsed <= HoursAvailable

Solver Options (Excel 2010):
  Make Variables Nonnegative
  Solving Method: Simplex LP
Solver Options (older Excel):
  Assume Nonnegative
  Assume Linear Model

	E
5	Hours
6	Used
7	=SUMPRODUCT(C7:D7,UnitsProduced)
8	=SUMPRODUCT(C8:D8,UnitsProduced)
9	=SUMPRODUCT(C9:D9,UnitsProduced)

	G
11	Total Profit
12	=SUMPRODUCT(Unit Profit,UnitsProduced)

Range Name	Cells
HoursAvailable	G7:G9
HoursUsed	E7:E9
HoursUsedPerUnitProduced	C7:D9
TotalProfit	G12
UnitProfit	C4:D4
UnitsProduced	C12:D12

columns C and D, the Hours Used per Unit Produced data use this same structure. This structure also is carried through to the changing cells (Units Produced). Similarly, the data for each plant (rows 7–9) are in the rows for both the Hours Used per Unit Produced data *and* the Hours Available data. Keeping the data oriented the same way is not only less confusing, but it also makes it possible to use the SUMPRODUCT function. Recall that the SUMPRODUCT function assumes that the two ranges are exactly the same shape (i.e., the same number of rows *and* columns). If the Unit Profit data and the Units Produced data had not been oriented the same way (e.g., one in a column and the other in a row), it would not have been possible to use the SUMPRODUCT function in the Total Profit calculation.

Similarly, for the Everglade problem (Figure 4.5), the five sets of data have been grouped into cells and tables and clearly labeled ST Rate, LT Rate, Start Balance, Cash Flow, and Minimum Cash. The units of the data are identified (cells F5:I5 specify that all cash figures are in millions of dollars), and all the tables make consistent use of rows and columns (years in the rows).

Enter Each Piece of Data into One Cell Only

Every formula using the same piece of data should refer to the same single data cell.

If a piece of data is needed in more than one formula, then refer to the original data cell rather than repeating the data in additional places. This makes the model much easier to modify. If the value of that piece of data changes, it only needs to be changed in one place. You do not need to search through the entire model to find all the places where the data value appears.

For example, in the Everglade problem (Figure 4.5), there is a company policy of maintaining a cash balance of at least $500,000 at all times. This translates into a constraint for the minimum balance of $500,000 at the end of each year. Rather than entering the minimum cash position of 0.5 (in millions of dollars) into all the cells in column L, it is entered once in MinimumCash (C7) and then referred to by the cells in MinimumBalance (L11:L21). Then, if this policy were to change to, say, a minimum of $200,000 cash, the number would need to be changed in only one place.

Separate Data from Formulas

Formulas should refer to data cells for any needed numbers.

Avoid using numbers directly in formulas. Instead, enter any needed numbers into data cells and then refer to the data cells as needed. For example, in the Everglade problem (Figure 4.5), all the data (the interest rates, starting balance, minimum cash, and projected cash flows) are entered into separate data cells on the spreadsheet. When these numbers are needed to calculate the interest charges (in columns F and G), loan payments (in column H and I), ending balances (column J), and minimum balances (column L), the data cells are referred to rather than entering these numbers directly in the formulas.

Separating the data from the formulas has a couple advantages. First, all the data are visible on the spreadsheet rather than buried in formulas. Seeing all the data makes the model easier to interpret. Second, the model is easier to modify since changing data only requires modifying the corresponding data cells. You don't need to modify any formulas. This proves to be very important when it comes time to perform what-if analysis to see what the effect would be if some of the estimates in the data cells were to take on other plausible values.

Keep It Simple

Make the spreadsheet as easy to interpret as possible.

Avoid the use of powerful Excel functions when simpler functions are available that are easier to interpret. As much as possible, stick to SUMPRODUCT or SUM functions. This makes the model easier to understand and also helps to ensure that the model will be linear. (Linear models are considerably easier to solve than others.) Try to keep formulas short and simple. If a complicated formula is required, break it out into intermediate calculations with subtotals. For example, in the Everglade spreadsheet, each element of the loan payments is broken out explicitly: LT Interest, ST Interest, LT Payback, and ST Payback. Some of these columns could have been combined (e.g., into two columns with LT Payments and ST Payments, or even into one column for all Loan Payments). However, this makes the formulas more complicated and also makes the model harder to test and debug. As laid out, the individual formulas for the loan payments are so simple that their values can be predicted easily without even looking at the formula. This simplifies the testing and debugging of the model.

Use Range Names

Range names make formulas much easier to interpret.

One way to refer to a block of related cells (or even a single cell) in a spreadsheet formula is to use its cell address (e.g., L11:L21 or C3). However, when reading the formula, this requires looking at that part of the spreadsheet to see what kind of information is given there. As mentioned previously in Sections 1.2 and 2.2, a better alternative is to assign a descriptive **range name** to the block of cells that immediately identifies what is there. (This is done by selecting the block of cells, clicking on the name box on the left of the formula bar above the spreadsheet, and then typing a name.) This is especially helpful when writing a formula for an output cell. Writing the formula in terms of range names instead of cell addresses makes the formula much easier to interpret. Range names also make the description of the model in the Solver dialogue box much easier to understand.

Figure 4.5 illustrates the use of range names for the Everglade spreadsheet model. For example, consider the formula for long-term interest in cell F12. Since the long-term rate is given in cell C3 and the long-term loan amount is in cell D11, the formula for the long-term interest could have been written as = −C3*D11. However, by using the range name LTRate for cell C3 and the range name LTLoan for cell D11, the formula instead becomes = −LTRate*LTLoan, which is much easier to interpret at a glance.

On the other hand, be aware that it is easy to get carried away with defining range names. Defining too many range names can be more trouble than it is worth. For example, when related data are grouped together in a table, we recommend giving a range name only for the entire table rather than for the individual rows and columns. In general, we suggest defining range names only for each group of data cells, the changing cells, the target cell, and both sides of each group of constraints (the left-hand side and the right-hand side).

Spaces are not allowed in range names. When a range name has more than one word, we have used capital letters to distinguish the start of each new word in a range name (e.g., MinimumBalance). Another way is to use the underscore character (e.g., Minimum_Balance).

Care also should be taken to assure that it is easy to quickly identify which cells are referred to by a particular range name. Use a name that corresponds exactly to the label on the spreadsheet. For example, in Figure 4.5, columns J and L are labeled Ending Balance and Minimum Balance on the spreadsheet, so we use the range names EndingBalance and MinimumBalance. Using exactly the same name as the label on the spreadsheet makes it quick and easy to find the cells that are referred to by a range name.

When desired, a list of all the range names and their corresponding cell addresses can be pasted directly into the spreadsheet by choosing Paste from the Use in Formula menu on the Formulas tab (for Excel 2007 or 2010) or Name\Paste from the Insert menu (for other versions of Excel), and then clicking Paste List. Such a list (after reformatting) is included below essentially all the spreadsheets displayed in this text.

When modifying an existing model that utilizes range names, care should be taken to assure that the range names continue to refer to the correct range of cells. When inserting a row or column into a spreadsheet model, it is helpful to insert the row or column into the middle of a range rather than at the end. For example, to add another product to a product-mix model with four products, add a column between products 2 and 3 rather than after product 4. This will automatically extend the relevant range names to span across all five columns since these range names will continue to refer to everything between product 1 and product 4, including the newly inserted column for the fifth product. Similarly, deleting a row or column from the middle of a range will contract the span of the relevant range names appropriately. You can double-check the cells that are referred to by a range name by choosing that range name from the name box (on the left of the formula bar above the spreadsheet). This will highlight the cells that are referred to by the chosen range name.

Use Relative and Absolute References to Simplify Copying Formulas

Excel's fill commands provide a quick and reliable way to replicate a formula into multiple cells.

Whenever multiple related formulas will be needed, try to enter the formula just once and then use Excel's fill commands to replicate the formula. Not only is this quicker than retyping the formula, but it is also less prone to error.

We saw a good example of this when discussing the expansion of the model to full-scale size in the preceding section. Starting with the two-year spreadsheet in Figure 4.3, fill commands were used to copy the formulas in columns F, G, I, J, and L for the remaining years to create the full-scale, 10-year spreadsheet in Figure 4.4.

Using relative and absolute references for related formulas not only aids in building a model but also makes it easier to modify an existing model or template. For example, suppose that you have formulated a spreadsheet model for a product-mix problem but now wish to modify the model to add another resource. This requires inserting a row into the spreadsheet. If the output cells are written with proper relative and absolute references, then it is simple to copy the existing formulas into the inserted row.

Use Borders, Shading, and Colors to Distinguish between Cell Types

It is important to be able to easily distinguish between the data cells, changing cells, output cells, and target cell in a spreadsheet. One way to do this is to use different borders and cell shading for each of these different types of cells. In the text, data cells appear lightly shaded, changing cells are shaded a medium amount with a light border, output cells appear with no shading, and the target cell is shaded darkly with a heavy border.

Make it easy to spot all the cells of the same type.

In the spreadsheet files in MS Courseware, data cells are light blue, changing cells are yellow, and the target cell is orange. Obviously, you may use any scheme that you like. The important thing is to be consistent, so that you can quickly recognize the types of cells. Then, when you want to examine the cells of a certain type, the color will immediately guide you there.

Show the Entire Model on the Spreadsheet

The Solver uses a combination of the spreadsheet and the Solver dialogue box to specify the model to be solved. Therefore, it is possible to include certain elements of the model (such as the $\leq$, $=$, or $\geq$ signs and/or the right-hand sides of the constraints) in the Solver dialogue box without displaying them in the spreadsheet. However, we strongly recommend that *every* element of the model be displayed *on the spreadsheet*. Every person using or adapting the model, or referring back to it later, needs to be able to interpret the model. This is much easier to do by viewing the model on the spreadsheet than by trying to decipher it from the Solver dialogue box. Furthermore, a printout of the spreadsheet does not include information from the Solver dialogue box.

In particular, all the elements of a constraint should be displayed on the spreadsheet. For each constraint, three adjacent cells should be used for the total of the left-hand side, the ≤, =, or ≥ sign in the middle, and the right-hand side. (Note in Figure 4.5 that this was done in columns J, K, and L of the spreadsheet for the Everglade problem.) As mentioned earlier, the changing cells and target cell should be highlighted in some manner (e.g., with borders and/or cell shading). A good test is that you should not need to go to the Solver dialogue box to determine any element of the model. You should be able to identify the changing cells, the target cell, and all the constraints in the model just by looking at the spreadsheet.

Display every element of the model on the spreadsheet rather than relying on only the Solver dialogue box to include certain elements.

A Poor Spreadsheet Model

It is certainly possible to set up a linear programming spreadsheet model without utilizing any of these ideas. Figure 4.7 shows an alternative spreadsheet formulation for the Everglade problem that violates nearly every one of these guidelines. This formulation can still be solved using Solver, which in fact yields the same optimal solution as in Figure 4.5. However,

FIGURE 4.7
A poor formulation of the spreadsheet model for the Everglade cash flow management problem.

	A	B	C	D	E	F
1		**A Poor Formulation of the Everglade Cash Flow Problem**				
2						
3			LT	ST	Ending	
4		Year	Loan	Loan	Balance	
5		2011	6.65	0.85	0.50	
6		2012		3.40	0.50	
7		2013		8.21	0.50	
8		2014		6.49	0.50	
9		2015		1.61	0.50	
10		2016		0	1.27	
11		2017		3.70	0.50	
12		2018		0	2.97	
13		2019		0	0.50	
14		2020		0	10.03	
15		2021			2.92	

Solver Parameters

Set Objective (Target Cell): E15
To: Max
By Changing (Variable) Cells:
   C5, D5:D14
Subject to the Constraints:
   E5:E15 >= 0.5

Solver Options (Excel 2010):
   Make Variables Nonnegative
   Solving Method: Simplex LP
Solver Options (older Excel):
   Assume Nonnegative
   Assume Linear Model

	E
3	Ending
4	Balance
5	=1–8+C5+D5
6	=E5–2+D6–$C$5*(0.07)–D5*(1.1)
7	=E6–4+D7–$C$5*(0.07)–D6*(1.1)
8	=E7+3+D8–$C$5*(0.07)–D7*(1.1)
9	=E8+6+D9–$C$5*(0.07)–D8*(1.1)
10	=E9+3+D10–$C$5*(0.07)–D9*(1.1)
11	=E10–4+D11–$C$5*(0.07)–D10*(1.1)
12	=E11+7+D12–$C$5*(0.07)–D11*(1.1)
13	=E12–2+D13–$C$5*(0.07)–D12*(1.1)
14	=E13+10+D14–$C$5*(0.07)–D13*(1.1)
15	=E14+D15–$C$5*(1.07)–D14*(1.1)

the formulation has many problems. It is not clear which cells yield the solution (borders and/or shading are not used to highlight the changing cells and target cell). Without going to the Solver dialogue box, the constraints in the model cannot be identified (the spreadsheet does not show the entire model). The spreadsheet also does not show most of the data. For example, to determine the data used for the projected cash flows, the interest rates, or the starting balance, you need to dig into the formulas in column E (the data are not separate from the formulas). If any of these data change, the actual formulas need to be modified rather than simply changing a number on the spreadsheet. Furthermore, the formulas and the model in the Solver dialogue box are difficult to interpret (range names are not utilized).

Compare Figures 4.5 and 4.7. Applying the guidelines for good spreadsheet models (as is done for Figure 4.5) results in a model that is easier to understand, easier to debug, and easier to modify. This is especially important for models that will have a long life span. If this model is going to be reused months later, the "good" model of Figure 4.5 immediately can be understood, modified, and reapplied as needed, whereas deciphering the spreadsheet model of Figure 4.7 again would be a great challenge.

Review
Questions

1. Which part of the model should be entered first on the spreadsheet?
2. Should numbers be included in formulas or entered separately in data cells?
3. How do range names make formulas and the model in the Solver dialogue box easier to interpret? How should range names be chosen?
4. What are some ways to distinguish data cells, changing cells, output cells, and target cells on a spreadsheet?
5. How many cells are needed to completely specify a constraint on a spreadsheet?

4.4   DEBUGGING A SPREADSHEET MODEL

Debugging a spreadsheet model sometimes is as challenging as debugging a computer program.

No matter how carefully it is planned and built, even a moderately complicated model usually will not be error-free the first time it is run. Often the mistakes are immediately obvious and quickly corrected. However, sometimes an error is harder to root out. Following the guidelines in Section 4.3 for developing a good spreadsheet model can make the model *much* easier to debug. Even so, much like debugging a computer program, debugging a spreadsheet model can be a difficult task. This section presents some tips and a variety of Excel features that can make debugging easier.

As a first step in debugging a spreadsheet model, test the model using the principles discussed in the first subsection on testing in Section 4.2. In particular, try different values for the changing cells for which you can predict the correct result in the output cells and see if they calculate as expected. Values of 0 are good ones to try initially because usually it is then obvious what should be in the output cells. Try other simple values, such as all 1s, where the correct results in the output cells are reasonably obvious. For more complicated values, break out a calculator and do some manual calculations to check the various output cells. Include some very large values for the changing cells to ensure that the calculations are behaving reasonably for these extreme cases.

If you have added rows or columns to the spreadsheet, make sure that each of the range names still refers to the correct cells.

If you have defined range names, be sure that they still refer to the correct cells. Sometimes they can become disjointed when you add rows or columns to the spreadsheet. To test the range names, you can either select the various range names in the name box, which will highlight the selected range in the spreadsheet, or paste the entire list of range names and their references into the spreadsheet.

toggle
The toggle feature in Excel is a great way to check the formulas for the output cells.

Carefully study each formula to be sure it is entered correctly. A very useful feature in Excel for checking formulas is the **toggle** to switch back and forth between viewing the formulas in the worksheet and viewing the resulting values in the output cells. By default, Excel shows the values that are calculated by the various output cells in the model. Typing control-~ switches the current worksheet to instead display the formulas in the output cells, as shown in Figure 4.8. Typing control-~ again switches back to the standard view of displaying the values in the output cells (like Figure 4.5).

FIGURE 4.8

The spreadsheet obtained by toggling the spreadsheet in Figure 4.5 once to replace the values in the output cells by the formulas entered into those cells. Using the toggle feature in Excel once more will restore the view of the spreadsheet shown in Figure 4.5.

	A	B	C	D	E	F	G	H	I	J	K	L
1	Everglade Cash Flow Management Problem											
2												
3		LT Rate	0.07									
4		ST Rate	0.1									
5						(all cash figures in millions of dollars)						
6		Start Balance	1									
7		Minimum Cash	0.5									
8												Minimum
9			Cash	LT	ST	LT	ST	LT	ST	Ending		Balance
10		Year	Flow	Loan	Loan	Interest	Interest	Payback	Payback	Balance		
11		2011	−8	6.64945	0.85054	=−LTRate*LTLoan	=−STRate*E11			=StartBalance+SUM(C11:I11)	≥	=MinimumCash
12		2012	−2		3.40105	=−LTRate*LTLoan	=−STRate*E12		=−E11	=J11+SUM(C12:I12)	≥	=MinimumCash
13		2013	−4		8.20662	=−LTRate*LTLoan	=−STRate*E13		=−E12	=J12+SUM(C13:I13)	≥	=MinimumCash
14		2014	3		6.49274	=−LTRate*LTLoan	=−STRate*E14		=−E13	=J13+SUM(C14:I14)	≥	=MinimumCash
15		2015	6		1.60748	=−LTRate*LTLoan	=−STRate*E15		=−E14	=J14+SUM(C15:I15)	≥	=MinimumCash
16		2016	3		0	=−LTRate*LTLoan	=−STRate*E16		=−E15	=J15+SUM(C16:I16)	≥	=MinimumCash
17		2017	−4		3.69915	=−LTRate*LTLoan	=−STRate*E17		=−E16	=J16+SUM(C17:I17)	≥	=MinimumCash
18		2018	7		0	=−LTRate*LTLoan	=−STRate*E18		=−E17	=J17+SUM(C18:I18)	≥	=MinimumCash
19		2019	−2		0	=−LTRate*LTLoan	=−STRate*E19		=−E18	=J18+SUM(C19:I19)	≥	=MinimumCash
20		2020	10		0	=−LTRate*LTLoan	=−STRate*E20		=−E19	=J19+SUM(C20:I20)	≥	=MinimumCash
21		2021				=−LTRate*LTLoan		=−LTLoan	=−E20	=J20+SUM(C21:I21)	≥	=MinimumCash

Excel Tip: Pressing control-~ on a PC (or command-~ on a Mac) toggles the worksheet between viewing values and viewing formulas in all the output cells.

Another useful set of features built into Excel are the **auditing tools.** The auditing tools are available in the Formula Auditing group of the Formulas Tab (for Excel 2007 or 2010) or under the Tools\Auditing menu (for other versions of Excel).

The auditing tools can be used to graphically display which cells make direct links to a given cell. For example, selecting LTLoan (D11) in Figure 4.5 and then Trace Dependents generates the arrows on the spreadsheet shown in Figure 4.9.

You now can immediately see that LTLoan (D11) is used in the calculation of LT Interest for every year in column F, in the calculation of LTPayback (H21), and in the calculation of the ending balance in 2011 (J11). This can be very illuminating. Think about what output cells LTLoan should impact directly. There should be an arrow to each of these cells. If, for example, LTLoan is missing from any of the formulas in column F, the error will be immediately revealed by the missing arrow. Similarly, if LTLoan is mistakenly entered in any of the short-term loan output cells, this will show up as extra arrows.

Excel's auditing tools enable you to either trace forward or backward to see the linkages between cells.

You also can trace backward to see which cells provide the data for any given cell. These can be displayed graphically by choosing Trace Precedents. For example, choosing Trace Precedents for the ST Interest cell for 2012 (G12) displays the arrows shown in Figure 4.10. These arrows indicate that the ST Interest cell for 2012 (G12) refers to the ST Loan in 2011 (E11) and to STRate (C4).

When you are done, choose Remove Arrows.

Review Questions

1. What is a good first step for debugging a spreadsheet model?
2. How do you toggle between viewing formulas and viewing values in output cells?
3. Which Excel tool can be used to trace the dependents or precedents for a given cell?

FIGURE 4.9

The spreadsheet obtained by using the Excel auditing tools to trace the dependents of the LT Loan value in cell D11 of the spreadsheet in Figure 4.5.

	A	B	C	D	E	F	G	H	I	J	K	L
1		**Everglade Cash Flow Management Problem**										
2												
3		LT Rate	7%									
4		ST Rate	10%									
5						(all cash figures in millions of dollars)						
6		Start Balance	1									
7		Minimum Cash	0.5									
8												
9			Cash	LT	ST	LT	ST	LT	ST	Ending		Minimum
10		Year	Flow	Loan	Loan	Interest	Interest	Payback	Payback	Balance		Balance
11		2011	–8	6.65	0.85					0.50	≥	0.5
12		2012	–2		3.40	–0.47	–0.09		–0.85	0.50	≥	0.5
13		2013	–4		8.21	–0.47	–0.34		–3.40	0.50	≥	0.5
14		2014	3		6.49	–0.47	–0.82		–8.21	0.50	≥	0.5
15		2015	6		1.61	–0.47	–0.65		–6.49	0.50	≥	0.5
16		2016	3		0	–0.47	–0.16		–1.61	1.27	≥	0.5
17		2017	–4		3.70	–0.47	0		0	0.50	≥	0.5
18		2018	7		0	–0.47	–0.37		–3.70	2.97	≥	0.5
19		2019	–2		0	–0.47	0		0	0.50	≥	0.5
20		2020	10		0	–0.47	0		0	10.03	≥	0.5
21		2021				–0.47	0	–6.65	0	2.92	≥	0.5

FIGURE 4.10

The spreadsheet obtained by using the Excel auditing tools to trace the precedents of the ST Interest (2012) calculation in cell G12 of the spreadsheet in Figure 4.5.

	A	B	C	D	E	F	G	H	I	J	K	L
1		**Everglade Cash Flow Management Problem**										
2												
3		LT Rate	7%									
4		ST Rate	10%									
5						(all cash figures in millions of dollars)						
6		Start Balance	1									
7		Minimum Cash	0.5									
8												
9			Cash	LT	ST	LT	ST	LT	ST	Ending		Minimum
10		Year	Flow	Loan	Loan	Interest	Interest	Payback	Payback	Balance		Balance
11		2011	−8	6.65	0.85					0.50	≥	0.5
12		2012	−2		3.40	−0.47	−0.09		−0.85	0.50	≥	0.5
13		2013	−4		8.21	−0.47	−0.34		−3.40	0.50	≥	0.5
14		2014	3		6.49	−0.47	−0.82		−8.21	0.50	≥	0.5
15		2015	6		1.61	−0.47	−0.65		−6.49	0.50	≥	0.5
16		2016	3		0	−0.47	−0.16		−1.61	1.27	≥	0.5
17		2017	−4		3.70	−0.47	0		0	0.50	≥	0.5
18		2018	7		0	−0.47	−0.37		−3.70	2.97	≥	0.5
19		2019	−2		0	−0.47	0		0	0.50	≥	0.5
20		2020	10		0	−0.47	0		0	10.03	≥	0.5
21		2021				−0.47	0	−6.65	0	2.92	≥	0.5

4.5 Summary

There is a considerable art to modeling well with spreadsheets. This chapter focuses on providing a foundation for learning this art.

The general process of modeling in spreadsheets has four major steps: (1) plan the spreadsheet model, (2) build the model, (3) test the model, and (4) analyze the model and its results. During the planning step, it is helpful to begin by visualizing where you want to finish and then doing some calculations by hand to clarify the needed computations before starting to sketch out a logical layout for the spreadsheet. Then, when you are ready to undertake the building step, it is a good idea to start by building a small, readily manageable version of the model before expanding the model to full-scale size. This enables you to test the small version first to get all the logic straightened out correctly before expanding to a full-scale model and undertaking a final test. After completing all of this, you are ready for the analysis step, which involves applying the model to evaluate proposed solutions and perhaps using Solver to optimize the model.

Using this plan-build-test-analyze process should yield a spreadsheet model, but it doesn't guarantee that you will obtain a good one. Section 4.3 describes in detail the following guidelines for building "good" spreadsheet models:

- Enter the data first.
- Organize and clearly identify the data.
- Enter each piece of data into one cell only.
- Separate data from formulas.
- Keep it simple.
- Use range names.
- Use relative and absolute references to simplify copying formulas.
- Use borders, shading, and colors to distinguish between cell types.
- Show the entire model on the spreadsheet.

Even if all these guidelines are followed, a thorough debugging process may be needed to eliminate the errors that lurk within the initial version of the model. It is important to check whether the output cells are giving correct results for various values of the changing cells. Other items to check include whether range names refer to the appropriate cells and whether formulas have been entered into output cells correctly. Excel provides a number of useful features to aid in the debugging process. One is the ability to toggle the worksheet between viewing the results in the output cells and the formulas entered into those output cells. Several other helpful features are available with Excel's auditing tools.

Glossary

auditing tools   A set of tools provided by Excel to aid in debugging a spreadsheet model. (Section 4.4), 137

range name   A descriptive name given to a range of cells that immediately identifies what is there. (Section 4.3), 132

toggle   The act of switching back and forth between viewing the results in the output cells and viewing the formulas entered into those output cells. (Section 4.4), 135

Learning Aids for This Chapter in Your MS Courseware

Chapter 4 Excel Files:

Everglade Case Study
Wyndor Example

Everglade Problem 4.12
Everglade Problem 4.13

Solved Problems (See the CD-ROM or Web site for the Solutions)

4.S1. Production and Inventory Planning Model

Surfs Up produces high-end surfboards. A challenge faced by Surfs Up is that their demand is highly seasonal. Demand exceeds production capacity during the warm summer months, but is very low in the winter months. To meet the high demand during the summer, Surfs Up typically produces more surfboards than are needed in the winter months and then carries inventory into the summer months. Their production facility can produce at most 50 boards per month using regular labor at a cost of $125 each. Up to 10 additional boards can be produced by utilizing overtime labor at a cost of $135 each. The boards are sold for $200. Because of storage cost and the opportunity cost of capital, each board held in inventory from one month to the next incurs a cost of $5 per board. Since demand is uncertain, Surfs Up would like to maintain an ending inventory (safety stock) of at least 10 boards during the warm months (May–September) and at least 5 boards during the other months (October–April). It is now the start of January and Surfs Up has 5 boards in inventory. The forecast of demand over the next 12 months is shown in the table below. Formulate and solve a linear programming model in a spreadsheet to determine how many surfboards should be produced each month to maximize total profit.

4.S2. Aggregate Planning: Manpower Hiring/Firing/Training

Cool Power produces air-conditioning units for large commercial properties. Because of the low cost and efficiency of its products, the company has been growing from year to year. Also, seasonality in construction and weather conditions create production requirements that vary from month to month. Cool Power currently has 10 fully trained employees working in manufacturing. Each trained employee can work 160 hours per month and is paid a monthly wage of $4,000. New trainees can be hired at the beginning of any month. Because of their lack of initial skills and required training, a new trainee provides only 100 hours of useful labor in the first month, but is still paid a full monthly wage of $4,000. Furthermore, because of required interviewing and training, there is a $2,500 hiring cost for each employee hired. After one month, a trainee is considered fully trained. An employee can be fired at the beginning of any month, but must be paid two weeks of severance pay ($2,000). Over the next 12 months, Cool Power forecasts the labor requirements shown in the table on the next page. Since management anticipates higher requirements next year, Cool Power would like to end the year with at least 12 fully trained employees. How many trainees should be hired and/or workers fired in each month to meet the labor requirements at the minimum possible cost? Formulate and solve a linear programming spreadsheet model.

Forecasted Demand

	Jan.	Feb.	Mar.	Apr.	May	June	July	Aug.	Sept.	Oct.	Nov.	Dec.
	10	14	15	20	45	65	85	85	40	30	15	15

Labor Requirements (hours)

Jan.	Feb.	Mar.	Apr.	May	June	July	Aug.	Sept.	Oct.	Nov.	Dec.
1,600	2,000	2,000	2,000	2,800	3,200	3,600	3,200	1,600	1,200	800	800

Problems

We have inserted the symbol E* (for Excel) to the left of each problem or part where Excel should be used. An asterisk on the problem number indicates that at least a partial answer is given in the back of the book.

E*4.1. Consider the Everglade cash flow problem discussed in this chapter. Suppose that extra cash is kept in an interest-bearing savings account. Assume that any cash left at the end of a year earns 3 percent interest the following year. Make any necessary modifications to the spreadsheet and re-solve. (The original spreadsheet for this problem is available on the CD-ROM.)

4.2.* The Pine Furniture Company makes fine country furniture. The company's current product lines consist of end tables, coffee tables, and dining room tables. The production of each of these tables requires 8, 15, and 80 pounds of pine wood, respectively. The tables are handmade and require one hour, two hours, and four hours, respectively. Each table sold generates $50, $100, and $220 profit, respectively. The company has 3,000 pounds of pine wood and 200 hours of labor available for the coming week's production. The chief operating officer (COO) has asked you to do some spreadsheet modeling with these data to analyze what the product mix should be for the coming week and make a recommendation.

    a. Visualize where you want to finish. What numbers will the COO need? What are the decisions that need to be made? What should the objective be?

    b. Suppose that Pine Furniture were to produce three end tables and three dining room tables. Calculate by hand the amount of pine wood and labor that would be required, as well as the profit generated from sales.

    c. Make a rough sketch of a spreadsheet model, with blocks laid out for the data cells, changing cells, output cells, and target cell.

  E* *d.* Build a spreadsheet model and then solve it.

4.3. Reboot, Inc., is a manufacturer of hiking boots. Demand for boots is highly seasonal. In particular, the demand in the next year is expected to be 3,000, 4,000, 8,000, and 7,000 pairs of boots in quarters 1, 2, 3, and 4, respectively. With its current production facility, the company can produce at most 6,000 pairs of boots in any quarter. Reboot would like to meet all the expected demand, so it will need to carry inventory to meet demand in the later quarters. Each pair of boots sold generates a profit of $20 per pair. Each pair of boots in inventory at the end of a quarter incurs $8 in storage and capital recovery costs. Reboot has 1,000 pairs of boots in inventory at the start of quarter 1. Reboot's top management has given you the assignment of doing some spreadsheet modeling to analyze what the production schedule should be for the next four quarters and make a recommendation.

    a. Visualize where you want to finish. What numbers will top management need? What are the decisions that need to be made? What should the objective be?

    b. Suppose that Reboot were to produce 5,000 pairs of boots in each of the first two quarters. Calculate by hand the ending inventory, profit from sales, and inventory costs for quarters 1 and 2.

    c. Make a rough sketch of a spreadsheet model, with blocks laid out for the data cells, changing cells, output cells, and target cell.

  E* *d.* Build a spreadsheet model for quarters 1 and 2, and then thoroughly test the model.

  E* *e.* Expand the model to full scale and then solve it.

E*4.4.* The Fairwinds Development Corporation is considering taking part in one or more of three different development projects—A, B, and C—that are about to be launched. Each project requires a significant investment over the next few years and then would be sold upon completion. The projected cash flows (in millions of dollars) associated with each project are shown in the table below.

Year	Project A	Project B	Project C
1	−4	−8	−10
2	−6	−8	−7
3	−6	−4	−7
4	24	−4	−5
5	0	30	−3
6	0	0	44

Fairwinds has $10 million available now and expects to receive $6 million from other projects by the end of each year (1 through 6) that would be available for the ongoing investments the following year in projects A, B, and C. By acting now, the company may participate in each project either fully, fractionally (with other development partners), or not at all. If Fairwinds participates at less than 100 percent, then all the cash flows associated with that project are reduced proportionally. Company policy requires ending each year with a cash balance of at least $1 million.

    a. Visualize where you want to finish. What numbers are needed? What are the decisions that need to be made? What should the objective be?

    b. Suppose that Fairwinds were to participate in Project A fully and in Project C at 50 percent. Calculate by hand what the ending cash positions would be after year 1 and year 2.

    c. Make a rough sketch of a spreadsheet model, with blocks laid out for the data cells, changing cells, output cells, and target cell.

  E* *d.* Build a spreadsheet model for years 1 and 2, and then thoroughly test the model.

  E* *e.* Expand the model to full scale, and then solve it.

4.5. Read the referenced article that fully describes the management science study summarized in the application vignette presented in Section 4.3. Briefly describe how spreadsheet modeling was applied in this study. Then list the various financial and nonfinancial benefits that resulted from this study.

4.6. Decorum, Inc., manufactures high-end ceiling fans. Their sales are seasonal with higher demand in the warmer summer months. Typically, sales average 400 units per month. However, in the hot summer months (June, July, and August), sales spike up to 600 units per month. Decorum can produce up to 500 units per month at a cost of $300 each. By bringing in temporary workers, Decorum can produce up to an additional 75 units at a cost of $350 each. Decorum sells the ceiling fans for $500 each. Decorum can carry inventory from one month to the next, but at a cost of $20 per ceiling fan per month. Decorum has 25 units in inventory at the start of January. Assuming Decorum must produce enough ceiling fans to meet demand, how many ceiling fans should Decorum produce each month (using their regular labor force and/or temporary workers) over the course of the next year so as to maximize their total profit?

   a. Visualize where you want to finish. What numbers will Decorum require? What are the decisions that need to be made? What should the objective be?

   b. Suppose Decorum builds 450 ceiling fans in January and 550 (utilizing temporary workers) in February. Calculate by hand the total costs for January and February.

   c. Make a rough sketch of a spreadsheet model, with blocks laid out for the data cells, changing cells, output cells, and target cell.

E*   *d.* Build a spreadsheet model for January and February and thoroughly test the model.

E*   *e.* Build and solve a linear programming spreadsheet model to maximize the profit over all 12 months.

4.7. Allen Furniture is a manufacturer of hand-crafted furniture. At the start of January, Allen employs 20 trained craftspeople. They have forecasted their labor needs over the next 12 months as shown in the table below. Each trained craftsperson provides 200 labor-hours per month and is paid a wage of $3,000 per month. Hiring new craftspeople requires advertising, interviewing, and then training at a cost of $2,500 per hire. New hires are called apprentices for their first month. Apprentices spend their first month observing and learning. They are paid $2,000 for the month, but provide no labor. In their second month, apprentices are reclassified as trained craftspeople. The union contract allows for firing a craftsperson at the beginning of a month, but $1,500 must be given in severance pay. Moreover, at most 10% of the trained craftspeople can be fired in any month. Allen would like to start next year with at least 25 trained craftspeople. How many apprentices should be hired and how many craftspeople should be fired in each month to meet the labor requirements at the minimum possible cost?

   a. Visualize where you want to finish. What numbers will Allen require? What are the decisions that need to be made? What should the objective be?

   b. Suppose one apprentice is hired in January. Calculate by hand how many labor-hours would be available in January and February. Calculate by hand the total costs in January and February.

   c. Make a rough sketch of a spreadsheet model, with blocks laid out for the data cells, changing cells, output cells, and target cell.

E*   *d.* Build a spreadsheet model for January and February and thoroughly test the model.

E*   *e.* Build and solve a linear programming spreadsheet model to maximize the profit over all 12 months.

4.8. Refer to the scenario described in Problem 3.13 (Chapter 3), but ignore the instructions given there. Focus instead on using spreadsheet modeling to address Web Mercantile's problem by doing the following.

   a. Visualize where you want to finish. What numbers will Web Mercantile require? What are the decisions that need to be made? What should the objective be?

   b. Suppose that Web Mercantile were to lease 30,000 square feet for all five months and then 20,000 additional square feet for the last three months. Calculate the total costs by hand.

   c. Make a rough sketch of a spreadsheet model, with blocks laid out for the data cells, changing cells, output cells, and target cell.

E*   *d.* Build a spreadsheet model for months 1 and 2, and then thoroughly test the model.

E*   *e.* Expand the model to full scale, and then solve it.

4.9.* Refer to the scenario described in Problem 3.15 (Chapter 3), but ignore the instructions given there. Focus instead on using spreadsheet modeling to address Larry Edison's problem by doing the following.

   a. Visualize where you want to finish. What numbers will Larry require? What are the decisions that need to be made? What should the objective be?

   b. Suppose that Larry were to hire three full-time workers for the morning shift, two for the afternoon shift, and four for the evening shift, as well as three part-time workers for each of the four shifts. Calculate by hand how many workers would be working at each time of the day and what the total cost would be for the entire day.

   c. Make a rough sketch of a spreadsheet model, with blocks laid out for the data cells, changing cells, output cells, and target cell.

E*   *d.* Build a spreadsheet model and then solve it.

4.10. Refer to the scenario described in Problem 3.18 (Chapter 3), but ignore the instructions given there. Focus instead on using spreadsheet modeling to address Al Ferris's problem by doing the following.

Labor Requirements (hours)

Jan.	Feb.	Mar.	Apr.	May	June	July	Aug.	Sep.	Oct.	Nov.	Dec.
4,000	4,000	4,200	4,200	3,000	2,800	3,000	4,000	4,500	5,000	5,200	4,800

a. Visualize where you want to finish. What numbers will Al require? What are the decisions that need to be made? What should the objective be?

b. Suppose that Al were to invest $20,000 each in investment *A* (year 1), investment *B* (year 2), and investment *C* (year 2). Calculate by hand what the ending cash position would be after each year.

c. Make a rough sketch of a spreadsheet model, with blocks laid out for the data cells, changing cells, output cells, and target cell.

E* d. Build a spreadsheet model for years 1 through 3, and then thoroughly test the model.

E* e. Expand the model to full scale, and then solve it.

4.11. In contrast to the spreadsheet model for the Wyndor Glass Co. product-mix problem shown in Figure 4.6, the spreadsheet given below is an example of a poorly formulated spreadsheet model for this same problem. Referring to Section 4.3, identify the guidelines violated by the model below. Then, explain how each guideline has been violated and why the model in Figure 4.6 is a better alternative.

E*4.12. Refer to the spreadsheet file named "Everglade Problem 4.12" contained on the CD-ROM. This file contains a formulation of the Everglade problem considered in this chapter. However, three errors are included in this formulation. Use the ideas presented in Section 4.4 for debugging a spreadsheet model to find the errors. In particular, try different trial values for which you can predict the correct results, use the toggle to examine all the formulas, and use the auditing tools to check precedence and dependence relationships among the various changing cells, data cells, and output cells. Describe the errors found and how you found them.

E*4.13. Refer to the spreadsheet file named "Everglade Problem 4.13" contained on the CD-ROM. This file contains a formulation of the Everglade problem considered in this chapter. However, three errors are included in this formulation. Use the ideas presented in Section 4.4 for debugging a spreadsheet model to find the errors. In particular, try different trial values for which you can predict the correct results, use the toggle to examine all the formulas, and use the auditing tools to check precedence and dependence relationships among the various changing cells, data cells, and output cells. Describe the errors found and how you found them.

	A	B	C	D
1		**Wyndor Glass Co. (Poor Formulation)**		
2				
3		Doors Produced	2	
4		Windows Produced	6	
5		Hours Used (Plant 1)	2	
6		Hours Used (Plant 2)	12	
7		Hours Used (Plant 3)	18	
8		Total Profit	$3,600	

Solver Parameters
Set Objective (Target Cell): C8
To: Max
By Changing (Variable) Cells:
  C3:C4
Subject to the Constraints:
  C5 <= 4
  C6 <= 12
  C7 <= 18
Solver Options (Excel 2010):
  Make Variables Nonnegative
  Solving Method: Simplex LP
Solver Options (older Excel):
  Assume Nonnegative
  Assume Linear Model

	B	C
5	Hours Used (Plant 1)	=1*C3+0*C4
6	Hours Used (Plant 2)	=0*C3+2*C4
7	Hours Used (Plant 3)	=3*C3+2*C4
8	Total Profit	=300*C3+500*C4

Partial Answers to Selected Problems

CHAPTER 4

4.2. *d.* 0 end tables, 40 coffee tables, 30 dining room tables. Profit = $10,600.

4.4. *e.* 19% participation in Project A, 0% participation in Project B, and 100% participation in Project C. Ending Balance = $59.5 million.

4.9. *d.* 4 FT (8AM–4PM), 4 FT (12PM–8PM), 4 FT (4PM–midnight), 2 PT (8AM–12PM), 0 PT (12PM–4PM), 4 PT (4PM–8PM), 2 PT (8PM–midnight). Total cost per day = $1,728.

CHAPTER 4
THE ART OF MODELING WITH SPREADSHEETS
SOLUTION TO SOLVED PROBLEMS

4.S1 Production and Inventory Planning Model

Surfs Up produces high-end surfboards. A challenge faced by Surfs Up is that their demand is highly seasonal. Demand exceeds production capacity during the warm summer months, but is very low in the winter months. To meet the high demand during the summer, Surfs Up typically produces more surfboards than are needed in the winter months and then carries inventory into the summer months. Their production facility can produce at most 50 boards per month using regular labor at a cost of $125 each. Up to 10 additional boards can be produced by utilizing overtime labor at a cost of $135 each. The boards are sold for $200. Because of storage cost and the opportunity cost of capital, each board held in inventory from one month to the next incurs a cost of $5 per board. Since demand is uncertain, Surfs Up would like to maintain an ending inventory (safety stock) of at least 10 boards during the warm months (May–September) and at least 5 boards during the other months (October–April). It is now the start of January and Surfs Up has 5 boards in inventory. The forecast of demand over the next 12 months is shown in the table below. Formulate and solve a linear programming model in a spreadsheet to determine how many surfboards should be produced each month to maximize total profit.

Jan	Feb	Mar	Apr	May	Jun	July	Aug	Sep	Oct	Nov	Dec
10	14	15	20	45	65	85	85	40	30	15	15

This is a dynamic problem with 12 time periods (months). The activities are the production quantities in each of the 12 months using regular labor and the production quantities in each of the 12 months using overtime labor.

To get started, we sketch a spreadsheet model. Each of the 12 months will be a separate column in the spreadsheet. For each month, the regular production quantity (a changing cell) must be no more than the maximum regular production (50). Similarly, for each month the overtime production quantity (a changing cell) must be no more than the maximum overtime production (10). Each month will generate revenue, incur regular and overtime production costs, inventory holding costs, and achieve a resulting profit. The goal will be to maximize the total profit over all 12 months. This leads to the following sketch of a spreadsheet model.

Unit Cost (Reg)
Unit Cost (OT)
Selling Price
Holding Cost
Starting Inventory

Jan Feb Mar Apr May Jun Jul Aug Sep Oct Nov Dec

Regular Production
<=
Max Regular
OT Production
<=
Max OT
Forecasted Sales
Ending Inventory
>=
Safety Stock

Revenue
Regular Production Cost
Overtime Production Cost
Holding Cost
Profit

The ending inventory each month will equal the starting inventory (the given starting inventory for January, or the previous month's ending inventory for future months) plus all production (regular and overtime) minus the forecasted sales. The ending inventory at the end of each month must be at least the minimum safety stock level. The revenue will equal the selling price times forecasted sales. The regular (or overtime) production cost will be the regular (or overtime) production quantity times the unit regular (or overtime) production cost. The holding cost will equal the ending inventory times the unit holding cost. The monthly profit will be revenue minus both production costs minus holding cost. Finally, the total profit will be the sum of the monthly profits. The final solved spreadsheet, formulas, and Solver information are shown below.

		Jan	Feb	Mar	Apr	May	Jun	Jul	Aug	Sep	Oct	Nov	Dec	Total
1	oduction and Inventory Planning at Surfs Up													
3	Unit Cost (Reg)	$125												
4	Unit Cost (OT)	$135												
5	Selling Price	$200												
6	Holding Cost	$5												
7	Starting Inventory	5												
9		Jan	Feb	Mar	Apr	May	Jun	Jul	Aug	Sep	Oct	Nov	Dec	
10	Regular Production	10	14	30	50	50	50	50	50	40	25	15	15	
11		<=	<=	<=	<=	<=	<=	<=	<=	<=	<=	<=	<=	
12	Max Regular	50	50	50	50	50	50	50	50	50	50	50	50	
14	OT Production	0	0	0	0	10	10	10	10	0	0	0	0	
15		<=	<=	<=	<=	<=	<=	<=	<=	<=	<=	<=	<=	
16	Max OT	10	10	10	10	10	10	10	10	10	10	10	10	
18	Forecasted Sales	10	14	15	20	45	65	85	85	40	30	15	15	
20	Ending Inventory	5	5	20	50	65	60	35	10	10	5	5	5	
21		>=	>=	>=	>=	>=	>=	>=	>=	>=	>=	>=	>=	
22	Safety Stock	5	5	5	5	10	10	10	10	10	5	5	5	
23														Total
24	Revenue	$2,000	$2,800	$3,000	$4,000	$9,000	$13,000	$17,000	$17,000	$8,000	$6,000	$3,000	$3,000	$87,800
25	Regular Production Cost	$1,250	$1,750	$3,750	$6,250	$6,250	$6,250	$6,250	$6,250	$5,000	$3,125	$1,875	$1,875	$49,875
26	Overtime Production Cost	$0	$0	$0	$0	$1,350	$1,350	$1,350	$1,350	$0	$0	$0	$0	$5,400
27	Holding Cost	$25	$25	$100	$250	$325	$300	$175	$50	$50	$25	$25	$25	$1,375
28	Profit	$725	$1,025	-$850	-$2,500	$1,075	$5,100	$9,225	$9,350	$2,950	$2,850	$1,100	$1,100	$31,150

2

Set Objective (Target Cell): TotalProfit
To: Max
By Changing (Variable) Cells:
  RegularProduction, OTProduction
Subject to the Constraints:
  RegularProduction <= MaxRegular
  OTProduction <= MaxOT
  EndingInventory >= SafetyStock

Solver Options (Excel 2010):
  Make Variables Nonnegative
  Solving Method: Simplex LP
Solver Options (older Excel):
  Assume Nonnegative
  Assume Linear Model

Range Name	Cells
EndingInventory	C20:N20
ForecastedSales	C18:N18
HoldingCost	C6
MaxOT	C16:N16
MaxRegular	C12:N12
OTProduction	C14:N14
RegularProduction	C10:N10
SafetyStock	C22:N22
SellingPrice	C5
StartingInventory	C7
TotalProfit	O29
UnitCostOT	C4
UnitCostReg	C3

	B	C	D		O
3	Unit Cost (Reg)	125			
4	Unit Cost (OT)	135			
5	Selling Price	200			
6	Holding Cost	5			
7	Starting Inventory	5			
8					
9		Jan	Feb		
10	Regular Production	10	14		
11		<=	<=		
12	Max Regular	50	50		
13					
14	OT Production	0	0		
15		<=	<=		
16	Max OT	10	10		
17					
18	Forecasted Sales	10	14		
19					
20	Ending Inventory	=StartingInventory+RegularProduction+OTProduction-ForecastedSales	=C20+RegularProduction+OTProduction-ForecastedSales		
21		>=	>=		
22	Safety Stock	5	5		
23					
24					Total
25	Revenue	=SellingPrice*ForecastedSales	=SellingPrice*ForecastedSales		=SUM(C25:N25)
26	Regular Production Cost	=UnitCostReg*RegularProduction	=UnitCostReg*RegularProduction		=SUM(C26:N26)
27	Overtime Production Cost	=UnitCostOT*OTProduction	=UnitCostOT*OTProduction		=SUM(C27:N27)
28	Holding Cost	=HoldingCost*EndingInventory	=HoldingCost*EndingInventory		=SUM(C28:N28)
29	Profit	=C25-C26-C27-C28	=D25-D26-D27-D28		=SUM(C29:N29)

The values in RegularProduction (C10:N10) and OTProduction (C14:N14) show how many surf boards Surfs Up should produce each month so as to achieve the maximum profit of $31,150.

4.S2 Aggregate Planning: Manpower Hiring/Firing/Training

Cool Power produces air conditioning units for large commercial properties. Due to the low cost and efficiency of its products, the company has been growing from year to year. Also, due to seasonality in construction and weather conditions, production requirements vary from month to month. Cool Power currently has 10 fully trained employees working in manufacturing. Each trained employee can work 160 hours per month and is paid a monthly wage of $4000. New trainees can be hired at the beginning of any month. Due to their lack of initial skills and required training, a new trainee only provides 100 hours of useful labor in their first month, but are still paid a full monthly wage of $4000. Furthermore, because of required interviewing and training, there is a $2500 hiring cost for each employee hired. After one month, a trainee is considered fully trained. An employee can be fired at the beginning of any month, but must be paid two weeks of severance pay ($2000). Over the next 12 months, Cool Power forecasts the labor requirements shown in the table below. Since management anticipates higher requirements next year, Cool Power would like to end the year with at least 12 fully trained employees. How many trainees should be hired and/or workers fired in each month to meet the labor requirements at the minimum possible cost? Formulate and solve a linear programming spreadsheet model.

Jan	Feb	Mar	Apr	May	Jun	Jul	Aug	Sep	Oct	Nov	Dec
1600	2000	2000	2000	2800	3200	3600	3200	1600	1200	800	800

This is a dynamic problem with 12 time periods (months). The activities are the number of workers to hire and fire in each of the 12 months.

To get started, we sketch a spreadsheet model. Each of the 12 months will be a separate column in the spreadsheet. For each month, there are changing cells for both the number of workers hired and fired. Based on the values of these changing cells, we can determine the number of trainees and trained employees. The number of labor hours generated by the employees must be at least the required labor hours each month. Finally, labor costs (for trainees and the trained workforce), hiring cost, and severance pay leads to a total monthly cost. The goal will be to minimize the total cost over all 12 months. This leads to the following sketch of a spreadsheet model.

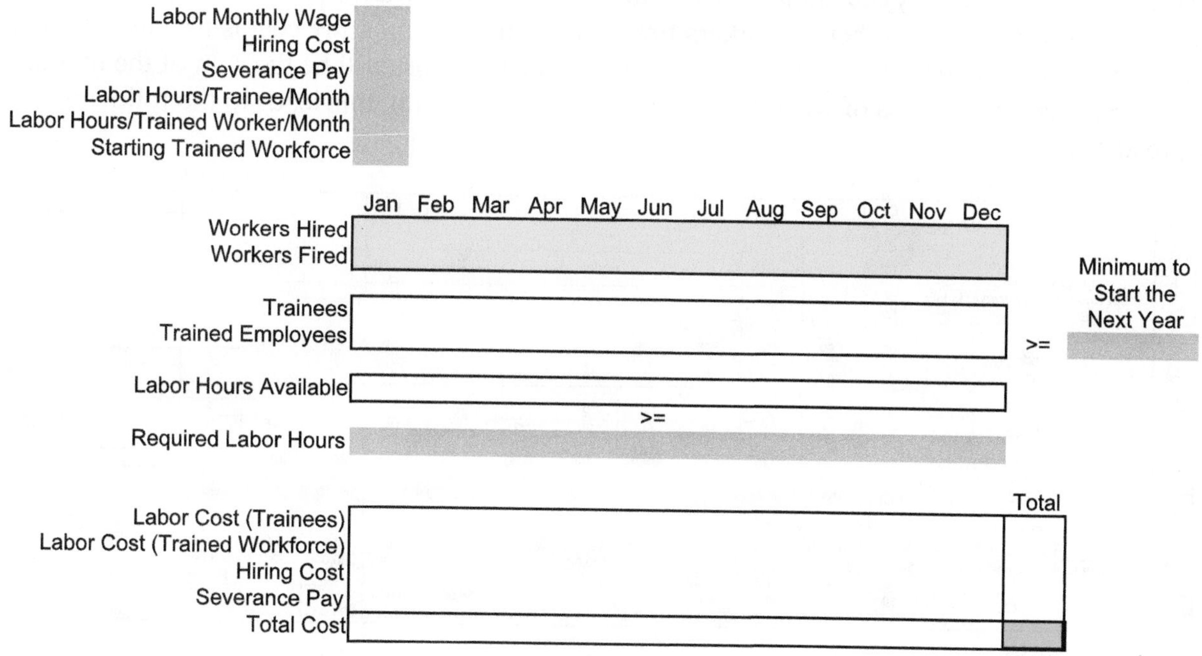

When an employee is first hired, he or she is a trainee for one month before becoming a fully-trained employee. Therefore, the number of trainees (row 14) is equal to the number of workers hired in that month, while the number of trained employees (row 15) is the number of trained employees and trainees from the previous month minus any employee that is fired. The labor hours available in each month equals the sumproduct of the labor hours provided by each type of worker (trained or trainees) with the number of each type of employee. The labor costs in each month are the monthly wage multiplied by the number of employees. The hiring cost is the unit hiring cost multiplied by the number of workers hired. The severance pay is the unit severance cost multiplied by the number of workers fired. Then, the total monthly cost is the sum of the labor costs, hiring cost, and severance pay. Finally, the total cost will be the sum of the monthly costs. For arbitrary values of workers hired and fired each month, this leads to the following spreadsheet.

	B	C	D	E	F	G	H	I	J	K	L	M	N	O	P
3	Labor Monthly Wage	$4,000													
4	Hiring Cost	$2,500													
5	Severance Pay	$2,000													
6	Labor Hours/Trainee/Month	100													
7	Labor Hours/Trained Worker/Month	160													
8	Starting Trained Workforce	10													
9															
10		Jan	Feb	Mar	Apr	May	Jun	Jul	Aug	Sep	Oct	Nov	Dec		
11	Workers Hired	2	2	2	2	2	2	2	0	0	0	2	2		Minimum to
12	Workers Fired	0	0	0	0	0	0	0	3	3	3	0	0		Start the
13															Next Year
14	Trainees	2	2	2	2	2	2	2	0	0	0	2	2	>=	12
15	Trained Employees	10	12	14	16	18	20	22	21	18	15	15	17		
16															
17	Labor Hours Available	1800	2120	2440	2760	3080	3400	3720	3360	2880	2400	2600	2920		
18		>=	>=	>=	>=	>=	>=	>=	>=	>=	>=	>=	>=		
19	Required Labor Hours	1600	2000	2000	2000	2800	3200	3600	3200	1600	1200	800	800		
20														Total	
21															
22	Labor Cost (Trainees)	$8,000	$8,000	$8,000	$8,000	$8,000	$8,000	$8,000	$0	$0	$0	$8,000	$8,000	$72,000	
23	Labor Cost (Trained Workforce)	$40,000	$48,000	$56,000	$64,000	$72,000	$80,000	$88,000	$84,000	$72,000	$60,000	$60,000	$68,000	$792,000	
24	Hiring Cost	$5,000	$5,000	$5,000	$5,000	$5,000	$5,000	$5,000	$0	$0	$0	$5,000	$5,000	$45,000	
25	Severance Pay	$0	$0	$0	$0	$0	$0	$0	$6,000	$6,000	$6,000	$0	$0	$18,000	
26	Total Cost	$53,000	$61,000	$69,000	$77,000	$85,000	$93,000	$101,000	$90,000	$78,000	$66,000	$73,000	$81,000	$927,000	

	B	C	O	P
3	Labor Monthly Wage	4000		
4	Hiring Cost	2500		
5	Severance Pay	2000		
6	Labor Hours/Trainee/Month	100		
7	Labor Hours/Trained Worker/Month	160		
8	Starting Trained Workforce	10		
9				
10		Jan		
11	Workers Hired	2		Minimum to
12	Workers Fired	0		Start the
13				Next Year
14	Trainees	=WorkersHired	>=	12
15	Trained Employees	=StartingTrainedWorkforce-WorkersFired		
16				
17	Labor Hours Available	=SUMPRODUCT(LaborHoursPerTrainee:LaborHoursPerTrainedWorker,C14:C15)		
18		>=		
19	Required Labor Hours	1600		
20			Total	
21				
22	Labor Cost (Trainees)	=LaborMonthlyWage*Trainees	=SUM(C22:N22)	
23	Labor Cost (Trained Workforce)	=LaborMonthlyWage*TrainedEmployees	=SUM(C23:N23)	
24	Hiring Cost	=HiringCost*WorkersHired	=SUM(C24:N24)	
25	Severance Pay	=SeverancePay*WorkersFired	=SUM(C25:N25)	
26	Total Cost	=SUM(C22:C25)	=SUM(C26:N26)	

The Solver information is shown below, followed by the solved spreadsheet.

	B	C	D	E	F	G	H	I	J	K	L	M	N	O	P
3	Labor Monthly Wage	$4,000													
4	Hiring Cost	$2,500													
5	Severance Pay	$2,000													
6	Labor Hours/Trainee/Month	100													
7	Labor Hours/Trained Worker/Month	160													
8	Starting Trained Workforce	10													
9															
10		Jan	Feb	Mar	Apr	May	Jun	Jul	Aug	Sep	Oct	Nov	Dec		
11	Workers Hired	2.1E-11	4	0	0	6	2	1	0	0	0	2	0		
12	Workers Fired	0	0	0	0	0	0	0	3	10	0	0	0		Minimum to
13															Start the
14	Trainees	2.1E-11	4	0	0	6	2	1	0	0	0	2	0		Next Year
15	Trained Employees	10	10	14	14	14	20	22	20	10	10	10	12	>=	12
16															
17	Labor Hours Available	1600	2000	2240	2240	2840	3400	3620	3200	1600	1600	1800	1920		
18		>=	>=	>=	>=	>=	>=	>=	>=	>=	>=	>=	>=		
19	Required Labor Hours	1600	2000	2000	2000	2800	3200	3600	3200	1600	1200	800	800		
20															
21														Total	
22	Labor Cost (Trainees)	$0	$16,000	$0	$0	$24,000	$8,000	$4,000	$0	$0	$0	$8,000	$0	$60,000	
23	Labor Cost (Trained Workforce)	$40,000	$40,000	$56,000	$56,000	$56,000	$80,000	$88,000	$80,000	$40,000	$40,000	$40,000	$48,000	$664,000	
24	Hiring Cost	$0	$10,000	$0	$0	$15,000	$5,000	$2,500	$0	$0	$0	$5,000	$0	$37,500	
25	Severance Pay	$0	$0	$0	$0	$0	$0	$0	$6,000	$20,000	$0	$0	$0	$26,000	
26	Total Cost	$40,000	$66,000	$56,000	$56,000	$95,000	$93,000	$94,500	$86,000	$60,000	$40,000	$53,000	$48,000	$787,500	

Solver Parameters

Set Objective (Target Cell): TotalCost
To: Min
By Changing (Variable) Cells:
  WorkersHired, WorkersFired
Subject to the Constraints:
  N15 >= MinimumToStartNextYear
  LaborHoursAvailable >= RequiredLaborHours
  WorkersFired = integer
  WorkersHired = integer

Solver Options (Excel 2010):
  Make Variables Nonnegative
  Solving Method: Simplex LP
Solver Options (older Excel):
  Assume Nonnegative
  Assume Linear Model

Range Name	Cells
HiringCost	C4
LaborHoursAvailable	C17:N17
LaborHoursPerTrainedWorker	C7
LaborHoursPerTrainee	C6
LaborMonthlyWage	C3
MinimumToStartNextYear	P15
RequiredLaborHours	C19:N19
SeverancePay	C5
StartingTrainedWorkforce	C8
TotalCost	O26
TrainedEmployees	C15:N15
Trainees	C14:N14
WorkersFired	C12:N12
WorkersHired	C11:N11

	B	C	...D:N...	O	P
3	Labor Monthly Wage	4000			
4	Hiring Cost	2500			
5	Severance Pay	2000			
6	Labor Hours/Trainee/Month	100			
7	Labor Hours/Trained Worker/Month	160			
8	Starting Trained Workforce	10			
9					
10		Jan	Balance		
11	Workers Hired	2			
12	Workers Fired	0			Minimum to
13					Start the
14	Trainees	=WorkersHired			Next Year
15	Trained Employees	=StartingTrainedWorkforce-WorkersFired		>=	12
16					
17	Labor Hours Available	=SUMPRODUCT(LaborHoursPerTrainee:LaborHoursPerTrainedWorker,C14:C15)			
18		>=			
19	Required Labor Hours	1600			
20					
21				Total	
22	Labor Cost (Trainees)	=LaborMonthlyWage*Trainees		=SUM(C22:N22)	
23	Labor Cost (Trained Workforce)	=LaborMonthlyWage*TrainedEmployees		=SUM(C23:N23)	
24	Hiring Cost	=HiringCost*WorkersHired		=SUM(C24:N24)	
25	Severance Pay	=SeverancePay*WorkersFired		=SUM(C25:N25)	
26	Total Cost	=SUM(C22:C25)		=SUM(C26:N26)	

Thus, WorkersHired (C11:N11) shows the number of workers Cool Power should hire each month and WorkersFired (C12:N12) shows the number of workers Cool Power should fire each month so as to achieve the minimum TotalCost (O26) of $787,500.

What-If Analysis for Linear Programming

Learning objectives

After completing this chapter, you should be able to

1. Explain what is meant by *what-if analysis.*
2. Summarize the benefits of what-if analysis.
3. Enumerate the different kinds of changes in the model that can be considered by what-if analysis.
4. Describe how the spreadsheet formulation of the problem can be used to perform any of these kinds of what-if analysis.
5. Use the Solver Table to systematically investigate the effect of changing either one or two data cells to various other trial values.
6. Find how much any single coefficient in the objective function can change without changing the optimal solution.
7. Evaluate simultaneous changes in objective function coefficients to determine whether the changes are small enough that the original optimal solution must still be optimal.
8. Predict how the value in the target cell would change if a small change were to be made in the right-hand side of one or more of the functional constraints.
9. Find how much the right-hand side of a single functional constraint can change before this prediction becomes no longer valid.
10. Evaluate simultaneous changes in right-hand sides to determine whether the changes are small enough that this prediction must still be valid.

Chapters 2 to 4 have described and illustrated how to formulate a linear programming model on a spreadsheet to represent a variety of managerial problems, and then how to use the Solver to find an optimal solution for this model. You might think that this would finish our story about linear programming: Once the manager learns the optimal solution, she would immediately implement this solution and then turn her attention to other matters. However, this is not the case. The enlightened manager demands much more from linear programming, and linear programming has much more to offer her—as you will discover in this chapter.

An optimal solution is only optimal with respect to a particular mathematical model that provides only a rough representation of the real problem. A manager is interested in much more than just finding such a solution. The purpose of a linear programming study is to help guide management's final decision by providing insights into the likely consequences of pursuing various managerial options under a variety of assumptions about future conditions. Most of the important insights are gained while conducting analysis *after* finding an optimal solution for the original version of the basic model. This analysis is commonly referred to as **what-if analysis** because it involves addressing some questions about *what* would happen to the optimal solution *if* different assumptions were made about future conditions. Spreadsheets play a central role in addressing these *what-if questions.*

This chapter focuses on the types of information provided by what-if analysis and why it is valuable to managers. The first section provides an overview. Section 5.2 returns to the Wyndor Glass Co. product-mix case study (Section 2.1) to describe the what-if analysis that is needed in this situation. The subsequent sections then perform this what-if analysis, using a variety of procedures that are applicable to any linear programming problem.

5.1   THE IMPORTANCE OF WHAT-IF ANALYSIS TO MANAGERS

In real applications, many of the numbers in the model may be only rough estimates.

The examples and problems in the preceding chapters on linear programming have provided the data needed to determine precisely all the numbers that should go into the data cells for the spreadsheet formulation of the linear programming model. (Recall that these numbers are referred to as the **parameters of the model**.) Real applications seldom are this straightforward. Substantial time and effort often are needed to track down the needed data. Even then, it may be possible to develop only rough estimates of the parameters of the model.

For example, in the Wyndor case study, two key parameters of the model are the coefficients in the objective function that represent the unit profits of the two new products. These parameters were estimated to be $300 for the doors and $500 for the windows. However, these unit profits depend on many factors—the costs of raw materials, production, shipping, advertising, and so on, as well as such things as the market reception to the new products and the amount of competition encountered. Some of these factors cannot be estimated with real accuracy until long after the linear programming study has been completed and the new products have been on the market for some time.

Therefore, before Wyndor's management makes a decision on the product mix, it will want to know what the effect would be if the unit profits turn out to differ significantly from the estimates. For example, would the optimal solution change if the unit profit for the doors turned out to be $200 instead of the estimate of $300? How inaccurate can the estimate be in either direction before the optimal solution changes?

Such questions are addressed in Section 5.3 when only one estimate is inaccurate. Section 5.4 will address similar questions when multiple estimates are inaccurate.

What happens to the optimal solution if an error is made in estimating a parameter of the model?

If the optimal solution will remain the same over a wide range of values for a particular coefficient in the objective function, then management will be content with a fairly rough estimate for this coefficient. On the other hand, if even a small error in the estimate would change the optimal solution, then management will want to take special care to refine this estimate. Management sometimes will get involved directly in adjusting such estimates to its satisfaction.

Here then is a summary of the first benefit of what-if analysis:

1. Typically, many of the parameters of a linear programming model are only *estimates* of quantities (e.g., unit profits) that cannot be determined precisely at this time. What-if analysis reveals how close each of these estimates needs to be to avoid obtaining an erroneous optimal solution, and therefore pinpoints the **sensitive parameters** (those parameters where extra care is needed to refine their estimates because even small changes in their values can change the optimal solution).

Several sections describe how what-if analysis provides this benefit for the most important parameters. Sections 5.3 and 5.4 do this for the coefficients in the objective function (these numbers typically appear in the spreadsheet in the row for the unit contribution of each activity toward the overall measure of performance). Sections 5.5 and 5.6 do the same for the *right-hand sides of the functional constraints* (these are the numbers that typically are in the right-hand column of the spreadsheet just to the right of the $\leq$, $\geq$, or $=$ signs).

Businesses operate in a dynamic environment. Even when management is satisfied with the current estimates and implements the corresponding optimal solution, conditions may change later. For example, suppose that Wyndor's management is satisfied with $300 as the estimate of the unit profit for the doors, but increased competition later forces a price reduction that reduces this unit profit. Does this change the optimal product mix? The what-if analysis shown in Section 5.3 immediately indicates in advance which new unit profits would leave the optimal product mix unchanged, which can help guide management in its

What happens to the
optimal solution if conditions change in the future?

new pricing decision. Furthermore, if the optimal product mix is unchanged, then there is no need to solve the model again with the new coefficient. Avoiding solving the model again is no big deal for the tiny two-variable Wyndor problem, but it is extremely welcome for real applications that may have hundreds or thousands of constraints and variables. In fact, for such large models, it may not even be practical to re-solve the model repeatedly to consider the many possible changes of interest.

Thus, here is the second benefit of what-if analysis:

2. If conditions change after the study has been completed (a common occurrence), what-if analysis leaves signposts that indicate (without solving the model again) whether a resulting change in a parameter of the model changes the optimal solution.

Again, several subsequent sections describe how what-if analysis does this.

These sections focus on studying how changes in the parameters of a linear programming model affect the optimal solution. This type of what-if analysis commonly is referred to as **sensitivity analysis,** because it involves checking how *sensitive* the optimal solution is to the value of each parameter. Sensitivity analysis is a vital part of what-if analysis.

However, rather than being content with the passive sensitivity analysis approach of checking the effect of parameter estimates being inaccurate, what-if analysis often goes further to take a proactive approach. An analysis may be made of various possible managerial actions that would result in changes to the model.

A prime example of this proactive approach arises when certain parameters of the model represent *managerial policy decisions* rather than quantities that are largely outside the control of management. For example, for the Wyndor product-mix problem, the right-hand sides of the three functional constraints (4, 12, 18) represent the number of hours of production time in the three respective plants being made available per week for the production of the two new products. Management can change these three resource amounts by altering the production levels for the old products in these plants. Therefore, after learning the optimal solution, management will want to know the impact on the profit from the new products if these resource amounts are changed in certain ways. One key question is how much this profit can be increased by increasing the available production time for the new products in just one of the plants. Another is how much this profit can be increased by simultaneously making helpful changes in the available production times in all the plants. If the profit from the new products can be increased enough to more than compensate for the profit lost by decreasing the production levels for certain old products, management probably will want to make the change.

What happens if managerial
policy decisions change?

We now can summarize the third benefit of what-if analysis:

3. When certain parameters of the model represent managerial policy decisions, what-if analysis provides valuable guidance to management regarding the impact of altering these policy decisions.

Sections 5.5 and 5.6 will explore this benefit further.

What-if analysis sometimes goes even further in providing helpful guidance to management, such as when analyzing alternate scenarios for how business conditions might evolve. However, this chapter will focus on the three benefits summarized above.

Review Questions

1. What are the *parameters* of a linear programming model?
2. How can inaccuracies arise in the parameters of a model?
3. What does what-if analysis reveal about the parameters of a model that are only estimates?
4. Is it always inappropriate to make only a fairly rough estimate for a parameter of a model? Why?
5. How is it possible for the parameters of a model to be accurate initially and then become inaccurate at a later date?
6. How does what-if analysis help management prepare for changing conditions?
7. What is meant by *sensitivity analysis?*
8. For what kinds of managerial policy decisions does what-if analysis provide guidance?

5.2 CONTINUING THE WYNDOR CASE STUDY

We now return to the case study introduced in Section 2.1 involving the Wyndor Glass Co. product-mix problem.

To review briefly, recall that the company is preparing to introduce two new products:

- An 8-foot glass door with aluminum framing.
- A 4-foot × 6-foot double-hung wood-framed window.

To analyze which mix of the two products would be most profitable, the company's Management Science Group introduced two decision variables:

D = Production rate of this new kind of door

W = Production rate of this new kind of window

where this rate measures the number of units produced per week. Three plants will be involved in the production of these products. Based on managerial decisions regarding how much these plants will continue to be used to produce current products, the number of hours of production time per week being made available in plants 1, 2, and 3 for the new products is 4, 12, and 18, respectively. After obtaining rough estimates that the profit per unit will be $300 for the doors and $500 for the windows, the Management Science Group then formulated the linear programming model shown in Figure 2.13 and repeated here in Figure 5.1, where the objective is to choose the values of D and W in the changing cells UnitsProduced (C12:D12) so as to maximize the total profit (per week) given in the target cell TotalProfit (G12). Applying the Solver to this model yielded the optimal solution shown on this spreadsheet and summarized as follows.

Optimal Solution

$D = 2$ (Produce 2 doors per week.)

$W = 6$ (Produce 6 windows per week.)

Profit = 3,600   (The estimated total weekly profit is $3,600.)

However, this optimal solution assumes that all the estimates that provide the parameters of the model (as shown in the UnitProfit (C4:D4), HoursUsedPerUnitProduced (C7:D9), and HoursAvailable (G7:G9) data cells) are accurate.

The head of the Management Science Group, Lisa Taylor, now is ready to meet with management to discuss the group's recommendation that the above product mix be used.

Management's Discussion of the Recommended Product Mix

Lisa Taylor (head of Management Science Group): I asked for this meeting so we could explore what questions the two of you would like us to pursue further. In particular, I am especially concerned that we weren't able to better pin down just what the numbers should be to go into our model. Which estimates do you think are the shakiest?

Bill Tasto (vice president for manufacturing): Without question, the estimates of the unit profits for the two products. Since the products haven't gone into production yet, all we could do is analyze the data from similar current products and then try to project what the changes would be for these new products. We have some numbers, but they are pretty rough. We would need to do a lot more work to pin down the numbers better.

John Hill (president): We may need to do that. Lisa, do you have a way of checking how far off one of these estimates can be without changing the optimal product mix?

The allowable range for a unit profit indicates how far its estimate can be off without affecting the optimal product mix.

Lisa: Yes, we do. We can quickly find what we call the *allowable range* for each unit profit. As long as the true value of the unit profit is within this allowable range, and the other unit profit is correct, the optimal product mix will not change. If this range is pretty wide, you don't need to worry about refining the estimate of the unit profit. However, if the range is quite narrow, then it is important to pin down the estimate more closely.

FIGURE 5.1

The spreadsheet model and its optimal solution for the original Wyndor problem before beginning what-if analysis.

	A	B	C	D	E	F	G
1		**Wyndor Glass Co. Product-Mix Problem**					
2							
3			Doors	Windows			
4		Unit Profit	$300	$500			
5					Hours		Hours
6			Hours Used per Unit Produced		Used		Available
7		Plant 1	1	0	2	≤	4
8		Plant 2	0	2	12	≤	12
9		Plant 3	3	2	18	≤	18
10							
11			Doors	Windows			Total Profit
12		Units Produced	2	6			$3,600

Solver Parameters

Set Objective (Target Cell): TotalProfit
To: Max
By Changing (Variable) Cells:
  UnitsProduced
Subject to the Constraints:
  HoursUsed <= HoursAvailable

Solver Options (Excel 2010):
  Make Variables Nonnegative
  Solving Method: Simplex LP
Solver Options (older Excel):
  Assume Nonnegative
  Assume Linear Model

	E
5	Hours
6	Used
7	=SUMPRODUCT(C7:D7, UnitsProduced)
8	=SUMPRODUCT(C8:D8, UnitsProduced)
9	=SUMPRODUCT(C9:D9, UnitsProduced)

	G
11	Total Profit
12	=SUMPRODUCT(UnitProfit, UnitsProduced)

Range Name	Cells
DoorsProduced	C12
HoursAvailable	G7:G9
HoursUsed	E7:E9
HoursUsedPerUnitProduced	C7:D9
TotalProfit	G12
UnitProfit	C4:D4
UnitsProduced	C12:D12
WindowsProduced	D12

John: What happens if both estimates are off?

Lisa: We can provide a way of checking whether the optimal product mix might change for any new combination of unit profits you think might be the true one.

John: Great. That's what we need. There's also one more thing. Bill gave you the numbers for how many hours of production time we're making available per week in the three plants for these new products. I noticed you used these numbers on your spreadsheet.

Lisa: Yes. They're the right-hand sides of our constraints. Is something wrong with these numbers?

John: No, not at all. I just wanted to let you know that we haven't made a final decision on whether these are the numbers we want to use. We would like your group to provide us with some analysis of what the effect would be if we change any of those numbers. How much more profit could we get from the new products for each additional hour of production time per week we provide in one of the plants? That sort of thing.

Lisa: Yes, we can get that analysis to you right away also.

John: We might also be interested in changing the available production hours for two or three of the plants.

Lisa: No problem. We'll give you information about that as well.

Summary of Management's What-If Questions

Here is a summary of John Hill's what-if questions that Lisa and her group will be addressing in the coming sections.

1. What happens if the estimate of the unit profit of one of Wyndor's new products is inaccurate? (Section 5.3)
2. What happens if the estimates of the unit profits of both of Wyndor's new products are inaccurate? (Section 5.4)
3. What happens if a change is made in the number of hours of production time per week being made available to Wyndor's new products in one of the plants? (Section 5.5)
4. What happens if simultaneous changes are made in the number of hours of production time per week being made available to Wyndor's new products in all the plants? (Section 5.6)

Review
Questions

1. Which estimates of the parameters in the linear programming model for the Wyndor problem are most questionable?
2. Which numbers in this model represent tentative managerial decisions that management might want to change after receiving the Management Science Group's analysis?

5.3   THE EFFECT OF CHANGES IN ONE OBJECTIVE FUNCTION COEFFICIENT

Section 5.1 began by discussing the fact that many of the parameters of a linear programming model typically are only *estimates* of quantities that cannot be determined precisely at the time. What-if analysis (or *sensitivity analysis* in particular) reveals how close each of these estimates needs to be to avoid obtaining an erroneous optimal solution.

We focus in this section on how sensitivity analysis does this when the parameters involved are *coefficients in the objective function*. (Recall that each of these coefficients gives the *unit contribution* of one of the activities toward the overall measure of performance.) In the process, we will address the first of the what-if questions posed by Wyndor management in the preceding section.

Question 1: What happens if the estimate of the unit profit of one of Wyndor's new products is inaccurate?

To start this process, first consider the question of what happens if the estimate of $300 for the unit profit for Wyndor's new kind of door is inaccurate. To address this question, let

P_D = Unit profit for the new kind of door

   = Cell C4 in the spreadsheet (see Figure 5.1)

Although P_D = $300 in the current version of Wyndor's linear programming model, we now want to explore how much larger or how much smaller P_D can be and still have $(D, W) = (2, 6)$ as the optimal solution. In other words, how much can the estimate of $300 for the unit profit for these doors be off before the model will give an erroneous optimal solution?

Using the Spreadsheet to Do Sensitivity Analysis

One of the great strengths of a spreadsheet is the ease with which it can be used interactively to perform various kinds of what-if analysis, including the sensitivity analysis being considered in this section. Once the Solver has been set up to obtain an optimal solution, you can immediately find out what would happen if one of the parameters of the model were to be changed to some other value. All you have to do is make this change on the spreadsheet and then click on the Solve button again.

To illustrate, Figure 5.2 shows what would happen if the unit profit for doors were to be decreased from P_D = $300 to P_D = $200. Comparing with Figure 5.1, there is no change at all in the optimal solution. In fact, the *only* changes in the new spreadsheet are the new value

Click on the Solve button again and the spreadsheet immediately reveals the effect of changing any values in the data cells.

FIGURE 5.2

The revised Wyndor problem where the estimate of the unit profit for doors has been decreased from $P_D = \$300$ to $P_D = \$200$, but no change occurs in the optimal solution.

	A	B	C	D	E	F	G
1		Wyndor Glass Co. Product-Mix Problem					
2							
3			Doors	Windows			
4		Unit Profit	$200	$500			
5					Hours		Hours
6			Hours Used per Unit Produced		Used		Available
7		Plant 1	1	0	2	≤	4
8		Plant 2	0	2	12	≤	12
9		Plant 3	3	2	18	≤	18
10							
11			Doors	Windows			Total Profit
12		Units Produced	2	6			$3,400

FIGURE 5.3

The revised Wyndor problem where the estimate of the unit profit for doors has been increased from $P_D = \$300$ to $P_D = \$500$, but no change occurs in the optimal solution.

	A	B	C	D	E	F	G
1		Wyndor Glass Co. Product-Mix Problem					
2							
3			Doors	Windows			
4		Unit Profit	$500	$500			
5					Hours		Hours
6			Hours Used per Unit Produced		Used		Available
7		Plant 1	1	0	2	≤	4
8		Plant 2	0	2	12	≤	12
9		Plant 3	3	2	18	≤	18
10							
11			Doors	Windows			Total Profit
12		Units Produced	2	6			$4,000

of P_D in cell C4 and a decrease of $200 in the total profit shown in cell G12 (because each of the two doors produced per week provides $100 less profit). Because the optimal solution does not change, we now know that the original estimate of $P_D = \$300$ can be considerably *too high* without invalidating the model's optimal solution.

But what happens if this estimate is *too low* instead? Figure 5.3 shows what would happen if P_D were to be increased to $P_D = \$500$. Again, there is no change in the optimal solution.

Because the original value of $P_D = \$300$ can be changed considerably in either direction without changing the optimal solution, P_D is said to be *not a sensitive parameter*. It is not necessary to pin down this estimate with great accuracy to have confidence that the model is providing the correct optimal solution.

This may be all the information that is needed about P_D. However, if there is a good possibility that the true value of P_D will turn out to be outside this broad range from $200 to $500, further investigation would be desirable. How much higher or lower can P_D be before the optimal solution would change?

Figure 5.4 demonstrates that the optimal solution would indeed change if P_D were increased all the way up to $P_D = \$1,000$. Thus, we now know that this change occurs somewhere between $500 and $1,000 during the process of increasing P_D.

Using the Solver Table to Do Sensitivity Analysis Systematically

To pin down just when the optimal solution will change, we could continue selecting new values of P_D at random. However, a better approach is to systematically consider a range of values of P_D. An Excel add-in developed by the authors, called the *Solver Table*, is designed to

FIGURE 5.4

The revised Wyndor problem where the estimate of the unit profit for doors has been increased from $P_D = \$300$ to $P_D = \$1,000$, which results in a change in the optimal solution.

	A	B	C	D	E	F	G
1		**Wyndor Glass Co. Product-Mix Problem**					
2							
3			Doors	Windows			
4		Unit Profit	$1,000	$500			
5					Hours		Hours
6			Hours Used per Unit Produced		Used		Available
7		Plant 1	1	0	4	≤	4
8		Plant 2	0	2	6	≤	12
9		Plant 3	3	2	18	≤	18
10							
11			Doors	Windows			Total Profit
12		Units Produced	4	3			$5,500

perform just this sort of analysis. It is available to you in your MS Courseware. Complete instructions for using the Solver Table are given in Appendix A.

The Solver Table re-solves the problem for a whole range of values of a data cell.

The Solver Table is used to show the results in the changing cells and/or certain output cells for various trial values in a data cell. For each trial value in the data cell, Solver is called on to re-solve the problem.

To use the Solver Table, first expand the original spreadsheet (Figure 5.1) to make a table with headings as shown in Figure 5.5. In the first column of the table (cells B19:B28), list the trial values for the data cell (the unit profit for doors), except leave the first row (cell B18) blank. The headings of the next columns specify which output will be evaluated. For each of these columns, use the first row of the table (cells C18:E18) to write an equation that refers to the relevant changing cell or output cell. In this case, the cells of interest are DoorsProduced (C12), WindowsProduced (D12), and TotalProfit (G12), so the equations for C18:E18 are those shown in Figure 5.5.

Excel Tip: When filling in the first column of a Solver Table with the trial values for the data cell of interest, skip the first row to leave room in the other columns for the equations referring to the changing cells and/or output cells of interest.

Next, select the entire table by clicking and dragging from cells B18 through E28, and then choose the Solver Table from the Add-Ins tab (for Excel 2007 or 2010) or Tools menu (for other versions of Excel). In the Solver Table dialogue box (as shown at the bottom of Figure 5.5), indicate the column input cell (C4), which refers to the data cell that is being changed in the first column of the table. Nothing is entered for the row input cell because no row is being used to list the trial values of a data cell in this case.

Clicking on the OK button then generates the Solver Table automatically. One at a time, the trial values listed in the first column of the table are put into the column input cell and then Solver Table calls on the Solver to re-solve the problem. Then, since the first row of the Solver Table has equations pointing to the output cells that now hold the new optimal solution, the first row of the Solver Table will now also show the optimal results for that particular trial value of the column input cell. Solver Table copies these results from the first row of the table into the corresponding row of the table for that trial value. This process is then repeated automatically for each remaining trial value in the first column of the table. The end result when Solver Table is finished (which happens very quickly for small problems) is that the Solver Table is completely filled in (as shown in Figure 5.6) and shows the optimal results for all trial values of the column input cell. (The numbers currently displayed in the first row of the table in Figure 5.6 come from the original solution in the spreadsheet before changing the original value in the column input cell.)

The allowable range for a coefficient in the objective function is the range of values for this coefficient over which the optimal solution for the original model remains optimal.

The table reveals that the optimal solution remains the same all the way from $P_D = \$100$ (and perhaps lower) to $P_D = \$700$, but that a change occurs somewhere between $700 and $800. We next could systematically consider values of P_D between $700 and $800 to determine more closely where the optimal solution changes. However, here is a shortcut. The range of values of P_D over which $(D, W) = (2, 6)$ remains as the optimal solution is referred to as the **allowable range for an objective function coefficient,** or just the

FIGURE 5.5

Expansion of the spreadsheet in Figure 5.1 to prepare for using the Solver Table to show the effect of systematically varying the estimate of the unit profit for doors in the Wyndor problem.

	A	B	C	D	E	F	G
1		**Wyndor Glass Co. Product-Mix Problem**					
2							
3			Doors	Windows			
4		Unit Profit	$300	$500			
5					Hours		Hours
6			Hours Used per Unit Produced		Used		Available
7		Plant 1	1	0	2	≤	4
8		Plant 2	0	2	12	≤	12
9		Plant 3	3	2	18	≤	18
10							
11			Doors	Windows			Total Profit
12		Units Produced	2	6			$3,600
13							
14							Select
15							these cells
16		Unit Profit	Optimal Units Produced		Total		(B18:E28)
17		for Doors	Doors	Windows	Profit		before
18			2	6	$3,600		choosing
19		$100					the Solver
20		$200					Table.
21		$300					
22		$400					
23		$500					
24		$600					
25		$700					
26		$800					
27		$900					
28		$1,000					

	C	D	E
16	Optimal Units Produced		Total
17	Doors	Windows	Profit
18	=DoorsProduced	=WindowsProduced	=TotalProfit

Range Name	Cells
DoorsProduced	C12
TotalProfit	G12
WindowsProduced	D12

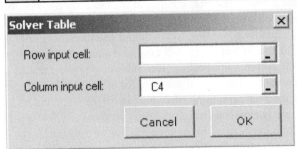

allowable range for short. Upon request, the Excel Solver will provide a report called the *sensitivity report* that reveals exactly what this allowable range is.

Using the Sensitivity Report to Find the Allowable Range

As was shown in Figure 2.12, when the Solver gives the message that it has found a solution, it also gives on the right a list of three reports that can be provided. By selecting the second one (labeled Sensitivity), you will obtain the sensitivity report.

FIGURE 5.6

An application of the Solver Table that shows the effect of systematically varying the estimate of the unit profit for doors in the Wyndor problem.

	B	C	D	E
16	Unit Profit	Optimal Units Produced		Total
17	for Doors	Doors	Windows	Profit
18		2	6	$3,600
19	$100	2	6	$3,200
20	$200	2	6	$3,400
21	$300	2	6	$3,600
22	$400	2	6	$3,800
23	$500	2	6	$4,000
24	$600	2	6	$4,200
25	$700	2	6	$4,400
26	$800	4	3	$4,700
27	$900	4	3	$5,100
28	$1,000	4	3	$5,500

FIGURE 5.7

Part of the sensitivity report generated by the Excel Solver for the original Wyndor problem (Figure 5.1), where the last three columns enable identifying the allowable ranges for the unit profits for doors and windows.

Reduced costs are described in the supplement to this chapter on the CD-ROM. Don't worry about this relatively technical subject (unless your instructor assigns this supplement).

The sensitivity report generated by the Excel Solver reveals the allowable range for each coefficient in the objective function.

Variable Cells

Cell	Name	Final Value	Reduced Cost	Objective Coefficient	Allowable Increase	Allowable Decrease
$C$12	DoorsProduced	2	0	300	450	300
$D$12	WindowsProduced	6	0	500	1E+30	300

Figure 5.7 shows the relevant part of this report for the Wyndor problem. The Final Value column indicates the optimal solution. The next column gives the *reduced costs,* which can provide some useful information when any of the changing cells equal zero in the optimal solution, which is not the case here. (For a zero-valued changing cell, the corresponding reduced cost can be used to determine what the effect would be of either increasing that changing cell or making a change in its coefficient in the objective function. Because of the relatively technical nature of these interpretations of reduced costs, we will not discuss them further here, but will provide a full explanation in the supplement to this chapter on the CD-ROM.) The next three columns provide the information needed to identify the *allowable range* for each coefficient in the objective function. The Objective Coefficient column gives the current value of each coefficient, and then the next two columns give the *allowable increase* and the *allowable decrease* from this value to remain within the allowable range.

For example, consider P_D, the coefficient of D in the objective function. Since D is the production rate for these special doors, the Doors row in the table provides the following information (without the dollar sign) about P_D:

Current value of P_D:	300	
Allowable increase in P_D:	450	So $P_D \leq 300 + 450 = 750$
Allowable decrease in P_D:	300	So $P_D \geq 300 - 300 = 0$
Allowable range for P_D:	$0 \leq P_D \leq 750$	

Therefore, if P_D is changed from its current value (without making any other change in the model), the current solution $(D, W) = (2, 6)$ will remain optimal so long as the new value of P_D is within this allowable range.

Figure 5.8 provides graphical insight into this allowable range. For the original value of $P_D = 300$, the solid line in the figure shows the slope of the objective function line passing through (2, 6). At the lower end of the allowable range, when $P_D = 0$, the objective function line that passes through (2, 6) now is line B in the figure, so every point on the line segment between (0, 6) and (2, 6) is an optimal solution. For any value of $P_D < 0$, the objective function line will have rotated even further so that (0, 6) becomes the only optimal solution. At the upper end of the allowable range, when $P_D = 750$, the objective function line that passes through

FIGURE 5.8

The two dashed lines that pass through solid constraint boundary lines are the objective function lines when P_D (the unit profit for doors) is at an endpoint of its allowable range, $0 \leq P_D \leq 750$, since either line or any objective function line in between still yields $(D, W) = (2, 6)$ as an optimal solution for the Wyndor problem.

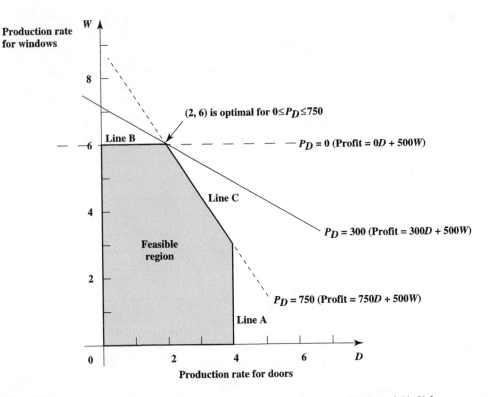

(2, 6) becomes line C, so every point on the line segment between (2, 6) and (4, 3) becomes an optimal solution. For any value of $P_D > 750$, the objective function line is even steeper than line C, so (4, 3) becomes the only optimal solution.

Check out this module in the Interactive Management Science Modules to gain graphical insight into the allowable range.

The module called *Graphical Linear Programming and Sensitivity Analysis* in the Interactive Management Science Modules (available at **www.mhhe.com/hillier4e/** or in your CD-ROM) is designed to help you perform this kind of graphical analysis. After you enter the model for the original Wyndor problem, the module provides you with the graph shown in Figure 5.8 (without the dashed lines). You then can simply drag one end of the objective function line up or down to see how far you can increase or decrease P_D before $(D, W) = (2, 6)$ will no longer be optimal.

Conclusion: The allowable range for P_D is $0 \leq P_D \leq 750$, because $(D, W) = (2, 6)$ remains optimal over this range but not beyond. (When $P_D = 0$ or $P_D = 750$, there are multiple optimal solutions, but $(D, W) = (2, 6)$ still is one of them.) With the range this wide around the original estimate of \$300 ($P_D = 300$) for the unit profit for doors, we can be quite confident of obtaining the correct optimal solution for the true unit profit even though the discussion in Section 5.2 indicates that this estimate is fairly rough.

The sensitivity report also can be used to find the allowable range for the unit profit for Wyndor's other new product. In particular, let

P_W = Unit profit for Wyndor's new kind of window

= Cell D4 in the spreadsheet

Referring to the Windows row of the sensitivity report (Figure 5.7), this row indicates that the allowable decrease in P_W is 300 (so $P_W \geq 500 - 300 = 200$) and the allowable increase is 1E+30. What is meant by 1E+30? This is shorthand in Excel for 10^{30} (1 with 30 zeroes after it). This tremendously huge number is used by Excel to represent *infinity*. Therefore, the allowable range of P_W is obtained from the sensitivity report as follows:

Current value of P_W:	500	
Allowable increase in P_W:	Unlimited	So P_W has no upper limit
Allowable decrease in P_W:	300	So $P_W \geq 500 - 300 = 200$
Allowable range:	$P_W \geq 200$	

The allowable range is quite wide for both objective function coefficients. Thus, even though $P_D = \$300$ and $P_W = \$500$ were only rough estimates of the true unit profit for the doors and windows, respectively, we can still be confident that we have obtained the correct optimal solution.

We are not always so lucky. For some linear programming problems, even a small change in the value of certain coefficients in the objective function can change the optimal solution. Such coefficients are referred to as *sensitive parameters*. The sensitivity report will immediately indicate which of the objective function coefficients (if any) are sensitive parameters. These are parameters that have a small allowable increase and/or a small allowable decrease. Hence, extra care should be taken to refine these estimates.

Once this has been done and the final version of the model has been solved, the allowable ranges continue to serve an important purpose. As indicated in Section 5.1, the second benefit of what-if analysis is that if conditions change after the study has been completed (a common occurrence), what-if analysis leaves signposts that indicate (without solving the model again) whether a resulting change in a parameter of the model changes the optimal solution. Thus, if weeks, months, or even years later, the unit profit for one of Wyndor's new products changes substantially, its allowable range indicates immediately whether the old optimal product mix still is the appropriate one to use. Being able to draw an affirmative conclusion without reconstructing and solving the revised model is extremely helpful for any linear programming problem, but especially so when the model is a large one.

> *A parameter is considered sensitive if even a small change in its value can change the optimal solution.*

Review Questions

1. What is meant by the *allowable range* for a coefficient in the objective function?
2. What is the significance if the true value for a coefficient in the objective function turns out to be so different from its estimate that it lies outside its allowable range?
3. In Excel's sensitivity report, what is the interpretation of the Objective Coefficient column? The Allowable Increase column? The Allowable Decrease column?

5.4 THE EFFECT OF SIMULTANEOUS CHANGES IN OBJECTIVE FUNCTION COEFFICIENTS

The coefficients in the objective function typically represent quantities (e.g., unit profits) that can only be estimated because of considerable uncertainty about what their true values will turn out to be. The allowable ranges described in the preceding section deal with this uncertainty by focusing on just one coefficient at a time. In effect, the allowable range for a particular coefficient assumes that the original estimates for all the other coefficients are completely accurate so that this coefficient is the only one whose true value may differ from its original estimate.

In actuality, the estimates for *all* the coefficients (or at least more than one of them) may be inaccurate simultaneously. The crucial question is whether this is likely to result in obtaining the wrong optimal solution. If so, greater care should be taken to refine these estimates as much as possible, at least for the more crucial coefficients. On the other hand, if what-if analysis reveals that the anticipated errors in estimating the coefficients are unlikely to affect the optimal solution, then management can be reassured that the current linear programming model and its results are providing appropriate guidance.

This section focuses on how to determine, without solving the problem again, whether the optimal solution might change if certain changes occur simultaneously in the coefficients of the objective function (due to their true values differing from their estimates). In the process, we will address the second of Wyndor management's what-if questions.

Question 2: What happens if the estimates of the unit profits of both of Wyndor's new products are inaccurate?

Using the Spreadsheet for This Analysis

Once again, a quick-and-easy way to address this kind of question is to simply try out different estimates on the spreadsheet formulation of the model and see what happens each time when clicking on the Solve button.

An Application Vignette

The **Pacific Lumber Company (PALCO)** is a large timber-holding company with headquarters in Scotia, California. The company has over 200,000 acres of highly productive forest lands that support five mills located in Humboldt County in northern California. The lands include some of the most spectacular redwood groves in the world that have been given or sold at low cost to be preserved as parks. PALCO manages the remaining lands intensively for sustained timber production, subject to strong forest practice laws. Since PALCO's forests are home to many species of wildlife, including endangered species such as spotted owls and marbled murrelets, the provisions of the federal Endangered Species Act also need to be carefully observed.

To obtain a sustained yield plan for the entire landholding, PALCO management contracted with a team of management science consultants to develop a 120-year, 12-period, long-term forest ecosystem management plan. The management science team performed this task by formulating and applying a linear programming model to optimize the company's overall timberland operations and profitability after satisfying the various constraints. The model was a huge one with approximately 8,500 functional constraints and 353,000 decision variables.

A major challenge in applying the linear programming model was the many uncertainties in estimating what the parameters of the model should be. The major factors causing these uncertainties were the continuing fluctuations in market supply and demand, logging costs, and environmental regulations. Therefore, the management science team made extensive use of *detailed sensitivity analysis*. The resulting sustained yield plan *increased the company's present net worth by over* **$398 million** while also generating a better mix of wildlife habitat acres.

Source: L. R. Fletcher, H. Alden, S. P. Holmen, D. P. Angelis, and M. J. Etzenhouser, "Long-Term Forest Ecosystem Planning at Pacific Lumber," *Interfaces* 29, no. 1 (January–February 1999), pp. 90–112. (A link to this article is provided on our Web site, **www.mhhe.com/hillier4e.**)

In this case, the optimal product mix indicated by the model is heavily weighted toward producing the windows (6 per week) rather than the doors (only 2 per week). Since there is equal enthusiasm for both new products, management is concerned about this imbalance. Therefore, management has raised a what-if question. What would happen if the estimate of the unit profit for the doors ($300) were too low and the corresponding estimate for the windows ($500) were too high? Management feels that the estimates could easily be off in these directions. If this were the case, would this lead to a more balanced product mix being the most profitable one?

This question can be answered in a matter of seconds simply by substituting new estimates of the unit profits in the original spreadsheet in Figure 5.1 and clicking on the Solve button. Figure 5.9 shows that new estimates of $450 for doors and $400 for windows causes no change at all in the solution for the optimal product mix. (The total profit does change, but this occurs only because of the changes in the unit profits.) Would even larger changes in the estimates of unit profits finally lead to a change in the optimal product mix? Figure 5.10 shows that this does happen, yielding a relatively balanced product mix of $(D, W) = (4, 3)$, when estimates of $600 for doors and $300 for windows are used.

FIGURE 5.9

The revised Wyndor problem where the estimates of the unit profits for doors and windows have been changed to $P_D = \$450$ and $P_W = \$400$, respectively, but no change occurs in the optimal solution.

	A	B	C	D	E	F	G
1		**Wyndor Glass Co. Product-Mix Problem**					
2							
3			Doors	Windows			
4		Unit Profit	$450	$400			
5					Hours		Hours
6			Hours Used per Unit Produced		Used		Available
7		Plant 1	1	0	2	≤	4
8		Plant 2	0	2	12	≤	12
9		Plant 3	3	2	18	≤	18
10							
11			Doors	Windows			Total Profit
12		Units Produced	2	6			$3,300

FIGURE 5.10

The revised Wyndor problem where the estimates of the unit profits for doors and windows have been changed to $600 and $300, respectively, which results in a change in the optimal solution.

	A	B	C	D	E	F	G
1		**Wyndor Glass Co. Product-Mix Problem**					
2							
3			Doors	Windows			
4		Unit Profit	$600	$300			
5					Hours		Hours
6			Hours Used per Unit Produced		Used		Available
7		Plant 1	1	0	4	≤	4
8		Plant 2	0	2	6	≤	12
9		Plant 3	3	2	18	≤	18
10							
11			Doors	Windows			Total Profit
12		Units Produced	4	3			$3,300

Unlike a *one-way* Solver Table (as in Figure 5.6) which shows results for trial values in a *single* data cell, a *two-way* Solver Table shows results for trial values in *two* data cells.

Using Two-way Solver Tables for This Analysis

A *two-way* Solver Table provides a way of systematically investigating the effect if the estimates of both unit profits are inaccurate. This kind of Solver Table shows the results in a single output cell for various trial values in two data cells. Therefore, it can be used to show how TotalProfit (G12) in Figure 5.1 varies over a range of trial values in the two data cells, UnitProfit (C4:D4). For each pair of trial values in these data cells, Solver is called on to re-solve the problem.

To create a two-way Solver Table for the Wyndor problem, expand the original spreadsheet (Figure 5.1) to make a table with column and row headings as shown in rows 16–21 of the spreadsheet in Figure 5.11. In the upper left-hand corner of the table (C17), write an equation that refers to the target cell (=TotalProfit). In the first column of the table (column C, below the equation in cell C17), insert various trial values for the first data cell of interest (the unit profit for doors). In the first row of the table (row 17, to the right of the equation in cell C17), insert various trial values for the second data cell of interest (the unit profit for windows).

Appendix A describes this same procedure and then provides a useful summary of the steps needed to create a two-way Solver Table.

Next, select the entire table (C17:H21) and choose Solver Table from the Add-Ins tab (for Excel 2007 or 2010) or Tools menu (for other versions of Excel). In the Solver Table dialogue box (shown at the bottom of Figure 5.11), indicate which data cells are being changed simultaneously. The column input cell C4 refers to the data cell whose various trial values are listed in the first column of the table (C18:C21), while the row input cell refers to the data cell whose various trial values are listed in the first row of the table (D17:H17).

Clicking on the OK button then generates the Solver Table automatically. One at a time, a pair of trial values listed in the first column and first row of the table are put into the column input cell and row input cell, respectively, and then the Solver Table calls on Solver to re-solve the problem. Then, since the cell in the upper left corner of the Solver Table (C17 for this example) has an equation referring to the output cell of interest (the target cell for this example) that now holds the new optimal solution, the cell in the upper left corner now also shows the optimal result for that particular pair of trial values. Solver Table copies this result into the corresponding entry in the row and column of the table for that trial value pair. This process is then repeated automatically for each remaining trial value pair. The end result when Solver Table is finished is that the Solver Table is completely filled in (as shown in Figure 5.12) and shows the optimal result for all trial value pairs. (The number currently displayed in C17 comes from the original solution in the spreadsheet before changing the original values in the column and row input cells.)

Although a two-way Solver Table is limited to showing results in a single cell of the table for each combination of trial values in two data cells, the & symbol can be used to show results from multiple cells of the original spreadsheet in this single cell.

Unlike a one-way Solver Table that can show the results of *multiple* changing cells and/or output cells for various trial values of a single data cell, a two-way Solver Table is limited to showing the results in a *single* cell for each pair of trial values in the two data cells of interest. However, there is a trick using the & symbol that enables the Solver Table to show the results

FIGURE 5.11

Expansion of the spreadsheet in Figure 5.1 to prepare for using a two-dimensional Solver Table to show the effect on total profit of systematically varying the estimates of the unit profits of doors and windows for the Wyndor problem.

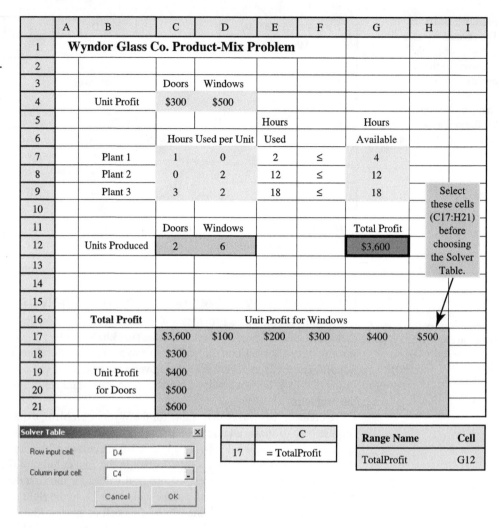

FIGURE 5.12

A two-dimensional application of the Solver Table that shows the effect on total profit of systematically varying the estimates of the unit profits of doors and windows for the Wyndor problem.

	B	C	D	E	F	G	H
16	**Total Profit**		Unit Profit for Windows				
17		$3,600	$100	$200	$300	$400	$500
18		$300	$1,500	$1,800	$2,400	$3,000	$3,600
19	Unit Profit	$400	$1,900	$2,200	$2,600	$3,200	$3,800
20	for Doors	$500	$2,300	$2,600	$2,900	$3,400	$4,000
21		$600	$2,700	$3,000	$3,300	$3,600	$4,200

from multiple changing cells and/or output cells within a single cell of the table. We utilize this trick in the Solver Table shown in Figure 5.13 to show the results for *both* changing cells DoorsProduced (C12) and WindowsProduced (D12) for each pair of trial values for Unit-Profit (C4:D4). The key formula is in cell C25:

C25 = "(" & DoorsProduced & ", " & WindowsProduced & ")"

Excel Tip: Any text that you would like a formula to display (such as the parentheses and commas in the formula in C25 of Figure 5.13) must be enclosed within quotation marks.

The & character tells Excel to concatenate, so the result will be a left parenthesis, followed by the value in DoorsProduced (C12), then a comma and the contents in WindowsProduced (D12), and finally a right parenthesis. If DoorsProduced = 2 and WindowsProduced = 6, the result is (2, 6). Thus, the results from *both* changing cells are displayed within a *single* cell of the table.

After the usual preliminaries in entering the information shown in rows 24–25 and columns B–C of Figure 5.13, along with the formula in C25, clicking on the OK button

FIGURE 5.13

A two-dimensional application of the Solver Table that shows the effect on the optimal solution of systematically varying the estimates of the unit profits of doors and windows for the Wyndor problem.

	B	C	D	E	F	G	H
24	**Units Produced (Doors, Windows)**			Unit Profit for Windows			
25		(2,6)	$100	$200	$300	$400	$500
26		$300	(4,3)	(4,3)	(2,6)	(2,6)	(2,6)
27	Unit Profit	$400	(4,3)	(4,3)	(2,6)	(2,6)	(2,6)
28	for Doors	$500	(4,3)	(4,3)	(4,3)	(2,6)	(2,6)
29		$600	(4,3)	(4,3)	(4,3)	(4,3)	(2,6)

	C
25	= "(" & DoorsProduced & "," & WindowsProduced & ")"

Range Name	Cell
DoorsProduced	C12
WindowsProduced	D12

Solver Table

Row input cell: D4

Column input cell: C4

Cancel   OK

automatically generates the entire Solver Table. Cells D26:H29 show the optimal solution for the various combinations of trial values for the unit profits of the doors and windows. The upper right-hand corner (cell H26) of this Solver Table gives the optimal solution of $(D, W) = (2, 6)$ when using the original unit-profit estimates of $300 for doors and $500 for windows. Moving down from this cell corresponds to increasing this estimate for doors, while moving to the left amounts to decreasing the estimate for windows. (The cells when moving up or to the right of H26 are not shown because these changes would only increase the attractiveness of $(D, W) = (2, 6)$ as the optimal solution.) Note that $(D, W) = (2, 6)$ continues to be the optimal solution for all the cells near H26. This indicates that the original estimates of unit profit would need to be very inaccurate indeed before the optimal product mix would change. Although the estimates are fairly rough, management is confident that they are not that inaccurate. Therefore, there is no need to expend the considerable effort that would be needed to refine the estimates.

What-if analysis shows that there is no need to refine Wyndor's estimates of the unit profits for doors and windows.

At this point, it continues to appear that $(D, W) = (2, 6)$ is the best product mix for initiating the production of the two new products (although additional what-if questions remain to be addressed in subsequent sections). However, we also now know from Figure 5.13 that as conditions change in the future, if the unit profits for both products change enough, it may be advisable to change the product mix later. We still need to leave clear signposts behind to signal when a future change in the product mix should be considered, as described next.

Gleaning Additional Information from the Sensitivity Report

The preceding section described how the data in the sensitivity report enable finding the allowable range for an individual coefficient in the objective function when that coefficient is the only one that changes from its original value. These same data (the allowable increase and allowable decrease in each coefficient) also can be used to analyze the effect of *simultaneous* changes in these coefficients. Here is how.

A sum ≤ 100 percent guarantees that the original optimal solution is still optimal.

The 100 Percent Rule for Simultaneous Changes in Objective Function Coefficients: If simultaneous changes are made in the coefficients of the objective function, calculate for each change the percentage of the allowable change (increase or decrease) for that coefficient to remain within its allowable range. If the *sum* of the percentage changes does *not* exceed 100 percent, the original optimal solution definitely will still be optimal. (If the sum *does* exceed 100 percent, then we cannot be sure.)

This rule does not spell out what happens if the sum of the percentage changes *does* exceed 100 percent. The consequence depends on the directions of the changes in the coefficients.

Exceeding 100 percent may or may not change the optimal solution, but so long as 100 percent is not exceeded, the original optimal solution *definitely* will still be optimal.

Keep in mind that we can safely use the entire allowable increase or decrease in a single objective function coefficient only if none of the other coefficients have changed at all. With simultaneous changes in the coefficients, we focus on the *percentage* of the allowable increase or decrease that is being used for each coefficient.

To illustrate, consider the Wyndor problem again, along with the information provided by the sensitivity report in Figure 5.7. Suppose conditions have changed after the initial study, and the unit profit for doors (P_D) has increased from \$300 to \$450 while the unit profit for windows (P_W) has decreased from \$500 to \$400. The calculations for the 100 percent rule then are

P_D: \$300 $\rightarrow$ \$450

$$\text{Percentage of allowable increase} = 100\left(\frac{450 - 300}{450}\right)\% = 33\tfrac{1}{3}\%$$

P_W: \$500 $\rightarrow$ \$400

$$\text{Percentage of allowable decrease} = 100\left(\frac{500 - 400}{300}\right)\% = 33\tfrac{1}{3}\%$$

$$\text{Sum} = \overline{66\tfrac{2}{3}\%}$$

Since the sum of the percentages does not exceed 100 percent, the original optimal solution $(D, W) = (2, 6)$ definitely is still optimal, just as we found earlier in Figure 5.9.

Now suppose conditions have changed even further, so P_D has increased from \$300 to \$600 while P_W has decreased from \$500 to \$300. The calculations for the 100 percent rule now are

P_D: \$300 $\rightarrow$ \$600

$$\text{Percentage of allowable increase} = 100\left(\frac{600 - 300}{450}\right)\% = 66\tfrac{2}{3}\%$$

P_W: \$500 $\rightarrow$ \$300

$$\text{Percentage of allowable decrease} = 100\left(\frac{500 - 300}{300}\right)\% = 66\tfrac{2}{3}\%$$

$$\text{Sum} = \overline{133\tfrac{1}{3}\%}$$

Since the sum of the percentages now exceeds 100 percent, the 100 percent rule says that we can no longer guarantee that $(D, W) = (2, 6)$ is still optimal. In fact, we found earlier in both Figures 5.10 and 5.13 that the optimal solution has changed to $(D, W) = (4, 3)$.

These results suggest how to find just where the optimal solution changes while P_D is being increased and P_W is being decreased in this way. Since 100 percent is midway between 66⅔ percent and 133⅓ percent, the sum of the percentage changes will equal 100 percent when the values of P_D and P_W are midway between their values in the above cases. In particular, $P_D = \$525$ is midway between \$450 and \$600 and $P_W = \$350$ is midway between \$400 and \$300. The corresponding calculations for the 100 percent rule are

P_D: \$300 $\rightarrow$ \$525

$$\text{Percentage of allowable increase} = 100\left(\frac{525 - 300}{450}\right)\% = 50\%$$

P_W: \$500 $\rightarrow$ \$350

$$\text{Percentage of allowable decrease} = 100\left(\frac{500 - 350}{300}\right)\% = 50\%$$

$$\text{Sum} = \overline{100\%}$$

FIGURE 5.14

When the estimates of the unit profits for doors and windows change to $P_D =$ $525 and $P_W =$ $350, which lies at the edge of what is allowed by the 100 percent rule, the graphical method shows that (D, W) = (2, 6) still is an optimal solution, but now every other point on the line segment between this solution and (4, 3) also is optimal.

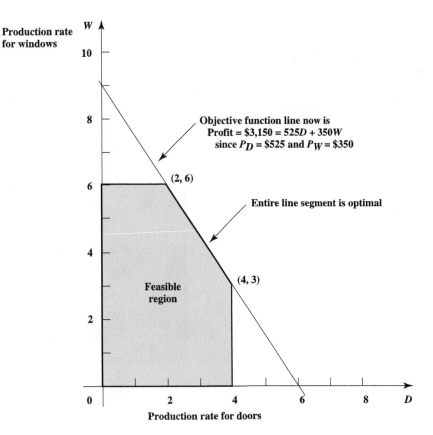

Although the sum of the percentages equals 100 percent, the fact that it does not *exceed* 100 percent guarantees that (D, W) = (2, 6) is still optimal. Figure 5.14 shows graphically that *both* (2, 6) and (4, 3) are now optimal, as well as all the points on the line segment connecting these two points. However, if P_D and P_W were to be changed any further from their original values (so that the sum of the percentages exceeds 100 percent), the objective function line would be rotated so far toward the vertical that (D, W) = (4, 3) would become the only optimal solution.

Here is an example where the original optimal solution is still optimal even though the sum exceeds 100 percent.

At the same time, keep in mind that having the sum of the percentages of allowable changes exceed 100 percent does not automatically mean that the optimal solution will change. For example, suppose that the estimates of both unit profits are halved. The resulting calculations for the 100 percent rule are

P_D: $300 → $150

$$\text{Percentage of allowable decrease} = 100\left(\frac{300 - 150}{300}\right)\% = 50\%$$

P_W: $500 → $250

$$\text{Percentage of allowable decrease} = 100\left(\frac{500 - 250}{300}\right)\% = 83\%$$

$$\text{Sum} = \overline{133\%}$$

Even though this sum exceeds 100 percent, Figure 5.15 shows that the original optimal solution is still optimal. In fact, the objective function line has the same slope as the original objective function line (the solid line in Figure 5.8). This happens whenever *proportional changes* are made to all the unit profits, which will automatically lead to the same optimal solution.

Comparisons

You now have seen three approaches to investigating what happens if simultaneous changes occur in the coefficients of the objective function: (1) try out changes directly on a spreadsheet, (2) use a two-way Solver Table, and (3) apply the 100 percent rule.

FIGURE 5.15

When the estimates of the unit profits for doors and windows change to $P_D =$ $150 and $P_W =$ $250 (half their original values), the graphical method shows that the optimal solution still is $(D, W) = (2, 6)$, even though the 100 percent rule says that the optimal solution might change.

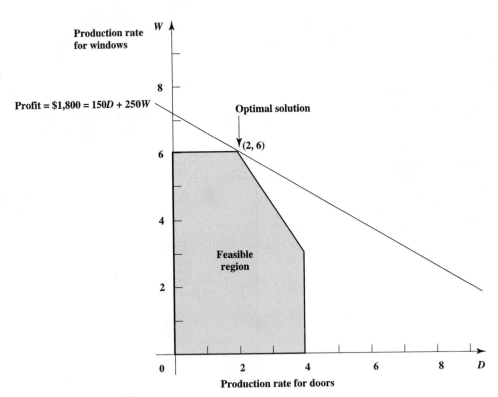

The spreadsheet approach is a good place to start, especially for less experienced modelers, because it is simple and quick. If you are only interested in checking one specific set of changes in the coefficients, you can immediately see what happens after making the changes in the spreadsheet.

More often, there will be numerous possibilities for what the true values of the coefficients will turn out to be, because of uncertainty in the original estimates of these coefficients. The Solver Table is useful for systematically checking a variety of possible changes in one or two objective function coefficients. Trying out representative possibilities on the spreadsheet may provide all the insight that is needed. Perhaps the optimal solution for the original model will remain optimal over nearly all these possibilities, so this solution can be confidently used. Or perhaps it will become clear that the original estimates need to be refined before selecting a solution.

When the spreadsheet approach and/or Solver Table does not provide a clear conclusion, the 100 percent rule can usefully complement this approach in the following ways:

- The 100 percent rule can be used to determine just how large the changes in the objective function coefficients need to be before the original optimal solution may no longer be optimal.
- When the model has a large number of decision variables (as is common for real problems), it may become impractical to use the spreadsheet approach to systematically try out a variety of simultaneous changes in many or all of the coefficients in the objective function because of the huge number of representative possibilities. The Solver Table can only be used to systematically check possible changes in—at most—two coefficients at a time. However, by dividing each coefficient's allowable increase or allowable decrease by the number of decision variables, the 100 percent rule immediately indicates how much each coefficient can be safely changed without invalidating the current optimal solution.
- After completing the study, if conditions change in the future that cause some or all of the coefficients in the objective function to change, the 100 percent rule quickly indicates whether the original optimal solution must remain optimal. If the answer is affirmative, there is no need to take all the time that may be required to reconstruct the (revised) spreadsheet model. The time saved can be very substantial for large models.

Review
Questions

1. In the 100 percent rule for simultaneous changes in objective function coefficients, what are the percentage changes that are being considered?
2. In this 100 percent rule, if the sum of the percentage changes does not exceed 100 percent, what does this say about the original optimal solution?
3. In this 100 percent rule, if the sum of the percentage changes exceeds 100 percent, does this mean that the original optimal solution is no longer optimal?

5.5   THE EFFECT OF SINGLE CHANGES IN A CONSTRAINT

We now turn our focus from the coefficients in the objective function to the effect of changing the functional constraints. The changes might occur either in the coefficients on the left-hand sides of the constraints or in the values of the right-hand sides.

We might be interested in the effect of such changes for the same reason we are interested in this effect for objective function coefficients, namely, that these parameters of the model are only *estimates* of quantities that cannot be determined precisely at this time so we want to determine the effect if these estimates are inaccurate.

When the right-hand sides represent managerial policy decisions, what-if analysis provides guidance regarding the effect of altering these decisions.

However, a more common reason for this interest is the one discussed at the end of Section 5.1, namely, that the right-hand sides of the functional constraints may well represent *managerial policy decisions* rather than quantities that are largely outside the control of management. Therefore, after the model has been solved, management will want to analyze the effect of altering these policy decisions in a variety of ways to see if these decisions can be improved. What-if analysis provides valuable guidance to management in determining the effect of altering these policy decisions. (Recall that this was cited as the third benefit of what-if analysis in Section 5.1.)

This section describes how to perform what-if analysis when making changes in just one spot (a coefficient or a right-hand side) of a single constraint. The next section then will deal with simultaneous changes in the constraints.

The procedure for determining the effect if a single change is made in a constraint is the same regardless of whether the change is in a coefficient on the left-hand side or in the value on the right-hand side. (The one exception is that the Excel sensitivity report provides information about changes in the right-hand side but does not do so for the left-hand side.) Therefore, we will illustrate the procedure by making changes in a right-hand side.

In particular, we return to the Wyndor case study to address the third what-if question posed by Wyndor management in Section 5.2.

Question 3: What happens if a change is made in the number of hours of production time per week being made available to Wyndor's new products in one of the plants?

The number of hours available in each plant is the value of the right-hand side for the corresponding constraint, so we want to investigate the effect of changing this right-hand side for one of the plants. With the original optimal solution, $(D, W) = (2, 6)$, only 2 of the 4 available hours in plant 1 are used, so changing this number of available hours (barring a large decrease) would have no effect on either the optimal solution or the resulting total profit from the two new products. However, it is unclear what would happen if the number of available hours in either plant 2 or plant 3 were to be changed. Let's start with plant 2.

Using the Spreadsheet for This Analysis

Referring back to Section 5.2, Figure 5.1 shows the spreadsheet model for the original Wyndor problem before beginning what-if analysis. The optimal solution is $(D, W) = (2, 6)$ with a total profit of $3,600 per week from the two new products. Cell G8 shows that 12 hours of production time per week are being made available for the new products in plant 2.

To see what happens if a specific change is made in this number of hours, all you need to do is substitute the new number in cell G8 and click on the Solve button again. For example, Figure 5.16 shows the result if the number of hours is increased from 12 to 13. The corresponding optimal solution in C12:D12 gives a total profit of $3,750. Thus, the resulting change in profit would be

$$\text{Incremental profit} = \$3,750 - \$3,600$$

$$= \$150$$

FIGURE 5.16

The revised Wyndor problem where the hours available in plant 2 per week have been increased from 12 (as in Figure 5.1) to 13, which results in an increase of $150 in the total profit per week from the two new products.

	A	B	C	D	E	F	G
1		**Wyndor Glass Co. Product-Mix Problem**					
2							
3			Doors	Windows			
4		Unit Profit	$300	$500			
5					Hours		Hours
6			Hours Used per Unit Produced		Used		Available
7		Plant 1	1	0	1.66667	≤	4
8		Plant 2	0	2	13	≤	13
9		Plant 3	3	2	18	≤	18
10							
11			Doors	Windows			Total Profit
12		Units Produced	1.667	6.5			$3,750

FIGURE 5.17

A further revision of the Wyndor problem in Figure 5.16 to further increase the hours available in plant 2 from 13 to 18, which results in a further increase in total profit of $750 (which is the $150 per hour added in plant 2).

	A	B	C	D	E	F	G
1		**Wyndor Glass Co. Product-Mix Problem**					
2							
3			Doors	Windows			
4		Unit Profit	$300	$500			
5					Hours		Hours
6			Hours Used per Unit Produced		Used		Available
7		Plant 1	1	0	0	≤	4
8		Plant 2	0	2	18	≤	18
9		Plant 3	3	2	18	≤	18
10							
11			Doors	Windows			Total Profit
12		Units Produced	0	9			$4,500

Since this increase in profit is obtained by adding just one more hour in plant 2, it would be interesting to see the effect of adding several more hours. Figure 5.17 shows the effect of adding five more hours. Comparing Figure 5.17 to Figure 5.16, the additional profit from providing five more hours would be

$$\text{Incremental profit} = \$4,500 - \$3,750$$
$$= \$750 \text{ from adding 5 hours}$$
$$= \$150 \text{ per hour added}$$

So far, each additional hour provided in plant 2 adds $150 to profit.

Would adding even more hours increase profit even further? Figure 5.18 shows what would happen if a total of 20 hours per week were made available to the new products in plant 2. Both the optimal solution and the total profit are the same as in Figure 5.17, so increasing from 18 to 20 hours would not help. (The reason is that the 18 hours available in plant 3 prevent producing more than 9 windows per week, so only 18 hours can be used in plant 2.) Thus, it appears that 18 hours is the maximum that should be considered for plant 2.

Now management needs to consider the trade-off between adding production time for the new products and decreasing it for other products.

However, the fact that the total profit from the two new products can be increased substantially by increasing the number of hours per week made available to the new products from 12 to 18 does not mean that these additional hours should be provided automatically. The production time made available for these two new products can be increased only if it is decreased for other products. Therefore, management will need to assess the disadvantages of decreasing the production time for any other products (including both lost profit and less tangible disadvantages) before

FIGURE 5.18

A further revision of the Wyndor problem in Figure 5.17 to further increase the hours available in plant 2 from 18 to 20, which results in no change in total profit because the optimal solution cannot make use of these additional hours.

	A	B	C	D	E	F	G
1		**Wyndor Glass Co. Product-Mix Problem**					
2							
3			Doors	Windows			
4		Unit Profit	$300	$500			
5					Hours		Hours
6			Hours Used per Unit Produced		Used		Available
7		Plant 1	1	0	0	≤	4
8		Plant 2	0	2	18	≤	20
9		Plant 3	3	2	18	≤	18
10							
11			Doors	Windows			Total Profit
12		Units Produced	0	9			$4,500

deciding whether to increase the production time for the new products. This analysis also might lead to *decreasing* the production time made available to the two new products in one or more of the plants.

Using the Solver Table for This Analysis

Complete instructions for using the Solver Table are given in Appendix A.

A Solver Table can be used to systematically determine the effect of making various changes in one of the parameters in a constraint. In Figure 5.19, we use the Solver Table to show how the changing cells and total profit change as the number of available hours in plant 2 range between 4 and 20. The trial values considered for this number are listed in the first column of the table (B19:B35). The output cells of interest are the DoorsProduced (C12), WindowsProduced (D12), and TotalProfit (G12), so equations referring to these cells are entered in the first row of the table (C18:E18). Running the Solver Table (with the column input cell as G8, the hours available in plant 2) then fills in the values in the body of the table (C19:E35). We also have calculated in column F the incremental profit, that is, the additional profit that was obtained by adding the last hour to the time available in plant 2.

An interesting pattern is apparent in the incremental profit column. Starting at 12 hours available at plant 2 (the current allotment), each additional hour allocated yields an additional $150 in profit (up to 18 hours). Similarly, if hours are taken away from plant 2, each hour lost causes a loss of $150 profit (down to six hours). This rate of change in the profit for increases

In general, the shadow price for a constraint reveals the rate at which the target cell can be increased by increasing the right-hand side of that constraint. This remains valid as long as the right-hand side is within its allowable range.

or decreases in the right-hand side of a constraint is known as the *shadow price*.

Given an optimal solution and the corresponding value of the objective function for a linear programming model, the **shadow price** for a functional constraint is the *rate* at which the value of the objective function can be increased by increasing the right-hand side of the constraint by a small amount.

This allowable range focuses on a right-hand side and the corresponding shadow price. In contrast to the allowable range for objective function coefficients described in Section 5.3, it does *not* indicate whether the original solution is still optimal, just whether the shadow price remains valid.

However, the shadow price of $150 for the plant 2 constraint is valid only within a range of values near 12 (in particular, between 6 hours and 18 hours). If the number of available hours is increased beyond 18 hours, then the incremental profit drops to zero. If the available hours are reduced below six hours, then profit drops at a faster rate of $250 per hour. Therefore, letting RHS denote the value of the right-hand side, the shadow price of $150 is valid for

$$6 \leq \text{RHS} \leq 18$$

This range is known as the **allowable range for the right-hand side** (or just **allowable range** for short).

The **allowable range for the right-hand side** of a functional constraint is the range of values for this right-hand side over which this constraint's shadow price remains valid.

FIGURE 5.19

An application of the Solver Table that shows the effect of varying the number of hours of production time being made available per week in plant 2 for Wyndor's new products.

	A	B	C	D	E	F	G
1		**Wyndor Glass Co. Product-Mix Problem**					
2							
3			Doors	Windows			
4		Unit Profit	$300	$500			
5					Hours		Hours
6			Hours Used per Unit Produced		Used		Available
7		Plant 1	1	0	2	≤	4
8		Plant 2	0	2	12	≤	12
9		Plant 3	3	2	18	≤	18
10							
11			Doors	Windows			Total Profit
12		Units Produced	2	6			$3,600
13							
14							
15							
16		Time Available in	Optimal Units Produced		Total	Incremental	
17		Plant 2 (hours)	Doors	Windows	Profit	Profit	
18			2	6	$3,600		
19		4	4	2	$2,200		
20		5	4	2.5	$2,450	$250	
21		6	4	3	$2,700	$250	
22		7	3.667	3.5	$2,850	$150	
23		8	3.333	4	$3,000	$150	
24		9	3	4.5	$3,150	$150	
25		10	2.667	5	$3,300	$150	
26		11	2.333	5.5	$3,450	$150	
27		12	2	6	$3,600	$150	
28		13	1.667	6.5	$3,750	$150	
29		14	1.333	7	$3,900	$150	
30		15	1	7.5	$4,050	$150	
31		16	0.667	8	$4,200	$150	
32		17	0.333	8.5	$4,350	$150	
33		18	0	9	$4,500	$150	
34		19	0	9	$4,500	$0	
35		20	0	9	$4,500	$0	

Select these cells (B18:E35) before choosing the Solver Table.

	C	D	E
16	Optimal Units Produced		Total
17	Doors	Windows	Profit
18	=DoorsProduced	=WindowsProduced	=TotalProfit

	F
16	Incremental
17	Profit
18	
19	
20	=E20-E19
21	=E21-E20
22	=E22-E21
23	=E23-E22

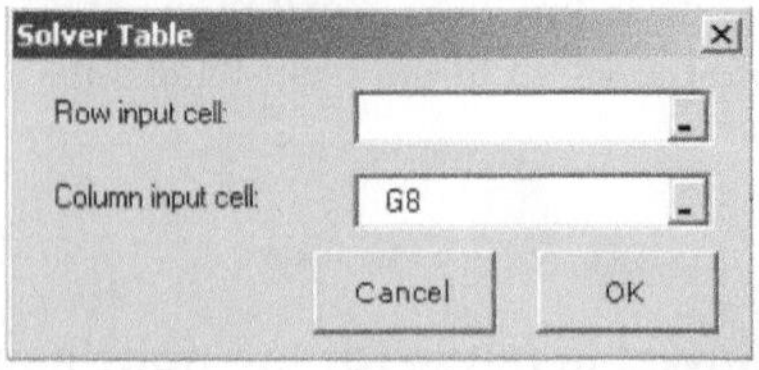

Solver Table

Row input cell:

Column input cell: G8

Cancel   OK

Range Name	Cell
DoorsProduced	C12
TotalProfit	G12
WindowsProduced	D12

Unlike the allowable range for objective function coefficients described in Section 5.3, a change that is within the allowable range for the right-hand side does *not* mean the original solution is still optimal. In fact, any time the shadow price is not zero, a change to a right-hand side leads to a change in the optimal solution. The shadow price indicates how much the value of the objective function will change as the optimal solution changes.

Using the Sensitivity Report to Obtain the Key Information

As illustrated earlier, it is straightforward to use the Solver Table to calculate the *shadow price* for a functional constraint, as well as to find (or at least closely approximate) the *allowable range* for the right-hand side of this constraint over which the shadow price remains valid. However, this same information also can be obtained immediately from Solver's sensitivity report for all the functional constraints. Figure 5.20 shows the full sensitivity report provided by the Solver for the original Wyndor problem after obtaining the optimal solution given in Figure 5.1. The top half is the part already shown in Figure 5.7 for finding allowable ranges for the objective function coefficients. The bottom half focuses on the functional constraints, including providing the shadow prices for these constraints in the fourth column. The first three columns remind us that (1) the output cells for these constraints in Figure 5.1 are cells E7 to E9, (2) these cells give the number of production hours used per week in the three plants, and (3) the final values in these cells are 2, 12, and 18 (as shown in column E of Figure 5.1). (We will discuss the last three columns a little later.)

The shadow price given in the fourth column for each constraint tells us how much the value of the objective function [target cell (G12) in Figure 5.1] would increase if the right-hand side of that constraint (cell G7, G8, or G9) were to be increased by 1. Conversely, it also tells us how much the value of the objective function would *decrease* if the right-hand side were to be decreased by 1. The shadow price for the plant 1 constraint is 0, because this plant already is using less hours (2) than are available (4) so there would be no benefit to making an additional hour available. However, plants 2 and 3 are using all the hours available to them for the two new products (with the product mix given by the changing cells). Thus, it is not surprising that the shadow prices indicate that the target cell would increase if the hours available in either plant 2 or plant 3 were to be increased.

To express this information in the language of management, the value of the objective function for this problem [target cell (G12) in Figure 5.1] represents the *total profit* in dollars per week from the two new products under consideration. The right-hand side of each functional constraint represents the number of hours of production time being made available per week for these products in the plant that corresponds to this constraint. Therefore, the shadow price for a functional constraint informs management as to how much the total profit from the two new products could be increased for each additional hour of production time made available to these products per week in the corresponding plant. Conversely, the shadow price indicates how much this profit would decrease for each reduction of an hour of production time in that plant. This interpretation of the shadow price remains valid as long as the change in the number of hours of production time is not very large.

The shadow prices reveal the relationship between profit and the amount of production time made available in the plants.

FIGURE 5.20
The complete sensitivity report generated by the Excel Solver for the original Wyndor problem as formulated in Figure 5.1.

Variable Cells

Cell	Name	Final Value	Reduced Cost	Objective Coefficient	Allowable Increase	Allowable Decrease
$C$12	DoorsProduced	2	0	300	450	300
$D$12	WindowsProduced	6	0	500	1E+30	300

Constraints

Cell	Name	Final Value	Shadow Price	Constraint R. H. Side	Allowable Increase	Allowable Decrease
$E$7	Plant 1 Used	2	0	4	1E+30	2
$E$8	Plant 2 Used	12	150	12	6	6
$E$9	Plant 3 Used	18	100	18	6	6

Here is how to find the allowable ranges for the right-hand sides from the sensitivity report.

Specifically, this interpretation of the shadow price remains valid as long as the number of hours of production time remains within its *allowable range*. The Solver's sensitivity report provides all the data needed to identify the allowable range of each functional constraint. Refer back to the bottom of this report given in Figure 5.20. The final three columns enable calculation of this range. The "Constraint R. H. Side" column indicates the original value of the right-hand side before any change is made. Adding the number in the "Allowable Increase" column to this original value then gives the upper endpoint of the allowable range. Similarly, subtracting the number in the "Allowable Decrease" column from this original value gives the lower endpoint. Using the fact that 1E+30 represents infinity (∞), these calculations of the allowable ranges are shown below, where a subscript has been added to each RHS to identify the constraint involved.

Plant 1 constraint: $\quad 4 - 2 \leq RHS_1 \leq 4 + \infty, \quad$ so $\quad 2 \leq RHS_1 \quad$ (no upper limit)

Plant 2 constraint: $\quad 12 - 6 \leq RHS_2 \leq 12 + 6, \quad$ so $\quad 6 \leq RHS_2 \leq 18$

Plant 3 constraint: $\quad 18 - 6 \leq RHS_3 \leq 18 + 6, \quad$ so $\quad 12 \leq RHS_3 \leq 24$

In the case of the plant 2 constraint, Figure 5.21 provides graphical insight into why $6 \leq RHS \leq 18$ is the range of validity for the shadow price. The optimal solution for the original problem, $(D, W) = (2, 6)$, lies at the intersection of line B and line C. The equation for line B is $2W = 12$ because this is the constraint boundary line for the plant 2 constraint ($2W \leq 12$). However, if the value of this right-hand side ($RHS_2 = 12$) is changed, line B will either shift upward (for a larger value of RHS_2) or downward (for a smaller value of RHS_2). As line B shifts, the boundary of the feasible region shifts accordingly and the optimal solution continues to lie at the intersection of the shifted line B and line C—provided the shift in line B is not so large that this intersection is no longer feasible. Each time RHS_2 is increased (or decreased) by 1, this intersection shifts enough to increase (or decrease) Profit by the amount of the shadow price ($150). Figure 5.21 indicates that this intersection remains feasible (and so optimal) as RHS_2 increases from 12 to 18, because the feasible region expands upward as line B shifts upward. However, for values of RHS_2 larger than 18, this intersection is no longer feasible

FIGURE 5.21

A graphical interpretation of the allowable range, $6 \leq RHS_2 \leq 18$, for the right-hand side of Wyndor's plant 2 constraint.

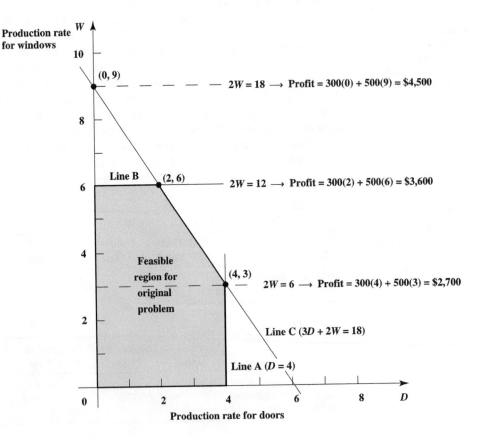

because it gives a negative value of D (the production rate for doors). Thus, each increase of 1 above 18 no longer increases Profit by the amount of the shadow price. Similarly, as RHS_2 decreases from 12 to 6, this intersection remains feasible (and so optimal) as line B shifts down accordingly. However, for values of RHS_2 less than 6, this intersection is no longer feasible because it violates the plant 1 constraint ($D \leq 4$) whose boundary line is line A. Hence, each decrease of 1 below 6 no longer decreases Profit by the amount of the shadow price. Consequently, $6 \leq RHS \leq 18$ is the allowable range over which the shadow price is valid.

Summary

Recall again that the right-hand side of each functional constraint represents the number of hours of production time per week in the corresponding plant that is being made available to the two new products. The *shadow price* for each constraint reveals how much the total profit from these new products would increase for each additional hour of production time made available in the corresponding plant for these products. This interpretation of the shadow price remains valid as long as the number of hours remains within its *allowable range*. Therefore, each shadow price can be applied by management to evaluate a change in its original decision regarding the number of hours as long as the new number is within the corresponding allowable range. This evaluation also would need to take into account how the change in the number of hours made available to the new products would impact the production rates and profits for the company's other products.

Review Questions

1. Why might it be of interest to investigate the effect of making changes in a functional constraint?
2. Why might it be possible to alter the right-hand side of a functional constraint?
3. What is meant by a *shadow price?*
4. How can a shadow price be found by using the spreadsheet? By using the Solver Table? By using Solver's sensitivity report?
5. Why are shadow prices of interest to managers?
6. Can shadow prices be used to determine the effect of *decreasing* rather than increasing the right-hand side of a functional constraint?
7. What does a shadow price of 0 tell a manager?
8. Which columns of the Solver's sensitivity report are used to find the allowable range for the right-hand side of a functional constraint?
9. Why are these allowable ranges of interest to managers?

5.6   THE EFFECT OF SIMULTANEOUS CHANGES IN THE CONSTRAINTS

The preceding section described how to perform what-if analysis to investigate the effect of changes in a single spot of a constraint. We now turn our consideration to the effect of simultaneous changes in the constraints.

The need to consider these simultaneous changes arises frequently. There may be considerable uncertainty about the estimates for a number of the parameters in the functional constraints, so questions will arise as to the effect if the true values of the parameters simultaneously deviate significantly from the estimates. Since the right-hand sides of the constraints often represent managerial policy decisions, questions will arise about what would happen if some of these decisions were to be changed. These decisions frequently are interrelated and so need to be considered simultaneously.

Managerial policy decisions involving right-hand sides frequently are interrelated, so changes in these decisions should be considered simultaneously.

We outline next how the usual three methods for performing what-if analysis can be applied to considering simultaneous changes in the constraints. The third one (using Solver's sensitivity report) is only helpful for changing right-hand sides. For the first two (using the spreadsheet and using the Solver Table), the procedure is the same regardless of whether the changes are in the coefficients on the left-hand sides or in the right-hand sides of the constraints (or both). Since changing the right-hand sides is the more important case, we will focus on this case.

In particular, we now will deal with the last of Wyndor management's what-if questions.

Question 4: What happens if simultaneous changes are made in the number of hours of production time per week being made available to Wyndor's new products in all the plants?

In particular, after seeing that the plant 2 constraint has the largest shadow price (150), versus a shadow price of 100 for the plant 3 constraint, management now is interested in exploring a specific type of simultaneous change in these production hours. By shifting the production of one of the company's current products from plant 2 to plant 3, it is possible to increase the number of production hours available to the new products in plant 2 by decreasing the number of production hours available in plant 3 by the same amount. Management wonders what would happen if these simultaneous changes in production hours were made.

Using the Spreadsheet for This Analysis

According to the shadow prices, the effect of shifting one hour of production time per week from plant 3 to plant 2 would be as follows.

$$RHS_2: \quad 12 \to 13 \qquad \text{Change in total profit} = \quad \text{Shadow price} = \$150$$

$$RHS_3: \quad 18 \to 17 \qquad \text{Change in total profit} = - \text{Shadow price} = -100$$

$$\text{Net increase in total profit} = \quad \$50$$

We now are checking to see whether the shadow prices remain valid for evaluating simultaneous changes in the right-hand sides.

However, we don't know if these shadow prices remain valid if *both* right-hand sides are changed by this amount.

A quick way to check this is to substitute the new right-hand sides into the original spreadsheet in Figure 5.1 and click on the Solve button again. The resulting spreadsheet in Figure 5.22 shows that the net increase in total profit (from \$3,600 to \$3,650) is indeed \$50, so the shadow prices are valid for these particular simultaneous changes in right-hand sides.

How long will these shadow prices remain valid if we continue shifting production hours from plant 3 to plant 2? We could continue checking this by substituting other combinations of right-hand sides into the spreadsheet and re-solving each time. However, a more systematic way of doing this is to use the Solver Table as described below.

Using the Solver Table for This Analysis

Complete instructions for using the Solver Table are given in Appendix A.

Since it can become tedious, or even impractical, to use the spreadsheet to investigate a large number of simultaneous changes in the right-hand sides, let us see how a Solver Table (provided in your MS Courseware) can be used to do this analysis more systematically.

We could use a two-way Solver Table to investigate how the profit and optimal production rates vary for different combinations of the number of hours available in plant 2 and plant 3. However, in this case we aren't interested in *all* combinations of hours in the two plants, but

FIGURE 5.22

The revised Wyndor problem where column G in Figure 5.1 has been changed by shifting one of the hours available in plant 3 to plant 2 and then re-solving.

	A	B	C	D	E	F	G
1		**Wyndor Glass Co. Product-Mix Problem**					
2							
3			Doors	Windows			
4		Unit Profit	\$300	\$500			
5					Hours		Hours
6			Hours Used per Unit Produced		Used		Available
7		Plant 1	1	0	1.33333	≤	4
8		Plant 2	0	2	13	≤	13
9		Plant 3	3	2	17	≤	17
10							
11			Doors	Windows			Total Profit
12		Units Produced	1.333	6.5			\$3,650

rather only those combinations that involve a simple *shifting* of available hours from plant 3 to plant 2. For this analysis, we will see that a one-way Solver Table is sufficient.

For each hour reduced in plant 3, an additional hour is made available in plant 2. Thus, the number of available hours in plant 2 is a function of the number of available hours in plant 3. In particular, since there are 30 total hours available at the two plants ($RHS_2 + RHS_3 = 30$), the number of available hours in plant 2 (RHS_2) is

$$RHS_2 = 30 - RHS_3$$

By entering a formula into one data cell in terms of another one, the one-way Solver Table is able to investigate interrelated trial values in both data cells.

Figure 5.23 shows the Wyndor Glass Co. spreadsheet with the data cell for the number of available hours in plant 2 replaced by the above formula. Because of this formula, whenever the number of available hours in plant 3 is reduced, the number of available hours in plant 2 will automatically increase by the same amount. Now a one-way Solver Table can be used to investigate various numbers of available hours in plant 3 (with the corresponding automatic adjustment made to the available hours at plant 2). The trial values for the number of hours available in plant 3 are shown in the Solver Table at the bottom of the spreadsheet in Figure 5.23 (C20:C26). We are interested in the output cells DoorsProduced (C12), WindowsProduced (D12), and TotalProfit (G12), so equations referring to these cells are entered in the first row of the table (D19:F19). Running the Solver Table (with the column input cell as G9, the hours available in plant 3) then fills in the values in the body of the table (D20:F26). We have calculated the incremental profit (in column G) for each hour shifted from plant 3 to plant 2.

Again there is a pattern to the incremental profit. For each hour shifted from plant 3 to plant 2 (up to 3 hours), an additional profit of $50 is achieved. However, if more than 3 hours are shifted, the incremental profit becomes $-$250. Thus, it appears worthwhile to shift up to 3 available hours from plant 3 to plant 2, but no more.

Although a one-way Solver Table is limited to enumerating trial values for only one data cell, you have just seen how such a Solver Table still can systematically investigate a large number of simultaneous changes in two data cells by entering a formula for the second data cell in terms of the first one. The two data cells considered above happened to be right-hand sides of constraints, but either or both could have been coefficients on the left-hand side instead. It is even possible to enter formulas for multiple data cells in terms of the one whose trial values are being enumerated. Furthermore, by using the two-way Solver Table, trial values can be enumerated simultaneously for two data cells, with the possibility of entering formulas for additional data cells in terms of these two.

Gleaning Additional Information from the Sensitivity Report

Despite the versatility of the Solver Table, it cannot handle a number of important cases. The most important one is where management wants to explore various possibilities for changing its policy decisions that correspond to changing several right-hand sides simultaneously in a variety of ways. Although the spreadsheet can be used to see the effect of any combination of simultaneous changes, it can take an exorbitant amount of time to systematically investigate a large number of simultaneous changes in right-hand sides in this way. Fortunately, Solver's sensitivity report provides valuable information for guiding such an investigation. In particular, there is a *100 percent rule* (analogous to the one presented in Section 5.4) that uses this information to conduct this kind of investigation.

Recall that the 100 percent rule described in Section 5.4 is used to investigate simultaneous changes in *objective function coefficients*. The new 100 percent rule presented next investigates simultaneous changes in *right-hand sides* in a similar way.

The data needed to apply the new 100 percent rule for the Wyndor problem are given by the last three columns in the bottom part of the sensitivity report in Figure 5.20. Keep in mind that we can safely use the entire allowable decrease or increase from the current value of a right-hand side only if none of the other right-hand sides are changed at all. With simultaneous changes in the right-hand sides, we focus for each change on the *percentage* of the allowable decrease or increase that is being used. As detailed next, the 100 percent rule basically says that we can safely make the simultaneous changes only if the *sum* of these percentages does not exceed 100 percent.

FIGURE 5.23

By inserting a formula into cell G8 that keeps the total number of hours available in plant 2 and plant 3 equal to 30, this one-dimensional application of the Solver Table shows the effect of shifting more and more of the hours available from plant 3 to plant 2.

	A	B	C	D	E	F	G	H
1		**Wyndor Glass Co. Product-Mix Problem**						
2								
3			Doors	Windows				
4		Unit Profit	$300	$500				
5					Hours		Hours	
6			Hours Used per Unit Produced		Used		Available	
7		Plant 1	1	0	2	≤	4	Total (Plants 2 & 3)
8		Plant 2	0	2	12	≤	12	30
9		Plant 3	3	2	18	≤	18	
10								
11			Doors	Windows			Total Profit	
12		Units Produced	2	6			$3,600	
13								
14								
15								
16								
17		Time Available in	Time Available in	Optimal Units Produced		Total	Incremental	
18		Plant 2 (hours)	Plant 3 (hours)	Doors	Windows	Profit	Profit	
19				2	6	$3,600		Select these cells (C19:F26), before choosing the Solver Table.
20		12	18	2	6	$3,600		
21		13	17	1.333	6.5	$3,650	$50	
22		14	16	0.667	7	$3,700	$50	
23		15	15	0	7.5	$3,750	$50	
24		16	14	0	7	$3,500	-$250	
25		17	13	0	6.5	$3,250	-$250	
26		18	12	0	6	$3,000	-$250	

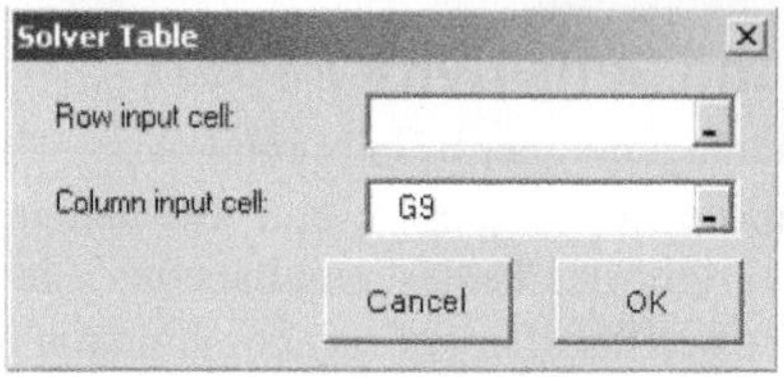

Solver Table

Row input cell: [ ]

Column input cell: [G9]

[Cancel] [OK]

Range Name	Cells
DoorsProduced	C12
TotalProfit	G12
WindowsProduced	D12

	G	H
5	Hours	
6	Available	
7	4	Total (Plants 2 & 3)
8	=H8-G9	30
9	18	

	B	C	D	E	F	G
17	Time Available in	Time Available in	Optimal Units Produced		Total	Incremental
18	Plant 2 (hours)	Plant 3 (hours)	Doors	Windows	Profit	Profit
19			=DoorsProduced	=WindowsProduced	=TotalProfit	
20	=$H$8-C20	18	2	6	$3,600	
21	=$H$8-C21	17	1.333	6.5	$3,650	=F21-F20
22	=$H$8-C22	16	0.667	7	$3,700	=F22-F21
23	=$H$8-C23	15	0	7.5	$3,750	=F23-F22
24	=$H$8-C24	14	0	7	$3,500	=F24-F23
25	=$H$8-C25	13	0	6.5	$3,250	=F25-F24
26	=$H$8-C26	12	0	6	$3,000	=F26-F25

This 100 percent rule reveals whether the simultaneous changes in the right-hand sides are small enough to guarantee that the shadow prices are still valid.

The 100 Percent Rule for Simultaneous Changes in Right-Hand Sides: The shadow prices remain valid for predicting the effect of simultaneously changing the right-hand sides of some of the functional constraints as long as the changes are not too large. To check whether the changes are small enough, calculate for each change the percentage of the allowable change (decrease or increase) for that right-hand side to remain within its allowable range. If the *sum* of the percentage changes does *not* exceed 100 percent, the shadow prices definitely will still be valid. (If the sum *does* exceed 100 percent, then we cannot be sure.)

To illustrate this rule, consider again the simultaneous changes (shifting one hour of production time per week from plant 3 to plant 2) that led to Figure 5.22. The calculations for the 100 percent rule in this case are

RHS_2: $12 \rightarrow 13$

$$\text{Percentage of allowable increase} = 100\left(\frac{13-12}{6}\right) = 16\frac{2}{3}\%$$

RHS_3: $18 \rightarrow 17$

$$\text{Percentage of allowable decrease} = 100\left(\frac{18-17}{6}\right) = 16\frac{2}{3}\%$$

$$\text{Sum} = \overline{33\frac{1}{3}\%}$$

Since the sum of $33\frac{1}{3}$ percent is less than 100 percent, the shadow prices definitely are valid for predicting the effect of these changes, as was illustrated with Figure 5.22.

The fact that $33\frac{1}{3}$ percent is one-third of 100 percent suggests that the changes can be three times as large as above without invalidating the shadow prices. To check this, let us apply the 100 percent rule with these larger changes.

RHS_2: $12 \rightarrow 15$

$$\text{Percentage of allowable increase} = \left(\frac{15-12}{6}\right)\% = 50\%$$

RHS_3: $18 \rightarrow 15$

$$\text{Percentage of allowable decrease} = \left(\frac{18-15}{6}\right)\% = 50\%$$

$$\text{Sum} = \overline{100\%}$$

Because the sum does *not exceed* 100 percent, the shadow prices are still valid, but these are the largest changes in the right-hand sides that can provide this guarantee. In fact, Figure 5.23 demonstrated that the shadow prices become invalid for larger changes.

Review Questions

1. Why might it be of interest to investigate the effect of making simultaneous changes in the functional constraints?
2. How can the spreadsheet be used to investigate simultaneous changes in the functional constraints?
3. What are the capabilities of the Solver Table for investigating simultaneous changes in the functional constraints?
4. Why might a manager be interested in considering simultaneous changes in right-hand sides?
5. What is the 100 percent rule for simultaneous changes in right-hand sides?
6. What are the data needed to apply the 100 percent rule for simultaneous changes in right-hand sides?
7. What is guaranteed if the sum of the percentages of allowable changes in the right-hand sides does not exceed 100 percent?
8. What is the conclusion if the sum of the percentages of allowable changes in the right-hand sides does exceed 100 percent?

5.7 Summary

What-if analysis is analysis done *after* finding an optimal solution for the original version of the basic model. This analysis provides important insights to help guide managerial decision making. This chapter describes how this is done when the basic model is a linear programming model. The spreadsheet for the model, the Solver Table provided in your MS Courseware, and the sensitivity report generated by the Excel Solver all play a central role in this process.

The coefficients in the objective function typically represent quantities that can only be roughly estimated when the model is formulated. Will the optimal solution obtained from the model be the correct one if the true value of one of these coefficients is significantly different from the estimate used in the model? The spreadsheet can be used to quickly check specific changes in the coefficient. The Solver Table enables the systematic investigation of many trial values for this coefficient. For a broader investigation, the *allowable range* for each coefficient identifies the interval within which the true value must lie in order for this solution to still be the correct optimal solution. These ranges are easily calculated from the data in the sensitivity report provided by the Excel Solver.

What happens if there are significant inaccuracies in the estimates of two or more coefficients in the objective function? Specific simultaneous changes can be checked with the spreadsheet. A two-way Solver Table can systematically investigate various simultaneous changes in two coefficients. To go further, the *100 percent rule for simultaneous changes in objective function coefficients* provides a convenient way of checking whole ranges of simultaneous changes, again by using the data in the Solver's sensitivity report.

What-if analysis usually extends to considering the effect of changes in the functional constraints as well. Occasionally, changes in the coefficients of these constraints will be considered because of the uncertainty in their original estimates. More frequently, the changes considered will be in the right-hand sides of the constraints. The right-hand sides frequently represent managerial policy decisions. In such cases, *shadow prices* provide valuable guidance to management about the potential effects of altering these policy decisions. The shadow price for each constraint is easily found by using the spreadsheet, the Solver Table, or the sensitivity report.

Shadow price analysis can be validly applied to investigate possible changes in right-hand sides as long as these changes are not too large. The *allowable range* for each right-hand side indicates just how far it can be changed, assuming no other changes are made. If other changes are made as well, the *100 percent rule for simultaneous changes in right-hand sides* enables checking whether the changes definitely are not too large. The Solver's sensitivity report provides the key information needed to find each allowable range or to apply this 100 percent rule. Both the spreadsheet and the Solver Table also can sometimes be used to help investigate these simultaneous changes.

Glossary

allowable range for an objective function coefficient   The range of values for a particular coefficient in the objective function over which the optimal solution for the original model remains optimal. (Section 5.3), 151

allowable range for the right-hand side   The range of values for the right-hand side of a functional constraint over which this constraint's shadow price remains valid. (Section 5.5), 165

parameters of the model   The parameters of a linear programming model are the constants (coefficients or right-hand sides) in the functional constraints and the objective function. (Section 5.1), 145

sensitive parameter   A parameter is considered sensitive if even a small change in its value can change the optimal solution. (Section 5.1), 145

sensitivity analysis   The part of what-if analysis that focuses on individual parameters of the model. It involves checking how sensitive the optimal solution is to the value of each parameter. (Section 5.1), 146

shadow price   The shadow price for a functional constraint is the rate at which the optimal value of the objective function can be increased by increasing the right-hand side of the constraint by a small amount. (Section 5.5), 165

what-if analysis   Analysis that addresses questions about what would happen to the optimal solution if different assumptions were made about future conditions. (Chapter introduction), 144

Learning Aids for This Chapter in Your MS Courseware

Chapter 5 Excel Files:
Wyndor Example
Profit & Gambit Example

Excel Add-in:
Solver Table

Interactive Management Science Modules:
Module for Graphical Linear Programming and Sensitivity Analysis

Supplement to Chapter 5 on the CD-ROM:
Reduced Costs

Solved Problem (See the CD-ROM or Web site for the Solution)

5.S1. Sensitivity Analysis at Stickley Furniture

Stickley Furniture is a manufacturer of fine hand-crafted furniture. During the next production period, management is considering producing dining room tables, dining room chairs, and/or bookcases. The time required for each item to go through the two stages of production (assembly and finishing), the amount of wood required (fine cherry wood), and the corresponding unit profits are given in the following table, along with the amount of each resource available in the upcoming production period.

	Tables	Chairs	Bookcases	Available
Assembly (minutes)	80	40	50	8,100
Finishing) (minutes)	30	20	30	4,500
Wood (pounds)	80	10	50	9,000
Unit profit	$360	$125	$300	

After formulating a linear programming model to determine the production levels that would maximize profit, the solved model and the corresponding sensitivity report are shown below.

a. Suppose the profit per table increases by $100. Will this change the optimal production quantities? What can be said about the change in total profit?

b. Suppose the profit per chair increases by $100. Will this change the optimal production quantities? What can be said about the change in total profit?

c. Suppose the profit per table increases by $90 and the profit per bookcase decreases by $50. Will this change the optimal production quantities? What can be said about the change in total profit?

d. Suppose a worker in the assembly department calls in sick, so eight fewer hours now are available in the assembly department. How much would this affect total profit? Would it change the optimal production quantities?

e. Explain why the shadow price for the wood constraint is zero.

f. A new worker has been hired who is trained to do both assembly and finishing. She will split her time between the two areas, so there now are four additional hours available in both assembly and finishing. How much would this affect total profit? Would this change the optimal production quantities?

	B	C	D	E	F	G	H
3		Tables	Chairs	Bookcases			
4	Unit Profit	$360	$125	$300			
5							
6		Resources Required per Unit			Used		Available
7	Assembly (minutes)	80	40	50	8,100	<=	8,100
8	Finishing (minutes)	30	20	30	4,500	<=	4,500
9	Woods (pounds)	80	10	50	8,100	<=	9,000
10							
11		Tables	Chairs	Bookcases			Total Profit
12	Production	20	0	130			$46,200

Variable Cells

Cell	Name	Final Value	Reduced Cost	Objective Coefficient	Allowable Increase	Allowable Decrease
$C$12	Production Tables	20	0	360	120	60
$D$12	Production Chairs	0	−88.333	125	88.333	1E+30
$E$12	Production Bookcases	130	0	300	60	75

Constraints

Cell	Name	Final Value	Shadow Price	Constraint R. H. Side	Allowable Increase	Allowable Decrease
$F$7	Assembly (minutes) Used	8,100	2	8,100	900	600
$F$8	Finishing (minutes) Used	4,500	6.67	4,500	360	1,462.5
$F$9	Wood (pounds) Used	8,100	0	9,000	1E+30	900

g. Based on the sensitivity report, is it wise to have the new worker in part *f* split her time equally between assembly and finishing, or would some other plan be better?

h. Use the Solver Table to determine how the optimal production quantities and total profit will change

depending on how the new worker in part *f* allocates her time between assembly and finishing. In particular, assume 0, 1, 2, . . . , or 8 hours are added to assembly, with a corresponding 8, 7, 6, . . . , or 0 hours added to finishing. (The original spreadsheet is contained on the CD included with the textbook.)

Problems

We have inserted the symbol E* to the left of each problem (or its parts) where Excel should be used (unless your instructor gives you contrary instructions). An asterisk on the problem number indicates that at least a partial answer is given in the back of the book.

5.1.*   One of the products of the G. A. Tanner Company is a special kind of toy that provides an estimated unit profit of $3. Because of a large demand for this toy, management would like to increase its production rate from the current level of 1,000 per day. However, a limited supply of two subassemblies (A and B) from vendors makes this difficult. Each toy requires two sub-assemblies of type A, but the vendor providing these subassemblies would only be able to increase its supply rate from the current 2,000 per day to a maximum of 3,000 per day. Each toy requires only one subassembly of type B, but the vendor providing these subassemblies would be unable to increase its supply rate above the current level of 1,000 per day.

Because no other vendors currently are available to provide these subassemblies, management is considering initiating a new production process internally that would simultaneously produce an equal number of subassemblies of the two types to supplement the supply from the two vendors. It is estimated that the company's cost for producing one subassembly of each type would be $2.50 more than the cost of purchasing these subassemblies from the two vendors. Management wants to determine both the production rate of the toy and the production rate of each pair of subassemblies (one A and one B) that would maximize the total profit.

Viewing this problem as a resource-allocation problem, one of the company's managers has organized its data as follows:

	Resource Usage per Unit of Each Activity		
Resource	Produce Toys	Produce Subassemblies	Amount of Resource Available
Subassembly A	2	−1	3,000
Subassembly B	1	−1	1,000
Unit profit	$3	−$2.50	

E*   a. Formulate and solve a spreadsheet model for this problem.

E*   b. Since the stated unit profits for the two activities are only estimates, management wants to know how much each of these estimates can be off before the

optimal solution would change. Begin exploring this question for the first activity (producing toys) by using the spreadsheet and Solver to manually generate a table that gives the optimal solution and total profit as the unit profit for this activity increases in 50¢ increments from $2.00 to $4.00. What conclusion can be drawn about how much the estimate of this unit profit can differ in each direction from its original value of $3.00 before the optimal solution would change?

E*   c. Repeat part *b* for the second activity (producing subassemblies) by generating a table as the unit profit for this activity increases in 50¢ increments from −$3.50 to −$1.50 (with the unit profit for the first activity fixed at $3).

E*   d. Use the Solver Table to systematically generate all the data requested in parts *b* and *c*, except use 25¢ increments instead of 50¢ increments. Use these data to refine your conclusions in parts *b* and *c*.

E*   e. Use Excel's sensitivity report to find the allowable range for the unit profit of each activity.

E*   f. Use a two-way Solver Table to systematically generate the total profit as the unit profits of the two activities are changed simultaneously as described in parts *b* and *c*.

g. Use the information provided by Excel's sensitivity report to describe how far the unit profits of the two activities can change simultaneously before the optimal solution might change.

5.2.   Consider a resource-allocation problem having the following data:

	Resource Usage per Unit of Each Activity		
Resource	1	2	Amount of Resource Available
1	1	2	10
2	1	3	12
Unit profit	$2	$5	

The objective is to determine the number of units of each activity to undertake so as to maximize the total profit.

While doing what-if analysis, you learn that the estimates of the unit profits are accurate only to within ± 50 percent. In other words, the ranges of *likely values* for these unit profits are $1 to $3 for activity 1 and $2.50 to $7.50 for activity 2.

E* a. Formulate a spreadsheet model for this problem based on the original estimates of the unit profits. Then use the Solver to find an optimal solution and to generate the sensitivity report.

E* b. Use the spreadsheet and Solver to check whether this optimal solution remains optimal if the unit profit for activity 1 changes from $2 to $1. From $2 to $3.

E* c. Also check whether the optimal solution remains optimal if the unit profit for activity 1 still is $2 but the unit profit for activity 2 changes from $5 to $2.50. From $5 to $7.50.

E* d. Use the Solver Table to systematically generate the optimal solution and total profit as the unit profit of activity 1 increases in 20¢ increments from $1 to $3 (without changing the unit profit of activity 2). Then do the same as the unit profit of activity 2 increases in 50¢ increments from $2.50 to $7.50 (without changing the unit profit of activity 1). Use these results to estimate the allowable range for the unit profit of each activity.

    e. Use the Graphical Linear Programming and Sensitivity Analysis module in your Interactive Management Science Modules to estimate the allowable range for the unit profit of each activity.

E* f. Use the sensitivity report to find the allowable range for the unit profit of each activity. Then use these ranges to check your results in parts *b–e*.

E* g. Use a two-way Solver Table to systematically generate the optimal solution as the unit profits of the two activities are changed simultaneously as described in part *d*.

    h. Use the Graphical Linear Programming and Sensitivity Analysis module to interpret the results in part *g* graphically.

E*5.3. Consider the Big M Co. problem presented in Section 3.5, including the spreadsheet in Figure 3.10 showing its formulation and optimal solution.

There is some uncertainty about what the unit costs will be for shipping through the various shipping lanes. Therefore, before adopting the optimal solution in Figure 3.10, management wants additional information about the effect of inaccuracies in estimating these unit costs.

Use the Excel Solver to generate the sensitivity report preparatory to addressing the following questions.

    a. Which of the unit shipping costs given in Table 3.9 has the smallest margin for error without invalidating the optimal solution given in Figure 3.10? Where should the greatest effort be placed in estimating the unit shipping costs?

    b. What is the allowable range for each of the unit shipping costs?

    c. How should the allowable range be interpreted to management?

    d. If the estimates change for more than one of the unit shipping costs, how can you use the sensitivity report to determine whether the optimal solution might change?

E*5.4.* Consider the Union Airways problem presented in Section 3.3, including the spreadsheet in Figure 3.5 showing its formulation and optimal solution.

Management is about to begin negotiations on a new contract with the union that represents the company's customer service agents. This might result in some small changes in the daily costs per agent given in Table 3.5 for the various shifts. Several possible changes listed below are being considered separately. In each case, management would like to know whether the change might result in the solution in Figure 3.5 no longer being optimal. Answer this question in parts *a* to *e* by using the spreadsheet and Solver directly. If the optimal solution changes, record the new solution.

    a. The daily cost per agent for shift 2 changes from $160 to $165.

    b. The daily cost per agent for shift 4 changes from $180 to $170.

    c. The changes in parts *a* and *b* both occur.

    d. The daily cost per agent increases by $4 for shifts 2, 4, and 5, but decreases by $4 for shifts 1 and 3.

    e. The daily cost per agent increases by 2 percent for each shift.

    f. Use the Solver to generate the sensitivity report for this problem. Suppose that the above changes are being considered later without having the spreadsheet model immediately available on a computer. Show in each case how the sensitivity report can be used to check whether the original optimal solution must still be optimal.

    g. For each of the five shifts in turn, use the Solver Table to systematically generate the optimal solution and total cost when the only change is that the daily cost per agent on that shift increases in $3 increments from $15 less than the current cost up to $15 more than the current cost.

E*5.5. Consider the Think-Big Development Co. problem presented in Section 3.2, including the spreadsheet in Figure 3.3 showing its formulation and optimal solution. In parts *a–g*, use the spreadsheet and Solver to check whether the optimal solution would change and, if so, what the new optimal solution would be, if the estimates in Table 3.3 of the net present values of the projects were to be changed in each of the following ways. (Consider each part by itself.)

    a. The net present value of project 1 (a high-rise office building) increases by $200,000.

    b. The net present value of project 2 (a hotel) increases by $200,000.

    c. The net present value of project 1 decreases by $5 million.

    d. The net present value of project 3 (a shopping center) decreases by $200,000.

    e. All three changes in parts *b*, *c*, and *d* occur simultaneously.

    f. The net present values of projects 1, 2, and 3 change to $46 million, $69 million, and $49 million, respectively.

g. The net present values of projects 1, 2, and 3 change to $54 million, $84 million, and $60 million, respectively.

h. Use the Solver to generate the sensitivity report for this problem. For each of the preceding parts, suppose that the change occurs later without having the spreadsheet model immediately available on a computer. Show in each case how the sensitivity report can be used to check whether the original optimal solution must still be optimal.

i. For each of the three projects in turn, use the Solver Table to systematically generate the optimal solution and the total net present value when the only change is that the net present value of that project increases in $1 million increments from $5 million less than the current value up to $5 million more than the current value.

5.6. Read the referenced article that fully describes the management science study summarized in the application vignette presented in Section 5.4. Briefly describe how what-if analysis was applied in this study. Then list the various financial and nonfinancial benefits that resulted from this study.

5.7. University Ceramics manufactures plates, mugs, and steins that include the campus name and logo for sale in campus bookstores. The time required for each item to go through the two stages of production (molding and finishing), the material required (clay), and the corresponding unit profits are given in the following table, along with the amount of each resource available in the upcoming production period.

	Plates	Mugs	Steins	Available
Molding (minutes)	4	6	3	2,400
Finishing (minutes)	8	14	12	7,200
Clay (ounces)	5	4	3	3,000
Unit Profit	$3.10	$4.75	$4.00	

A linear programming model has been formulated in a spreadsheet to determine the production levels that would maximize profit. The solved spreadsheet model and corresponding sensitivity report are shown below.

For each of the following parts, answer the question as specifically and completely as is possible without re-solving the problem

	A	B	C	D	E	F	G
1		Plates	Mugs	Steins			
2	Unit Profit	$3.10	$4.75	$4.00			
3							
4		Resource Required per Unit			Used		Available
5	Molding (minutes)	4	6	3	2,400	<=	2,400
6	Finishing (minutes)	8	14	12	7,200	<=	7,200
7	Clay (ounces)	5	4	3	2,700	<=	3,000
8							
9		Plates	Mugs	Steins			Total Profit
10	Production	300	0	400			$2,530

Variable Cells

Cell	Name	Final Value	Reduced Cost	Objective Coefficient	Allowable Increase	Allowable Decrease
$B$10	Production Plates	300	0	3.10	2.23	0.37
$C$10	Production Mugs	0	−0.46	4.75	0.46	
$D$10	Production Steins	400	0	4.00	0.65	1.37

Constraints

Cell	Name	Final Value	Shadow Price	Constraint R. H. Side	Allowable Increase	Allowable Decrease
$E$5	Molding (minutes) Used	2,400	0.22	2400	200	600
$E$6	Finishing (minutes) Used	7,200	0.28	7200	2400	2400
$E$7	Cream (ounces) Used	2,700	0	3000	1E+30	

with the Excel Solver. *Note*: Each part is independent (i.e., any change made in one part does not apply to any other parts).

a. Suppose the profit per plate decreases from $3.10 to $2.80. Will this change the optimal production quantities? What can be said about the change in total profit?

b. Suppose the profit per stein *increases* by $0.30 and the profit per plate *decreases* by $0.25. Will this change the optimal production quantities? What can be said about the change in total profit?

c. Suppose a worker in the molding department calls in sick. Now eight fewer hours are available that day in the molding department. How much would this affect total profit? Would it change the optimal production quantities?

d. Suppose one of the workers in the molding department is also trained to do finishing. Would it be a good idea to have this worker shift some of her time from the molding department to the finishing department? Indicate the rate at which this would increase or decrease total profit per minute shifted. How many minutes can be shifted before this rate might change?

e. The allowable decrease for the mugs' objective coefficient and for the available clay constraint are both missing from the sensitivity report. What numbers should be there? Explain how you were able to deduce each number.

5.8. Ken and Larry, Inc., supplies its ice cream parlors with three flavors of ice cream: chocolate, vanilla, and banana. Due to extremely hot weather and a high demand for its products, the company has run short of its supply of ingredients: milk, sugar,

and cream. Hence, they will not be able to fill all the orders received from their retail outlets, the ice cream parlors. Due to these circumstances, the company has decided to choose the amount of each flavor to produce that will maximize total profit, given the constraints on the supply of the basic ingredients.

The chocolate, vanilla, and banana flavors generate, respectively, $1.00, $0.90, and $0.95 of profit per gallon sold. The company has only 200 gallons of milk, 150 pounds of sugar, and 60 gallons of cream left in its inventory. The linear programming formulation for this problem is shown below in algebraic form.

Let

C = Gallons of chocolate ice cream produced

V = Gallons of vanilla ice cream produced

B = Gallons of banana ice cream produced

Maximize   Profit = $1.00C + 0.90V + 0.95B$

subject to

Milk: $0.45C + 0.50V + 0.40B \le 200$ gallons

Sugar: $0.50C + 0.40V + 0.40B \le 150$ pounds

Cream: $0.10C + 0.15V + 0.20B \le 60$ gallons

and

$$C \ge 0 \quad V \ge 0 \quad B \ge 0$$

This problem was solved using the Excel Solver. The spreadsheet (already solved) and the sensitivity report are shown below. (Note: The numbers in the sensitivity report for the milk constraint are missing on purpose, since you will be asked to fill in these numbers in part *f*.)

For each of the following parts, answer the question as specifically and completely as possible without solving the

	A	B	C	D	E	F	G
1		Chocolate	Vanilla	Banana			
2	Unit Profit	$1.00	$0.90	$0.95			
3							
4	Resource	Resources Used per Gallon Produced			Used		Available
5	Milk	0.45	0.5	0.4	180	≤	200
6	Sugar	0.5	0.4	0.4	150	≤	150
7	Cream	0.1	0.15	0.2	60	≤	60
8							
9		Chocolate	Vanilla	Banana			Total Profit
10	Gallons Produced	0	300	75			$341.25

Variable Cells

Cell	Name	Final Value	Reduced Cost	Objective Coefficient	Allowable Increase	Allowable Decrease
$B$10	Gallons Produced Chocolate	0	−0.0375	1	0.0375	1E+30
$C$10	Gallons Produced Vanilla	300	0	0.9	0.05	0.0125
$D$10	Gallons Produced Banana	75	0	0.95	0.0214	0.05

Constraints

Cell	Name	Final Value	Shadow Price	Constraint R. H. Side	Allowable Increase	Allowable Decrease
$E$5	Milk Used					
$E$6	Sugar Used	150	1.875	150	10	30
$E$7	Cream Used	60	1	60	15	3.75

problem again with the Excel Solver. Note: Each part is independent (i.e., any change made to the model in one part does not apply to any other parts).

    a. What is the optimal solution and total profit?

    b. Suppose the profit per gallon of banana changes to $1.00. Will the optimal solution change and what can be said about the effect on total profit?

    c. Suppose the profit per gallon of banana changes to 92¢. Will the optimal solution change and what can be said about the effect on total profit?

    d. Suppose the company discovers that three gallons of cream have gone sour and so must be thrown out. Will the optimal solution change and what can be said about the effect on total profit?

    e. Suppose the company has the opportunity to buy an additional 15 pounds of sugar at a total cost of $15. Should it do so? Explain.

    f. Fill in all the sensitivity report information for the milk constraint, given just the optimal solution for the problem. Explain how you were able to deduce each number.

5.9.   Colonial Furniture produces hand-crafted colonial style furniture. Plans are now being made for the production of rocking chairs, dining room tables, and/or armoires over the next week. These products go through two stages of production (assembly and finishing). The following table gives the time required for each item to go through these two stages, the amount of wood required (fine cherry wood), and the corresponding unit profits, along with the amount of each resource available next week.

	Rocking Chair	Dining Room Table	Armoire	Available
Assembly (minutes)	100	180	120	3,600
Finishing (minutes)	60	80	80	2,000
Wood (pounds)	30	180	120	4,000
Unit Profit	$240	$720	$600	

    A linear programming model has been formulated in a spreadsheet to determine the production levels that would maximize profit. The solved spreadsheet model and corresponding sensitivity report are shown below.

    For each of the following parts, answer the question as specifically and completely as is possible without re-solving the problem with the Solver. *Note:* Each part is independent (i.e., any change made in one problem part does not apply to any other parts).

    a. Suppose the profit per armoire decreases by $50. Will this change the optimal production

	A	B	C	D	E	F	G
1		Rocking	Dining Room				
2		Chair	Table	Armoire			
3	Unit Profit	$240	$720	$600			
4							
5		Resource Required per Unit			Used		Available
6	Assembly (minutes)	100	180	120	3,600	<=	3,600
7	Finishing (minutes)	60	80	80	2,000	<=	2,000
8	Wood (pounds)	30	180	120	3,600	<=	4,000
9							
10		Rocking	Dining Room				
11		Chair	Table	Armoire			Total Profit
12	Production	0	10	15			$16,200

Variable Cells

Cell	Name	Final Value	Reduced Cost	Objective Coefficient	Allowable Increase	Allowable Decrease
$B$12	Production Chair	0	−230	240	230	1E+30
$C$12	Production Table	10	0	720	180	120
$D$12	Production Armoire	15	0	600	120	120

Constraints

Cell	Name	Final Value	Shadow Price	Constraint R. H. Side	Allowable Increase	Allowable Decrease
$E$6	Assembly (minutes) Used	3,600	2.00	3,600	400	600
$E$7	Finishing (minutes) Used	2,000	4.50	2,000	400	400
$E$8	Wood (pounds) Used	3,600		4,000		

quantities? What can be said about the change in total profit?

b. Suppose the profit per table decreases by $60 and the profit per armoire increases by $90. Will this change the optimal production quantities? What can be said about the change in total profit?

c. Suppose a part-time worker in the assembly department calls in sick, so that now four fewer hours are available that day in the assembly department. How much would this affect total profit? Would it change the optimal production quantities?

d. Suppose one of the workers in the assembly department is also trained to do finishing. Would it be a good idea to have this worker shift some of his time from the assembly department to the finishing department? Indicate the rate at which this would increase or decrease total profit per minute shifted. How many minutes can be shifted before this rate might change?

e. The shadow price and allowable range for the wood constraint are missing from the sensitivity report. What numbers should be there? Explain how you were able to deduce each number.

5.10. David, LaDeana, and Lydia are the sole partners and workers in a company that produces fine clocks. David and LaDeana are each available to work a maximum of 40 hours per week at the company, while Lydia is available to work a maximum of 20 hours per week.

The company makes two different types of clocks: a grandfather clock and a wall clock. To make a clock, David (a mechanical engineer) assembles the inside mechanical parts of the clock while LaDeana (a woodworker) produces the hand-carved wood casings. Lydia is responsible for taking orders and shipping the clocks. The amount of time required for each of these tasks is shown next.

| Task | Time Required | |
	Grandfather Clock	Wall Clock
Assemble clock mechanism	6 hours	4 hours
Carve wood casing	8 hours	4 hours
Shipping	3 hours	3 hours

Each grandfather clock built and shipped yields a profit of $300, while each wall clock yields a profit of $200.

The three partners now want to determine how many clocks of each type should be produced per week to maximize the total profit.

a. Formulate a linear programming model in algebraic form for this problem.

b. Use the Graphical Linear Programming and Sensitivity Analysis module in your Interactive Management Science Modules to solve the model. Then use this module to check if the optimal solution would change if the unit profit for grandfather clocks were changed from $300 to $375 (with no other changes

in the model). Then check if the optimal solution would change if, in addition to this change in the unit profit for grandfather clocks, the estimated unit profit for wall clocks also changed from $200 to $175.

E* c. Formulate and solve the original version of this model on a spreadsheet.

E* d. Use the Excel Solver to check the effect of the changes specified in part b.

E* e. Use the Solver Table to systematically generate the optimal solution and total profit as the unit profit for grandfather clocks is increased in $20 increments from $150 to $450 (with no change in the unit profit for wall clocks). Then do the same as the unit profit for wall clocks is increased in $20 increments from $50 to $350 (with no change in the unit profit for grandfather clocks). Use this information to estimate the allowable range for the unit profit of each type of clock.

E* f. Use a two-way Solver Table to systematically generate the optimal solution (similar to Figure 5.13) as the unit profits for the two types of clocks are changed simultaneously as specified in part e, except use $50 increments instead of $20 increments.

E* g. For each of the three partners in turn, use the Excel Solver to determine the effect on the optimal solution and the total profit if that partner alone were to increase his or her maximum number of work hours available per week by 5 hours.

E* h. Use the Solver Table to systematically generate the optimal solution and the total profit when the only change is that David's maximum number of hours available to work per week changes to each of the following values: 35, 37, 39, 41, 43, 45. Then do the same when the only change is that LaDeana's maximum number of hours available to work per week changes in the same way. Then do the same when the only change is that Lydia's maximum number of hours available to work per week changes to each of the following values: 15, 17, 19, 21, 23, 25.

E* i. Generate the Excel sensitivity report and use it to determine the allowable range for the unit profit for each type of clock and the allowable range for the maximum number of hours each partner is available to work per week.

j. To increase the total profit, the three partners have agreed that one of them will slightly increase the maximum number of hours available to work per week. The choice of which one will be based on which one would increase the total profit the most. Use the sensitivity report to make this choice. (Assume no change in the original estimates of the unit profits.)

k. Explain why one of the shadow prices is equal to zero.

l. Can the shadow prices in the sensitivity report be validly used to determine the effect if Lydia were to change her maximum number of hours available to work per week from 20 to 25? If so, what would be the increase in the total profit?

m. Repeat part *l* if, in addition to the change for Lydia, David also were to change his maximum number of hours available to work per week from 40 to 35.

n. Use graphical analysis to verify your answer in part *m.*

E*5.11.* Reconsider Problem 5.1. After further negotiations with each vendor, management of the G.A. Tanner Company has learned that either of them would be willing to consider increasing their supply of their respective subassemblies over the previously stated maxima (3,000 subassemblies of type A per day and 1,000 of type B per day) if the company would pay a small premium over the regular price for the extra subassemblies. The size of the premium for each type of subassembly remains to be negotiated. The demand for the toy being produced is sufficiently high that 2,500 per day could be sold if the supply of subassemblies could be increased enough to support this production rate. Assume that the original estimates of unit profits given in Problem 5.1 are accurate.

a. Formulate and solve a spreadsheet model for this problem with the original maximum supply levels and the additional constraint that no more than 2,500 toys should be produced per day.

b. Without considering the premium, use the spreadsheet and Solver to determine the shadow price for the subassembly A constraint by solving the model again after increasing the maximum supply by one. Use this shadow price to determine the maximum premium that the company should be willing to pay for each subassembly of this type.

c. Repeat part *b* for the subassembly B constraint.

d. Estimate how much the maximum supply of subassemblies of type A could be increased before the shadow price (and the corresponding premium) found in part *b* would no longer be valid by using the Solver Table to generate the optimal solution and total profit (excluding the premium) as the maximum supply increases in increments of 100 from 3,000 to 4,000.

e. Repeat part *d* for subassemblies of type B by using the Solver Table as the maximum supply increases in increments of 100 from 1,000 to 2,000.

f. Use the Solver's sensitivity report to determine the shadow price for each of the subassembly constraints and the allowable range for the right-hand side of each of these constraints.

E*5.12. Reconsider the model given in Problem 5.2. While doing what-if analysis, you learn that the estimates of the right-hand sides of the two functional constraints are accurate only to within ± 50 percent. In other words, the ranges of *likely values* for these parameters are 5 to 15 for the first right-hand side and 6 to 18 for the second right-hand side.

a. After solving the original spreadsheet model, determine the shadow price for the first functional constraint by increasing its right-hand side by one and solving again.

b. Use the Solver Table to generate the optimal solution and total profit as the right-hand side of the first functional constraint is incremented by 1 from 5 to 15. Use this table to estimate the allowable range for this right-hand side, that is, the range over which the shadow price obtained in part *a* is valid.

c. Repeat part *a* for the second functional constraint.

d. Repeat part *b* for the second functional constraint where its right-hand side is incremented by 1 from 6 to 18.

e. Use the Solver's sensitivity report to determine the shadow price for each functional constraint and the allowable range for the right-hand side of each of these constraints.

5.13. Consider a resource-allocation problem having the following data:

	Resource Usage per Unit of Each Activity		
Resource	1	2	Amount of Resource Available
1	1	3	8
2	1	1	4
Unit profit	$1	$2	

The objective is to determine the number of units of each activity to undertake so as to maximize the total profit.

a. Use the graphical method to solve this model.

b. Use graphical analysis to determine the shadow price for each of these resources by solving again after increasing the amount of the resource available by one.

E* *c.* Use the spreadsheet model and the Solver instead to do parts *a* and *b*.

E* *d.* For each resource in turn, use the Solver Table to systematically generate the optimal solution and the total profit when the only change is that the amount of that resource available increases in increments of 1 from 4 less than the original value up to 6 more than the original value. Use these results to estimate the allowable range for the amount available for each resource.

E* *e.* Use the Solver's sensitivity report to obtain the shadow prices. Also use this report to find the range for the amount of each resource available over which the corresponding shadow price remains valid.

f. Describe why these shadow prices are useful when management has the flexibility to change the amounts of the resources being made available.

5.14. Follow the instructions of Problem 5.13 for a resource-allocation problem that again has the objective of maximizing total profit and that has the following data:

Resource	Resource Usage per Unit of Each Activity		Amount of Resource Available
	1	2	
1	1	0	4
2	1	3	15
3	2	1	10
Unit profit	$3	$2	

E*5.15.* Consider the Super Grain Corp. case study as presented in Section 3.1, including the spreadsheet in Figure 3.1 showing its formulation and optimal solution. Use the Excel Solver to generate the sensitivity report. Then use this report to independently address each of the following questions.

    a. How much could the total expected number of exposures be increased for each additional $1,000 added to the advertising budget?

    b. Your answer in part *a* would remain valid for how large of an increase in the advertising budget?

    c. How much could the total expected number of exposures be increased for each additional $1,000 added to the planning budget?

    d. Your answer in part *c* would remain valid for how large of an increase in the planning budget?

    e. Would your answers in parts *a* and *c* definitely remain valid if *both* the advertising budget and planning budget were increased by $100,000 each?

    f. If only $100,000 can be added to *either* the advertising budget or the planning budget, where should it be added to do the most good?

    g. If $100,000 must be *removed* from either the advertising budget or the planning budget, from which budget should it be removed to do the least harm?

E*5.16.* Follow the instructions of Problem 5.15 for the continuation of the Super Grain Corp. case study as presented in Section 3.4 including the spreadsheet in Figure 3.7 showing its formulation and optimal solution.

E*5.17.* Consider the Union Airways problem presented in Section 3.3, including the spreadsheet in Figure 3.5 showing its formulation and optimal solution.

    Management now is considering increasing the level of service provided to customers by increasing one or more of the numbers in the rightmost column of Table 3.5 for the minimum number of agents needed in the various time periods. To guide them in making this decision, they would like to know what impact this change would have on total cost.

    Use the Excel Solver to generate the sensitivity report in preparation for addressing the following questions.

    a. Which of the numbers in the rightmost column of Table 3.5 can be increased without increasing total cost? In each case, indicate how much it can be increased (if it is the only one being changed) without increasing total cost.

    b. For each of the other numbers, how much would the total cost increase per increase of 1 in the number? For each answer, indicate how much the number can be increased (if it is the only one being changed) before the answer is no longer valid.

    c. Do your answers in part *b* definitely remain valid if all the numbers considered in part *b* are simultaneously increased by 1?

    d. Do your answers in part *b* definitely remain valid if all 10 numbers are simultaneously increased by 1?

    e. How far can all 10 numbers be simultaneously increased by the same amount before your answers in part *b* may no longer be valid?

Partial Answers to Selected Problems

CHAPTER 5

    5.1.   *e.* Allowable range for unit profit from producing toys: $2.50 to $5.00.

                Allowable range for unit profit from producing subassemblies: −$3.00 to −$1.50.

5.4. *f.* (*Part a*)

Optimal solution does not change (within allowable increase of $10).

(*Part b*)

Optimal solution does change (outside of allowable decrease of $5).

(*Part c*)

By the 100% rule for simultaneous changes in the objective function, the optimal solution may or may not change.

C_{8AM}: $160 → $165   % of allowable increase = $100 \left(\dfrac{165 - 160}{10} \right) = 50\%$

C_{4PM}: $180 → $170   % of allowable decrease = $100 \left(\dfrac{180 - 170}{5} \right) = \underline{200\%}$

$\text{Sum} = 250\%$

5.11. *a.* Produce 2,000 toys and 1,000 sets of subassemblies. Profit = $3,500.

b. The shadow price for subassembly A is $0.50, which is the maximum premium that the company should be willing to pay.

5.15. *a.* The total expected number of exposures could be increased by 3,000 for each additional $1,000 added to the advertising budget.

b. This remains valid for increases of up to $250,000.

e. By the 100% rule for simultaneous changes in right-hand sides, the shadow prices are still valid. Using units of thousands of dollars,

C_A: $4,000 → $4,100   % of allowable increase = $100 \left(\dfrac{4,100 - 4,000}{250} \right) = 40\%$

C_P: $1,000 → $1,100   % of allowable increase = $100 \left(\dfrac{1,100 - 1,000}{450} \right) = \underline{22\%}$

$\text{Sum} = 62\%$

5.S1 Sensitivity Analysis at Stickley Furniture

Stickley Furniture is a manufacturer of fine hand-crafted furniture. During the next production period, management is considering producing dining room tables, dining room chairs, and/or bookcases. The time required for each item to go through the two stages of production (assembly and finishing), the amount of wood required (fine cherry wood), and the corresponding unit profits are given in the following table, along with the amount of each resource available in the upcoming production period.

	Tables	Chairs	Bookcases	Available
Assembly (minutes)	80	40	50	8100
Finishing (minutes)	30	20	30	4500
Wood (pounds)	80	10	50	9000
Unit Profit	$360	$125	$300	

After formulating a linear programming model to determine the production levels that would maximize profit, the solved model and the corresponding sensitivity report are shown below.

	B	C	D	E	F	G	H
3		Tables	Chairs	Bookcases			
4	Unit Profit	$360	$125	$300			
5							
6		Resource Required per Unit			Used		Available
7	Assembly (minutes)	80	40	50	8,100	<=	8,100
8	Finishing (minutes)	30	20	30	4,500	<=	4,500
9	Wood (pounds)	80	10	50	8,100	<=	9,000
10							
11		Tables	Chairs	Bookcases			Total Profit
12	Production	20	0	130			$46,200

	A	B	C	D	E	F	G	H
6		Variable Cells						
7				Final	Reduced	Objective	Allowable	Allowable
8		Cell	Name	Value	Cost	Coefficient	Increase	Decrease
9		$C$12	Production Tables	20	0	360	120	60
10		$D$12	Production Chairs	0	-88.333	125	88.333	1E+30
11		$E$12	Production Bookcases	130	0	300	60	75
12								
13		Constraints						
14				Final	Shadow	Constraint	Allowable	Allowable
15		Cell	Name	Value	Price	R.H. Side	Increase	Decrease
16		$F$7	Assembly (minutes) Used	8,100	2	8100	900	600
17		$F$8	Finishing (minutes) Used	4,500	6.67	4500	360	1462.5
18		$F$9	Wood (pounds) Used	8,100	0	9000	1E+30	900

a. *Suppose the profit per table increases by $100. Will this change the optimal production quantities? What can be said about the change in total profit?*

No. The increase of $100 is less than the allowable increase for the profit per table of $120. Therefore, the optimal production quantities will stay the same. The total profit will increase by $100 per table produced, or (20)($100) = $2000, to a total profit of $48,200.

b. *Suppose the profit per chair increases by $100. Will this change the optimal production quantities? What can be said about the change in total profit?*

Yes. The increase of $100 is more than the allowable increase for the profit per chair of $88.33. Therefore, the optimal production quantities will change. The total profit will likely increase, but the amount it will increase cannot be determined without re-solving.

c. *Suppose the profit per table increases by $90 and the profit per bookcase decreases by $50. Will this change the optimal production quantities? What can be said about the change in total profit?*

$90 is 90/120 = 75% of the allowable increase for tables. $50 is 50/75 = 66.7% of the allowable decrease for bookcases. 75% + 66.7% > 100%. Therefore, the optimal solution may or may not change. We can't determine the new profit without re-solving.

d. *Suppose a worker in the assembly department calls in sick, so eight fewer hours now are available in the assembly department. How much would this affect total profit? Would it change the optimal production quantities?*

The decrease of 8 hours = 480 minutes is within the allowable decrease for assembly of 600 minutes. Therefore the shadow price of $2 is valid. The change in profit is equal to the shadow price times the change in the right-hand-side or ($2)(–480 minutes) = –$960. Therefore, the total profit decreases by $960 to $45,240. The current optimal solution used all of the available assembly time, so the production quantities must change with the decrease in available assembly time.

e. *Explain why the shadow price for the wood constraint is zero.*

The current optimal solution uses only 8,100 out of the available 9,000 pounds of wood. Therefore, there are 900 pounds of slack in this constraint. Adding more wood or taking a small amount of wood away will not change the optimal solution or the total profit because the current optimal solution isn't using all of the wood anyway.

f. *A new worker has been hired who is trained to do both assembly and finishing. She will split her time between the two areas, so there now are four additional hours available in both assembly and finishing. How much would this affect total profit? Would this change the optimal production quantities?*

4 hours = 240 minutes is 240/900 = 26.7% of the allowable increase for assembly time. 4 hours = 240 minutes is 240/360 = 66.7% of the allowable increase for finishing. 26.7% + 66.7% < 100%, so the 100% rule says that both shadow prices are valid. The increase in profit is therefore

Change in Profit = (Shadow Price)(Change in Right-Hand-Side)
= ($2)(240) + ($6.67)(240)
= $480 + $1,600
= $2,080.

Therefore, profit will increase by $2,080 to $48,280. The optimal production quantities will change to take advantage of the extra hours and this increased profit.

g. *Based on the sensitivity report, is it wise to have the new worker in part f split her time equally between assembly and finishing, or would some other plan be better?*

The shadow price is higher for finishing than assembly. Thus, the profit will increase if more hours are devoted to finishing rather than assembly. However, after 360 minutes (6 hours) are added to assembly, the allowable increase is exceeded and the shadow price will change. Depending on what the shadow price changes to, it would either be advisable to devote all 8 hours to assembly (if the new shadow price is still greater than $2), or devote 6 hours to assembly and 2 hours to finishing (if the new shadow price is less than $2).

h. *Use the Solver Table to determine how the optimal production quantities and total profit will change depending on how the new worker in part f allocates her time between assembly and finishing. In particular, assume 0, 1, 2, ..., or 8 hours are added to assembly, with a corresponding 8, 7, 6, ..., or 0 hours added to finishing. (The original spreadsheet is contained on the CD included with the textbook.)*

The original spreadsheet needs to be modified to account for the extra minutes available in assembly and finishing. The extra minutes for assembly are put into a data cell in J7. The extra minutes left over for finishing are then calculated in J8. These extra minutes are accounted for in the total available minutes in H7:H8.

Next, a Solver Table is run. The different trial values for the extra minutes for assembly are listed in the first column of the table (B18:B26). In the first row of the table (C17:G17), write an equation referring to the output cells and changing cells of interest (the extra finishing minutes from J8, the changing cells in C12, D12, and E12, and the total profit in H12). Next select the entire table and choose Solver Table from the Add-Ins tab (for Excel 2007) or the Tools menu (for earlier versions of Excel). J7 is chosen as the column input cell. The Solver Table is then generated automatically.

From the Solver Table, the highest profit is achieved when 1 hour is allocated to assembly and 7 hours to finishing. A little trial and error reveals that the highest profit is achieved with 75 minutes allocated to assembly and 405 minutes allocated to finishing.

	B	C	D	E	F	G	H	I	J
2									Total Extra
3		Tables	Chairs	Bookcases					480
4	Unit Profit	$360	$125	$300			Total	Original	Extra
5					Used		Available	Available	Available
6		Resource Required per Unit							
7	Assembly (minutes)	80	40	50	8,175	<=	8,175	8,100	75
8	Finishing (minutes)	30	20	30	4,905	<=	4,905	4,500	405
9	Wood (pounds)	80	10	50	8,175	<=	9,000	9,000	
10									
11		Tables	Chairs	Bookcases			Total Profit		
12	Production	0	0	163.5			$49,050		
13									
14									
15	Extra to	Extra to							
16	Assembly	Finishing	Tables	Chairs	Bookcases	Total Profit			
17		405	0	0	163.5	$49,050			
18	0	480	0	0	162	$48,600			
19	60	420	0	0	163.2	$48,960			
20	120	360	4	0	158	$48,840			
21	180	300	9.33333333	0	150.66667	$48,560			
22	240	240	14.6666667	0	143.33333	$48,280			
23	300	180	20	0	136	$48,000			
24	360	120	25.3333333	0	128.66667	$47,720			
25	420	60	30.6666667	0	121.33333	$47,440			
26	480	0	36	0	114	$47,160			

	C	D	E	F	G
15	Extra to				
16	Finishing	Tables	Chairs	Bookcases	Total Profit
17	=J8	=C12	=D12	=E12	=H12

	H	I	J
2			Total Extra
3			480
4			
5	Total	Original	Extra
6	Available	Available	Available
7	=I7+J7	8100	0
8	=I8+J8	4500	=J3-J7
9	=I9	9000	

Network Optimization Problems

Learning objectives

After completing this chapter, you should be able to

1. Formulate network models for various types of network optimization problems.
2. Describe the characteristics of minimum-cost flow problems, maximum flow problems, and shortest path problems.
3. Identify some areas of application for these types of problems.
4. Identify several categories of network optimization problems that are special types of minimum-cost flow problems.
5. Formulate and solve a spreadsheet model for a minimum-cost flow problem, a maximum flow problem, or a shortest path problem from a description of the problem.

Networks arise in numerous settings and in a variety of guises. Transportation, electrical, and communication networks pervade our daily lives. Network representations also are widely used for problems in such diverse areas as production, distribution, project planning, facilities location, resource management, and financial planning—to name just a few examples. In fact, a network representation provides such a powerful visual and conceptual aid for portraying the relationships between the components of systems that it is used in virtually every field of scientific, social, and economic endeavor.

One of the most exciting developments in management science in recent years has been the unusually rapid advance in both the methodology and application of network optimization problems. A number of algorithmic breakthroughs have had a major impact, as have ideas from computer science concerning data structures and efficient data manipulation. Consequently, algorithms and software now are available and are being used to solve huge problems on a routine basis that would have been completely intractable a few decades ago.

This chapter presents the network optimization problems that have been particularly helpful in dealing with managerial issues. We focus on the nature of these problems and their applications rather than on the technical details and the algorithms used to solve the problems.

You already have seen some examples of network optimization problems in Chapter 3. In particular, transportation problems (described in Section 3.5) have a network representation, as illustrated in Figure 3.9, and assignment problems (Section 3.6) have a similar network representation (as described in Chapter 15 on the CD-ROM). Therefore, both transportation problems and assignment problems are simple types of network optimization problems.

Like transportation problems and assignment problems, many other network optimization problems (including all the types considered in this chapter) also are special types of *linear programming* problems. Consequently, after formulating a spreadsheet model for these problems, they can be readily solved by the Excel Solver.

Section 6.1 discusses an especially important type of network optimization problem called a *minimum-cost flow problem*. A typical application involves minimizing the cost of shipping goods through a distribution network.

Section 6.3 presents *maximum flow problems,* which are concerned with such issues as how to maximize the flow of goods through a distribution network. Section 6.2 lays the groundwork by introducing a case study of a maximum flow problem.

Section 6.4 considers *shortest path problems.* In their simplest form, the objective is to find the shortest route between two locations.

A supplement to this chapter on the CD-ROM discusses *minimum spanning-tree problems,* which are concerned with minimizing the cost of providing connections between all users of a system. This is the only network optimization problem considered in this book that is not, in fact, a special type of linear programming problem.

6.1 MINIMUM-COST FLOW PROBLEMS

Before describing the general characteristics of minimum-cost flow problems, let us first look at a typical example.

An Example: The Distribution Unlimited Co. Problem

The **Distribution Unlimited Co.** has two factories producing a product that needs to be shipped to two warehouses. Here are some details.

Factory 1 is producing 80 units.

Factory 2 is producing 70 units.

Warehouse 1 needs 60 units.

Warehouse 2 needs 90 units.

(Each unit corresponds to a full truckload of the product.)

Figure 6.1 shows the distribution network available for shipping this product, where F1 and F2 are the two factories, W1 and W2 are the two warehouses, and DC is a distribution center. The arrows show feasible shipping lanes. In particular, there is a rail link from factory 1 to warehouse 1 and another from factory 2 to warehouse 2. (Any amounts can be shipped along these rail links.) In addition, independent truckers are available to ship up to 50 units from each factory to the distribution center, and then to ship up to 50 units from the distribution center to each warehouse. (Whatever is shipped to the distribution center must subsequently be shipped on to the warehouses.) Management's objective is to determine the shipping plan (how many units to ship along each shipping lane) that will minimize the total shipping cost.

The objective is to minimize the total shipping cost through the distribution network.

The shipping costs differ considerably among these shipping lanes. The cost per unit shipped through each lane is shown above the corresponding arrow in the *network* in Figure 6.2.

To make the network less crowded, the problem usually is presented even more compactly, as shown in Figure 6.3. The number in square brackets next to the location of each facility

FIGURE 6.1

The distribution network for the Distribution Unlimited Co. problem, where each feasible shipping lane is represented by an arrow.

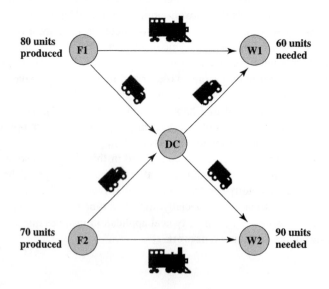

FIGURE 6.2

The data for the distribution network for the Distribution Unlimited Co. problem.

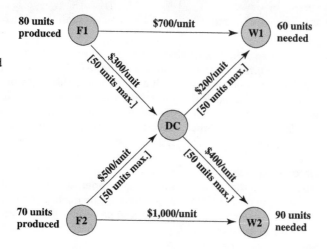

indicates the net number of units (outflow minus inflow) generated there. Thus, the number of units terminating at each warehouse is shown as a negative number. The number at the distribution center is 0 since the number of units leaving *minus* the number of units arriving must equal 0. The number on top of each arrow shows the unit shipping cost along that shipping lane. Any number in square brackets underneath an arrow gives the maximum number of units that can be shipped along that shipping lane. (The absence of a number in square brackets underneath an arrow implies that there is no limit on the shipping amount there.) This network provides a complete representation of the problem, including all the necessary data, so it constitutes a *network model* for this minimum-cost flow problem.

Figure 6.3 illustrates how a minimum-cost flow problem can be completely depicted by a network.

Since this is such a tiny problem, you probably can see what the optimal solution must be. (Try it.) This solution is shown in Figure 6.4, where the shipping amount along each shipping lane is given in parentheses. (To avoid confusion, we delete the unit shipping costs and shipping capacities in this figure.) Combining these shipping amounts with the unit shipping costs given in Figures 6.2 and 6.3, the total shipping cost for this solution (when starting by listing the costs from F1, then from F2, and then from DC) is

$$\text{Total shipping cost} = 30(\$700) + 50(\$300) + 30(\$500) + 40(\$1,000)$$
$$+ 30(\$200) + 50(\$400)$$
$$= \$117,000$$

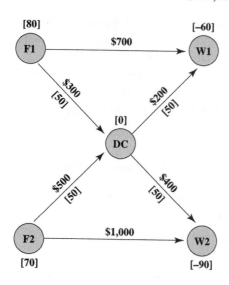

FIGURE 6.3

A network model for the Distribution Unlimited Co. problem as a minimum-cost flow problem.

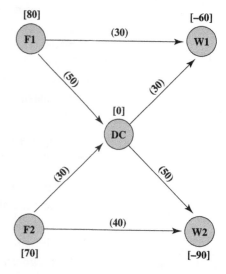

FIGURE 6.4

The optimal solution for the Distribution Unlimited Co. problem, where the shipping amounts are shown in parentheses over the arrows.

An Application Vignette

An especially challenging problem encountered daily by any major airline company is how to compensate effectively for disruptions in the airline's flight schedules. Bad weather can disrupt flight arrivals and departures. So can mechanical problems. Each delay or cancellation involving a particular airplane can then cause subsequent delays or cancellations because that airplane is not available on time for its next scheduled flights.

An airline has two primary ways of compensating for delays or cancellations. One is to swap aircraft so that an airplane scheduled for a later flight can take the place of the delayed or canceled airplane. The other is to use a spare airplane (often after flying it in) to replace the delayed or canceled airplane. However, it is a real challenge to quickly make good decisions of these types when a considerable number of delays or cancellations occur throughout the day.

United Airlines has led the way in applying management science to this problem. This is done by formulating and solving the problem as a *minimum-cost flow problem* where each node in the network represents an airport and each arc represents the route of a flight. The objective of the model then is to keep the airplanes flowing through the network in a way that minimizes the cost incurred by having delays or cancellations. When a status monitor subsystem alerts an operations controller of impending delays or cancellations, the controller provides the necessary input into the model and then solves it in order to provide the updated operating plan in a matter of minutes. This application of the minimum-cost flow problem has resulted in *reducing passenger delays by about 50 percent.*

Source: A. Rakshit, N. Krishnamurthy, and G. Yu, "System Operations Advisor: A Real-Time Decision Support System for Managing Airline Operations at United Airlines," *Interfaces* 26, no. 2 (March–April 1996), pp. 50–58. (A link to this article is provided on our Web site, **www.mhhe.com/hillier4e.**)

General Characteristics

This example possesses all the general characteristics of any minimum-cost flow problem. Before summarizing these characteristics, here is the terminology you will need.

Terminology

1. The model for any minimum-cost flow problem is represented by a *network* with flow passing through it.
2. The circles in the network are called **nodes.**

A supply node has net flow going out whereas a demand node has net flow coming in.

3. Each node where the net amount of flow generated (outflow minus inflow) is a fixed *positive* number is a **supply node.** (Thus, F1 and F2 are the supply nodes in Figure 6.3.)
4. Each node where the net amount of flow generated is a fixed *negative* number is a **demand node.** (Consequently, W1 and W2 are the demand nodes in the example.)
5. Any node where the net amount of flow generated is fixed at *zero* is a **transshipment node.** (Thus, DC is the transshipment node in the example.) Having the amount of flow out of the node equal the amount of flow into the node is referred to as **conservation of flow.**
6. The arrows in the network are called **arcs.**
7. The maximum amount of flow allowed through an arc is referred to as the **capacity** of that arc.

Using this terminology, the general characteristics of minimum-cost flow problems (the model for this type of problem) can be described in terms of the following assumptions.

Assumptions of a Minimum-Cost Flow Problem

1. *At least one* of the nodes is a *supply node.*
2. *At least one* of the other nodes is a *demand node.*
3. All the remaining nodes are *transshipment nodes.*

Since the arrowhead on an arc indicates the direction in which flow is allowed, a pair of arcs pointing in opposite directions is used if flow can occur in both directions.

4. Flow through an arc is only allowed in the direction indicated by the arrowhead, where the maximum amount of flow is given by the *capacity* of that arc. (If flow can occur in both directions, this would be represented by a pair of arcs pointing in opposite directions.)
5. The network has enough arcs with sufficient capacity to enable all the flow generated at the *supply nodes* to reach all the *demand nodes.*

6. The cost of the flow through each arc is *proportional* to the amount of that flow, where the cost per unit flow is known.

7. The objective is to minimize the total cost of sending the available supply through the network to satisfy the given demand. (An alternative objective is to maximize the total profit from doing this.)

The objective is to minimize the total cost of supplying the demand nodes.

A *solution* for this kind of problem needs to specify how much flow is going through each arc. To be a *feasible* solution, the amount of flow through each arc cannot exceed the capacity of that arc and the net amount of flow generated at each node must equal the specified amount for that node. The following property indicates when the problem will have feasible solutions.

The Feasible Solutions Property: Under the above assumptions, a minimum-cost flow problem will have feasible solutions if and only if the sum of the supplies from its supply nodes *equals* the sum of the demands at its demand nodes.

Note that this property holds for the Distribution Unlimited Co. problem, because the sum of its supplies is $80 + 70 = 150$ and the sum of its demands is $60 + 90 = 150$.

For many applications of minimum-cost flow problems, management desires a solution with *integer* values for all the flow quantities (e.g., integer numbers of *full* truckloads along each shipping lane). The model does not include any constraints that require this for feasible solutions. Fortunately, such constraints are not needed because of the following property.

Integer Solutions Property: As long as all its supplies, demands, and arc capacities have integer values, any minimum-cost flow problem with feasible solutions is guaranteed to have an optimal solution with integer values for all its flow quantities.

See in Figures 6.2 and 6.4 that this property holds for the Distribution Unlimited Co. problem. All the supplies (80 and 70), demands (60 and 90), and arc capacities (50) have integer values. Therefore, all the flow quantities in the optimal solution given in Figure 6.4 (30 three times, 50 two times, and 40) have integer values. This ensures that only full truckloads will be shipped into and out of the distribution center. (Remember that each unit corresponds to a full truckload of the product.)

Now let us see how to obtain an optimal solution for the Distribution Unlimited Co. problem by formulating a spreadsheet model and then applying the Excel Solver.

Using Excel to Formulate and Solve Minimum-Cost Flow Problems

Figure 6.5 shows a spreadsheet model that is based directly on the network representation of the problem in Figure 6.3. The arcs are listed in columns B and C, along with their capacities (unless unlimited) in column F and their costs per unit flow in column G. The changing cells Ship (D4:D9) show the flow amounts through these arcs and the target cell TotalCost (D11) provides the total cost of this flow by using the equation

$$D11 = \text{SUMPRODUCT(Ship,UnitCost)}$$

The first set of constraints in the Solver Parameters box, D5:D8 ≤ Capacity (F5:F8), ensures that the arc capacities are not exceeded.

Capacity constraints like these are needed in any minimum-cost flow problem that has any arcs with limited capacity.

Similarly, Column I lists the nodes, column J calculates the actual net flow generated at each node (given the flows in the changing cells), and column L specifies the net amount of flow that needs to be generated at each node. Thus, the second set of constraints in the Solver Parameters box is NetFlow (J4:J8) = SupplyDemand (L4:L8), requiring that the actual net amount of flow generated at each node must equal the specified amount.

Any minimum-cost flow problem needs net flow constraints like this for every node.

The equations entered into NetFlow (J4:J8) use the difference of two SUMIF functions to calculate the net flow (outflow minus inflow) generated at each node. In each case, the first SUMIF function calculates the flow leaving the node and the second one calculates the flow entering the node. For example, consider the F1 node (I4). SUMIF(From,I4,Ship) sums each individual entry in Ship (D4:D9) if that entry is in a row where the entry in From (B4:B9) is the same as in I4. Since I4 = F1 and the only rows that have F1 in the From column are rows 4 and 5, the sum in the Ship column is only over these same rows, so this sum is D4 + D5. Similarly, SUMIF(To,I4,Ship) sums each individual entry in Ship (D4:D9) if that entry is in a

Excel Tip: SUMIF(A, B, C) adds up each entry in the range C for which the corresponding entry in range A equals B. This function is especially useful in network problems for calculating the net flow generated at a node.

FIGURE 6.5

A spreadsheet model for the Distribution Unlimited Co. minimum-cost flow problem, including the target cell TotalCost (D11) and the other output cells NetFlow (J4:J8), as well as the equations entered into these cells and the other specifications needed to set up the model. The changing cells Ship (D4:D9) show the optimal shipping quantities through the distribution network obtained by the Solver.

	A	B	C	D	E	F	G	H	I	J	K	L
1		**Distribution Unlimited Co. Minimum Cost Flow Problem**										
2												
3		**From**	**To**	**Ship**		**Capacity**	**Unit Cost**		**Nodes**	**Net Flow**		**Supply/Demand**
4		F1	W1	30			$700		F1	80	=	80
5		F1	DC	50	≤	50	$300		F2	70	=	70
6		DC	W1	30	≤	50	$200		DC	0	=	0
7		DC	W2	50	≤	50	$400		W1	-60	=	-60
8		F2	DC	30	≤	50	$500		W2	-90	=	-90
9		F2	W2	40			$1,000					
10												
11			**Total Cost**	$117,000								

Solver Parameters
Set Objective (Target Cell): TotalCost
To: Min
By Changing (Variable) Cells:
Ship
Subject to the Constraints:
D5:D8 <= Capacity
NetFlow = SupplyDemand
Solver Options (Excel 2010):
Make Variables Nonnegative
Solving Method: Simplex LP
Solver Options (older Excel):
Assume Nonnegative
Assume Linear Model

Range Name	Cells
Capacity	F5:F8
From	B4:B9
NetFlow	J4:J8
Nodes	I4:I8
Ship	D4:D9
SupplyDemand	L4:L8
To	C4:C9
TotalCost	D11
UnitCost	G4:G9

	J
3	**Net Flow**
4	=SUMIF(From,I4,Ship)-SUMIF(To,I4,Ship)
5	=SUMIF(From,I5,Ship)-SUMIF(To,I5,Ship)
6	=SUMIF(From,I6,Ship)-SUMIF(To,I6,Ship)
7	=SUMIF(From,I7,Ship)-SUMIF(To,I7,Ship)
8	=SUMIF(From,I8,Ship)-SUMIF(To,I8,Ship)

	C	D
11	**Total Cost**	=SUMPRODUCT(Ship,UnitCost)

row where the entry in To (C4:C9) is the same as in I4. However, F1 never appears in the To column, so this sum is 0. Therefore, the overall equation for J4 yields J4 = D4 + D5 = 30 + 50 = 80, which is the net flow generated at the F1 node.

While it appears more complicated to use the SUMIF function rather than just entering J4 = D4 + D5, J5 = D8 + D9, J6 = D6 + D7 − D5 − D8, and so on, it is actually simpler. The SUMIF formula only needs to be entered once (in cell J4). It can then be copied down into the remaining cells in NetFlow (J5:J8). For a problem with many nodes, this is much quicker and (perhaps more significantly) less prone to error. In a large problem, it is all too easy to miss an arc when determining which cells in the Ship column to add and subtract to calculate the net flow for a given node.

The first Solver option specifies that the flow amounts cannot be negative. The second acknowledges that this is still a linear programming problem.

Clicking on the Solve button gives the optimal solution shown in Ship (D4:D9). This is the same solution as displayed in Figure 6.4.

Solving Large Minimum-Cost Flow Problems More Efficiently

Because minimum-cost flow problems are a special type of linear programming problem, and the *simplex method* can solve any linear programming problem, it also can solve any minimum-cost flow problem in the standard way. For example, the Excel Solver uses the simplex method to solve this type (or any other type) of linear programming problem. This works fine for small problems, like the Distribution Unlimited Co. problem, and for considerably larger ones as well. Therefore, the approach illustrated in Figure 6.5 will serve you well for any minimum-cost flow problem encountered in this book and for many that you will encounter subsequently.

However, we should mention that a different approach is sometimes needed in practice to solve really big problems. Because of the special form of minimum-cost flow problems, it is possible to greatly *streamline* the simplex method to solve them far more quickly. In particular, rather than going through all the algebra of the simplex method, it is possible to execute the same steps far more quickly by working directly with the network for the problem.

This streamlined version of the simplex method is called the **network simplex method.** The network simplex method can solve some huge problems that are much too large for the simplex method.

Like the simplex method, the network simplex method not only finds an optimal solution but also can be a valuable aid to managers in conducting the kinds of what-if analyses described in Chapter 5.

Many companies now use the network simplex method to solve their minimum-cost flow problems. Some of these problems are huge, with many tens of thousands of nodes and arcs. Occasionally, the number of arcs will even be far larger, perhaps into the millions.

Although the Excel Solver does not, other commercial software packages for linear programming commonly include the network simplex method.

An important advance in recent years has been the development of excellent *graphical interfaces* for modeling minimum-cost flow problems. These interfaces make the design of the model and the interpretation of the output of the network simplex method completely visual and intuitive with no mathematics involved. This is very helpful for managerial decision making.

network simplex method
The network simplex method can solve much larger minimum-cost flow problems (sometimes with millions of nodes and arcs) than can the simplex method used by the Excel Solver.

Some Applications

Probably the most important kind of application of minimum-cost flow problems is to the operation of a distribution network, such as the one depicted in Figures 6.1–6.4 for the Distribution Unlimited Co. problem. As summarized in the first row of Table 6.1, this kind of application involves determining a plan for shipping goods from their *sources* (factories, etc.) to *intermediate storage facilities* (as needed) and then on to the *customers.*

For some applications of minimum-cost flow problems, all the transshipment nodes are *processing facilities* rather than intermediate storage facilities. This is the case for *solid waste management,* as indicated in Table 6.1. Here, the flow of materials through the network begins at the sources of the solid waste, then goes to the facilities for processing these waste materials into a form suitable for landfill, and then sends them on to the various landfill locations. However, the objective still is to determine the flow plan that minimizes the total cost, where the cost now is for both shipping and processing.

In other applications, the *demand nodes* might be processing facilities. For example, in the third row of Table 6.1, the objective is to find the minimum-cost plan for obtaining supplies from various possible vendors, storing these goods in warehouses (as needed), and then shipping the supplies to the company's processing facilities (factories, etc.).

The next kind of application in Table 6.1 (coordinating product mixes at plants) illustrates that arcs can represent something other than a shipping lane for a physical flow of materials.

TABLE 6.1   Typical Kinds of Applications of Minimum-Cost Flow Problems

Kind of Application	Supply Nodes	Transshipment Nodes	Demand Nodes
Operation of a distribution network	Sources of goods	Intermediate storage facilities	Customers
Solid waste management	Sources of solid waste	Processing facilities	Landfill locations
Operation of a supply network	Vendors	Intermediate warehouses	Processing facilities
Coordinating product mixes at plants	Plants	Production of a specific product	Market for a specific product
Cash flow management	Sources of cash at a specific time	Short-term investment options	Needs for cash at a specific time

This application involves a company with several plants (the supply nodes) that can produce the same products but at different costs. Each arc from a supply node represents the production of one of the possible products at that plant, where this arc leads to the transshipment node that corresponds to this product. Thus, this transshipment node has an arc coming in from each plant capable of producing this product, and then the arcs leading out of this node go to the respective customers (the demand nodes) for this product. The objective is to determine how to divide each plant's production capacity among the products so as to minimize the total cost of meeting the demand for the various products.

The last application in Table 6.1 (cash flow management) illustrates that different nodes can represent some event that occurs at different times. In this case, each supply node represents a specific time (or time period) when some cash will become available to the company (through maturing accounts, notes receivable, sales of securities, borrowing, etc.). The supply at each of these nodes is the amount of cash that will become available then. Similarly, each demand node represents a specific time (or time period) when the company will need to draw on its cash reserves. The demand at each such node is the amount of cash that will be needed then. The objective is to maximize the company's income from investing the cash between each time it becomes available and when it will be used. Therefore, each transshipment node represents the choice of a specific short-term investment option (e.g., purchasing a certificate of deposit from a bank) over a specific time interval. The resulting network will have a succession of flows representing a schedule for cash becoming available, being invested, and then being used after the maturing of the investment.

Special Types of Minimum-Cost Flow Problems

There are five important categories of network problems that turn out to be special types of minimum-cost flow problems.

One is the **transportation problems** discussed in section 3.5. Figure 3.9 shows the network representation of a typical transportation problem. In our current terminology, the sources and destinations of a transportation problem are the supply nodes and demand nodes, respectively. Thus, a transportation problem is just a minimum-cost flow problem without any transshipment nodes and without any capacity constraints on the arcs (all of which go directly from a supply node to a demand node).

A second category is the **assignment problems** discussed in Section 3.6. Recall that this kind of problem involves assigning a group of people (or other operational units) to a group of tasks where each person is to perform a single task. An assignment problem can be viewed as a special type of transportation problem whose sources are the assignees and whose destinations are the tasks. This then makes the assignment problem also a special type of minimum-cost flow problem with the characteristics described in the preceding paragraph. In addition, each person is a supply node with a supply of 1 and each task is a demand node with a demand of 1.

transshipment problem

A transshipment problem is just a minimum-cost flow problem that has unlimited capacities for all its arcs.

A third special type of minimum-cost flow problem is **transshipment problems.** This kind of problem is just like a transportation problem except for the additional feature that the shipments from the sources (supply nodes) to the destinations (demand nodes) might also pass through intermediate transfer points (transshipment nodes) such as distribution centers. Like a transportation problem, there are no capacity constraints on the arcs. Consequently, any minimum-cost flow problem where each arc can carry any desired amount of flow is a transshipment problem. For example, if the data in Figure 6.2 were altered so that any amounts (within the ranges of the supplies and demands) could be shipped into and out of the distribution center, the Distribution Unlimited Co. would become just a transshipment problem.[1]

Because of their close relationship to a general minimum-cost flow problem, we will not discuss transshipment problems further.

The other two important special types of minimum-cost flow problems are **maximum flow problems** and **shortest path problems,** which will be described in Sections 6.3 and 6.4 after presenting a case study of a maximum flow problem in the next section.

---

[1] Be aware that a minimum-cost flow problem that does have capacity constraints on the arcs is sometimes referred to as a *capacitated transshipment problem*. We will not use this terminology.

The network simplex
method can be used to solve
huge problems of any of
these five special types.

In case you are wondering why we are bothering to point out that these five kinds of problems are special types of minimum-cost flow problems, here is one very important reason. It means that the *network simplex method* can be used to solve large problems of any of these types that might be difficult or impossible for the simplex method to solve. It is true that other efficient *special-purpose algorithms* also are available for each of these kinds of problems. However, recent implementations of the network simplex method have become so powerful that it now provides an excellent alternative to these other algorithms in most cases. This is especially valuable when the available software package includes the network simplex method but not another relevant special-purpose algorithm. Furthermore, even after finding an optimal solution, the network simplex method can continue to be helpful in aiding managerial what-if sessions along the lines discussed in Chapter 5.

Review
Questions

1. Name and describe the three kinds of nodes in a minimum-cost flow problem.
2. What is meant by the *capacity* of an arc?
3. What is the usual objective for a minimum-cost flow problem?
4. What property is necessary for a minimum-cost flow problem to have feasible solutions?
5. What is the integer solutions property for minimum-cost flow problems?
6. What is the name of the streamlined version of the simplex method that is designed to solve minimum-cost flow problems very efficiently?
7. What are a few typical kinds of applications of minimum-cost flow problems?
8. Name five important categories of network optimization problems that turn out to be special types of minimum-cost flow problems.

6.2   A CASE STUDY: THE BMZ CO. MAXIMUM FLOW PROBLEM

What a day! First being called into his boss's office and then receiving an urgent telephone call from the company president himself. Fortunately, he was able to reassure them that he has the situation under control.

Although his official title is Supply Chain Manager for the BMZ Company, Karl Schmidt often tells his friends that he really is the company's *crisis manager.* One crisis after another. The supplies needed to keep the production lines going haven't arrived yet. Or the supplies have arrived but are unusable because they are the wrong size. Or an urgent shipment to a key customer has been delayed. This current crisis is typical. One of the company's most important distribution centers—the one in Los Angeles—urgently needs an increased flow of shipments from the company.

Karl was chosen for this key position because he is considered a rising young star. Having just received his MBA degree from a top American business school four years ago, he is the youngest member of upper-level management in the entire company. His business school training in the latest management science techniques has proven invaluable in improving supply chain management throughout the company. The crises still occur, but the frequent chaos of past years has been eliminated.

Karl has a plan for dealing with the current crisis. This will mean calling on management science once again.

Background

The **BMZ Company** is a European manufacturer of luxury automobiles. Although its cars sell well in all the developed countries, its exports to the United States are particularly important to the company.

BMZ has a well-deserved reputation for providing excellent service. One key to maintaining this reputation is having a plentiful supply of automobile replacement parts readily available to the company's numerous dealerships and authorized repair shops. These parts are mainly stored in the company's distribution centers and then delivered promptly when needed. One of Karl Schmidt's top priorities is avoiding shortages at these distribution centers.

The company has several distribution centers in the United States. However, the closest one to the Los Angeles center is over 1,000 miles away in Seattle. Since BMZ cars are becoming especially popular in California, it is particularly important to keep the Los Angeles center well supplied. Therefore, the fact that supplies there are currently dwindling is a matter of real concern to BMZ top management—as Karl learned forcefully today.

Most of the automobile replacement parts are produced at the company's main factory in Stuttgart, Germany, along with the production of new cars. It is this factory that has been supplying the Los Angeles center with spare parts. Some of these parts are bulky, and very large numbers of certain parts are needed, so the total volume of the supplies has been relatively massive—over 300,000 cubic feet of goods arriving monthly. Now a much larger amount will be needed over the next month to replenish the dwindling inventory.

The Problem

The problem is to maximize the flow of automobile replacement parts from the factory in Stuttgart, Germany, to the distribution center in Los Angeles.

Karl needs to execute a plan quickly for shipping as much as possible from the main factory to the distribution center in Los Angeles over the next month. He already has recognized that this is a *maximum flow problem*—a problem of maximizing the flow of replacement parts from the factory to this distribution center.

The factory is producing far more than can be shipped to this one distribution center. Therefore, the limiting factor on how much can be shipped is the limited capacity of the company's distribution network.

This distribution network is depicted in Figure 6.6, where the nodes labeled ST and LA are the factory in Stuttgart and the distribution center in Los Angeles, respectively. There is a rail head at the factory, so shipments first go by rail to one of three European ports: Rotterdam (node RO), Bordeaux (node BO), and Lisbon (node LI). They then go by ship to ports in the United States, either New York (node NY) or New Orleans (node NO). Finally, they are shipped by truck from these ports to the distribution center in Los Angeles.

The organizations operating these railroads, ships, and trucks are independently owned companies that ship goods for numerous firms. Because of prior commitments to their regular customers, these companies are unable to drastically increase the allocation of space to any single customer on short notice. Therefore, the BMZ Co. is only able to secure a limited amount of shipping space along each shipping lane over the next month. The amounts available are given in Figure 6.6, using units of *hundreds of cubic meters*. (Since each unit of 100 cubic meters is a little over 3,500 cubic feet, these are large volumes of goods that need to be moved.)

FIGURE 6.6

The BMZ Co. distribution network from its main factory in Stuttgart, Germany, to a distribution center in Los Angeles.

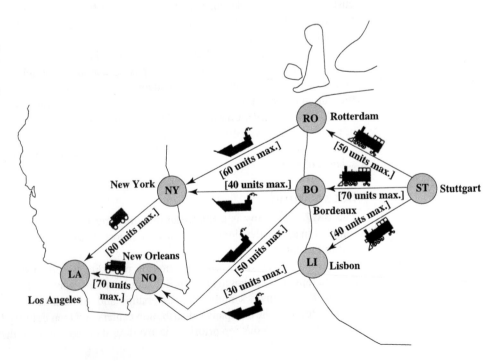

FIGURE 6.7

A network model for the BMZ Co. problem as a maximum flow problem, where the number in square brackets below each arc is the capacity of that arc.

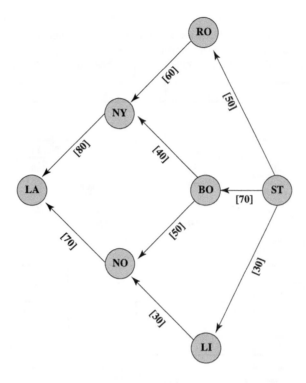

Model Formulation

Figure 6.7 shows the *network model* for this maximum flow problem. Rather than showing the geographical layout of the distribution network, this network simply lines up the nodes (representing the cities) in evenly spaced columns. The arcs represent the shipping lanes, where the capacity of each arc (given in square brackets under the arc) is the amount of shipping space available along that shipping lane. The objective is to determine how much flow to send through each arc (how many units to ship through each shipping lane) to maximize the total number of units flowing from the factory in Stuttgart to the distribution center in Los Angeles.

Figure 6.8 shows the corresponding spreadsheet model for this problem when using the format introduced in Figure 6.5. The main difference from the model in Figure 6.5 is the change in the objective. Since we are no longer minimizing the total cost of the flow through the network, column G in Figure 6.5 can be deleted in Figure 6.8. The target cell MaxFlow (D14) in Figure 6.8 now needs to give the total number of units flowing from Stuttgart to Los Angeles. Thus, the equations at the bottom of the figure include D14 = I4, where I4 gives the net flow leaving Stuttgart to go to Los Angeles. As in Figure 6.5, the equations in Figure 6.8 entered into NetFlow (I4:I10) again use the difference of two SUMIF functions to calculate the net flow generated at each node. Since the objective is to maximize the flow shown in MaxFlow (D14), the Solver Parameters box specifies that this target cell is to be maximized. After clicking on the Solve button, the optimal solution shown in the changing cells Ship (D4:D12) is obtained for the amount that BMZ should ship through each shipping lane.

In contrast to the spreadsheet model in Figure 6.5, which *minimizes* TotalCost (D11), the spreadsheet model in Figure 6.8 *maximizes* the target cell MaxFlow (D14).

However, Karl is not completely satisfied with this solution. He has an idea for doing even better. This will require formulating and solving another maximum flow problem. (This story continues in the middle of the next section.)

Review Questions

1. What is the current crisis facing the BMZ Co.?
2. When formulating this problem in network terms, what is flowing through BMZ's distribution network? From where to where?
3. What is the objective of the resulting maximum flow problem?

FIGURE 6.8
A spreadsheet model for the BMZ Co. maximum flow problem, including the equations entered into the target cell MaxFlow (D14) and the other output cells NetFlow (I4:I10), as well as the other specifications needed to set up the model. The changing cells Ship (D4:D12) show the optimal shipping quantities through the distribution network obtained by the Solver.

	A	B	C	D	E	F	G	H	I	J	K
1	**BMZ Co. Maximum Flow Problem**										
2											
3		**From**	**To**	**Ship**		**Capacity**		**Nodes**	**Net Flow**		**Supply/Demand**
4		Stuttgart	Rotterdam	50	≤	50		Stuttgart	150		
5		Stuttgart	Bordeaux	70	≤	70		Rotterdam	0	=	0
6		Stuttgart	Lisbon	30	≤	40		Bordeaux	0	=	0
7		Rotterdam	New York	50	≤	60		Lisbon	0	=	0
8		Bordeaux	New York	30	≤	40		New York	0	=	0
9		Bordeaux	New Orleans	40	≤	50		New Orleans	0	=	0
10		Lisbon	New Orleans	30	≤	30		Los Angeles	-150		
11		New York	Los Angeles	80	≤	80					
12		New Orleans	Los Angeles	70	≤	70					
13											
14			**Maximum Flow**	150							

Solver Parameters
Set Objective (Target Cell): MaxFlow
To: Max
By Changing (Variable) Cells:
Ship
Subject to the Constraints:
I5:I9 = SupplyDemand
Ship <= Capacity

Solver Options (Excel 2010):
Make Variables Nonnegative
Solving Method: Simplex LP
Solver Options (older Excel):
Assume Nonnegative
Assume Linear Model

Range Name	Cells
Capacity	F4:F12
From	B4:B12
MaxFlow	D14
NetFlow	I4:I10
Nodes	H4:H10
Ship	D4:D12
SupplyDemand	K5:K9
To	C4:C12

	I
3	**Net Flow**
4	=SUMIF(From,H4,Ship)-SUMIF(To,H4,Ship)
5	=SUMIF(From,H5,Ship)-SUMIF(To,H5,Ship)
6	=SUMIF(From,H6,Ship)-SUMIF(To,H6,Ship)
7	=SUMIF(From,H7,Ship)-SUMIF(To,H7,Ship)
8	=SUMIF(From,H8,Ship)-SUMIF(To,H8,Ship)
9	=SUMIF(From,H9,Ship)-SUMIF(To,H9,Ship)
10	=SUMIF(From,H10,Ship)-SUMIF(To,H10,Ship)

	C	D
14	**Maximum Flow**	=I4

6.3 MAXIMUM FLOW PROBLEMS

Like a minimum-cost flow problem, a maximum flow problem is concerned with *flow through a network.* However, the objective now is different. Rather than minimizing the cost of the flow, the objective now is to find a flow plan that maximizes the amount flowing through the network. This is how Karl Schmidt was able to find a flow plan that maximizes the number of units of automobile replacement parts flowing through BMZ's distribution network from its factory in Stuttgart to the distribution center in Los Angeles.

General Characteristics

Except for the difference in objective (maximize flow versus minimize cost), the characteristics of the maximum flow problem are quite similar to those for the minimum-cost flow problem. However, there are some minor differences, as we will discuss after summarizing the assumptions.

Assumptions of a Maximum Flow Problem

1. All flow through the network originates at one node, called the **source,** and terminates at one other node, called the **sink.** (The source and sink in the BMZ problem are the factory and the distribution center, respectively.)

The network for transport of natural gas on the Norwegian Continental Shelf, with approximately 5,000 miles of subsea pipelines, is the world's largest offshore pipeline network. **Gassco** is a company entirely owned by the Norwegian state, which operates this network. Another company that is largely state owned, **StatoilHydro**, is the main Norwegian supplier of natural gas to markets throughout Europe and elsewhere.

Gassco and StatoilHydro together use management science techniques to optimize both the configuration of the network and the routing of the natural gas. The main model used for this routing is a multicommodity network-flow model in which the different hydrocarbons and contaminants in natural gas constitute the commodities. The objective function for the model is to *maximize the total flow* of the natural gas from the supply points (the offshore drilling platforms) to the demand points (typically import terminals). However, in addition to the usual supply-and-demand constraints, the model also includes constraints involving pressure-flow relationships, maximum delivery pressures, and technical pressure bounds on pipelines. Therefore, this model is a generalization of the model for the maximum flow problem described in this section.

This key application of management science, along with a few others, has had a dramatic impact on the efficiency of the operation of this offshore pipeline network. The resulting *accumulated savings* were estimated to be approximately **$2 billion** in the period 1995–2008.

Source: F. Rømo, A. Tomasgard, L. Hellemo, M. Fodstad, B. H. Eidesen, and B. Pedersen, "Optimizing the Norwegian Natural Gas Production and Transport," *Interfaces* 39, no. 1 (January–February 2009), pp. 46–56. (A link to this article is provided on our Web site, **www.mhhe.com/hillier4e.**)

2. All the remaining nodes are *transshipment nodes.* (These are nodes RO, BO, LI, NY, and NO in the BMZ problem.)
3. Flow through an arc is only allowed in the direction indicated by the arrowhead, where the maximum amount of flow is given by the *capacity* of that arc. At the *source,* all arcs point away from the node. At the *sink,* all arcs point into the node.
4. The objective is to maximize the total amount of flow from the source to the sink. This amount is measured in either of two equivalent ways, namely, either the amount *leaving the source* or the amount *entering the sink.* (Cells D14 and I4 in Figure 6.8 use the amount leaving the source.)

> The objective is to find a flow plan that maximizes the flow from the source to the sink.

The source and sink of a maximum flow problem are analogous to the supply nodes and demand nodes of a minimum-cost flow problem. These are the only nodes in both problems that do not have conservation of flow (flow out equals flow in). Like the supply nodes, the source *generates flow.* Like the demand nodes, the sink *absorbs flow.*

However, there are two differences between these nodes in a minimum-cost flow problem and the corresponding nodes in a maximum flow problem.

One difference is that, whereas supply nodes have fixed supplies and demand nodes have fixed demands, the source and sink do not. The reason is that the objective is to maximize the flow leaving the source and entering the sink rather than fixing this amount.

> Although a maximum flow problem has only a single source and a single sink, variants with multiple sources and sinks also can be solved, as illustrated in the next subsection.

The second difference is that, whereas the number of supply nodes and the number of demand nodes in a minimum-cost flow problem may be *more than one,* there can be *only one* source and *only one* sink in a maximum flow problem. However, variants of maximum flow problems that have multiple sources and sinks can still be solved by the Excel Solver, as you now will see illustrated by the BMZ case study introduced in the preceding section.

Continuing the Case Study with Multiple Supply Points and Multiple Demand Points

Here is Karl Schmidt's idea for how to improve upon the flow plan obtained at the end of Section 6.2 (as given in column D of Figure 6.8).

The company has a second, smaller factory in Berlin, north of its Stuttgart factory, for producing automobile parts. Although this factory normally is used to help supply distribution centers in northern Europe, Canada, and the northern United States (including one in Seattle), it also is able to ship to the distribution center in Los Angeles. Furthermore, the distribution center in Seattle has the capability of supplying parts to the customers of the distribution center in Los Angeles when shortages occur at the latter center.

FIGURE 6.9

A network model for the expanded BMZ Co. problem as a variant of a maximum flow problem, where the number in square brackets below each arc is the capacity of that arc.

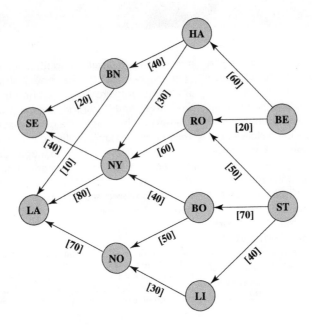

In this light, Karl now has developed a better plan for addressing the current inventory shortages in Los Angeles. Rather than simply maximizing shipments from the Stuttgart factory to Los Angeles, he has decided to maximize shipments from both factories to the distribution centers in both Los Angeles and Seattle.

Figure 6.9 shows the network model representing the expanded distribution network that encompasses both factories and both distribution centers. In addition to the nodes shown in Figures 6.6 and 6.7, node BE is the second, smaller factory in Berlin; nodes HA and BN are additional ports used by this factory in Hamburg and Boston, respectively; and node SE is the distribution center in Seattle. As before, the arcs represent the shipping lanes, where the number in square brackets below each arc is the capacity of that arc, that is, the maximum number of units that can be shipped through that shipping lane over the next month.

The corresponding spreadsheet model is displayed in Figure 6.10. The format is the same as in Figure 6.8. However, the target cell MaxFlow (D21) now gives the total flow from Stuttgart and Berlin, so D21 = I4 + I5 (as shown by the equation for this target cell given at the bottom of the figure).

The changing cells Ship (D4:D19) in this figure show the optimal solution obtained for the number of units to ship through each shipping lane over the next month. Comparing this solution with the one in Figure 6.8 shows the impact of Karl Schmidt's decision to expand the distribution network to include the second factory and the distribution center in Seattle. As indicated in column I of the two figures, the number of units going to Los Angeles directly has been increased from 150 to 160, in addition to the 60 units going to Seattle as a backup for the inventory shortage in Los Angeles. This plan solved the crisis in Los Angeles and won Karl commendations from top management.

Some Applications

The applications of maximum flow problems and their variants are somewhat similar to those for minimum-cost flow problems described in the preceding section when management's objective is to *maximize flow* rather than to *minimize cost*. Here are some typical kinds of applications.

1. Maximize the flow through a distribution network, as for the BMZ Co. problem.
2. Maximize the flow through a company's supply network from its vendors to its processing facilities.
3. Maximize the flow of oil through a system of pipelines.
4. Maximize the flow of water through a system of aqueducts.
5. Maximize the flow of vehicles through a transportation network.

FIGURE 6.10

A spreadsheet model for the expanded BMZ Co. problem as a variant of a maximum flow problem with sources in both Stuttgart and Berlin and sinks in both Los Angeles and Seattle. Using the target cell MaxFlow (D21) to maximize the total flow from the two sources to the two sinks, the Solver yields the optimal shipping plan shown in the changing cells Ship (D4:D19).

	A	B	C	D	E	F	G	H	I	J	K
1		**BMZ Co. Expanded Maximum Flow Problem**									
2											
3		**From**	**To**	**Ship**		**Capacity**		**Nodes**	**Net Flow**		**Supply/Demand**
4		Stuttgart	Rotterdam	40	≤	50		Stuttgart	140		
5		Stuttgart	Bordeaux	70	≤	70		Berlin	80		
6		Stuttgart	Lisbon	30	≤	40		Hamburg	0	=	0
7		Berlin	Rotterdam	20	≤	20		Rotterdam	0	=	0
8		Berlin	Hamburg	60	≤	60		Bordeaux	0	=	0
9		Rotterdam	New York	60	≤	60		Lisbon	0	=	0
10		Bordeaux	New York	30	≤	40		Boston	0	=	0
11		Bordeaux	New Orleans	40	≤	50		New York	0	=	0
12		Lisbon	New Orleans	30	≤	30		New Orleans	0	=	0
13		Hamburg	New York	30	≤	30		Los Angeles	-160		
14		Hamburg	Boston	30	≤	40		Seattle	-60		
15		New Orleans	Los Angeles	70	≤	70					
16		New York	Los Angeles	80	≤	80					
17		New York	Seattle	40	≤	40					
18		Boston	Los Angeles	10	≤	10					
19		Boston	Seattle	20	≤	20					
20											
21			**Maximum Flow**	220							

Solver Parameters
Set Objective (Target Cell): MaxFlow
To: Max
By Changing (Variable) Cells:
Ship
Subject to the Constraints:
I6:I12 = SupplyDemand
Ship <= Capacity
Solver Options (Excel 2010):
Make Variables Nonnegative
Solving Method: Simplex LP
Solver Options (older Excel):
Assume Nonnegative
Assume Linear Model

Range Name	Cells
Capacity	F4:F19
From	B4:B19
MaxFlow	D21
NetFlow	I4:I14
Nodes	H4:H14
Ship	D4:D19
SupplyDemand	K6:K12
To	C4:C19

	I
3	**Net Flow**
4	=SUMIF(From,H4,Ship)-SUMIF(To,H4,Ship)
5	=SUMIF(From,H5,Ship)-SUMIF(To,H5,Ship)
6	=SUMIF(From,H6,Ship)-SUMIF(To,H6,Ship)
7	=SUMIF(From,H7,Ship)-SUMIF(To,H7,Ship)
8	=SUMIF(From,H8,Ship)-SUMIF(To,H8,Ship)
9	=SUMIF(From,H9,Ship)-SUMIF(To,H9,Ship)
10	=SUMIF(From,H10,Ship)-SUMIF(To,H10,Ship)
11	=SUMIF(From,H11,Ship)-SUMIF(To,H11,Ship)
12	=SUMIF(From,H12,Ship)-SUMIF(To,H12,Ship)
13	=SUMIF(From,H13,Ship)-SUMIF(To,H13,Ship)
14	=SUMIF(From,H14,Ship)-SUMIF(To,H14,Ship)

	C	D
21	**Maximum Flow**	=I4+I5

Solving Very Large Problems

The expanded BMZ network in Figure 6.9 has 11 nodes and 16 arcs. However, the networks for most real applications are considerably larger, and occasionally vastly larger. As the number of nodes and arcs grows into the hundreds or thousands, the formulation and solution approach illustrated in Figures 6.8 and 6.10 quickly becomes impractical.

Fortunately, management scientists have other techniques available for formulating and solving huge problems with many tens of thousands of nodes and arcs. One technique is to reformulate a variant of a maximum flow problem so that an extremely efficient special-purpose algorithm for maximum flow problems still can be applied. Another is to reformulate the problem to fit the format for a minimum-cost flow problem so that the network simplex method can be applied. These special algorithms are available in some software packages, but not in the Excel Solver. Thus, if you should ever encounter a maximum flow problem or a variant that is beyond the scope of the Excel Solver (which won't happen in this book), rest assured that it probably can be formulated and solved in another way.

Review Questions

1. How does the objective of a maximum flow problem differ from that for a minimum-cost flow problem?
2. What are the *source* and the *sink* for a maximum flow problem? For each, in what direction do all their arcs point?
3. What are the two equivalent ways in which the total amount of flow from the source to the sink can be measured?
4. The source and sink of a maximum flow problem are different from the supply nodes and demand nodes of a minimum-cost flow problem in what two ways?
5. What are a few typical kinds of applications of maximum flow problems?

6.4 SHORTEST PATH PROBLEMS

The most common applications of shortest path problems are for what the name suggests—finding the *shortest path* between two points. Here is an example.

An Example: The Littletown Fire Department Problem

Littletown is a small town in a rural area. Its fire department serves a relatively large geographical area that includes many farming communities. Since there are numerous roads throughout the area, many possible routes may be available for traveling to any given farming community from the fire station. Since time is of the essence in reaching a fire, the fire chief wishes to determine in advance the *shortest path* from the fire station to each of the farming communities.

The objective is to find the shortest route from the fire station to the farming community.

Figure 6.11 shows the road system connecting the fire station to one of the farming communities, including the mileage along each road. Can you find which route from the fire station to the farming community minimizes the total number of miles?

Model Formulation for the Littletown Problem

Figure 6.12 gives the network representation of this problem, which ignores the geographical layout and the curves in the roads. This network model is the usual way of representing a shortest path problem. The junctions now are nodes of the network, where the fire station and farming community are two additional nodes labeled as O (for *origin*) and T (for *destination*), respectively. Since travel (flow) can go in either direction between the nodes, the lines

FIGURE 6.11

The road system between the Littletown Fire Station and a certain farming community, where A, B, . . . , H are junctions and the number next to each road shows its distance in miles.

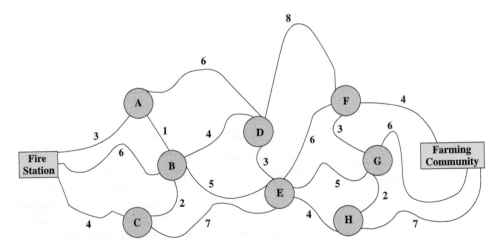

An Application Vignette

Incorporated in 1881, **Canadian Pacific Railway (CPR)** was North America's first transcontinental railway. CPR transports rail freight over a 14,000-mile network extending from Montreal to Vancouver and throughout the U.S. Northwest and Midwest. Alliances with other carriers extend CPR's market reach into the major business centers of Mexico as well.

Every day CPR receives approximately 7,000 new shipments from its customers going to destinations across North America and for export. It must route and move these shipments in railcars over the network of track, where a railcar may be switched a number of times from one locomotive engine to another before reaching its destination. CPR must coordinate the shipments with its operational plans for 1,600 locomotives, 65,000 railcars, over 5,000 train crew members, and 250 train yards.

CPR management turned to a management science consulting firm, MultiModal Applied Systems, to work with CPR employees in developing a management science approach to this problem. A variety of management science techniques were used to create a new operating strategy. However, the foundation of the approach was to represent the flow of blocks of railcars as flow through a network where each node corresponds to both a location and a point in time. This representation then enabled the application of network optimization techniques. For example, numerous *shortest path problems* are solved each day as part of the overall approach.

This application of management science is *saving CPR roughly* **US$100 million** *per year*. Labor productivity, locomotive productivity, fuel consumption, and railcar velocity have improved very substantially. In addition, CPR now provides its customers with reliable delivery times and has received many awards for its improvement in service. This application of network optimization techniques also led to CPR winning the prestigious First Prize in the 2003 international competition for the Franz Edelman Award for Achievement in Operations Research and the Management Sciences.

Source: P. Ireland, R. Case, J. Fallis, C. Van Dyke, J. Kuehn, and M. Meketon, "The Canadian Pacific Railway Transforms Operations by Using Models to Develop Its Operating Plans," *Interfaces* 34, no. 1 (January–February 2004), pp. 5–14. (A link to this article is provided on our Web site, **www.mhhe.com/hillier4e.**)

links

In a shortest path problem, travel goes from the origin to the destination through a series of links (such as roads) that connect pairs of nodes (junctions) in the network.

connecting the nodes now are referred to as **links**[2] instead of *arcs*. A link between a pair of nodes allows travel in either direction, whereas an arc allows travel in only the direction indicated by an arrowhead, so the lines in Figure 6.12 need to be links instead of arcs. (Notice that the links do not have an arrowhead at either end.)

Have you found the shortest path from the origin to the destination yet? (Try it now before reading further.) It is

$$O \rightarrow A \rightarrow B \rightarrow E \rightarrow F \rightarrow T$$

with a total distance of 19 miles.

This problem (like any shortest path problem) can be thought of as a special kind of minimum-cost flow problem (Section 6.1) where the *miles traveled* now are interpreted to be the *cost* of flow through the network. A trip from the fire station to the farming community is interpreted to be a flow of 1 on the chosen path through the network, so minimizing the cost of this flow is equivalent to minimizing the number of miles traveled. The fire station is considered to be the one supply node, with a supply of 1 to represent the start of this trip. The farming community is the one demand node, with a demand of 1 to represent the completion of this trip. All the other nodes in Figure 6.12 are transshipment nodes, so the net flow generated at each is 0.

Figure 6.13 shows the spreadsheet model that results from this interpretation. The format is basically the same as for the minimum-cost flow problem formulated in Figure 6.5, except now

FIGURE 6.12

The network representation of Figure 6.11 as a shortest path problem.

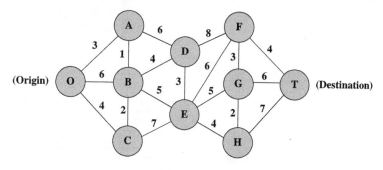

[2] Another name sometimes used is *undirected arc,* but we will not use this terminology.

FIGURE 6.13

A spreadsheet model for the Littletown Fire Department shortest path problem, including the equations entered into the target cell TotalDistance (D29) and the other output cells SupplyDemand (K4:K13). The values of 1 in the changing cells OnRoute (D4:D27) reveal the optimal solution obtained by the Solver for the shortest path (19 miles) from the fire station to the farming community.

	A	B	C	D	E	F	G	H	I	J	K
1		**Littletown Fire Department Shortest Path Problem**									
2											
3		**From**	**To**	**On Route**		**Distance**		**Nodes**	**Net Flow**		**Supply/Demand**
4		Fire St.	A	1		3		Fire St.	1	=	1
5		Fire St.	B	0		6		A	0	=	0
6		Fire St.	C	0		4		B	0	=	0
7		A	B	1		1		C	0	=	0
8		A	D	0		6		D	0	=	0
9		B	A	0		1		E	0	=	0
10		B	C	0		2		F	0	=	0
11		B	D	0		4		G	0	=	0
12		B	E	1		5		H	0	=	0
13		C	B	0		2		Farm Com.	-1	=	-1
14		C	E	0		7					
15		D	E	0		3					
16		D	F	0		8					
17		E	D	0		3					
18		E	F	1		6					
19		E	G	0		5					
20		E	H	0		4					
21		F	G	0		3					
22		F	Farm Com.	1		4					
23		G	F	0		3					
24		G	H	0		2					
25		G	Farm Com.	0		6					
26		H	G	0		2					
27		H	Farm Com.	0		7					
28											
29			**Total Distance**	19							

Set Objective (Target Cell): TotalDistance
To: Min
By Changing (Variable) Cells:
  OnRoute
Subject to the Constraints:
  NetFlow = SupplyDemand

Solver Options (Excel 2010):
  Make Variables Nonnegative
  Solving Method: Simplex LP
Solver Options (older Excel):
  Assume Nonnegative
  Assume Linear Model

Range Name	Cells
Distance	F4:F27
From	B4:B27
NetFlow	I4:I13
Nodes	H4:H13
OnRoute	D4:D27
SupplyDemand	K4:K13
To	C4:C27
TotalDistance	D29

	I
3	**Net Flow**
4	=SUMIF(From,H4,OnRoute)-SUMIF(To,H4,OnRoute)
5	=SUMIF(From,H5,OnRoute)-SUMIF(To,H5,OnRoute)
6	=SUMIF(From,H6,OnRoute)-SUMIF(To,H6,OnRoute)
7	=SUMIF(From,H7,OnRoute)-SUMIF(To,H7,OnRoute)
8	=SUMIF(From,H8,OnRoute)-SUMIF(To,H8,OnRoute)
9	=SUMIF(From,H9,OnRoute)-SUMIF(To,H9,OnRoute)
10	=SUMIF(From,H10,OnRoute)-SUMIF(To,H10,OnRoute)
11	=SUMIF(From,H11,OnRoute)-SUMIF(To,H11,OnRoute)
12	=SUMIF(From,H12,OnRoute)-SUMIF(To,H12,OnRoute)
13	=SUMIF(From,H13,OnRoute)-SUMIF(To,H13,OnRoute)

	C	D
29	**Total Distance**	=SUMPRODUCT(OnRoute,Distance)

there are no arc capacity constraints and the unit cost column is replaced by a column of distances in miles. The flow quantities given by the changing cells OnRoute (D4:D27) are 1 for each arc that is on the chosen path from the fire station to the farming community and 0 otherwise. The target cell TotalDistance (D29) gives the total distance of this path in miles. (See the equation for this cell at the bottom of the figure.) Columns B and C together list all the vertical links in Figure 6.12 twice, once as a downward arc and once as an upward arc, since either direction might be on the chosen path. The other links are only listed as left-to-right arcs, since this is the only direction of interest for choosing a shortest path from the origin to the destination.

Column K shows the net flow that needs to be generated at each of the nodes. Using the equations at the bottom of the figure, each column I cell then calculates the *actual* net flow at that node by adding the flow out and subtracting the flow in. The corresponding constraints, Nodes (H4:H13) = SupplyDemand (K4:K13), are specified in the Solver Parameters box.

The solution shown in OnRoute (D4:D27) is the optimal solution obtained after clicking on the Solve button. It is exactly the same as the shortest path given earlier.

Just as for minimum-cost flow problems and maximum flow problems, special algorithms are available for solving large shortest path problems very efficiently, but these algorithms are not included in the Excel Solver. Using a spreadsheet formulation and the Solver is fine for problems of the size of the Littletown problem and somewhat larger, but you should be aware that vastly larger problems can still be solved by other means.

General Characteristics

Except for more complicated variations beyond the scope of this book, all shortest path problems share the characteristics illustrated by the Littletown problem. Here are the basic assumptions.

Assumptions of a Shortest Path Problem

1. You need to choose a path through the network that starts at a certain node, called the **origin,** and ends at another certain node, called the **destination.**
2. The lines connecting certain pairs of nodes commonly are *links* (which allow travel in either direction), although arcs (which only permit travel in one direction) also are allowed.
3. Associated with each link (or arc) is a nonnegative number called its **length.** (Be aware that the drawing of each link in the network typically makes no effort to show its true length other than giving the correct number next to the link.)
4. The objective is to find the shortest path (the path with the minimum total length) from the origin to the destination.

Some Applications

Not all applications of shortest path problems involve minimizing the distance traveled from the origin to the destination. In fact, they might not even involve travel at all. The links (or arcs) might instead represent activities of some other kind, so choosing a path through the network corresponds to selecting the best sequence of activities. The numbers giving the "lengths" of the links might then be, for example, the costs of the activities, in which case the objective would be to determine which sequence of activities minimizes the total cost.

Here are three categories of applications.

1. Minimize the total *distance* traveled, as in the Littletown example.
2. Minimize the total *cost* of a sequence of activities, as in the example that follows in the subsection below.
3. Minimize the total *time* of a sequence of activities, as in the example involving the Quick Company at the end of this section.

An Example of Minimizing Total Cost

Sarah has just graduated from high school. As a graduation present, her parents have given her a car fund of $21,000 to help purchase and maintain a certain three-year-old used car for college. Since operating and maintenance costs go up rapidly as the car ages, Sarah's parents tell her that she will be welcome to trade in her car on another three-year-old car one or more times during the next three summers if she determines that this would minimize her total net cost.

This spreadsheet model is like one for a minimum-cost flow problem with no arc capacity constraints except that distances replace unit costs and travel on a chosen path is interpreted as a flow of 1 through this path.

The objective is to find the shortest path from the origin to the destination.

They also inform her that they will give her a new car in four years as a college graduation present, so she should definitely plan to trade in her car then. (These are pretty nice parents!)

Table 6.2 gives the relevant data for *each* time Sarah purchases a three-year-old car. For example, if she trades in her car after two years, the next car will be in ownership year 1 during her junior year, and so forth.

When should Sarah trade in her car (if at all) during the next three summers to minimize her total net cost of purchasing, operating, and maintaining the car(s) over her four years of college?

Figure 6.14 shows the network formulation of this problem as a shortest path problem. Nodes 1, 2, 3, and 4 are the end of Sarah's first, second, third, and fourth years of college, respectively. Node 0 is now, before starting college. Each arc from one node to a second node corresponds to the activity of purchasing a car at the time indicated by the first of these two nodes and then trading it in at the time indicated by the second node. Sarah begins by purchasing a car now, and she ends by trading in a car at the end of year 4, so node 0 is the *origin* and node 4 is the *destination*.

The number of arcs on the path chosen from the origin to the destination indicates how many times Sarah will purchase and trade in a car. For example, consider the path

Sarah needs a schedule for trading in her car that will minimize her total net cost.

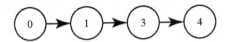

This corresponds to purchasing a car now, then trading it in at the end of year 1 to purchase a second car, then trading in the second car at the end of year 3 to purchase a third car, and then trading in this third car at the end of year 4.

Since Sarah wants to minimize her total net cost from now (node 0) to the end of year 4 (node 4), each arc length needs to measure the net cost of that arc's cycle of purchasing, maintaining, and trading in a car. Therefore,

$$\text{Arc length} = \text{Purchase price} + \text{Operating and maintenance costs} - \text{Trade-in value}$$

For example, consider the arc from node 1 to node 3. This arc corresponds to purchasing a car at the end of year 1, operating and maintaining it during ownership years 1 and 2, and then trading it in at the end of ownership year 2. Consequently,

$$\text{Length of arc from } \textcircled{1} \text{ to } \textcircled{3} = 12,000 + 2,000 + 3,000 - 6,500$$
$$= 10,500 \quad \text{(in dollars)}$$

TABLE 6.2
Sarah's Data Each Time She Purchases a Three-Year-Old Car

Purchase Price	Operating and Maintenance Costs for Ownership Year				Trade-in Value at End of Ownership Year			
	1	2	3	4	1	2	3	4
$12,000	$2,000	$3,000	$4,500	$6,500	$8,500	$6,500	$4,500	$3,000

FIGURE 6.14
Formulation of the problem of when Sarah should trade in her car as a shortest path problem. The node labels measure the number of years from now. Each arc represents purchasing a car and then trading it in later.

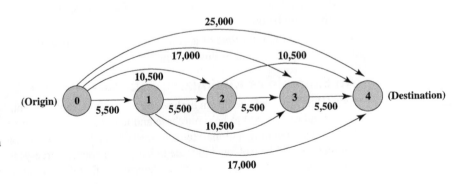

The sum of the arc lengths on any path through this network gives the total net cost of the corresponding plan for trading in cars.

The arc lengths calculated in this way are shown next to the arcs in Figure 6.14. Adding up the lengths of the arcs on any path from node 0 to node 4 then gives the total net cost for that particular plan for trading in cars over the next four years. Therefore, finding the shortest path from the origin to the destination identifies the plan that will minimize Sarah's total net cost.

The target cell now is TotalCost instead of TotalDistance.

Figure 6.15 shows the corresponding spreadsheet model, formulated in just the same way as for Figure 6.13 except that distances are now costs. Thus, the target cell TotalCost (D23) now gives the total cost that is to be minimized. The changing cells OnRoute (D12:D21) in the figure display the optimal solution obtained after having clicked on the Solve button. Since values of 1 indicate the path being followed, the shortest path turns out to be

Trade in the first car at the end of year 2.

Trade in the second car at the end of year 4.

The length of this path is 10,500 + 10,500 = 21,000, so Sarah's total net cost is $21,000, as given by the target cell. Recall that this is exactly the amount in Sarah's car fund provided by her parents. (These are *really* nice parents!)

An Example of Minimizing Total Time

The **Quick Company** has learned that a competitor is planning to come out with a new kind of product with great sales potential. Quick has been working on a similar product that had been scheduled to come to market in 20 months. However, research is nearly complete and Quick's management now wishes to rush the product out to meet the competition.

There are four nonoverlapping phases left to be accomplished, including the remaining research (the first phase) that currently is being conducted at a normal pace. However, each phase can instead be conducted at a priority or crash level to expedite completion. These are the only levels that will be considered for the last three phases, whereas both the normal level and these two levels will be considered for the first phase. The times required at these levels are shown in Table 6.3.

Management now has allocated $30 million for these four phases. The cost of each phase at the levels under consideration is shown in Table 6.4.

The objective is to minimize the total time for the project.

Management wishes to determine at which level to conduct each of the four phases to minimize the total time until the product can be marketed, subject to the budget restriction of $30 million.

Figure 6.16 shows the network formulation of this problem as a shortest path problem. Each node indicates the situation at that point in time. Except for the destination, a node is identified by two numbers:

1. The number of phases completed.
2. The number of millions of dollars left for the remaining phases.

The sum of the arc lengths on any path through this network gives the total time of the corresponding plan for preparing the new product.

The origin is *now,* when 0 phases have been completed and the entire budget of $30 million is left. Each arc represents the choice of a particular level of effort (identified in parentheses below the arc) for that phase. [There are no crash arcs emanating from the (2, 12) and (3, 3) nodes because this level of effort would require exceeding the budget of $30 million for the four phases.] The *time* (in months) required to perform the phase with this level of effort then is the *length* of the arc (shown above the arc). Time is chosen as the measure of arc length because the objective is to minimize the total time for all four phases. Summing the arc lengths for any particular path through the network gives the total time for the plan corresponding to that path. Therefore, the shortest path through the network identifies the plan that minimizes total time.

FIGURE 6.15

A spreadsheet model that formulates Sarah's problem as a shortest path problem where the objective is to minimize the total cost instead of the total distance. The bottom of the figure shows the equations entered in the target cell TotalCost (D23) and the other output cells Cost (E12:E21) and NetFlow (H12:H16). After applying the Solver, the values of 1 in the changing cells OnRoute (D12:D21) identify the shortest (least expensive) path for scheduling trade-ins.

	A	B	C	D	E	F	G	H	I	J
1		**Sarah's Car Purchasing Problem**								
2										
3			Operating &	Trade-in Value at End	Purchase					
4			Maint. Cost	of Year	Price					
5		Year 1	$2,000	$8,500	$12,000					
6		Year 2	$3,000	$6,500						
7		Year 3	$4,500	$4,500						
8		Year 4	$6,500	$3,000						
9										
10										
11		**From**	**To**	**On Route**	**Cost**		**Nodes**	**Net Flow**		**Supply/Demand**
12		Year 0	Year 1	0	$5,500		Year 0	1	=	1
13		Year 0	Year 2	1	$10,500		Year 1	0	=	0
14		Year 0	Year 3	0	$17,000		Year 2	0	=	0
15		Year 0	Year 4	0	$25,000		Year 3	0	=	0
16		Year 1	Year 2	0	$5,500		Year 4	-1	=	-1
17		Year 1	Year 3	0	$10,500					
18		Year 1	Year 4	0	$17,000					
19		Year 2	Year 3	0	$5,500					
20		Year 2	Year 4	1	$10,500					
21		Year 3	Year 4	0	$5,500					
22										
23			**Total Cost**	$21,000						

Range Name	Cells
Cost	E12:E21
From	B12:B21
NetFlow	H12:H16
Nodes	G12:G16
OnRoute	D12:D21
OpMaint1	C5
OpMaint2	C6
OpMaint3	C7
OpMaint4	C8
PurchasePrice	E5
SupplyDemand	J12:J16
To	C12:C21
TotalCost	D23
TradeIn1	D5
TradeIn2	D6
TradeIn3	D7
TradeIn4	D8

	E
11	Cost
12	=PurchasePrice+OpMaint1-TradeIn1
13	=PurchasePrice+OpMaint1+OpMaint2-TradeIn2
14	=PurchasePrice+OpMaint1+OpMaint2+OpMaint3-TradeIn3
15	=PurchasePrice+OpMaint1+OpMaint2+OpMaint3+OpMaint4-TradeIn4
16	=PurchasePrice+OpMaint1-TradeIn1
17	=PurchasePrice+OpMaint1+OpMaint2-TradeIn2
18	=PurchasePrice+OpMaint1+OpMaint2+OpMaint3-TradeIn3
19	=PurchasePrice+OpMaint1-TradeIn1
20	=PurchasePrice+OpMaint1+OpMaint2-TradeIn2
21	=PurchasePrice+OpMaint1-TradeIn1

	H
11	Net Flow
12	=SUMIF(From,G12,OnRoute)-SUMIF(To,G12,OnRoute)
13	=SUMIF(From,G13,OnRoute)-SUMIF(To,G13,OnRoute)
14	=SUMIF(From,G14,OnRoute)-SUMIF(To,G14,OnRoute)
15	=SUMIF(From,G15,OnRoute)-SUMIF(To,G15,OnRoute)
16	=SUMIF(From,G16,OnRoute)-SUMIF(To,G16,OnRoute)

	C	D
23	Total Cost	=SUMPRODUCT(OnRoute,Cost)

Solver Parameters

Set Objective (Target Cell): TotalCost
To: Min
By Changing (Variable) Cells:
  OnRoute
Subject to the Constraints:
  NetFlow = SupplyDemand

Solver Options (Excel 2010):
  Make Variables Nonnegative
  Solving Method: Simplex LP
Solver Options (older Excel):
  Assume Nonnegative
  Assume Linear Model

TABLE 6.3
Time Required for the
Phases of Preparing
Quick Co.'s New Product

Level	Remaining Research	Development	Design of Manufacturing System	Initiate Production and Distribution
Normal	5 months	—	—	—
Priority	4 months	3 months	5 months	2 months
Crash	2 months	2 months	3 months	1 month

TABLE 6.4
Cost for the Phases of
Preparing Quick Co.'s
New Product

Level	Remaining Research	Development	Design of Manufacturing System	Initiate Production and Distribution
Normal	$3 million	—	—	—
Priority	6 million	$6 million	$ 9 million	$3 million
Crash	9 million	9 million	12 million	6 million

FIGURE 6.16
Formulation of the Quick
Co. problem as a shortest
path problem. Except for
the dummy destination,
the arc labels indicate,
first, the number of
phases completed and,
second, the amount of
money left (in millions of
dollars) for the remaining
phases. Each arc length
gives the time (in months)
to perform that phase.

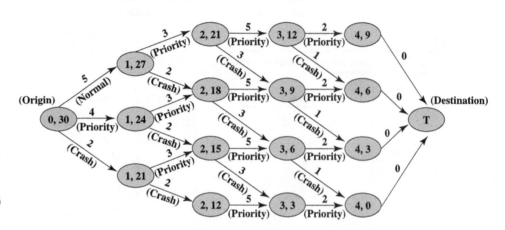

All four phases have been completed as soon as any one of the four nodes with a first label of 4 has been reached. So why doesn't the network just end with these four nodes rather than having an arc coming out of each one? The reason is that a shortest path problem is required to have only a single destination. Consequently, a dummy destination is added at the right-hand side.

> When real travel through a network can end at more than one node, an arc with length 0 is inserted from each of these nodes to a **dummy destination** so that the network will have just a single destination.

Since each of the arcs into the dummy destination has length 0, this addition to the network does not affect the total length of a path from the origin to its ending point.

The target cell now is TotalTime instead of TotalDistance.

Figure 6.17 displays the spreadsheet model for this problem. Once again, the format is the same as in Figures 6.13 and 6.15, except now the quantity of concern in column F and the target cell TotalTime (D32) is time rather than distance or cost. Since the Solve button has already been clicked, the changing cells OnRoute (D4:D30) indicate which arcs lie on the path that minimizes the total time. Thus, the shortest path is

with a total length of 2 + 3 + 3 + 2 + 0 = 10 months, as given by TotalTime (D32). The resulting plan for the four phases is shown in Table 6.5. Although this plan does consume the entire budget of $30 million, it reduces the time until the product can be brought to market from the originally planned 20 months down to just 10 months.

Given this information, Quick's management now must decide whether this plan provides the best trade-off between time and cost. What would be the effect on total time of spending a few million more dollars? What would be the effect of reducing the spending somewhat instead? It is easy to provide management with this information as well by quickly solving some shortest path problems that correspond to budgets different from $30 million. The ultimate decision regarding which plan provides the best time–cost trade-off then is a judgment decision that only management can make.

FIGURE 6.17

A spreadsheet model that formulates the Quick Co. problem as a shortest path problem where the objective is to minimize the total time instead of the total distance, so the target cell is TotalTime (D32). The other output cells are NetFlow (I4:I20). The values of 1 in the changing cells OnRoute (D4:D30) reveal the shortest (quickest) path obtained by the Solver.

	A	B	C	D	E	F	G	H	I	J	K
1		**Quick Co. Product Development Scheduling Problem**									
2											
3		**From**	**To**	**On Route**		**Time**		**Nodes**	**Net Flow**		**Supply/Demand**
4		(0, 30)	(1, 27)	0		5		(0, 30)	1	=	1
5		(0, 30)	(1, 24)	0		4		(1, 27)	0	=	0
6		(0, 30)	(1, 21)	1		2		(1, 24)	0	=	0
7		(1, 27)	(2, 21)	0		3		(1, 21)	0	=	0
8		(1, 27)	(2, 18)	0		2		(2, 21)	0	=	0
9		(1, 24)	(2, 18)	0		3		(2, 18)	0	=	0
10		(1, 24)	(2, 15)	0		2		(2, 15)	0	=	0
11		(1, 21)	(2, 15)	1		3		(2, 12)	0	=	0
12		(1, 21)	(2, 12)	0		2		(3, 12)	0	=	0
13		(2, 21)	(3, 12)	0		5		(3, 9)	0	=	0
14		(2, 21)	(3, 9)	0		3		(3, 6)	0	=	0
15		(2, 18)	(3, 9)	0		5		(3, 3)	0	=	0
16		(2, 18)	(3, 6)	0		3		(4, 9)	0	=	0
17		(2, 15)	(3, 6)	0		5		(4, 6)	0	=	0
18		(2, 15)	(3, 3)	1		3		(4, 3)	0	=	0
19		(2, 12)	(3, 3)	0		5		(4, 0)	0	=	0
20		(3, 12)	(4, 9)	0		2		(T)	-1	=	-1
21		(3, 12)	(4, 6)	0		1					
22		(3, 9)	(4, 6)	0		2					
23		(3, 9)	(4, 3)	0		1					
24		(3, 6)	(4, 3)	0		2					
25		(3, 6)	(4, 0)	0		1					
26		(3, 3)	(4, 0)	1		2					
27		(4, 9)	(T)	0		0					
28		(4, 6)	(T)	0		0					
29		(4, 3)	(T)	0		0					
30		(4, 0)	(T)	1		0					
31											
32			**Total Time**	10							

(continued)

FIGURE 6.17 *(continued)*

Range Name	Cells
From	B4:B30
NetFlow	I4:I20
Nodes	H4:H20
OnRoute	D4:D30
SupplyDemand	K4:K20
Time	F4:F30
To	C4:C30
TotalTime	D32

Solver Parameters

Set Objective (Target Cell): TotalTime
To: Min
By Changing (Variable) Cells:
    OnRoute
Subject to the Constraints:
    NetFlow = SupplyDemand

Solver Options (Excel 2010):
    Make Variables Nonnegative
    Solving Method: Simplex LP
Solver Options (older Excel):
    Assume Nonnegative
    Assume Linear Model

	I
3	**Net Flow**
4	=SUMIF(From,H4,OnRoute)-SUMIF(To,H4,OnRoute)
5	=SUMIF(From,H5,OnRoute)-SUMIF(To,H5,OnRoute)
6	=SUMIF(From,H6,OnRoute)-SUMIF(To,H6,OnRoute)
7	=SUMIF(From,H7, OnRoute)-SUMIF(To,H7,OnRoute)
8	=SUMIF(From,H8,OnRoute)-SUMIF(To,H8,OnRoute)
9	=SUMIF(From,H9,OnRoute)-SUMIF(To,H9,OnRoute)
10	=SUMIF(From,H10,OnRoute)-SUMIF(To,H10,OnRoute)
11	=SUMIF(From,H11,OnRoute)-SUMIF(To,H11,OnRoute)
12	=SUMIF(From,H12,OnRoute)-SUMIF(To,H12,OnRoute)
13	=SUMIF(From,H13,OnRoute)-SUMIF(To,H13,OnRoute)
14	=SUMIF(From,H14,OnRoute)-SUMIF(To,H14,OnRoute)
15	=SUMIF(From,H15,OnRoute)-SUMIF(To,H15,OnRoute)
16	=SUMIF(From,H16,OnRoute)-SUMIF(To,H16,OnRoute)
17	=SUMIF(From,H17,OnRoute)-SUMIF(To,H17,OnRoute)
18	=SUMIF(From,H18,OnRoute)-SUMIF(To,H18,OnRoute)
19	=SUMIF(From,H19,OnRoute)-SUMIF(To,H19,OnRoute)
20	=SUMIF(From,H20,OnRoute)-SUMIF(To,H20,OnRoute)

	C	D
32	**Total Time**	=SUMPRODUCT(OnRoute,Time)

TABLE 6.5
The Optimal Solution Obtained by the Excel Solver for Quick Co.'s Shortest Path Problem

Phase	Level	Time	Cost
Remaining research	Crash	2 months	$ 9 million
Development	Priority	3 months	6 million
Design of manufacturing system	Crash	3 months	12 million
Initiate production and distribution	Priority	2 months	3 million
Total		10 months	$30 million

Review Questions

1. What are the origin and the destination in the Littletown Fire Department example?
2. What is the distinction between an arc and a link?
3. What are the supply node and the demand node when a shortest path problem is interpreted as a minimum-cost flow problem? With what supply and demand?
4. What are three measures of the length of a link (or arc) that lead to three categories of applications of shortest path problems?
5. What is the objective for Sarah's shortest path problem?
6. When does a dummy destination need to be added to the formulation of a shortest path problem?
7. What kind of trade-off does the management of the Quick Co. need to consider in making its final decision about how to expedite its new product to market?

6.5 Summary

Networks of some type arise in a wide variety of contexts. Network representations are very useful for portraying the relationships and connections between the components of systems. Each component is represented by a point in the network called a *node,* and then the connections between components (nodes) are represented by lines called *arcs* (for one-way travel) or *links* (for two-way travel).

Frequently, a flow of some type must be sent through a network, so a decision needs to be made about the best way to do this. The kinds of network optimization models introduced in this chapter provide a powerful tool for making such decisions.

The model for minimum-cost flow problems plays a central role among these network optimization models, both because it is so broadly applicable and because it can be readily solved. The Excel Solver solves spreadsheet formulations of reasonable size, and the network simplex method can be used to solve larger problems, including huge problems with tens of thousands of nodes and arcs. A minimum-cost flow problem typically is concerned with optimizing the flow of goods through a network from their points of origin (the *supply nodes*) to where they are needed (the *demand nodes*). The objective is to minimize the total cost of sending the available supply through the network to satisfy the given demand. One typical application (among several) is to optimize the operation of a distribution network.

Special types of minimum-cost flow problems include transportation problems and assignment problems (discussed in Chapter 3) as well as two prominent types introduced in this chapter: maximum flow problems and shortest path problems.

Given the limited capacities of the arcs in the network, the objective of a maximum flow problem is to maximize the total amount of flow from a particular point of origin (the *source*) to a particular terminal point (the *sink*). For example, this might involve maximizing the flow of goods through a company's supply network from its vendors to its processing facilities.

A shortest path problem also has a beginning point (the *origin*) and an ending point (the *destination*), but now the objective is to find a path from the origin to the destination that has the minimum total *length*. For some applications, length refers to distance, so the objective is to minimize the total distance traveled. However, some applications instead involve minimizing either the total cost or the total time of a sequence of activities.

Glossary

arc   A channel through which flow may occur from one node to another, shown as an arrow between the nodes pointing in the direction in which flow is allowed. (Section 6.1), 192

capacity of an arc   The maximum amount of flow allowed through the arc. (Section 6.1), 192

conservation of flow   Having the amount of flow out of a node equal the amount of flow into that node. (Section 6.1), 192

demand node   A node where the net amount of flow generated (outflow minus inflow) is a fixed negative number, so that flow is absorbed there. (Section 6.1), 192

destination   The node at which travel through the network is assumed to end for a shortest path problem. (Section 6.4), 207

dummy destination   A fictitious destination introduced into the formulation of a shortest path problem with multiple possible termination points to satisfy the requirement that there be just a single destination. (Section 6.4), 211

length of a link or arc   The number (typically a distance, a cost, or a time) associated with including the link or arc in the selected path for a shortest path problem. (Section 6.4), 207

link   A channel through which flow may occur in either direction between a pair of

nodes, shown as a line between the nodes. (Section 6.4), 205

network simplex method   A streamlined version of the simplex method for solving minimum-cost flow problems very efficiently. (Section 6.1), 195

node   A junction point of a network, shown as a labeled circle. (Section 6.1), 192

origin   The node at which travel through the network is assumed to start for a shortest path problem. (Section 6.4), 207

sink   The node for a maximum flow problem at which all flow through the network terminates. (Section 6.3), 200

source   The node for a maximum flow problem at which all flow through the network originates. (Section 6.3), 200

supply node   A node where the net amount of flow generated (outflow minus inflow) is a fixed positive number. (Section 6.1), 192

transshipment node   A node where the amount of flow out equals the amount of flow in. (Section 6.1), 192

transshipment problem   A special type of minimum-cost flow problem where there are no capacity constraints on the arcs. (Section 6.1), 196

Learning Aids for This Chapter in Your MS Courseware

Chapter 6 Excel Files:

Distribution Unlimited Example
BMZ Example
Expanded BMZ Example
Littletown Fire Department Example

Sarah Example
Quick Example

Supplement to Chapter 6 on the CD-ROM:

Minimum Spanning-Tree Problems

Solved Problems (See the CD-ROM or Web site for the Solutions)

6.S1. Distribution at Heart Beats

Heart Beats is a manufacturer of medical equipment. The company's primary product is a device used to monitor the heart during medical procedures. This device is produced in two factories and shipped to two warehouses. The product is then shipped on demand to four third-party wholesalers. All shipping is done by truck. The product distribution network is shown below. The annual production capacity at factories 1 and 2 is 400 and 250, respectively. The annual demand at wholesalers 1, 2, 3, and 4 is 200, 100, 150, and 200, respectively. The cost of shipping one unit in each shipping lane is shown on the arcs. Because of limited truck capacity, at most 250 units can be shipped from factory 1 to warehouse 1 each year. Formulate and solve a network optimization model in a spreadsheet to determine how to distribute the product at the lowest possible annual cost.

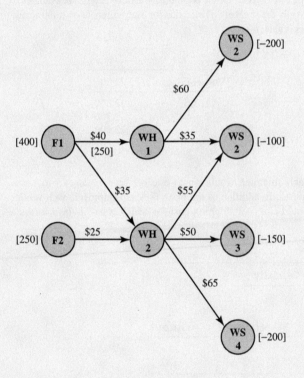

6.S2. Assessing the Capacity of a Pipeline Network

Exxo 76 is an oil company that operates the pipeline network shown below, where each pipeline is labeled with its maximum flow rate in million cubic feet (MMcf) per day. A new oil well has been constructed near A. They would like to transport oil from the well near A to their refinery at G. Formulate and solve a network optimization model to determine the maximum flow rate from A to G.

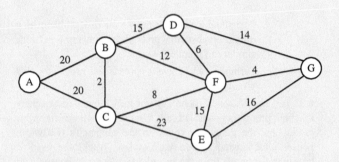

6.S3. Driving to the Mile-High City

Sarah and Jennifer have just graduated from college at the University of Washington in Seattle and want to go on a road trip. They have always wanted to see the mile-high city of Denver. Their road atlas shows the driving time (in hours) between various city pairs, as shown below. Formulate and solve a network optimization model to find the quickest route from Seattle to Denver.

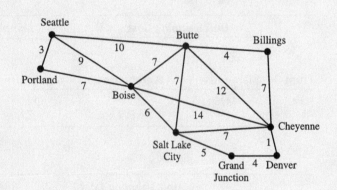

Problems

We have inserted the symbol E* to the left of each problem (or its parts) where Excel should be used (unless your instructor gives you contrary instructions). An asterisk on the problem number indicates that at least a partial answer is given in the back of the book.

6.1.   Read the referenced article that fully describes the management science study summarized in the application vignette presented in Section 6.1. Briefly describe how the model for the minimum-cost flow problem was applied in this study. Then list the various financial and nonfinancial benefits that resulted from this study.

6.2.* Consider the transportation problem having the following data.

	Destination			
	1	**2**	**3**	**Supply**
Source				
1	6	7	4	40
2	5	8	6	60
Demand	30	40	30	

a. Formulate a network model for this problem as a minimum-cost flow problem by drawing a network similar to Figure 6.3.

E* *b.* Formulate and solve a spreadsheet model for this problem.

6.3. The Makonsel Company is a fully integrated company that both produces goods and sells them at its retail outlets. After production, the goods are stored in the company's two warehouses until needed by the retail outlets. Trucks are used to transport the goods from the two plants to the warehouses, and then from the warehouses to the three retail outlets.

Using units of full truckloads, the first table below shows each plant's monthly output, its shipping cost per truckload sent to each warehouse, and the maximum amount that it can ship per month to each warehouse.

For each retail outlet (RO), the second table below shows its monthly demand, its shipping cost per truckload from each warehouse, and the maximum amount that can be shipped per month from each warehouse.

Management now wants to determine a distribution plan (number of truckloads shipped per month from each plant to each warehouse and from each warehouse to each retail outlet) that will minimize the total shipping cost.

a. Draw a network that depicts the company's distribution network. Identify the supply nodes, transshipment nodes, and demand nodes in this network.

b. Formulate a network model for this problem as a minimum-cost flow problem by inserting all the necessary data into the network drawn in part *a*. (Use the format depicted in Figure 6.3 to display these data.)

E* *c.* Formulate and solve a spreadsheet model for this problem.

6.4. The Audiofile Company produces boomboxes. However, management has decided to subcontract out the production of the speakers needed for the boomboxes. Three vendors are available to supply the speakers. Their price for each shipment of 1,000 speakers is shown below.

Vendor	Price
1	$22,500
2	22,700
3	22,300

Each shipment would go to one of the company's two warehouses. In addition to the price for each shipment, each vendor would charge a shipping cost for which it has its own formula

	Unit Shipping Cost		Shipping Capacity		
To From	**Warehouse 1**	**Warehouse 2**	**Warehouse 1**	**Warehouse 2**	**Output**
Plant 1	$425	$560	125	150	200
Plant 2	510	600	175	200	300

	Unit Shipping Cost			Shipping Capacity		
To From	**RO1**	**RO2**	**RO3**	**RO1**	**RO2**	**RO3**
Warehouse 1	$470	$505	$490	100	150	100
Warehouse 2	390	410	440	125	150	75
Demand	150	200	150	150	200	150

based on the mileage to the warehouse. These formulas and the mileage data are shown below.

Vendor	Charge per Shipment	Warehouse 1	Warehouse 2
1	$300 + 40¢/mile	1,600 miles	400 miles
2	$200 + 50¢/mile	500 miles	600 miles
3	$500 + 20¢/mile	2,000 miles	1,000 miles

Whenever one of the company's two factories needs a shipment of speakers to assemble into the boomboxes, the company hires a trucker to bring the shipment in from one of the warehouses. The cost per shipment is given next, along with the number of shipments needed per month at each factory.

	Unit Shipping Cost	
	Factory 1	Factory 2
Warehouse 1	$200	$700
Warehouse 2	400	500
Monthly demand	10	6

Each vendor is able to supply as many as 10 shipments per month. However, because of shipping limitations, each vendor is only able to send a maximum of six shipments per month to each warehouse. Similarly, each warehouse is only able to send a maximum of six shipments per month to each factory.

Management now wants to develop a plan for each month regarding how many shipments (if any) to order from each vendor, how many of those shipments should go to each warehouse, and then how many shipments each warehouse should send to each factory. The objective is to minimize the sum of the purchase costs (including the shipping charge) and the shipping costs from the warehouses to the factories.

a. Draw a network that depicts the company's supply network. Identify the supply nodes, transshipment nodes, and demand nodes in this network.

b. This problem is only a *variant* of a minimum-cost flow problem because the supply from each vendor is a *maximum* of 10 rather than a fixed amount of 10. However, it can be converted to a full-fledged minimum-cost flow problem by adding a dummy demand node that receives (at zero cost) all the unused supply capacity at the vendors. Formulate a network model for this minimum-cost flow problem by inserting all the necessary data into the network drawn in part *a* supplemented by this dummy demand node. (Use the format depicted in Figure 6.3 to display these data.)

E* *c.* Formulate and solve a spreadsheet model for the company's problem.

6.5.* Consider Figure 6.9 (in Section 6.3), which depicts the BMZ Co. distribution network from its factories in Stuttgart and Berlin to the distribution centers in both Los Angeles and Seattle. This figure also gives in brackets the maximum amount that can be shipped through each shipping lane.

In the weeks following the crisis described in Section 6.2, the distribution center in Los Angeles has successfully replenished its inventory. Therefore, Karl Schmidt (the supply chain manager for the BMZ Co.) has concluded that it will be sufficient hereafter to ship 130 units per month to Los Angeles and 50 units per month to Seattle. (One unit is a hundred cubic meters of automobile replacement parts.) The Stuttgart factory (node ST in the figure) will allocate 130 units per month and the Berlin factory (node BE) will allocate 50 units per month out of their total production to cover these shipments. However, rather than resuming the past practice of supplying the Los Angeles distribution center from only the Stuttgart factory and supplying the Seattle distribution center from only the Berlin factory, Karl has decided to allow either factory to supply either distribution center. He feels that this additional flexibility is likely to reduce the total shipping cost.

The following table gives the shipping cost per unit through each of these shipping lanes.

	Unit Shipping Cost to Node								
From \ To	LI	BO	RO	HA	NO	NY	BN	LA	SE
Node									
ST	$3,200	$2,500	$2,900	—	—	—	—	—	—
BE	—	—	$2,400	$2,000	—	—	—	—	—
LI	—	—	—	—	$6,100	—	—	—	—
BO	—	—	—	—	$6,800	$5,400	—	—	—
RO	—	—	—	—	—	$5,900	—	—	—
HA	—	—	—	—	—	$6,300	$5,700	—	—
NO	—	—	—	—	—	—	—	$3,100	—
NY	—	—	—	—	—	—	—	$4,200	$4,000
BN	—	—	—	—	—	—	—	$3,400	$3,000

Karl wants to determine the shipping plan that will minimize the total shipping cost.

  a. Formulate a network model for this problem as a minimum-cost flow problem by inserting all the necessary data into the distribution network shown in Figure 6.9. (Use the format depicted in Figure 6.3 to display these data.)

E* b. Formulate and solve a spreadsheet model for this problem.

  c. What is the total shipping cost for this optimal solution?

6.6. Reconsider Problem 6.5. Suppose now that, for administrative convenience, management has decided that all 130 units per month needed at the distribution center in Los Angeles must come from the Stuttgart factory (node ST) and all 50 units per month needed at the distribution center in Seattle must come from the Berlin factory (node BE). For each of these distribution centers, Karl Schmidt wants to determine the shipping plan that will minimize the total shipping cost.

  a. For the distribution center in Los Angeles, formulate a network model for this problem as a minimum-cost flow problem by inserting all the necessary data into the distribution network shown in Figure 6.6. (Use the format depicted in Figure 6.3 to display these data.)

E* b. Formulate and solve a spreadsheet model for the problem formulated in part *a*.

  c. For the distribution center in Seattle, draw its distribution network emanating from the Berlin factory at node BE.

  d. Repeat part *a* for the distribution center in Seattle by using the network drawn in part *c*.

E* e. Formulate and solve a spreadsheet model for the problem formulated in part *d*.

  f. Add the total shipping costs obtained in parts *b* and *e*. Compare this sum with the total shipping cost obtained in part *c* of Problem 6.5 (as given in the back of the book).

6.7. Consider the maximum flow problem formulated in Figures 6.7 and 6.8 for the BMZ case study. Redraw Figure 6.7 and insert the optimal shipping quantities (cells D4:D12 in Figure 6.8) in parentheses above the respective arcs. Examine the capacities of these arcs. Explain why these arc capacities ensure that the shipping quantities in parentheses must be an optimal solution because the maximum flow cannot exceed 150.

6.8. Read the referenced article that fully describes the management science study summarized in the application vignette presented in Section 6.3. Briefly describe how a generalization of the model for the maximum flow problem was applied in this study. Then list the various financial and nonfinancial benefits that resulted from this study.

E*6.9. Formulate and solve a spreadsheet model for the maximum flow problem shown at the top of the next column, where node A is the source, node F is the sink, and the arc capacities are the numbers in square brackets shown next to the arcs.

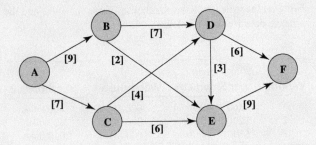

6.10. The diagram depicts a system of aqueducts that originate at three rivers (nodes R1, R2, and R3) and terminate at a major city (node T), where the other nodes are junction points in the system.

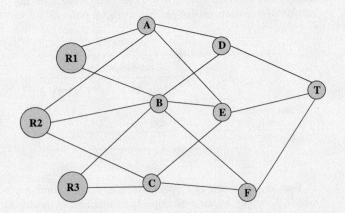

Using units of thousands of acre feet, the following tables show the maximum amount of water that can be pumped through each aqueduct per day.

To From	A	B	C
R1	75	65	—
R2	40	50	60
R3	—	80	70

To From	D	E	F
A	60	45	—
B	70	55	45
C	—	70	90

To From	T
D	120
E	190
F	130

The city water manager wants to determine a flow plan that will maximize the flow of water to the city.

  a. Formulate this problem as a maximum flow problem by identifying a source, a sink, and the transshipment nodes, and then drawing the complete network that shows the capacity of each arc.

E* b. Formulate and solve a spreadsheet model for this problem.

6.11. The Texago Corporation has four oil fields, four refineries, and four distribution centers in the locations identified in the next tables. A major strike involving the transportation industries now has sharply curtailed Texago's capacity to ship oil from the four oil fields to the four refineries and to ship petroleum products from the refineries to the distribution centers. Using units of thousands of barrels of crude oil (and its equivalent in refined products), the following tables show the maximum number of units that can be shipped per day from each oil field to each refinery and from each refinery to each distribution center.

	Refinery			
Oil Field	**New Orleans**	**Charleston**	**Seattle**	**St. Louis**
Texas	11	7	2	8
California	5	4	8	7
Alaska	7	3	12	6
Middle East	8	9	4	15

	Distribution Center			
Refinery	**Pittsburgh**	**Atlanta**	**Kansas City**	**San Francisco**
New Orleans	5	9	6	4
Charleston	8	7	9	5
Seattle	4	6	7	8
St. Louis	12	11	9	7

The Texago management now wants to determine a plan for how many units to ship from each oil field to each refinery and from each refinery to each distribution center that will maximize the total number of units reaching the distribution centers.

    a. Draw a rough map that shows the location of Texago's oil fields, refineries, and distribution centers. Add arrows to show the flow of crude oil and then petroleum products through this distribution network.

    b. Redraw this distribution network by lining up all the nodes representing oil fields in one column, all the nodes representing refineries in a second column, and all the nodes representing distribution centers in a third column. Then add arcs to show the possible flow.

    c. Use the distribution network from part *b* to formulate a network model for Texago's problem as a variant of a maximum flow problem.

E*   *d.* Formulate and solve a spreadsheet model for this problem.

6.12 Read the referenced article that fully describes the management science study summarized in the application vignette presented in Section 6.4. Briefly describe how network optimization models (including for shortest path problems)

were applied in this study. Then list the various financial and nonfinancial benefits that resulted from this study.

E*6.13. Reconsider the Littletown Fire Department problem presented in Section 6.4 and depicted in Figure 6.11. Due to maintenance work on the one-mile road between nodes A and B, a detour currently must be taken that extends the trip between these nodes to four miles.

Formulate and solve a spreadsheet model for this revised problem to find the new shortest path from the fire station to the farming community.

6.14. You need to take a trip by car to another town that you have never visited before. Therefore, you are studying a map to determine the shortest route to your destination. Depending on which route you choose, there are five other towns (call them A, B, C, D, E) through which you might pass on the way. The map shows the mileage along each road that directly connects two towns without any intervening towns. These numbers are summarized in the following table, where a dash indicates that there is no road directly connecting these two towns without going through any other towns.

	Miles between Adjacent Towns					
Town	**A**	**B**	**C**	**D**	**E**	**Destination**
Origin	40	60	50	—	—	—
A		10	—	70	—	—
B			20	55	40	—
C				—	50	—
D					10	60
E						80

    a. Formulate a network model for this problem as a shortest path problem by drawing a network where nodes represent towns, links represent roads, and numbers indicate the length of each link in miles.

E*   *b.* Formulate and solve a spreadsheet model for this problem.

    c. Use part *b* to identify your shortest route.

    d. If each number in the table represented your *cost* (in dollars) for driving your car from one town to the next, would the answer in part *c* now give your minimum-cost route?

    e. If each number in the table represented your *time* (in minutes) for driving your car from one town to the next, would the answer in part *c* now give your minimum-time route?

6.15.* At a small but growing airport, the local airline company is purchasing a new tractor for a tractor-trailer train to bring luggage to and from the airplanes. A new mechanized luggage system will be installed in three years, so the tractor will not be needed after that. However, because it will receive heavy use, so that the running and maintenance costs will increase rapidly as it ages, it may still be more economical to replace the tractor after one or two years. The following table gives the total net discounted cost associated with purchasing a tractor (purchase price minus trade-in allowance, plus running and maintenance costs) at the end of year i and trading it in at the end of year j (where year 0 is now).

	j		
	1	**2**	**3**
i			
0	$8,000	$18,000	$31,000
1		10,000	21,000
2			12,000

Management wishes to determine at what times (if any) the tractor should be replaced to minimize the total cost for the tractor(s) over three years.

      a. Formulate a network model for this problem as a shortest path problem.

E*   b. Formulate and solve a spreadsheet model for this problem.

6.16.   One of Speedy Airlines's flights is about to take off from Seattle for a nonstop flight to London. There is some flexibility in choosing the precise route to be taken, depending upon weather conditions. The following network depicts the possible routes under consideration, where SE and LN are Seattle and London, respectively, and the other nodes represent various intermediate locations.

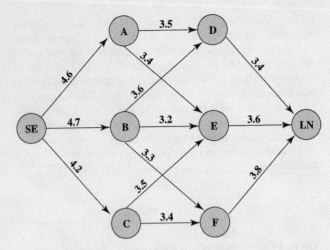

The winds along each arc greatly affect the flying time (and so the fuel consumption). Based on current meteorological reports, the flying times (in hours) for this particular flight are shown next to the arcs. Because the fuel consumed is so expensive, the management of Speedy Airlines has established a policy of choosing the route that minimizes the total flight time.

      a. What plays the role of distances in interpreting this problem to be a shortest path problem?

E*   b. Formulate and solve a spreadsheet model for this problem.

Partial Answers to Selected Problems

CHAPTER 6

6.2. *b.* 0 S1-D1, 10 S1-D2, 30 S1-D3, 30 S2-D1, 30 S2-D2, 0 S2-D3. Total cost = $580.

6.5. *c.* $2,187,000.

6.9. Maximum flow = 15.

6.15. *b.* Replace after year 1. Total cost = $29,000.

6.S1 Distribution at Heart Beats

Heart Beats is a manufacturer of medical equipment. The company's primary product is a device used to monitor the heart during medical procedures. This device is produced in two factories and shipped to two warehouses. The product is then shipped on demand to four third-party wholesalers. All shipping is done by truck. The product distribution network is shown below. The annual production capacity at Factories 1 and 2 is 400 and 250, respectively. The annual demand at Wholesalers 1, 2, 3, and 4 is 200, 100, 150, and 200, respectively. The cost of shipping one unit in each shipping lane is shown on the arcs. Due to limited truck capacity, at most 250 units can be shipped from Factory 1 to Warehouse 1 each year. Formulate and solve a network optimization model in a spreadsheet to determine how to distribute the product at the lowest possible annual cost.

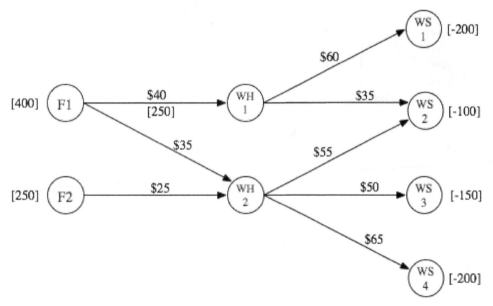

This is a minimum-cost flow problem. To set up a spreadsheet model, first list all of the arcs as shown in B4:C11, along with their capacity (F4) and unit cost (G4:G11). Only the arc from F1 to WH1 is capacitated. Then list all of the nodes as shown in I4:I11 along with each node's supply or demand (L4:L11).

1

	B	C	D	E	F	G	H	I	J	K	L
3	From	To			Capacity	Unit Cost		Nodes			Supply/Demand
4	F1	WH1			250	$40		F1			400
5	F1	WH2				$35		F2			250
6	F2	WH2				$25		WH1			0
7	WH1	WS1				$60		WH2			0
8	WH1	WS2				$35		WS1			-200
9	WH2	WS2				$55		WS2			-100
10	WH2	WS3				$50		WS3			-150
11	WH2	WS4				$65		WS4			-200

The changing cells are the amount of flow to send through each arc. These are shown in Flow (D4:D11) below, with an arbitrary value of 10 entered for each. The flow through the arc from F1 to WH1 must be less than the capacity of 250, as indicated by the constraint D4 <= F4.

	B	C	D	E	F	G
3	From	To	Flow		Capacity	Unit Cost
4	F1	WH1	10	<=	250	$40
5	F1	WH2	10			$35
6	F2	WH2	10			$25
7	WH1	WS1	10			$60
8	WH1	WS2	10			$35
9	WH2	WS2	10			$55
10	WH2	WS3	10			$50
11	WH2	WS4	10			$65

For each node, calculate the net flow as a function of the changing cells. This can be done using the SUMIF function. In each case, the first SUMIF function calculates the flow leaving the node and the second one calculates the flow entering the node. For example, consider the F1 node (I4). SUMIF(From, Nodes, Flow) sums each individual entry in Flow (the changing cells in D4:D11) if that entry is in a row where the entry in From (B4:B11) is the same as in that row of Nodes (i.e., F1). Since I4 = F1 and the only rows that have F1 in From (B4:B11) are rows 4 and 5, the sum in the ship column is only over these same rows, so this sum is D4+D5.

	B	C	D	E	F	G	H	I	J	K	L
3	From	To	Flow		Capacity	Unit Cost		Nodes	Net Flow		Supply/Demand
4	F1	WH1	10	<=	250	$40		F1	20	=	400
5	F1	WH2	10			$35		F2	10	=	250
6	F2	WH2	10			$25		WH1	10	=	0
7	WH1	WS1	10			$60		WH2	10	=	0
8	WH1	WS2	10			$35		WS1	-10	=	-200
9	WH2	WS2	10			$55		WS2	-20	=	-100
10	WH2	WS3	10			$50		WS3	-10	=	-150
11	WH2	WS4	10			$65		WS4	-10	=	-200

	J
3	Net Flow
4	=SUMIF(From,Nodes,Flow)-SUMIF(To,Nodes,Flow)
5	=SUMIF(From,Nodes,Flow)-SUMIF(To,Nodes,Flow)
6	=SUMIF(From,Nodes,Flow)-SUMIF(To,Nodes,Flow)
7	=SUMIF(From,Nodes,Flow)-SUMIF(To,Nodes,Flow)
8	=SUMIF(From,Nodes,Flow)-SUMIF(To,Nodes,Flow)
9	=SUMIF(From,Nodes,Flow)-SUMIF(To,Nodes,Flow)
10	=SUMIF(From,Nodes,Flow)-SUMIF(To,Nodes,Flow)
11	=SUMIF(From,Nodes,Flow)-SUMIF(To,Nodes,Flow)

The goal is to minimize the total cost of shipping the product from the factories to the wholesalers. The cost is the SUMPRODUCT of the Unit Costs with the Flow, or Total Cost = SUMPRODUCT(UnitCost, Flow). This formula is entered into TotalCost (D13).

	B	C	D	E	F	G	H	I	J	K	L
3	From	To	Flow		Capacity	Unit Cost		Nodes	Net Flow		Supply/Demand
4	F1	WH1	10	<=	250	$40		F1	20	=	400
5	F1	WH2	10			$35		F2	10	=	250
6	F2	WH2	10			$25		WH1	10	=	0
7	WH1	WS1	10			$60		WH2	10	=	0
8	WH1	WS2	10			$35		WS1	-10	=	-200
9	WH2	WS2	10			$55		WS2	-20	=	-100
10	WH2	WS3	10			$50		WS3	-10	=	-150
11	WH2	WS4	10			$65		WS4	-10	=	-200
12											
13		Total Cost	$3,650								

	C	D
13	Total Cost	=SUMPRODUCT(UnitCost,Flow)

The Solver information and solved spreadsheet are shown below.

	B	C	D	E	F	G	H	I	J	K	L
3	From	To	Flow		Capacity	Unit Cost		Nodes	Net Flow		Supply/Demand
4	F1	WH1	250	<=	250	$40		F1	400	=	400
5	F1	WH2	150			$35		F2	250	=	250
6	F2	WH2	250			$25		WH1	0	=	0
7	WH1	WS1	200			$60		WH2	0	=	0
8	WH1	WS2	50			$35		WS1	-200	=	-200
9	WH2	WS2	50			$55		WS2	-100	=	-100
10	WH2	WS3	150			$50		WS3	-150	=	-150
11	WH2	WS4	200			$65		WS4	-200	=	-200
12											
13	Total Cost		$58,500								

Solver Parameters

Set Objective (Target Cell): TotalCost
To: Min
By Changing (Variable) Cells:
    Flow
Subject to the Constraints:
    D4 <= Capacity
    NetFlow = SupplyDemand

Solver Options (Excel 2010):
    Make Variables Nonnegative
    Solving Method: Simplex LP
Solver Options (older Excel):
    Assume Nonnegative
    Assume Linear Model

Range Name	Cells
Capacity	F4
Flow	D4:D11
From	B4:B11
NetFlow	J4:J11
Nodes	I4:I11
SupplyDemand	L4:L11
To	C4:C11
TotalCost	D13
UnitCost	G4:G11

	J
3	**Net Flow**
4	=SUMIF(From,Nodes,Flow)-SUMIF(To,Nodes,Flow)
5	=SUMIF(From,Nodes,Flow)-SUMIF(To,Nodes,Flow)
6	=SUMIF(From,Nodes,Flow)-SUMIF(To,Nodes,Flow)
7	=SUMIF(From,Nodes,Flow)-SUMIF(To,Nodes,Flow)
8	=SUMIF(From,Nodes,Flow)-SUMIF(To,Nodes,Flow)
9	=SUMIF(From,Nodes,Flow)-SUMIF(To,Nodes,Flow)
10	=SUMIF(From,Nodes,Flow)-SUMIF(To,Nodes,Flow)
11	=SUMIF(From,Nodes,Flow)-SUMIF(To,Nodes,Flow)

	C	D
13	Total Cost	=SUMPRODUCT(UnitCost,Flow)

Thus, Flow (D4:D11) indicates how to distribute the product so as to achieve the minimum Total Cost (D13) of $58,500.

6.S2 Assessing the Capacity of a Pipeline Network

Exxo 76 is an oil company that operates the pipeline network shown below, where each pipeline is labeled with its maximum flow rate in million cubic feet (MMcf) per day. A new oil well has been constructed near A. They would like to transport oil from the well near A to their refinery at G. Formulate and solve a network optimization model to determine the maximum flow rate from A to G.

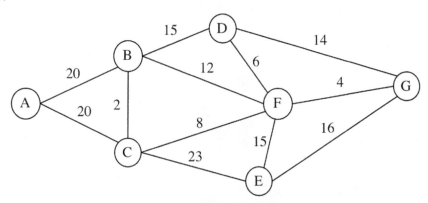

This is a minimum-cost flow problem. Associated with each pipe in the network will be an arc (or, for pipes which might flow in either direction, two arcs, one in each direction). To set up a spreadsheet model, first list all of the arcs as shown in B5:C19, along with their capacity (F5:F19). Then list all of the nodes as shown in H5:H11. All the transshipment nodes (every node except the start node A and the end node G) will be constrained to have net flow = 0 (Supply/Demand = 0). The start node (A) and end node (G) are left unconstrained. We want to maximize the net flow out of node A.

	B	C	D	E	F	G	H	I	J	K
4	From	To			Capacity		Nodes			Supply/Demand
5	A	B			20		A			
6	A	C			20		B		=	0
7	B	C			2		C		=	0
8	B	D			15		D		=	0
9	B	F			12		E		=	0
10	C	B			2		F		=	0
11	C	E			23		G			
12	C	F			8					
13	D	F			6					
14	D	G			14					
15	E	F			15					
16	E	G			16					
17	F	D			6					
18	F	E			15					
19	F	G			4					

The changing cells are the amount of flow to send through each pipe (arc). These are shown in Flow (D5:D19) below, with an arbitrary value of 0 entered for each. The flow through each arc is capacitated as indicated by the <= in E5:E19.

	B	C	D	E	F
3			thousands of gallons / hour		
4	From	To	Flow		Capacity
5	A	B	0	<=	20
6	A	C	0	<=	20
7	B	C	0	<=	2
8	B	D	0	<=	15
9	B	F	0	<=	12
10	C	B	0	<=	2
11	C	E	0	<=	23
12	C	F	0	<=	8
13	D	F	0	<=	6
14	D	G	0	<=	14
15	E	F	0	<=	15
16	E	G	0	<=	16
17	F	D	0	<=	6
18	F	E	0	<=	15
19	F	G	0	<=	4

For each node, calculate the net flow as a function of the changing cells. This can be done using the SUMIF function. In each case, the first SUMIF function calculates the flow leaving the node and the second one calculates the flow entering the node. For example, consider the A node (H5). SUMIF(From, Nodes, Flow) in I5 sums each individual entry in Flow (the changing cells in D5:D19) if that entry is in a row where the entry in From (B5:B19) is the same as in the entry in that row of Nodes (i.e., A). Since the only rows that have A in From (B5:B19) are rows 5 and 6, the sum in the ship column is only over these same rows, so this sum is D5+D6.

	B	C	D	E	F	G	H	I	J	K
3			thousands of gallons / hour					thousands of gallons / hour		
4	From	To	Flow		Capacity		Nodes	Net Flow		Supply/Demand
5	A	B	0	<=	20		A	0		
6	A	C	0	<=	20		B	0	=	0
7	B	C	0	<=	2		C	0	=	0
8	B	D	0	<=	15		D	0	=	0
9	B	F	0	<=	12		E	0	=	0
10	C	B	0	<=	2		F	0	=	0
11	C	E	0	<=	23		G	0		
12	C	F	0	<=	8					
13	D	F	0	<=	6					
14	D	G	0	<=	14					
15	E	F	0	<=	15					
16	E	G	0	<=	16					
17	F	D	0	<=	6					
18	F	E	0	<=	15					
19	F	G	0	<=	4					

	I
4	Net Flow
5	=SUMIF(From,Nodes,Flow)-SUMIF(To,Nodes,Flow)
6	=SUMIF(From,Nodes,Flow)-SUMIF(To,Nodes,Flow)
7	=SUMIF(From,Nodes,Flow)-SUMIF(To,Nodes,Flow)
8	=SUMIF(From,Nodes,Flow)-SUMIF(To,Nodes,Flow)
9	=SUMIF(From,Nodes,Flow)-SUMIF(To,Nodes,Flow)
10	=SUMIF(From,Nodes,Flow)-SUMIF(To,Nodes,Flow)
11	=SUMIF(From,Nodes,Flow)-SUMIF(To,Nodes,Flow)

The goal is to maximize the amount shipped from A to G. Since nodes B through F are transshipment nodes (net flow = 0), any amount that leaves A must enter G. Thus, maximizing the flow out of A will achieve our goal. Thus, the formula entered into the target cell MaximumFlow (D21) is =I5.

	B	C	D	E	F	G	H	I	J	K
3			thousands of gallons / hour					thousands of gallons / hour		
4	From	To	Flow		Capacity		Nodes	Net Flow		Supply/Demand
5	A	B	0	<=	20		A	0		
6	A	C	0	<=	20		B	0	=	0
7	B	C	0	<=	2		C	0	=	0
8	B	D	0	<=	15		D	0	=	0
9	B	F	0	<=	12		E	0	=	0
10	C	B	0	<=	2		F	0	=	0
11	C	E	0	<=	23		G	0		
12	C	F	0	<=	8					
13	D	F	0	<=	6					
14	D	G	0	<=	14					
15	E	F	0	<=	15					
16	E	G	0	<=	16					
17	F	D	0	<=	6					
18	F	E	0	<=	15					
19	F	G	0	<=	4					
20										
21	Maximum Flow		0							

	C	D
21	Maximum Flow	=I5

The Solver information and solved spreadsheet are shown below.

	B	C	D	E	F	G	H	I	J	K
3			thousands of gallons / hour					thousands of gallons / hour		
4	From	To	Flow		Capacity		Nodes	Net Flow		Supply/Demand
5	A	B	20	<=	20		A	34		
6	A	C	14	<=	20		B	0	=	0
7	B	C	0	<=	2		C	0	=	0
8	B	D	14	<=	15		D	0	=	0
9	B	F	8	<=	12		E	0	=	0
10	C	B	2	<=	2		F	0	=	0
11	C	E	12	<=	23		G	-34		
12	C	F	0	<=	8					
13	D	F	0	<=	6					
14	D	G	14	<=	14					
15	E	F	0	<=	15					
16	E	G	16	<=	16					
17	F	D	0	<=	6					
18	F	E	4	<=	15					
19	F	G	4	<=	4					
20										
21	Maximum Flow		34							

Solver Parameters

Set Objective (Target Cell): MaximumFlow
To: Max
By Changing (Variable) Cells:
    Flow
Subject to the Constraints:
    Flow <= Capacity
    NetFlow = SupplyDemand

Solver Options (Excel 2010):
    Make Variables Nonnegative
    Solving Method: Simplex LP
Solver Options (older Excel):
    Assume Nonnegative
    Assume Linear Model

Range Name	Cells
Capacity	F5:F19
Flow	D5:D19
From	B5:B19
MaximumFlow	D21
NetFlow	I6:I10
Nodes	H5:H11
SupplyDemand	K6:K10
To	C5:C19

	I
4	Net Flow
5	=SUMIF(From,Nodes,Flow)-SUMIF(To,Nodes,Flow)
6	=SUMIF(From,Nodes,Flow)-SUMIF(To,Nodes,Flow)
7	=SUMIF(From,Nodes,Flow)-SUMIF(To,Nodes,Flow)
8	=SUMIF(From,Nodes,Flow)-SUMIF(To,Nodes,Flow)
9	=SUMIF(From,Nodes,Flow)-SUMIF(To,Nodes,Flow)
10	=SUMIF(From,Nodes,Flow)-SUMIF(To,Nodes,Flow)
11	=SUMIF(From,Nodes,Flow)-SUMIF(To,Nodes,Flow)

	C	D
21	Maximum Flow	=I5

Thus, Flow (D5:D19) indicates how to send oil through the network so as to achieve the Maximum Flow (D21) of 34 thousand gallons/hour.

6.S3 Driving to the Mile-High City

Sarah and Jennifer have just graduated from college at the University of Washington in Seattle and want to go on a road trip. They have always wanted to see the mile-high city of Denver. Their road atlas shows the driving time (in hours) between various city pairs, as shown below. Formulate and solve a network optimization model to find the quickest route from Seattle to Denver?

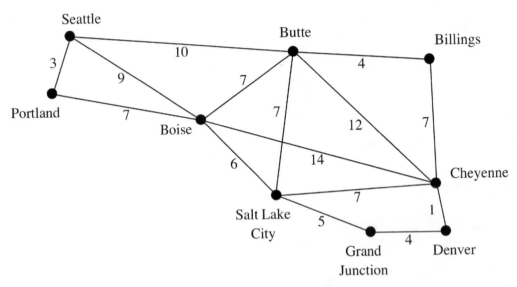

This is a shortest path problem. To set up a spreadsheet model, first list all of the arcs as shown in B4:C11, along with their capacity (F4). Only the arc from F1 to WH1 is capacitated. Then list all of the nodes as shown in I4:I11 along with each node's supply or demand (L4:L11).

	B	C	D	E	F	G	H	I	J	K	L
3	**From**	**To**			**Capacity**	**Unit Cost**		**Nodes**			**Supply/Demand**
4	F1	WH1			250	$40		F1			400
5	F1	WH2				$35		F2			250
6	F2	WH2				$25		WH1			0
7	WH1	WS1				$60		WH2			0
8	WH1	WS2				$35		WS1			-200
9	WH2	WS2				$55		WS2			-100
10	WH2	WS3				$50		WS3			-150
11	WH2	WS4				$65		WS4			-200

The changing cells are the amount of flow to send through each arc. These are shown in Flow (D4:D11) below, with an arbitrary value of 10 entered for each. The flow through the arc from F1 to WH1 must be less than the capacity of 250, as indicated by the constraint D4 <= F4.

	B	C	D	E	F	G
3	**From**	**To**	**Flow**		**Capacity**	**Unit Cost**
4	F1	WH1	10	<=	250	$40
5	F1	WH2	10			$35
6	F2	WH2	10			$25
7	WH1	WS1	10			$60
8	WH1	WS2	10			$35
9	WH2	WS2	10			$55
10	WH2	WS3	10			$50
11	WH2	WS4	10			$65

For each node, calculate the net flow as a function of the changing cells. This can be done using the SUMIF function. In each case, the first SUMIF function calculates the flow leaving the node and the second one calculates the flow entering the node. For example, consider the F1 node (I4). SUMIF(From, I4, Flow) sums each individual entry in Flow (the changing cells in D4:D11) if that entry is in a row where the entry in From (B4:B11) is the same as in I4 (i.e., F1). Since I4 = F1 and the only rows that have F1 in From (B4:B11) are rows 4 and 5, the sum in the ship column is only over these same rows, so this sum is D4+D5.

	B	C	D	E	F	G	H	I	J	K	L
3	**From**	**To**	**Flow**		**Capacity**	**Unit Cost**		**Nodes**	**Net Flow**		**Supply/Demand**
4	F1	WH1	10	<=	250	$40		F1	20	=	400
5	F1	WH2	10			$35		F2	10	=	250
6	F2	WH2	10			$25		WH1	10	=	0
7	WH1	WS1	10			$60		WH2	10	=	0
8	WH1	WS2	10			$35		WS1	-10	=	-200
9	WH2	WS2	10			$55		WS2	-20	=	-100
10	WH2	WS3	10			$50		WS3	-10	=	-150
11	WH2	WS4	10			$65		WS4	-10	=	-200

	J
3	**Net Flow**
4	=SUMIF(From,Nodes,Flow)-SUMIF(To,Nodes,Flow)
5	=SUMIF(From,Nodes,Flow)-SUMIF(To,Nodes,Flow)
6	=SUMIF(From,Nodes,Flow)-SUMIF(To,Nodes,Flow)
7	=SUMIF(From,Nodes,Flow)-SUMIF(To,Nodes,Flow)
8	=SUMIF(From,Nodes,Flow)-SUMIF(To,Nodes,Flow)
9	=SUMIF(From,Nodes,Flow)-SUMIF(To,Nodes,Flow)
10	=SUMIF(From,Nodes,Flow)-SUMIF(To,Nodes,Flow)
11	=SUMIF(From,Nodes,Flow)-SUMIF(To,Nodes,Flow)

The goal is to minimize the total cost of shipping the product from the factories to the wholesalers. The cost is the SUMPRODUCT of the Unit Costs with the Flow, or Total Cost = SUMPRODUCT(UnitCost, Flow). This formula is entered into TotalCost (D13).

	B	C	D	E	F	G	H	I	J	K	L
3	From	To	Flow		Capacity	Unit Cost		Nodes	Net Flow		Supply/Demand
4	F1	WH1	10	<=	250	$40		F1	20	=	400
5	F1	WH2	10			$35		F2	10	=	250
6	F2	WH2	10			$25		WH1	10	=	0
7	WH1	WS1	10			$60		WH2	10	=	0
8	WH1	WS2	10			$35		WS1	-10	=	-200
9	WH2	WS2	10			$55		WS2	-20	=	-100
10	WH2	WS3	10			$50		WS3	-10	=	-150
11	WH2	WS4	10			$65		WS4	-10	=	-200
12											
13	Total Cost		$3,650								

	C	D
13	Total Cost	=SUMPRODUCT(UnitCost,Flow)

The Solver information and solved spreadsheet are shown below.

	B	C	D	E	F	G	H	I	J	K	L
3	From	To	Flow		Capacity	Unit Cost		Nodes	Net Flow		Supply/Demand
4	F1	WH1	250	<=	250	$40		F1	400	=	400
5	F1	WH2	150			$35		F2	250	=	250
6	F2	WH2	250			$25		WH1	0	=	0
7	WH1	WS1	200			$60		WH2	0	=	0
8	WH1	WS2	50			$35		WS1	-200	=	-200
9	WH2	WS2	50			$55		WS2	-100	=	-100
10	WH2	WS3	150			$50		WS3	-150	=	-150
11	WH2	WS4	200			$65		WS4	-200	=	-200
12											
13		Total Cost	$58,500								

Solver Parameters

Set Objective (Target Cell): TotalCost
To: Min
By Changing (Variable) Cells:
   Flow
Subject to the Constraints:
   D4 <= Capacity
   NetFlow = SupplyDemand

Solver Options (Excel 2010):
   Make Variables Nonnegative
   Solving Method: Simplex LP
Solver Options (older Excel):
   Assume Nonnegative
   Assume Linear Model

Range Name	Cells
Capacity	F4
Flow	D4:D11
From	B4:B11
NetFlow	J4:J11
Nodes	I4:I11
SupplyDemand	L4:L11
To	C4:C11
TotalCost	D13
UnitCost	G4:G11

	J
3	**Net Flow**
4	=SUMIF(From,Nodes,Flow)-SUMIF(To,Nodes,Flow)
5	=SUMIF(From,Nodes,Flow)-SUMIF(To,Nodes,Flow)
6	=SUMIF(From,Nodes,Flow)-SUMIF(To,Nodes,Flow)
7	=SUMIF(From,Nodes,Flow)-SUMIF(To,Nodes,Flow)
8	=SUMIF(From,Nodes,Flow)-SUMIF(To,Nodes,Flow)
9	=SUMIF(From,Nodes,Flow)-SUMIF(To,Nodes,Flow)
10	=SUMIF(From,Nodes,Flow)-SUMIF(To,Nodes,Flow)
11	=SUMIF(From,Nodes,Flow)-SUMIF(To,Nodes,Flow)

	C	D
13	Total Cost	=SUMPRODUCT(UnitCost,Flow)

Thus, Flow (D4:D11) indicates how to distribute the product so as to achieve the minimum Total Cost (D13) of $58,500.

Using Binary Integer Programming to Deal with Yes-or-No Decisions

Learning objectives

After completing this chapter, you should be able to

1. Describe how binary decision variables are used to represent yes-or-no decisions.
2. Use binary decision variables to formulate constraints for mutually exclusive alternatives and contingent decisions.
3. Formulate a binary integer programming model for the selection of projects.
4. Formulate a binary integer programming model for the selection of sites for facilities.
5. Formulate a binary integer programming model for crew scheduling in the travel industry.
6. Formulate other basic binary integer programming models from a description of the problems.
7. Use mixed binary integer programming to deal with setup costs for initiating the production of a product.

The preceding chapters have considered various kinds of problems where decisions need to be made about *how much to do* of various activities. Thus, the decision variables in the resulting model represent the *level* of the corresponding activities.

We turn now to a common type of problem where, instead of *how-much decisions,* the decisions to be made are **yes-or-no decisions.** A yes-or-no decision arises when a particular option is being considered and the only possible choices are yes, go ahead with this option, or no, decline this option.

The natural choice of a decision variable for a yes-or-no decision is a *binary variable.* **Binary variables** are variables whose only possible values are 0 and 1. Thus, when representing a yes-or-no decision, a **binary decision variable** is assigned a value of 1 for choosing yes and a value of 0 for choosing no.

Models that fit linear programming except that they use binary decision variables are called **binary integer programming (BIP)** models. (We hereafter will use the **BIP** abbreviation.) A **pure BIP** model is one where all the variables are binary variables, whereas a **mixed BIP** model is one where only some of the variables are binary variables.

A BIP model can be considered to be a special type of *integer programming model.* A general integer programming model is simply a linear programming model except for also having constraints that some or all of the decision variables must have integer values (0, 1, 2, . . .). A BIP model further restricts these integer values to be *only* 0 or 1.

However, BIP problems are quite different from general integer programming problems because of the difference in the nature of the decisions involved. Like linear programming problems, general integer programming problems involve how-much decisions, but where these decisions make sense only if they have integer values. For example, the TBA Airlines problem presented in Section 3.2 is a general integer programming problem because it is essentially a linear programming problem except that its how-much decisions (how many small airplanes and how many large airplanes to purchase) only make sense if they have integer values. By contrast, BIP problems involve yes-or-no decisions instead of how-much decisions.

The preceding chapters already have focused on problems involving how-much decisions and how such techniques as linear programming or integer programming can be used to analyze these problems. Therefore, this chapter will be devoted instead to problems involving yes-or-no decisions and how BIP models can be used to analyze this special category of problems.

BIP problems arise with considerable frequency in a wide variety of applications. To illustrate this, we begin with a case study and then present some more examples in the subsequent sections. One of the supplements to this chapter on the CD-ROM also provides additional formulation examples for BIP problems.

You will see throughout this chapter that BIP problems can be formulated on a spreadsheet just as readily as linear programming problems. The Excel Solver also can solve BIP problems of modest size. You normally will have no problem solving the small BIP problems found in this book, but Solver may fail on somewhat larger problems. To provide some perspective on this issue, we include another supplement on the CD-ROM that is entitled Some Perspectives on Solving Binary Integer Programming Problems. The algorithms available for solving BIP problems (including the one used by the Excel Solver) are not nearly as efficient as those for linear programming, so this supplement discusses some of the difficulties and pitfalls involved in solving large BIP problems. One option with any large problem that fits linear programming except that it has decision variables that are restricted to integer values (but not necessarily just 0 and 1) is to ignore the integer constraints and then to round the solution obtained to integer values. This is a reasonable option in some cases but not in others. The supplement emphasizes that this is a particularly dangerous shortcut with BIP problems.

7.1 A CASE STUDY: THE CALIFORNIA MANUFACTURING CO. PROBLEM

"OK, Steve here is the situation. With our growing business, we are strongly considering building a new factory. Maybe even two. The factory needs to be close to a large, skilled labor force, so we are looking at Los Angeles and San Francisco as the potential sites. We also are considering building one new warehouse. Not more than one. This warehouse would make sense in saving shipping costs only if it is in the same city as the new factory. Either Los Angeles or San Francisco. If we decide not to build a new factory at all, we definitely don't want the warehouse either. Is this clear, so far?"

"Yes, Armando, I understand," Steve Chan responds. "What are your criteria for making these decisions?"

"Well, all the other members of top management have joined me in addressing this issue," Armando Ortega replies. "We have concluded that these two potential sites are very comparable on nonfinancial grounds. Therefore, we feel that these decisions should be based mainly on financial considerations. We have $10 million of capital available for this expansion and we want it to go as far as possible in improving our bottom line. Which feasible combination of investments in factories and warehouses in which locations will be most profitable for the company in the long run? In your language, we want to maximize the total net present value of these investments."

What is the most profitable combination of investments?

"That's very clear. It sounds like a classical management science problem."

"That's why I called you in, Steve. I would like you to conduct a quick management science study to determine the most profitable combination of investments. I also would like you to take a look at the amount of capital being made available and its effect on how much profit we can get from these investments. The decision to make $10 million available is only a tentative one. That amount is stretching us, because we now are investigating some other interesting project proposals that would require quite a bit of capital, so we would prefer to use less than $10 million on these particular investments if the last few million don't buy us much. On the other hand, this expansion into either Los Angeles or San Francisco, or maybe both of these key cities, is our number one priority. It will have a real positive impact on the future of

An Application Vignette

With headquarters in Houston, Texas, **Waste Management, Inc.** (a Fortune 100 company), is the leading provider of comprehensive waste-management services in North America. Its network of operations includes 293 active landfill disposal sites, 16 waste-to-energy plants, 72 landfill gas-to-energy facilities, 146 recycling plants, 346 transfer stations, and 435 collection operations (depots) to provide services to nearly 20 million residential customers and 2 million commercial customers throughout the United States and Canada.

The company's collection-and-transfer vehicles need to follow nearly 20,000 daily routes. With an annual operating cost of nearly $120,000 per vehicle, management wanted to have a comprehensive route-management system that would make every route as profitable and efficient as possible. Therefore, a management science team that included a number of consultants was formed to attack this problem.

The heart of the route-management system developed by this team is a *huge mixed BIP model* that optimizes the routes assigned to the respective collection-and-transfer

vehicles. Although the objective function takes several factors into account, the primary goal is the minimization of total travel time. The main decision variables are binary variables that equal 1 if the route assigned to a particular vehicle includes a particular possible leg and that equal 0 otherwise. A geographical information system (GIS) provides the data about the distance and time required to go between any two points. All of this is imbedded within a Web-based Java application that is integrated with the company's other systems.

It is estimated that the recent implementation of this comprehensive route-management system will *increase the company's cash flow by* **$648 million** *over a five-year period*, largely because of *savings of* **$498 million** in operational expenses over this same period. It also is providing better customer service.

Source: S. Sahoo, S. Kim, B.-I. Kim, B. Krass, and A. Popov, Jr., "Routing Optimization for Waste Management," *Interfaces* 35, no. 1 (January–February 2005), pp. 24–36. (A link to this article is provided on our Web site, **www.mhhe.com/hillier4e.**)

this company. So we are willing to go out and raise some more capital if it would give us a lot of bang for the buck. Therefore, we would like you to do some what-if analysis to tell us what the effect would be if we were to change the amount of capital being made available to anything between $5 million and $15 million."

"Sure, Armando, we do that kind of what-if analysis all the time. We refer to it as sensitivity analysis because it involves checking how sensitive the outcome is to the amount of capital being made available."

"Good. Now, Steve, I need your input within the next couple weeks. Can you do it?"

"Well, Armando, as usual, the one question is whether we can gather all the necessary data that quickly. We'll need to get good estimates of the net present value of each of the possible investments. I'll need a lot of help in digging out that information."

"I thought you would say that. I already have my staff working hard on developing those estimates. I can get you together with them this afternoon."

"Great. I'll get right on it."

As president of the California Manufacturing Company, Armando Ortega has had many similar conversations in the past with Steve Chan, the company's top management scientist. Armando is confident that Steve will come through for him again.

Background

The **California Manufacturing Company** is a diversified company with several factories and warehouses throughout California, but none yet in Los Angeles or San Francisco. Because the company is enjoying increasing sales and earnings, management feels that the time may be ripe to expand into one or both of those prime locations. A basic issue is whether to build a new factory in either Los Angeles or San Francisco, or perhaps even in both cities. Management also is considering building at most one new warehouse, but will restrict the choice of location to a city where a new factory is being built.

The decisions to be made are listed in the second column of Table 7.1 in the form of yes-or-no questions. In each case, giving an answer of yes to the question corresponds to the decision to make the investment to build the indicated facility (a factory or a warehouse) in the indicated location (Los Angeles or San Francisco). The capital required for the investment is given in the rightmost column, where management has made the tentative decision that the total amount of capital being made available for all the investments is $10 million. (Note that this amount is inadequate for some of the combinations of investments.) The fourth column shows the estimated *net present value* (net long-run profit considering

TABLE 7.1
Data for the California Manufacturing Co. Problem

Decision Number	Yes-or-No Question	Decision Variable	Net Present Value (Millions)	Capital Required (Millions)
1	Build a factory in Los Angeles?	x_1	$8	$6
2	Build a factory in San Francisco?	x_2	5	3
3	Build a warehouse in Los Angeles?	x_3	6	5
4	Build a warehouse in San Francisco?	x_4	4	2
			Capital available: $10 million	

the time value of money) if the corresponding investment is made. (The net present value is 0 if the investment is not made.) Much of the work of Steve Chan's management science study (with substantial help from the president's staff) goes into developing these estimates of the net present values. As specified by the company's president, Armando Ortega, the objective now is to find the feasible combination of investments that maximizes the total net present value.

Introducing Binary Decision Variables for the Yes-or-No Decisions

As summarized in the second column of Table 7.1, the problem facing management is to make four interrelated *yes-or-no decisions*. To formulate a mathematical model for this problem, Steve Chan needs to introduce a decision variable for each of these decisions. Since each decision has just two alternatives, choose yes or choose no, the corresponding decision variable only needs to have two values (one for each alternative). Therefore, Steve uses a *binary variable*, whose only possible values are 0 and 1, where 1 corresponds to the decision to choose yes and 0 corresponds to choosing no.

These decision variables are shown in the second column of Table 7.2. The final two columns give the interpretation of a value of 1 and 0, respectively.

Dealing with Interrelationships between the Decisions

Recall that management wants no more than one new warehouse to be built. In terms of the corresponding decision variables, x_3 and x_4, this means that no more than one of these variables is allowed to have the value 1. Therefore, these variables must satisfy the constraint

$$x_3 + x_4 \leq 1$$

as part of the mathematical model for the problem.

These two alternatives (build a warehouse in Los Angeles or build a warehouse in San Francisco) are referred to as **mutually exclusive alternatives** because choosing one of these alternatives excludes choosing the other. Groups of two or more mutually exclusive alternatives arise commonly in BIP problems. For each such group where at most one of the alternatives can be chosen, the constraint on the corresponding binary decision variables has the form shown above, namely, the sum of these variables must be *less than or equal to* 1. For some groups of mutually exclusive alternatives, management will exclude the possibility of choosing *none* of the alternatives, in which case the constraint will set the sum of the corresponding binary decision variables *equal* to 1.

The California Manufacturing Co. problem also has another important kind of restriction. Management will allow a warehouse to be built in a particular city only if a factory also is being built in that city. For example, consider the situation for Los Angeles (LA).

With a group of mutually exclusive alternatives, only one of the corresponding binary decision variables can equal 1.

TABLE 7.2 Binary Decision Variables for the California Manufacturing Co. Problem

Decision Number	Decision Variable	Possible Value	Interpretation of a Value of 1	Interpretation of a Value of 0
1	x_1	0 or 1	Build a factory in Los Angeles	Do not build this factory
2	x_2	0 or 1	Build a factory in San Francisco	Do not build this factory
3	x_3	0 or 1	Build a warehouse in Los Angeles	Do not build this warehouse
4	x_4	0 or 1	Build a warehouse in San Francisco	Do not build this warehouse

If decide no, do not build a factory in LA (i.e., if choose $x_1 = 0$),
  then cannot build a warehouse in LA (i.e., must choose $x_3 = 0$).

If decide yes, do build a factory in LA (i.e., if choose $x_1 = 1$),
  then can either build a warehouse in LA or not (i.e., can choose either $x_3 = 1$ or 0).

How can these interrelationships between the factory and warehouse decisions for LA be expressed in a constraint for a mathematical model? The key is to note that, for either value of x_1, the permissible value or values of x_3 are less than or equal to x_1. Since x_1 and x_3 are binary variables, the constraint

$$x_3 \leq x_1$$

forces x_3 to take on a permissible value given the value of x_1.

Exactly the same reasoning leads to

$$x_4 \leq x_2$$

as the corresponding constraint for San Francisco. Just as for Los Angeles, this constraint forces having no warehouse in San Francisco ($x_4 = 0$) if a factory will not be built there ($x_2 = 0$), whereas going ahead with the factory there ($x_2 = 1$) leaves open the decision to build the warehouse there ($x_4 = 0$ or 1).

One yes-or-no decision is contingent on another yes-or-no decision if the first one is allowed to be yes only if the other one is yes.

For either city, the warehouse decision is referred to as a **contingent decision**, because the decision depends on a prior decision regarding whether to build a factory there. In general, one yes-or-no decision is said to be contingent on another yes-or-no decision if it is allowed to be yes *only if* the other is yes. As above, the mathematical constraint expressing this relationship requires that the binary variable for the former decision must be less than or equal to the binary variable for the latter decision.

The rightmost column of Table 7.1 reveals one more interrelationship between the four decisions, namely, that the amount of capital expended on the four facilities under consideration cannot exceed the amount available ($10 million). Therefore, the model needs to include a constraint that requires

Capital expended ≤ $10 million

How can the amount of capital expended be expressed in terms of the four binary decision variables? To start this process, consider the first yes-or-no decision (build a factory in Los Angeles?). Combining the information in the rightmost column of Table 7.1 and the first row of Table 7.2,

$$\text{Capital expended on factory in Los Angeles} = \begin{cases} \$6 \text{ million} & \text{if } x_1 = 1 \\ 0 & \text{if } x_1 = 0 \end{cases}$$

$$= \$6 \text{ million } times \ x_1$$

By the same reasoning, the amount of capital expended on the other three investment opportunities (in units of millions of dollars) is $3x_2$, $5x_3$, and $2x_4$, respectively. Consequently,

Capital expended $= 6x_1 + 3x_2 + 5x_3 + 2x_4$ (in millions of dollars)

Excel Tip: Beware that rounding errors can occur with Excel. Therefore, even when you add a constraint that a changing cell has to be binary, Excel occasionally will return a noninteger value very close to an integer (e.g., 1.23E-10, meaning 0.000000000123). When this happens, you then can replace the noninteger value with the proper integer value.

Therefore, the constraint becomes

$$6x_1 + 3x_2 + 5x_3 + 2x_4 \leq 10$$

The BIP Model

As indicated by Armando Ortega in his conversation with Steve Chan, management's objective is to find the feasible combination of investments that *maximizes* the total net present value of these investments. Thus, the value of the objective function should be

NPV = Total net present value

If the investment is made to build a particular facility (so that the corresponding decision variable has a value of 1), the estimated net present value from that investment is given in the

FIGURE 7.1

A spreadsheet formulation of the BIP model for the California Manufacturing Co. case study where the changing cells BuildFactory? (C18:D18) and BuildWarehouse? (C16:D16) give the optimal solution obtained by using the Excel Solver.

	A	B	C	D	E	F	G
1		**California Manufacturing Co. Facility Location Problem**					
2							
3		**NPV ($millions)**	LA	SF			
4		Warehouse	6	4			
5							
6		Factory	8	5			
7							
8		**Capital Required**					
9		**($millions)**	LA	SF			
10		Warehouse	5	2	Capital		Capital
11					Spent		Available
12		Factory	6	3	9	?	10
13							
14					Total		Maximum
15		**Build?**	LA	SF	Warehouses		Warehouses
16		Warehouse	0	0	0	?	1
17			?	?			
18		Factory	1	1			
19							
20		Total NPV ($millions)	$13				

Excel Tip: In the Solver Options of Excel 2010, the *Integer Optimality (%)* setting (1 percent by default) causes Solver to stop solving an integer programming problem when it finds a feasible solution whose objective function value is within the specified percentage of being optimal. (In earlier versions of Excel, this option is referred to as *Tolerance*, and the default is 5 percent.) This is useful for very large BIP problems since it may enable finding a near-optimal solution when finding an optimal solution in a reasonable period of time is not possible. For smaller problems (e.g., all the problems in this book), this option should be set to 0 to guarantee finding an optimal solution.

Solver Parameters

Set Objective (Target Cell): TotalNPV
To: Max
By Changing (Variable) Cells:
    BuildWarehouse?, BuildFactory?
Subject to the Constraints:
    BuildFactory? = binary
    BuildWarehouse? = binary
    BuildWarehouse? <= BuildFactory?
    CapitalSpent <= CapitalAvailable
    TotalWarehouses <= MaxWarehouses

Solver Options (Excel 2010):
    Make Variables Nonnegative
    Solving Method: Simplex LP
Solver Options (older Excel):
    Assume Nonnegative
    Assume Linear Model

	E
10	Capital
11	Spent
12	= SUMPRODUCT(CapitalRequired,Build?)
13	
14	Total
15	Warehouses
16	= SUM(BuildWarehouse?)

Range Name	Cells
Build?	C16:D18
BuildWarehouse?	C16:D16
BuildFactory?	C18:D18
CapitalAvailable	G12
CapitalRequired	C10:D12
CapitalSpent	E12
MaxWarehouses	G16
NPV	C4:D6
TotalNPV	D20
TotalWarehouses	E16

	C	D
20	Total NPV ($millions)	=SUMPRODUCT(NPV,Build?)

fourth column of Table 7.1. If the investment is not made (so the decision variable equals 0), the net present value is 0. Therefore, continuing to use units of millions of dollars,

$$NPV = 8x_1 + 5x_2 + 6x_3 + 4x_4$$

is the quantity to enter into the target cell to be maximized.

Incorporating the constraints developed in the preceding subsection, the complete BIP model then is shown in Figure 7.1. The format is basically the same as for linear programming models. The one key difference arises when using the Solver dialogue box. Each of the decision variables (cells C18:D18 and C16:D16) is constrained to be binary. This is accomplished in the Add Constraint dialogue box by choosing each range of variables as the left-hand side and then choosing bin from the pop-up menu. The other constraints shown in the Solver dialogue box (see the lower left-hand side of Figure 7.1) have been made quite intuitive by using the suggestive range names given in the lower right-hand side of the figure. For convenience, the equations entered into the output cells in E12 and D20 use a SUMPRODUCT function that includes C17:D17 and either C11:D11 or C5:D5 because the blanks or ≤ signs in these rows are interpreted as zeroes by the Solver.

The Excel Solver gives the optimal solution shown in C18:D18 and C16:D16 of the spreadsheet, namely, build factories in *both* Los Angeles and San Francisco, but do not build any warehouses. The target cell (D20) indicates that the total net present value from building these two factories is estimated to be $13 million.

> Note how helpful the range names are for interpreting this BIP spreadsheet model.

Performing Sensitivity Analysis

Now that Steve Chan has used the BIP model to determine what should be done when the amount of capital being made available to these investments is $10 million, his next task is to perform *what-if analysis* on this amount. Recall that Armando Ortega wants him to determine *what* the effect would be *if* this amount were changed to anything else between $5 million and $15 million.

In Chapter 5, we described three different methods of performing what-if analysis on a linear programming spreadsheet model when there is a change in a constraint: using trial and error with the spreadsheet, applying the Solver Table, or referring to the Excel sensitivity report. The first two of these can be used on integer programming problems in exactly the same way as for linear programming problems. The third method, however, does not work. The sensitivity report is not available for integer programming problems. This is because the concept of a shadow price and allowable range no longer applies. In contrast to linear programming, the objective function values for an integer programming problem do not change in a predictable manner when the right-hand side of a constraint is changed.

> The Excel sensitivity report is *not* available for integer programming problems.

It is straightforward to determine the impact of changing the amount of available capital by trial and error. Simply try different values in the data cell CapitalAvailable (G12) and click Solve in the Solver. However, a more systematic way to perform this analysis is to use an Excel add-in in your MS Courseware called the *Solver Table*. The Solver Table works for integer programming models in exactly the same way as it does for linear programming models (as described in Section 5.3 in the subsection entitled *Using the Solver Table to Do Sensitivity Analysis Systematically*). Appendix A describes the use of the Solver Table in detail.

> Trial-and-error and/or the Solver Table can be used to perform sensitivity analysis for integer programming problems. See Section 5.3 and Appendix A for more details on using the Solver Table.

After expanding the original spreadsheet (Figure 7.1) to make room, the Solver Table has been used to generate the results shown in Figure 7.2 by executing the series of steps outlined in Section 5.3 and Appendix A. Note how Figure 7.2 shows the effect on the optimal solution and the resulting total net present value of varying the amount of capital being made available.

What-if analysis also could be performed on any of the other data cells—NPV (C4:D6), CapitalRequired (C10:D12), and MaxWarehouses (G16)—in a similar way with the Solver Table (or by using trial and error with the spreadsheet). However, a careful job was done in developing good estimates of the net present value of each of the possible investments, and there is little uncertainty in the values entered in the other data cells, so Steve Chan decides that further what-if analysis is not needed.

Management's Conclusion

Steve Chan's report is delivered to Armando Ortega within the two-week deadline. The report recommends the plan presented in Figure 7.1 (build a factory in both Los Angeles and San Francisco but no warehouses) if management decides to stick with its tentative decision to make $10 million of capital available for these investments. One advantage of this plan is that it only uses $9 million of this capital, which frees up $1 million of capital for other project proposals currently being investigated. The report also highlights the results shown in Figure 7.2 while emphasizing two points. One is that a heavy penalty would be paid (a reduction in the total net present value from $13 million to $9 million) if the amount of capital being made available were to be reduced below $9 million. The other is that *increasing* the amount of capital being made available by just $1 million (from $10 million to $11 million) would enable a

FIGURE 7.2

An application of the Solver Table that shows the effect on the optimal solution and the resulting total net present value of systematically varying the amount of capital being made available for these investments.

	B	C	D	E	F	G	H
23	Capital Available	Warehouse	Warehouse	Factory	Factory	Total NPV	
24	($millions)	in LA?	in SF?	in LA?	in SF?	($millions)	
25		0	0	1	1	13	
26	5	0	1	0	1	9	
27	6	0	1	0	1	9	Select the entire table (B25:G36), before choosing Solver Table from the Tools menu.
28	7	0	1	0	1	9	
29	8	0	1	0	1	9	
30	9	0	0	1	1	13	
31	10	0	0	1	1	13	
32	11	0	1	1	1	17	
33	12	0	1	1	1	17	
34	13	0	1	1	1	17	
35	14	1	0	1	1	19	
36	15	1	0	1	1	19	

	B	C	D	E	F	G
23	Capital Available	Warehouse	Warehouse	Factory	Factory	Total NPV
24	($millions)	in LA?	in SF?	in LA?	in SF?	($millions)
25		=C16	=D16	=C18	=D18	=TotalNPV

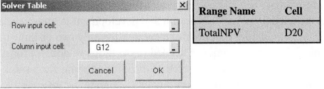

Range Name	Cell
TotalNPV	D20

Solver Table

Row input cell: _____

Column input cell: G12

Cancel   OK

substantial increase of $4 million in the total net present value (from $13 million to $17 million). However, a much larger further increase in the amount of capital being made available (from $11 million to $14 million) would be needed to enable a considerably smaller further increase in the total net present value (from $17 million to $19 million).

Armando Ortega deliberates with other members of top management before making a decision. It is quickly concluded that increasing the amount of capital being made available all the way up to $14 million would be stretching the company's financial resources too dangerously to justify the relatively small payoff. However, there is considerable discussion of the pros and cons of the two options of using either $9 million or $11 million of capital. Because of the large payoff from the latter option (an additional $4 million in total net present value), management finally decides to adopt the plan presented in row 32 of Figure 7.2. Thus, the company will build new factories in both Los Angeles and San Francisco as well as a new warehouse in San Francisco, with an estimated total net present value of $17 million. However, because of the large capital requirements of this plan, management also decides to defer building the warehouse until the two factories are completed so that their profits can help finance the construction of the warehouse.

Review Questions

1. What are the four interrelated decisions that need to be made by the management of the California Manufacturing Co.?
2. Why are binary decision variables appropriate to represent these decisions?
3. What is the objective specified by management for this problem?
4. What are the mutually exclusive alternatives in this problem? What is the form of the resulting constraint in the BIP model?
5. What are the contingent decisions in this problem? For each one, what is the form of the resulting constraint in the BIP model?
6. What is the tentative managerial decision on which sensitivity analysis needs to be performed?

7.2 USING BIP FOR PROJECT SELECTION: THE TAZER CORP. PROBLEM

The California Manufacturing Co. case study focused on four proposed projects: (1) build a factory in Los Angeles, (2) build a factory in San Francisco, (3) build a warehouse in Los Angeles, and (4) build a warehouse in San Francisco. Management needed to make yes-or-no decisions on which of these projects to select. This is typical of many applications of BIP. However, the nature of the projects may vary considerably from one application to the next. Instead of the proposed construction projects in the case study, our next example involves the selection of research and development projects.

This example is adapted from both Case 3-7 and its continuation in the supplement to Chapter 13, but all the relevant information is repeated below.

The Tazer Corp. Problem

Tazer Corp., a pharmaceutical manufacturing company, is beginning the search for a new breakthrough drug. The following five potential research and development projects have been identified for attempting to develop such a drug.

Project Up:	Develop a more effective antidepressant that does not cause serious mood swings.
Project Stable:	Develop a drug that addresses manic depression.
Project Choice:	Develop a less intrusive birth control method for women.
Project Hope:	Develop a vaccine to prevent HIV infection.
Project Release:	Develop a more effective drug to lower blood pressure.

In contrast to Case 3-7, Tazer management now has concluded that the company cannot devote enough money to research and development to undertake all of these projects. Only $1.2 billion is available, which will be enough for only two or three of the projects. The first row of Table 7.3 shows the amount needed (in millions of dollars) for each of these projects. The second row estimates each project's probability of being successful. If a project is successful, it is estimated that the resulting drug would generate the revenue shown in the third row. Thus, the *expected revenue* (in the statistical sense) from a potential drug is the product of its numbers in the second and third rows, whereas its *expected profit* is this expected revenue minus the investment given in the first row. These expected profits are shown in the bottom row of Table 7.3.

The objective is to choose the projects that will maximize the expected profit while satisfying the budget constraint.

Tazer management now wants to determine which of these projects should be undertaken to maximize their expected total profit.

Formulation with Binary Variables

Because the decision for each of the five proposed research and development projects is a yes-or-no decision, the corresponding decision variables are binary variables. Thus, the decision variable for each project has the following interpretation.

$$\text{Decision Variable} = \begin{cases} 1, & \text{if approve the project} \\ 0, & \text{if reject the project} \end{cases}$$

Let $x_1, x_2, x_3, x_4,$ and x_5 denote the decision variables for the respective projects in the order in which they are listed in Table 7.3.

If a project is rejected, there is neither any profit nor any loss, whereas the expected profit if a project is approved is given in the bottom row of Table 7.3. Using units of millions of dollars, the expected total profit is

$$P = 300x_1 + 120x_2 + 170x_3 + 100x_4 + 70x_5$$

TABLE 7.3
Data for the Tazer Project Selection Problem

	Project				
	1 (Up)	**2 (Stable)**	**3 (Choice)**	**4 (Hope)**	**5 (Release)**
R&D investment ($million)	400	300	600	500	200
Success rate	50%	35%	35%	20%	45%
Revenue if successful ($million)	1,400	1,200	2,200	3,000	600
Expected profit ($million)	300	120	170	100	70

The objective is to select the projects to approve that will maximize this expected total profit while satisfying the budget constraint.

Other than requiring the decision variables to be binary, the budget constraint limiting the total investment to no more than $1.2 billion is the only constraint that has been imposed by Tazer management on the selection of these research and development projects. Referring to the first row of Table 7.3, this constraint can be expressed in terms of the decision variables as

$$400x_1 + 300x_2 + 600x_3 + 500x_4 + 200x_5 \leq 1,200$$

With this background, the stage now is set for formulating a BIP spreadsheet model for this problem.

A BIP Spreadsheet Model for the Tazer Problem

Figure 7.3 shows a BIP spreadsheet model for this problem. The data in Table 7.3 have been transferred into cells C5:G8. The changing cells are DoProject? (C10:G10) and the target cell is TotalExpectedProfit (H8). The one functional constraint is depicted in cells H5:J5. The Add

FIGURE 7.3

A spreadsheet formulation of the BIP model for the Tazer Corp. project selection problem where the changing cells DoProject? (C10:G10) give the optimal solution obtained by the Excel Solver.

	A	B	C	D	E	F	G	H	I	J
1		**Tazer Corp. Project Selection Problem**								
2										
3										
4			Up	Stable	Choice	Hope	Release	Total		Budget
5		R&D Investment ($million)	400	300	600	500	200	1,200	<=	1,200
6		Success Rate	50%	35%	35%	20%	45%			
7		Revenue If Successful ($million)	1,400	1,200	2,200	3,000	600			
8		Expected Profit ($million)	300	120	170	100	70	540		
9										
10		Do Project?	1	0	1	0	1			

	B	C	D	E	F	G
8	Expected Profit ($million)	=C7*C6-C5	=D7*D6-D5	=E7*E6-E5	=F7*F6-F5	=G7*G6-G5

Range Name	Cells
Budget	J5
DoProject?	C10:G10
ExpectedProfit	C8:G8
RandDInvestment	C5:G5
Revenue	C7:G7
SuccessRate	C6:G6
TotalExpectedProfit	H8
TotalRandD	H5

	H
4	Total
5	=SUMPRODUCT(RandDInvestment,DoProject?)
6	
7	
8	=SUMPRODUCT(ExpectedProfit,DoProject?)

Solver Parameters
Set Objective (Target Cell): TotalExpectedProfit
To: Max
By Changing (Variable) Cells:
    DoProject?
Subject to the Constraints:
    DoProject? = binary
    TotalRandD <= Budget

Solver Options (Excel 2010):
    Make Variables Nonnegative
    Solving Method: Simplex LP
Solver Options (older Excel):
    Assume Nonnegative
    Assume Linear Model

Constraint dialogue box has been used to officially enter both this constraint and the DoProject? = binary constraints into the model, as shown in the Solver Parameters box.

The changing cells DoProject? (C10:G10) in Figure 7.3 show the optimal solution that has been obtained by the Excel Solver, namely,

Choose Project Up, Project Choice, and Project Release.

The target cell indicates that the resulting total expected profit is $540 million.

Review Questions

1. How are binary variables used to represent managerial decisions on which projects from a group of proposed projects should be selected for approval?
2. What types of projects are under consideration in the Tazer Corp. problem?
3. What is the objective for this problem?

7.3 USING BIP FOR THE SELECTION OF SITES FOR EMERGENCY SERVICES FACILITIES: THE CALIENTE CITY PROBLEM

Although the problem encountered in the California Manufacturing Co. case study can be described as a *project selection* problem (as was done at the beginning of the preceding section), it could just as well have been called a *site selection* problem. Recall that the company's management needed to select a site (Los Angeles or San Francisco) for its new factory as well as for its possible new warehouse. For either of the possible sites for the new factory (or the warehouse), there is a *yes-or-no decision* for whether that site should be selected, so it becomes natural to represent each such decision by a binary decision variable.

Various kinds of site selection problems are one of the most common types of applications of BIP. The kinds of facilities for which sites need to be selected can be of any type. In some cases, several sites are to be selected for several facilities of a particular type, whereas only a single site is to be selected in other cases.

We will focus here on the selection of sites for emergency services facilities. These facilities might be fire stations, police stations, ambulance centers, and so forth. In any of these cases, the overriding concern commonly is to provide facilities close enough to each part of the area being served that the response time to an emergency anywhere in the area will be sufficiently small. The form of the BIP model then will be basically the same regardless of the specific type of emergency services being considered.

To illustrate, let us consider an example where sites are being selected for fire stations. For simplicity, this example will divide the area being served into only eight tracts instead of the many dozens or hundreds that would be typical in real applications.

The Caliente City Problem

Caliente City is located in a particularly warm and arid part of the United States, so it is especially prone to the occurrence of fires. The city has become a popular place for senior citizens to move to after retirement, so it has been growing rapidly and spreading well beyond its original borders. However, the city still has only one fire station, located in the congested center of the original town site. The result has been some long delays in fire trucks reaching fires in the outer parts of the city, causing much more damage than would have occurred with a prompt response. The city's residents are very unhappy about this, so the city council has directed the city manager to develop a plan for locating multiple fire stations throughout the city (including perhaps moving the current fire station) that would greatly reduce the response time to any fire. In particular, the city council has adopted the following policy about the maximum acceptable response time for fire trucks to reach a fire anywhere in the city after being notified about the fire.

Response time ≤ 10 minutes

Having had a management science course in college, the city manager recognizes that BIP provides her with a powerful tool for analyzing this problem. To get started, she divides the city

TABLE 7.4 **Response Time and Cost Data for the Caliente City Problem**

		Fire Station in Tract							
		1	**2**	**3**	**4**	**5**	**6**	**7**	**8**
Response	1	2	8	18	9	23	22	16	28
times	2	9	3	10	12	16	14	21	25
(minutes)	3	17	8	4	20	21	8	22	17
for a fire	4	10	13	19	2	18	21	6	12
in tract	5	21	12	16	13	5	11	9	12
	6	25	15	7	21	15	3	14	8
	7	14	22	18	7	13	15	2	9
	8	30	24	15	14	17	9	8	3
Cost of station ($thousands)		350	250	450	300	50	400	300	200

into eight tracts and then gathers data on the estimated response time for a fire in each tract from a potential fire station in each of the eight tracts. These data are shown in Table 7.4. For example, if a decision were to be made to locate a fire station in tract 1 and if that fire station were to be used to respond to a fire in any of the tracts, the second column of Table 7.4 shows what the (estimated) response time would be. (Since the response time would exceed 10 minutes for a fire in tracts 3, 5, 6, 7, or 8, a fire station actually would need to be located nearer to each of these tracts to satisfy the city council's new policy.) The bottom row of Table 7.4 shows what the cost would be of acquiring the land and constructing a fire station in any of the eight tracts. (The cost is far less for tract 5 because the current fire station already is there so only a modest renovation is needed if the decision is made to retain a fire station there.)

> The objective is to minimize the total cost of ensuring a response time of no more than 10 minutes.

The objective now is to determine which tracts should receive a fire station to minimize the total cost of the stations while ensuring that each tract has at least one station close enough to respond to a fire in no more than 10 minutes.

Formulation with Binary Variables

For each of the eight tracts, there is a yes-or-no decision as to whether that tract should receive a fire station. Therefore, we let $x_1, x_2, \ldots, x_8$ denote the corresponding binary decision variables, where

$$x_j = \begin{cases} 1, & \text{if tract } j \text{ is selected to receive a fire station} \\ 0, & \text{if not} \end{cases}$$

for $j = 1, 2, \ldots, 8$.

Since the objective is to minimize the total cost of the fire stations that will satisfy the city council's new policy on response times, the total cost needs to be expressed in terms of these decision variables. Using units of thousands of dollars while referring to the bottom row of Table 7.4, the total cost is

$$C = 350x_1 + 250x_2 + 450x_3 + 300x_4 + 50x_5 + 400x_6 + 300x_7 + 200x_8$$

We also need to formulate constraints in terms of these decision variables that will ensure that no response times exceed 10 minutes. For example, consider tract 1. When a fire occurs there, the row for tract 1 in Table 7.4 indicates that the only tracts close enough that a fire station would provide a response time not exceeding 10 minutes are tract 1 itself, tract 2, and tract 4. Thus, at least one of these three tracts needs to have a fire station. This requirement is expressed in the constraint

> This constraint ensures that the response time for a fire in tract 1 will be no more than 10 minutes.

$$x_1 + x_2 + x_4 \geq 1$$

Incidentally, this constraint is called a **set covering constraint** because it *covers* the requirement of having a fire station located in at least one member of the *set* of tracts (tracts 1, 2, and 4) that are within 10 minutes of tract 1. In general, any constraint where a sum of binary variables is required to be greater-than-or-equal-to one is referred to as a set covering constraint.

Applying the above reasoning for tract 1 to all the tracts leads to the following constraints.

Tract 1:	x_1	$+x_2$		$+x_4$				≥ 1
Tract 2:	x_1	$+x_2$	$+x_3$					≥ 1
Tract 3:		x_2	$+x_3$		$+x_6$			≥ 1
Tract 4:	x_1			$+x_4$		$+x_7$		≥ 1
Tract 5:					$+x_5$	$+x_7$		≥ 1
Tract 6:			x_3		$+x_6$		$+x_8$	≥ 1
Tract 7:				x_4		$+x_7$	$+x_8$	≥ 1
Tract 8:					x_6	$+x_7$	$+x_8$	≥ 1

These *set covering constraints* (along with requiring the variables to be binary) are all that is needed to ensure that each tract has at least one fire station close enough to respond to a fire in no more than 10 minutes.

This type of BIP model (minimizing total cost where all the functional constraints are set covering constraints) is called a **set covering problem.** Such problems arise fairly frequently. In fact, you will see another example of a set covering problem in Section 7.4.

Having identified the nature of the constraints for the Caliente City problem, it now is fairly straightforward to formulate its BIP spreadsheet model.

A BIP Spreadsheet Model for the Caliente City Problem

Figure 7.4 shows a BIP spreadsheet model for this problem. The data cells ResponseTime (D5:K12) show all the response times given in Table 7.4 and CostOfStation (D14:K14) provides the cost data from the bottom row of this table. There is a yes-or-no decision for each tract as to whether a fire station should be located there, so the changing cells are StationIn-Tract? (D29:K29). The objective is to minimize total cost, so the target cell is TotalCost (N29). The set covering constraints are displayed in cells L17:N24. The Add Constraint dialogue box has been used to officially enter both these constraints and the StationInTract? = binary constraints into the model, as can be seen in the Solver Parameters box.

After clicking on Solve, the optimal solution shown in the changing cells StationInTract? (D29:K29) in Figure 7.4 is obtained, namely,

Select tracts 2, 7, and 8 as the sites for fire stations.

The target cell TotalCost (N29) indicates that the resulting total cost is $750,000.

Review Questions

1. How are binary variables used to represent managerial decisions regarding which site or sites should be selected for new facilities?
2. What are some types of emergency services facilities for which sites may need to be selected?
3. What was the objective for the Caliente City problem?
4. What is a set covering constraint and what is a set covering problem?

7.4 USING BIP FOR CREW SCHEDULING: THE SOUTHWESTERN AIRWAYS PROBLEM

Throughout the travel industry (airlines, rail travel, cruise ships, tour companies, etc.), one of the most challenging problems in maintaining an efficient operation is the scheduling of its crews who serve customers during their travels. Given many feasible overlapping sequences of trips for a crew, to which ones should a crew be assigned so as to cover all the trips at a minimum cost? Thus, for each feasible sequence of trips, there is a *yes-or-no decision* as to whether a crew should be assigned to that sequence, so a binary decision variable can be used to represent that decision.

FIGURE 7.4

A spreadsheet formulation of the BIP model for the Caliente City site selection problem where the changing cells StationInTract? (D29:K29) show the optimal solution obtained by the Excel Solver.

	A	B	C	D	E	F	G	H	I	J	K	L	M	N
1		**Caliente City Fire Station Location Problem**												
2														
3						Fire Station in Tract								
4				1	2	3	4	5	6	7	8			
5			1	2	8	18	9	23	22	16	28			
6		Response	2	9	3	10	12	16	14	21	25			
7		Times	3	17	8	4	20	21	8	22	17			
8		(minutes)	4	10	13	19	2	18	21	6	12			
9		for a Fire	5	21	12	16	13	5	11	9	12			
10		in Tract	6	25	15	7	21	15	3	14	8			
11			7	14	22	18	7	13	15	2	9			
12			8	30	24	15	14	17	9	8	3			
13														
14		Cost of Station		350	250	450	300	50	400	300	200			
15		($thousands)										Number		
16												Covering		
17			1	1	1	0	1	0	0	0	0	1	>=	1
18		Response	2	1	1	1	0	0	0	0	0	1	>=	1
19		Time	3	0	1	1	0	0	1	0	0	1	>=	1
20		<=	4	1	0	0	1	0	0	1	0	1	>=	1
21		10	5	0	0	0	0	1	0	1	0	1	>=	1
22		Minutes?	6	0	0	1	0	0	1	0	1	1	>=	1
23			7	0	0	0	1	0	0	1	1	2	>=	1
24			8	0	0	0	0	0	1	1	1	2	>=	1
25														
26														Total
27						Fire Station in Tract								Cost
28				1	2	3	4	5	6	7	8			($thousands)
29		Station in Tract?		0	1	0	0	0	0	1	1			750

	J	K	L
15			
16			Number
			Covering
17	=IF(J5<=MaxResponseTime,1,0)	=IF(K5<=MaxResponseTime,1,0)	=SUMPRODUCT(D17:K17,StationInTract?)
18	=IF(J6<=MaxResponseTime,1,0)	=IF(K6<=MaxResponseTime,1,0)	=SUMPRODUCT(D18:K18,StationInTract?)
19	=IF(J7<=MaxResponseTime,1,0)	=IF(K7<=MaxResponseTime,1,0)	=SUMPRODUCT(D19:K19,StationInTract?)

Solver Parameters

Set Objective (Target Cell): TotalCost
To: Min
By Changing (Variable) Cells:
  StationInTract?
Subject to the Constraints:
  StationInTract? = binary
  NumberCovering >= One

Solver Options (Excel 2010):
  Make Variables Nonnegative
  Solving Method: Simplex LP
Solver Options (older Excel):
  Assume Nonnegative
  Assume Linear Model

Range Name	Cells
CostOfStation	D14:K14
MaxResponseTime	B21
NumberCovering	L17:L24
One	N17:N24
ResponseTime	D5:K12
StationInTract?	D29:K29
TotalCost	N29

	N
26	Total
27	Cost
28	($thousands)
29	=SUMPRODUCT(CostOfStation,StationInTract?)

An Application Vignette

Netherlands Railways (Nederlandse Spoorwegen Reizigers) is the main Dutch railway operator of passenger trains. In this densely populated country, about 5,500 passenger trains currently transport approximately 1.1 million passengers on an average workday. The company's operating revenues are approximately 1.5 billion euros (approximately $2 billion) per year.

The amount of passenger transport on the Dutch railway network has steadily increased over the years, so a national study in 2002 concluded that three major infrastructure extensions should be undertaken. As a result, a new national timetable for the Dutch railway system, specifying the planned departure and arrival times of every train at every station, would need to be developed. Therefore, the management of Netherlands Railways directed that an extensive management science study should be conducted over the next few years to develop an optimal overall plan for both the new timetable and the usage of the available resources (rolling-stock units and train crews) for meeting this timetable. A task force consisting of several members of the company's Department of Logistics and several prominent management science scholars from European universities or a software company was formed to conduct this study.

The new timetable was launched in December 2006, along with a new system for scheduling the allocation of rolling-stock units (various kinds of passenger cars and other train units) to the trains meeting this timetable. A new system also was implemented for scheduling the assignment of crews (with a driver and a number of conductors in each crew) to the trains. *Binary integer programming* and related techniques were used to do all of this. For example, the BIP model used for crew scheduling closely resembles (except for its vastly larger size) the one shown in this section for the Southwestern Airlines problem.

This application of management science immediately resulted in *an additional annual profit of approximately $60 million* for the company and this additional profit is expected to increase to **$105 million** annually in the coming years. These dramatic results led to Netherlands Railways winning the prestigious First Prize in the 2008 international competition for the Franz Edelman Award for Achievement in Operations Research and the Management Sciences.

Source: L. Kroon, D. Huisman, E. Abbink, P.-J. Fioole, M. Fischetti, G. Maróti, A. Schrijver, A. Steenbeck, and R. Ybema, "The New Dutch Timetable: The OR Revolution," *Interfaces* 39, no. 1 (January–February 2009), pp. 6–17. (A link to this article is provided on our Web site, www.mhhe.com/hillier4e.)

For many years, airline companies have been using BIP models to determine how to do their crew scheduling in the most cost-efficient way. Some airlines have saved many millions of dollars annually through this application of BIP. Consequently, other segments of the travel industry now are also using BIP in this way. For example, the application vignette in this section describes how Netherlands Railways achieved a dramatic increase in profits by applying BIP (and related techniques) in a variety of ways, including crew scheduling.

To illustrate the approach, consider the following miniature example of airline crew scheduling.

The Southwestern Airways Problem

Southwestern Airways needs to assign its crews to cover all its upcoming flights. We will focus on the problem of assigning three crews based in San Francisco (SFO) to the 11 flights shown in Figure 7.5. These same flights are listed in the first column of Table 7.5. The other

FIGURE 7.5

The arrows show the 11 Southwestern Airways flights that need to be covered by the three crews based in San Francisco.

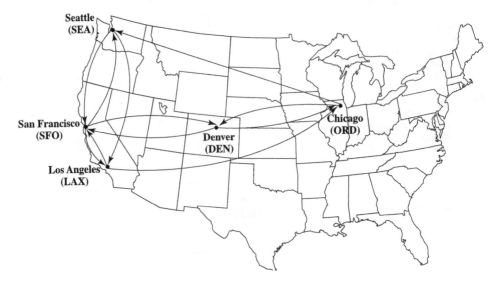

TABLE 7.5   Data for the Southwestern Airways Problem

Flight		Feasible Sequence of Flights											
		1	2	3	4	5	6	7	8	9	10	11	12
1.	San Francisco to Los Angeles (SFO–LAX)	1			1			1			1		
2.	San Francisco to Denver (SFO–DEN)		1			1			1			1	
3.	San Francisco to Seattle (SFO–SEA)			1			1			1			1
4.	Los Angeles to Chicago (LAX–ORD)				2			2		3	2		3
5.	Los Angeles to San Francisco (LAX–SFO)	2					3				5	5	
6.	Chicago to Denver (ORD–DEN)				3	3				4			
7.	Chicago to Seattle (ORD–SEA)							3	3		3	3	4
8.	Denver to San Francisco (DEN–SFO)			2		4	4			5			
9.	Denver to Chicago (DEN–ORD)						2		2			2	
10.	Seattle to San Francisco (SEA–SFO)			2				4	4				5
11.	Seattle to Los Angeles (SEA–LAX)						2			2	4	4	2
Cost, $1,000s		2	3	4	6	7	5	7	8	9	9	8	9

12 columns show the 12 feasible sequences of flights for a crew. (The numbers in each column indicate the order of the flights.) At most, three of the sequences need to be chosen (one per crew) in such a way that every flight is covered. (It is permissible to have more than one crew on a flight, where the extra crews would fly as passengers, but union contracts require that the extra crews still be paid for their time as if they were working.) The cost of assigning a crew to a particular sequence of flights is given (in thousands of dollars) in the bottom row of the table. The objective is to minimize the total cost of the crew assignments that cover all the flights.

Formulation with Binary Variables

With 12 feasible sequences of flights, we have 12 yes-or-no decisions:

Should sequence j be assigned to a crew? $(j = 1, 2, \ldots, 12)$

Therefore, we use 12 binary variables to represent these respective decisions:

$$x_j = \begin{cases} 1, & \text{if sequence } j \text{ is assigned to a crew} \\ 0, & \text{otherwise} \end{cases}$$

Since the objective is to minimize the total cost of the three crew assignments, we now need to express the total cost in terms of these binary decision variables. Referring to the bottom row of Table 7.5, this total cost (in units of thousands of dollars) is

$$C = 2x_1 + 3x_2 + 4x_3 + 6x_4 + 7x_5 + 5x_6 + 7x_7 + 8x_8 + 9x_9 + 9x_{10} + 8x_{11} + 9x_{12}$$

With only three crews available to cover the flights, we also need the constraint

$$x_1 + x_2 + \cdots + x_{12} \leq 3$$

The most interesting part of this formulation is the nature of each constraint that ensures that a corresponding flight is covered. For example, consider the last flight in Table 7.5 (Seattle to Los Angeles). Five sequences (namely, sequences 6, 9, 10, 11, and 12) include this flight. Therefore, at least one of these five sequences must be chosen. The resulting constraint is

$$x_6 + x_9 + x_{10} + x_{11} + x_{12} \geq 1$$

For each of the 11 flights, the constraint that ensures that the flight is covered is constructed in the same way from Table 7.5 by requiring that at least one of the flight sequences that includes that flight is assigned to a crew. Thus, 11 constraints of the following form are needed.

These are set covering constraints, just like the constraints in the Caliente City problem in Section 7.3.

Flight 1: $x_1 + x_4 + x_7 + x_{10} \geq 1$

Flight 2: $x_2 + x_5 + x_8 + x_{11} \geq 1$

.

.

.

Flight 11: $x_6 + x_9 + x_{10} + x_{11} + x_{12} \geq 1$

Note that these constraints have the same form as the constraints for the Caliente City problem in Section 7.3 (a sum of certain binary variables ≥ 1), so these too are *set covering constraints*. Therefore, this crew scheduling problem is another example of a *set covering problem* (where this particular set covering problem also includes the side constraint that $x_1 + x_2 + \cdots + x_{12} \leq 3$).

Having identified the nature of the constraints, the stage now is set for formulating a BIP spreadsheet model for this problem.

A BIP Spreadsheet Model for the Southwestern Airways Problem

Figure 7.6 shows a spreadsheet formulation of the complete BIP model for this problem. The changing cells FlySequence? (C22:N22) contain the values of the 12 binary decision variables. The data in IncludesSegment? (C8:N18) and Cost (C5:N5) come directly from Table 7.5. The last three columns of the spreadsheet are used to show the set covering constraints, Total $\geq$ AtLeastOne, and the side constraint, TotalSequences $\leq$ NumberOfCrews. The Add Constraint dialogue box has been used to officially enter both these constraints and the constraints, FlySequence? = binary, into the model, as shown in the Solver Parameters box.

The Excel Solver provides the optimal solution shown in FlySequence? (C22:N22). In terms of the x_j variables, this solution is

$x_3 = 1$ (assign sequence 3 to a crew)

$x_4 = 1$ (assign sequence 4 to a crew)

$x_{11} = 1$ (assign sequence 11 to a crew)

and all other $x_j = 0$, for a total cost of \$18,000 as given by TotalCost (Q24). (Another optimal solution is $x_1 = 1$, $x_5 = 1$, $x_{12} = 1$, and all other $x_j = 0$.)

Many airlines are solving huge BIP models of this kind.

We should point out that this BIP model is a tiny one compared to the ones typically used in actual practice. Airline crew scheduling problems involving thousands of possible flight sequences now are being solved by using models similar to the one shown above but with thousands of binary variables rather than just a dozen.

Review Questions

1. What is the crew scheduling problem that is encountered by companies in the travel industry?
2. What are the yes-or-no decisions that need to be made when addressing a crew scheduling problem?
3. For the Southwestern Airways problem, there is a constraint for each flight to ensure that this flight is covered by a crew. Describe the mathematical form of this constraint. Then explain in words what this constraint is saying.

7.5   USING MIXED BIP TO DEAL WITH SETUP COSTS FOR INITIATING PRODUCTION: THE REVISED WYNDOR PROBLEM

All of the examples considered thus far in this chapter have been *pure BIP problems* (problems where all the decision variables are binary variables). However, *mixed BIP problems* (problems where only some of the decision variables are binary variables) also arise quite

FIGURE 7.6

A spreadsheet formulation of the BIP model for the Southwestern Airways crew scheduling problem, where FlySequence (C22:N22) shows the optimal solution obtained by the Excel Solver. The list of flight sequences under consideration is given in cells A25:D37.

	A	B	C	D	E	F	G	H	I	J	K	L	M	N	O	P	Q
1		**Southwestern Airways Crew Scheduling Problem**															
2																	
3							Flight Sequence										
4			1	2	3	4	5	6	7	8	9	10	11	12			
5		Cost ($thousands)	2	3	4	6	7	5	7	8	9	9	8	9			At
6																	Least
7		**Includes Segment?**													Total		One
8		SFO–LAX	1	0	0	1	0	0	1	0	0	1	0	0	1	≥	1
9		SFO–DEN	0	1	0	0	1	0	0	1	0	0	1	0	1	≥	1
10		SFO–SEA	0	0	1	0	0	1	0	0	1	0	0	1	1	≥	1
11		LAX–ORD	0	0	0	1	0	0	1	0	1	1	0	1	1	≥	1
12		LAX–SFO	1	0	0	0	0	1	0	0	0	1	1	0	1	≥	1
13		ORD–DEN	0	0	0	1	1	0	0	0	1	0	0	0	1	≥	1
14		ORD–SEA	0	0	0	0	0	0	1	1	0	1	1	1	1	≥	1
15		DEN–SFO	0	1	0	1	1	0	0	0	1	0	0	0	1	≥	1
16		DEN–ORD	0	0	0	0	1	0	0	1	0	0	1	0	1	≥	1
17		SEA–SFO	0	0	1	0	0	0	1	1	0	0	0	1	1	≥	1
18		SEA–LAX	0	0	0	0	0	1	0	0	1	1	1	1	1	≥	1
19																	
20															Total		Number
21			1	2	3	4	5	6	7	8	9	10	11	12	Sequences		of Crews
22		Fly Sequence?	0	0	1	1	0	0	0	0	0	0	1	0	3	≤	3
23																	
24														Total Cost ($thousands)		18

25		**Flight Sequence Key**
26	1	SFO-LAX
27	2	SFO-DEN-SFO
28	3	SFO-SEA-SFO
29	4	SFO-LAX-ORD-DEN-SFO
30	5	SFO-DEN-ORD-DEN-SFO
31	6	SFO-SEA-LAX-SFO
32	7	SFO-LAX-ORD-SEA-SFO
33	8	SFO-DEN-ORD-SEA-SFO
34	9	SFO-SEA-LAX-ORD-DEN-SFO
35	10	SFO-LAX-ORD-SEA-LAX-SFO
36	11	SFO-DEN-ORD-SEA-LAX-SFO
37	12	SFO-SEA-LAX-ORD-SEA-SFO

Solver Parameters

Set Objective (Target Cell): TotalCost
To: Min
By Changing (Variable) Cells:
  FlySequence?
Subject to the Constraints:
  FlySequence? = binary
  Total >= AtLeastOne
  TotalSequences <= NumberOfCrews

Solver Options (Excel 2010):
  Make Variables Nonnegative
  Solving Method: Simplex LP
Solver Options (older Excel):
  Assume Nonnegative
  Assume Linear Model

	O
7	Total
8	=SUMPRODUCT(C8:N8,FlySequence?)
9	=SUMPRODUCT(C9:N9,FlySequence?)
10	=SUMPRODUCT(C10:N10,FlySequence?)
11	=SUMPRODUCT(C11:N11,FlySequence?)
12	=SUMPRODUCT(C12:N12,FlySequence?)
13	=SUMPRODUCT(C13:N13,FlySequence?)
14	=SUMPRODUCT(C14:N14,FlySequence?)
15	=SUMPRODUCT(C15:N15,FlySequence?)
16	=SUMPRODUCT(C16:N16,FlySequence?)
17	=SUMPRODUCT(C17:N17,FlySequence?)
18	=SUMPRODUCT(C18:N18,FlySequence?)
19	
20	Total
21	Sequences
22	=SUM(FlySequence?)

	P	Q
24	Total Cost ($thousands)	=SUMPRODUCT(Cost,FlySequence?)

Range Name	Cells
AtLeastOne	Q8:Q18
Cost	C5:N5
FlySequence?	C22:N22
IncludesSegment?	C8:N18
NumberOfCrews	Q22
Total	O8:O18
TotalCost	Q24
TotalSequences	O22

frequently because only some of the decisions to be made are yes-or-no decisions and the rest are how-much decisions.

One important example of this type is the *product-mix problem* introduced in Chapter 2, but now with the added complication that a setup cost must be incurred to initiate the production of each product. Therefore, in addition to the *how-much decisions* of how much to produce of each product, there also is a prior yes-or-no decision for each product of whether to perform a setup to enable initiating its production.

To illustrate this type of problem, we will consider a revised version of the Wyndor Glass Co. product-mix problem that was described in Section 2.1 and analyzed throughout most of Chapter 2.

The Revised Wyndor Problem with Setup Costs

Suppose now that the **Wyndor Glass Co.** will only devote one week each month to the production of the special doors and windows described in Section 2.1, so the question now is *how many* doors and windows to produce during each of these week-long production runs. Since the decisions to be made are no longer the *rates* of production for doors and windows, but rather *how many* doors and windows to produce in individual production runs, these quantities now are required to be *integer*.

Each time Wyndor's plants convert from the production of other products to the production of these doors and windows for a week, the following setup costs would be incurred to initiate this production.

Setup cost to produce doors = $700

Setup cost to produce windows = $1,300

Otherwise, all the original data given in Table 2.2 still apply, including a unit profit of $300 for doors and $500 for windows when disregarding these setup costs.

Table 7.6 shows the resulting net profit from producing any feasible quantity for either product. Note that the large setup cost for either product makes it unprofitable to produce less than three units of that product.

The dots in Figure 7.7 show the feasible solutions for this problem. By adding the appropriate entries in Table 7.6, the figure also shows the calculation of the total net profit P for each of the corner points. The optimal solution turns out to be

$$(D, W) = (0, 6) \quad \text{with} \quad P = 1,700$$

By contrast, the original solution

$$(D, W) = (2, 6) \quad \text{with} \quad P = 1,600$$

now gives a smaller value of P. The reason that this original solution (which gave $P = 3,600$ for the original problem) is no longer optimal is that the setup costs reduce the total net profit so much:

$$P = 3,600 - 700 - 1,300 = 1,600$$

TABLE 7.6
Net Profit ($) for the Revised Wyndor Problem

Number of Units Produced	Net Profit ($)	
	Doors	**Windows**
0	0 (300) − 0 = 0	0 (500) − 0 = 0
1	1 (300) − 700 = −400	1 (500) − 1,300 = −800
2	2 (300) − 700 = −100	2 (500) − 1,300 = −300
3	3 (300) − 700 = 200	3 (500) − 1,300 = 200
4	4 (300) − 700 = 500	4 (500) − 1,300 = 700
5	Not feasible	5 (500) − 1,300 = 1,200
6	Not feasible	6 (500) − 1,300 = 1,700

FIGURE 7.7

The dots are the feasible solutions for the revised Wyndor problem. Also shown is the calculation of the total net profit P (in dollars) for each corner point from the net profits given in Table 7.6.

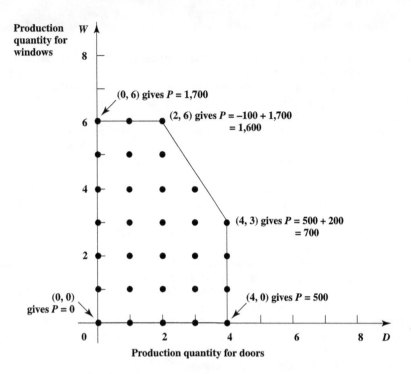

Therefore, the graphical method for linear programming can no longer be used to find the optimal solution for this new problem with setup costs.

How can we formulate a model for this problem so that it fits a standard kind of model that can be solved by the Excel Solver? Table 7.6 shows that the net profit for either product is no longer *directly proportional* to the number of units produced. Therefore, as it stands, the problem no longer fits either linear programming or BIP. Before, for the original problem without setup costs, the objective function was simply $P = 300D + 500W$. Now we need to subtract from this expression each setup cost *if* the corresponding product will be produced, but we should not subtract the setup cost if the product will not be produced. This is where *binary variables* come to the rescue.

Formulation with Binary Variables

For each product, there is a *yes-or-no decision* regarding whether to perform the setup that would enable initiating the production of the product, so the setup cost is incurred only if the decision is *yes*. Therefore, we can introduce a *binary variable* for each setup cost and associate each value of the binary variable with one of the two possibilities for the setup cost. In particular, let

These binary variables enable subtracting each setup cost only if the setup is performed.

$$y_1 = \begin{cases} 1, & \text{if perform the setup to produce doors} \\ 0, & \text{if not} \end{cases}$$

$$y_2 = \begin{cases} 1, & \text{if perform the setup to produce windows} \\ 0, & \text{if not} \end{cases}$$

Therefore, the objective function now can be written as

$$P = 300D + 500W - 700y_1 - 1{,}300y_2$$

which fits the format for mixed BIP.

Since a setup is required to produce the corresponding product, these binary variables can be related directly to the production quantities as follows.

Continental Airlines is a major United States air carrier that transports passengers, cargo, and mail. It operates more than 2,000 daily departures to well over 100 domestic destinations and nearly 100 foreign destinations.

Airlines like Continental face schedule disruptions daily because of unexpected events, including inclement weather, aircraft mechanical problems, and crew unavailability. These disruptions can cause flight delays and cancellations. The application vignette in Section 6.1 describes how United Airlines led the way in applying management science to determine how to most effectively reassign airplanes to flights when these disruptions occur. However, another consequence of such disruptions is that crews may not be in positions to service their remaining scheduled flights. Airlines must reassign crews quickly to cover open flights and to return them to their original schedules in a cost-effective manner while honoring all government regulations, contractual obligations, and quality-of-life requirements.

To address such problems, a management science team at Continental Airlines developed a detailed *mixed BIP model* for reassigning crews to flights as soon as such emergencies arise. Because the airline has thousands of crews and daily flights, the model needed to be huge to consider all possible pairings of crews with flights. Therefore, the model has *millions of decision variables* and *many thousands of constraints*. (Most of these decision variables are *binary variables* and the rest are general integer variables). In its first year of use (mainly in 2001), the model was applied four times to recover from major schedule disruptions (two snowstorms, a flood, and the September 11 terrorist attacks). This led to *savings of approximately* **$40 million**. Subsequent applications extended to many daily minor disruptions as well.

Although other airlines subsequently scrambled to apply management science in a similar way, this initial advantage over other airlines in being able to recover more quickly from schedule disruptions with fewer delays and cancelled flights left Continental Airlines in a relatively strong position as the airline industry struggled through a difficult period during the initial years of the 21st century. This initiative led to Continental winning the prestigious First Prize in the 2002 international competition for the Franz Edelman Award for Achievement in Operations Research and the Management Sciences.

Source: G. Yu, M. Argüello, C. Song, S. M. McGowan, and A. White, "A New Era for Crew Recovery at Continental Airlines," *Interfaces* 33, no. 1 (January–February 2003), pp. 5–22. (A link to this article is provided on our Web site, www.mhhe.com/hillier4e.)

$$y_1 = \begin{cases} 1, & \text{if } D > 0 \text{ can hold (can produce doors)} \\ 0, & \text{if } D = 0 \text{ must hold (cannot produce doors)} \end{cases}$$

$$y_2 = \begin{cases} 1, & \text{if } W > 0 \text{ can hold (can produce windows)} \\ 0, & \text{if } W = 0 \text{ must hold (cannot produce windows)} \end{cases}$$

We need to include constraints in the model that will ensure that these relationships will hold. (An algorithm solving the model only recognizes the objective function and the constraints, not the definitions of the variables.)

So what are the constraints of the model? We still need all the constraints of the original model. We also need constraints that D and W are integers, and that y_1 and y_2 are binary. In addition, we need some ordinary linear programming constraints that will ensure the following relationships:

If $y_1 = 0$, then $D = 0$.

If $y_2 = 0$, then W $= 0$.

(If $y_1 = 1$ or $y_2 = 1$, no restrictions are placed on D or W other than those already imposed by the other constraints.)

It is possible with Excel to use the IF function to represent this relationship between y_1 and D and between y_2 and W. Unfortunately, the IF function does not fit the assumptions of linear programming. Consequently, the Excel Solver has difficulty solving spreadsheet models that use this function. This is why another formulation with ordinary linear programming constraints is needed instead to express these relationships.

Since the other constraints impose bounds on D and W of $0 \leq D \leq 4$ and $0 \leq W \leq 6$, here are some ordinary linear programming constraints that ensure these relationships.

$$D \leq 4y_1$$

$$W \leq 6y_2$$

FIGURE 7.8

A spreadsheet model for the revised Wyndor problem, where the Excel Solver gives the optimal solution shown in the changing cells, UnitsProduced (C14:D14) and Setup? (C17:D17).

	A	B	C	D	E	F	G	H
1		**Wyndor Glass Co. Product-Mix with Setup Costs**						
2								
3			Doors	Windows				
4		Unit Profit	$300	$500				
5		Setup Cost	$700	$1,300				
6								
7					Hours		Hours	
8			Hours Used per Unit Produced		Used		Available	
9		Plant 1	1	0	0	?	4	
10		Plant 2	0	2	12	?	12	
11		Plant 3	3	2	12	?	18	
12								
13			Doors	Windows				
14		Units Prod'd	0	6				
15			?	?			Production Profit	$3,000
16		Only if Set Up	0	99			−Total Setup Cost	$1,300
17		Setup?	0	1			Total Profit	$1,700

Solver Parameters

Set Objective (Target Cell): TotalProfit
To: Max
By Changing (Variable) Cells:
  UnitsProduced, Setup?
Subject to the Constraints:
  Setup? = binary
  UnitsProduced = integer
  HoursUsed <= HoursAvailable
  UnitsProduced <= OnlyIfSetup

Solver Options (Excel 2010):
  Make Variables Nonnegative
  Solving Method: Simplex LP
Solver Options (older Excel):
  Assume Nonnegative
  Assume Linear Model

Range Name	Cells
HoursAvailable	G9:G11
HoursUsed	E9:E11
HoursUsedPerUnitProduced	C9:D11
OnlyIfSetup	C16:D16
ProductionProfit	H15
Setup?	C17:D17
SetupCost	C5:D5
TotalProfit	H17
TotalSetupCost	H16
UnitProfit	C4:D4
UnitsProduced	C14:D14

	E
7	Hours
8	Used
9	=SUMPRODUCT(C9:D9,UnitsProduced)
10	=SUMPRODUCT(C10:D10,UnitsProduced)
11	=SUMPRODUCT(C11:D11,UnitsProduced)

	B	C	D
16	Only if Set Up	=99*C17	=99*D17

	G	H
15	Production Profit	=SUMPRODUCT(UnitProfit,UnitsProduced)
16	−Total Setup Cost	=SUMPRODUCT(SetupCost,Setup?)
17	Total Profit	=ProductionProfit − TotalSetupCost

These constraints force the model to refuse production if the corresponding setup is not performed.

Note that setting $y_1 = 0$ gives $D \leq 0$, which forces the nonnegative D to be $D = 0$, whereas setting $y_1 = 1$ gives $D \leq 4$, which allows all the values of D already allowed by the other constraints. Then check that the same conclusions apply for W when setting $y_2 = 0$ and $y_2 = 1$.

It was not necessary to choose 4 and 6 for the respective coefficients of y_1 and y_2 in these two constraints. Any coefficients *larger* than 4 and 6 would have the same effect. You just need to avoid *smaller* coefficients, since this would impose undesired restrictions on D and W when $y_1 = 1$ and $y_2 = 1$.

If a *how-much* decision x can only be done (i.e., $x > 0$) if a corresponding *yes-no* decision y is done (i.e., $y = 1$), this can be enforced with a big-number constraint such as $x \leq 99y$. If $y = 0$, this becomes $x \leq 0$. If $y = 1$, then this becomes $x \leq 99$. The big number (99 in this example) is chosen to be big enough so that it is safely larger than x could ever become.

On larger problems, it is sometimes difficult to determine the smallest acceptable coefficients for these binary variables. Therefore, it is common to formulate the model by just using a reasonably large number (say, 99 in this case) that is safely larger than the smallest acceptable coefficient.

With this background, we now are ready to formulate a mixed BIP spreadsheet model for this problem that uses the number 99 in these constraints.

A Mixed BIP Spreadsheet Model for the Revised Wyndor Problem

Figure 7.8 shows one way of formulating this model. The format for the first 14 rows is the same as for the original Wyndor problem, so the difference arises in rows 15–17 of the spreadsheet. The values of the binary variables, y_1 and y_2, appear in the new changing cells, Setup? (C17:D17). The bottom of the figure identifies the equations entered into the output cells in row 16, C16 = 99*C17 and D16 = 99*D17. Consequently, the constraints, UnitsProduced (C14:D14) ≤ OnlyIfSetup (C16:D16), impose the relationships that $D \leq 99y_1$ and $W \leq 99y_2$.

The changing cells in this spreadsheet show the optimal solution obtained after applying the Excel Solver. Thus, this solution is to not produce any doors ($y_1 = 0$ and $D = 0$) but to perform the setup to enable producing 6 windows ($y_2 = 1$ and $W = 6$) to obtain a net profit of $1,700.

Note that this optimal solution does indeed satisfy the requirements that $D = 0$ must hold when $y_1 = 0$ and that $W > 0$ can hold when $y_2 = 1$. The constraints do permit performing a setup to produce a product and then not producing any units ($y_1 = 1$ with $D = 0$ or $y_2 = 1$ with $W = 0$), but the objective function causes an optimal solution automatically to avoid this foolish option of incurring the setup cost for no purpose.

Review Questions

1. How does a mixed BIP problem differ from a pure BIP problem?
2. Why is a linear programming formulation no longer valid for a product-mix problem when there are setup costs for initiating production?
3. How can a binary variable be defined in terms of whether a setup is performed to initiate the production of a certain product?
4. What caused the optimal solution for the revised Wyndor problem to differ from that for the original Wyndor problem?

7.6 Summary

Managers frequently must make yes-or-no decisions, where the only two possible choices are yes, go ahead with a particular option, or no, decline this option. A binary integer programming (BIP) model considers many options simultaneously, with a binary decision variable for each option. Mixed BIP models include some continuous decision variables as well.

The California Manufacturing Co. case study involves yes-or-no decisions on whether a new factory should be built in certain cities and then whether a new warehouse also should be built in certain cities. This case study also introduced the modeling of mutually exclusive alternatives and contingent decisions, as well as the performance of sensitivity analysis for BIP models.

Many companies have saved millions of dollars by formulating and solving BIP models for a wide variety of applications. We have described and illustrated some of the most important types, including the selection of projects (e.g., research and development projects), the selection of sites for facilities (e.g., emergency services facilities such as fire stations), and crew scheduling in the travel industry (e.g., airlines). We also have discussed how to use mixed BIP to deal with setup costs for initiating production when addressing product-mix problems.

Glossary

binary decision variable   A binary variable that represents a yes-or-no decision by assigning a value of 1 for choosing yes and a value of 0 for choosing no. (Introduction), 228

binary integer programming   A type of problem or model that fits linear programming except that it uses binary decision variables. (Introduction), 228

binary variable   A variable whose only possible values are 0 and 1. (Introduction), 228

BIP   Abbreviation for binary integer programming. (Introduction), 228

contingent decision   A yes-or-no decision is a contingent decision if it can be yes only if a certain other yes-or-no decision is yes. (Section 7.1), 232

mixed BIP model   A BIP model where only some of the variables are restricted to be binary variables. (Introduction), 228

mutually exclusive alternatives   A group of alternatives where choosing any one alternative excludes choosing any of the others. (Section 7.1), 231

pure BIP model   A BIP model where all the variables are restricted to be binary variables. (Introduction), 228

set covering constraint   A constraint that requires the sum of certain binary variables

to be greater than or equal to 1. (Section 7.3), 239

set covering problem   A type of BIP model where the objective is to minimize some quantity such as total cost and all the functional constraints are set covering constraints. (Section 7.3), 240

yes-or-no decision   A decision whose only possible choices are (1) yes, go ahead with a certain option, or (2) no, decline this option. (Introduction), 228

Learning Aids for This Chapter in Your MS Courseware

Chapter 7 Excel Files:

California Mfg. Case Study

Tazer Corp. example

Caliente City example

Southwestern Airways Example

Revised Wyndor example

Excel Add-in:

Solver Table

Supplements to This Chapter on the CD-ROM:

Advanced Formulation Techniques for Binary Integer Programming

Some Perspectives on Solving Binary Integer Programming Problems

Solved Problems (See the CD-ROM or Web site for the Solutions)

7.S1. Capital Budgeting with Contingency Constraints

A company is planning its capital budget over the next several years. There are eight potential projects under consideration. A calculation has been made of the expected net present value of each project, along with the cash outflow that would be required over the next four years. These data, along with the cash that is available each year, are shown in the next table. There also are the following contingency constraints: (a) at least one of project 1, 2, or 3 must be done, (b) projects 6 and 7 cannot both be done, and (c) project 5 can only be done if project 6 is done. Formulate and solve a BIP model in a spreadsheet to determine which projects should be pursued to maximize the total expected net present value.

7.S2. Locating Search and Rescue Teams

The Washington State legislature is trying to decide on locations at which to base search-and-rescue teams. The teams are expensive, so the legislature would like as few as possible while still providing the desired level of service. In particular, since response time is critical, the legislature would like every county to either have a team located in that county or in an adjacent county. (The locations and names of the counties are shown at the top of the next page.) Formulate and solve a BIP model in a spreadsheet to determine where the teams should be located.

	Cash Outflow Required ($million)								Cash Available ($million)
	Project								
	1	**2**	**3**	**4**	**5**	**6**	**7**	**8**	
Year 1	1	3	0	3	3	7	2	5	20
Year 2	2	2	2	2	2	3	3	4	20
Year 3	2	3	4	2	3	3	6	2	20
Year 4	2	1	0	5	4	2	1	2	20
NPV ($mil)	10	12	11	15	24	17	16	18	

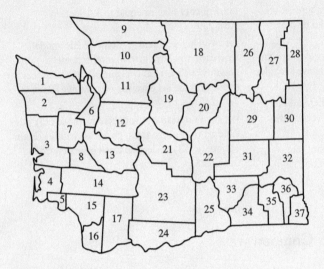

Counties

1. Clallum	19. Chelan
2. Jefferson	20. Douglas
3. Grays Harbor	21. Kittitas
4. Pacific	22. Grant
5. Wahkiakum	23. Yakima
6. Kitsap	24. Klickitat
7. Mason	25. Benton
8. Thurston	26. Ferry
9. Whatcom	27. Stevens
10. Skagit	28. Pend Oreille
11. Snohomish	29. Lincoln
12. King	30. Spokane
13. Pierce	31. Adams
14. Lewis	32. Whitman
15. Cowlitz	33. Franklin
16. Clark	34. Walla Walla
17. Skamania	35. Columbia
18. Okanogan	36. Garfield
	37. Asotin

7.S3. Warehouse Site Selection

Consider a small company that produces a single product in two plants and serves customers in five different regions.

The company has been using a make-to-order policy of producing the product only in the quantities needed to fill the orders that have come in from the various regions. However, because of the problems caused by the sporadic production schedule, management has decided to smooth out the production rate and ship the product to one or more storage warehouses, which then will use inventory to fill the incoming regional orders. Management now needs to decide where to locate the company's new warehouse(s). There are three locations under consideration. For each location, there is a fixed monthly cost associated with leasing and operating the warehouse there. Furthermore, each potential warehouse location has a maximum capacity for monthly shipments restricted primarily by the number of trucking docks at the site. The product costs $400 to produce at plant 1 and $300 to produce at plant 2. The shipping cost from each plant to each potential warehouse location is shown in the first table below. The fixed leasing and operating cost (if open), the shipping costs, and the capacity (maximum monthly shipments) of each potential warehouse location are shown in the second table below. The monthly demand in each of the customer regions is expected to be 200, 225, 100, 150, and 175 units, respectively. Formulate and solve a BIP model in a spreadsheet to determine which warehouse(s) should be used and how the product should be distributed from plant to warehouse(s) to customer.

Shipping Costs and Capacity of the Plants

	Shipping Cost (per unit)			Capacity (units/month)
	WH 1	WH 2	WH 3	
Plant 1	$25	$50	$75	500
Plant 2	$50	$75	$25	400

Fixed Cost, Shipping Costs, and Capacity of the Warehouses

	Fixed Cost (per month)	Shipping Cost (per unit)					Capacity (units/month)
		Region 1	Region 2	Region 3	Region 4	Region 5	
WH 1	$50,000	$30	$70	$75	$55	$40	700
WH 2	$30,000	$55	$30	$45	$45	$70	500
WH 3	$70,000	$70	$30	$50	$60	$55	1,000

Problems

To the left of the problems (or their parts), we have inserted an E* whenever Excel should be used (unless your instructor gives you contrary instructions). An asterisk on the problem number indicates that at least a partial answer is given in the back of the book.

7.1. Read the referenced article that fully describes the management science study summarized in the application vignette presented in Section 7.1. Briefly describe how mixed BIP was applied in this study. Then list the various financial and nonfinancial benefits that resulted from this study.

7.2. Reconsider the California Manufacturing Co. case study presented in Section 7.1. The mayor of San Diego now has contacted the company's president, Armando Ortega, to try to persuade him to build a factory and perhaps a warehouse in that city. With the tax incentives being offered the company, Armando's staff estimates that the net present value of building a factory in San Diego would be $7 million and the amount of capital required to do this would be $4 million. The net present value of building a warehouse there would be $5 million and the capital required would be $3 million. (This option will only be considered if a factory also is being built there.)

Armando has asked Steve Chan to revise his previous management science study to incorporate these new alternatives into the overall problem. The objective still is to find the feasible combination of investments that maximizes the total net present value, given that the amount of capital available for these investments is $10 million.

    a. Formulate a BIP model in algebraic form for this problem.

E* *b.* Formulate and solve this model on a spreadsheet.

7.3.* A young couple, Eve and Steven, want to divide their main household chores (marketing, cooking, dishwashing, and laundering) between them so that each has two tasks but the total time they spend on household duties is kept to a minimum. Their efficiencies on these tasks differ, where the time each would need to perform the task is given by the following table:

	Time Needed per Week (Hours)			
	Marketing	**Cooking**	**Dish Washing**	**Laundry**
Eve	4.5	7.8	3.6	2.9
Steven	4.9	7.2	4.3	3.1

    a. Formulate a BIP model in algebraic form for this problem.

E* *b.* Formulate and solve this model on a spreadsheet.

7.4. A real-estate development firm, Peterson and Johnson, is considering five possible development projects. Using units of millions of dollars, the following table shows the estimated long-run profit (net present value) that each project would generate, as well as the amount of investment required to undertake the project.

	Development Project				
	1	**2**	**3**	**4**	**5**
Estimated profit (millions)	$1	$ 1.8	$ 1.6	$0.8	$1.4
Capital required (millions)	6	12	10	4	8

The owners of the firm, Dave Peterson and Ron Johnson, have raised $20 million of investment capital for these projects. Dave and Ron now want to select the combination of projects that will maximize their total estimated long-run profit (net present value) without investing more than $20 million.

    a. Formulate a BIP model in algebraic form for this problem.

E* *b.* Formulate and solve this model on a spreadsheet.

E* *c.* Perform sensitivity analysis on the amount of investment capital made available for the development projects by using the Solver Table to solve the model with the following amounts of investment capital (in millions of dollars): 16, 18, 20, 22, 24, 26, 28, and 30. Include both the changing cells and the target cell as output cells in the Solver Table.

E*7.5. The board of directors of General Wheels Co. is considering seven large capital investments. Each investment can be made only once. These investments differ in the estimated long-run profit (net present value) that they will generate as well as in the amount of capital required, as shown by the following table:

Investment Opportunity	Estimated Profit (millions)	Capital Required (millions)
1	$17	$43
2	10	28
3	15	34
4	19	48
5	7	17
6	13	32
7	9	23

The total amount of capital available for these investments is $100 million. Investment opportunities 1 and 2 are mutually exclusive, and so are 3 and 4. Furthermore, neither 3 nor 4 can be undertaken unless one of the first two opportunities is undertaken. There are no such restrictions on investment opportunities 5, 6, and 7. The objective is to select the combination of capital investments that will maximize the total estimated long-run profit (net present value).

    a. Formulate and solve a BIP model on a spreadsheet for this problem.

    b. Perform sensitivity analysis on the amount of capital made available for the investment opportunities by using the Solver Table to solve the model with the following amounts of capital (in millions of dollars): 80, 90, 100, 110, . . . , and 200. Include both the changing cells and the target cell as output cells in the Solver Table.

E*7.6. The Fly-Right Airplane Company builds small jet airplanes to sell to corporations for use by their executives. To meet the needs of these executives, the company's customers sometimes order a custom design of the airplanes being purchased. When this occurs, a substantial start-up cost is incurred to initiate the production of these airplanes.

Fly-Right has recently received purchase requests from three customers with short deadlines. However, because the company's production facilities already are almost completely tied up filling previous orders, it will not be able to accept all three orders. Therefore, a decision now needs to be made on the number of airplanes the company will agree to produce (if any) for each of the three customers.

The relevant data are given in the next table. The first row gives the start-up cost required to initiate the production of the airplanes for each customer. Once production is under way, the marginal net revenue (which is the purchase price minus the marginal production cost) from each airplane produced is shown in the second row. The third row gives the percentage of the available production capacity that would be used for each airplane produced. The last row indicates the maximum number of airplanes requested by each customer (but less will be accepted).

	Customer		
	1	**2**	**3**
Start-up cost	$3 million	$2 million	0
Marginal net revenue	$2 million	$3 million	$0.8 million
Capacity used per plane	20%	40%	20%
Maximum order	3 planes	2 planes	5 planes

Fly-Right now wants to determine how many airplanes to produce for each customer (if any) to maximize the company's total profit (total net revenue minus start-up costs). Formulate and solve a spreadsheet model with both integer variables and binary variables for this problem.

E*7.7. Consider the following special type of shortest path problem (discussed in Section 6.4) where the nodes are in columns and the only paths considered always move forward one column at a time.

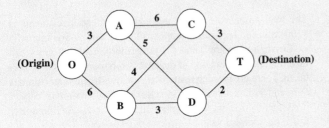

The numbers along the links represent distances (in miles), and the objective is to find the shortest path from the origin to the destination.

This problem also can be formulated as a BIP model involving both mutually exclusive alternatives and contingent decisions. Formulate and solve this BIP model on a spreadsheet. Identify the constraints for (1) mutually exclusive alternatives and (2) contingent decisions.

7.8. Read the referenced article that fully describes the management science study summarized in the application vignette presented in Section 7.4. Briefly describe how BIP and related techniques were applied in this study. Then list the various financial and nonfinancial benefits that resulted from this study.

7.9. Speedy Delivery provides two-day delivery service of large parcels across the United States. Each morning at each collection center, the parcels that have arrived overnight are loaded onto several trucks for delivery throughout the area. Since the competitive battlefield in this business is speed of delivery, the parcels are divided among the trucks according to their geographical destinations to minimize the average time needed to make the deliveries.

On this particular morning, the dispatcher for the Blue River Valley Collection Center, Sharon Lofton, is hard at work. Her three drivers will be arriving in less than an hour to make the day's deliveries. There are nine parcels to be delivered, all at locations many miles apart. As usual, Sharon has loaded these locations into her computer. She is using her company's special software package, a decision support system called Dispatcher. The first thing Dispatcher does is use these locations to generate a considerable number of attractive possible routes for the individual delivery trucks. These routes are shown in the table below (where the numbers in each column indicate the order of the deliveries), along with the estimated time required to traverse the route.

Dispatcher is an interactive system that shows these routes to Sharon for her approval or modification. (For example, the computer may not know that flooding has made a particular route infeasible.) After Sharon approves these routes as attractive possibilities with reasonable time estimates, Dispatcher next formulates and solves a BIP model for selecting three routes that minimize their total time while including each delivery location on exactly one route.

Delivery Location	Attractive Possible Route									
	1	**2**	**3**	**4**	**5**	**6**	**7**	**8**	**9**	**10**
A	1				1				1	
B		2		1		2			2	2
C			3	3			3		3	
D	2					1		1		
E				2	2	3				
F			1		2					
G	3						1	2		3
H				1		3				1
I		3		4			2			
Time (in hours)	6	4	7	5	4	6	5	3	7	6

E* a. Using the data in the table, demonstrate how Dispatcher can formulate and solve this BIP model on a spreadsheet.

b. Describe how the problem addressed in part *a* is analogous to the crew scheduling problem described in Section 7.4.

E*7.10. An increasing number of Americans are moving to a warmer climate when they retire. To take advantage of this trend, Sunny Skies Unlimited is undertaking a major real-estate development project. The project is to develop a completely new retirement community (to be called Pilgrim Haven) that will cover several square miles. One of the decisions to be made is where to locate the two paramedic stations that have been allocated to the community to respond to medical emergencies. For planning purposes, Pilgrim Haven has been divided into five tracts, with no more than one paramedic station to be located in any given tract. Each station is to respond to *all* the medical emergencies that occur in the tract in which it is located as well as in the other tracts that are assigned to this station. Thus, the decisions to be made consist of (1) the tracts to receive a paramedic station and (2) the assignment of each of the other tracts to one of the paramedic stations. The objective is to minimize the overall average of the *response times* to medical emergencies.

The following table gives the average response time to a medical emergency in each tract (the rows) if that tract is served by a station in a given tract (the columns). The last column gives the forecasted average number of medical emergencies that will occur in each of the tracts per day.

| | | \multicolumn{5}{c}{Fire Station in Tract} | Average Frequency of Medical Emergencies per Day |
		1	2	3	4	5	
Response	1	5	20	15	25	10	2
times (min.)	2	12	4	20	15	25	1
to a medical	3	30	15	6	25	15	3
emergency	4	20	10	15	4	12	1
in tract	5	15	25	12	10	5	3

Formulate and solve a BIP model on a spreadsheet for this problem. Identify any constraints that correspond to mutually exclusive alternatives or contingent decisions.

7.11. Reconsider Problem 7.10. The management of Sunny Skies Unlimited now has decided that the decision regarding the locations of the paramedic stations should be based mainly on costs.

The cost of locating a paramedic station in a tract is $200,000 for tract 1, $250,000 for tract 2, $400,000 for tract 3, $300,000 for tract 4, and $500,000 for tract 5. Management's objective now is to determine which tracts should receive a station to minimize the total cost of stations while ensuring that each tract has at least one station close enough to respond to a medical emergency in no more than 15 minutes (on the average). In contrast to the original problem, note that the total number of paramedic stations is no longer fixed. Furthermore, if a tract without a station has more than one station within 15 minutes, it is no longer necessary to assign this tract to just one of these stations.

  a. Formulate the algebraic form of a pure BIP model with five binary variables for this problem.
E* b. Display and solve this model on a spreadsheet.

7.12. Reconsider the Southwestern Airlines crew scheduling problem presented in Section 7.4. Because of a blizzard in the Chicago area, all the flights into and out of Chicago (including flights 4, 6, 7, and 9 in Table 7.5) have been canceled for the time being, so a new crew scheduling plan needs to be developed to cover the seven remaining flights in Table 7.5.

The 12 feasible sequences of flights still are the ones shown in Table 7.5 after deleting the canceled flights. When flights into and out of Chicago had originally been part of a sequence, a crew now would fly as passengers on a Southwestern Airways flight to the next city in the sequence to cover the remaining flights in the sequence. For example, flight sequence 4 now would be San Francisco to Los Angeles to Denver to San Francisco, where a crew would fly as passengers on a flight from Los Angeles to Denver (not shown in the table) to enable serving as the crew from Denver to San Francisco. (Since the original sequence 5 included a round-trip from Denver to Chicago and back, a crew assigned to this sequence now would simply lay over in Denver to await the flight from Denver to San Francisco.) The cost of assigning a crew to any sequence still would be the same as shown in the bottom row of Table 7.5.

The objective still is to minimize the total cost of the crew assignments that cover all the flights. The fact that only 7 flights now need to be covered instead of 11 increases the chance that fewer than three crews will need to be assigned to a flight sequence this time. (The flights where these crews fly as passengers do not need to be covered since they already are assigned to crews that are not based in San Francisco.)

  a. Formulate a BIP model in algebraic form for this problem.
E* b. Formulate and solve this problem on a spreadsheet.

7.13. Yakima Construction Corporation (YCC) is considering a number of different development projects. The cash outflows that would be required to complete each project are indicated in the table below, along with the expected net present value of each project (all values in millions of dollars).

| | \multicolumn{5}{c}{Project} |
	1	2	3	4	5
Year 1	$8	$10	$12	$4	$14
Year 2	6	8	6	3	6
Year 3	3	7	6	2	5
Year 4	0	5	6	0	7
NPV	$12	$15	$20	$9	$23

Each project must be done in full (with the corresponding cash flows for all four years) or not done at all. Furthermore, there are the following additional considerations. Project 1 cannot be done unless project 2 is also undertaken, and projects 3 and 4 would compete with each other, so they should not both be chosen. YCC expects to have the following cash available to invest in these projects: $40 million for year 1, $25 million for year 2, $16 million for year 3, and $12 million for year 4. Any available money not spent in a given year is then available to spend the following year. YCC's policy is to choose their projects so as to maximize their total expected NPV.

   a. Formulate a BIP model in algebraic form for this problem.

E*   *b.* Formulate and solve this model on a spreadsheet.

7.14.   Read the referenced article that fully describes the management science study summarized in the application vignette presented in Section 7.5. Briefly describe how mixed BIP was applied in this study. Then list the various financial and nonfinancial benefits that resulted from this study.

7.15.   An electrical utility needs to generate 6,500 megawatts of electricity today. It has five generators. If any electricity is generated by a given generator, that generator must be started up and a fixed start-up cost is incurred. There is an additional cost for each megawatt generated by a generator. These costs, as well as the maximum capacity of each generator, are shown in the following table. The objective is to determine the minimum cost plan that meets the electrical needs for today.

computer and a fixed delivery and installation cost for these large sales to school districts. The table below shows these charges as well as the capacity (the maximum number of computers that can be sold from the limited inventory) for each of the companies.

	Educomp	Macwin	McElectronics
Capacity	700	700	1,000
Fixed cost	$45,000	$35,000	$50,000
Variable cost	$750	$775	$700

The school board wants to determine the minimum-cost plan for meeting its computer needs.

   a. Formulate a BIP model in algebraic form for this problem.

E*   *b.* Formulate and solve this model on a spreadsheet.

E*   *c.* Now suppose that Macwin has not submitted its final bid yet, so the per computer cost is not known with certainty. Generate a Solver Table to show the optimal order quantities and total cost of the optimal solution when the cost per computer for Macwin is $680, $690, $700, $710, . . . , $790, or $800.

E*7.17.   Noble Amazon sells books online. Management is trying to determine the best sites for the company's warehouses. Five

	Generator				
	A	**B**	**C**	**D**	**E**
Fixed start-up cost	$3,000	$2,000	$2,500	$1,500	$1,000
Cost per megawatt generated	$5	$4	$6	$6	$7
Maximum capacity (MW)	2,100	1,800	2,500	1,500	3,000

   a. Formulate a BIP model in algebraic form for this problem.

E*   *b.* Formulate and solve this model on a spreadsheet.

7.16.   The school board for the Bellevue School District has made the decision to purchase 1,350 additional Macintosh computers for computer laboratories in all its schools. Based on past experience, the school board also has directed that these computers should be purchased from some combination of three companies—Educomp, Macwin, and McElectronics. In all three cases, the companies charge a discounted variable cost per

potential sites are under consideration. Most of the sales come from customers in the United States. The average weekly demand from each region of the country, the average shipping cost from each warehouse site to each region of the country, the fixed cost per week of each warehouse if it is operated, and the maximum capacity of each warehouse (if it is operated) are shown in the table below. Formulate and solve a mixed BIP model in a spreadsheet to determine which warehouse sites Noble Amazon should operate and how books should be distributed from each warehouse to each region of the country to minimize total cost.

	Average Shipping Cost ($/book)					Fixed Cost (per week)	Warehouse Capacity (books/week)
Warehouse Site	**Northwest**	**Southwest**	**Midwest**	**Southeast**	**Northeast**		
Spokane, WA	$2.40	$3.50	$4.80	$6.80	$5.75	$40,000	20,000
Reno, NV	$3.25	$2.30	$3.40	$5.25	$6.00	$30,000	20,000
Omaha, NE	$4.05	$3.25	$2.85	$4.30	$4.75	$25,000	15,000
Harrisburg, PA	$5.25	$6.05	$4.30	$3.25	$2.75	$40,000	25,000
Jacksonville, FL	$6.95	$5.85	$4.80	$2.10	$3.50	$30,000	15,000
Customer demand (per week)	8,000	12,000	9,000	14,000	17,000		

E*7.18. Aberdeen Computer Corp. (ACC) is located in Aberdeen, Washington. The company has developed the Web-Surfer, a low-cost e-mail and Web-surfing appliance. This product is manufactured at four plants, located in Atlanta, Kansas City, Aberdeen, and Austin. After production, the WebSurfers are shipped to three warehouses, located in Nashville, San Jose, and Houston. ACC sells the WebSurfers through the retail channel. In particular, five different retailers currently sell the WebSurfer—Sears, Best Buy, Fry's, Comp USA, and Office Max. ACC makes weekly shipments to the main warehouses of these five retailers. The shipping cost from each plant to each warehouse, along with the production cost and weekly production capacity at each plant, are given in the table below.

Plant	Fixed Cost ($/week)
Atlanta	$8,000
Kansas City	$9,000
Aberdeen	$9,000
Austin	$10,000

Warehouse	Fixed Cost ($/week)
Nashville	$4,000
San Jose	$5,000
Houston	$5,000

Plant	Shipping Cost ($/unit) Nashville	Shipping Cost ($/unit) San Jose	Shipping Cost ($/unit) Houston	Production Cost ($/unit)	Capacity (units/week)
Atlanta	$30	$40	$50	$208	200
Kansas City	$25	$45	$40	$214	300
Aberdeen	$45	$30	$55	$215	300
Austin	$30	$50	$30	$210	400

The shipping cost from each warehouse to each customer, the variable cost (cost per unit moved through the warehouse), the capacity (maximum number of units that can be moved through the warehouse per week) for each warehouse, and the weekly demand for each customer are given in the table below.

b. Now suppose that ACC is considering saving money by closing some of its production facilities and/or warehouses. Suppose there is a fixed cost to operate each plant and each warehouse as indicated in the tables above. Add binary variables to your

Warehouse	Shipping Cost ($/unit) Sears	Shipping Cost ($/unit) Best Buy	Shipping Cost ($/unit) Fry's	Shipping Cost ($/unit) Comp USA	Shipping Cost ($/unit) Office Max	Variable Cost ($/unit)	Capacity (units/week)
Nashville	$40	$45	$30	$25	$20	$4	300
San Jose	$15	$50	$25	$15	$40	$5	500
Houston	$50	$35	$15	$40	$50	$5	500
Customer demand (per week)	100	50	75	300	150		

a. Formulate and solve a linear programming model in a spreadsheet to determine the plan for weekly production and distribution of the WebSurfer from the various plants, through the warehouses, to the customers that will minimize total costs.

model in part *a* to incorporate the decision of which plants and warehouses to keep open so as to minimize total cost (including the fixed costs for any plant or warehouse that is operated).

Partial Answers to Selected Problems

CHAPTER 7

7.3. *b.* Marketing and dishwashing by Eve, cooking and laundry by Steven. Total time = 18.4 hours.

7.7. Optimal path = OADT. Total distance = 10 miles.

7.S1 Capital Budgeting with Contingency Constraints

A company is planning its capital budget over the next several years. There are eight potential projects under consideration. A calculation has been made of the expected net present value of each project, along with the cash outflow that would be required over the next four years. These data, along with the cash that is available each year, are shown in the table below. There also are the following contingency constraints: (a) at least one of project 1, 2, or 3 must be done, (b) project 6 and 7 cannot both be done, and (c) project 5 can only be done if project 6 is done. Formulate and solve a BIP model in a spreadsheet to determine which projects should be pursued to maximize the total expected net present value.

	Cash Outflow Required ($million)								Cash Available ($million)
	Project								
	1	2	3	4	5	6	7	8	
Year 1	1	3	0	3	3	7	2	5	20
Year 2	2	2	2	2	2	3	3	4	20
Year 3	2	3	4	2	3	3	6	2	20
Year 4	2	1	0	5	4	2	1	2	20
NPV ($mil)	10	12	11	15	24	17	16	18	

This is a resource-allocation problem. The activities are the various projects and the limited resources are the available cash in each year. We will therefore build a spreadsheet following the template for resource-allocation problems in Figure 3.4. Start by entering the data. The data for this problem are the NPV for each project, the cash outflow for the projects, and the cash available each year. Following the template, the data in the spreadsheet would be entered as displayed below, where range names of NPV (C5:J5) and TotalAvailable (M8:M11) are assigned to the corresponding data cells.

	B	C	D	E	F	G	H	I	J	K	L	M
3		Project	Project	Project	Project	Project	Project	Project	Project			
4		1	2	3	4	5	6	7	8			
5	NPV ($million)	10	12	11	15	24	17	16	18			
6												Total
7	Cash Outflow Required ($million)											Available
8	Year 1	1	3	0	3	3	7	2	5			20
9	Year 2	2	2	2	2	2	3	3	4			20
10	Year 3	2	3	4	2	3	3	6	2			20
11	Year 4	2	1	0	5	4	2	1	2			20

The decisions to be made in this problem are whether or not to do each project. Thus, a binary variable is defined for each project in the changing cells Undertake? (C15:J15). The values in Undertake? (C15:J15) will eventually be determined by the Solver. For now, arbitrary values are entered.

	B	C	D	E	F	G	H	I	J	K	L	M
3		Project	Project	Project	Project	Project	Project	Project	Project			
4		1	2	3	4	5	6	7	8			
5	NPV ($million)	10	12	11	15	24	17	16	18			
6												Total
7	Cash Outflow Required ($million)											Available
8	Year 1	1	3	0	3	3	7	2	5			20
9	Year 2	2	2	2	2	2	3	3	4			20
10	Year 3	2	3	4	2	3	3	6	2			20
11	Year 4	2	1	0	5	4	2	1	2			20
12												
13		Project	Project	Project	Project	Project	Project	Project	Project			
14		1	2	3	4	5	6	7	8			
15	Undertake?	1	0	1	0	1	0	1	0			

The goal is to maximize the total expected NPV. Thus, the target cell should calculate the total NPV. In this case, the total NPV will be

Total NPV = SUMPRODUCT(NPV, Undertake?).

This formula is entered into TotalNPV (M15).

	B	C	D	E	F	G	H	I	J	K	L	M
3		Project	Project	Project	Project	Project	Project	Project	Project			
4		1	2	3	4	5	6	7	8			
5	NPV ($million)	10	12	11	15	24	17	16	18			
6												Total
7	Cash Outflow Required ($million)											Available
8	Year 1	1	3	0	3	3	7	2	5			20
9	Year 2	2	2	2	2	2	3	3	4			20
10	Year 3	2	3	4	2	3	3	6	2			20
11	Year 4	2	1	0	5	4	2	1	2			20
12												
13		Project	Project	Project	Project	Project	Project	Project	Project			Total NPV
14		1	2	3	4	5	6	7	8			($million)
15	Undertake?	1	0	1	0	1	0	1	0			61

	M
13	Total NPV
14	($million)
15	=SUMPRODUCT(NPV, Undertake?)

The functional constraints in this problem take into account the limited resources of the cash available each year. Given Undertake? (the changing cells in C15:J15), we calculate the total outflow in (K8:K11). For year 1, this will be =SUMPRODUCT(C8:J8, Undertake?). Using a range name or an absolute reference for Undertake?, this formula can be copied into cells K9:K11 to calculate the total outflow in years 2, 3, and 4. The TotalOutflow (K8:K11) must be <= TotalAvailable (M8:M11), as indicated by the <= in L8:L11.

Furthermore, there are three contingency constraints.

a) At least one of projects 1, 2, or 3 must be done. Therefore, we add the changing cells for projects 1, 2, and 3 in C18 and constrain C18 >= 1.

b) Project 6 and 7 cannot both be done. Therefore, we add the changing cells for projects 6 and 7 in C19 and constrain C19 <= 1.

c) Project 5 can only be done if project 6 is done. Therefore we constrain the changing cell for Project 5 to be <= the changing cell for Project 6 in C20:E20.

	B	C	D	E	F	G	H	I	J	K	L	M
3		Project	Project	Project	Project	Project	Project	Project	Project			
4		1	2	3	4	5	6	7	8			
5	NPV ($million)	10	12	11	15	24	17	16	18			
6										Total		Total
7	Cash Outflow Required ($million)									Outflow		Available
8	Year 1	1	3	0	3	3	7	2	5	6	<=	20
9	Year 2	2	2	2	2	2	3	3	4	9	<=	20
10	Year 3	2	3	4	2	3	3	6	2	15	<=	20
11	Year 4	2	1	0	5	4	2	1	2	7	<=	20
12												
13		Project	Project	Project	Project	Project	Project	Project	Project			Total NPV
14		1	2	3	4	5	6	7	8			($million)
15	Undertake?	1	0	1	0	1	0	1	0			61
16												
17	Contingency Constraints											
18	Project 1,2,3	2	>=	1								
19	Project 6,7	1	<=	1								
20	Project 5	1	<=	0	Project 6							

	K
6	Total
7	Outflow
8	=SUMPRODUCT(C8:J8,Undertake?)
9	=SUMPRODUCT(C9:J9,Undertake?)
10	=SUMPRODUCT(C10:J10,Undertake?)
11	=SUMPRODUCT(C11:J11,Undertake?)

	B	C	D	E	F
18	Project 1,2,3	=SUM(C15:E15)	>=	1	
19	Project 6,7	=SUM(H15:I15)	<=	1	
20	Project 5	=G15	<=	=H15	Project 6

The Solver information and solved spreadsheet are shown below.

	A	B	C	D	E	F	G	H	I	J	K	L	M
1		**Capital Budgeting with Contingency Constraints**											
2													
3			Project	Project	Project	Project	Project	Project	Project	Project			
4			1	2	3	4	5	6	7	8			
5		NPV ($million)	10	12	11	15	24	17	16	18			
6											Total		Total
7		Cash Outflow Required ($million)									Outflow		Available
8		Year 1	1	3	0	3	3	7	2	5	19	<=	20
9		Year 2	2	2	2	2	2	3	3	4	15	<=	20
10		Year 3	2	3	4	2	3	3	6	2	16	<=	20
11		Year 4	2	1	0	5	4	2	1	2	15	<=	20
12													
13			Project	Project	Project	Project	Project	Project	Project	Project			Total NPV
14			1	2	3	4	5	6	7	8			($million)
15		Undertake?	1	0	1	1	1	1	0	1			95
16													
17		Contingency Constraints											
18		Project 1,2,3	2	>=	1								
19		Project 6,7	1	<=	1								
20		Project 5	1	<=	1	Project 6							

	K
6	Total
7	Outflow
8	=SUMPRODUCT(C8:J8,Undertake?)
9	=SUMPRODUCT(C9:J9,Undertake?)
10	=SUMPRODUCT(C10:J10,Undertake?)
11	=SUMPRODUCT(C11:J11,Undertake?)

	M
13	Total NPV
14	($million)
15	=SUMPRODUCT(NPV, Undertake?)

	B	C	D	E	F
18	Project 1,2,3	=SUM(C15:E15)	>=	1	
19	Project 6,7	=SUM(H15:I15)	<=	1	
20	Project 5	=G15	<=	=H15	Project 6

Thus, they should undertake projects 1, 3, 4, 5, 6, and 8 to obtain a total expected NPV of $95 million.

7.S2 Locating Search and Rescue Teams

The Washington State legislature is trying to decide on locations at which to base search-and-rescue teams. The teams are expensive, so the legislature would like as few as possible while still providing the desired level of service. In particular, since response time is critical, the legislature would like every county to either have a team located in that county or in an adjacent county. Formulate and solve a BIP model in a spreadsheet to determine where the teams should be located.

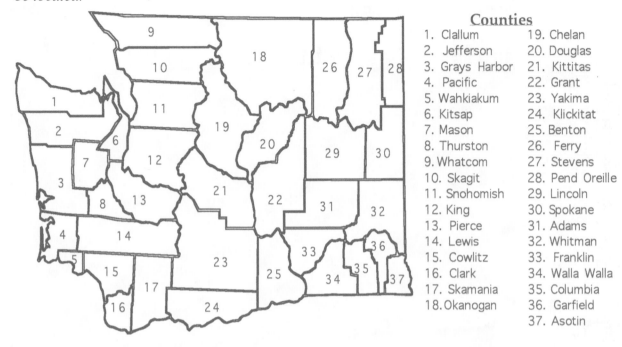

Counties

1. Clallum
2. Jefferson
3. Grays Harbor
4. Pacific
5. Wahkiakum
6. Kitsap
7. Mason
8. Thurston
9. Whatcom
10. Skagit
11. Snohomish
12. King
13. Pierce
14. Lewis
15. Cowlitz
16. Clark
17. Skamania
18. Okanogan
19. Chelan
20. Douglas
21. Kittitas
22. Grant
23. Yakima
24. Klickitat
25. Benton
26. Ferry
27. Stevens
28. Pend Oreille
29. Lincoln
30. Spokane
31. Adams
32. Whitman
33. Franklin
34. Walla Walla
35. Columbia
36. Garfield
37. Asotin

This is a set covering problem. The decisions to be made are whether to locate a team in each county. The requirement for each county is that there be a team nearby, where nearby is defined as in that county or an adjacent county. The data for this problem are the coverage data. In particular, in the row representing each county, there is a 1 in every column that would satisfy the coverage of the row's county if there were a team there. For example, Clallum county would be covered if there is a team in either Clallum or Jefferson county.

County Nearby? — columns 1–37 correspond (in order) to: 1 Clallum, 2 Jefferson, 3 Grays Harbor, 4 Pacific, 5 Wahkiakum, 6 Kitsap, 7 Mason, 8 Thurston, 9 Whatcom, 10 Skagit, 11 Snohomish, 12 King, 13 Pierce, 14 Lewis, 15 Cowlitz, 16 Clark, 17 Skamania, 18 Okanogan, 19 Chelan, 20 Douglas, 21 Kittitas, 22 Grant, 23 Yakima, 24 Klickitat, 25 Benton, 26 Ferry, 27 Stevens, 28 Pend Oreille, 29 Lincoln, 30 Spokane, 31 Adams, 32 Whitman, 33 Franklin, 34 Walla Walla, 35 Columbia, 36 Garfield, 37 Asotin.

#	County	1	2	3	4	5	6	7	8	9	10	11	12	13	14	15	16	17	18	19	20	21	22	23	24	25	26	27	28	29	30	31	32	33	34	35	36	37
1	Clallum	1	1																																			
2	Jefferson	1	1	1			1	1																														
3	Grays Harbor		1	1	1			1	1						1																							
4	Pacific			1	1	1									1	1																						
5	Wahkiakum				1	1									1	1																						
6	Kitsap		1				1	1					1	1																								
7	Mason		1	1			1	1	1					1																								
8	Thurston			1				1	1					1	1																							
9	Whatcom									1	1								1																			
10	Skagit									1	1	1							1	1																		
11	Snohomish										1	1	1							1																		
12	King						1					1	1	1						1		1																
13	Pierce						1	1	1				1	1	1							1		1														
14	Lewis			1	1	1			1					1	1	1		1						1														
15	Cowlitz				1	1									1	1	1	1																				
16	Clark															1	1	1																				
17	Skamania														1	1	1	1						1	1													
18	Okanogan									1	1								1	1	1						1											
19	Chelan										1	1	1						1	1	1	1																
20	Douglas																		1	1	1	1	1							1								
21	Kittitas												1	1						1	1	1	1	1														
22	Grant																				1	1	1	1		1				1		1		1				
23	Yakima													1	1			1				1	1	1	1	1												
24	Klickitat																	1						1	1	1												
25	Benton																						1	1	1	1								1	1			
26	Ferry																		1								1	1		1								
27	Stevens																										1	1	1	1	1							
28	Pend Oreille																											1	1		1							
29	Lincoln																				1		1				1	1		1	1	1						
30	Spokane																											1	1	1	1	1	1					
31	Adams																						1							1	1	1	1	1				
32	Whitman																														1	1	1	1		1	1	1
33	Franklin																						1			1						1		1	1			
34	Walla Walla																									1								1	1	1		
35	Columbia																																1		1	1	1	
36	Garfield																																1			1	1	1
37	Asotin																																1				1	1

The decisions to be made in this problem are whether or not to place a team in each county. Thus, a binary variable is defined for each county in the changing cells Team? (D44:AN44). The values in Team? (D44:AN44) will eventually be determined by the Solver. For now, arbitrary values are entered.

The goal is to minimize the total number of teams. Thus, the target cell should calculate this total:

Total Teams = SUM(Teams?).

This formula is entered into TotalTeams (AQ44).

#	County	1	2	3	4	5	6	7	8	9	10	11	12	13	14	15	16	17	18	19	20	21	22	23	24	25	26	27	28	29	30	31	32	33	34	35	36	37
		Clallam	Jefferson	Grays Harbor	Pacific	Wahkiakum	Kitsap	Mason	Thurston	Whatcom	Skagit	Snohomish	King	Pierce	Lewis	Cowlitz	Clark	Skamania	Okanogan	Chelan	Douglas	Kittitas	Grant	Yakima	Klickitat	Benton	Ferry	Stevens	Pend Oreille	Lincoln	Spokane	Adams	Whitman	Franklin	Walla Walla	Columbia	Garfield	Asotin
1	Clallum	1	1																																			
2	Jefferson	1	1	1			1	1																														
3	Grays Harbor		1	1	1			1	1						1																							
4	Pacific			1	1	1									1	1																						
5	Wahkiakum				1	1										1																						
6	Kitsap		1				1	1					1	1																								
7	Mason		1	1			1	1	1					1																								
8	Thurston			1				1	1					1	1																							
9	Whatcom									1	1								1																			
10	Skagit									1	1	1							1	1																		
11	Snohomish										1	1	1							1		1																
12	King						1					1	1	1								1																
13	Pierce						1	1	1				1	1	1							1		1														
14	Lewis			1	1				1					1	1	1		1						1														
15	Cowlitz				1	1									1	1	1	1																				
16	Clark															1	1	1																				
17	Skamania														1	1	1	1						1	1													
18	Okanogan									1	1								1	1	1		1				1											
19	Chelan										1	1							1	1	1	1	1															
20	Douglas																		1	1	1		1							1								
21	Kittitas											1	1	1						1	1	1	1	1														
22	Grant																		1	1	1	1	1	1		1				1		1		1				
23	Yakima													1	1			1				1	1	1	1	1												
24	Klickitat																	1						1	1	1												
25	Benton																						1	1	1	1								1				
26	Ferry																		1								1	1		1	1							
27	Stevens																										1	1	1	1	1							
28	Pend Oreille																											1	1		1							
29	Lincoln																				1		1				1			1	1	1						
30	Spokane																										1	1	1	1	1	1	1					
31	Adams																						1							1	1	1	1	1				
32	Whitman																														1	1	1	1			1	1
33	Franklin																						1			1						1		1	1	1		
34	Walla Walla																																	1	1	1	1	
35	Columbia																																		1	1	1	
36	Garfield																																1			1	1	1
37	Asotin																																1				1	1
	Team?	1	0	1	0	1	0	1	0	1	0	1	0	1	0	1	0	1	0	1	0	1	0	1	0	1	0	1	0	1	0	1	0	1	0	1	0	1

Total Teams: 19

	AQ
43	Total Teams
44	=SUM(Team?)

7

The functional constraints in this problem are that each county must have at least one team nearby. Given Teams? (D44:AN44), we calculate the number of teams nearby in TeamsNearby(AO5:AO41). For Clallum county, this will be =SUMPRODUCT(D5:AN5, Team?). Using a range name or an absolute reference for Team?, this formula can be copied into cells AO6:AO41 to calculate the number of teams nearby for the other counties. The TeamsNearby (AO5:AO41) must be >= 1, as indicated by the >= in AP5:AP41.

	B	C	D	E	F	G	H	I	J	K	L	M	N	O	P	Q	R	S	T	U	V	W	X	Y	Z	AA	AB	AC	AD	AE	AF	AG	AH	AI	AJ	AK	AL	AM	AN	AO	AP	AQ
2																		County Nearby?																								
3			1	2	3	4	5	6	7	8	9	10	11	12	13	14	15	16	17	18	19	20	21	22	23	24	25	26	27	28	29	30	31	32	33	34	35	36	37			
4		County	Clallum	Jefferson	Grays Harbor	Pacific	Wahkiakum	Kitsap	Mason	Thurston	Whatcom	Skagit	Snohomish	King	Pierce	Lewis	Cowlitz	Clark	Skamania	Okanogan	Chelan	Douglas	Kittitas	Grant	Yakima	Klickitat	Benton	Ferry	Stevens	Pend Oreille	Lincoln	Spokane	Adams	Whitman	Franklin	Walla Walla	Columbia	Garfield	Asotin	Teams nearby		Needed
5	1	Clallum |1|1|																																							1	>=	1
6	2	Jefferson	1	1	1			1	1																																			3	>=	1
7	3	Grays Harbor		1	1	1			1	1						1																										2	>=	1
8	4	Pacific			1	1	1									1																										2	>=	1
9	5	Wahkiakum				1	1									1	1																									2	>=	1
10	6	Kitsap		1				1	1					1	1																											2	>=	1
11	7	Mason		1	1			1	1	1					1																											3	>=	1
12	8	Thurston			1				1	1					1	1																										3	>=	1
13	9	Whatcom									1	1								1																						1	>=	1
14	10	Skagit									1	1	1							1	1																					3	>=	1
15	11	Snohomish										1	1	1							1																					2	>=	1
16	12	King						1					1	1	1						1		1																			4	>=	1
17	13	Pierce						1	1	1				1	1	1							1		1																	4	>=	1
18	14	Lewis			1	1	1			1					1	1	1		1						1																	6	>=	1
19	15	Cowlitz					1									1	1		1																							3	>=	1
20	16	Clark															1	1	1																							2	>=	1
21	17	Skamania														1	1	1	1						1	1																3	>=	1
22	18	Okanogan									1	1								1	1	1						1			1											3	>=	1
23	19	Chelan										1	1	1						1	1	1	1																			3	>=	1
24	20	Douglas																		1	1	1	1	1																		2	>=	1
25	21	Kittitas												1	1						1	1	1	1	1																	4	>=	1
26	22	Grant																				1	1	1	1		1				1		1		1							6	>=	1
27	23	Yakima													1	1			1				1	1	1	1	1															5	>=	1
28	24	Klickitat																	1						1	1	1															3	>=	1
29	25	Benton																						1	1	1	1								1	1						3	>=	1
30	26	Ferry																		1								1	1		1											2	>=	1
31	27	Stevens																										1	1	1	1	1										2	>=	1
32	28	Pend Oreille																											1	1		1										1	>=	1
33	29	Lincoln																		1				1				1	1		1	1	1	1								3	>=	1
34	30	Spokane																											1	1	1	1		1								2	>=	1
35	31	Adams																						1							1		1	1	1							3	>=	1
36	32	Whitman																													1	1	1	1	1		1	1	1	5	>=	1
37	33	Franklin																						1			1						1	1	1	1					3	>=	1
38	34	Walla Walla																									1								1	1	1				3	>=	1
39	35	Columbia																																1		1	1	1			1	>=	1
40	36	Garfield																																1			1	1	1	2	>=	1
41	37	Asotin																																1				1	1	1	>=	1
42																																											
43																																											Total Teams
44		Team?	1	0	1	0	1	0	1	0	1	0	1	0	1	0	1	0	1	0	1	0	1	0	1	0	1	0	1	0	1	0	1	0	1	0	1	0	1			19

	AO
4	Teams nearby
5	=SUMPRODUCT(D5:AN5,Team?)
6	=SUMPRODUCT(D6:AN6,Team?)
7	=SUMPRODUCT(D7:AN7,Team?)
8	:
9	:

The Solver information and solved spreadsheet are shown below.

Search & Rescue Location

	#	County	1 Clallam	2 Jefferson	3 Grays Harbor	4 Pacific	5 Wahkiakum	6 Kitsap	7 Mason	8 Thurston	9 Whatcom	10 Skagit	11 Snohomish	12 King	13 Pierce	14 Lewis	15 Cowlitz	16 Clark	17 Skamania	18 Okanogan	19 Chelan	20 Douglas	21 Kittitas	22 Grant	23 Yakima	24 Klickitat	25 Benton	26 Ferry	27 Stevens	28 Pend Oreille	29 Lincoln	30 Spokane	31 Adams	32 Whitman	33 Franklin	34 Walla Walla	35 Columbia	36 Garfield	37 Asotin	Teams nearby		Needed
5	1	Clallam	1	1																																				1	>=	1
6	2	Jefferson	1	1				1	1																															1	>=	1
7	3	Grays Harbor			1	1	1		1	1						1																								2	>=	1
8	4	Pacific			1	1	1									1																								1	>=	1
9	5	Wahkiakum				1	1									1	1																							1	>=	1
10	6	Kitsap	1					1	1	1				1	1																									2	>=	1
11	7	Mason	1	1	1			1	1	1					1																									1	>=	1
12	8	Thurston		1	1				1	1					1	1																								1	>=	1
13	9	Whatcom									1	1								1																				1	>=	1
14	10	Skagit									1	1	1								1																			1	>=	1
15	11	Snohomish										1	1	1							1																			1	>=	1
16	12	King						1					1	1	1						1		1																	1	>=	1
17	13	Pierce						1	1	1				1	1								1		1															2	>=	1
18	14	Lewis			1	1	1			1					1	1	1		1						1															1	>=	1
19	15	Cowlitz					1									1	1	1	1																					1	>=	1
20	16	Clark															1	1	1																					1	>=	1
21	17	Skamania														1	1	1	1						1	1														2	>=	1
22	18	Okanogan									1	1								1	1	1		1				1												1	>=	1
23	19	Chelan										1	1	1						1	1	1	1	1																2	>=	1
24	20	Douglas																		1	1	1	1	1							1									1	>=	1
25	21	Kittitas												1	1						1	1	1	1	1															1	>=	1
26	22	Grant																		1	1	1	1	1	1		1				1		1							1	>=	1
27	23	Yakima													1	1			1				1	1	1	1	1													2	>=	1
28	24	Klickitat																	1						1	1	1													1	>=	1
29	25	Benton																						1	1	1	1								1	1				1	>=	1
30	26	Ferry																		1								1	1		1									1	>=	1
31	27	Stevens																										1	1	1	1	1								1	>=	1
32	28	Pend Oreille																											1	1		1								1	>=	1
33	29	Lincoln																		1		1		1				1	1		1	1	1							3	>=	1
34	30	Spokane																											1	1	1	1	1	1						2	>=	1
35	31	Adams																						1							1	1	1	1	1					1	>=	1
36	32	Whitman																														1	1	1	1		1	1	1	2	>=	1
37	33	Franklin																						1			1						1	1	1	1				2	>=	1
38	34	Walla Walla																									1								1	1	1			1	>=	1
39	35	Columbia																																1		1	1	1		1	>=	1
40	36	Garfield																																1			1	1	1	1	>=	1
41	37	Asotin																																1				1	1	1	>=	1

| | Team? | 0 | 1 | 0 | 0 | 0 | 0 | 0 | 0 | 0 | 0 | 0 | 1 | 0 | 1 | 0 | 1 | 0 | 1 | 0 | 0 | 0 | 0 | 0 | 0 | 1 | 0 | 0 | 0 | 0 | 1 | 0 | 1 | 0 | 0 | 0 | 0 | 0 | | | Total Teams: 8 |

Solver Parameters

Set Objective (Target Cell): TotalTeams
To: Min
By Changing (Variable) Cells:
  Team?
Subject to the Constraints:
  Team? = binary
  TeamsNearby >= Needed

Solver Options (Excel 2010):
  Make Variables Nonnegative
  Solving Method: Simplex LP
Solver Options (older Excel):
  Assume Nonnegative
  Assume Linear Model

	AO
4	Teams nearby
5	=SUMPRODUCT(D5:AN5,Team?)
6	=SUMPRODUCT(D6:AN6,Team?)
7	=SUMPRODUCT(D7:AN7,Team?)
8	:
9	:

Range Name	Cells
Needed	AQ5:AQ41
Team?	D44:AN44
TeamsNearby	AO5:AO41
TotalTeams	AQ44

	AQ
43	Total Teams
44	=SUM(Team?)

Thus, they should locate a team in Jefferson, King, Lewis, Clark, Okanagan, Blanton, Spokane, and Whitman counties, for a total of 8 teams. (There are multiple optimal solutions for this problem.)

7.S3 Warehouse Site Selection

Consider a small company that produces a single product in two plants and serves customers in five different regions. The company has been using a make-to-order policy of producing the product only in the quantities needed to fill the orders that have come in from the various regions. However, because of the problems caused by the sporadic production schedule, management has decided to smooth out the production rate and ship the product to one or more storage warehouses, which then will use inventory to fill the incoming regional orders. Management now needs to decide where to locate the company's new warehouse(s). There are three locations under consideration. For each location, there is a fixed monthly cost associated with leasing and operating the warehouse there. Furthermore, each potential warehouse location has a maximum capacity for monthly shipments restricted primarily by the number of trucking docks at the site. The product costs $400 to produce at plant 1 and $300 to produce at plant 2. The shipping cost from each plant to each potential warehouse location is shown in the first table below. The fixed leasing and operating cost (if open), the shipping costs, and the capacity (maximum monthly shipments) of each potential warehouse location are shown in the second table below. The monthly demand in each of the customer regions is expected to be 200, 225, 100, 150, and 175 units, respectively. Formulate and solve a BIP model in a spreadsheet to determine which warehouse(s) should be used and how the product should be distributed from plant to warehouse(s) to customer.

| | Shipping Cost (per unit) | | | Capacity |
	WH #1	WH #2	WH #3	(units/month)
Plant 1	$25	$50	$75	500
Plant 2	$50	$75	$25	400

Shipping Costs and Capacity of the Plants

| | Fixed Cost | Shipping Cost (per unit) | | | | | Capacity |
	(per month)	Region 1	Region 2	Region 3	Region 4	Region 5	(units/mo.)
WH#1	$50,000	$30	$70	$75	$55	$40	700
WH#2	$30,000	$55	$30	$45	$45	$70	500
WH#3	$70,000	$70	$30	$50	$60	$55	1000

Fixed Cost, Shipping Costs, and Capacity of the Warehouses

Basically this problem is two linked transportation problems: (1) How much to ship from each plant to each warehouse, and (2) how much to ship from each warehouse to each region.

The first transportation problem is set up as follows. The decisions are how much to ship from each plant to each warehouse: PtoWShipments (D11:F12). The production cost and shipping cost are combined in PtoWCost (D6:F7). The PlantTotalShipped (G11:G12) must be <= PlantCapacity (I11:I12). The PtoWShipments (D11:F12) values will eventually be determined by the Solver. For now, arbitrary values are entered.

	B	C	D	E	F	G	H	I
3	**Plant to Warehouse**							
4		**Shipping + Production**						
5		**Cost**	Warehouse 1	Warehouse 2	Warehouse 3			
6		Plant 1	$425	$450	$475			
7		Plant 2	$350	$375	$325			
8						Plant		
9		**Shipment**				Total		Plant
10		**Quantities**	Warehouse 1	Warehouse 2	Warehouse 3	Shipped		Capacity
11		Plant 1	100	100	100	300	<=	500
12		Plant 2	100	100	100	300	<=	400
13		Total Shipped	200	200	200			

	C	D	E	F
13	Total Shipped	=SUM(D11:D12)	=SUM(E11:E12)	=SUM(F11:F12)

	G
8	Plant
9	Total
10	Shipped
11	=SUM(D11:F11)
12	=SUM(D12:F12)

The second transportation problem is set up as follows. The decisions are how much to ship from each warehouse to each region: WtoRShipments (D24:H26). The shipping costs are entered in WtoRCost (D18:H20). The total ShippedOut (I24:I26) must be <= ShippedIn (K24:K26), which are a function of the amounts shipped to the warehouses in the first transportation problem. Furtheremore, the amount ShippedIn (K24:K26) must be <= the capacity of the warehouse. The capacity of the warehouse will be Capacity(L18:L20) if that warehouse is open. Binary decision variables, Open? (N24:N26) are defined to make the yes-or-no decision of whether or not to open that warehouse. The actual capacity will then equal the capacity multiplied by the corresponding binary variable. For example, for warehouse 1, Actual Capacity = M24*N24. The WtoRShipments (D24:H26) values and Open? (N24:N26) will eventually be determined by the Solver. For now, arbitrary values are entered.

	B	C	D	E	F	G	H	I	J	K	L	M	N
15		Warehouse to Region								Fixed			
16		Shipping								Cost	Capacity		
17		Cost	Region 1	Region 2	Region 3	Region 4	Region 5			Cost	Capacity		
18		Warehouse 1	$30	$70	$75	$55	$40			$50,000	700		
19		Warehouse 2	$55	$30	$45	$45	$70			$30,000	500		
20		Warehouse 3	$70	$30	$50	$60	$55			$70,000	1000		
21													
22		Shipment						Shipped		Shipped		Actual	
23		Quantities	Region 1	Region 2	Region 3	Region 4	Region 5	Out		In		Capacity	Open?
24		Warehouse 1	100	100	0	0	0	200	<=	200	<=	700	1
25		Warehouse 2	0	0	100	100	0	200	<=	200	<=	500	1
26		Warehouse 3	0	0	0	0	0	0	<=	200	<=	0	0
27		Total Shipped	100	100	100	100	0						
28			>=	>=	>=	>=	>=						
29		Needed	200	225	100	150	175						

	I	J	K	L	M	N
22	Shipped		Shipped		Actual	
23	Out		In		Capacity	Open?
24	=SUM(D24:	<=	=D13	<=	=N24*L18	1
25	=SUM(D25:	<=	=E13	<=	=N25*L19	1
26	=SUM(D26:	<=	=F13	<=	=N26*L20	0

	C	D	E	F	G	H
27	Total Shipped	=SUM(D24:D26)	=SUM(E24:E26)	=SUM(F24:F26)	=SUM(G24:G26)	=SUM(H24:H26)

The goal is to minimize the total cost. This includes the shipping cost from plant to warehouse, shipping cost from warehouse to region, and the fixed cost of operating the open warehouses. These are calculated as follows.

Shipping Cost (Plants → Warehouses) = SUMPRODUCT(PtoWCost, PtoWShipments)
Shipping Cost (Warehouses → Regions) = SUMPRODUCT(WtoRCost, WtoRShipments)
Fixed Cost of Warehouses = SUMPRODUCT(FixedCost, Open?)

These values are calculated in N9:N11, and summed to calculate TotalCost (N12).

The Solver information and solved spreadsheet are shown below.

	A	B	C	D	E	F	G	H	I	J	K	L	M	N
1	**Warehouse Site Selection**													
2														
3			**Plant to Warehouse**											
4			Shipping + Production											
5			Cost	Warehouse 1	Warehouse 2	Warehouse 3								
6			Plant 1	$425	$450	$475								
7			Plant 2	$350	$375	$325								
8							Plant							**Total Costs**
9			Shipment				Total		Plant			Shipping Cost (P-->W)		$339,375
10			Quantities	Warehouse 1	Warehouse 2	Warehouse 3	Shipped		Capacity			Shipping Cost (W-->R)		$32,500
11			Plant 1	125	325	0	450	<=	500			Fixed Cost (W)		$80,000
12			Plant 2	400	0	0	400	<=	400			Total Cost		$451,875
13			Total Shipped	525	325	0								
14														
15			**Warehouse to Region**											
16			Shipping							Fixed				
17			Cost	Region 1	Region 2	Region 3	Region 4	Region 5		Cost		Capacity		
18			Warehouse 1	$30	$70	$75	$55	$40		$50,000		700		
19			Warehouse 2	$55	$30	$45	$45	$70		$30,000		500		
20			Warehouse 3	$70	$30	$50	$60	$55		$70,000		1000		
21														
22			Shipment						Shipped		Shipped		Actual	
23			Quantities	Region 1	Region 2	Region 3	Region 4	Region 5	Out		In		Capacity	Open?
24			Warehouse 1	200	0	0	150	175	525	<=	525	<=	700	1
25			Warehouse 2	0	225	100	0	0	325	<=	325	<=	500	1
26			Warehouse 3	0	0	0	0	0	0	<=	0	<=	0	0
27			Total Shipped	200	225	100	150	175						
28				>=	>=	>=	>=	>=						
29			Needed	200	225	100	150	175						

Solver Parameters

Set Objective (Target Cell): TotalCost
To: Min
By Changing (Variable) Cells:
   PtoWShipments, WtoRShipments, Open?
Subject to the Constraints:
   Open? = binary
   PlantTotalShipped <= PlantCapacity
   ShippedIn <= ActualCapacity
   ShippedOut <= ShippedIn
   TotalShippedToRegion >= NeededInRegion

Solver Options (Excel 2010):
   Make Variables Nonnegative
   Solving Method: Simplex LP
Solver Options (older Excel):
   Assume Nonnegative
   Assume Linear Model

Range Name	Cells
ActualCapacity	M24:M26
Capacity	L18:L20
FixedCost	J18:J20
NeededInRegion	D29:H29
Open?	N24:N26
PlantCapacity	I11:I12
PlantTotalShipped	G11:G12
PtoWCost	D6:F7
PtoWShipments	D11:F12
ShippedIn	K24:K26
ShippedOut	I24:I26
TotalCost	N12
TotalShippedToRegion	D27:H27
WtoRCost	D18:H20
WtoRShipments	D24:H26

	B	C	D	E	F	G	H	I	J	K	L	M	N
3	Plant												
4		Shipping + Prod											
5		Cost	Warehouse 1	Warehouse 2	Warehouse 3								
6		Plant 1	425	450	475								
7		Plant 2	350	375	325								
8						Plant							**Total Costs**
9		Shipment				Total		Plant			Shipping Cost (P-->W)		=SUMPRODUCT(PtoWCost,PtoWShipments)
10		Quantities	Warehouse 1	Warehouse 2	Warehouse 3	Shipped		Capacity			Shipping Cost (W-->R)		=SUMPRODUCT(WtoRCost,WtoRShipments)
11		Plant 1	125	325	0	=SUM(D11:F11)	<=	500			Fixed Cost (W)		=SUMPRODUCT(FixedCost,Open?)
12		Plant 2	400	0	0	=SUM(D12:F12)	<=	400			Total Cost		=SUM(N9:N11)
13		Total Shipped	=SUM(D11:D12)	=SUM(E11:E12)	=SUM(F11:F12)								
14													
15	Wareh												
16		Shipping							Fixed				
17		Cost	Region 1	Region 2	Region 3	Region 4	Region 5		Cost		Capacity		
18		Warehouse 1	30	70	75	55	40		50000		700		
19		Warehouse 2	55	30	45	45	70		30000		500		
20		Warehouse 3	70	30	50	60	55		70000		1000		
21													
22		Shipment						Shipped		Shipped		Actual	
23		Quantities	Region 1	Region 2	Region 3	Region 4	Region 5	Out		In		Capacity	Open?
24		Warehouse 1	200	0	0	150	175	=SUM(D24:H24)	<=	=D13	<=	=Open?*L18	1
25		Warehouse 2	0	225	100	0	0	=SUM(D25:H25)	<=	=E13	<=	=Open?*L19	1
26		Warehouse 3	0	0	0	0	0	=SUM(D26:H26)	<=	=F13	<=	=Open?*L20	0
27		Total Shipped	=SUM(D24:D26)	=SUM(E24:E26)	=SUM(F24:F26)	=SUM(G24:G26)	=SUM(H24:H26)						
28			>=	>=	>=	>=	>=						
29		Needed	200	225	100	150	175						

Thus, they should use warehouse 1 and 2, and ship product as indicated in PtoWShipments (D11:F12) and WtoRShipments (D24:H26), at a total cost of $451,875.

Chapter **Thirteen**

Computer Simulation with Crystal Ball

Learning objectives

After completing this chapter, you should be able to

1. Describe the role of Crystal Ball in performing computer simulations.
2. Use Crystal Ball to perform various basic computer simulations that cannot be readily performed with the standard Excel package.
3. Interpret the results generated by Crystal Ball when performing a computer simulation.
4. Use a Crystal Ball feature that enables stopping a simulation run after achieving the desired level of precision.
5. Describe the characteristics of many of the probability distributions that can be incorporated into a computer simulation when using Crystal Ball.
6. Use a Crystal Ball procedure that identifies the continuous distribution that best fits historical data.
7. Use a Crystal Ball feature that generates both a decision table and a trend chart as an aid to decision making.
8. Use a Crystal Ball tool called OptQuest that automatically searches for an optimal solution for a simulation model.

The preceding chapter presented the basic concepts of computer simulation. Its emphasis throughout was on the use of spreadsheet modeling to perform basic computer simulations. Except for the use of the Queueing Simulator to deal with queueing systems, all of the computer simulations in Chapter 12 were executed using nothing more than the standard Excel package.

Although the standard Excel package has some basic simulation capabilities, an exciting development in recent years has been the development of powerful Excel add-ins that greatly extend these capabilities. An especially popular one is *Crystal Ball,* which is a product of Oracle, Inc. Oracle has generously provided a license to download and use the latest version of Crystal Ball on a 140-day trial basis. (The license code and download instructions are on a card included at the back of this book.) In addition to its strong functionality for performing computer simulations, Crystal Ball also includes two other modules. One is CB Predictor, which is used for generating forecasts from time-series data, as described and illustrated in Section 10.4. The other is OptQuest, which enhances Crystal Ball by using its output from a series of simulation runs to automatically search for an optimal solution for a simulation model.

This chapter focuses on describing and illustrating the advances in spreadsheet simulation modeling that are made possible by Crystal Ball. (Other Excel add-ins for spreadsheet simulation modeling provide some of the same functionality.) Section 13.1 begins with a case study that will be revisited in Sections 13.7–13.8. Sections 13.2–13.6 present several other examples of important business problems that can be effectively addressed by using computer simulations with Crystal Ball. Section 13.7 focuses on how to choose the right probability distributions as inputs for a computer simulation. Section 13.8 then describes how decision tables (which work much like data tables or like Solver Table in your MS Courseware) can be constructed and applied to make a decision about the problem being simulated. Finally, Section 13.9 discusses and illustrates the powerful optimization tool provided by OptQuest.

13.1   A CASE STUDY: FREDDIE THE NEWSBOY'S PROBLEM

This case study concerns a newsstand in a prominent downtown location of a major city. The newsstand has been there longer than most people can remember. It has always been run by a well-known character named Freddie. (Nobody seems to know his last name.) His many customers refer to him affectionately as Freddie the newsboy, even though he is considerably older than most of them.

Freddie sells a wide variety of newspapers and magazines. The most expensive of the newspapers is a large national daily called the *Financial Journal*. Our case study involves this newspaper.

Freddie's Problem

The day's copies of the *Financial Journal* are brought to the newsstand early each morning by a distributor. Any copies unsold at the end of the day are returned to the distributor the next morning. However, to encourage ordering a large number of copies, the distributor does give a small refund for unsold copies.

Here are Freddie's cost figures.

Freddie pays $1.50 per copy delivered.

Freddie charges $2.50 per copy.

Freddie's refund is $0.50 per unsold copy.

Partially because of the refund, Freddie always has taken a plentiful supply. However, he has become concerned about paying so much for copies that then have to be returned unsold, particularly since this has been occurring nearly every day. He now thinks he might be better off ordering only a minimal number of copies and saving this extra cost.

To investigate this further, Freddie has been keeping a record of his daily sales. This is what he has found.

- Freddie sells anywhere between 40 and 70 copies on any given day.
- The frequency of the numbers between 40 and 70 are roughly equal.

Freddie's problem involves determining the order quantity that will maximize his average daily profit.

Freddie needs to determine how many copies to order per day from the distributor. His objective is to maximize his average daily profit.

If you have previously studied inventory management in an operations management course, you might recognize this problem as being an example of what is called the *newsvendor problem*. In fact, we use a basic inventory model to analyze a simplified version of this same case study in Chapter 19 (one of the supplementary chapters on the CD-ROM). However, we will use computer simulation to analyze this problem in this chapter.

A Spreadsheet Model for This Problem

Figure 13.1 shows a spreadsheet model for this problem. Given the data cells C4:C6, the decision variable is the order quantity to be entered in cell C9. (The number 60 has been entered arbitrarily in this figure as a first guess of a reasonable value.) The bottom of the figure shows the equations used to calculate the output cells C14:C16. These output cells are then used to calculate the output cell Profit (C18).

A day's demand for the Financial Journal appears to have a discrete uniform distribution between 40 and 70.

The only uncertain input quantity in this spreadsheet is the day's demand in cell C12. This quantity can be anywhere between 40 and 70. Since the frequency of the numbers between 40 and 70 are about the same, the probability distribution of the day's demand can be reasonably assumed to be a *discrete uniform distribution* between 40 and 70 (so all integer values between 40 and 70 are assumed to be equally likely), as indicated in cells D12:F12. Rather than enter a single number permanently into Demand (C12), what Crystal Ball does is enter this probability distribution into this cell. (Before turning to Crystal Ball, an arbitrary number 55 has been entered temporarily into this cell in Figure 13.1.) By using Crystal Ball to generate a *random observation* from this probability distribution, the spreadsheet can calculate the output cells in the usual way. Each time this is done is referred to as a **trial** by Crystal Ball. By

FIGURE 13.1

A spreadsheet model for applying computer simulation to the case study that involves Freddie the newsboy. The assumption cell is Demand (C12), the forecast cell is Profit (C18), and the decision variable is OrderQuantity (C9).

	A	B	C	D	E	F
1		**Freddie the Newsboy**				
2						
3			**Data**			
4		Unit Sale Price	$2.50			
5		Unit Purchase Cost	$1.50			
6		Unit Salvage Value	$0.50			
7						
8			**Decision Variable**			
9		Order Quantity	60			
10						
11			**Simulation**		Minimum	Maximum
12		Demand	55	*Discrete Uniform*	40	70
13						
14		Sales Revenue	$137.50			
15		Purchasing Cost	$90.00			
16		Salvage Value	$2.50			
17						
18		Profit	$50.00			

	B	C
14	Sales Revenue	=UnitSalePrice*MIN(OrderQuantity,Demand)
15	Purchasing Cost	=UnitPurchaseCost*OrderQuantity
16	Salvage Value	=UnitSalvageValue*MAX(OrderQuantity-Demand,0)
17		
18	Profit	=SalesRevenue-PurchasingCost+SalvageValue

Range Name	Cell
Demand	C12
OrderQuantity	C9
Profit	C18
PurchasingCost	C15
SalesRevenue	C14
SalvageValue	C16
UnitPurchaseCost	C5
UnitSalePrice	C4
UnitSalvageValue	C6

running the number of trials specified by the user (typically hundreds or thousands), the computer simulation thereby generates the same number of random observations of the values in the output cells. Crystal Ball records this information for the output cell(s) of particular interest (Freddie's daily profit) and then, at the end, displays it in a variety of convenient forms that reveal an estimate of the underlying probability distribution of Freddie's daily profit. (More about this later.)

The Application of Crystal Ball

Four steps must be taken to use the spreadsheet in Figure 13.1 to perform the computer simulation with Crystal Ball. They are:

1. Define the random input cells.
2. Define the output cells to forecast.
3. Set the run preferences.
4. Run the simulation.

We now describe each of these four steps in turn.

Define the Random Input Cells

Crystal Ball Tip: Before defining an assumption cell, the cell must contain a value. Any number can be entered, since it will not be used during the actual simulation. When a simulation run is completed, Crystal Ball restores the same value.

A random input cell is an input cell that has a random value (such as the daily demand for the *Financial Journal*). Therefore, an assumed probability distribution must be entered into the cell instead of permanently entering a single number. The only random input cell in

Figure 13.1 is Demand (C12). Crystal Ball refers to each such random input cell as an **assumption cell.**

The following procedure is used to define an assumption cell.

Procedure for Defining an Assumption Cell

1. Select the cell by clicking on it.
2. If the cell does not already contain a value, enter *any* number into the cell.
3. Click on the Define Assumption button ( ) in the Crystal Ball tab (for Excel 2007 or 2010) or toolbar (for earlier versions of Excel).
4. Select a probability distribution to enter into the cell by clicking on this distribution in the Distribution Gallery shown in Figure 13.2.
5. Click on OK (or double click on the distribution) to bring up a dialogue box for the selected distribution.
6. Use this dialogue box to enter the parameters for the distribution, preferably by referring to the cells in the spreadsheet that contain the values of these parameters. If desired, a name also can be entered for the assumption cell. (If the cell already has a name next to it or above it on the spreadsheet, that name will appear in the dialogue box.)

The Distribution Gallery includes 21 probability distributions.

7. Click on OK.

The **Distribution Gallery** mentioned in step 4 provides a wide variety of 21 probability distributions from which to choose. Figure 13.2 displays six basic distributions, but 15 more also are available by clicking on the All button. (Section 13.7 will focus on the question of how to choose the right distribution.)

Which distribution is appropriate in Freddie's case? Since the frequency of sales between 40 and 70 are all roughly equal, the two uniform distributions are possibilities. The uniform distribution assumes *all* values (including fractional values) between some minimum and maximum value are equally likely. The discrete uniform distribution assumes just the *integer* values are possible, but that the integer values between the minimum and maximum are equally likely. Since newspaper sales are always integer, the discrete uniform distribution is the appropriate distribution for Freddie.

Double-clicking on the discrete uniform distribution in the Distribution Gallery brings up the Discrete Uniform Distribution dialogue box shown in Figure 13.3, which is used to enter

FIGURE 13.2

The Crystal Ball Distribution Gallery dialogue box showing the basic distributions. In addition to the 6 distributions displayed here, 15 more distributions can be accessed by clicking on the All button.

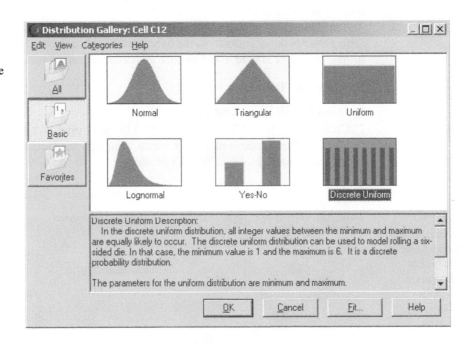

FIGURE 13.3

The Crystal Ball Discrete Uniform Distribution dialogue box. It is being used here to enter a discrete uniform distribution with the parameters 40(=E12) and 70(=F12) into the assumption cell Demand (C12) in the spreadsheet model in Figure 13.1.

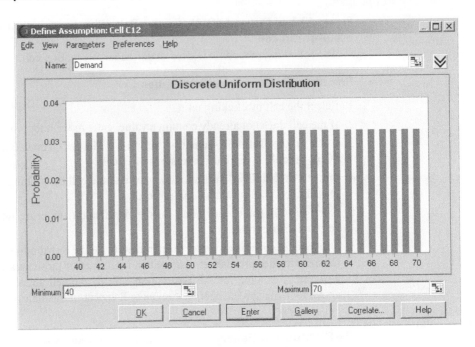

Crystal Ball Tip: Rather than entering raw numbers, use cell references for the distribution parameters (e.g., type =E12 and =F12). This allows changes to be made directly on the spreadsheet rather than having to dig into Crystal Ball dialogue boxes.

the parameters of the distribution. For each of the parameters (Minimum and Maximum), we refer to the data cells in E12 and F12 on the spreadsheet by typing the formulas =E12 and =F12 for Minimum and Maximum, respectively. After entering the cell references, the dialogue box will show the actual value of the parameter based on the cell reference (40 and 70 as shown in Figure 13.3). To see or make a change to a cell reference, clicking on the parameter will show the underlying cell reference.

Define the Output Cells to Forecast

Crystal Ball refers to the output of a computer simulation as a *forecast,* since it is forecasting the underlying probability distribution for the performance of the system (now being simulated) when it actually is in operation. Thus, each output cell that is being used by a computer simulation to forecast a measure of performance is referred to as a **forecast cell.** The spreadsheet model for a computer simulation does not include a target cell, but a forecast cell plays roughly the same role.

The measure of performance of interest to Freddie the newsboy is his daily profit from selling the *Financial Journal,* so the only forecast cell in Figure 13.1 is Profit (C18). The following procedure is used to define such an output cell as a forecast cell.

Procedure for Defining a Forecast Cell

1. Select the cell by clicking on it.
2. Click on the Define Forecast button ( ) in the Crystal Ball tab (Excel 2007 or 2010) or toolbar (other versions of Excel), which brings up the Define Forecast dialogue box (as shown in Figure 13.4 for Freddie's problem).

FIGURE 13.4

The Crystal Ball Define Forecast dialogue box. It is being used here to define the forecast cell Profit (C18) in the spreadsheet model in Figure 13.1.

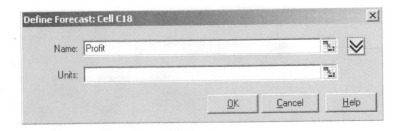

FIGURE 13.5

The Crystal Ball Run Preferences dialogue box after selecting the Trials tab.

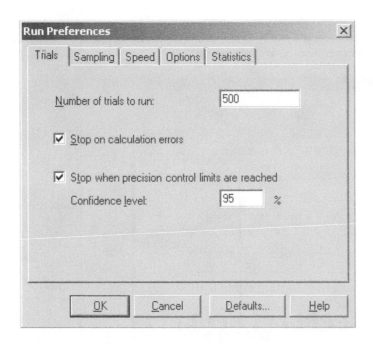

3. This dialogue box can be used to define a name and (optionally) units for the forecast cell. (If a range name already has been assigned to the cell, that name will appear as the default choice in the dialogue box.)
4. Click on OK.

Set the Run Preferences

The third step—setting run preferences—refers to such things as choosing the number of trials to run and deciding on other options regarding how to perform the computer simulation. This step begins by clicking on Run Preferences in the Crystal Ball tab (Excel 2007 or 2010) or toolbar (earlier versions of Excel). The Run Preferences dialogue box has the five tabs shown on the top of Figure 13.5. By clicking on these tabs, you can enter or change any of the specifications controlled by that tab for how to run the computer simulation. For example, Figure 13.5 shows the version of the dialogue box that is obtained by selecting the Trials tab. This figure indicates that 500 has been chosen as the maximum number of trials for the computer simulation. (The other option in the Run Preferences Trials dialogue box—Stop when precision control limits are reached—will be described later.)

Run the Simulation

At this point, the stage is set to begin running the computer simulation. To start, you only need to click on the Start Simulation button (▷). However, if a computer simulation has been run previously, you should first click on the Reset Simulation button (◁◁) to reset the simulation before starting a new one.

Once started, a forecast window displays the results of the computer simulation as it runs. Figure 13.6 shows the forecast for Profit (Freddie's daily profit from selling the *Financial Journal*) after all 500 trials have been completed. The default view of the forecast is the frequency chart shown on the left side of the figure. The height of the vertical lines in the frequency chart indicates the relative frequency of the various profit values that were obtained during the simulation run. For example, consider the tall vertical line at $60. The right-hand side of the chart indicates a frequency of about 175 there, which means that about 175 of the 500 trials led to a profit of $60. Thus, the left-hand side of the chart indicates that the estimated probability of a profit of $60 is 175/500 = 0.350. This is the profit that results whenever the demand equals or exceeds the order quantity of 60. The remainder of the time, the profit was scattered fairly evenly between $20 and $60. These profit values correspond to trials where the demand was between 40 and 60 units, with lower profit values corresponding to

FIGURE 13.6

The frequency chart and statistics table provided by Crystal Ball to summarize the results of running the simulation model in Figure 13.1 for the case study that involves Freddie the newsboy.

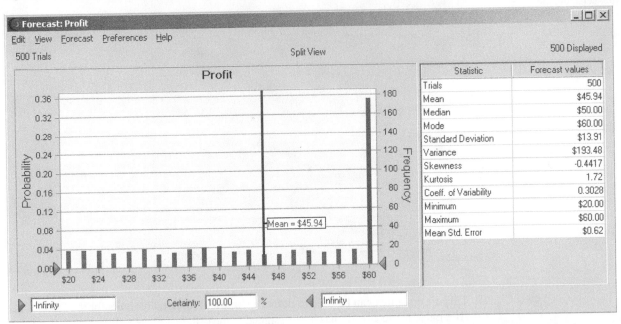

demands closer to 40 and higher profit values corresponding to demands closer to 60. The mean of the 500 profit values is $45.94, as indicated by the *mean line* at this point.

Crystal Ball Tip: To display the mean line on the frequency chart, as in Figure 13.6, choose this option in "Chart . . . " under the Preferences menu on the Chart Type tab.

The statistics table in Figure 13.6 is obtained by choosing Statistics from the View menu. These statistics summarize the outcome of the 500 trials of the computer simulation. These 500 trials provide a sample of 500 random observations from the underlying probability distribution of Freddie's daily profit. The most interesting statistics about this sample provided by the table include the *mean* of $45.94, the *median* of $50.00 (indicating that $50 was the middle profit value from the 500 trials when listing the profits from smallest to largest), the *mode* of $60 (meaning that this was the profit value that occurred most frequently), and the *standard deviation* of $13.91 (a measure of the variability of the profit values from the trials). The information near the bottom of the table regarding the *minimum* and *maximum* profit values also is particularly useful.

Crystal Ball Tip: To view more than one chart or table in the same window (e.g., a frequency chart and statistics, as shown in Figure 13.6), choose Split View from the View menu of the forecast window. Any combination of charts and tables can then be selected in the View menu to appear in the split view.

In general, the *x* percent percentile is the dividing line between the smallest *x* percent of the values and the rest of the values.

In addition to the frequency chart and statistics table presented in Figure 13.6, the View menu provides some other useful ways of displaying the results of a simulation run, including a percentiles table, a cumulative chart, and a reverse cumulative chart. These alternative displays are shown in a split view in Figure 13.7. The percentiles table is based on listing the profit values generated by the 500 trials from smallest to largest, dividing this list into 10 equal parts (50 values in each), and then recording the value at the end of each part. Thus, the value 10 percent through the list is $24, the value 20 percent through the list is $30, and so forth. (For example, the intuitive interpretation of the 10 percent percentile of $24 is that 10 percent of the trials have profit values less than or equal to $24 and the other 90 percent of the trials have profit values greater than or equal to $24, so $24 is the dividing line between the smallest 10 percent of the values and the largest 90 percent.) The cumulative chart on the top left of Figure 13.7 provides similar (but more detailed) information about this same list of the smallest-to-largest profit values. The horizontal axis shows the entire range of values from the smallest possible profit value ($20) to the largest possible profit value ($60). For each value in this range, the chart cumulates the number of actual profits generated by the 500 trials that are less than or equal to that value. This number equals the frequency shown on the right or, when divided by the number of trials, the probability shown on the left. The reverse cumulative chart on the bottom left of Figure 13.7 is constructed in the same way as the cumulative chart except for the following crucial difference. For each value in the range from $20 to $60, the reverse cumulative chart cumulates the number of actual profits generated by the 500 trials that are *greater* than or equal to that value.

FIGURE 13.7

Three more forms in which Crystal Ball displays the results of running the simulation model in Figure 13.1 for the case study that involves Freddie the newsboy.

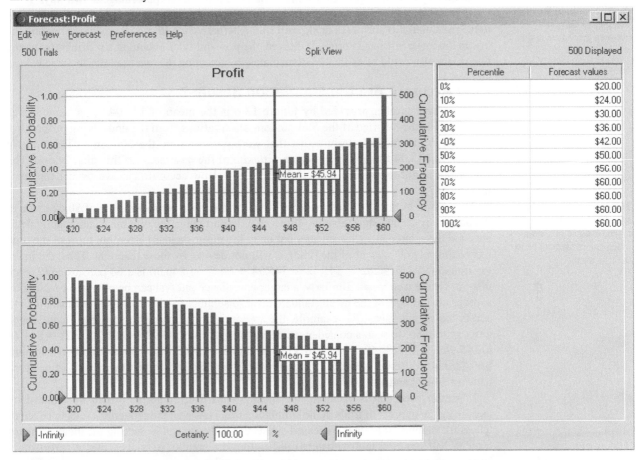

FIGURE 13.8

After setting a lower bound of $40 for desirable profit values, the Certainty box below this frequency chart reveals that 65.80 percent of the trials in Freddie's simulation run provided a profit at least this high.

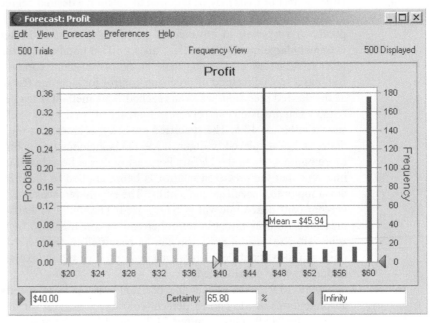

Figure 13.8 illustrates another of the many helpful ways provided by Crystal Ball for extracting helpful information from the results of a simulation run. Freddie the newsboy feels that he has had a reasonably successful day if he obtains a profit of at least $40 from selling the *Financial Journal*. Therefore, he would like to know the percentage of days that he could

expect to achieve this much profit if he were to adopt the order quantity currently being analyzed (60). An estimate of this percentage (65.80 percent) is shown in the Certainty box below the frequency chart in Figure 13.8. Crystal Ball can provide this percentage in two ways. First, the user can drag the triangle on the left just under the chart (originally at $20 in Figure 13.6) to the right until it is at $40 (as in Figure 13.8). Alternatively, $40 can be typed directly into the box in the lower left-hand corner. If desired, the probability of obtaining a profit between any two values also could be estimated immediately by dragging the two triangles to those values.

> The Certainty box gives the percentage of the trials that generated values between the values in the adjacent boxes.

How Accurate Are the Simulation Results?

An important number provided by Figure 13.6 is the mean of $45.94. This number was calculated as the *average* of the 500 random observations from the underlying probability distribution of Freddie's daily profit that were generated by the 500 trials. This *sample average* of $45.94 thereby provides an *estimate* of the *true mean* of this distribution. The true mean might deviate somewhat from $45.94. How accurate can we expect this estimate to be?

> The *mean standard error* specifies how close the mean obtained in a simulation run is likely to be to the true mean.

The answer to this key question is provided by the *mean standard error* of $0.62 given at the bottom of the statistics table in Figure 13.6. In particular, the true mean can readily deviate from the sample mean by any amount up to the mean standard error, but most of the time (approximately 68 percent of the time), it will not deviate by more than that. Thus, the interval from $45.94 − $0.62 = $45.32 to $45.94 + $0.62 = $46.56 is a 68 percent *confidence interval* for the true mean. Similarly, a larger confidence interval can be obtained by using an appropriate multiple of the mean standard error to subtract from the sample mean and then to add to the sample mean. For example, the appropriate multiple for a 95 percent confidence interval is 1.965, so such a confidence interval ranges from $45.94 − 1.965($0.62) = $44.72 to $45.94 + 1.965($0.62) = $47.16. (This multiple of 1.965 will change slightly if the number of trials is different from 500.) Therefore, it is very likely that the true mean is somewhere between $44.72 and $47.16.

If greater precision is required, the mean standard error normally can be reduced by increasing the number of trials in the simulation run. However, the reduction tends to be small unless the number of trials is increased substantially. For example, cutting the mean standard error in half requires approximately quadrupling the number of trials. Thus, a surprisingly large number of trials may be required to obtain the desired degree of precision.

Since the number of trials required to obtain the desired degree of accuracy cannot be predicted very well in advance of the simulation run, the temptation is to specify an extremely large number of trials. This specified number may turn out to be many times as large as necessary and thereby cause an excessively long computer run. Fortunately, Crystal Ball has a special method of precision control for stopping the simulation run early as soon as the desired precision has been reached. This method is triggered by choosing the option "Stop when precision control limits are reached" in the Run Preferences Trials dialogue box shown in Figure 13.5. The specified precision is entered in the Expanded Define Forecast dialogue box displayed in Figure 13.9. (This dialogue box is brought up by clicking on the More button (⌄) in the Define Forecast dialogue box shown in Figure 13.4.) Figure 13.9 indicates that the precision control is being applied to the mean (but not to the standard deviation or to a specified percentile). The run preferences in Figure 13.5 indicate that a 95 percent confidence interval is being used. The width of half of the confidence interval, measured from its midpoint to either end, is considered to be the precision that has been achieved. The desired precision can be specified in either absolute terms (using the same units as for the confidence interval) or in relative terms (expressed as a percentage of the midpoint of the confidence interval).

Figure 13.9 indicates that the decision was made to specify the desired precision in absolute terms as $1. The 95 percent confidence interval for the mean after 500 trials was found to be $45.94 plus-or-minus $1.22, so $1.22 is the precision that was achieved after all these trials. Crystal Ball also calculates the confidence interval (and so the current precision) periodically to check whether the current precision is under $1, in which case the run would be stopped. However, this never happened, so Crystal Ball allowed the simulation to run until the maximum number of trials (500) was reached.

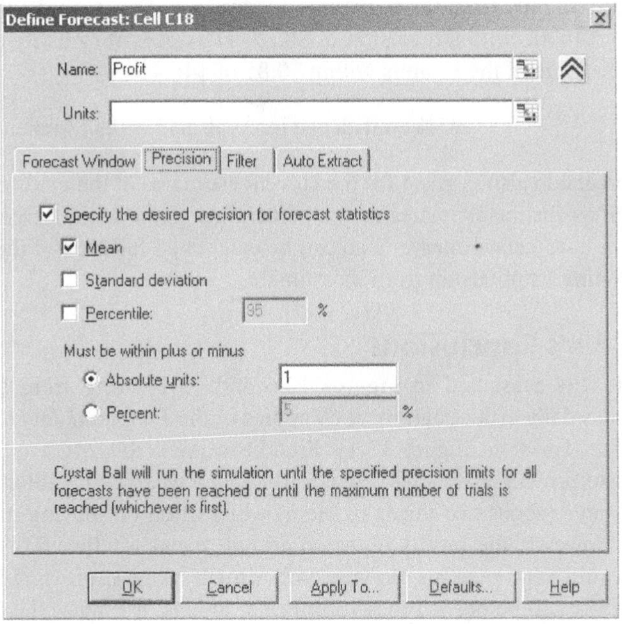

FIGURE 13.9

This Expanded Define Forecast dialogue box is being used to specify how much precision is desired in Freddie's simulation run.

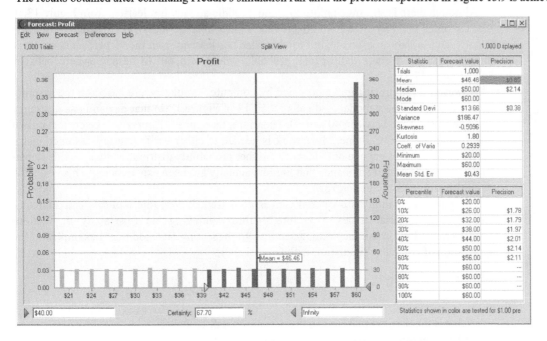

FIGURE 13.10

The results obtained after continuing Freddie's simulation run until the precision specified in Figure 13.9 is achieved.

To obtain the desired precision, the simulation would need to be restarted to generate additional trials. This is done by entering a larger number (such as 5,000) for the maximum number of trials (including the 500 already obtained) in the Run Preferences dialogue box (shown in Figure 13.5) and then clicking on the Start Simulation button (▷). Figure 13.10 shows the results of doing this. The first row indicates that the desired precision was obtained after only 500 additional trials, for a total of 1,000 trials. (The default value for the frequency of checking the precision is every 500 trials, so the precision of $1 actually was reached somewhere between 500 and 1,000 trials.) Because of the additional trials, some of the statistics have

1,000 trials were needed to have 95 percent confidence that the true value of the mean is within $1 of the mean obtained in the simulation run.

changed slightly from those given in Figure 13.6. For example, the best estimate of the mean now is $46.46, with a precision of $0.85. Thus, it is very likely (95 percent confidence) that the true value of the mean is within $0.85 of $46.46.

$$\text{95\% confidence interval: } \$45.61 \leq \text{Mean} \leq \$47.31$$

The precision also is given for the current estimates of the median and the standard deviation, as well as for the estimates of the percentiles given in the percentiles table. Therefore, a 95 percent confidence interval also can be calculated for each of these quantities by adding and subtracting its precision from its estimate.

Freddie's Conclusions

The results presented in Figures 13.6 and 13.10 were from a simulation run that fixed Freddie's daily order quantity at 60 copies of the *Financial Journal* (as indicated in cell C9 of the spreadsheet in Figure 13.1). Freddie wanted this order quantity tried first because it seems to provide a reasonable compromise between being able to fully meet the demand on many days (about two-thirds of them) while often not having many unsold copies on those days. However, the results obtained do not reveal whether 60 is the *optimal* order quantity that would maximize his average daily profit. Many more simulation runs with other order quantities will be needed to determine (or at least estimate) the optimal order quantity. Section 13.8 will describe how this search for the optimal order quantity can be done for Freddie with the help of a decision table and a trend chart. Section 13.9 then describes how the OptQuest module in your Crystal Ball software package uses a powerful optimization technique to search systematically for the optimal order quantity. That presentation will bring the case study to a close.

Freddie now has 95 percent confidence that an order quantity of 60 would provide an average daily profit between $45.61 and $47.31 in the long run.

Although there is still much more to come, Freddie already has learned from Figure 13.10 that an order quantity of 60 would provide a nice average daily profit of approximately $46.46. This is only an estimate, but Freddie also has learned from the 95 percent confidence interval that the average daily profit probably would turn out to be somewhere between $45.61 and $47.31.

However, these profit figures provided by computer simulation are based on the assumption in the spreadsheet model (see cells D12:F12 in Figure 13.1) that demand has a discrete uniform distribution between 40 and 70. Therefore, these profit figures will be correct only if this assumption is a valid one. More work is needed to either verify that this assumed distribution is the appropriate one or to identify another probability distribution that provides a better fit to the data of daily demands that Freddie actually has been experiencing. This issue will be explored further in Section 13.7.

Computer simulation with Crystal Ball is an extremely versatile tool that can address a myriad of managerial issues. Therefore, before continuing the case study in Sections 13.7–13.8, we turn in the intervening sections to presenting five additional examples of the application of computer simulation with Crystal Ball.

Review Questions

1. What is the decision that Freddie the newsboy needs to make?
2. What is an *assumption cell* when using Crystal Ball?
3. What is entered into the assumption cell in Freddie's spreadsheet model?
4. What is a *forecast cell* when using Crystal Ball?
5. What is entered into the forecast cell in Freddie's spreadsheet model?
6. What kind of information is provided by a frequency chart when using Crystal Ball?
7. What are the key statistics provided by the statistics table when using Crystal Ball?
8. What is the significance of the *mean standard error* of the results from a computer simulation?
9. What provision does Crystal Ball provide for perhaps stopping a simulation run before the specified number of trials have been completed?
10. What has Freddie the newsboy learned so far about what his order quantity should be?

13.2 BIDDING FOR A CONSTRUCTION PROJECT: A PRELUDE TO THE RELIABLE CONSTRUCTION CO. CASE STUDY

Managers frequently must make decisions whose outcomes will be greatly affected by the corresponding decisions being made by the management of competitor firms. For example, marketing decisions often fall into this category. To illustrate, consider the case in which a manager must determine the price for a new product being brought to market. How well this decision works out will depend greatly on the pricing decisions being made nearly simultaneously by other firms marketing competitive new products. Similarly, the success of a decision on how soon to market a product under development will be determined largely by whether this product reaches the market before competitive products are released by other firms.

When a decision must be made before learning the corresponding decisions being made by competitors, the analysis needs to take into account the uncertainty surrounding what competitors' decisions will be. Computer simulation provides a natural way of doing this by using assumption cells to represent competitors' decisions.

The following example illustrates this process by considering a situation where the decision being made is the bid to submit on a construction project while three other companies are simultaneously preparing their own bids.

The Reliable Construction Co. Bidding Problem

The case study carried throughout Chapter 16 on the CD-ROM involves the Reliable Construction Co. and its project to construct a new plant for a major manufacturer. That chapter describes how the project manager (David Perty) made extensive use of PERT/CPM models to help guide his management of the project.

As the opening sentence of Section 16.1 indicates, this case study begins as the company has just made the winning bid of $5.4 million to do this project. We now will back up in time to describe how the company's management used computer simulation with Crystal Ball to guide its choice of $5.4 million as its bid for the project. You will not need to review the case study in Chapter 16 to follow this example.

This section reveals how the company chose the bid of $5.4 million, which won the contract.

Reliable's first step in this process was to estimate what the company's total cost would be if it were to undertake the project. This was determined to be $4.55 million. (This amount excludes the penalty for missing the deadline for completion of the project, as well as the bonus for completion well before the deadline, since management considers either event to be relatively unlikely.) There also is an additional cost of approximately $50,000 for preparing the bid, including estimating the project cost and analyzing the bidding strategies of the competition.

Three other construction companies also were invited to submit bids for this project. All three have been long-standing competitors of the Reliable Construction Co., so the company has had a great deal of experience in observing their bidding strategies. A veteran analyst in the bid preparation office has taken on the task of estimating what bid each of these competitors will submit. Since there is so much uncertainty in this process, the analyst has determined that each of these estimates needs to be in the form of a probability distribution. Competitor 1 is known to use a 30 percent profit margin above the total (direct) cost of a project in setting its bid. However, competitor 1 also is a particularly unpredictable bidder because of an inability to estimate the true costs of a project with much accuracy. Its actual profit margin on past bids has ranged from as low as minus 5 percent to as high as 60 percent. Competitor 2 uses a 25 percent profit margin and is somewhat more accurate than competitor 1 in estimating project costs, but it still has set bids in the past that have missed this profit margin by as much as 15 percent in either direction. On the other hand, competitor 3 is unusually accurate in estimating project costs (as is the Reliable Construction Co.). Competitor 3 also is adept at adjusting its bidding strategy, so it is equally likely to set its profit margin anywhere between 20 and 30 percent, depending on its assessment of the competition, its current backlog of work, and various other factors. Therefore, the estimated probability distributions of the bids that the three competitors will submit, expressed as a percentage of Reliable's assessment of the total project cost, are as follows.

Competitor 1: A triangular distribution with a minimum value of 95 percent, a most likely value of 130 percent, and a maximum value of 160 percent.

Competitor 2: A triangular distribution with a minimum value of 110 percent, a most likely value of 125 percent, and a maximum value of 140 percent.

Competitor 3: A uniform distribution between 120 percent and 130 percent.

A Spreadsheet Model for Applying Computer Simulation

Figure 13.11 shows the spreadsheet model that has been formulated to evaluate any possible bid that Reliable might submit. Since there is uncertainty about what the competitors' bids will be, this model needs CompetitorBids (C8:E8) to be *assumption cells,* so the above probability

FIGURE 13.11

A spreadsheet model for applying computer simulation to the Reliable Construction Co.'s contract bidding problem. The assumption cells are CompetitorBids (C8:E8), the forecast cell is Profit (C29), and the decision variable is OurBid (C25).

	A	B	C	D	E
1		**Reliable Construction Co. Contract Bidding**			
2					
3		**Data**			
4		Our Project Cost ($million)	4.550		
5		Our Bid Cost ($million)	0.050		
6					
7		**Competitor Bids**	Competitor 1	Competitor 2	Competitor 3
8		Bid ($million)	5.839	5.688	5.688
9					
10		Distribution	*Triangular*	*Triangular*	*Uniform*
11					
12		Competitor Distribution Parameters (Proportion of Our Project Cost)			
13		Minimum	95%	110%	120%
14		Most Likely	130%	125%	
15		Maximum	160%	140%	130%
16					
17		Competitor Distribution Parameters ($million)			
18		Minimum	4.323	5.005	5.460
19		Most Likely	5.915	5.688	
20		Maximum	7.280	6.370	5.915
21					
22		**Minimum Competitor**			
23		Bid ($million)	5.688		
24					
25		**Our Bid ($million)**	5.400		
26					
27		**Win Bid?**	1	(1=yes, 0=no)	
28					
29		**Profit ($million)**	0.800		

Range Name	Cells
CompetitorBids	C8:E8
MinimumCompetitorBid	C23
OurBid	C25
OurBidCost	C5
OurProjectCost	C4
Profit	C29
WinBid?	C27

	B	C	D	E
18	Minimum	=OurProjectCost*C13	=OurProjectCost*D13	=OurProjectCost*E13
19	Most Likely	=OurProjectCost*C14	=OurProjectCost*D14	
20	Maximum	=OurProjectCost*C15	=OurProjectCost*D15	=OurProjectCost*E15

	B	C
22	**Minimum Competitor**	
23	Bid ($million)	=MIN(C8:E8)
24		
25	**Our Bid ($million)**	5.4
26		
27	**Win Bid?**	=IF(OurBid<MinimumCompetitorBid,1,0)
28		
29	**Profit ($million)**	=WinBid?*(OurBid-OurProjectCost)-OurBidCost

FIGURE 13.12

The Triangular Distribution dialogue box. It is being used here to enter a triangular distribution with the parameters 4.323 (=C18), 5.915 (=C19), and 7.280 (=C20) into the assumption cell C8 in the spreadsheet model in Figure 13.11.

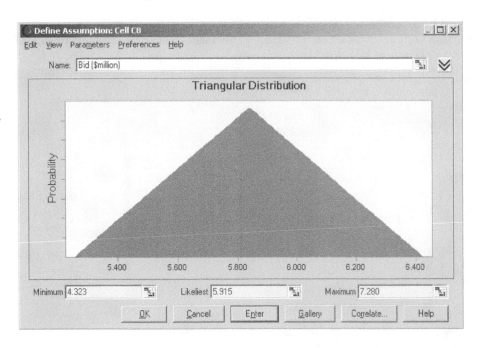

The bids that other companies will submit are uncertain, so they need to be assumption cells.

distributions are entered into these cells. As described in the preceding section, this is done by selecting each cell in turn, entering any number into the cell, and then clicking on the appropriate distribution in the Distribution Gallery, which brings up the dialogue box for that distribution. Figure 13.12 shows the Triangular Distribution dialogue box that has been used to set the parameter values (Minimum, Likeliest, and Maximum) for competitor 1, and competitor 2 would be handled similarly. These parameter values for competitor 1 come from cells C18:C20, where the parameters in percentage terms (cells C13:C15) have been converted to dollars by multiplying them by OurProjectCost (C4). The Uniform Distribution dialogue box is used instead to set the parameter values for cell E8.

MinimumCompetitorBid (C23) records the smallest of the competitors' bids for each trial of the computer simulation. The company wins the bid on a given trial only if the quantity entered into OurBid (C25) is less than the smallest of the competitors' bids. The IF function entered into WinBid? (C27) then returns a 1 if this occurs and a 0 otherwise.

The objective is to determine the bid that would maximize the resulting expected profit.

Since management wants to maximize the expected profit from the entire process of determining a bid (if the bid wins) and then doing the project, the forecast cell in this model is Profit (C29). The profit achieved on a given trial depends on whether the company wins the bid. If not, the profit actually is a loss of $50,000 (the bid cost). However, if the bid wins, the profit is the amount by which the bid exceeds the sum of the project cost and the bid cost. The equation entered into Profit (C29) performs this calculation for whichever case applies.

Here is a summary of the key cells in this model.

Assumption cells:	CompetitorBids (C8:E8)
Decision variable:	OurBid (C25)
Forecast cell:	Profit (C29)

The Simulation Results

To evaluate a possible bid of $5.4 million entered into OurBid (C25), a computer simulation of this model ran for 1,000 trials. Figure 13.13 shows the results in the form of a frequency chart and a statistics table, while Figure 13.14 displays the corresponding percentiles table and cumulative chart. Using units of millions of dollars, the profit on each trial has only two possible values, namely, a loss shown as −0.050 in these figures (if the bid loses) or a profit of 0.800 (if the bid wins). The frequency chart indicates that this loss of $50,000 occurred on about 380 of the 1,000 trials whereas the profit of $800,000 occurred on the other 620 trials.

FIGURE 13.13

The frequency chart and statistics table that summarize the results of running the simulation model in Figure 13.11 for the Reliable Construction Co. contract bidding problem.

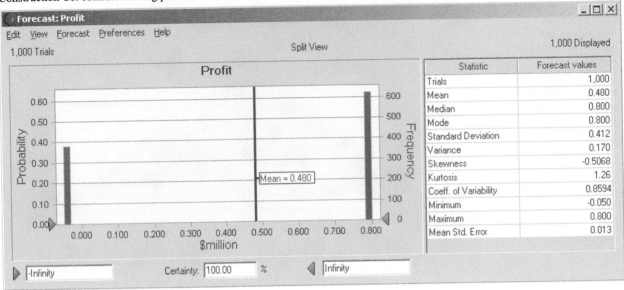

FIGURE 13.14

Further results for the Reliable Construction Co. contract bidding problem.

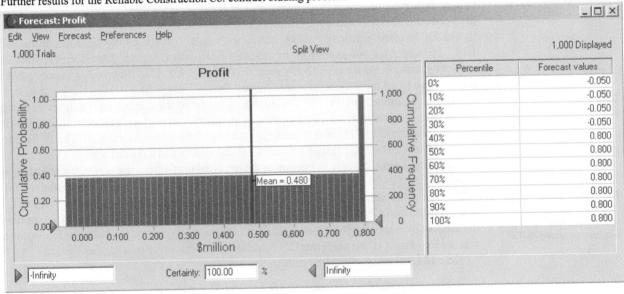

This resulted in a mean profit of 0.480 ($480,000) from all 1,000 trials, as well as the other statistics recorded in the statistics table. In Figure 13.14, note how the possibility of only two profit values results in only these values appearing in the percentiles table and also results in having a flat cumulative chart until the upper value is reached.

By themselves, these results do not show that $5.4 million is the best bid to submit. We still need to estimate with additional simulation runs whether a larger expected profit could be obtained with another bid value. Section 13.8 will describe how doing this with a decision table leads to choosing $5.4 million as the bid. This turned out to be the winning bid for the Reliable Construction Co., which then led into the case study for Chapter 16.

This story will continue in Section 13.8.

Review
Questions

1. What is the project for which the Reliable Construction Co. is submitting a bid?
2. The bids of the competitors are being estimated in what form?
3. What are the quantities in the assumption cells in this example's spreadsheet model for applying computer simulation?
4. What quantity appears in the forecast cell for this spreadsheet model?
5. What are the possible outcomes on each trial of this computer simulation?

13.3   PROJECT MANAGEMENT: REVISITING THE RELIABLE CONSTRUCTION CO. CASE STUDY

Computer simulation improves upon a PERT/CPM method for estimating the probability of completing a project by the deadline.

One of the most important responsibilities of a project manager is to meet the deadline that has been set for the project. Therefore, a skillful project manager will revise the plan for conducting the project as needed to ensure a strong likelihood of meeting the deadline. But how does the project manager estimate the probability of meeting the deadline with any particular plan? Section 16.4 describes one method provided by PERT/CPM. We now will illustrate how computer simulation provides a better method.

This example illustrates a common role for computer simulation—refining the results from a preliminary analysis conducted with approximate mathematical models. You also will get a first look at assumption cells where the random inputs are *times*. Another interesting feature of this example is its use of a special kind of Crystal Ball chart called the *sensitivity chart*. This chart will provide a key insight into how the project plan should be revised.

The Problem Being Addressed

Like the example in the preceding section, this one also revolves around the Reliable Construction Co. case study introduced in Section 16.1 and continued throughout Chapter 16. However, rather than preceding the part of the story described in Chapter 16, this example arises in the middle of the case study. In particular, Section 16.4 discusses how a PERT/CPM procedure was used to obtain a rough approximation of the probability of meeting the deadline for the Reliable Construction Co. project. It then was pointed out that computer simulation could be used to obtain a better approximation. We now are in a position to describe how this is done.

The deadline for completing the project is 47 weeks from now.

Here are the essential facts about the case study that are needed for the current example. (There is no need for you to refer to Chapter 16 for further details.) The Reliable Construction Company has just made the winning bid to construct a new plant for a major manufacturer. However, the contract includes a large penalty if construction is not completed by the deadline 47 weeks from now. Therefore, a key element in evaluating alternative construction plans is the *probability of meeting this deadline* under each plan. There are 14 major activities involved in carrying out this construction project, as listed on the right-hand side of Figure 13.15 (which repeats Figure 16.1 for your convenience). The project network in this figure depicts the precedence relationships between the activities. Thus, there are six sequences of activities (paths through the network), all of which must be completed to finish the project. These six sequences are listed below.

Path 1:   Start → A → B → C → D → G → H → M → Finish
Path 2:   Start → A → B → C → E → H → M → Finish
Path 3:   Start → A → B → C → E → F → J → K → N → Finish
Path 4:   Start → A → B → C → E → F → J → L → N → Finish
Path 5:   Start → A → B → C → I → J → K → N → Finish
Path 6:   Start → A → B → C → I → J → L → N → Finish

The numbers next to the activities in the project network represent the *estimates* of the number of weeks the activities will take if they are carried out in the normal manner with the usual

FIGURE 13.15

The project network for
the Reliable Construction
Co. project.

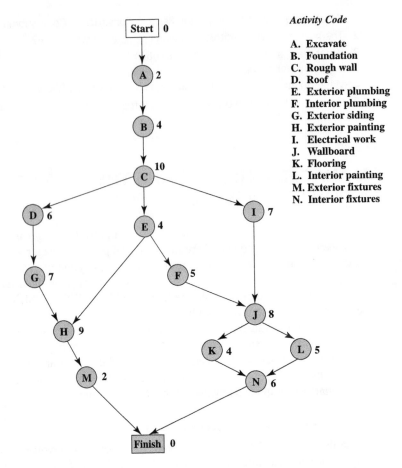

Activity Code

A. Excavate
B. Foundation
C. Rough wall
D. Roof
E. Exterior plumbing
F. Interior plumbing
G. Exterior siding
H. Exterior painting
I. Electrical work
J. Wallboard
K. Flooring
L. Interior painting
M. Exterior fixtures
N. Interior fixtures

crew sizes, and so forth. Adding these times over each of the paths (as was done in Table 16.2) reveals that path 4 is the *longest path,* requiring a total of 44 weeks. Since the project is finished as soon as its longest path is completed, this indicates that the project can be completed in 44 weeks, 3 weeks before the deadline.

Now we come to the crux of the problem. The times for the activities in Figure 13.15 are only estimates, and there actually is considerable uncertainty about what the duration of each activity will be. Therefore, the duration of the entire project could well differ substantially from the estimate of 44 weeks, so there is a distinct possibility of missing the deadline of 47 weeks. What is the *probability* of missing this deadline? To estimate this probability, we need to learn more about the probability distribution of the duration of the project.

This is the reason for the PERT three-estimate approach described in Section 16.4. This approach involves obtaining three estimates—a *most likely estimate,* an *optimistic estimate,* and a *pessimistic estimate*—of the duration of each activity. (Table 16.4 lists these estimates for all 14 activities for the project under consideration.) These three quantities are intended to estimate the most likely duration, the minimum duration, and the maximum duration, respectively. Using these three quantities, PERT assumes (somewhat arbitrarily) that the form of the probability distribution of the duration of an activity is a *beta distribution.* By also making three simplifying approximations (described in Section 16.4), this leads to an analytical method for roughly approximating the probability of meeting the project deadline.

Computer simulation has two key advantages over analytical methods like PERT/CPM.

One key advantage of computer simulation is that it does not need to make most of the simplifying approximations that may be required by analytical methods. Another is that there is great flexibility about which probability distributions to use. It is not necessary to choose an analytically convenient one.

When dealing with the duration of an activity, computer simulations commonly use a *triangular distribution* as the distribution of this duration. A triangular distribution for the

FIGURE 13.16

The shape of a triangular distribution for the duration of an activity, where the minimum lies at the optimistic estimate o, the most likely value lies at the most likely estimate m, and the maximum lies at the pessimistic estimate p.

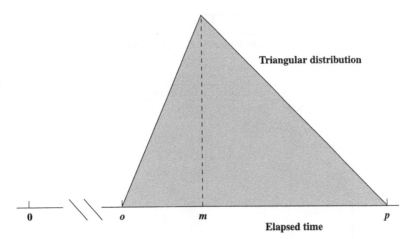

duration of an activity has the shape shown in Figure 13.16, where o, m, and p are the labels for the optimistic estimate, the most likely estimate, and the pessimistic estimate, respectively. For each *assumption cell* containing this distribution, a Triangular Distribution dialogue box (such as the one shown in Figure 13.12) is used to enter the values of o, m, and p by entering their respective cell references into the Minimum, Likeliest, and Maximum boxes.

A Spreadsheet Model for Applying Computer Simulation

Figure 13.17 shows a spreadsheet model for simulating the duration of the Reliable Construction Co. project. The values of o, m, and p in columns D, E, and F are obtained directly from Table 16.4. The equations entered into the cells in columns G and I give the start times and finish times for the respective activities. For each trial of the simulation, the maximum of the finish times for the last two activities (M and N) gives the duration of the project (in weeks), which goes into the forecast cell ProjectCompletion (I21).

Since the activity times generally are variable, the cells H6:H19 all need to be *assumption cells* with the one exception of cell H16. Since $o = m = p = 4$ for activity K, its activity time actually is a constant 4, so this constant is entered into cell H16. (Crystal Ball would give an error message if cell H16 were specified to be an assumption cell with a triangular distribution where Minimum = Likeliest = Maximum.) Figure 13.18 shows the Triangular Distribution dialogue box after it has been used to specify the parameters for the first assumption cell H6. Rather than repeating this process for all the other assumption cells, it is quicker to simply copy and paste the parameters for the other assumption cells. This is begun by selecting cell H6 and clicking on the Copy Data button on the Crystal Ball tab or toolbar. Then select the cells in which to paste the data (H7:H15 and H17:H19) and choose Paste Data by clicking this button on the Crystal Ball tab or toolbar. The cell references for the parameters in Figure 13.18 are entered as =D6, =E6, and =F6 (relative references without $ signs). Therefore, the row numbers will update appropriately to refer to the data cells in the correct row during this copy-and-paste process. For example, the cell references for the parameters of the triangular distribution in cell H7 will update to =D7, =E7, and =F7.

Here is a summary of the key cells in this model.

Assumption cells: Cells H6:H15 and H17:H19

Forecast cell: ProjectCompletion (I21)

The Simulation Results

We now are ready to undertake a computer simulation of the spreadsheet model in Figure 13.17. Using the Run Preferences dialogue box to specify 1,000 trials, Figure 13.19 shows the results in the form of a frequency chart, a statistics table, and a percentiles table. These results show a very wide range of possible project durations. Out of the 1,000 trials, both the statistics table and percentiles table indicate that one trial had a duration as short as 35.98 weeks

Variable activity times need to be assumption cells.

FIGURE 13.17

A spreadsheet model for applying computer simulation to the Reliable Construction Co. project scheduling problem. The assumption cells are cells H6:H15 and H17:H19. The forecast cell is ProjectCompletion (I21).

Simulation of Reliable Construction Co. Project

	Activity	Immediate Predecessor	Time Estimates o	m	p	Activity Start Time	Activity Time (triangular)	Activity Finish Time
A	A	—	1	2	3	0	2	2
B	B	A	2	3.5	8	2	4.5	6.5
C	C	B	6	9	18	6.5	11	17.5
D	D	C	4	5.5	10	17.5	6.5	24
E	E	C	1	4.5	5	17.5	3.5	21
F	F	E	4	4	10	21	6	27
G	G	D	5	6.5	11	24	7.5	31.5
H	H	E, G	5	8	17	31.5	10	41.5
I	I	C	3	7.5	9	17.5	6.5	24
J	J	F, I	3	9	9	27	7	34
K	K	J	4	4	4	34	4	38
L	L	J	1	5.5	7	34	4.5	38.5
M	M	H	1	2	3	41.5	2	43.5
N	N	K, L	5	5.5	9	38.5	6.5	45

Project Completion: **45**

Range Name	Cell
AFinish	I6
AStart	G6
ATime	H6
BFinish	I7
BStart	G7
BTime	H7
CFinish	I8
CStart	G8
CTime	H8
DFinish	I9
DStart	G9
DTime	H9
EFinish	I10
EStart	G10
ETime	H10
FFinish	I11
FStart	G11
FTime	H11
GFinish	I12
GStart	G12
GTime	H12
HFinish	I13
HStart	G13
HTime	H13
IFinish	I14
IStart	G14
ITime	H14
JFinish	I15
JStart	G15
JTime	H15
KFinish	I16
KStart	G16
KTime	H16
LFinish	I17
LStart	G17
LTime	H17
MFinish	I18
MStart	G18
MTime	H18
NFinish	I19
NStart	G19
NTime	H19
ProjectCompletion	I21

	G Start Time	H Activity Time (triangular)	I Finish Time
6	0	2	=AStart+ATime
7	=AFinish	4.5	=BStart+BTime
8	=BFinish	11	=CStart+CTime
9	=CFinish	6.5	=DStart+DTime
10	=CFinish	3.5	=EStart+ETime
11	=EFinish	6	=FStart+FTime
12	=DFinish	7.5	=GStart+GTime
13	=MAX(EFinish,GFinish)	10	=HStart+HTime
14	=CFinish	6.5	=IStart+ITime
15	=MAX(FFinish,IFinish)	7	=JStart+JTime
16	=JFinish	4	=KStart+KTime
17	=JFinish	4.5	=LStart+LTime
18	=HFinish	2	=MStart+MTime
19	=MAX(KFinish,LFinish)	6.5	=NStart+NTime
20			
21		Project Completion	=MAX(MFinish,NFinish)

while another was as long as 58.81 weeks. The frequency chart indicates that the duration that occurred most frequently during the 1,000 trials is close to 47 weeks (the project deadline), but that many other durations up to a few weeks either shorter or longer than this also occurred with considerable frequency. The mean is 46.20 weeks, which is much too close to the deadline of 47 weeks to leave much margin for slippage in the project schedule. (The small mean standard error of 0.12 weeks reported at the bottom of the statistics table shows that the sample average of 46.20 weeks from the 1,000 trials probably is extremely close to the true mean of the underlying probability distribution of project duration.) The 70 percent percentile of 48.05 weeks in the percentiles table reveals that 30 percent of the trials missed the deadline by at least a week.

FIGURE 13.18

A triangular distribution with parameters 1 (=D6), 2 (=E6), and 3 (=F6) is being entered into the first assumption cell H6 in the spreadsheet model in Figure 13.17.

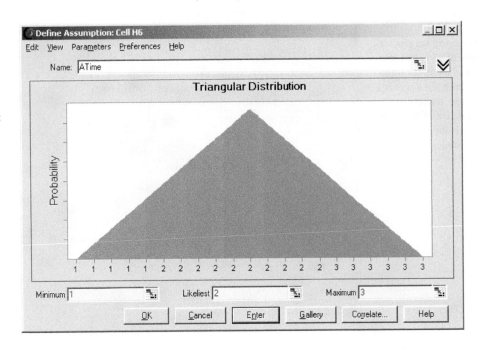

FIGURE 13.19

The frequency chart, statistics table, and percentiles table that summarize the results of running the simulation model in Figure 13.17 for the Reliable Construction Co. project scheduling problem.

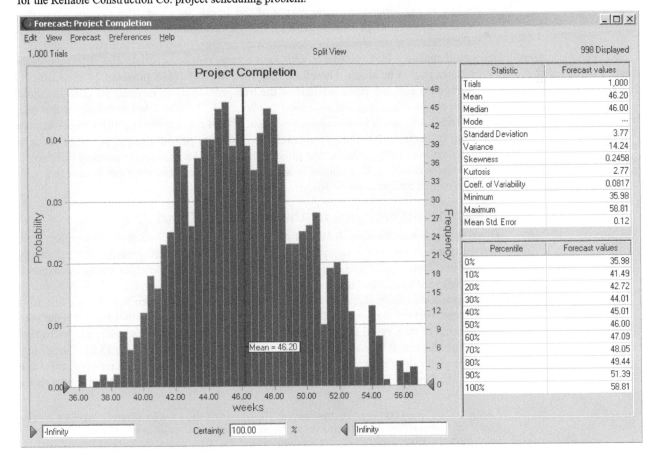

FIGURE 13.20

After entering the project deadline of 47 weeks into the box in the lower right-hand corner, the Certainty box reveals that about 58.88 percent of the trials resulted in the project being completed by the deadline.

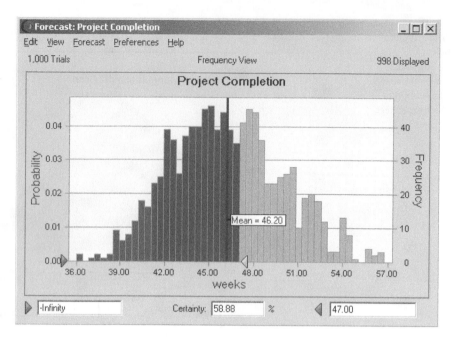

A statistic of special interest to Reliable's management is the probability of meeting the deadline of 47 weeks under the current project plan. (Remember that the contract includes a severe penalty of $300,000 for missing this deadline.) The 60 percent percentile of 47.09 weeks in the percentiles table suggests that slightly under 60 percent of the trials made the deadline, but nothing else in Figure 13.19 pins down this percentage any closer. Figure 13.20 shows that all you need to do to identify the exact percentage is to type the deadline of 47.00 in the box in the lower right-hand corner of the frequency chart. The Certainty box then reveals that about 58.88 percent of the trials met the deadline.[1]

If the simulation run were to be repeated with another 1,000 trials, this percentage probably would change a little. However, with such a large number of trials, the difference in the percentages should be slight. Therefore, the probability of 0.588 provided by the Certainty box in Figure 13.20 is a close estimate of the true probability of meeting the deadline under the assumptions of the spreadsheet model in Figure 13.17. Note how much smaller this relatively precise estimate is than the rough estimate of 0.84 obtained by the PERT three-estimate approach in Section 16.4. Thus, the simulation estimate provides much better guidance to management in deciding whether the project plan should be changed to improve the chances of meeting the deadline. This illustrates how useful computer simulation can be in refining the results obtained by approximate analytical results.

Computer simulation provides a close estimate of the probability of meeting the project deadline (0.588) that is much smaller than the rough PERT/CPM estimate (0.84).

A Key Insight Provided by the Sensitivity Chart

Given such a low probability (0.588) of meeting the project deadline, Reliable's project manager (David Perty) will want to revise the project plan to improve the probability substantially. Crystal Ball has another tool, called the *sensitivity chart,* that provides strong guidance in identifying which revisions in the project plan would be most beneficial.

To open a sensitivity chart after running a simulation, choose Open Sensitivity Chart from the Forecast menu of the Forecast Chart dialogue box, or choose Sensitivity Chart from the View Charts menu of the Crystal Ball tab or toolbar. Both a contribution to variance chart and a rank correlation chart are then available under the View menu, as shown in Figure 13.21. Using range names, the left side of both charts identify various assumption cells (activity times) in column H of the spreadsheet model in Figure 13.17. The other key cell in the spreadsheet model that is

---

[1] Actually 588 of the 1,000 trials met the deadline. The certainty is shown as 58.88 rather than 58.8 because Crystal Ball further refines the certainty estimate based on where the 47-week deadline falls relative to the 588th longest trial (which just barely met the deadline) and the 589th longest (which just barely did not).

FIGURE 13.21

This sensitivity chart shows how strongly various activity times in the Reliable Construction Co. project are influencing the project completion time.

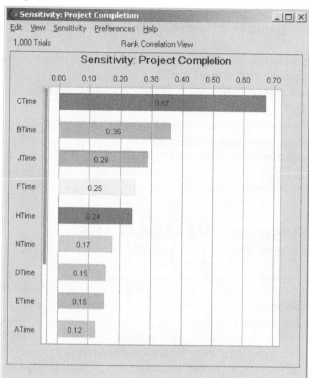 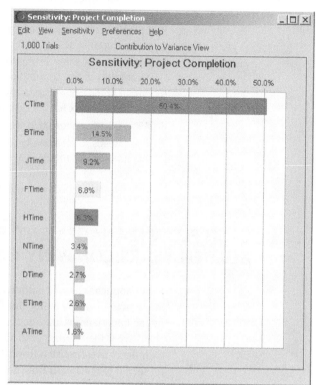

considered in the sensitivity charts (as indicated at the top of both charts) is the forecast cell Project Completion (I21) that gives the duration of the project. The contribution to variance chart indicates what percentage of the variability that exists in the forecast cell is due to the variability of each assumption cell. The rows in the chart are listed in descending order. For example, roughly half the variability in project completion time is due to variability in CTime (the time to complete Activity C: Rough Wall).

The rank correlation chart gives the correlation coefficient (based on rank values) between each assumption cell and the forecast cell. A correlation coefficient between two variables measures the strength of the relationship between those variables. Thus, each correlation coefficient in Figure 13.21 measures how strongly that activity time is influencing the project completion time. The higher the correlation coefficient, the stronger is this influence. Therefore, the activities with the highest correlation coefficients are those where the greatest effort should be made to reduce their activity times.

Figure 13.21 indicates that CTime has a far higher contribution to variance and correlation coefficient than the times for any of the other activities. An examination of Figures 13.15 and 13.17 suggests why. Figure 13.15 shows that activity C precedes *all* the other activities except activities A and B, so any delay in completing activity C would delay the start time for all these other activities. Furthermore, cells D8:F8 in Figure 13.17 indicate that CTime is highly variable, with an unusually large spread of 9 weeks between its most likely estimate and its pessimistic estimate, so long delays beyond the most likely estimate may well occur.

The sensitivity chart reveals that reducing the time for activity C would most improve the chances of completing the project before the deadline.

This very high contribution to variance and correlation coefficient for CTime suggest that the best way to reduce the project completion time (and its variability) is to focus on reducing this activity time (and its variability). This can be accomplished by revising the project plan to assign activity C more personnel, better equipment, stronger supervision, and so forth. Crystal Ball's sensitivity chart clearly highlights this insight into where the project plan needs to be revised.

Review Questions

1. What is the project that is being considered in this section's example?
2. A PERT/CPM procedure can obtain only a rough approximation of a certain key quantity, so computer simulation is used to obtain a much closer estimate of the quantity. What is this quantity?
3. Computer simulations commonly use which kind of probability distribution as the distribution of the duration of an activity?
4. What are the three estimates provided by the PERT three-estimate approach that give the parameters of this distribution of the duration of an activity?
5. What can be done to quickly enter these parameters into all the assumption cells after using the dialogue box for the distribution of the duration of only the first activity?
6. What quantity appears in the forecast cell of the spreadsheet model for this example?
7. What needs to be done to identify the exact percentage of trials of a computer simulation of this spreadsheet model that will result in meeting the project completion deadline?
8. What kind of chart is used to highlight where a project plan needs to be revised to best improve the chances of meeting the project deadline?

13.4 CASH FLOW MANAGEMENT: REVISITING THE EVERGLADE GOLDEN YEARS COMPANY CASE STUDY

Many applications of computer simulation involve scenarios that evolve far into the future. Since nobody can predict the future with certainty, computer simulation is needed to take future uncertainties into account. For example, businesses typically have great uncertainty about what their future cash flows will be. An attempt often is made to predict these future cash flows as a first step toward making decisions about what should be done (e.g., arranging for loans) to meet cash flow needs. However, effective cash management requires going a step further to consider the effect of the uncertainty in the future cash flows. This is where computer simulation comes in, with assumption cells being used for the cash flows in various future periods. This process is illustrated by the following example.

The Everglade Cash Flow Management Problem

The case study analyzed in Chapter 4 involves the Everglade Golden Years Company (which operates upscale retirement communities) and its efforts to manage its cash flow problems. In particular, because of both a temporary decline in business and some current or future construction costs, the company is facing some negative cash flows in the next few years as well as in some more distant years. As first provided in Table 4.1, Table 13.1 shows the projected net cash flows over the next 10 years (2011 to 2020). The company has some new retirement communities opening within the 10 years, so it is anticipated (or at least hoped) that a large positive cash flow will occur in 2020. Therefore, the problem confronting Everglade management is how to best arrange Everglade's financing to tide the company over until its investments in new retirement communities can start to pay off.

TABLE 13.1
Projected Net Cash Flows for the Everglade Golden Years Company over the Next 10 Years

Year	Projected Net Cash Flow (millions of dollars)
2011	−8
2012	−2
2013	−4
2014	3
2015	6
2016	3
2017	−4
2018	7
2019	−2
2020	10

Chapter 4 describes how a decision was made to combine taking a long-term (10-year) loan now (the beginning of 2011) and a series of short-term (1-year) loans as needed to maintain a positive cash balance of at least $500,000 (as dictated by company policy) throughout the 10 years. Assuming no deviation from the projected cash flows shown in Table 13.1, linear programming was used to optimize the size of both the long-term loan and the short-term loans so as to maximize the company's cash balance at the beginning of 2021 when all of the loans have been paid off. Figure 4.5 in Chapter 4 shows the complete spreadsheet model after using the Excel Solver to obtain the optimal solution. For your convenience, Figure 4.5 is repeated here as Figure 13.22. The changing cells, LTLoan (D11) and STLoan (E11:E20), give the sizes of the long-term loan and the short-term loans at the beginning of the various years. The target cell EndBalance (J21) indicates that the resulting cash balance at the end of the 10 years (the beginning of 2021) would be $2.92 million. Since this is the cell that is being maximized, any other plan for the sizes of the loans would result in a smaller cash balance at the end of the 10 years.

The drawback of the linear programming solution in Figure 13.22 is that it does not assess the effect of the great uncertainty regarding future cash flows, so computer simulation is needed to do this.

Obtaining the "optimal" financing plan presented in Figure 13.22 is an excellent first step in developing a final plan. However, the drawback of the spreadsheet model in Figure 13.22 is that it makes no allowance for the inevitable deviations from the projected cash flows shown in Table 13.1. The actual cash flow for the first year (2011) probably will turn out to be quite close to the projection. However, it is difficult to predict the cash flows in even the second and third years with much accuracy, let alone up to 10 years into the future. Computer simulation is needed to assess the effect of these uncertainties.

A Spreadsheet Model for Applying Computer Simulation

Figure 13.23 shows the modification of the spreadsheet model in Figure 13.22 that is needed to apply computer simulation. One key difference is that the constants in CashFlow (C11:C20) in Figure 13.22 have turned into random inputs in CashFlow (F12:F21) in Figure 13.23. Thus, the latter cells, CashFlow (F12:F21), are *assumption cells*. (The numbers appearing in these cells have been entered arbitrarily as a first step in defining these assumption cells.) As indicated in cells D9:E9, the assumption has been made that each of the cash flows has a triangular distribution. Estimates have been made of the three parameters of this distribution (minimum, most likely, and maximum) for each of the years, as presented in cells C12:E21.

The uncertain future cash flows need to be assumption cells.

The number 6.65 entered into LTLoan (G12) is the size of the long-term loan (in millions of dollars) that was obtained in Figure 13.22. However, because of the variability in the cash flows, it no longer makes sense to lock in the sizes of the short-term loans that were obtained in STLoan (E11:E20) in Figure 13.22. It is better to be flexible and adjust these sizes based on the actual cash flows that occur in the preceding years. If the balance at the beginning of a year (as calculated in BalanceBeforeSTLoan [L12:L22]) already exceeds the required minimum balance of $0.50 million, then there is no need to take any short-term loan at that point. However, if the balance is not this large, then a sufficiently large short-term loan should be taken to bring the balance up to $0.50 million. This is what is done by the equations entered into STLoan (M12:M22) that are shown at the bottom of Figure 13.23.

The target cell EndBalance (J21) in Figure 13.22 becomes the forecast cell EndBalance (N22) in Figure 13.23. On any trial of the computer simulation, if the simulated cash flows in CashFlow (F12:F21) in Figure 13.23 are more favorable than the projected cash flows given in Table 13.1 (as is the case for the current numbers in Figure 13.23), then EndBalance (N22) in Figure 13.23 would be larger than EndBalance (J21) in Figure 13.22. However, if the simulated cash flows are less favorable than the projections, then EndBalance (N22) in Figure 13.23 might even be a negative number. For example, if all the simulated cash flows are close to the corresponding minimum values given in cells C12:C21, then the required short-term loans will become so large that paying off the last one at the beginning of 2021 (along with paying off the long-term loan then) will result in a very large negative number in EndBalance (N22). This would spell serious trouble for the company. Computer simulation will reveal the relative likelihood of this occurring versus a favorable outcome.

A key question is the likelihood of achieving a positive cash balance at the end of the 10 years.

Here is a summary of the key cells in this model.

FIGURE 13.22
The spreadsheet model that used linear programming in Chapter 4 (Figure 4.5) to analyze the Everglade Golden Years Company cash flow management problem without taking the uncertainty in future cash flows into account.

	A	B	C	D	E	F	G	H	I	J	K	L
1		**Everglade Cash Flow Management Problem When Applying Linear Programming**										
2												
3		LT Rate	7%									
4		ST Rate	10%									
5												
6		Start Balance	1			(all cash figures in millions of dollars)						
7		Minimum Cash	0.5									
8												
9			Cash	LT	ST	LT	ST	LT	ST	Ending		Minimum
10		Year	Flow	Loan	Loan	Interest	Interest	Payback	Payback	Balance		Balance
11		2011	-8	6.65	0.85					0.50	≥	0.5
12		2012	-2		3.40	-0.47	-0.09		-0.85	0.50	≥	0.5
13		2013	-4		8.21	-0.47	-0.34		-3.40	0.50	≥	0.5
14		2014	3		6.49	-0.47	-0.82		-8.21	0.50	≥	0.5
15		2015	6		1.61	-0.47	-0.65		-6.49	0.50	≥	0.5
16		2016	3		0	-0.47	-0.16		-1.61	1.27	≥	0.5
17		2017	-4		3.70	-0.47	0		0	0.50	≥	0.5
18		2018	7		0	-0.47	-0.37		-3.70	2.97	≥	0.5
19		2019	-2		0	-0.47	0		0	0.50	≥	0.5
20		2020	10		0	-0.47	0		0	10.03	≥	0.5
21		2021				-0.47	0	-6.65	0	2.92	≥	0.5

Range Name	Cells
CashFlow	C11:C20
EndBalance	J21
EndingBalance	J11:J21
LTLoan	D11
LTRate	C3
MinimumBalance	L11:L21
MinimumCash	C7
StartBalance	C6
STLoan	E11:E20
STRate	C4

Solver Parameters

Set Target Cell: EndBalance

Equal To: (•) Max ( ) Min

By Changing Cells:

LTLoan,STLoan

Subject to the Constraints:

EndingBalance >= MinimumBalance

Solver Options

☑ Assume Linear Model

☑ Assume Non-Negative

	F	G	H	I	J	K	L
9	LT	ST	LT	ST	Ending		Minimum
10	Interest	Interest	Payback	Payback	Balance		Balance
11					=StartBalance+SUM(C11:I11)	≥	=MinimumCash
12	=–LTRate*LTLoan	=–STRate*E11		=–E11	=J11+SUM(C12:I12)	≥	=MinimumCash
13	=–LTRate*LTLoan	=–STRate*E12		=–E12	=J12+SUM(C13:I13)	≥	=MinimumCash
14	=–LTRate*LTLoan	=–STRate*E13		=–E13	=J13+SUM(C14:I14)	≥	=MinimumCash
15	=–LTRate*LTLoan	=–STRate*E14		=–E14	=J14+SUM(C15:I15)	≥	=MinimumCash
16	=–LTRate*LTLoan	=–STRate*E15		=–E15	=J15+SUM(C16:I16)	≥	=MinimumCash
17	=–LTRate*LTLoan	=–STRate*E16		=–E16	=J16+SUM(C17:I17)	≥	=MinimumCash
18	=–LTRate*LTLoan	=–STRate*E17		=–E17	=J17+SUM(C18:I18)	≥	=MinimumCash
19	=–LTRate*LTLoan	=–STRate*E18		=–E18	=J18+SUM(C19:I19)	≥	=MinimumCash
20	=–LTRate*LTLoan	=–STRate*E19		=–E19	=J19+SUM(C20:I20)	≥	=MinimumCash
21	=-LTRate*LTLoan	=–STRate*E20	=–LTLoan	=–E20	=J20+SUM(C21:I21)	≥	=MinimumCash

FIGURE 13.23

A spreadsheet model for applying computer simulation to the Everglade Golden Years Company cash flow management problem. The assumption cells are CashFlow (F12:F21) and the forecast cell is EndBalance (N22).

Everglade Cash Flow Management Problem When Applying Simulation

LT Rate	7%		
ST Rate	10%		
Start Balance	1		
Minimum Cash	0.5		

(all cash figures in millions of dollars)

Year	Cash Flow (Triangular Distribution) Minimum	Most Likely	Maximum	Simulated Cash Flow	LT Loan	LT Interest	ST Interest	LT Payback	ST Payback	Balance Before ST Loan	ST Loan	Ending Balance	≥	Minimum Balance
2011	-9	-8	-7	-8.00	6.65					-0.35	0.85	0.50	≥	0.50
2012	-4	-2	1	-1.67		-0.47	-0.09		-0.85	-2.57	3.07	0.50	≥	0.50
2013	-7	-4	0	-3.67		-0.47	-0.31		-3.07	-7.01	7.51	0.50	≥	0.50
2014	0	3	7	1.33		-0.47	-0.75		-7.51	-4.89	5.39	0.50	≥	0.50
2015	3	6	9	6.00		-0.47	-0.54		-5.39	0.11	0.39	0.50	≥	0.50
2016	1	3	5	3.00		-0.47	-0.04		-0.39	2.60	0.00	2.60	≥	0.50
2017	-6	-4	-2	-4.00		-0.47	0		0	-1.86	2.36	0.50	≥	0.50
2018	4	7	12	7.67		-0.47	-0.24		-2.36	5.10	0.00	5.10	≥	0.50
2019	-5	-2	4	-1.00		-0.47	0		0	3.64	0.00	3.64	≥	0.50
2020	5	10	18	11.00		-0.47	0		0	14.17	0.00	14.17	≥	0.50
2021						-0.47	0	-6.65	0	7.05	0.00	7.05	≥	0.50

Range Name	Cells
BalanceBeforeSTLoan	L12:L22
CashFlow	F12:F21
EndBalance	N22
EndingBalance	N12:N22
LTLoan	G12
LTRate	C3
MinimumBalance	P12:P22
MinimumCash	C7
StartBalance	C6
STLoan	M12:M22
STRate	C4

	H LT Interest	I ST Interest	J LT Payback	K ST Payback	L Balance Before ST Loan
12					=StartBalance+SUM(F12:K12)
13	=-LTRate*LTLoan	=-STRate*M12		=-M12	=N12+SUM(F13:K13)
14	=-LTRate*LTLoan	=-STRate*M13		=-M13	=N13+SUM(F14:K14)
15	=-LTRate*LTLoan	=-STRate*M14		=-M14	=N14+SUM(F15:K15)
16	=-LTRate*LTLoan	=-STRate*M15		=-M15	=N15+SUM(F16:K16)
17	=-LTRate*LTLoan	=-STRate*M16		=-M16	=N16+SUM(F17:K17)
18	=-LTRate*LTLoan	=-STRate*M17		=-M17	=N17+SUM(F18:K18)
19	=-LTRate*LTLoan	=-STRate*M18		=-M18	=N18+SUM(F19:K19)
20	=-LTRate*LTLoan	=-STRate*M19		=-M19	=N19+SUM(F20:K20)
21	=-LTRate*LTLoan	=-STRate*M20		=-M20	=N20+SUM(F21:K21)
22	=-LTRate*LTLoan	=-STRate*M21	=-LTLoan	=-M21	=N21+SUM(F22:K22)

	M ST Loan	N Ending Balance	O	P Minimum Balance
12	=MAX(MinimumBalance-BalanceBeforeSTLoan,0)	=BalanceBeforeSTLoan+STLoan	≥	=MinimumCash
13	=MAX(MinimumBalance-BalanceBeforeSTLoan,0)	=BalanceBeforeSTLoan+STLoan	≥	=MinimumCash
14	=MAX(MinimumBalance-BalanceBeforeSTLoan,0)	=BalanceBeforeSTLoan+STLoan	≥	=MinimumCash
15	=MAX(MinimumBalance-BalanceBeforeSTLoan,0)	=BalanceBeforeSTLoan+STLoan	≥	=MinimumCash
16	=MAX(MinimumBalance-BalanceBeforeSTLoan,0)	=BalanceBeforeSTLoan+STLoan	≥	=MinimumCash
17	=MAX(MinimumBalance-BalanceBeforeSTLoan,0)	=BalanceBeforeSTLoan+STLoan	≥	=MinimumCash
18	=MAX(MinimumBalance-BalanceBeforeSTLoan,0)	=BalanceBeforeSTLoan+STLoan	≥	=MinimumCash
19	=MAX(MinimumBalance-BalanceBeforeSTLoan,0)	=BalanceBeforeSTLoan+STLoan	≥	=MinimumCash
20	=MAX(MinimumBalance-BalanceBeforeSTLoan,0)	=BalanceBeforeSTLoan+STLoan	≥	=MinimumCash
21	=MAX(MinimumBalance-BalanceBeforeSTLoan,0)	=BalanceBeforeSTLoan+STLoan	≥	=MinimumCash
22	=MAX(MinimumBalance-BalanceBeforeSTLoan,0)	=BalanceBeforeSTLoan+STLoan	≥	=MinimumCash

FIGURE 13.24

The frequency chart and cumulative chart that summarize the results of running the simulation model in Figure 13.23 for the Everglade Golden Years cash flow management problem.

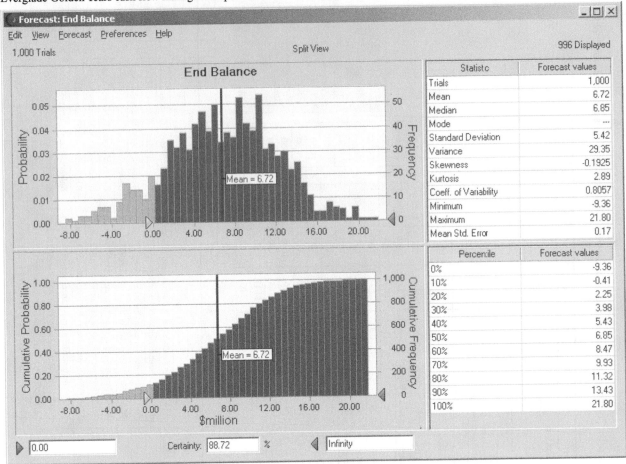

Assumption cells: CashFlow (F12:F21)

Forecast cell: EndBalance (N22)

The Simulation Results

The Certainty box in the frequency chart reveals that nearly 89 percent of the trials resulted in a positive cash balance at the end of the 10 years.

Figure 13.24 shows the results from applying computer simulation with 1,000 trials. Because Everglade management is particularly interested in learning how likely it is that the current financing plan would result in a positive cash balance at the end of the 10 years, the number 0 has been entered into the lower left-hand box in the frequency chart. The Certainty box in the lower middle box then indicates that nearly 89 percent of the trials resulted in a positive cash balance at the end. Furthermore, both the frequency chart and the cumulative chart show that many of these positive cash balances are reasonably large, with some exceeding $10 million. The overall mean is $6.72 million.

On the other hand, it is worrisome that more than 11 percent of the trials resulted in a negative cash balance at the end. Although huge losses were rare, most of these negative cash balances were quite significant, ranging from $1 million to $3 million.

Conclusions

Everglade management is pleased that the simulation results indicate that the proposed financing plan is likely to lead to a favorable outcome at the end of the 10 years. At the same time, management feels that it would be prudent to take steps to reduce the 11 percent chance of an unfavorable outcome.

One possibility would be to increase the size of the long-term loan, since this would reduce the sizes of the higher interest short-term loans that would be needed in the later years if the cash flows are not as good as currently projected. This possibility is investigated in Problem 13.19.

The scenarios that would lead to a negative cash balance at the end of the 10 years are those where the company's retirement communities fail to achieve full occupancy because of overestimating the demand for this service. Therefore, Everglade management concludes that it should take a more cautious approach in moving forward with its current plans to build more retirement communities over the next 10 years. In each case, the final decisions regarding the start date for construction and the size of the retirement community should be made only after obtaining and carefully assessing a detailed forecast of the trends in the demand for this service.

After adopting this policy, Everglade management approves the financing plan that is incorporated into the spreadsheet model in Figure 13.23. In particular, a 10-year loan of $6.65 million will be taken now (the beginning of 2011). In addition, a one-year loan will be taken at the beginning of each year from 2011 to 2020 if it is needed to bring the cash balance for that year up to the level of $500,000 required by company policy.

A more cautious expansion plan is needed to improve the chances of ending with a positive cash balance.

Review Questions

1. What is the cash flow management problem that is currently confronting the management of the Everglade Golden Years Company?
2. Which management science technique was previously used to address this cash flow management problem before applying computer simulation?
3. What aspect of the problem does computer simulation take into account that this prior management science technique could not?
4. What are the quantities in the assumption cells in this example's spreadsheet model for applying computer simulation?
5. How are the sizes of the short-term loans determined in this spreadsheet model?
6. What can happen in a trial of the computer simulation that would result in a negative cash balance at the end of 10 years?
7. What percentage of the trials actually resulted in a negative cash balance at the end of 10 years?
8. What policy did Everglade management adopt to reduce the possibility of having a negative cash balance at the end of 10 years?

13.5   FINANCIAL RISK ANALYSIS: REVISITING THE THINK-BIG DEVELOPMENT CO. PROBLEM

One of the earliest areas of application of computer simulation, dating back to the 1960s, was *financial risk analysis.* This continues today to be one of the most important areas of application.

When assessing any financial investment (or a portfolio of investments), the key trade-off is between the *return* from the investment and the *risk* associated with the investment. Of these two quantities, the less difficult one to determine is the return that would be obtained if everything evolves as currently projected. However, assessing the risk is relatively difficult. Fortunately, computer simulation is ideally suited to perform this risk analysis by obtaining a **risk profile,** namely, a *frequency distribution* of the return from the investment. The portion of the frequency distribution that reflects an unfavorable return clearly describes the risk associated with the investment.

The following example illustrates this approach in the context of real estate investments. Like the Everglade example in the preceding section, you will see computer simulation being used to refine prior analysis done by linear programming because this prior analysis was unable to take the uncertainty in future cash flows into account.

The Think-Big Financial Risk Analysis Problem

As introduced in Section 3.2, the Think-Big Development Co. is a major investor in commercial real estate development projects. It has been considering taking a share in three large construction projects—a high-rise office building, a hotel, and a shopping center. In each case,

For nearly a century after its founding in 1914, **Merrill Lynch** was a leading full-service financial service firm that strove to bring Wall Street to Main Street by making financial markets accessible to everyone. It then was purchased in 2008 by the Bank of America Corporation and given the new name of *Merrill Lynch Wealth Management* as part of the merged corporate and investment bank now called *Bank of America Merrill Lynch*.

Prior to this merger, Merrill Lynch employed a highly trained salesforce of over 15,000 financial advisors throughout the United States as well as operating in 36 countries. A Fortune 100 company with net revenues of $26 billion in 2005, it managed client assets that totaled over $1.7 trillion.

Faced with increasing competition from discount brokerage firms and electronic brokerage firms, a task force was formed in late 1998 to recommend a product or service response to the marketplace challenge. Merrill Lynch's strong management science group was charged with doing the detailed analysis of two potential new pricing options for clients. One option would replace charging for trades individually by charging a fixed percentage of a client's assets at Merrill Lynch and then allowing an unlimited number of free trades and complete access to a financial advisor. The other option would allow self-directed investors to invest online directly for a fixed low fee per trade without consulting a financial advisor.

The great challenge facing the management science group was to determine a "sweet spot" for the prices for these options that would be likely to grow the firm's business and increase its revenues while minimizing the risk of losing revenue instead. A key tool in attacking this problem proved to be *computer simulation*. To undertake a major computer simulation study, the group assembled and evaluated an extensive volume of data on the assets and trading activity of the firm's 5 million clients. For each segment of the client base, a careful analysis was done of its offer-adoption behavior by using managerial judgment, market research, and experience with clients. With this input, the group then formulated and ran a *computer simulation model* with various pricing scenarios to identify the pricing sweet spot.

The implementation of these results had a profound impact on Merrill Lynch's competitive position, restoring it to a leadership role in the industry. Instead of continuing to lose ground to the fierce new competition, *client assets managed by the company had increased by* **$22 billion** *and its incremental revenue reached* **$80 million** *within 18 months*. The CEO of Merrill Lynch called the new strategy "the most important decision we as a firm have made (in the last 20 years)."

Source: S. Altschuler, D. Batavia, J. Bennett, R. Labe, B. Liao, R. Nigam, and J. Oh, "Pricing Analysis for Merrill Lynch Integrated Choice," *Interfaces* 32, no. 1 (January–February 2002), pp. 5–19. (A link to this article is provided on our Web site, **www.mhhe.com/hillier4e**.)

the partners in the project would spend three years with the construction, then retain ownership for three years while establishing the property, and then sell the property in the seventh year. By using estimates of expected cash flows, Section 3.2 describes how linear programming has been applied to obtain the following proposal for how big a share Think-Big should take in each of these projects.

Proposal

Do not take any share of the high-rise building project.

Take a 16.50 percent share of the hotel project.

Take a 13.11 percent share of the shopping center project.

This proposal is estimated to return a *net present value* (NPV) of $18.11 million to Think-Big.

However, Think-Big management understands very well that such decisions should not be made without taking risk into account. These are very risky projects since it is unclear how well these properties will compete in the marketplace when they go into operation in a few years. Although the construction costs during the first three years can be estimated fairly roughly, the net incomes during the following three years of operation are very uncertain. Consequently, there is an extremely wide range of possible values for each sale price in year 7. Therefore, management wants *risk analysis* to be performed in the usual way (with computer simulation) to obtain a *risk profile* of what the total NPV might actually turn out to be with this proposal.

To perform this risk analysis, Think-Big staff now has devoted considerable time to estimating the amount of uncertainty in the cash flows for each project over the next seven years. These data are summarized in Table 13.2 (in units of millions of dollars) for a 100 percent share of each project. Thus, when taking a smaller percentage share of a project, the numbers in the table should be reduced proportionally to obtain the relevant numbers for Think-Big. In years 1 through 6 for each project, the probability distribution of cash flow is assumed to be a

Management needs a risk profile of the proposal to assess whether the likelihood of a sizable profit justifies the risk of possible large losses.

TABLE 13.2
The Estimated Cash Flows for 100 Percent of the Hotel and Shopping Center Projects

	Hotel Project		Shopping Center Project
Year	Cash Flow ($1,000,000s)	Year	Cash Flow ($1,000,000s)
0	−80	0	−90
1	Normal (−80, 5)	1	Normal (−50, 5)
2	Normal (−80, 10)	2	Normal (−20, 5)
3	Normal (−70, 15)	3	Normal (−60, 10)
4	Normal (+30, 20)	4	Normal (+15, 15)
5	Normal (+40, 20)	5	Normal (+25, 15)
6	Normal (+50, 20)	6	Normal (+40, 15)
7	Uniform (+200, 844)	7	Uniform (160, 600)

normal distribution, where the first number shown is the estimated *mean* and the second number is the estimated *standard deviation* of the distribution. In year 7, the income from the sale of the property is assumed to have a *uniform distribution* over the range from the first number shown to the second number shown.

To compute NPV, a cost of capital of 10 percent per annum is being used. Thus, the cash flow in year n is divided by 1.1^n before adding these discounted cash flows to obtain NPV.

A Spreadsheet Model for Applying Computer Simulation

A spreadsheet model has been formulated for this problem in Figure 13.25. There is no uncertainty about the immediate (Year 0) cash flows appearing in cells D6 and D16, so these are data cells. However, because of the uncertainty for Years 1–7, cells D7:D13 and D17:D23 containing the simulated cash flows for these years need to be assumption cells. (The numbers in these cells in Figure 13.25 happen to be mean values that were entered merely to start the process of defining these assumption cells.) Table 13.2 specifies the probability distributions and their parameters that have been estimated for these cash flows, so the form of the distributions has been recorded in cells E7:E13 and E17:E23 while entering the corresponding parameters in cells F7:G13 and F17:G23. Figure 13.26 shows the Normal Distribution dialogue box that is used to enter the parameters (mean and standard deviation) for the normal distribution into the first assumption cell D7 by referencing cells F7 and G7. The parameters for the other normal distributions are then copied and pasted into the corresponding assumption cells. The Uniform Distribution dialogue box (like the similar one displayed earlier in Figure 13.3 for a discrete uniform distribution) is used in a similar way to enter the parameters (minimum and maximum) for this kind of distribution into the assumption cells D13 and D23.

The simulated cash flows in cells D6:D13 and D16:D23 are for 100 percent of the hotel project and the shopping center project, respectively, so Think-Big's share of these cash flows needs to be reduced proportionally based on its shares in these projects. The proposal being analyzed is to take the shares shown in cells H28:H29. The equations entered into cells D28:D35 (see the bottom of Figure 13.25) then gives Think-Big's total cash flow in the respective years for its share of the two projects.

Excel Tip: The NPV (*discount rate, cash flows*) function calculates the net present value of a stream of *future* cash flows at regular intervals (e.g., annually) in a range of cells (*cash flows*) using the specified *discount rate* per interval.

Think-Big's management wants to obtain a risk profile of what the total net present value (NPV) might be with this proposal. Therefore, the forecast cell is NetPresent Value (D37).

Here is a summary of the key cells in this model.

Assumption cells: Cells D7:D13 and D17:D23

Decision variables: HotelShare (H28) and ShoppingCenterShare (H29)

Forecast cell: NetPresentValue (D37)

The Simulation Results

The frequency chart provides the risk profile for the proposal.

Using the Run Preferences dialogue box to specify 1,000 trials, Figure 13.27 shows the results of applying computer simulation to the spreadsheet model in Figure 13.25. The frequency chart in Figure 13.27 provides the risk profile for the proposal since it shows the relative likelihood of the various values of NPV, including those where NPV is negative. The mean is $18.117 million, which is very attractive. However, the 1,000 trials generated an extremely wide range of

FIGURE 13.25

A spreadsheet model for applying computer simulation to the Think-Big Development Co. financial risk analysis problem. The assumption cells are cells D7:D13 and D17:D23, the forecast cell is NetPresentValue (D37), and the decision variables are HotelShare (H28) and ShoppingCenterShare (H29).

	A	B	C	D	E	F	G	H
1		**Simulation of Think-Big Development Co. Problem**						
2								
3				**Project Simulated**				
4				**Cash Flow**				
5		**Hotel Project:**		**($millions)**				
6		Construction Costs:	Year 0	−80				
7			Year 1	−80	*Normal*	−80	5	(mean, st. dev.)
8			Year 2	−80	*Normal*	−80	10	(mean, st. dev.)
9			Year 3	−70	*Normal*	−70	15	(mean, st. dev.)
10		Revenue per Share	Year 4	30	*Normal*	30	20	(mean, st. dev.)
11			Year 5	40	*Normal*	40	20	(mean, st. dev.)
12			Year 6	50	*Normal*	50	20	(mean, st. dev.)
13		Selling Price per Share	Year 7	522	*Uniform*	200	844	(min,max)
14								
15		**Shopping Center Project**						
16		Construction Costs:	Year 0	−90				
17			Year 1	−50	*Normal*	−50	5	(mean, st. dev.)
18			Year 2	−20	*Normal*	−20	5	(mean, st. dev.)
19			Year 3	−60	*Normal*	−60	10	(mean, st. dev.)
20		Revenue per Share	Year 4	15	*Normal*	15	15	(mean, st. dev.)
21			Year 5	25	*Normal*	25	15	(mean, st. dev.)
22			Year 6	40	*Normal*	40	15	(mean, st. dev.)
23		Selling Price per Share	Year 7	387.5	*Uniform*	160	615	(min,max)
24								
25				**Think-Big's**				
26				**Simulated Cash Flow**				
27				**($millions)**				**Share**
28			Year 0	−24.999			Hotel	16.50%
29			Year 1	−19.755		Shopping Center		13.11%
30			Year 2	−15.822				
31			Year 3	−19.416		Cost of Capital		10%
32			Year 4	6.917				
33			Year 5	9.878				
34			Year 6	13.494				
35			Year 7	136.931				
36								
37		Net present Value ($millions)		18.120				

	C	D
25		**Total Simulated**
26		**Cash Flow**
27		**($millions)**
28	Year 0	=HotelShare*D6+ShoppingCenterShare*D16
29	Year 1	=HotelShare*D7+ShoppingCenterShare*D17
30	Year 2	=HotelShare*D8+ShoppingCenterShare*D18
31	Year 3	=HotelShare*D9+ShoppingCenterShare*D19
32	Year 4	=HotelShare*D10+ShoppingCenterShare*D20
33	Year 5	=HotelShare*D11+ShoppingCenterShare*D21
34	Year 6	=HotelShare*D12+ShoppingCenterShare*D22
35	Year 7	=HotelShare*D13+ShoppingCenterShare*D23
36		
37	Net Present Value ($millions)	=CashFlowYear0+NPV(CostOfCapital,CashFlowYear1To7)

Range Name	Cells
CashFlowYear0	D28
CashFlowYear1To7	D29:D35
CostOfCapital	H31
HotelShare	H28
NetPresentValue	D37
ShoppingCenterShare	H29

FIGURE 13.26

A normal distribution with parameters −80 (=F7) and 5 (=G7) is being entered into the first assumption cell D7 in the spreadsheet model in Figure 13.25.

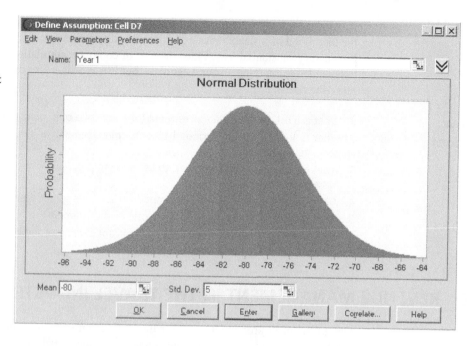

FIGURE 13.27

The frequency chart and percentiles table that summarize the results of running the simulation model in Figure 13.25 for the Think-Big Development Co. financial risk analysis problem. The Certainty box under the frequency chart reveals that 81.39 percent of the trials resulted in a positive value of the net present value.

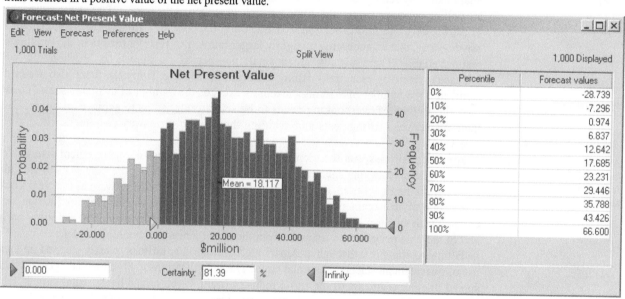

NPV values, all the way from about −$29 million to over $66 million. Thus, there is a significant chance of incurring a huge loss. By entering 0 into the box in the lower left-hand corner of the frequency chart, the Certainty box indicates that 81.39 percent of the trials resulted in a profit (a positive value of NPV). This also gives the bad news that there is nearly a 19 percent chance of incurring a loss of some size. The lightly shaded portion of the chart to the left of 0 shows that most of the trials with losses involved losses up to about $10 million, but that quite a few trials had losses that ranged from $10 million to nearly $30 million.

The percentiles table in Figure 13.27 also provides management with some specific numbers for better assessing the risk. The 10 percent percentile of −7.296 indicates a 10 percent chance of incurring a loss greater than about $7.3 million. On the other hand, the 90 percent percentile of 43.426 indicates a 10 percent chance of achieving a huge profit (NPV) exceeding $43.4 million.

Armed with all this information, a managerial decision now can be made about whether the likelihood of a sizable profit justifies the significant risk of incurring a loss and perhaps even a very substantial loss. Thus, the role of computer simulation is to provide the information needed for making a sound decision, but it is management that uses its best judgment to make the decision.

Review Questions

1. What is a *risk profile* for an investment (or a portfolio of investments)?
2. What is the investment proposal that the management of the Think-Big Development Co. needs to evaluate?
3. What are the estimates that need to be made to prepare for applying computer simulation to this example?
4. What quantities appear in the assumption cells of the spreadsheet model for this example?
5. What quantity appears in the forecast cell for this example?
6. Does computer simulation indicate a significant chance of incurring a loss if Think-Big management approves the investment proposal?

13.6 REVENUE MANAGEMENT IN THE TRAVEL INDUSTRY

One of the most prominent areas for the application of management science in recent years has been in improving *revenue management* in the travel industry. Revenue management refers to the various ways of increasing the flow of revenues through such devices as setting up different fare classes for different categories of customers. The objective is to maximize total income by setting fares that are at the upper edge of what the different market segments are willing to pay and then allocating seats appropriately to the various fare classes.

As the example in this section will illustrate, one key area of revenue management is *overbooking*, that is, accepting a slightly larger number of reservations than the number of seats available. There usually are a small number of no-shows, so overbooking will increase revenue by essentially filling the available seating. However, there also are costs incurred if the number of arriving customers exceeds the number of available seats. Therefore, the amount of overbooking needs to be set carefully so as to achieve an appropriate trade-off between filling seats and avoiding the need to turn away customers who have a reservation.

American Airlines was the pioneer in making extensive use of management science for improving its revenue management. The guiding motto was "selling the right seats to the right customers at the right time." This work won the 1991 Franz Edelman Award as that year's best application of management science anywhere throughout the world. This application was credited with increasing annual revenues for American Airlines by over $500 million. Nearly half of these increased revenues came from the use of a new overbooking model.

Following this breakthrough at American Airlines, other airlines quickly stepped up their use of management science in similar ways. These applications to revenue management then spread to other segments of the travel industry (train travel, cruise lines, rental cars, hotels, etc.) around the world. Our example below involves overbooking by an airline company.

A new overbooking model increased annual revenues for American Airlines by about $225 million.

The Transcontinental Airlines Overbooking Problem

Transcontinental Airlines has a daily flight (excluding weekends) from San Francisco to Chicago that is mainly used by business travelers. There are 150 seats available in the single cabin. The average fare per seat is $300. This is a nonrefundable fare, so no-shows forfeit the entire fare. The fixed cost for operating the flight is $30,000, so more than 100 reservations are needed to make a profit on any particular day.

For most of these flights, the number of requests for reservations considerably exceeds the number of seats available. The company's management science group has been compiling data on the number of reservation requests per flight for the past several months. The average number has been 195, but with considerable variation from flight to flight on both sides of this average. Plotting a frequency chart for these data suggests that they roughly follow a bell-shaped curve. Therefore, the group estimates that the number of reservation requests per flight has a *normal distribution* with a mean of 195. A calculation from the data estimates that the standard deviation is 30.

An unusually high 20 percent no-show rate requires developing a special overbooking policy for this particular flight.

The company's policy is to accept 10 percent more reservations than the number of seats available on nearly all its flights, since roughly 10 percent of all its customers making reservations end up being no-shows. However, if its experience with a particular flight is much different from this, then an exception is made and the management science group is called in to analyze what the overbooking policy should be for that particular flight. This is what has just happened regarding the daily flight from San Francisco to Chicago. Even when the full quota of 165 reservations has been reached (which happens for most of the flights), there usually are a significant number of empty seats. While gathering its data, the management science group has discovered the reason why. On the average, only 80 percent of the customers who make reservations for this flight actually show up to take the flight. The other 20 percent forfeit the fare (or, in most cases, allow their company to do so) because their plans have changed.

Now that the data have been gathered, the management science group decides to begin its analysis by investigating the option of increasing the number of reservations to accept for this flight to 190. If the number of reservation requests for a particular day actually reaches this level, then this number should be large enough to avoid many, if any, empty seats. Furthermore, this number should be small enough that there will not be many occasions when a significant number of customers need to be bumped from the flight because the number of arrivals exceeds the number of seats available (150). Thus, 190 appears to be a good first guess for an appropriate trade-off between avoiding many empty seats and avoiding bumping many customers.

When a customer is bumped from this flight, Transcontinental Airlines arranges to put the customer on the next available flight to Chicago on another airline. The company's average cost for doing this is $150. In addition, the company gives the customer a voucher worth $200 for use on a future flight. The company also feels that an additional $100 should be assessed for the intangible cost of a loss of goodwill on the part of the bumped customer. Therefore, the total cost of bumping a customer is estimated to be $450.

The management science group now wants to investigate the option of accepting 190 reservations by using computer simulation to generate frequency charts for the following three measures of performance for each day's flight:

1. The profit.
2. The number of filled seats.
3. The number of customers denied boarding.

A Spreadsheet Model for Applying Computer Simulation

Having three measures of performance means that the simulation model needs three forecast cells.

Figure 13.28 shows a spreadsheet model for this problem. Because there are three measures of interest here, the spreadsheet model needs three forecast cells. These forecast cells are Profit (F23), NumberOfFilledSeats (C20), and NumberDeniedBoarding (C21). The decision variable ReservationsToAccept (C13) has been set at 190 for investigating this current option. Some basic data have been entered near the top of the spreadsheet in cells C4:C7.

Each trial of the computer simulation will correspond to one day's flight. There are two random inputs associated with each flight, namely, the number of customers requesting reservations (abbreviated as Ticket Demand in cell B10) and the number of customers who actually arrive to take the flight (abbreviated as Number That Show in cell B17). Thus, the two assumption cells in this model are SimulatedTicketDemand (C10) and NumberThatShow (C17).

Excel Tip: The Excel function ROUND(x, 0) rounds the value x to the nearest integer. The zero specifies that 0 digits after the decimal point should be included when rounding.

Since the management science group has estimated that the number of customers requesting reservations has a normal distribution with a mean of 195 and a standard deviation of 30, this information has been entered into cells D10:F10. The Normal Distribution dialogue box (shown earlier in Figure 13.26) then has been used to enter this distribution with these parameters into SimulatedTicketDemand (C10). Because the normal distribution is a continuous distribution, whereas the number of reservations must have an integer value, Demand (C11) uses Excel's ROUND function to round the number in SimulatedTicketDemand (C10) to the nearest integer.

FIGURE 13.28

A spreadsheet model for applying computer simulation to the Transcontinental Airlines overbooking problem. The assumption cells are SimulatedTicketDemand (C10) and NumberThatShow (C17). The forecast cells are Profit (F23), NumberOfFilledSeats (C20), and NumberDeniedBoarding (C21). The decision variable is ReservationsToAccept (C13).

	A	B	C	D	E	F
1		**Airline Overbooking**				
2						
3			**Data**			
4		Available Seats	150			
5		Fixed Cost	$30,000			
6		Avg. Fare / Seat	$300			
7		Cost of Bumping	$450			
8						
9					Mean	Standard Dev.
10		Ticket Demand	195	*Normal*	195	30
11		Demand (rounded)	195			
12						
13		Reservations to Accept	190			
14						
15					Tickets	Probability
16					Purchased	to Show Up
17		Number That Show	152	*Binomial*	190	80%
18						
19						
20		Number of Filled Seats	150		Ticket Revenue	$45,000
21		Number Denied Boarding	2		Bumping Cost	$900
22					Fixed Cost	$30,000
23					Profit	$14,100

	B	C
11	Demand (rounded)	=ROUND(SimulatedTicketDemand,0)

	E
15	Tickets
16	Purchased
17	=MIN(Demand,ReservationsToAccept)

Range Name	Cell
AvailableSeats	C4
AverageFare	C6
BumpingCost	F21
CostOfBumping	C7
Demand	C11
FixedCost	C5
NumberDeniedBoarding	C21
NumberOfFilledSeats	C20
NumberThatShow	C17
Profit	F23
ReservationsToAccept	C13
SimulatedTicketDemand	C10
TicketRevenue	F20
TicketsPurchased	E17

	B	C
20	Number of Filled Seats	=MIN(AvailableSeats,NumberThatShow)
21	Number Denied Boarding	=MAX(0,NumberThatShow–AvailableSeats)

	E	F
20	Ticket Revenue	=AverageFare*NumberOfFilledSeats
21	Bumping Cost	=CostOfBumping*NumberDeniedBoarding
22	Fixed Cost	=FixedCost
23	Profit	=TicketRevenue–BumpingCost–FixedCost

The random input for the second assumption cell NumberThatShow (C17) depends on two key quantities. One is TicketsPurchased (E17), which is the minimum of Demand (C11) and ReservationsToAccept (C13). The other key quantity is the probability that an individual making a reservation actually will show up to take the flight. This probability has been set at 80 percent in cell F17 since this is the *average* percentage of those who have shown up for the flight in recent months.

However, the *actual* percentage of those who show up on any particular day may vary somewhat on either side of this average percentage. Therefore, even though NumberThatShow (C17)

FIGURE 13.29

A binomial distribution
with parameters
0.8 (=F17) and
190 (=E17) is being
entered into the
assumption cell
NumberThatShow (C17).

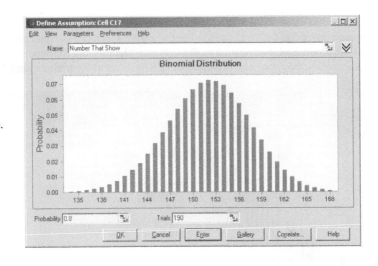

These characteristics of
the binomial distribution
are just what is needed for
the assumption cell
NumberThatShow (C17).

would be expected to be fairly close to the product of cells E17 and F17, there will be some variation according to some probability distribution. What is the appropriate distribution for this assumption cell? Section 13.7 will describe the characteristics of various distributions. The one that has the characteristics to fit this assumption cell turns out to be the *binomial distribution.*

As indicated in Section 13.7, the binomial distribution gives the distribution of the number of times a particular event occurs out of a certain number of opportunities. In this case, the *event* of interest is a passenger showing up to take the flight. The *opportunity* for this event to occur arises when a customer makes a reservation for the flight. These opportunities are conventionally referred to as *trials* (not to be confused with a trial of a computer simulation). The binomial distribution assumes that the trials are statistically independent and that, on each trial, there is a fixed probability (80 percent in this case) that the event will occur. The parameters of the distribution are this fixed probability and the number of trials.

Figure 13.29 displays the Binomial Distribution dialogue box that enters this distribution into NumberThatShow (C17) by referencing the parameters in cells F17 and E17. The actual value in Trials for the binomial distribution will vary from simulation trial to simulation trial because it depends on the number of tickets purchased which in turn depends on the ticket demand which is random. Crystal Ball therefore must determine the value for TicketsPurchased (E17) *before* it can randomly generate NumberThatShow (C17). Fortunately, Crystal Ball automatically takes care of the order in which to generate the various assumption cells so that this is not a problem.

The equations entered into all the output cells and forecast cells are given at the bottom of Figure 13.28.

Here is a summary of the key cells in this model.

Assumption cells:	SimulatedTicketDemand (C10) and NumberThatShow (C17)
Decision variable:	ReservationsToAccept (C13)
Forecast cells:	Profit (F23), NumberOfFilledSeats (C20), and NumberDeniedBoarding (C21)

The Simulation Results

Figure 13.30 shows the frequency chart obtained for each of the three forecast cells after applying computer simulation for 1,000 trials to the spreadsheet model in Figure 13.28, with ReservationsToAccept (C13) set at 190.

The profit results estimate that the mean profit per flight would be $11,693. However, this mean is a little less than the profits that had the highest frequencies. The reason is that a small number of trials had profits far below the mean, including even a few that incurred losses, which dragged the mean down somewhat. By entering 0 into the lower left-hand box, the Certainty box reports that 98.87 percent of the trials resulted in a profit for that day's flight.

FIGURE 13.30

The frequency charts that summarize the results for the respective forecast cells—Profit (F23), NumberOfFilledSeats (C20), and NumberDeniedBoarding (C21)—from running the simulation model in Figure 13.28 for the Transcontinental Airlines overbooking problem. The Certainty box below the first frequency chart reveals that 98.87 percent of the trials resulted in a positive profit.

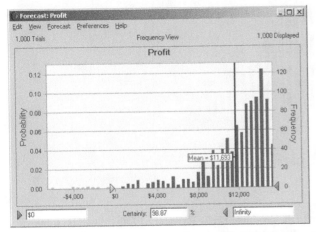

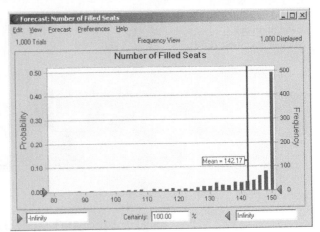

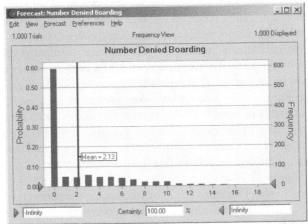

The frequency chart for NumberOfFilledSeats (C20) indicates that almost half of the 1,000 trials resulted in all 150 seats being filled. Furthermore, most of the remaining trials had at least 130 seats filled. The fact that the mean of 142.17 is so close to 150 shows that a policy of accepting 190 reservations would do an excellent job of filling seats.

The price that would be paid for filling seats so well is that a few customers would need to be bumped from some of the flights. The frequency chart for NumberDeniedBoarding (C21) indicates that this occurred over 40 percent of the time. On nearly all of these trials, the number ranged between 1 and 10. Considering that no customers were denied boarding for 60 percent of the trials, the mean number is only 2.13.

We will return to this example in Section 13.8 to further evaluate how many reservations to accept.

Although these results suggest that a policy of accepting 190 reservations would be an attractive option for the most part, they do not demonstrate that this is necessarily the best option. Additional simulation runs are needed with other numbers entered in ReservationsTo Accept (C13) to pin down the optimal value of this decision variable. We will demonstrate how to do this efficiently with the help of a decision table in Section 13.8.

Review Questions

1. What is meant by *revenue management* in the travel industry?
2. In the pioneering application of management science to revenue management at American Airlines, what increase in annual revenues was achieved?
3. What problem is being addressed by the management science group at Transcontinental Airlines in this section's example?
4. What trade-off must be considered in addressing this problem?

5. What is the decision variable for this problem?
6. What quantities appear in the forecast cells of the spreadsheet model for this problem?
7. What quantities appear in the assumption cells of the spreadsheet model?
8. What are the parameters of a binomial distribution?
9. Did the simulation results obtained in this section determine how many reservations should be accepted for the flight under consideration?

13.7   CHOOSING THE RIGHT DISTRIBUTION

As mentioned in Section 13.1, Crystal Ball's **Distribution Gallery** provides a wealth of choices. Any of 21 probability distributions can be selected as the one to be entered into any assumption cell. In the preceding sections, we have illustrated the use of five of these distributions (the discrete uniform, uniform, triangular, normal, and binomial distributions). However, not much was said about *why* any particular distribution was chosen.

In this section, we focus on the issue of how to choose the right distribution. We begin by surveying the characteristics of many of the 21 distributions and how these characteristics help to identify the best choice. We next describe a special feature of Crystal Ball for creating a custom distribution when none of the other 20 choices in the Distribution Gallery will do. We then return to the case study presented in Section 13.1 to illustrate another special feature of Crystal Ball. When historical data are available, this feature will identify which of the available continuous distributions provides the best fit to these data while also estimating the parameters of this distribution. If you do not like this choice, it will even identify which of the distributions provides the second best fit, the third best fit, and so on.

Characteristics of the Available Distributions

The probability distribution of any random variable describes the relative likelihood of the possible values of the random variable. A *continuous* distribution is used if *any* values are possible, including both integer and fractional numbers, over the entire range of possible values. A *discrete* distribution is used if only certain specific values (e.g., only the integer numbers over some range) are possible. However, if the only possible values are integer numbers over a relatively broad range, a continuous distribution may be used as an approximation by rounding any fractional value to the nearest integer. (This approximation was used in cells C10:C11 of the spreadsheet model in Figure 13.28.) Crystal Ball's Distribution Gallery includes both continuous and discrete distributions. We will begin by looking at the continuous distributions.

The right-hand side of Figure 13.31 shows the dialogue box for three popular continuous distributions from the Distribution Gallery. The dark figure in each dialogue box displays a typical *probability density function* for that distribution. The height of the probability density function at the various points shows the relative likelihood of the corresponding values along the horizontal axis. Each of these distributions has a most likely value where the probability density function reaches a peak. Furthermore, all the other relatively high points are near the peak. This indicates that there is a tendency for one of the central values located near the most likely value to be the one that occurs. Therefore, these distributions are referred as *central-tendency distributions*. The characteristics of each of these distributions are listed on the left-hand side of Figure 13.31.

The Normal Distribution

The normal distribution is widely used by both management scientists and others because it describes so many natural phenomena. One reason that it arises so frequently is that the sum of many random variables tends to have a normal distribution (approximately) even when the individual random variables do not. Using this distribution requires estimating the mean and the standard deviation. The mean coincides with the most likely value because this is a symmetric distribution. Thus, the mean is a very intuitive quantity that can be readily estimated,

FIGURE 13.31

The characteristics and dialogue boxes for three popular central-tendency distributions in Crystal Ball's Distribution Gallery: (1) the normal distribution, (2) the triangular distribution, and (3) the lognormal distribution.

Popular Central-Tendency Distributions

Normal Distribution:
- Some value most likely (the mean)
- Values close to mean more likely
- Symmetric (as likely above as below mean)
- Extreme values possible, but rare

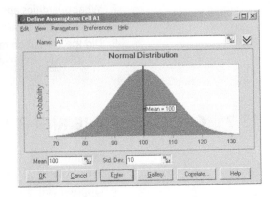

Triangular Distribution:
- Some value most likely
- Values close to most likely value more common
- Can be asymmetric
- Fixed upper and lower bound

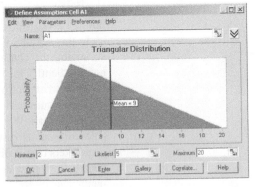

Lognormal Distribution:
- Some value most likely
- Positively skewed (below mean more likely)
- Values cannot fall below zero
- Extreme values (high end only) possible, but rare

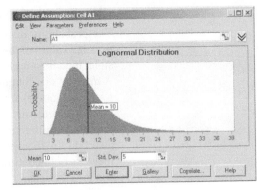

but the standard deviation is not. About two-thirds of the distribution lies within one standard deviation of the mean. Therefore, if historical data are not available for calculating an estimate of the standard deviation, a rough estimate can be elicited from a knowledgeable individual by asking for an amount such that the random value will be within that amount of the mean about two-thirds of the time.

One danger with using the normal distribution for some applications is that it can give negative values even when such values actually are impossible. Fortunately, it can give negative values with significant frequency only if the mean is less than three standard deviations. For example, consider the situation where a normal distribution was entered into an assumption cell in Figure 13.28 to represent the number of customers requesting a reservation. A negative number would make no sense in this case, but this was no problem since the mean (195) was much larger than three standard deviations ($3 \times 30 = 90$) so a negative value essentially could never occur. (When normal distributions were entered into assumption cells in Figure 13.25 to represent cash flows, the means were small or even negative, but this also was no problem since cash flows can be either negative or positive.)

The normal distribution allows negative values, which is not appropriate for some applications.

The Triangular Distribution

A comparison of the shapes of the triangular and normal distributions in Figure 13.31 reveals some key differences. One is that the triangular distribution has a fixed minimum value and a fixed maximum value, whereas the normal distribution allows rare extreme values far into the tails. Another is that the triangular distribution can be asymmetric (as shown in the figure), because the most likely value does not need to be midway between the bounds, whereas the normal distribution always is symmetric. This provides additional flexibility to the triangular distribution. Another key difference is that all its parameters (the minimum value, most likely value, and maximum value) are intuitive ones, so they are relatively easy to estimate.

These advantages have made the triangular distribution a popular choice for computer simulations. They are the reason why this distribution was used in previous examples to represent competitors' bids for a construction contract (in Figure 13.11), activity times (in Figure 13.17), and cash flows (in Figure 13.23).

However, the triangular distribution also has certain disadvantages. One is that, in many situations, rare extreme values far into the tails are possible, so it is quite artificial to have fixed minimum and maximum values. This also makes it difficult to develop meaningful estimates of the bounds. Still another disadvantage is that a curve with a gradually changing slope, such as the bell-shaped curve for the normal distribution, should describe the true distribution more accurately than the straight line segments in the triangular distribution.

The Lognormal Distribution

The lognormal distribution shown at the bottom of Figure 13.31 combines some of the advantages of the normal and triangular distributions. It has a curve with a gradually changing slope. It also allows rare extreme values on the high side. At the same time, it does not allow negative values, so it automatically fits situations where this is needed. This is particularly advantageous when the mean is less than three standard deviations and the normal distribution should not be used.

This distribution always is "positively skewed," meaning that the long tail always is to the right. This forces the most likely value to be toward the left side (so the mean is on its right), so this distribution is less flexible than the triangular distribution. Another disadvantage is that it has the same parameters as the normal distribution (the mean and the standard deviation), so the less intuitive one (the standard deviation) is difficult to estimate unless historical data are available.

When a positively skewed distribution that does not allow negative values is needed, the lognormal distribution provides an attractive option. That is why this distribution frequently is used to represent stock prices or real estate prices.

The Uniform and Discrete Uniform Distributions

Although the preceding three distributions are all central-tendency distributions, the uniform distributions shown in Figure 13.32 definitely are not. They have a fixed minimum value and a fixed maximum value. Otherwise, they say that no value between these bounds is any more likely than any other possible value. Therefore, these distributions have more variability than the central-tendency distributions with the same range of possible values (excluding rare extreme values).

The choice between these two distributions depends on which values between the minimum and maximum values are possible. If *any* values in this range are possible, including even *fractional* values, then the uniform distribution would be preferred over the discrete uniform distribution. If only integer values are possible, then the discrete uniform distribution would be the preferable one.

Either of these distributions is a particularly convenient one because it has only two parameters (the minimum value and the maximum value) and both are very intuitive. These distributions receive considerable use for this reason. Earlier in this chapter, the discrete uniform distribution was used to represent the demand for a newspaper (in Figure 13.1), whereas the uniform distribution was used to generate the bid for a construction

FIGURE 13.32

The characteristics and dialogue box for the uniform distribution in Crystal Ball's Distribution Gallery.

Uniform Distribution:

- Fixed minimum and maximum value
- All values equally likely

Uniform and Discrete Uniform Distribution

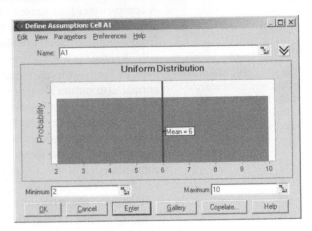

Discrete Uniform Distribution:

- Fixed minimum and maximum value
- All integer values equally likely

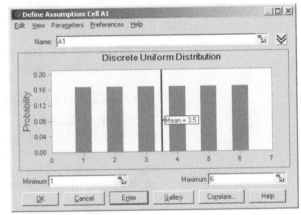

project by one competitor (in Figure 13.11), and the future sale price for real estate property (in Figure 13.25).

The uniform distribution is easy to use but usually is only a rough approximation of the true distribution.

The disadvantage of this distribution is that it usually is only a rough approximation of the true distribution. It is uncommon for either the minimum value or the maximum value to be just as likely as any other value between these bounds while any value barely outside these bounds is impossible.

The Weibull and Beta Distributions

We will describe the Weibull and beta distributions together because, as suggested by their similar shapes in Figure 13.33, these two distributions have similar characteristics. In contrast to the uniform distribution, both are central-tendency distributions. In contrast to the normal, lognormal, and uniform distributions, both have more than two parameters. The three (for the Weibull) or four (for the beta) parameters provide great flexibility in adjusting the shape of the curve to fit the situation. This enables making the distribution positively skewed, symmetric, or negatively skewed as desired. This flexibility is the key advantage of these distributions. Another advantage is that they have a minimum value, so negative values can be avoided. The location parameter sets the minimum value for the Weibull distribution. The Weibull distribution allows rare extreme values to the right, whereas the beta distribution has a fixed maximum value.

Certain parameters, such as the location parameter mentioned above for the Weibull distribution, or the minimum and maximum parameter for the beta distribution, have an intuitive interpretation. The scale parameter for the Weibull distribution simply sets the width of the distribution (excluding rare extreme values). However, neither the shape parameter for

FIGURE 13.33

The characteristics and dialogue boxes for three- and four-parameter distributions in Crystal Ball's Distribution Gallery: (1) the Weibull distribution and (2) the beta distribution.

Three- and Four-Parameter Distributions

Weibull Distribution:

- Random value above some number (location)
- Shape > 0 (usually ≤10)
- Shape < 3 becomes more positively skewed (below mean more likely) until it resembles exponential distribution (equivalent at Shape = 1)
- Symmetrical at Shape = 3.25, becomes more negatively skewed above that
- Scale defines width

Beta Distribution:

- Random value between some minimum and maximum
- Shape specified using two positive values (alpha, beta)
- Alpha < beta: positively skewed (below mean more likely)
- Beta < alpha: negatively skewed

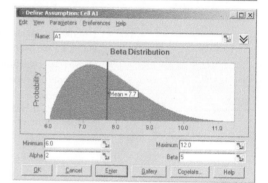

The Weibull and beta distributions are flexible enough to fit many situations, but they usually require historical data in order to calculate good estimates of their parameters.

the Weibull distribution nor the alpha and beta parameters for the beta distribution are particularly intuitive. Therefore, these distributions are mainly used only when historical data are available for calculating estimates of these parameters. (One exception is the innovative use of the beta distribution by the PERT three-estimate approach described in Section 16.4, which uses the minimum, most likely, and maximum values to calculate approximate values of the mean and standard deviation.) With historical data available, the choice between these two distributions (and other options as well) then can be based on which one provides the best fit with the data after obtaining statistical estimates of its parameters. We will describe a little later how Crystal Ball can do all of this for you.

The Exponential Distribution

If you have studied Chapter 11 on queueing models, you hopefully will recall that the most commonly used queueing models assume that the time between consecutive arrivals of customers to receive a particular service has an exponential distribution. The reason for this assumption is that, in most such situations, the arrivals of customers are random events and the exponential distribution is the probability distribution of the time between random events. Section 11.1 describes this property of the exponential distribution in some detail.

As first depicted in Figure 11.3, this distribution has the unusual shape shown in Figure 13.34. In particular, the peak is at 0 but there is a long tail to the right. This indicates that the most likely times are short ones well below the mean but that very long times also are possible. This is the nature of the time between random events.

Since the only parameter is the rate at which the random events occur on the average, this distribution is a relatively easy one to use.

The Poisson Distribution

Although the exponential distribution (like most of the preceding ones) is a continuous distribution, the Poisson distribution is a discrete distribution. The only possible values are nonnegative integers: 0, 1, 2. . . . However, it is natural to pair this distribution with the exponential

FIGURE 13.34

The characteristics and dialogue boxes for two distributions that involve random events. These distributions in Crystal Ball's Distribution Gallery are (1) the exponential distribution and (2) the Poisson distribution.

Distributions for Random Events

Exponential Distribution:

- Widely used to describe time between random events (e.g., time between arrivals)
- Events are independent
- Rate = average number of events per unit time (e.g., arrivals per hour)

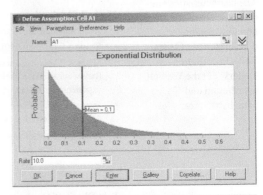

Poisson Distribution:

- Describes the number of times an event occurs during a given period of time or space
- Occurrences are independent
- Any number of events is possible
- Rate = average number of events during period of time (e.g., arrivals per hour), assumed constant over time

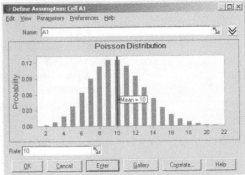

distribution for the following reason. If the time between consecutive events has an exponential distribution (i.e., the events are occurring at random), then the number of events that occur within a certain period of time has a Poisson distribution. This distribution has some other applications as well.

When considering the number of events that occur within a certain period of time, the "Rate" to be entered into the one parameter field in the dialogue box should be the average number of events that occur within that period of time.

The Yes–No and Binomial Distributions

The yes–no distribution is a very simple discrete distribution with only two possible values (1 or 0) as shown in Figure 13.35. It is used to simulate whether a particular event occurs or not. The only parameter of the distribution is the probability that the event occurs. The yes–no distribution gives a value of 1 (representing yes) with this probability; otherwise, it gives a value of 0 (representing no).

The binomial distribution is an extension of the yes–no distribution for when an event might occur a number of times. The binomial distribution gives the probability distribution of the number of *times* a particular event occurs, given the number of independent opportunities (called trials) for the event to occur, where the probability of the event occurring remains the same from trial to trial. For example, if the event of interest is getting heads on the flip of a coin, the binomial distribution (with Prob. = 0.5) gives the distribution of the number of heads in a given number of flips of the coin. Each flip constitutes a trial where there is an opportunity for the event (heads) to occur with a fixed probability (0.5). The binomial distribution is equivalent to the yes–no distribution when the number of trials is equal to 1.

You have seen another example in the preceding section when the binomial distribution was entered into the assumption cell NumberThatShow (C17) in Figure 13.28. In this airline overbooking example, the events are customers showing up for the flight and the trials are customers making reservations, where there is a fixed probability that a customer making a reservation actually will arrive to take the flight.

FIGURE 13.35

The characteristics and dialogue box for the yes–no and binomial distributions in Crystal Ball's Distribution Gallery.

Distributions for Number of Times an Event Occurs

Yes–No Distribution:

- Describes whether an event occurs or not

- Two possible outcomes: 1 (Yes) or 0 (No)

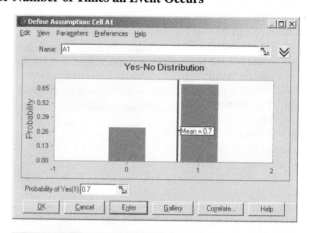

Binomial Distribution:

- Describes number of times an event occurs in a fixed number of trials (e.g., number of heads in 10 flips of a coin)

- For each trial, only two outcomes possible

- Trials independent

- Probability remains same for each trial

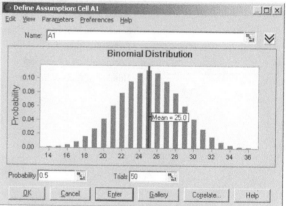

The only parameters for this distribution are the number of trials and the probability of the event occurring on a trial.

The Geometric and Negative Binomial Distributions

These two distributions displayed in Figure 13.36 are related to the binomial distribution because they again involve trials where there is a fixed probability on each trial that the event will occur. The *geometric distribution* gives the distribution of the number of trials until the event occurs for the first time. After entering a positive integer into the Shape field in its dialogue box, the *negative binomial distribution* gives the distribution of the number of trials until the event occurs the number of times specified in the Shape field. Thus, shape is a parameter for this distribution and the fixed probability of the event occurring on a trial is a parameter for both distributions.

To illustrate these distributions, suppose you are again interested in the event of getting heads on a flip of a coin (a trial). The geometric distribution (with Prob. = 0.5) gives the distribution of the number of flips until the first head occurs. If you want five heads, the negative binomial distribution (with Prob. = 0.5 and Shape = 5) gives the distribution of the number of flips until heads have occurred five times.

Similarly, consider a production process with a 50 percent yield, so each unit produced has an 0.5 probability of being acceptable. The geometric distribution (with Prob. = 0.5) gives the distribution of the number of units that need to be produced to obtain one acceptable unit. If a customer has ordered five units, the negative binomial distribution (with Prob. = 0.5 and Shape = 5) gives the distribution of the production run size that is needed to fulfill this order.

Other Distributions

The Distribution Gallery includes eight additional distributions: gamma, max extreme, min extreme, logistic, student's-t, Pareto, hypergeometric, and custom.

FIGURE 13.36

The characteristics and dialogue boxes for two distributions that involve the number of trials until events occur. These distributions in Crystal Ball's Distribution Gallery are (1) the geometric distribution and (2) the negative binomial distribution.

Distributions for Number of Trials Until Event Occurs

Geometric Distribution:

• Describes number of trials until an event occurs (e.g., number of times to spin roulette wheel until you win)
• Probability same for each trial
• Continue until succeed
• Number of trials unlimited

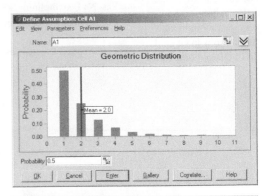

Negative Binomial Distribution:

• Describes number of trials until an event occurs *n* times
• Same as geometric when Shape = *n* = 1
• Probability same for each trial
• Continue until *n*th success
• Number of trials unlimited

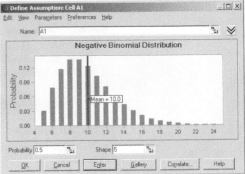

The custom distribution is an especially useful one because it enables you to design your own distribution when none of the other 20 distributions in the Distribution Gallery will do. The next subsection will focus on how this is done.

The remaining seven distributions are not widely used in computer simulations, so they will not be discussed further.

The Custom Distribution

Of the 21 probability distributions included in the Distribution Gallery, 20 of them are standard types that might be discussed in a course on probability and statistics. In most cases, one of these standard distributions will be just what is needed for an assumption cell. However, unique circumstances occasionally arise where none of the standard distributions fit the situation. This is where the 21st member of the Distribution Gallery, called the "custom distribution," enters the picture.

Choosing the custom distribution from the Distribution Gallery enables you to custom-design your own distribution to fit a special situation.

The custom distribution actually is not a probability distribution until you make it one. Rather, choosing this member of the Distribution Gallery triggers a process that enables you to custom-design your own probability distribution to fit almost any unique situation you might encounter. In designing your distribution, you are given five choices under the Parameters menu: unweighted values, weighted values, continuous ranges, discrete ranges, and sloping ranges. The choice determines how many parameters are available. For unweighted values, there is just one parameter (*Value*). A list of values are entered and each of these values are assumed to be equally likely. For weighted values, there are two parameters (*Value* and *Probability*) allowing each value to have a different probability. Continuous ranges have three parameters (*Minimum, Maximum,* and *Probability*) to specify the range (or ranges) of the distribution and the total probability of each range. Discrete ranges add a fourth parameter (*Step*) to specify the distance between the possible discrete values in the range. Finally, sloping ranges have two parameters (*Height of Minimum* and *Height of Maximum*) to allow the distribution to slope from the minimum to the maximum. Furthermore, these values or ranges can be combined in any possible way, such as combining a set of discrete values with a continuous range. We will show two examples.

FIGURE 13.37

Following the instructions to its left, this dialogue box illustrates how Crystal Ball's custom distribution can enable you to custom-design your own distribution to enter a set of discrete values and their probabilities.

- Enter set of values with varying probabilities

- For each discrete value, enter *Value* and *Probability*

Custom Distribution (Weighted Values)

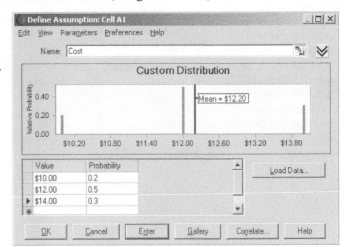

In the first example, a company is developing a new product but it is unclear which of three production processes will be needed to produce the product. The unit production cost will be $10, $12, or $14, depending on which process is needed. The probabilities for these individual discrete values of the cost are the following.

20 percent chance of $10

50 percent chance of $12

30 percent chance of $14

To enter this distribution, first choose weighted values under the Parameters menu in the Custom Distribution dialogue box. Each discrete value and probability (expressed as a decimal number) is then entered in the Value and Probability columns as shown in Figure 13.37.

The other distribution types (unweighted values, continuous ranges, discrete ranges, and sloping ranges) are entered in a similar fashion by choosing the appropriate option under the Parameter menu. We next illustrate how to enter a combination of a weighted value and a continuous range.

The example in this case is a variation of the probability distribution of the revenue from drilling for oil in the Goferbroke Company case study introduced in Section 9.1. In that case study, there was a probability of 0.75 of not finding oil (so a revenue of $0) and a probability of 0.25 of finding oil, in which case the revenue would be $800,000. However, there actually is some uncertainty about how much revenue would be received if oil were found, so the following distribution would be more realistic.

Revenue of $0 has probability 0.75

A range of revenue values: $600,000 to $1,000,000

The values over this range are equally likely

Probability of a value in this range: 0.25

This distribution combines a single discrete value at $0 with a continuous portion between $600,000 and $1,000,000. To enter such a combination distribution, choose the member of the combination under the Parameters menu with the most parameters needed. The weighted value requires two parameters (*Value* and *Probability*) while the continuous range requires three (*Minimum, Maximum,* and *Probability*), so choose Continuous Range under the Parameters menu. This leads to the Custom Distribution dialogue box with three columns for data (*Minimum, Maximum,* and *Probability*), as shown in Figure 13.38.

FIGURE 13.38

Following the instructions to its left, this dialogue box for the custom distribution demonstrates combining two of the options in Figure 13.37: (1) enter a discrete value at $0 and (2) enter a uniform distribution between $600,000 and $1,000,000.

Combinations with the Custom Distribution

For discrete values, enter
- Value and Probability

For continuous range, enter
- Minimum, Maximum, and Probability

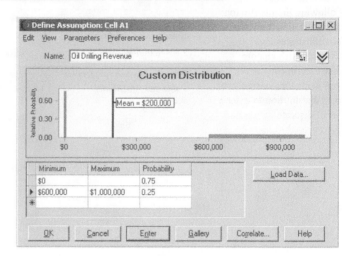

For a discrete value, only two parameters are needed (*Value* = $0 and *Probability* = 0.75), so the middle column is left blank in the first row of the box of data in Figure 13.38. For the continuous range, we enter the *Minimum* ($600,000), *Maximum* ($1,000,000), and *Probability* (0.25) in the second row of the data box in Figure 13.38.

Identifying the Continuous Distribution That Best Fits Historical Data

If you don't know which continuous distribution should be chosen for an assumption cell, Crystal Ball can do it for you if historical data are available.

We now have at least mentioned all 21 types of probability distributions in the Distribution Gallery and have described the characteristics of many of them. This brings us to the question of how to identify which distribution is best for a particular assumption cell. When historical data are available, Crystal Ball provides a powerful feature for doing this by using the Fit button on the Distribution Gallery dialogue box shown in Figure 13.2. We will illustrate this feature next by returning to the case study presented in Section 13.1.

Recall that one of the most popular newspapers that Freddie the newsboy sells from his newsstand is the daily *Financial Journal*. Freddie purchases copies from his distributor early each morning. Since excess copies left over at the end of the day represent a loss for Freddie, he is trying to decide what his order quantity should be in the future. This led to the spreadsheet model in Figure 13.1 that was shown earlier in Section 13.1. This model includes the assumption cell Demand (C12). To get started, a discrete uniform distribution between 40 and 70 has been entered into this assumption cell.

To better guide his decision on what the order quantity should be, Freddie has been keeping a record of the *demand* (the number of customers requesting a copy) for this newspaper each day. Figure 13.39 shows a portion of the data he has gathered over the last 60 days in cells F4:F63, along with part of the original spreadsheet model from Figure 13.1. These data indicate a lot of variation in sales from day to day—ranging from about 40 copies to 70 copies. However, it is difficult to tell from these numbers which distribution in the Distribution Gallery best fits these data.

Crystal Ball provides the following procedure for addressing this issue.

Procedure for Fitting the Best Distribution to Data

1. Gather the data needed to identify the best distribution to enter into an assumption cell.
2. Enter the data into the spreadsheet containing your simulation model.
3. Select the cell that you want to define as an assumption cell that contains the distribution that best fits the data.
4. Choose Define Assumption from the Crystal Ball tab or toolbar, which brings up the Distribution Gallery dialogue box.
5. Click the Fit button on this dialogue box, which brings up the Fit Distribution dialogue box.

FIGURE 13.39

Cells F4:F63 contain the historical demand data that have been collected for the case study involving Freddie the newsboy that was introduced in Section 13.1. Columns B and C come from the simulation model for this case study in Figure 13.1.

	A	B	C	D	E	F
1		**Freddie the Newsboy**				Historical
2						Demand
3			**Data**		Day	Data
4		Unit Sale Price	$2.50		1	62
5		Unit Purchase Cost	$1.50		2	45
6		Unit Salvage Value	$0.50		3	59
7					4	65
8			**Decision Variable**		5	50
9		Order Quantity	60		6	64
10					7	56
11			**Simulation**		8	51
12		Simulated Demand	55		9	55
13		Demand (rounded)	55		10	61
14					11	40
15		Sales Revenue	$137.50		12	47
16		Purchasing Cost	$90.00		13	63
17		Salvage Value	$2.50		14	68
18					15	67
19		Profit	$50.00		16	67
20					17	68
58					55	41
59					56	42
60					57	64
61					58	45
62					59	59
63					60	70

6. Use the Range box in this dialogue box to enter the range of the historical data in your worksheet.

7. Specify which distributions are being considered for fitting.

8. Also use this dialogue box to select which ranking method should be used to evaluate how well a distribution fits the data. (The default is the chi-square test, since this is the most popular choice.)

9. Click OK, which brings up the comparison chart that identifies the distribution (including its parameter values) that best fits the data.

10. If desired, the Next button can be clicked repeatedly for identifying the other types of distributions (including their parameter values) that are next in line for fitting the data well.

11. After choosing the distribution (from steps 9 and 10) that you want to use, click the Accept button while that distribution is showing. This will enter the appropriate parameters into the dialogue box for this distribution. Clicking OK then enters this distribution into the assumption cell.

Since Figure 13.39 already includes the needed data in cells F4:F63, applying this procedure to Freddie's problem begins by selecting SimulatedDemand (C12) as the cell we want to define as an assumption cell that contains the distribution that best fits the data. Then applying steps 4 and 5 brings up the Fit Distribution dialogue box displayed in Figure 13.40. The range F4:F63 of the data in Figure 13.39 is entered into the Range box of this dialogue box. When deciding which distributions should be considered for fitting, the default option of considering all the continuous distributions in the Distribution Gallery has been selected here. The default choice of the chi-square test also has been selected for the ranking method. Clicking OK then brings up the comparison chart displayed in Figure 13.41.

FIGURE 13.40

The Fit Distribution dialogue box specifies the range of the data in Figure 13.39 for the case study, which continuous distributions will be considered (all) and which ranking method will be used (the chi-square test) to evaluate how well each of the distributions fit the data.

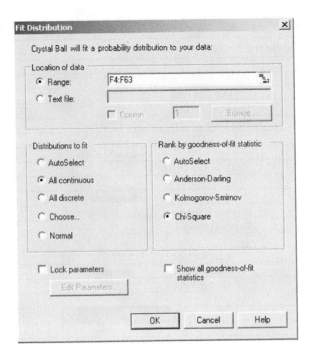

FIGURE 13.41

On the right, this comparison chart identifies the continuous distribution that provides the best fit with the historical demand data in Figure 13.39. This distribution then is plotted (the horizontal line) so that it can be compared with the frequency distribution of the historical demand data.

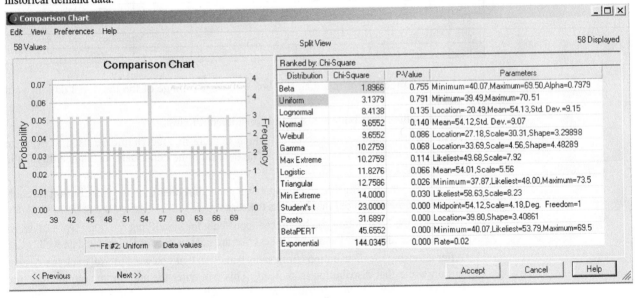

The left side of the comparison chart in Figure 13.41 shows the frequency chart for the data in Figure 13.39. The right side of the comparison chart identifies the best-fitting distributions, ranked according to the Chi-Square test. This is a widely used test in statistics where smaller values indicate a better fit. The *p*-value is also shown. The *p*-value is a statistical measure of how much evidence there is that the data does *not* fit the given distribution. A small *p*-value (e.g., less than 0.05 or 0.01) means there is strong statistical evidence that the data does not fit the distribution. A large *p*-value (e.g., greater than 0.5) indicates a good fit. Based on the *p*-values, it appears that either the beta distribution or the uniform distribution would be a good fit. In combination with the fact that demand must be integer, this confirms that the choice made in Freddie's original spreadsheet model in Figure 13.1 to enter the discrete uniform distribution into the assumption cell Demand (C12) was reasonable.

Review Questions

1. How many probability distributions are available in Crystal Ball's Distribution Gallery?
2. What is the difference between a continuous distribution and a discrete distribution?
3. What is a possible danger with choosing the normal distribution to enter into an assumption cell?
4. What are some advantages of choosing the triangular distribution instead?
5. How does the lognormal distribution compare with the normal and triangular distributions?
6. Why is the uniform distribution sometimes a convenient choice for an assumption cell?
7. What would be the key advantage of choosing either the Weibull distribution or a beta distribution for an assumption cell?
8. The binomial distribution gives the probability distribution of what?
9. What does choosing the custom distribution from the Distribution Gallery enable you to do?
10. What procedure does Crystal Ball provide for helping to identify the best distribution to enter into an assumption cell?

Solved Problem (See the CD-ROM or Web site for the Solution)

13.S1. Saving for Retirement

Patrick Gordon is 10 years away from retirement. He has accumulated a $100,000 nest egg that he would like to invest for his golden years. Furthermore, he is confident that he can invest $10,000 more each year until retirement. He is curious about what kind of nest egg he can expect to have accumulated at retirement 10 years from now.

Patrick plans to split his investments evenly among four investments: a money market fund, a domestic stock fund, a global stock fund, and an aggressive growth fund. On the basis of past performance, Patrick expects each of these funds to earn a return in each of the upcoming 10 years according to the distributions shown in the following table.

Fund	Distribution
Money market	Uniform (minimum = 2%, maximum = 5%)
Domestic stock	Normal (mean = 6%, standard deviation = 5%)
Global stock	Normal (mean = 8%, standard deviation = 10%)
Aggressive growth	Normal (mean = 11%, standard deviation = 16%)

Assume that the initial nest egg ($100,000) and the first year's investment ($10,000) are made right now (year 0) and are split evenly among the four funds (i.e., $27,500 in each fund). The returns of each fund are allowed to accumulate (i.e., are reinvested) in the same fund and no redistribution will be done before retirement. Furthermore, nine additional investments of $10,000 will be made and split evenly among the four funds ($2,500 each) at year 1, year 2, . . . , year 9.

A financial advisor told Patrick that he can retire comfortably if he can accumulate $300,000 by year 10 to supplement his

other sources of retirement income. Use a 2000-trial Crystal Ball simulation to estimate each of the following.

a. What will be the expected value (mean) of Patrick's nest egg at year 10?

b. What will be the standard deviation of Patrick's nest egg at year 10?

c. What is the probability that the total nest egg at year 10 will be at least $300,000?

Problems

Crystal Ball should be used for all of the following problems. An asterisk on the problem number indicates that a partial answer is given in the back of the book.

13.1.   The results from a simulation run are inherently random. This problem will demonstrate this fact and investigate the impact of the number of trials on this randomness. Consider the case study involving Freddie the newsboy that was introduced in Section 13.1. The spreadsheet model is available on your MS Courseware CD-ROM. Make sure that the "Use Same Sequence of Random Numbers" option is *not* checked and that the Monte-Carlo Sampling Method is selected in the Sampling tab of Run Preferences. Use an order quantity of 60.

a. Set the number of trials to 100 in Run Preferences and run the simulation of Freddie's problem five times. Note the mean profit for each simulation run.

b. Repeat part *a* except set the number of trials to 1,000 in Run Preferences.

c. Compare the results from part *a* and part *b* and comment on any differences.

13.2.   Consider the Reliable Construction Co. project scheduling example presented in Section 13.3. Recall that computer simulation was used to estimate the probability of meeting the deadline and that Figure 13.20 revealed that the deadline was met on 58.88 percent of the trials from one simulation run. As discussed while interpreting this result, the percentage of trials on which the project is completed by the deadline will vary from simulation run to simulation run. This problem will demonstrate this fact and investigate the impact of the number of trials on this randomness. The spreadsheet model is available on your MS Courseware CD-ROM. Make sure that the "Use Same Sequence of Random Numbers" option is *not* checked and that the Monte-Carlo Sampling Method is selected in the Sampling tab of Run Preferences.

a. Set the number of trials to 100 in Run Preferences and run the simulation of the project five times. Note the mean completion time and the percentage of trials on which the project is completed within the deadline of 47 weeks for each simulation run.

b. Repeat part *a* except set the number of trials to 1,000 in Run Preferences.

c. Compare the results from part *a* and part *b* and comment on any differences.

13.3.*   Consider the historical data contained in the Excel File "Sales Data 1" on your MS Courseware CD-ROM. Use Crystal Ball to fit all continuous distributions to these data.

a. Which distribution provides the closest fit to the data? What are the parameters of the distribution?

b. Which distribution provides the second-closest fit to the data? What are the parameters of the distribution?

13.4.   Consider the historical data contained in the Excel File "Sales Data 2" on your MS Courseware CD-ROM. Use Crystal Ball to fit all continuous distributions to these data.

a. Which distribution provides the closest fit to the data? What are the parameters of the distribution?

b. Which distribution provides the second-closest fit to the data? What are the parameters of the distribution?

13.5.   The Aberdeen Development Corporation (ADC) is reconsidering the Aberdeen Resort Hotel project. It would be located on the picturesque banks of Grays Harbor and have its own championship-level golf course.

The cost to purchase the land would be $1 million, payable now. Construction costs would be approximately $2 million, payable at the end of year 1. However, the construction costs are uncertain. These costs could be up to 20 percent higher or lower than the estimate of $2 million. Assume that the construction costs would follow a triangular distribution.

ADC is very uncertain about the annual operating profits (or losses) that would be generated once the hotel is constructed. Its best estimate for the annual operating profit that would be generated in years 2, 3, 4, and 5 is $700,000. Due to the great uncertainty, the estimate of the standard deviation of the annual operating profit in each year also is $700,000. Assume that the yearly profits are statistically independent and follow the normal distribution.

After year 5, ADC plans to sell the hotel. The selling price is likely to be somewhere between $4 and $8 million (assume a uniform distribution). ADC uses a 10 percent discount rate for calculating net present value. (For purposes of this calculation, assume that each year's profits are received at year-end.) Use Crystal Ball to perform 1,000 trials of a computer simulation of this project on a spreadsheet.

a. What is the mean net present value (NPV) of the project? (*Hint:* The NPV (rate, cash stream) function in Excel returns the NPV of a stream of cash flows assumed to start one year from now. For example, NPV(10%, C5:F5) returns the NPV at a 10% discount rate when C5 is a cash flow at the end of year 1, D5 at the end of year 2, E5 at the end of year 3, and F5 at the end of year 4.)

b. What is the estimated probability that the project will yield an NPV greater than $2 million?

c. ADC also is concerned about cash flow in years 2, 3, 4, and 5. Use Crystal Ball to generate a forecast of the distribution of the *minimum* annual operating profit (undiscounted) earned in any of the four years. What is the mean value of the minimum annual operating profit over the four years?

d. What is the probability that the annual operating profit will be at least $0 in all four years of operation?

13.6. Ivy University is planning to construct a new building for its business school. This project will require completing all of the activities in the table below. For most of these activities, a set of predecessor activities must be completed before the activity begins. For example, the foundation cannot be laid until the building is designed and the site prepared.

Activity	Predecessors
A. Secure funding	—
B. Design building	A
C. Site preparation	A
D. Foundation	B,C
E. Framing	D
F. Electrical	E
G. Plumbing	E
H. Walls and roof	F, G
I. Finish construction	H
J. Landscaping	H

Obtaining funding likely will take approximately six months (with a standard deviation of one month). Assume that this time has a normal distribution. The architect has estimated that the time required to design the building could be anywhere between 6 and 10 months. Assume that this time has a uniform distribution. The general contractor has provided three estimates for each of the construction tasks—an optimistic scenario (minimum time required if the weather is good and all goes well), a most likely scenario, and a pessimistic scenario (maximum time required if there are weather and other problems). These estimates are provided in the table that follows. Assume that each of these construction times has a triangular distribution. Finally, the landscaper has guaranteed that his work will be completed in five months.

Construction Time Estimates (months)

Activity	Optimistic Scenario	Most Likely Scenario	Pessimistic Scenario
C. Site preparation	1.5	2	2.5
D. Foundation	1.5	2	3
E. Framing	3	4	6
F. Electrical	2	3	5
G. Plumbing	3	4	5
H. Walls and roof	4	5	7
I. Do the finish work	5	6	7

Use Crystal Ball to generate 1,000 trials of a computer simulation for this project. Use the results to answer the following questions.

a. What is the mean project completion time?

b. What is the probability that the project will be completed in 36 months or less?

c. Generate a sensitivity chart. Based on this chart, which activities have the largest impact on the variability in the project completion time?

13.7.* Consider Problem 16.12 (see Chapter 16 on the CD-ROM), which involves estimating both the duration of a project and the probability that it will be completed by the deadline. Assume now that the duration of each activity has a triangular distribution that is based on the three estimates shown in Problem 16.12. Use Crystal Ball to perform 1,000 trials of a computer simulation of the project on a spreadsheet.

a. What is the mean project completion time?

b. What is the probability that the project can be completed within 22 months?

c. Generate a sensitivity chart. Based on this chart, which two activities have the largest impact on the variability in the project completion time?

13.8. The employees of General Manufacturing Corp. receive health insurance through a group plan issued by Wellnet. During the past year, 40 percent of the employees did not file any health insurance claims, 30 percent filed only a small claim, and 20 percent filed a large claim. The small claims were spread uniformly between 0 and $2,000, whereas the large claims were spread uniformly between $2,000 and $20,000.

Based on this experience, Wellnet now is negotiating the corporation's premium payment per employee for the upcoming year. To obtain a close estimate of the average cost of insurance coverage for the corporation's employees, use Crystal Ball with a spreadsheet to perform 500 trials of a computer simulation of an employee's health insurance experience. Generate a frequency chart and a statistics table.

13.9. Reconsider the Heavy Duty Co. problem that was presented as Example 2 in Section 12.1. For each of the following three options in parts *a* through *c*, obtain an estimate of the expected cost per day by using Crystal Ball to perform 1,000 trials of a computer simulation of the problem on a spreadsheet. Generate a frequency chart and a statistics table.

a. The option of not replacing a motor until a breakdown occurs.

b. The option of scheduling the replacement of a motor after four days (but replacing it sooner if a breakdown occurs).

c. The option of scheduling the replacement of a motor after five days (but replacing it sooner if a breakdown occurs).

d. An analytical result of $2,000 per day is available for the expected cost per day if a motor is replaced every three days. Comparing this option and the above three, which one appears to minimize the expected cost per day?

13.10. The Avery Co. factory has been having a maintenance problem with the control panel for one of its production processes. This control panel contains four identical electromechanical relays that have been the cause of the trouble. The problem is that the relays fail fairly frequently, thereby forcing the control panel (and the production process it controls) to be shut down while a replacement is made. The current practice is to replace the relays only when they fail. The average total cost of doing this has been $3.19 per hour. To attempt to reduce this cost, a proposal has been made to replace all four relays whenever any one of them fails to reduce the frequency with which the control panel must be shut down. Would this actually reduce the cost?

The pertinent data are the following. For each relay, the operating time until failure has approximately a uniform distribution from 1,000 to 2,000 hours. The control panel must be shut down for one hour to replace one relay or for two hours to replace all four relays. The total cost associated with shutting down the control panel and replacing relays is $1,000 per hour plus $200 for each new relay.

Use computer simulation on a spreadsheet to evaluate the cost of the proposal and compare it to the current practice. Use Crystal Ball to perform 1,000 trials (where the end of each trial coincides with the end of a shutdown of the control panel) and determine the average cost per hour.

13.11. For one new product produced by the Aplus Company, bushings need to be drilled into a metal block and cylindrical shafts need to be inserted into the bushings. The shafts are required to have a radius of at least 1.0000 inch, but the radius should be as little larger than this as possible. With the proposed production process for producing the shafts, the probability distribution of the radius of a shaft has a triangular distribution with a minimum of 1.0000 inch, a most likely value of 1.0010 inches, and a maximum value of 1.0020 inches. With the proposed method of drilling the bushings, the probability distribution of the radius of a bushing has a normal distribution with a mean of 1.0020 inches and a standard deviation of 0.0010 inches. The clearance between a bushing and a shaft is the difference in their radii. Because they are selected at random, there occasionally is interference (i.e., negative clearance) between a bushing and a shaft to be mated.

Management is concerned about the disruption in the production of the new product that would be caused by this occasional interference. Perhaps the production processes for the shafts and bushings should be improved (at considerable cost) to lessen the chance of interference. To evaluate the need for such improvements, management has asked you to determine how frequently interference is likely to occur with the currently proposed production processes.

Estimate the probability of interference by using Crystal Ball to perform 500 trials of a computer simulation on a spreadsheet.

13.12. Refer to the financial risk analysis example presented in Section 13.5, including its results shown in Figure 13.27. Think-Big management is quite concerned about the risk profile for the proposal. Two statistics are causing particular concern. One is that there is nearly a 20 percent chance of losing money (a negative NPV). Second, there is a 10 percent chance of losing more than a third ($7 million) as much as the mean gain ($18 million). Therefore, management is wondering whether it would be more

prudent to go ahead with just one of the two projects. Thus, in addition to option 1 (the proposal), option 2 is to take a 16.50 percent share of the hotel project only (so no participation in the shopping center project) and option 3 is to take a 13.11 percent share of the shopping center only (so no participation in the hotel project). Management wants to choose one of the three options. Risk profiles now are needed to evaluate the latter two.

   a. Generate a frequency chart and a percentiles table for option 2 after performing a computer simulation with 1,000 trials for this option.

   b. Repeat part *a* for option 3.

   c. Suppose *you* were the CEO of the Think-Big Development Co. Use the results in Figure 13.27 for option 1 along with the corresponding results obtained for the other two options as the basis for a managerial decision on which of the three options to choose. Justify your answer.

13.13. Reconsider Problem 12.5 involving the game of craps. Now the objective is to estimate the probability of winning a play of this game. If the probability is greater than 0.5, you will want to go to Las Vegas to play the game numerous times until you eventually win a considerable amount of money. However, if the probability is less than 0.5, you will stay home.

You have decided to perform computer simulation on a spreadsheet to estimate this probability. Use Crystal Ball to perform the number of trials (plays of the game) indicated below.

   a. 100 trials.

   b. 1,000 trials.

   c. 10,000 trials.

   d. The true probability is 0.493. Based upon the above simulation runs, what number of trials appears to be needed to give reasonable assurance of obtaining an estimate that is within 0.007 of the true probability?

13.14. Consider the case study involving Freddie the newsboy that was introduced in Section 13.1. The spreadsheet model is available on your MS Courseware CD-ROM. The Decision Table generated in Section 13.8 (see Figure 13.44) for Freddie's problem suggests that 55 is the best order quantity, but this table only considered order quantities that were a multiple of 5. Refine the search by generating a Decision Table for Freddie's problem that considers all integer order quantities between 50 and 60.

13.15.* Michael Wise operates a newsstand at a busy intersection downtown. Demand for the Sunday *Times* averages 300 copies with a standard deviation of 50 copies (assume a normal distribution). Michael purchases the papers for $0.75 and sells them for $1.25. Any papers left over at the end of the day are recycled with no monetary return.

   a. Suppose that Michael buys 350 copies for his newsstand each Sunday morning. Use Crystal Ball to perform 500 trials of a computer simulation on a spreadsheet. What will be Michael's mean profit from selling the Sunday *Times?* What is the probability that Michael will make at least $0 profit?

   b. Generate a Decision Table to consider five possible order quantities between 250 and 350. Which order quantity maximizes Michael's mean profit?

   c. Generate a trend chart for the five order quantities considered in part *b.*

d. Use OptQuest to search for the order quantity that maximizes Michael's mean profit.

13.16. Susan is a ticket scalper. She buys tickets for Los Angeles Lakers games before the beginning of the season for $100 each. Since the games all sell out, Susan is able to sell the tickets for $150 on game day. Tickets that Susan is unable to sell on game day have no value. Based on past experience, Susan has predicted the probability distribution for how many tickets she will be able to sell, as shown in the following table.

Tickets	Probability
10	0.05
11	0.10
12	0.10
13	0.15
14	0.20
15	0.15
16	0.10
17	0.10
18	0.05

a. Suppose that Susan buys 14 tickets for each game. Use Crystal Ball to perform 500 trials of a computer simulation on a spreadsheet. What will be Susan's mean profit from selling the tickets? What is the probability that Susan will make at least $0 profit? (*Hint:* Use the Custom Distribution to simulate the demand for tickets.)

b. Generate a Decision Table to consider all nine possible quantities of tickets to purchase between 10 and 18. Which purchase quantity maximizes Susan's mean profit?

c. Generate a trend chart for the nine purchase quantities considered in part *b*.

d. Use OptQuest to search for the purchase quantity that maximizes Susan's mean profit.

13.17. Consider the Reliable Construction Co. bidding problem discussed in Section 13.2. The spreadsheet Model is available on your MS Courseware CD-ROM. The Decision Table generated in Section 13.8 (see Figure 13.49) for this problem suggests that $5.4 million is the best bid, but this table only considered bids that were a multiple of $0.2 million.

a. Refine the search by generating a Decision Table for this bidding problem that considers all bids between $5.2 million and $5.6 million in multiples of $0.05 million.

b. Use OptQuest to search for the bid that maximizes Reliable Construction Co.'s mean profit. Assume that the bid may be any value between $4.8 million and $5.8 million.

13.18. Road Pavers, Inc., (RPI) is considering bidding on a county road construction project. RPI has estimated that the cost of this particular job would be $5 million. The cost of putting together a bid is estimated to be $50,000. The county also will receive four other bids on the project from competitors of RPI. Past experience with these competitors suggests that each competitor's bid is most likely to be 20 percent over cost, but could be as low as 5 percent over or as much as 40 percent over cost. Assume a triangular distribution for each of these bids.

a. Suppose that RPI bids $5.7 million on the project. Use Crystal Ball to perform 500 trials of a computer simulation on a spreadsheet. What is the probability that RPI will win the bid? What is RPI's mean profit?

b. Generate a Decision Table to consider eight possible bids between $5.3 million and $6 million and forecast RPI's mean profit. Which bid maximizes RPI's mean profit?

c. Generate a trend chart for the eight bids considered in part *b*.

d. Use OptQuest to search for the bid that maximizes RPI's mean profit.

13.19. Consider the Everglade cash flow problem analyzed in Section 13.4. The spreadsheet model is available on your MS Courseware CD-ROM.

a. Generate a Decision Table to consider five possible long-term loan amounts between $0 million and $20 million and forecast Everglade's mean ending balance. Which long-term loan amount maximizes Everglade's mean ending balance?

b. Generate a trend chart for the five long-term loan amounts considered in part *a*.

c. Use OptQuest to search for the long-term loan amount that maximizes Evergreen's mean ending balance.

13.20. Read the referenced article that fully describes the management science study summarized in the application vignette presented in Section 13.5. Briefly describe how computer simulation was applied in this study. Then list the various financial and nonfinancial benefits that resulted from this study.

13.21. Consider the airline overbooking problem discussed in Section 13.6. The spreadsheet model is available on the MS Courseware CD-ROM packaged with the textbook. The Decision Table generated in Section 13.8 (see Figure 13.50) for this problem suggests that 185 is the best number of reservations to accept in order to maximize profit, but the only numbers considered were a multiple of five.

a. Refine the search by generating a Decision Table for this overbooking problem that considers all integer values for the number of reservations to accept between 180 and 190.

b. Generate a trend chart for the 11 forecasts considered in part *a*.

c. Use OptQuest to search for the number of reservations to accept that maximizes the airline's mean profit. Assume that the number of reservations to accept may be any integer value between 150 and 200.

13.22. Flight 120 between Seattle and San Francisco is a popular flight among both leisure and business travelers. The airplane holds 112 passengers in a single cabin. Both a discount 7-day advance fare and a full-price fare are offered. The airline's management is trying to decide (1) how many seats to allocate to its discount 7-day advance fare and (2) how many tickets to issue in total.

The discount ticket sells for $150 and is nonrefundable. Demand for the 7-day advance fares is typically between 50 and 150, but is most likely to be near 90. (Assume a triangular distribution.) The full-price fare (no advance purchase requirement and fully refundable prior to check-in time) is $400. Excluding customers who purchase this ticket and then cancel prior to check-in time, demand is equally likely to be anywhere between 30 and 70 for these tickets (with essentially all of the demand occurring within one week of the flight). The average no-show rate is 5 percent for the nonrefundable discount tickets and 15 percent for the refundable full-price tickets. If more ticketed passengers show up than there are seats available, the extra passengers must be bumped. A bumped passenger is rebooked on another flight and given a voucher for a free ticket on a future flight. The total cost to the airline for bumping a passenger is $600. There is a fixed cost of $10,000 to operate the flight.

There are two decisions to be made. First, prior to one week before flight time, how many tickets should be made available at the discount fare? Too many and the airline risks losing out on potential full-fare passengers. Too few and the airline may have a less-than-full flight. Second, how many tickets should be issued in total? Too many and the airline risks needing to bump passengers. Too few and the airline risks having a less-than-full flight.

a. Suppose that the airline makes available a maximum of 75 tickets for the discount fare and a maximum of 120 tickets in total. Use Crystal Ball to generate a 1,000 trial forecast of the distribution of the profit, the number of seats filled, and the number of passengers bumped.

b. Generate a two-dimensional Decision Table that gives the mean profit for all combinations of the following values of the two decision variables: (1) the maximum number of tickets made available at the discount fare is a multiple of 10 between 50 and 90 and (2) the maximum number of tickets made available for either fare is 112, 117, 122, 127, or 132.

c. Use OptQuest to try to determine the maximum number of discount fare tickets and the maximum total number of tickets to make available so as to maximize the airline's expected profit.

13.23. Now that Jennifer is in middle school, her parents have decided that they really must start saving for her college education. They have $6,000 to invest right now. Furthermore, they plan to save another $4,000 each year until Jennifer starts college in five years. They plan to split their investment evenly between a stock fund and a bond fund. Historically, the stock fund has had an average annual return of 8 percent with a standard deviation of 6 percent. The bond fund has had an average annual return of 4 percent with a standard deviation of 3 percent. (Assume a normal distribution for both.)

Assume that the initial investment ($6,000) and the first year's investment ($4,000) are made right now (year 0) and are split evenly between the two funds (i.e., $5,000 in each fund). The returns of each fund are allowed to accumulate (i.e., are reinvested) in the same fund and no redistribution will be done before Jennifer starts college. Furthermore, four additional investments of $4,000 will be made and split evenly between both funds ($2,000 each) at year 1, year 2, year 3, and year 4. Use a 1000-trial Crystal Ball simulation to estimate each of the following.

a. What will be the expected value (mean) of the college fund at year 5?

b. What will be the standard deviation of the college fund at year 5?

c. What is the probability that the college fund at year 5 will be at least $30,000?

d. What is the probability that the college fund at year 5 will be at least $35,000?

Partial Answers to Selected Problems

CHAPTER 13

13.3.   a. Triangular distribution (Min = 293.51, Likeliest = 501.00, Max = 599.72).

13.7.   a. The mean project completion time should be approximately 33 months.

    ·c. Activities B and J have the greatest impact on the variability in the project completion time.

13.15.   a. Mean profit should be around $107, with about a 96.5% chance of making at least $0.

13.S1 Saving for Retirement

Patrick Gordon is ten years away from retirement. He has accumulated a $100,000 nest egg that he would like to invest for his golden years. Furthermore, he is confident that he can invest $10,000 more each year until retirement. He is curious about what kind of nest egg he can expect to have accumulated at retirement ten years from now.

Patrick plans to split his investments evenly among four investments: a Money Market Fund, a Domestic Stock Fund, a Global Stock Fund, and an Aggressive Growth Fund. Based on past performance, Patrick expects each of these funds to earn a return in each of the upcoming ten years according to the distributions shown in the following table.

Fund	Distribution
Money Market	*Uniform (Minimum = 2%, Maximum = 5%)*
Domestic Stock	*Normal (Mean = 6%, Standard Deviation = 5%)*
Global Stock	*Normal (Mean = 8%, Standard Deviation = 10%)*
Aggressive Growth	*Normal (Mean = 11%, Standard Deviation = 16%)*

Assume that the initial nest egg ($100,000) and the first year's investment ($10,000) are made right now (year 0) and are split evenly among the four funds (i.e., $27,500 in each fund). The returns of each fund are allowed to accumulate (i.e., are re-invested) in the same fund and no redistribution will be done before retirement. Furthermore, nine additional investments of $10,000 will be made and split evenly among the four funds ($2,500 each) at year 1, year 2, ..., year 9.

A financial advisor has told Patrick that he can retire comfortably if he can accumulate $300,000 by year 10 to supplement his other sources of retirement income. Use a 2000-trial Crystal Ball simulation to estimate each of the following.

The uncertain elements in this problem are the annual return of each investment over the next 10 years (Year 0 through Year 9). To simulate this, we define an assumption cell for the annual return of each investment in each year. These assumption cells are defined in rows 12, 17, 22, and 27 of the spreadsheet below.

To track the investments, we calculate their balances in each year. Row 10, 15, 20, and 25 show the investment made by Patrick in each year.

Rows 11, 16, 21, and 26 calculate the balance in each fund at the start of the year. For Year 0 in each fund, this will simply be the initial investment ($25,000) plus the annual investment ($2,500). For each future year, it will be the balance at the end of the preceding year plus the annual investment. For example, for Year 1 of the money market fund, the starting balance is D11 = C13 + D10.

Rows 13, 18, 23, and 28 calculate the year-end balance for each fund. This will be the starting balance times the net return. For example, for the money market fund in Year 0 this will be C13 = C11*(1+C12).

Finally, the Year 10 totals are added up in M30 to calculate Patrick's final nest egg. This cell is defined as a forecast cell in Crystal Ball.

	A	B	C	D	E	K	L	M	N	O	P	Q
1		Saving for Retirement										
2												
3		Investments	Initial	Annual								
4		Money Market Fund	$25,000	$2,500								
5		Income Fund	$25,000	$2,500								
6		Growth & Income	$25,000	$2,500								
7		Aggressive Growth Fund	$25,000	$2,500								
8												
9			Year 0	Year 1	Year 2	Year 8	Year 9	Year 10				
10		Money Market Investment	$27,500	$2,500	$2,500	$2,500	$2,500					
11		Money Market Start	$27,500	$30,963	$34,546	$58,841	$63,401	$65,620				
12		Money Market Return (%)	3.5%	3.5%	3.5%	3.5%	3.5%		Uniform	2%	5%	(Min, Max)
13		Money Market End	$28,463	$32,046	$35,755	$60,901	$65,620					
14												
15		Income Fund Investment	$27,500	$2,500	$2,500	$2,500	$2,500					
16		Income Fund Start	$27,500	$31,650	$36,049	$68,574	$75,189	$79,700				
17		Income Fund Return (%)	6.0%	6.0%	6.0%	6.0%	6.0%		Normal	6%	5%	(Mean, St. Dev.)
18		Income Fund End	$29,150	$33,549	$38,212	$72,689	$79,700					
19												
20		Growth & Income Investment	$27,500	$2,500	$2,500	$2,500	$2,500					
21		Growth & Income Start	$27,500	$32,200	$37,276	$77,492	$86,192	$93,087				
22		Growth & Income Return (%)	8.0%	8.0%	8.0%	8.0%	8.0%		Normal	8%	10%	(Mean, St. Dev.)
23		Growth & Income End	$29,700	$34,776	$40,258	$83,692	$93,087					
24												
25		Aggressive Growth Investment	$27,500	$2,500	$2,500	$2,500	$2,500					
26		Aggressive Growth Start	$27,500	$33,025	$39,158	$93,023	$105,756	$117,389				
27		Aggressive Growth Return (%)	11.0%	11.0%	11.0%	11.0%	11.0%		Normal	11%	16%	(Mean, St. Dev.)
28		Aggressive Growth End	$30,525	$36,658	$43,465	$103,256	$117,389					
29												
30							Total	$355,796				

	B	C	D	E	K	L	M
3	Investments	Initial	Annual				
4	Money Market Fund	25000	2500				
5	Income Fund	25000	2500				
6	Growth & Income	25000	2500				
7	Aggressive Growth Fund	25000	2500				
8							
9		Year 0	Year 1	Year 2	Year 8	Year 9	Year 10
10	Money Market Investment	=C4+D4	=$D$4	=$D$4	=$D$4	=$D$4	
11	Money Market Start	=C10	=C13+D10	=D13+E10	=J13+K10	=K13+L10	=L13+M10
12	Money Market Return (%)	0.035	0.035	0.035	0.035	0.035	
13	Money Market End	=C11*(1+C12)	=D11*(1+D12)	=E11*(1+E12)	=K11*(1+K12)	=L11*(1+L12)	
14							
15	Income Fund Investment	=C5+D5	=$D$5	=$D$5	=$D$5	=$D$5	
16	Income Fund Start	=C15	=C18+D15	=D18+E15	=J18+K15	=K18+L15	=L18+M15
17	Income Fund Return (%)	0.06	0.06	0.06	0.06	0.06	
18	Income Fund End	=C16*(1+C17)	=D16*(1+D17)	=E16*(1+E17)	=K16*(1+K17)	=L16*(1+L17)	
19							
20	Growth & Income Investment	=C6+D6	=$D$6	=$D$6	=$D$6	=$D$6	
21	Growth & Income Start	=C20	=C23+D20	=D23+E20	=J23+K20	=K23+L20	=L23+M20
22	Growth & Income Return (%)	0.08	0.08	0.08	0.08	0.08	
23	Growth & Income End	=C21*(1+C22)	=D21*(1+D22)	=E21*(1+E22)	=K21*(1+K22)	=L21*(1+L22)	
24							
25	Aggressive Growth Investment	=C7+D7	=$D$7	=$D$7	=$D$7	=$D$7	
26	Aggressive Growth Start	=C25	=C28+D25	=D28+E25	=J28+K25	=K28+L25	=L28+M25
27	Aggressive Growth Return (%)	0.11	0.11	0.11	0.11	0.11	
28	Aggressive Growth End	=C26*(1+C27)	=D26*(1+D27)	=E26*(1+E27)	=K26*(1+K27)	=L26*(1+L27)	
29							
30						Total	=M11+M16+M21+M26

The results of a 2000-trial simulation run are shown below.

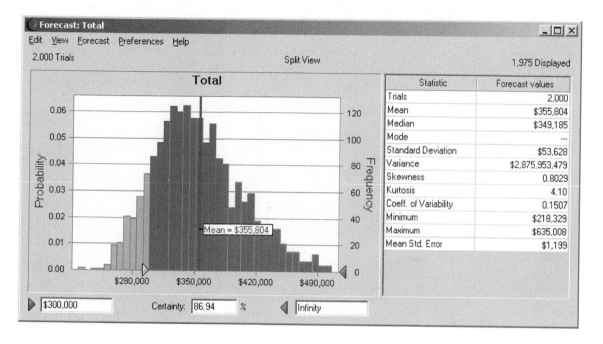

a. *What will be the expected value (mean) of Patrick's nest egg at year 10?*
The mean of the nest egg at year 10 is nearly $356 thousand.

b. *What will be the standard deviation of Patrick's nest egg at year 10?*
The standard deviation of Patrick's nest egg at year 10 is nearly $54 thousand.

c. *What is the probability that the total nest egg at year 10 will be at least $300,000?*
There is nearly an 87% chance that the total nest egg at year 10 will be at least $300,000.

Tips for Using Microsoft Excel for Modeling

Microsoft Excel is a powerful and flexible tool with a myriad of features. It is certainly not necessary to master all the features of Excel in order to successfully build models in spreadsheets. However, there are some features of Excel that are particularly useful for modeling that we will highlight here. This appendix is not designed to be a basic tutorial for Excel. It is designed instead for someone with a working knowledge of Excel (at least at a basic level) who wants to take advantage of some of the more advanced features of Excel that are useful for building models more efficiently.

ANATOMY OF THE MICROSOFT EXCEL WINDOW

When Microsoft Excel is first opened (e.g., by choosing Microsoft Excel from the Start menu), a blank spreadsheet appears in an Excel window. The various components of the Excel window are labeled in Figure B.1.

The Excel file is called a *workbook*. A workbook consists of a number of *worksheets* or *spreadsheets*, identified in the sheet tabs at the bottom of the screen (Sheet1, Sheet2, and Sheet3 in Figure B.1). Only one spreadsheet at a time is shown in the window, with the currently displayed spreadsheet highlighted in the sheet tab (Sheet1 in Figure B.1). To show a different spreadsheet (e.g., Sheet2 or Sheet3), click on the appropriate sheet tab.

Each spreadsheet consists of a huge grid, with many rows and columns. The rows are labeled on the left of the grid by numbers (1, 2, 3, . . .). The columns are labeled on the top of the grid by letters (A, B, C, . . .). Each element of the grid is referred to as a *cell*, and is referred to by its row and column label (e.g., cell C7). The currently selected cell is highlighted by the cell cursor (a dark or colored border). A different cell can be selected either by clicking on it or by moving the cell cursor with the arrow keys.

Only a portion of the spreadsheet is shown at any one time. For example, in Figure B.1 only the first 9 columns and first 17 rows are shown. The scroll bars can be used to show a different portion of the spreadsheet.

WORKING WITH WORKBOOKS

When Microsoft Excel is first opened (e.g., by choosing Microsoft Excel from the Start menu), a new workbook is created and given a default name that is visible in the Title Bar (e.g., Book1 in Figure B.1). To give the workbook a different name, save it under whatever name you desire by choosing Save As under the Office Button (for Excel 2007 or 2010) or File menu (for other versions of Excel).

To open an existing workbook that has been saved previously, choose Open from the Office Button (Excel 2007 or 2010) or Edit menu (other versions). It is possible to have more than one workbook open at a time within Excel. This may be desirable if you want to copy worksheets

FIGURE B.1

The Microsoft Excel window for Excel 2010 is on top (Excel 2007's is similar). The window on the bottom is representative of other Excel versions (e.g., Excel 2003).

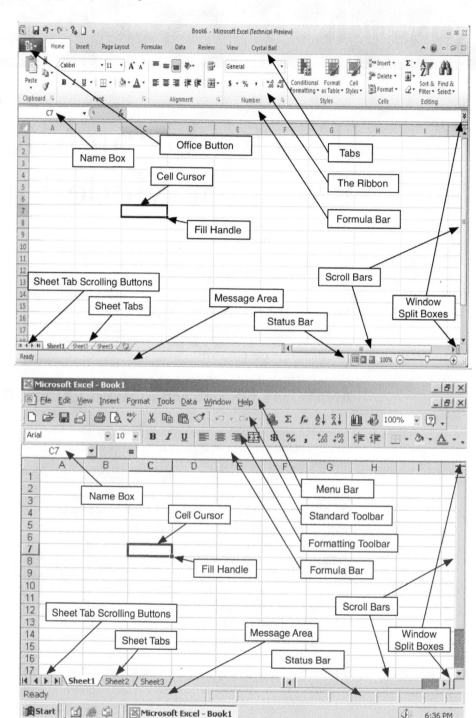

from one workbook to another or if you want to see the contents of another workbook while you are working on an existing workbook. When multiple workbooks are open, some of the workbooks can become hidden behind another workbook that is being displayed. To bring any workbook to the front, select it under the Switch Windows menu on the View tab (Excel 2007 or 2010) or the Window menu (other versions). The workbooks also can be arranged on the screen (e.g., one over the other, or one next to the other) by choosing Arrange All on the View tab (Excel 2007 or 2010) or Arrrange under the Window menu (other versions).

WORKING WITH WORKSHEETS

By default, a new Excel workbook consists of a few worksheets titled Sheet1, Sheet2, Sheet3, and so on. The currently displayed sheet is highlighted in the sheet tabs. To display a different sheet, click on the appropriate tab. If the desired tab is not visible because there are more tabs than can be displayed, the list of tabs can be scrolled using the sheet tab scroll buttons.

The sheets can be given descriptive names by double-clicking on the sheet tab and typing a new name. A new sheet can be added to the workbook by choosing Insert Sheet from the Insert menu of the Cells group on the Home tab (for Excel 2007 or 2010) or choosing Worksheet from the Insert menu (for other versions of Excel). The sheet tabs can be reordered by clicking and dragging a tab to a new location. To make a copy of a sheet, control-click (option-click on a Mac) and drag the tab. If multiple workbooks are open, you can also click (or control-click) and drag a sheet tab to a different workbook to move (or copy) a sheet to a different workbook.

Using Worksheets with Solver

A model must be confined to a single sheet. When using the Excel Solver, all cell references (e.g., the target cell, changing cells, etc.) must be on the currently displayed sheet. Thus, the different components of the Solver model cannot be spread among different sheets.

The Solver information is saved with the sheet. When data are entered in the Solver dialogue box (e.g., the target cell, changing cells, etc.), all of that information is saved with the sheet when the workbook is saved.

Separate sheets can contain separate models. Separate Solver dialogue box information (e.g., the target cell, changing cells, etc.) is kept for each sheet in the workbook. Thus, each sheet in a workbook can contain a separate and independent model. When the Solve button is clicked in Solver, only the model on the currently displayed sheet is solved.

Copy the whole sheet rather than just the relevant cells to copy models. To copy a model to another workbook or within the current workbook, it is important to control-click and drag the worksheet tab rather than simply selecting the cells containing the model and using copy and paste. Copying the sheet (by control-clicking and dragging the sheet tab) will copy *all* the contents of the sheet (formulas, data, *and* the Solver dialog box information). Using copy and paste copies only the formulas and data, but does *not* include the Solver dialogue box information.

Using Worksheets with TreePlan

Separate sheets can contain separate TreePlan decision trees. If the currently displayed sheet does not contain an existing TreePlan decision tree, then choosing Decision Tree under the Add-Ins tab (for Excel 2007 or 2010) or Tools menu (for other versions of Excel) will present the option of adding a new tree to the existing sheet. However, if a decision tree already exists on the sheet, then choosing Decision Tree instead presents options for modifying the existing tree. To create a new decision tree, first switch to (or add) a new sheet. A workbook can contain separate decision trees so long as they are on separate sheets.

Using Worksheets with Crystal Ball

The entire workbook is treated as a single model for Crystal Ball. In contrast with the Solver and TreePlan, Crystal Ball treats the entire workbook as part of a single model. Assumption cells, decision variables, and forecast cells can be defined on any or all of the different sheets of the workbook. When a simulation is run, all assumption cells are randomly generated and a forecast window is shown for all forecast cells regardless of whether they are on the currently displayed sheet. This can be an advantage with complicated simulation models, since it allows splitting the model into separate manageable components on different sheets.

Although it is possible to create separate models on different sheets for applying Crystal Ball in the same workbook, it would be confusing to do so. When you start running a simulation in a workbook containing separate models on different sheets, *all* the models on *all* the sheets will be run. To avoid this confusion, it is best to keep separate simulation models for applying Crystal Ball in separate workbooks and only keep a single workbook open at a time.

WORKING WITH CELLS

Selecting Cells

To make any changes to a cell or range of cells, such as entering or editing data or changing the formatting, the cell or cells involved first need to be selected. The cell cursor shows the currently selected cell (or range of cells). To select a different single cell, either click on it or use the arrow keys to move the cell cursor to that location. To select an entire row or an entire column, click the row or column heading (i.e., the A, B, C along the top of the spreadsheet, or the 1, 2, 3 along the left of the spreadsheet). To select the entire spreadsheet, click in the blank box at the upper left corner of the worksheet.

There are three ways to select a range of cells within a spreadsheet, which we will illustrate by considering the 3-by-3 range of cells from A1 to C3:

1. Click on one corner of the range (A1) and, without releasing the mouse button, drag to the other corner of the range (C3).
2. Click on one corner of the range (A1) and then hold down the SHIFT key and click on the other corner of the range (C3).
3. Click on one corner of the range (A1), hold down SHIFT or press F8 to turn on the extend mode, use the arrow keys to extend the range to the other corner (C3), and then either release the SHIFT key or press F8 again to turn the extend mode off.

Entering or Editing Data, Text, and Formulas into Cells

There are a number of ways to enter and edit the contents of a cell:

1. **Use the Formula Bar:** The contents of the currently selected cell appear in the formula bar (see Figure B.1). To enter data, text, or a formula into a cell, click on the cell and type or edit the contents in the formula bar. Press Enter when you are done.
2. **Double-click:** Double-clicking on a cell (or pressing F2) will display the contents of the cell and allow typing or editing directly within the cell on the spreadsheet. If the cell contains a formula, the cells referred to in the formula will be highlighted in different colors on the spreadsheet. The formula can be modified either by clicking and typing within the cell or by dragging the highlighted cell markers to new locations.
3. **Insert Function:** In an empty cell, pressing the f_x button next to the formula bar (for Excel 2007 or 2010) or on the standard toolbar (for other versions of Excel) will bring up a dialogue box showing all of the functions available in Excel sorted by type. After choosing a function from the list, the function is inserted into the cell and all the parameters of the function are shown in a small window.

Moving or Copying Cells

To move a cell or range of cells on the spreadsheet, first select the cell(s). To move the cell(s) a short distance on the spreadsheet (e.g., down a few rows), it is usually most convenient to use the dragging method. Click on an edge of the cell cursor and, without releasing the mouse button, drag the cell(s) to the new location. To move the cell(s) a large distance (e.g., down 100 rows, or to a different worksheet), it is usually more convenient to use Cut and Paste from the Home tab (for Excel 2007 or 2010) or Edit menu (for other versions of Excel).

Similar methods can be used to make a copy of a cell or range of cells. To copy a cell (or range of cells), press ctrl (option on a Mac) while clicking on the edge of the cell cursor and dragging, or use Copy and Paste from the Home tab (Excel 2007 or 2010) or Edit menu (other versions).

Filling Cells

When building a spreadsheet, it is common to need a series of numbers or dates in a row or column. For example, Figure B.2 shows a spreadsheet that calculates the projected annual

FIGURE B.2

A simple spreadsheet to calculate projected annual cash flow and tax due.

	A	B	C	D	E	F	G	H	I	J	K	L	M	N	O
1						Cash Flow ($000)								Annual	Tax
2		Jan	Feb	Mar	Apr	May	Jun	Jul	Aug	Sep	Oct	Nov	Dec	Cash Flow	Due
3	2011	10	−2	4	5	4	6	8	10	12	3	−4	8	64	16.0
4	2012	15	3	−4	3	10	4	6	10	3	6	−2	12	66	16.5
5	2013	8	4	2	−3	−5	7	4	8	8	11	−3	11	52	13.0
6	2014	7	5	5	3	2	6	10	12	14	8	2	8	82	20.5
7	2015	5	2	2	−4	9	7	12	14	3	−4	6	10	62	15.5
8															
9														Tax Rate	25%

	N	O
1	Annual	Tax
2	Cash Flow	Due
3	=SUM(B3:M3)	=N3*$O$9
4	=SUM(B4:M4)	=N4*$O$9
5	=SUM(B5:M5)	=N5*$O$9
6	=SUM(B6:M6)	=N6*$O$9
7	=SUM(B7:M7)	=N7*$O$9
8		
9	Tax Rate	0.25

cash flow and taxes due for 2011 through 2015, based upon monthly cash flows. Rather than typing all 12 column labels for the months in cells B2:M2, the fill handle (the small box on the lower right corner of the cell cursor) can be used to fill in the series. After entering the first couple of elements of the series, for example Jan in cell B2 and Feb in cell C2, select cells B2:C2 and then click and drag the fill handle to cell M2. The remainder of the series (Mar, Apr, May, etc.) will be filled in automatically. The year labels in cells A3:A7 can be filled in a similar fashion. After entering the first couple of years, 2011 in A3 and 2012 in A4, select cells A3:A4 and then click and drag the fill handle down to A7. On the basis of the data in the cells selected, the fill handle will try to guess the remainder of the series.

The fill handle is also useful for copying similar formulas into adjacent cells in a row or a column. For example, the formula to calculate the annual cash flows in N3:N7 is basically the same formula for every year. After entering the formula for 2011 in cell N3, select cell N3 and then click and drag the fill handle to copy the formula down through cell N7. Similarly, the taxes due formula in cell O3 can be copied down to cells O4:O7. In fact, both the annual cash flow and tax due formulas can be copied at once by selecting both cells N3 and O3 (the range N3:O3) and then dragging the fill handle down to cell O7. This will fill both formulas down into the cells N4:O7.

Relative and Absolute References

When using the fill handle, it is important to understand the difference between relative and absolute references. Consider the formula in cell N3 (=SUM(B3:M3)). The references to cells in the formula (B3:M3) are based upon their relative position to the cell containing the formula. Thus, B3:M3 are treated as the 12 cells immediately to the left. This is known as a **relative reference.** When this formula is copied to new cells using the fill handle, the references are automatically adjusted to refer to the new cell(s) at the same relative location (the 12 cells immediately to the left). For example, the formula in N4 becomes =SUM(B4:M4), the formula in N5 becomes =SUM(B5:M5), and so on.

In contrast, the reference to the tax rate ($O$9) in the formula in cell O3 is called an **absolute reference.** These references do not change when they are filled into other cells. Thus, when the formula in cell O3 is copied into cells O4:O7, the reference still refers to cell O9.

To make an absolute reference, put $ signs in front of the letter and number of the cell reference (e.g., $O$9). Similarly, you can make the column absolute and the row relative (or vice versa) by putting a $ sign in front of only the letter (or number) of the cell reference. After entering a cell reference, repeatedly pressing the F4 key (or command-T on a Mac) will rotate among the four possibilities of relative and absolute references (e.g., O9, $O$9, O$9, $O9).

Using Range Names

A block of related cells can be given a range name. Then, rather than referring to the cells by their cell addresses (e.g., L11:L21 or C3), a more descriptive name can be used (e.g., Total-Profit). To give a cell or range of cells a range name, first select the cell(s). Then click in the Name Box (see Figure B.1) and type a name. For example, for the spreadsheet in Figure B.2 we could define a range name for the tax rate by selecting cell O9 and typing TaxRate into the name box. Spaces are not allowed in range names, so use capital letters or underscore characters to separate words in a name.

Once a range name is defined, rather than typing the cell reference (e.g., O9) when it is used in a formula, the range name can be used instead (e.g., TaxRate). If you click on a cell (or cells) to use it in a formula, the range name is automatically used rather than the cell reference. This can make the formula easier to interpret (e.g., =SUM(B3:M3)*TaxRate, rather than =SUM(B3:M3)*$O$9). When using a range name in a formula, it is treated as an absolute reference. To make a relative reference to a cell that has a range name, type the cell address (e.g., O9) rather than either typing the range name or clicking on the cell (which then automatically uses the range name).

Formatting Cells

To make formatting changes to a cell or range of cells, first select the cell(s). If a range of cells is selected, any formatting changes will apply to every cell in the range. Most common types of formatting of cells, for example, changing the font, making text bold or italic, or changing the borders or shading of a cell, can be done by using the Home tab (for Excel 2007 or 2010) or the formatting toolbar (for other versions of Excel).

Clicking on the **.0→.00** or **.00→.0** buttons changes the number of decimal places shown in a cell. Note that this only changes how the number is displayed, since Excel always uses the full precision when this cell is used in other formulas.

For more advanced types of formatting, choose Format Cells under the Format menu of the Cells group on the Home tab (Excel 2007 or 2010) or Cells under the Format menu (other versions). A shortcut is to press ctrl-1 on a PC or command-1 on a Mac. This brings up the Format cells dialogue box, as shown in Figure B.3. Under the Numbers tab you can choose to display the contents in a cell as a number with any number of decimal places (e.g., 123.4 or 123.486), as currency (e.g., $1,234.10), as a date (e.g., 12/10/2013 or Dec 2013), and so on.

FIGURE B.3
The Format Cells
dialogue box.

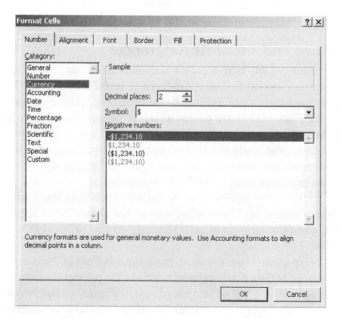

The other tabs are used to change the alignment of the text (e.g., left or right justified, printed vertically or horizontally, etc.), the font, the borders, the patterns, and the protection.

If a cell displays ####, this means that the column width is not wide enough to show the contents of the cell. To change column widths or row heights, click and drag the vertical or horizontal lines between the column or row labels. Double-clicking on the vertical line between column labels will make the column just wide enough to show the entire contents of every cell in the column.